JEWISH SPIRITUAL PRACTICES

JEWISH SPIRITUAL PRACTICES

Yitzhak Buxbaum

A Jason Aronson Book

ROWMAN & LITTLEFIELD PUBLISHERS, INC.
Lanham • Boulder • New York • Toronto • Oxford

A JASON ARONSON BOOK

ROWMAN & LITTLEFIELD PUBLISHERS, INC.

Published in the United States of America
by Rowman & Littlefield Publishers, Inc.
A wholly owned subsidiary of The Rowman & Littlefield Publishing Group, Inc.
4501 Forbes Boulevard, Suite 200, Lanham, Maryland 20706
www.rowmanlittlefield.com

PO Box 317
Oxford
OX2 9RU, UK

First Rowman & Littlefield edition 2005

British Library Cataloguing in Publication Information Available

Library of Congress Cataloging-in-Publication Data

Buxbaum, Yitzhak.
Jewish spiritual practices / Yitzhak Buxbaum.
p. cm.
Bibliography : p.
Includes index.
ISBN 1-56821-206-2
1. Spiritual life—Judaism. 2. Jewish way of life. 3. Hasidism. I. Title.
BM723.B84 1990
296.7'4—dc20 89-35141
CIP

Printed in the United States of America

The paper used in this publication meets the minimum requirements of American National Standard for Information Sciences—Permanence of Paper for Printed Library Materials, ANSI/NISO Z39.48-1992.

For my beloved father, Mac Buxbaum, of blessed memory, who is a model for me of goodness and humane wisdom.

And for my dear mother, Jeanette Buxbaum, may her light continue to shine strongly, who is the embodiment of loving patience and understanding.

Contents

NOTE

In Part II of this book the reader will find in the margin a system of numeration to indicate the outline form of the material. Thus, if Chapter 4 has five major sections, they will be 4:1, 4:2, and so on to 4:5. If section 4:1 has three parts, they will be 4:1:1, 4:1:2, and 4:1:3. The system was devised to assist the reader, and for ease of access to cross-references.

Acknowledgment

I would like to express my appreciation for the devoted efforts of my mother, Jeanette Buxbaum, who spent countless hours working on the manuscript of this book. I also want to acknowledge with gratitude the help and encouragement of Rabbi Meir Fund, the dynamic and vibrant spiritual leader of the Flatbush Minyan community in Brooklyn. Rabbi Fund graciously made himself available to answer questions relating to philosophical and halachic matters. He was also kind enough to read a number of chapters of the book and make valuable suggestions for improvement.

JEWISH SPIRITUAL PRACTICES

PART I

The General Principles of Hasidic Spirituality

The aim of this book is to make available to the reader some part of the wealth of Jewish spiritual practices whose goal is the attainment of God-consciousness.

1

D'vekut

GOD-CONSCIOUSNESS AND THE LOVE OF GOD

In Hasidism the goal of religious practice is often spoken of as *d'vekut*. Literally, this Hebrew word means "attachment," "cleaving," or "clinging," the full phrase usually being "cleaving to the *Shechinah*," the Divine Presence. This most important concept has two main aspects. On the one hand, *d'vekut* is the intensification of love of God until that love is so strong that you cleave to Him without separation. The other side of *d'vekut* is that it implies a direct awareness of God. For although sometimes it simply means the most passionate attachment motivated by love, *d'vekut* usually refers to the mind, the state of consciousness when a person is aware of God and His Presence.

Sefer Haredim says that *d'vekut* is

> the most intense love, such that you are not separated from God for even a moment. (chap. 9, #10)

And in teaching how we are to love God, *Reshit Hochmah* explains a phrase in the *Zohar* about *d'vekut* this way:

> "To cleave to Him"—this means the cleaving of the mind to Him, for there is no *d'vekut* except that of the mind and the meditation of the heart. (Sh'ar ha-Ahavah, chap. 6, #14)

Since *d'vekut*, in the Hebrew, is more pleasant and suggestive than the somewhat literal English words commonly used for it (attachment, cleaving, etc.), it has sometimes been left untranslated; otherwise, I have often translated it as God-consciousness, for that more accurately expresses its real meaning. But it should always be remembered that *d'vekut* is a God-consciousness imbued with love.

LOVE AND THE FEAR OF SEPARATION

The master of Kabbalah, Rabbi Eleazar Azikri, speaks of the *d'vekut* of the hasidim this way:

> [They] concentrate their thoughts on the Lord of all, blessed be He, with fear and love. (*Sefer Haredim*, chap. 65)

The goal of hasidic religious practice is to develop and cultivate fear of God, and higher than that, love of God. We are to strive to attain, not only continuous God-consciousness, but the love and fear which are its necessary emotional coloring.

The rabbis always talk about the balance of love and fear in our relation to God. There are higher and lower manifestations of each of these qualities, and the interaction between them varies. Ordinarily, fear acts contrary to love, in enforcing separation, for we feel a distance between ourselves and what we fear. But on the higher level of love, where all our being is passionately directed to cleaving to God without cease, fear in the normal sense disappears. The fear that comes from the higher love is altogether sweetened, for when love is intense, the fear subsumed under it is not the fear of punishment or even the fear and awe of God due to His greatness, but the fear of separation itself, and the fear of alienating the affection of the One loved.

> A person should have a fear of God which comes from his love for Him, blessed be He, for he should be afraid to sin lest he alienate

> himself from His love, God forbid. (Rabbi Eli Melech of Lizensk, Vayigash, beginning, p. 21b)

> When someone's fear of God is fear of punishment, either in this world or in the next, in hell, he is very far from love of God. But you should fear God, blessed be He, in the way of someone who loves his wife [who also loves him], and is afraid to do anything at all against her wishes, lest he lose her love. So here, when you are consumed with the burning coals of love for God, blessed be He, you should fear transgressing His commandments, lest you lose His love . . . and that is the fear which comes from love. (*Orchot Tzaddikim*, Gate 5, p. 41)

In *d'vekut*, love is supreme, love is as strong as death, and the "fear" which grows out of it is the fear of the death of separating from God for even a minute.

The fiery love of man and woman is often used (as in the previous quote) as the best metaphor for how intense our love of God should be, and how much we should yearn for Him and be agonized at separation from Him.[1]

The Rambam (Maimonides):

> What is the way that we should love God? We should love Him with an overwhelming and unlimited love, until our soul becomes permanently bound in the love of God, like one who is love-sick and cannot take his mind off the woman he loves, but always thinks of her—when lying down or rising up, when eating or drinking. Even greater than this should be the love of God in the hearts of those who love Him, thinking about Him constantly, as He commanded us, "And thou shalt love the Lord thy God with all thine heart and with all thy soul" [Deuteronomy 6:5]. This is what Solomon meant when he said allegorically, "for I am sick with love" [Song of Songs 2:5]; and the whole Song of Songs is an allegory on this subject. (*Code*, T'shuvah, x. 3)

BECOMING A CHARIOT OF GOD

The key verse in the Torah regarding *d'vekut* is Deuteronomy 11:22: "to love the Lord your God, to walk in all His ways, and to cleave unto Him [to be in a state of *d'vekut* with Him]. The Ramban (Nachmanides) says about this verse:

> One way to understand this is to say that *d'vekut* means to remember God and your love for Him always and at all times, so that you never remove your mind from Him, when you are walking on the way or lying down or rising up—until even when you are conversing with other people, in your innermost heart you are not with them but are in the presence of God. And it can be said about those who are on this exalted level of spiritual attainment, that their souls are bound up in the bond of life, and that they share in eternal life even in this world, for they are themselves a dwelling place for the *Shechinah*. (Commentary on *Chumash*)

It is through *d'vekut* that the Divine Presence comes to dwell within you, and you become a chariot for God.

> Who is a hasid? He who acts with love of his Creator, striving to give Him pleasure, and whose whole intention is to cleave to Him in *d'vekut* for the sake of His great name, becoming thereby a chariot for God. (Rabbi Isaiah Horowitz, *Kitzur Shnei Luchot ha-Brit*, Sh'ar ha-Ahavah, p. 11)

Jewish mysticism is called the Account of the Divine Chariot (*Maaseh Merkavah*). And of the Patriarchs, who are models for religious attainment, and who represent all the perfected *tzaddikim*, it is said:

> The Fathers—they indeed are the Chariot.[2] (*Bereshit Rabba* 82–7)

The idea is that a chariot is directed in all its movements by the charioteer who comes within it, and whose hands are on the reins. This is one expression of the ideal of Jewish spiritual practice, that all your actions, speech, and thoughts be directed by God, who is within you. The person who has attained to this high level will have continuous God–consciousness at all times. This is the level of the holy spirit. This is the level of Elijah, a great figure in Jewish mysticism.

Elijah was directed as a chariot of God, and only went when and where the holy spirit directed him.[3] The Torah tells how Elijah, as he walked along in conversation with his disciple, the prophet Elisha, was taken up to heaven in a chariot of fire (2 Kings 2:11). That Elijah was himself a chariot of devotional fire is one of the inner meanings of this story. As the rabbis said about his conversation at that moment before his departure from this world, when he was giving his closest disciple and successor his most intimate teaching:

He was then discussing with Elisha the Account of the Divine Chariot. (*Yerushalmi Berachot* 5-2)

The meaning of Elijah's ascent to heaven in the chariot is that when, through your fiery devotion to God, you become His chariot, you can then rise into heaven and attain mystic experience. Many of the hasidic *rebbes*, entering a spiritual state where the soul separates from the body, would make "soul-ascents" to heaven (*aliyot neshamah*). There is a famous account of one such ascent made by the Baal Shem Tov, which he himself described in detail in a personal letter (*Keter Shem Tov*, very beginning).

THE *MITZVOT* AS COUNSELS TO ATTAIN GOD-CONSCIOUSNESS

God-consciousness is the purpose of the many *mitzvot* of the Torah, when they are performed with complete intentionality.

> As it says in the holy *Zohar*, all the 613 *mitzvot* of the Torah are 613 counsels how to attain God-consciousness.[4] (*Or ha-Ganuz l'Tzaddikim*, p. 11)
>
> [Contrarily] sins separate you from God and God-consciousness, because a transgression is a barrier of separation. (*Or ha-Ganuz l'Tzaddikim*, pp. 17, 51, 95)

What the Kabbalah teaches in the *Zohar* is a perspective different from that of God as ordering, and the *mitzvot* as commandments. The *mitzvot* can be seen as counsels of advice (*aytzot*). A commandment is done because of the authority of the one who orders it, but advice is followed because of the help it offers in achieving our own purpose. In our religious life, that purpose should be to attain the love of God and God-consciousness. *Mitzvot* are done, then, to advance in love of God and in God-consciousness; sins are avoided not just because God says "No," but because they are barriers keeping us from *d'vekut*.[5]

The hasid does not limit himself to the prescribed *mitzvot*, however, for every act should be directed to the goal, and all deeds will then become accounted as *mitzvot*. And this desire for *d'vekut* becomes the standard of action.

> The main effort and work is to see in everything you are considering doing, whether it is a good counsel for achieving *d'vekut*. If so, do it; but if it does not bring you to God-consciousness, refrain. (*Or ha-Ganuz l'Tzaddikim*, p. 73)

According to this standard, you can decide by experiment and experience when to sleep and when to wake, what and what not to eat, how much to eat, where to go, whom to see, and everything else.

Rabbi Yehiel Michal, the Zlotchover Maggid (preacher), explaining the rabbinic tradition that Abraham was able to keep all of the Torah's commandments even before it had been given at Sinai, said:

> He was always conscious of God, and any action that would disrupt his attachment to God he refrained from doing; and any action that he saw would increase his attachment to God he realized it was a *mitzvah*, and that he would do. (*Yeshuot Malko*, p. 100)

Certainly this was the Zlotchover Maggid's own standard. He makes the application elsewhere:

> You should be attached to God continuously, and your love for Him should be constant. The test to know what His will is is this: If you want to do something, and see that this action will increase your God-consciousness and love of God, then know that this is a *mitzvah* and God's will. But if you see that this action will decrease your love and God-consciousness, then know that it is a transgression, and do not do it. (*Yeshuot Malko*, p. 19)

HANHAGOT—SPIRITUAL PRACTICES

There are many valuable and effective practices in the tradition that are not *mitzvot* in the ordinary sense. They are not commanded as such in the written or oral Torah, and need not be performed by everyone. But they are done as an expression of personal piety and as part of the spiritual practice of the individual. They are usually called *hanhagot* in Hebrew (singular, *hanhaga*). While some of them are basically separate practices in themselves, others are in the nature of enhancements of the *mitzvot*. It is all these *hanhagot* that are the subject of this book.

WHY THIS BOOK IS NEEDED

In contrast to some of the other aspects of Jewish religiosity, there is very little available to the English reader in learning about *hanhagot.* Even in Hebrew there are difficulties in acquiring knowledge about spiritual practices that go beyond the standard or the conventional. The information is scattered about—one practice is mentioned in one place and another practice in another—and in the few collections of *hanhagot* available, the information is not arranged topically. Moreover, the spiritual principles underlying the practices are often left unexplained, or the explanation is found elsewhere.

This book is based largely on the collections of *hanhagot* already made, but also includes many things found isolated in various holy texts. Most of the material is of hasidic origin, and it is the hasidic *hanhagot,* especially, that have a great resonance today.

Every age must have its own form of piety and in our modern time of great turmoil and spiritual confusion something new is needed. Just as the Baal Shem Tov, hundreds of years ago, developed a new form of Hasidism to meet the challenges of his time, so do we today need a new piety. But the best place to start in our search for it is in the holy ways of the Hasidism which has come down to us from earlier times.

In many of the original sources, *hanhagot* are discussed and recommended in the briefest way, in a sentence or two. But in this book, since so many are unfamiliar with the background of the various *hanhagot* and the way that they fit into the larger picture of hasidic spiritual practice, it will be necessary, more often than not, to provide that background and context, to expand and explain.

In Part I of this book I will attempt to give an outline of the general principles that underlie hasidic spirituality.

CONTINUAL GOD-CONSCIOUSNESS AND THE GARDEN OF EDEN

To attain *d'vekut* with the Divine Presence and the high level of being a chariot of the *Shechinah,* a person must more and more deepen his heart's devotion and commitment to God, and more and more increase those of his activities which are infused with God-consciousness and put in tune with God's will.

The goal of hasidic *d'vekut* is *continual* God-consciousness, not just when you are being "religious"—learning Torah, praying, doing *mitzvot*—but continual, at all times and at every moment, without the least cessation whatsoever. Whenever *d'vekut* is spoken about, the phrase "without a moment's cessation" regularly recurs. The idea is to be "religious" twenty-four hours a day—all the time. This is an essential point, which is most important to understand.

A basic statement of the hasidic ideal, referred to again and again, is in Psalm 16:8: "I have placed the Lord before me *always*." (Italics added.)

> You should fulfill "I have placed the Lord before me always," so that you do not turn your mind from God-consciousness for even one minute. (Rabbi Moshe Teitelbaum, *Hanhagot Tzaddikim*, p. 48, #19)

Our usual (and false) religious attitude is that we do something "religious"—study Torah, pray, or whatever—and then we forget about God. But the truth is that our goal must be *continual* remembrance of God.

Normally, we live in this (material) world and change our perspective and consciousness in order to "be religious" for a while. The purpose of continuous involvement in spiritual practices is that, as we spend more and more time in the other (spiritual) world, we finally come to where *that* is our true "home," where, at some point, there is a "flip" from the material state of consciousness to God-consciousness. It is as if a light bulb were turned on in a dark room. We become established in God-consciousness and that is our ordinary state of mind. Our relation to spirituality is no longer that it provides us with flashes or brief periods of illumination, but that we are in a world of light and everything we see and experience is spiritual.

> This material world is transient, but there is another, spiritual, world which is eternal and always-present. So you should separate yourself altogether from the things of this world, from its pleasures, from its hatred and its fierce competitiveness, and even from speaking about worldly matters. And when you think that you no longer belong to this [lower] world, you will not speak about it; rather, all your conversation will be about Torah and *mitzvot*, for they are of the upper, spiritual world. So, too, will all your thoughts be in the Upper World, for it is what is important to the soul. Why should you trouble your mind about things that not only are of no value or

> benefit to your soul, but will cause it harm? So it is good for a person [to practice being in this state, and] when he is involved in prayer or Torah to think that he is not [standing] in this material world, but in the spiritual world, in the Garden of Eden, before the Divine Presence—and through this he will purify his mind [until that is his actual experience always].[6] (*Reshit Hochmah*, Sh'ar ha-Kedushah, chap. 4, #23)

Reshit Hochmah speaks of two levels in spiritual attainment, where the key to the higher attainment is the dedication of the mind:

> The holiness we are to have vis-à-vis this world is that we are to separate from it and from the things of this world, and be sanctified to spirituality—as if we were not part of this world at all. But the higher level of holiness depends on the sanctification [not only of our action, but] of our mind, that it be totally involved in spiritual things and clinging in *d'vekut* to the upper, spiritual world. . . . Those who attain this higher state are not on the same level as the rest of the people who just do Torah and *mitzvot* without the inner elevation and are on the level of the Lower Garden of Eden; for these other *tzaddikim* ascend [to the Upper Garden of Eden]. (Sh'ar ha-Kedushah, chap. 4, #21)

Our spirituality should become more and more complete until we live in a spiritual world, until we are always in the Garden of Eden, in the presence of God. As alluded to in *Reshit Hochmah*, there are meditations (particularly for the times of prayer, Torah study, and eating) where we think of ourselves as being in the presence of the *Shechinah*. But this meditation is to be engaged in not only then, but whenever possible. As Rabbi Nachman of Bratzlav said in his striking and paradoxical way:

> You should accustom yourself to being in the World to Come. (*Sichot ha-Ran*, #96)

We will see that the World to Come is here now. For what is the World to Come? It is the spiritual world, the Garden of Eden that will one day "come" and be revealed to all eyes.

Whereas most people and even many *tzaddikim* have to exert themselves to rise to the upper, spiritual world, those *tzaddikim* who have achieved perfection and who are established in God-consciousness, on the contrary, have to force themselves down to involve themselves with the things of this lower, material world.

Rabbi Shalom, the Prince of Peace, of Belz, said:

> There are two levels of *tzaddikim*: one, the higher of the two, is a *tzaddik* who has purified all his limbs for the sake of heaven, so that he no longer has any connection with materiality at all. He no longer derives any enjoyment from physical pleasures, and when he needs to do something physical in this world he has to exert himself with all his energy to force a little materiality into himself.
>
> The second and lower level of *tzaddik* has not purified his limbs to that extent, and he has to exert all his energy to act with holiness and purity, such that he will not derive enjoyment from something physical [but only from what is spiritual]. (*Admorei Belz*, vol. 1, p. 8)

According to *Reshit Hochmah*, we are to consider ourselves as spiritual beings altogether, as if we belong to the upper, spiritual world. The following teaching of the Baal Shem Tov refers specifically to the matter of speech and conversation, but its application (as we know from elsewhere) is to all worldly activities that tend to pull the mind away from concentration on God.

> When you have to converse with someone about worldly things, you should have it in your mind that you are going from the Upper World below, like a person who is leaving his home, but whose intention is to return immediately at the first opportunity. And as he is going on his way he is thinking continuously about when he will be able to come back.
>
> So should you think—that the Upper World is your real home, with God, blessed be He—even when you are talking about things of this world. And when you are finished with your worldly business, return immediately to cling to God and to God-consciousness. (*Tzavaat ha-Ribash*, Kehot edition p. 12)

The level of fulfillment described in *Reshit Hochmah* of complete immersion in spirituality is that of being in the Garden of Eden. For the Garden of Eden is here now, and though a person has been "expelled," he can return along the way of the Tree of Life, which is the way of the Torah.

> For there is no other Tree of Life than the Torah. (*Berachot* 32, referring to Proverbs 3:18)

Rabbi Abraham of Slonim taught about the necessity to fix one's mind on God without wavering, and to become firmly established in loving God-consciousness:

"And the flaming sword which turns every which way and guards the entrance to the path to the Tree of Life." [Genesis 3:24] When a person serves God, blessed be He, continually, and not just from time to time, now yes—now no, he is on the level of the Lower Garden of Eden. And when he merits that his service is not only continual, but also with deep joy and delight, with the higher love and fear of God, he is on the level of the Upper Garden of Eden. But when he serves God just from time to time, and every minute or hour is changing, now he is a man, an Adam, now he is an animal without consciousness of God . . . drawn after his lower desires . . . this is the level of "the flaming sword [of the mind] that turns every which way." (*Torat Avot*, p. 38)

When a *tzaddik* is on the spiritual level of being in the Upper Garden of Eden he experiences great joy and delight. "Eden" in Hebrew means "delight," and the Garden of Eden is the pleasure-garden of the king, his garden of delights.[7] In this state of consciousness the *tzaddik* experiences now, in this world, the essence of the World to Come. For him, the Garden of Eden, the World to Come, is here now. The world of nature is not a wild growth, but is revealed to his eyes as the well-ordered garden of the King of the Universe, a pleasure-garden full of spiritual delights for those who are in His presence and who "tend the garden" according to His divine will (Genesis 2:15).

When a person so desires, he can taste in this world the delight of the Garden of Eden and the World to Come. (*Shema Shlomo*, Bereshit, #5)

Rabbi Elimelech of Lizensk:

The *tzaddik* attaches himself way Above, to eternal life, and even when he is in this world he experiences the delight of the Upper World and of eternal life. That is what the *Gemara* means when it says [as an expression of blessing], "May you see your [eternal] world in your lifetime"—that through all his deeds and movements being done with holiness and purity, with *d'vekut* and joy, and with love and fear of God, he will experience the delight of the Upper World in this world. (*Noam Elimelech*, Bereshit, p. 1a)

There are two kinds of *tzaddikim*, according to Rabbi Elimelech, on two levels, one higher than the other:

There is a *tzaddik* who serves God with *mitzvot*, and guards himself from transgressing, God forbid, any small *mitzvah*, but rather

> exerts himself to do it as it should be done. But he is not on the level where, by means of the *mitzvot*, he can come to *d'vekut* with God, blessed be He, and have great love and longing for Him, blessed be He. A *tzaddik* like this will look forward to his reward in the World to Come.
>
> The other kind of *tzaddik* serves God with thoughts altogether pure, and, by means of the *mitzvot* cleaves to God, blessed be He, with *d'vekut*, and great love and longing; he always sees God's exaltedness, blessed be He. A *tzaddik* like this draws to himself the delights of the World to Come, and he, as it were, enjoys the radiance of the *Shechinah* in this world. So he does not look forward to the World to Come, for he experiences the delights of the World to Come in this world. This is what is said in *Berachot*, where the rabbis give the blessing, "May you see your world in your lifetime"—that you merit to be such a *tzaddik*, that you be in *d'vekut* always, and experience the delights of the World to Come in your lifetime. (*Noam Elimelech* Terumah, p. 41b)

When someone performs a *mitzvah* or good deed he often does not experience the full meaning of what he is doing. A doctor, for example, who helps others in such wonderful ways, would also have to be a holy man to truly feel and experience the greatness of his actions.

> For example, a person does a great *mitzvah* and, as is well known, at the time when he is involved in it he is clothed in a surrounding light, an aura, a great and wonderful light. But often, due to his lower state, and the descent into materiality caused by his involvement in low bodily desires, this light is hidden from him, and he does not feel it or experience it—until the future time in the World to Come . . . when the lights of everyone's good deeds will be revealed to him.
>
> But all this is not true of the *tzaddik* of whom it is said, "May you see your world in your lifetime." [*Berachot* 17a] For he, while he is alive, experiences the surrounding light, that pure and sweet light, which comes with the fulfillment of the *mitzvot* of God. And all the physical delights and pleasures of this world do not even begin to touch the wonderful delights that the *tzaddik* feels in serving God. About this does the verse say, "Taste and see that the Lord is good." [Psalm 34:9] Happy are those who seek Him and revere Him. (Reb Arele Roth, *Shomer Emunim*, p. 139a)

What gives one access to this spiritual delight is the *d'vekut* that makes one aware of God's presence. For the essence of *d'vekut* is bliss.

> In this world the *tzaddikim* experience the delight of the World to Come because of the bliss inherent in God-consciousness. (*Or ha-Ganuz l'Tzaddikim*, p. 83)
>
> A person whose mind is always attached to the service of God, blessed be He, continuously . . . enjoys great delight at every moment, for the root of his soul is attached Above. As a result, if he were to cease serving for even a moment he would immediately feel the absence of this great pleasure. Knowing that, he will make sure not to separate himself from God's service for even the briefest moment, so as not to be exposed to the harshness of that deprivation. (*Likkutim Yekarim*, p. 9b)

When people are in this blissful state of *d'vekut* they can seem as if they are drunk or even insane. In his letter defending Rabbi Levi Yitzhak of Berditchev from those who did not understand his sometimes strange ways (for, in the ecstasy of *d'vekut*, he would run, and dance wildly on the tables, and fall and roll on the floor), Rabbi Eleazar (the son of Rabbi Elimelech of Lizensk) says:

> When a *tzaddik* serves God from fear and from love—that love can bring him to what almost seems like madness—as it is written, "In her love you will always be ravished," and err as if insane. This is what we find with King David [when he led the procession bringing the Ark up to Jerusalem], "And David danced and leaped with all his might." (*Noam Elimelech*, p. 966, Igeret ha-Kodesh)

Why is it important that we know all this? The answer is that if a person believes that happiness is to be found in possessions and physical pleasures, then his attention will be attached entirely to those things, and that is what he will focus on and run after. But if he comes to understand the truth, that God is the source of all pleasure, and that the experience of His presence provides the deepest happiness and joy, he will turn himself to spiritual things and seek the light of the Face of the Living God.

For who would knowingly give up the deep happiness of God's presence for the sake of a transient physical pleasure? Would Adam and Eve have eaten the apple—although it was "good for food and a delight for the eyes" (Genesis 3:6)—if they had known that because of it they would be removing themselves from the Garden of Eden?

Again and again, however, the hasidic *rebbes* teach that this spiritual joy of *d'vekut* only comes through continual and uninterrupted divine service.

Rabbi Shmuel of Slonim[8] said:

> The reason why many people do not feel a closeness to God, blessed be He, from their Torah study and prayer, is that they have no real continuity in their service of God, which they engage in in an off-and-on manner—now they become enthused to do something and then they stop—then again they become enthused and again they stop. But if you serve Him, blessed be He, always, without cease, certainly that is when you will feel a real attachment and closeness to Him, blessed be He. (*Divrei Shmuel*, p. 211, #90)

The Maggid of Mezritch said:

> If you see that someone sometimes serves God and sometimes does not, you can be sure that he has never really served God as he should. For if he had served God even once as he should, then he would serve Him continuously. (*Or ha-Emet*, p. 48)

Being in the Garden of Eden means not only serving God continually, but also having a constant awareness that everything that happens to you comes from God, and everything that God does is for the good. We are taught by the rabbis that whenever something happens that seems to be bad, we should say, "Everything the Merciful One does is for good" or "This also is for good."

Rabbi Pinhas of Koretz:

> When you believe that everything is from Him, blessed be He, then there is no evil or bad at all—there is just all good. (*Tosefta l'Midrash Pinhas*, #187)

When we reach the high level where we realize that everything is for good, and we see clearly with our mind's eye that everything that happens to us is coming to us directly from God's hand, then we are on the level of the Garden of Eden and of the World to Come. There is nothing bad anymore; everything is unified and everything we experience is good.

Rabbi Nachman of Bratzlav says:

> The *d'vekut* of a person with the Infinite One must be according to the way of "running and returning" [you "run" to unite with God in mystical experience, through prayer, meditation, etc., where you lose consciousness of self, and then you "return" to this world, to do God's will], so that you do not completely lose yourself and die before your time from the mystic nullification of self. Then, afterward, when you are on the level of "returning," when you have

returned to your this-world self-consciousness and self-existence, an impression of the wonderful Light of that higher *d'vekut* yet remains with you, and that impression allows you to see and to know the unity of the Infinite One in this world and His goodness, so that you know that everything is good and that everything is one. And this level is like that of the World to Come. (*Likkutei Aytzot*—Hasagot, #2)

IN THE PRESENCE OF GOD AND SEEING GOD

When a person reaches the state of consciousness where he is continuously in the presence of God, he sees God everywhere. This is the "seeing God" mentioned in various places in the Torah (Psalms 11:7, 24:6, etc.). Just as God-consciousness is to become normal, our "home," and material consciousness a "descent," so will a person see the spiritual side of things with more reality than he sees the physical aspect.

Rabbi Shlomo of Karlin said:

What is there that can obstruct our vision of God and hide Him from us? Are not all the worlds like a mere mustard seed before Him? How can a mustard seed get in the way of the Creator of the Universe, the Infinite One, blessed be He? So Moses [a paradigm for the *tzaddik*] had nothing between him and God, and he had God before him always. (*Shema Shlomo I*, p. 5, Bereshit, #3)

The Baal Shem Tov:

It is a high level of spiritual attainment when someone is always aware of God's presence—that He surrounds him on all sides—and his *d'vekut* with God is so great that he does not need to remind himself again and again that God, blessed be He, is there and present with him, but he sees God with the eyes of his mind, for He is the Place of the world.

What this means is that He was before He created the world, and the world exists within the Creator, blessed be He. If so, a person's *d'vekut* with God should be so great that what he primarily sees is God, blessed be He. It should not be that his vision is primarily of the world and then, by the way, of God. No—but his sight should be primarily of God. And when a person is on this level, all the Shells [the unholy forces which surround and block what is Divine] disperse and remove themselves from him, for it is they that darken his vision and the eyes of his mind so that he cannot see God,[9] blessed be He. (*Likkutei Yekarim*, quoted in *Midrash Ribash Tov*, p. 62)

A hasidic story tells us how this was the leading thought of the Baal Shem Tov. In the Besht's own words he tells of his closeness to his father when he was a child (his father passed away when he was just five years old), and says:

Before his death he called me to him and said to me, "My child, always remember that God is with you. Never let this thought out of your mind. Go deeper and deeper into it every hour and every minute, and in every place." These words of his are still fixed in my heart and engraved in my mind. And after my father's death I always went off alone in seclusion, in forests and fields, to strengthen this holy thought in my mind—that the glory of the Holy One, blessed be He, fills all the earth, and that He is actually with me. (*Ikkarei Emunah*, p. 11)

Other than generally increasing our level of devotion more and more, God-sight can be practiced and developed as the Besht did by his intense meditation on God's presence. There are various ways of connecting what our physical eyes see with God. One way is by understanding that all we see is brought into being and kept in being by God, that it is all part of Him.[10] Regular meditation on this will lead to the point where we actually come to see this, and Him, with our mind's eye.

The Peasetzna Rebbe explained how deep meditation leads to vision:

Many times during the day, at home and outside on the street, think, with a broken heart: "All the world is Godliness, even the particles of earth beneath my feet, as well as the air I breathe within me—and the reality of all that exists is Godliness. Why then have I alone separated myself from all this great camp of the *Shechinah*, to be independent unto myself?—Master of the World! Draw me close to You, surrounded with all Your blessings, and in complete repentance!" (*B'nai Machshavah Tovah*, Seder Hadracha v'Klalim, #7)

Elsewhere, he says:

But even before the exalted vision [of God] is actually revealed to you, where you see that all the world is Godliness . . . nevertheless, immerse yourself each day deeper in the thought: "I do not see it, but does not God's glory fill the world, and did He not create it from Godliness? Am I not also filled with Godliness, and are not even the particles of earth on which I walk [Godliness]?

> All the world is included in the holiness of His Godliness in total nullification; everything that exists does His will. Just I alone, in my own willfulness, have removed myself as a separate thing, far from Him, blessed be He, to wander outside this great camp of the *Shechinah*.
>
> When you meditate on this continually, and fix it in your mind, then you force this thought on yourself . . . and it is impossible that through this the holy vision not be revealed in your soul. For by itself this is what your soul always sees—it is just the body that obscures its holy vision. And when you force this thought on your body, meditating on it continuously, your soul emerges and sees. If not always, at least there will be exalted moments and hours when you will see. (*B'nai Machshavah Tovah*, Seder Emtzai v'Yesod ha-Hevrah, #14)

(The teaching of Rabbi Meshullam Feibush of Zabrizha about how intense meditation and longing for God lead to vision is also relevant here. See the quote in "Yearning for God" on p. 23.)

Just as we are to see God, we should know that He always sees us. Here is the teaching of the Baal Shem Tov:

> It is a high level to continually see God with the eye of your mind, just as you would see a person. And you should be aware that God is also looking at you, just as a man would look at you. . . . Always be joyful, believing with complete faith that the Divine Presence is by you and guards you. Meditate on this at all times. You should always be looking at God and seeing Him, and He is always looking at you. (*Tzavaat ha-Ribash*, p. 23)

(See "Meditation" 17:7 for more about seeing God and being seen by Him.)

BEING A SON OR DAUGHTER OF GOD

When you are always in the presence of God, seeing Him everywhere and knowing that He is also looking at you—and when you actually experience an intense personal relationship with God, aware that everything that comes to you from Him is good, and that He always protects you from all evil—that is the level of being a child of God.

The relationships with God traditionally spoken of are those of being a servant of God, or of being His son. How real these relationships become to you will determine the extent of their positive effect and influence. It is one thing to talk intellectually about being a servant or son of God, and another thing to make that relationship real—by practice and effort—so that you feel yourself as such in truth and act accordingly.

> The main purpose and task in the work of the Baal Shem Tov and his holy disciples was to strengthen the cords of love [binding the people to God], and to renew the feeling and awareness of what it means that we are children of God. (*Ish ha-Pele*, Preface, p. 9)

If you would be a son or daughter of God it is good to use language, in prayer and to yourself, that reflects that relationship. Call God "Master of the World," with an awareness of His greatness and the obligation we have to do His will. Call him "Father" or "Father in Heaven,"* with true belief that He really is your Father, in that He brought you into being, and loves you and cares for you always.

The Maggid of Mezritch taught that:

> A man should always call out and cry out to the Holy One, blessed be He, "Father!" until He becomes his father. (*Eser Orot*, p. 28, #21)

It is a practice, then, of some *tzaddikim* and hasidim to call out to God during prayer or when eating, "Father, Father!" and "Master of the World!"

In general, calling out to God is a way to remember Him always and to keep love for Him alive in our hearts.

> Rabbi Levi Yitzhak of Berditchev was always immersed in *d'vekut* . . . and would frequently call out "Merciful One!"* (*Midor Dor*, vol. 1, #579)

Although there are many things to say about the connections between the relationships to God as servant and son, the ideal is expressed in Malachi (3:18), of being a "son who serves Him."

Rabbi Levi Yitzhak of Berditchev:

> Serving God from fear is the level of a servant, and serving Him from love is the level of a son. (*Kedushat Levi*, Yitro, p. 36)

We must have both love and fear of God, but the rabbis teach us that love is always higher. And we must strive for the higher level of being a

*Asterisks denote corresponding Hebrew to be found in Appendix.

son or daughter of our Father in Heaven—to love Him and do His will. One of the most common motives in Hasidism is to give pleasure (*nahas*) to your Father in Heaven.

How can we increase our love for God? One way is by continuous remembrance of our eternal relation to Him as His children, that He is our Father in Heaven who is the source of all goodness that comes to us, and that He is always with us to protect us from harm. For love is latent within the awareness of this relationship and remembrance of the relationship draws it out. But one way or another, we must somehow make God our own.

> He is our true Father . . . who loves us and is always giving us good things, who has compassion on us and saves us in our time of trouble.
>
> When you think about this more and more, and about God's great goodness to you, love for Him will become fixed in your heart; you will long for Him, and your soul will become aroused to give pleasure to Him by doing His will. (*Beit Middot*, p. 24)

When we establish a relationship with God, such as being a son who serves Him, it will be a powerful aid in helping us to concentrate our mind on Him and to love Him and fear Him.

> And so you should remember your love and fear of God always, so that your mind not be diverted from Him for even one minute. And at every moment you should imagine that you are standing before Him to serve Him. (*Beit Middot*, p. 57)

This is one way to be in the presence of God always, by having just one leading thought before all others. Another example of a leading thought is to say to yourself always: "I am a son of God, and my only thought and desire and will is to do my Father's will—and to be in His presence at all times."

Although humility is at the center of the hasidic path, we are taught that there is one use for pride, as it says (2 Chronicles 17:6), "And his heart was lifted up in the ways of the Lord." Say to yourself: "I am a son of my Heavenly Father. How can I not act the right way?"

But a relationship of love is two-way. Just as it is important that we love God, it is equally important that we are aware of His love for us. All of our actions should be for love of God. At the same time, we should be aware of how all of God's actions are for love of us—that is the secret of the blessings. When we reach the level of being a son of God we will not only feel true love for our Father in Heaven, but also feel and experience His love for us.

The secret of prayer is to make our relationship to our Father in Heaven real. We should trust that we can go to Him for everything we need.

> The prayers should raise man in the purest perfection to be as a child towards his Father in heaven, perceiving the Father everywhere, allowing everything to be permeated by the thought of the Father, resolving the whole world, and the whole of life, in a single relationship of Father and child. (Rabbi Samson Rafael Hirsch, *Horeb*, vol. 2, #688, p. 544)

When you become a son or daughter to your Father in Heaven you will finally be at home in this world.

The Peasetzna Rebbe taught that we should aspire to be children of God, and yearn for God-vision, to see the *Shechinah* eye-to-eye. The Peasetzner, speaking for the hasidim of his fellowship, said that like all Jews they wanted to serve God with all their heart, soul, and might. He went on with this prayer:

> But, our Father, our merciful Father, have compassion on us and enlighten our hearts with a spark of desire and knowledge, so that we will know that it is not enough for us to be like a servant, the son of a maid-servant, who also serves the king, just that his work is done grinding behind the grindstones, far from the king. He does not hear his words, and he does not enjoy and delight in the radiance of his presence. His work is done with a closed mind and a dull heart.
>
> Our desire and longing is to be on the level of a son, as it says: "Sons are you to the Lord your God." And our fervent hope is, in our service to God—whether in Torah or prayer or the other *mitzvot*—to feel our closeness to God, like a son who is so happy to see his father again after being separated from him for years, and after suffering great longing for his father. So too will we, in the hour of our service to God, feel how our soul runs toward its Father, for whom it yearns all day and all night, how it runs and melts, as it is poured out into the bosom of its Father in Heaven.
>
> And not just in prayer and Divine service alone will we feel our closeness to God, and delight in the radiance of His glory, blessed be He, but our minds will always be so clear and strong and tied to His holiness that they will be able to dominate our senses. Not

only will our senses not have the power to confuse and entice our minds and to say to us, "It is the world that you see, and materiality that you perceive and feel," but even our senses will be subdued to the thought of our heart, and they too will see the holiness of God, which is spread out over all existence. And eye-to-eye we will see that we are in the Garden of God in Eden, before the Throne of His Glory, blessed be He. (*B'nai Machshavah Tovah*, beginning)

YEARNING FOR GOD

Yearning for God will lead us to see His Light.
Rabbi Meshullam Feibush of Zabrizha:

There is no reality in the world other than God's, blessed be He. Before the creation everything existent was within the potential of His power, and He emanated His powers and created [all things] . . . and at any moment it is within His hand, and a matter of His will, to return every existent thing to nonexistence as at the first, and He alone would remain. Therefore, there is nothing in the world but Him and His powers, which are one, and without that nothing exists. Although it appears that there are other things, it is all His existence and His powers.

But it is impossible to understand, to truly understand this, without constant meditation on the Creator, blessed be He, and on this matter—as we are indeed commanded to do, in the commandments to have faith, to love and fear Him, and to accept His unity. There is no special time for these *mitzvot*, but we are to be engaged in them all our lives, at every moment. You should not cease from them for even one minute. . . .

If we merit having this *d'vekut*, then we will come to be aware of God with a pure heart—not as so many people think nowadays, that they understand this (but without understanding at all). For real understanding means that you will actually see this . . . through the *d'vekut* and thoughts of your mind, which is constantly engaged in thinking of God. If a person does not meditate on God continually, even though he believes in all this, nevertheless, it is not actually visible to him—for what he sees is the world without any awareness of God. But someone who has God in his mind and thoughts continually, does not think of the world at all as separately existing, but with everything he sees, he thinks of how this depends on God. And he is full of longing for God.

There is a good parable to explain this:

It is like someone who looks at the beautiful clothes a woman is wearing. When he is attached to lust for women, God forbid, he pays no attention to the gold embroidery that beautifies her clothes—but immediately his mind turns to lust for the woman who is wearing them. But someone whose heart is pure and without this lust looks just at the garment. So the two are looking at one and the same thing, but each is seeing something different.

Similarly (making a distinction of one thousand times between what is impure and what is pure and is about a matter of holiness), when someone always yearns for God, blessed be He, he sees God and His powers in whatever he sees in the world, for His powers give life to everything that exists. . . . While someone who does not yearn for God sees just the physical. And although if you reminded him and asked him, he would say that God enlivens and gives existence to everything, he is not really attached to that understanding. Consider this parable well, for it is very similar to its application. (*Yosher Divrei Emet*, #11 end, and #12)

Rabbi Kalman of Cracow:

While a person is living in this world, of necessity he has to eat and drink and have clothes and a place to live, and many other needs of his also have to be fulfilled. But the Way of Truth is that all the direction of your soul in all your doings should be just for God alone, in order to view the Beauty of God, and your soul should thirst to taste the sweetness, closeness, and delight of His Godliness [the *Shechinah*]. All the days of your life you should say to yourself, in longing, "When will I come and see the Light of the Living King?"

. . . If you keep up a continuous effort in longing, and every day strengthen and increase your yearning and desire for *d'vekut* with God, blessed be He, your body itself will become purified, and even its materiality will become transformed into something spiritual. (*Maor v'Shemesh*, Pinhas, quoted in *Hachsharat ha-Abrechim*, p. 28b)

The words spoken in longing, referred to in this quote, are an allusion to Psalm 42:3, where David says, "My soul thirsts for God, for the living God. When will I come and see the face of God?"[12]

The Baal Shem Tov:

Attach your mind always in intimacy with the Divine Presence, such that you always think only of your love for Her, and cleave to Her. And you should always say to yourself, "When will I be

> worthy that the Light of the *Shechinah* dwell with me?"[13] (*Tzavaat ha-Ribash*, p. 2)

In the quotes above there are expressions of longing and yearning for God: "When will I see the Light of the Living King?" or "When will I be worthy that the Light of the *Shechinah* dwell with me?" Then there are the words of David from the Psalm: "When will I come and see the face of God?" Phrases such as these and others should be rolled over in the mind and even said aloud, many times during the day.

But the strength of such longing is in its focus and intensity.

Rabbi Mordechai of Tchernobil:

> You must break all your desires and desire *d'vekut* with the Supernal Light of the Creator, blessed be His name, with love and longing and yearning, until your soul is about to expire from the sweetness of the *d'vekut*.[14] This should be every minute and second, and you should not cease from this for one minute. (*Likkutei Torah*, Hadracha 1)

We should make every effort to cultivate our devotion and increase our love of God through longing. Rabbi Natan of Nemirov (Rabbi Nachman of Bratzlav's great disciple) often emphasized that we should always have words of the yearning for God on our lips:

> Accustom yourself to verbalize holy longings. (*Aytzot Yesharot*, Ratzon, #4)

Through perseverance in devotion, such feelings will eventually enter deeply into your heart and become a part of you. It is told about Rabbi Yehiel, a leading disciple of Rabbi Mordechai of Lechovitz:

> It was his holy way to sleep about two hours, no more, and even then he always had in his mouth words of the longing of his soul for God, such as "My soul thirsts for You," and "Whenever I speak of Your glory, my heart is aswirl with Your love," and "My heart desires You in the night hours," and others like this—all in the middle of sleep.[15] (*Torat Avot*, p. 284)

If he was saying these things while asleep, certainly he said their like during the day; but then, of course, due to the hidden and modest ways of the *tzaddikim*, no one could know of it.

TEFILLIN

The goal of continuous God-consciousness is represented by the *tefillin* worn on the head and arm.

Rabbi Elimelech of Lizensk:

> The *tefillin* symbolize *d'vekut*. (*Noam Elimelech*, Mishpatim, p. 40b; cf. Korach, p. 70a)

Rabbi Nachman of Bratzlav:

> A person should examine himself every moment to see if he has *d'vekut* with God, blessed be He. And the symbol for *d'vekut* is the *tefillin*. (*Likkutei Aytzot*, Tefillin, #2)

Hovot ha-Levavot—(*Duties of the Heart*):

> [The *tefillin*] are to arouse us to remembrance of God, to love Him with all our heart, and to long for Him—as a lover makes a sign for himself, so he will not forget his beloved, and even wears it on his body; as it says in the Song of Songs, "Put me as a seal upon thy heart, as a seal upon thy arm (8:6)." (Quoted in *Reshit Hochmah*,[16] Sh'ar ha-Kedushah, chap. 6, #76)

The head *tefillin* next to the brain is to help us keep God in our minds and thoughts, and to direct us to use all our senses and powers in His service. The arm *tefillin* reminds us that all our actions should be for the sake of heaven, and the box of the arm *tefillin* is next to the heart so our hearts will turn to God in love and fear.

In the time of the rabbis of the Talmud, *tefillin* were worn by pious people throughout the day as a constant physical reminder of God. Only later was their use restricted basically to just the time of the Morning Prayer. But eventually, after the passage of generations, the extended wearing of *tefillin* returned as a practice of devout people. However, unlike former times, they are not generally worn outside on the street or when engaged in work and worldly activity.[17]

Wearing *tefillin* whenever possible, during times of Torah and prayer, etc., can be a valuable aid in devotion.

> It is good to have *tefillin* on continually, the whole day if possible, or most of the day, or part of it, not only during the time of [the Morning] Prayer. (*Reshit Hochmah*, Sh'ar ha-Kedushah, chap. 6, #54)

> You should have fear of God throughout the whole day. And what reminds a person of the fear of God is that he have on *tefillin* the whole day if possible, or at least during the hours when he is occupied with Torah study, for then he is separated from worldly involvements. (*Reshit Hochmah*, Sh'ar ha-Yirah, chap. 15, #82)

> It was the custom of the Rebbe Reb Shmelke of Nikolsburg to be adorned in *tallit* and *tefillin* the whole day. (*Shemen ha-Tov*, p. 63, #16)

Among the practices that Rabbi Moshe Teitelbaum committed himself to when he became the rabbi of Shinova was:

> To go around in *tzitzit* [that is, *tallit*] and *tefillin* the whole day. (*Ha-Gaon ha-Kadosh Baal Yismach Moshe*, p. 53)

When you have on *tefillin*, which are holy objects, you are required to be in a more elevated state of God-consciousness.

> You should not say a word of worldly conversation while you have the *tefillin* on. (Rabbi Moshe Teitelbaum, *Hanhagot Tzaddikim*, p. 48, #9)

We are not to divert our attention from them and, to help us remember their presence, we touch them frequently and kiss our fingers. The point in remembering the *tefillin*, then, is that we remember God.[18]

Those who are on a high spiritual level know the holiness of that which is holy—and are affected by it. Once, when a *tzaddik* came to visit Rabbi Israel of Rizhin, after having been with Rabbi Zusya of Hanipol, the Rizhiner asked him what he had seen there. He said:

> When I entered his room he was wrapped in a *tallit* and crowned with *tefillin*, and the upper half of his body was burning as if on fire. Only after he removed the *tefillin* did he slowly begin to take on the appearance of a man of flesh and blood. (*Beit Rizhin*, p. 277)

There are those who are able to devote the whole day to religious activity and to have *tefillin* on for much of the day; but for most of us, our purpose when putting on the *tefillin*, a most important practice, is (after the holy influence from them they have when they are on) the symbolic one of expressing our commitment that during the day we will strive to have continuous consciousness and remembrance of God. It is a good practice when removing the *tefillin* to declare a strong intention and determination to achieve that which they symbolize.

2

Remembrance of God

GOD-CONSCIOUSNESS AND THE REMEMBRANCE OF GOD

When you truly love someone, you have him constantly in remembrance. Love for God is expressed in always having His name in your mind and on your lips. When you love God and long for Him, His name will be sweet to you and you will want to have it always on your tongue. *Sefer Haredim*:

> There are *mitzvot* which require no special occasion or time, but you are obliged to do them always, so that you not cease from them for even one minute all your life. These are they:
>
> 1. To believe in the existence of God and in His care and providence, and in His unlimited ability and power.
> 2. To believe that He is one.
> 3. To fear Him.
> 4. To love Him.
> 5. To cleave to Him in *d'vekut*.
> 6. To remember Him always.
>
> (Preface to the Mitzvot—2)

[Elsewhere, *Sefer Haredim* speaks of the *mitzvah*] to remember God always—in the way of "I have placed the Lord before me always." The holy poet said, "How sweet is Your name on my tongue, like the sweetest honey is its taste." And it is written, "For Your name and for the remembrance of You does my soul long." [Isaiah 26:8] And . . . it is written, "Take care, lest you forget the Lord your God." [Deuteronomy 8:11] Rabbeinu Yonah [Shaarei Tshuvah, Gate 3, #27] wrote that this refers to the negative commandment not to forget His great name for one minute. In *Sifre*, in a number of places, we are taught that we are "not to forget [God]"—in our hearts, and we are "to remember [Him]"—with our mouths. And it is an obligation for a man, every day, from time to time, to arouse and recall to himself his love for God and to speak with his mouth, aloud, a verse that is about the remembrance of our Creator and the fear due Him, blessed be He—such as "The whole earth is full of His glory" [Isaiah 6:3], or the verse "[God,] great in counsel and mighty in deed, whose eyes are open to see all the ways and doings of men" [Jeremiah 32:19], or "The everlasting God, the Lord" [Isaiah 40:28], and other verses like this.

And such indeed was the practice of my own teacher, the pious rabbi, our wonderful and holy master, Rabbi Yosef Sagis, his memory for a blessing for the life of the World to Come. In his great love for God, he was accustomed to speak aloud the verse from the prayers of *Rosh HaShanah* [*Musaf*], "Happy is the man who never forgets You, and the one who seeks His strength in You!"* (chap. 12, #51)

About Rabbi Hayim of Tzanz we are told that:

He would often walk back and forth in a room, totally absorbed in his holy thoughts and meditations, immersed in loving awareness of the Lord his God, blessed be He. And he would cry out, "There is no place where He is not!" or "He fills all worlds and surrounds all worlds!"* Or, sometimes he would call out the Thirteen Articles of Faith. (*Mekor Hayim*, p. 122, #412)

Rabbi Tzadok ha-Cohen of Lublin:

The essence of the whole Torah is the remembrance of God; the rest is just myriad counsels for every time and place and situation, how to come to that remembrance. But the intention in all of them is that your awareness of God's presence shall not depart for a minute, and that forgetfulness will not conquer you, God forbid. (*Tzidkat ha-Tzaddik*, #232, last sentence)

All of the *mitzvot* are "counsels" for how to ward off forgetfulness. But there are also many *hanhagot* by means of which we can cultivate this continuous remembrance of God in ourselves.

EVERYTHING THAT HAPPENS, EVERYTHING WE SEE AND HEAR, SHOULD REMIND US OF GOD

One hasidic practice is to work to fix in our minds the realization that everything that happens to us comes to us from God, and that everything we see and hear has been put before us by God for a purpose: to remind us of Him. There are many ways this can be done. One of them relates to the God–vision discussed previously, where we reflect particularly on the created existence of what we see.

Rabbi Tzadok ha-Cohen of Lublin:

> Everything that happens to a man, and all created things, are to remind him that there is a Creator . . . as it says, "The earth is full of Your possessions" [Psalm 104:24], that is, through all the created things in the world you can acquire and "possess" God. And God brings things and events to you every day . . . perhaps you will be brought to remembrance through them. (*Tzidkat ha-Tzaddik*, #232)

One version of this kind of meditation and reflection sees to the source of the qualities of all created things, and how they have their root in God.

The Maggid of Mezritch:

> You should have complete faith that everything you see has been put before your eyes so that you will remember the Holy One, blessed be He. You should look at whatever you see stripped of its material veil. For example, if you see a nice object, such as a beautiful vase, say to yourself, "From where did this thing get such beauty if not from Him?" And by that thought you will remember God's Beauty. (*Or ha-Emet*, p. 15)

Rabbi Elimelech of Lizensk:

> Everything that Jacob [a paradigm of the *tzaddik*] saw or heard or did or ate, he would take whatever there was in it of beauty or glory and attributed it to God, blessed be He. For example, if he ate some

delicious food he thought to himself, "Who created this food, and who put in it its sweet taste? Was it not the Creator, blessed be He?" . . . Such was his way in everything . . . and everything good or wonderful that Jacob saw, he would use as a way to attain *d'vekut* with Him, blessed be He and blessed be His name. So, for example, when he saw Rachel and how beautiful she was, he realized that her beauty was from God, and came to *d'vekut* with God through that. (*Noam Elimelech*, Beshallach, p. 34a)

Everything is seen with its spiritual reality foremost.

Rabbi Moshe Vorshiver, of blessed memory, asked the holy Rabbi Eleazar of Koznitz, "How did you merit to become a [hasidic] *rebbe*?" He responded, "One, I never prayed for myself alone without including others; two, from everything that I saw I took a lesson; three, in everything that I saw, I did not see its materiality, but its spiritual reality."

[To illustrate this latter point] he told a story of how he once traveled with a young Torah scholar to Warsaw. And when he went to be with the hasidim, the other young man stayed behind at the inn. When he returned there later, he asked where the young man, his traveling companion, was, and they said to him, "He's sitting over there." But to the rabbi, he appeared to be a goose. He looked at him closely and realized that, indeed, that was he. And he asked him, "What have you been doing?" He answered, "I've been enjoying myself eating—I had a delicious meal of goose." There was also a fourth thing that the rabbi said—he said that he never put his faith and trust in anyone but in God alone. (*Sifran Shel Tzaddikim*, p. 68)

The point of this little story is that in becoming immersed in the act of eating, and in "meditating," so to speak, on the goose, the young man had "become" a goose spiritually. The rabbi only saw the spiritual reality of things, and so he saw his spiritual state rather than his human form that the physical eye sees.

Rabbi Hayim Heikel of Amdur:

Never look at anything without taking from it some spiritual lesson. And never look at the materiality of anything in the world, but only at its spiritual aspect. (*Tiferet Shlomo*, Likkutim Hadashim)

Rabbi Elimelech of Lizensk:

All things in this world were created for His glory—for all things are parables and hints from which to derive some spiritual lesson.

> . . . You can even take such a lesson from the doings of worldly men. For example, seeing how much they exert themselves for the things of this world—how much more then should you exert yourself for spiritual things.[1] (*Noam Elimelech*, Likkutei Shoshanah)

The Holy Jew of Pshischa told how he learned this very lesson from a smith.

> The Holy Jew said that he merited all his greatness and spiritual levels because of a blacksmith. When he was a young man living in his father-in-law's house in Apta, there was a certain smith living close by. And when it was time to go to sleep, that smith would still be at work pounding on his anvil. The Holy Jew said that he thought to himself, "If this smith works so hard and for such long hours without letting himself sleep for the transient things of this world, how can I go to sleep and waste time that I could be devoting to eternal things?"
>
> It was the same thing in the morning, for the smith would get up early, before sunrise, to work. And the Holy Jew could not allow himself to sleep late, for he thought, "If the smith can get up so early just to earn money, how can I sleep?" (*Niflaot ha-Yehudi*, p. 59)

You can certainly remember God when seeing the good deeds of good people (their charity, their kindness, etc.), and take a lesson for yourself from their ways. But you can also from seeing others' faults and bad deeds.

The Baal Shem Tov said that when you are made aware of another person's faults, it is not the time for you to judge him, but to judge yourself:

> When you see someone doing something wrong, or hear people talk about it, you should take it as certain that there is at least a trace of the same thing in you . . . and that God, blessed be He, brought this seeing or hearing before you [so that you will be reminded of *your* fault, and so that you will repent]. For your responsibility is to fix what needs fixing in *you*. (*Arvai Nehal*, quoted in *Milei d'Avot*, p. 63, #14)

The Baal Shem Tov's grandson remarked:

> If you will consider this well, you will see that through this teaching you can understand how to remind yourself of God, blessed be He, so that you not forget Him when you are surrounded by the swirl of worldly vanities.[2] (*Milei d'Avot*, p. 63, #12)

Since we are supposed to remember God continuously, the Maggid of Mezritch explains, God has given us loved ones who are always in our presence and in our home, so that through them we can be reminded of Him at all times:

> With everything we are to serve God. So if you derive pleasure from something, it should lead you to love of God. And if you fear something, you should remember fear of God, blessed be He. [For that is why God has brought before you these things you love and fear: to remind you of how you should love and fear Him.]
>
> Now the service of God is to be in singleness, and continual. And so God, blessed be He, has given you something that will be with you continually for the sake of remembrance. For example, when a man has a son who is precious to him and whom he loves very much, he should by that remember the love of God. For the Holy One, blessed be He, has given him this son so that he will always be reminded of the love of God, blessed be He. (*Or ha-Emet*, p. 25)

Thus, instead of the overwhelming love and devotion of a parent for his child distracting him from his remembrance of God, on the contrary, it can serve as a constant reminder: "Who gave me this daughter I love so much? And what is the source of my happiness and joy?"

Everything that is holy or in some special way connected with God, such as synagogues, holy books, and holy objects, should arouse us to remembrance of God. We should also learn to cultivate this reaction in ourselves. But our effort should be to have even profane and "vain" sights call us to remembrance. The *Kav ha-Yashar* taught how we can sanctify our eyes by working to have everything we see remind us of God's commandments.

> King David, peace be upon him, said in the Psalms, "Keep my eyes from seeing vain things; enliven me in Your ways." A man should realize that many important things depend on what we see with our eyes. So it seems to me a good practice that as soon as you get up in the morning and, let us say, see your house and those of others, you should think of how God gave us the *mitzvah* of making a parapet for the roof of the house. . . . If you walk out onto the street and happen upon some clean animals, which are fit to be sacrificed in the Temple, think to yourself how God commanded us to offer sacrifices. Or, if you see some unclean animals, think of how He forbade us to eat them. (*Kav ha-Yashar*, chap. 2, beginning)

Not only does such a practice sanctify one's eyes and sight, but it leads to continuous remembrance of God.

One of the purposes of the *tzitzit*, the fringes on the *tallit*, is that when we see them we will be reminded of God and His commandments, and do them (Numbers 15:39).

> Make it a practice to look at the *tzitzit* often, so that you always remind yourself of the love and fear of God, and of the need for God-consciousness. (Rabbi Nahum of Tchernobil, *Hanhagot Tzaddikim*, p. 36, #16)

In the Talmud, Rabbi Meir spoke about the beautiful sea-blue thread among the many white ones of the *tzitzit*:

> Why was the color blue chosen from all the other colors?
> Because the blue resembles the sea,
> the sea resembles the sky,
> and the sky resembles the Throne of Glory. (*Sotah* 17a)

(In Exodus 24:10, part of the Throne is said to be "like sapphire stone, and as the sky itself for clearness." The sapphire is a transparent blue, and so, of course, is the sky.)

One lesson to be derived from this teaching is that love leads to remembrance. When you love someone, you remember him. When a man has a great love for a woman, everything reminds him of her, even though the connection is farfetched.

If we deepen our devotion to God, and cultivate the habit, many, many things will remind us of Him. For example, when you see an animal with horns, you may be reminded of the *shofar* (the ram's horn) and of the High Holidays and all they signify; or when you see a body of water, you may be reminded of how God split the Red Sea for our ancestors. This is a slight touch of love-madness for God. As in the words of the Rambam (quoted earlier), in our love for God we should be like someone "who is love-sick, and cannot take his mind off the woman he loves."

The Maggid of Mezritch (speaking about the way the Patriarchs would serve God in thought):

> For example, when he would see the water bubbling from a spring, he would be reminded of the Source of Living Water in the river

that goes out from Eden [to water the Garden]. (*Imrei Tzaddikim*, p. 83)

Like the *tzitzit*, the *mezuzah* also serves to remind us of God (when we walk in and out of buildings, for example). It is written about the original Lubavitcher *rebbe*, Rabbi Shneur Zalman of Ladi, that:

> He always had a *mezuzah* lying near him to look at and so remember God, according to the verse, "I have placed the Lord before me always." He would also often look at the sky [which reminds one of God, as in the quote above: "The sky resembles the Throne of Glory."][3] (*Beit Rabbi*, I, chap. 28, p. 178)

This practice of the *rebbe's* with the *mezuzah* (which would usually be attached to the doorpost, but here is not) can, of course, be imitated.

The *tzaddikim* are reminded of God, blessed be He, and His service by everything they see:

> The secret of smoke is the secret of the binding of the worlds to God, blessed be He, and this is the meaning of the incense burnt in the Temple. And so too do we find in the *Zohar*, that when they saw smoke, the *tzaddikim* would be aroused to Divine reflection and would talk about smoke as a symbol of what was taking place Above in the spiritual realm.
>
> When a person learns in the books of the pious and the masters of Kabbalah, he is able to become spiritually aroused through all the things that he sees (which are not evil, God forbid, but are just in the material world), and are representations of spiritual things and symbolize their hints and secrets. (*Darkei Tzedek*, p. 19)

Just as with seeing, what we hear can also remind us of God if we teach ourselves how to hear. Every conversation, even what is overheard, contains Divine messages and hints.

> Whenever people speak to them, even when ordinary people speak to them about ordinary and worldly things, the *tzaddikim* hear just the spiritual lesson for their own selves, taking whatever they can from what they hear. (*Divrei Hayim*, MiKaitz, quoted in *DhTvhY*, II, p. 37, Dibbur #25)

For example, in parting, someone says to you, "Take care." But you might hear in this God's message, reminding you of all the things connected with holiness you should take care of today.[4]

AIDS TO REMEMBRANCE—GOD'S NAME BEFORE OUR EYES AND REPETITION OF A HOLY SENTENCE

Specific practices and aids can be used to help one keep up the constant remembrance of God that is so integral a part of true devotion. We have already mentioned the *tzitzit*, and the function of the *tefillin* as a physical reminder, like tying a string around your finger. There is also the personal custom, mentioned earlier, of the Ladier Rebbe always having the *mezuzah* near him.

Another aid to remembrance is the practice of continually visualizing before your eyes, on the field of your vision, the name of God, YHVH, as if it were written on a television screen. This is taken as a literal fulfillment of the verse, "I have placed the Lord [YHVH] before me always." The Holy Jew, the Yehudi said that:

> From the time that he had a mind of his own, the name Havaya [YHVH], blessed be He, was never absent from before his eyes. (*Meir Einei ha-Golah*, p. 20)

> Once, on an extremely cold winter day, the holy rabbi, Rabbi Yitzhak of Drobitch, was on the road traveling (for he would go from town to town to preach). Some Jews passed by in a carriage, and, having compassion on him they took him with them. In the middle of the journey they suddenly came upon a river, and without warning Rabbi Yitzhak jumped down from the carriage, took off his clothes, and went into the freezing water and stayed there. The others stared in astonishment and did not move until he came out, dressed, and got back up into the carriage with them. When they asked him why he had done this, he answered, "My practice is to always have the name YHVH, blessed be He, before my eyes, in black fire on a background of white fire. And at that moment it disappeared from before me. So I went into the river and said, 'Master of the World! If you return it to me, good; but if not, why should I live any longer?' And it was returned to me."[5] (*Mishnat Hasidim*, p. 415, #7)

Parallel to this continuity of sight (in having God's name before your eyes) is the practice of establishing a continuity of sound as an aural reminder, by the continuous repetition or chanting of a holy sentence or Torah verse. *Rachmei ha-Av* teaches the frequent repetition of holy phrases and words as a reminder for *d'vekut*:

> You should have continuous *d'vekut* with God, blessed be He, and you should not lose it for even one minute, either when you are just waking, or just before you fall asleep. Immediately when you wake up you should accustom yourself to say continually, "Blessed is the One and Only One,"* and the verse, "I have placed the Lord before me always" [*Shivitti HaShem l'negdi tamid*]—or at least the word *Shivitti* [I have placed]. (*Rachmei ha-Av*, #16, D'vekut)

A disciple of the Besht, Rabbi Yaakov Koppel Hasid

> would verbally repeat at all hours of the day, nonstop, "I have placed the Lord before me always" even during the hours of work and business. (*Tiferet Beit David*, p. 103)

REMEMBERING HIM THROUGH BLESSINGS AND PRAISES, AND BY PRAYING FOR OUR NEEDS

The important practice of making blessings also leads to a loving remembrance of God.

> All the blessings . . . were ordained so that a person would remember the Creator, blessed be He, and His Godliness at all times and at every moment. (*Yesod v'Shoresh ha-Avodah*, Gate 2, chap. 4, p. 27)

The many blessings we are obliged to make on enjoyments and benefits, such as food, for example, train us to see how all the good things that come to us are from God and are expressions of His love for us. This awareness should awaken our love. *Reshit Hochmah* teaches that when we make blessings of enjoyment we should express our love for God and say them with joy:

> When you make blessings of enjoyment, you should intend to praise and give thanks to the Cause of all, who created that thing. And through that praise you will cleave in love to the Creator, recognizing His greatness and exaltedness. . . . The flow of His goodness and light is without cease, and for that reason are we obliged to bless Him. That is why it was established . . . that we say blessings on everything, so that we remember the greatness and exaltedness of the Holy One, blessed be He, and His love and continual care for us at all times. For he created this thing . . . so

> that His creatures would benefit and derive enjoyment from the flow of His Divine goodness. And through these blessings we will cleave to Him always. (Sh'ar ha-Ahavah, chap. 10, #45)

We are to take the "suggestion" of the blessings that are ordained in the tradition and expand the practice to all aspects of our personal life. We should turn to God frequently as we perceive His goodness to us throughout the day, and verbalize our own improvised blessings[6] of thankfulness and appreciation (at least until higher spiritual levels are reached, the mental intention alone is not enough, and these added blessings should be spoken). In this way, every day will contain a great and full series of such blessings along with their attendant God-consciousness.

> For anything that the rabbis did not establish a blessing . . . but that still gives you pleasure, enjoyment, or benefit, you should give thanks to God, blessed be He, in any language that you understand—for the pleasure that He created. And so wrote . . . the holy rabbi, the great master of Kabbalah, Rabbi Tzvi Hirsh of Ziditchov, the memory of a *tzaddik* and a holy man for a blessing, who taught wisdom to his disciples, that for all enjoyments for which there are no prescribed blessings, such as before sexual intercourse, they should give thanks to God, in their spoken language, for the pleasure that He created. (*Yifrach biYamav Tzaddik*, p. 48b)

> We should bless and give thanks to God for His goodness for every good thing that He does for us. For example, if you have a good piece of clothing, or a good and warm place to live . . . you should think, "How many righteous people there are, better than I, who do not have this thing that God, in His goodness, has given me." So accustom yourself to say about every thing: "Blessed be God who is so kind to me."* (*Rachmei ha-Av*, Beracha #7)

Thanking God for our clothes or for our house is not something that is to be done just once, but again and again. Rabbi Alexander Ziskind says in his ethical will (writing about himself in the past tense):

> When I put on good clothes I gave thanks to God with great joy, aloud, saying, "My Maker and Creator, blessed be Your name, I thank You that You have given me these good clothes, not according to my good deeds, but according to Your great mercy and kindness." For I thought to myself, "How many great *tzaddikim* are there, to whose ankles I do not reach, who do not have such clothes." (*Tzva'a Yekara*, #29)

And he says:

> Whenever I came home, morning or evening, and reached my house, I always offered thanks to God, aloud, for this [that out of His great kindness He had given me this house, for me and my family, though I did not deserve it]. (*Tzva'a Yekara*, #27)

We can thank God for the good things in our life again and again. When each day we see more and more and appreciate God's goodness to us, we will become happier:

> Every blessing is about the goodness of God and His great and unlimited kindness to us, in spiritual and material things. And we should pay attention and recognize this with our mind and our heart, everyone according to his own level, and as a result your heart will become happier and more joyful."[7] (Rabbi Aaron of Karlin, *Hanhagot Tzaddikim*, p. 19)

As you become aware of good things in your life, "blessings" that you might formerly have taken for granted, your happiness will grow and deepen. When we further come to understand that even what seems bad is for our good, and bless God for that too, then everything is good and the world becomes a Garden of Eden.

To achieve the true purpose of a blessing we should reach to its depth of meaning. A blessing of enjoyment or benefit is essentially a short meditation. When making the blessing we *first* turn our thought to the fact that this goodness is *from God, then* that it is an expression of His love for us, and that He loves us because we are His children, and, *last*, we direct our love, in return, to Him. (The point here is not so much the sequence of thought but the connection of ideas.) Just as we strive to actively love God, we should attend to the importance of developing a more passive and receptive awareness of His love for us. Not only does such an awareness sweeten our lives, but it itself fosters our love for our Father in Heaven and makes us feel His presence and His closeness.

The regular practice of blessings leads us to remembrance of God throughout the day so that we continually have His name on our tongue and His presence in our mind and heart. It is very important to know that when we remember God, when making blessings or at any other time, we are to do so with feelings of love directed to Him and an awareness of His love for us. Our continuous meditation on God is not a mind meditation alone, but an emotion meditation, a meditation of love, so that we become fully absorbed in remembrance of our relation of love to Him.

When we remember Him, then, we are to do so with love. And when we remember God, it is also in order to put ourselves at that time in tune with His will.

The religious belief and understanding which lies behind the practice of blessings can also be made into a continuing meditation that can be done on its own at any time:

> You should accustom yourself to think all the time and continually of the greatness of God, and the full extent of His freely given goodness to His creatures and to us—all due to His mercy. For according to our many sins we do not deserve His wonderful goodness. He is the Root of all and He is our true Father . . . who loves us and is always giving us things, and has compassion on us and saves us in our time of trouble.
>
> When you think about this more and more, and about God's great goodness to you, love for Him will become fixed in your heart. You will long for Him and your soul will become aroused to give pleasure to Him by doing His will. . . .
>
> The remembrance of His name, blessed be He, should not cease from your lips, and the remembrance of His greatness should not depart from your thoughts. . . . If a person's heart and mind were always aroused to think thoughts of God's wonderful lovingkindness and His great power, continually—and if he were to place God always before him, as if he were actually in God's presence,[8] then would his love for God be what it is supposed to be. (*Beit Middot*, p. 24)

Our ever-present awareness of God comes not only through the good, but also through the bad. For, in the words of Job, "Shall we receive good at the hand of the Lord, and shall we not receive bad?" (Job 2:10) The rabbis taught: Just as you bless God for the good that comes to you, so should you bless Him for the bad. (*Berachot* 48)

That was what Job did in saying, "The Lord gave and the Lord has taken away; blessed be the name of the Lord." (Job 1:21) These very words of Job can indeed be used by us also. Just as receiving good things should lead us to a recognition of God as the giver, so is there a similar lesson when we lose something. (In the storehouse of traditional language there are many pious expressions and phrases like that of Job, which serve to remind us regularly, in the specific situations where their use is called for, of God.)

Just as when we have some pleasure or when some good comes to us we bless God, we must also recognize His hand when something adverse happens. Our response should be to turn to Him, knowing that this comes from Him, in love, for our good. So we should also receive it in love, and repent and pray that it be an atonement for our sins.[9] Since our day is as full of mishaps and reverses as it is of good, such a practice will, equally with blessings for good, direct us to an unceasing remembrance of God.

In the words of Reb Arele Roth:

> Just as we are to give thanks to God even when afflictions come upon us, God save us from them, so, of course, are we to have this awareness and give thanks for each and every kindness that comes to us from God, blessed be He. . . . And the author of *Yesod v'Shoresh ha-Avodah* [Rabbi Alexander Ziskind] was especially immersed in this service of God—of giving thanks to God, which is the sign of our awareness of His continuous and full providence over us. This *tzaddik* would give thanks to God for even the smallest things that God did for him. For example, if a glass dropped and did not break, he thanked God for His kindness, or if he had to pass under an unsteady wall—or did so without realizing it and then saw it—and it did not fall on him, he thanked God for His kindness. This service of his was indeed great and awesome as attested to by our holy master, the Seer of Lublin, who said that it was revealed to him from heaven that this practice of this *tzaddik*, and his great and holy simplicity, was very precious in the eyes of God. For he would always be aware to have complete faith in God's Divine providence in all his affairs and doings.
>
> This was also the service of Joseph the Tzaddik, as it says, "And his master saw that God was with him." [Genesis 39:3] This is explained in *Midrash Tanhuma*: "Was then the wicked Potiphar actually able to see God, as it says that he 'saw that God was with him?' What does it mean when it says 'that God was with him?' It means that the name of God never left Joseph's mouth. When he entered his master's presence to serve him, he whispered a prayer: 'Master of the World! You are the only one whom I put my trust in; You are the only one on whom I rely. Let me find grace and favor in Your eyes, and in the eyes of all who see me, and in the eyes of Potiphar my master.'" . . . Joseph the Tzaddik would pray to God about everything that he needed, big or small, and he would give thanks to God for everything that happened, big or small—and the name of God never ceased from his lips, but was in his mouth continually. (*Shomer Emunim*, p. 135)

Of course, the teaching of the rabbis about Joseph or any other biblical hero reflects their own ways and is intended as a lesson for us and our practice.

Just as we are to be reminded of God by the blessings offered for enjoyments, so are we brought to remembrance by the prayers we make for our needs.

Hear this teaching of Rabbi Nachman of Bratzlav (reported by his disciple Rabbi Natan):

> The Rebbe once spoke to one of his disciples about clothing. He said, "You must pray for everything. If your garment is torn and must be replaced, pray to God for a new one. Do this for everything. Make it a habit to pray for all your needs, large or small. Your main prayers should be for fundamentals, that God help you in your devotion, that you be worthy of coming close to Him. Still, you should also pray even for trivial things. God may give food and clothing and everything else you need even though you do not ask for them. But then you are like an animal. God gives every living thing its bread without being asked. He can also give it to you that way. But if you do not draw your life through prayer, then it is like that of a beast. For a *man* must draw all necessities of life from God only through prayer."
>
> Once [continues Rabbi Natan] I had a slight need for some insignificant thing. When I mentioned it to the Rebbe, he said, "Pray to God for it." I was quite astonished to learn that I must even pray to God for such trivial things, especially in a case like this, where it was not even a necessity. Seeing my surprise, the Rebbe asked me, "Is it beneath your dignity to pray to God for a minor thing like this?"
>
> . . . The main lesson is that you must pray for everything, even the most trivial things (*Rabbi Nachman's Wisdom*, p. 367, *Sichos HaRan* #233)

> The moment it occurs to you that you need anything, great or small, ask God that He bring it to you, and only afterwards look for a means of getting the thing—and not the other way around. (*Alpha Beta* of Rabbi Tzvi Hirsh, Tzorech *Hanhagot Tzaddikim* [III], vol. 1, p. 381, #55)

When we pray for everything we need, even the smallest things, we will come to the palpable realization that everything we need comes from God.

One of the main ways to remember God is of course by continual immersion in the study of the holy Torah, for the Torah is all about His doings in the world, and about His people, His servants, and those who love Him.

The great hasidic *rebbe*, Rabbi Simha Bunim of Pshischa, said though, that at times when you cannot study Torah, because of the difficulties of working for a livelihood, for instance, a good way to remain in God-consciousness is by spontaneous prayer for your needs:

> Accustom yourself to pray and ask God for everything, big or small. Do not think that you have to be enclothed in a *tallit* and *tefillin* and off in a quiet place to pray. No, but in any place you are, even in the middle of the noisy marketplace, as long as you first see that the place is clean and fit for prayer . . . turn to God in prayer, and certainly He who hears the prayer of every mouth will fulfill your desire. And by this means you will be in continual God-consciousness . . . through this continual prayer. (*Hedvat Simha*, p. 64)

We can see from these quotes that through prayer for our needs, and thanks for their fulfillment, we will be engaged throughout the day in a running conversation with our Father in Heaven.

As in the previous quote from *Shomer Emunim*, Joseph "would pray to God about everything that he needed, big or small, and he would give thanks to God for everything that happened—big or small—and [as a result] the name of God never ceased from his lips, but was in his mouth continually."

What lies behind these teachings about blessings and spontaneous prayers of petition and thanks is the goal of coming to recognize our complete dependence on God for everything. When we also place our full trust in the goodness of our Father in Heaven, we will know ourselves as His children in actual experience, and feel His presence and His closeness always.[10]

In a similar way, we should recognize our dependence on our Father in Heaven even when it comes to our own activities, and we should accustom ourselves to remember God regularly by turning to Him in prayer at all times to give us direction.

> You should continually pray that God direct you, even though you may be full of the Torah's wisdom, for you are still able to stumble in your performance and fulfillment. (*Darkei Tzedek*, p. 19)
>
> A person should accustom himself to say this prayer every hour and every minute: "Master of the World! You are the One who helps

> those who come to be purified. Help me, then, that Your *mitzvot* not be hidden from my eyes." (Rabbi David of Lida, *Hanhagot Tzaddikim* [III], vol. 2, p. 129, #36)

We should pray that God make known to us His will, and guide us in our actions that they be done according to His will. We should also pray that what we do is successful, for nothing can succeed without His help.

> Make an effort to develop the habit of praying to God at all times about each and every thing—*about every action of yours* and about everything that happens to you. Also praise and thank Him each time for all the goodness and kindness He does for you at every moment. (Rabbi Shmuel Tefillinsky, *Hanhagot Tzaddikim* [III], vol. 2, p. 811) (Italics mine)

REMEMBER HIM BY DOING EVERYTHING IN HIS NAME AND BY STATED INTENTIONS

The ideal of always placing God before you should be manifested in thought, speech, and deed. One should constantly have God and His name in remembrance. Your thoughts should always be returning to Him. You should always have His name on your tongue. All your acts should be done in His name.

Of course, acting in the name of God means, first and foremost, that everything we do should be in the service of God. But the *Zohar* adds to this meaning the dimension of speech.

> All the actions of a man should be done for the sake of the Holy Name. And what does this mean, "for the sake of the Holy Name?" It means to mention with your mouth [through a blessing, invocation, stated intention, etc.] the Holy Name in connection with everything that you do. (*Zohar*, Ki Tazria, p. 91)

Kitzur Shnei Luchot ha-Brit (p. 20) discusses this saying from the *Zohar* and explains how we should always say "for everything we do—'God willing,' or 'With God's help,' or 'I am doing this for God.'"*

Let us consider this last suggestion more closely, that you should say that you are doing each act for God.

We have said something about blessings over enjoyments and benefits, and how we should learn from the prescribed blessings to improvise our own blessings throughout the day, to express our thanks for God's goodness. There are also the many blessings that have been ordained to be said not for passive enjoyments, but when we are active and do various *mitzvot*, like before Torah study, before lighting Sabbath candles, or putting on *tefillin*. Here, too, we should expand this practice, for as we said earlier, the hasid turns everything he does into *mitzvot*. And one way to accomplish this is by means of spoken intentions. By verbalizing the intention before each act, and explicitly expressing its purpose in the service of God, we bring that intention to a greater degree of concentration and intensity, and keep God's name on our lips and in our remembrance.

> It is said in the holy books that the early hasidim would express their *kavvanah* verbally [before the act]. (Rabbi Rafael of Bershad, *Pe'er l'Yesharim*, p. 15a, #157)

These stated intentions can be general or specific. For example, a general one to be used before every act would be "I am doing this for God," or "I am doing this to give pleasure to my Father in Heaven." A specific stated intention would be to say before eating, "I am eating so that my body will be healthy and strong to serve God." Often the two kinds, general and specific, can be combined and used together.[12]

REMEMBRANCE IN THE MIND ALONE; MEDITATION

Just as there are many ways to remember God through the use of speech, so are there numerous ways to remember Him through meditation and mental activity alone. Some of them have already been discussed. Here are further suggestions:

> You should not allow your mind to be diverted from God for even a split second, for even the blink of an eye. The *tzaddikim* . . . who serve God in their hearts and minds . . . are able to serve Him unceasingly, at all times, through the remembrance of His glorious name. Thus, they can serve Him mentally even without any action.
>
> For example, whatever joy comes to a *tzaddik*, he can turn it into a holy joy—if a son is born to him, he will be happy and rejoice that he can raise him up to be a servant of God, that he, too, should be added to the number of those who serve God, blessed be He. If he

> or a relative becomes rich, he will be happy and rejoice that with this money he can do more *mitzvot* [such as charity]. . . .
> Therefore you should remember your love and fear of God always, so that your mind not be diverted from Him for even one minute, and at every moment you should imagine that you are standing before Him to serve Him. (*Beit Middot*, p. 57)

Rabbi Hayim Heikel of Amdur:

> You should see that every day, in your mind [through meditation], you attach yourself to God, just you and Him, and draw onto yourself awe and reverence for Him in light of His awesome greatness. Do this until you are so accustomed to be together with Him and in His presence that even when you speak with another person in conversation you will not forget God. (*Hanhagot Tzaddikim*, p. 43)

Remembering God even during conversation with others is difficult to attain and is always recognized as a very high level.

PRAY FOR REMEMBRANCE

Even with all the spiritual practices in the world and all our own efforts, we always need God's help to succeed in anything, and certainly to succeed in remembering Him. So we should always pray to Him: "My Father in Heaven, let me not forget You for one minute or for one second. Let me forget everything else, but let me not forget You!"

BE HAPPY WHEN YOU REMEMBER AND SAD THAT YOU FORGOT; STRUGGLE AND PERSEVERANCE; RELIANCE ON GOD

Another way to cultivate remembrance of God in ourselves is by rejoicing when we remember Him, and by feeling anxiety that until then we forgot Him.

> It is a main pillar of religious practice that you should see to it that when you remember God you arouse yourself to a passionate

> enthusiasm and joy, and think to yourself, "Isn't this so good that I have remembered God—for I know that I have no life-energy but that which comes from Him." Be like a person who has just found something valuable, who has just lost some great treasure and then found it again—how great is his happiness. So should you rejoice when you remember God, because you know that this remembrance leads you to good in this world and the next. And you should also be sad and feel unhappiness that you forgot God until now, and should pray, concerning the future, that you not forget Him again. (*Seder ha-Yom ha-Katzar*, p. 5)

You should also give thanks to God when you remember Him. For no one remembers God if God has not remembered him first.

Arouse yourself to feel disturbed and grieved when your *d'vekut* is interrupted; sigh and groan and speak words of distress to God. For when love is such that separation produces anguish, you will cleave to Him all the more strongly, and the mind will be prevented from forgetfulness by the distress it causes.[13]

Rabbi Shneur Zalman of Ladi:

> You should remember God, blessed be He, always, as it says, "I have placed the Lord before me always." The Besht taught, if you forget Him for even a moment consider it a sin, and this will spur you not to forget. Happy is such a one. (*Kitvei Kodesh*, p. 24)

> Once, when the holy Rabbi Meir of Kretchnif, the memory of a *tzaddik* for a blessing for the life of the World to Come, was giving instruction to his children, he said to them, "My children, I can tell you that when I was young, if I ever forgot God, blessed be He, for a single minute—I cannot say so for a second, because it is just a second—but I never forgot God, blessed be He, for a minute without my whole body being shaken." He continued, "I can tell you that this is all a matter of habit. And if you accustom yourself to this, you can converse with someone about everything under the sun, but you will not forget Him for the briefest moment." (*Raza d'Uvda*, Sh'ar ha-Otiyot, p. 20, #5)

The Seer of Lublin was on a level where his anguish at forgetting God for the briefest moment was heartfelt. He once said:

> If a man forgets to cleave to God for one second of the 3,600 seconds in an hour, it would be better if he remained like a body without a soul, and be called dead. (*Niflaot ha-Rebbe*, p. 55, #130)

And this story is told:

> The Holy Jew, of blessed memory, once came to his master, the holy Rabbi of Lublin, of blessed memory, and found him disturbed and sighing deeply. When the Holy Jew asked why he was sighing so, the *rebbe* told him that he had transgressed the prohibition of "Guard yourself well, lest you forget the Lord your God"—for he had forgotten God for a moment. But the Holy Jew, of blessed memory, comforted his *rebbe* with the teaching of the *halacha*—that if a farmer left behind in the field a large measure of grain, a whole omer, it is not considered as if he had forgotten it [in which case it could be taken by the poor], even though it did pass from his mind momentarily. For, it is so important to him that he is sure to remember it afterwards.[14] "So too here," he told the *rebbe*, "it is not a transgression of the prohibition not to forget—for [He is so important to you that even if you forget momentarily] you are sure to remember God soon." Hearing this, the *rebbe* was relieved. (*Seder ha-Yom ha-Katzar*, p. 11)

It had been the Seer of Lublin himself who, when he was a disciple of Rabbi Shmelke of Nikolsburg, had served his master, at his request, by sitting by him as he studied Torah, to remind him, lest, through his intense concentration, he momentarily forget God. The story goes that the single time he thought his *rebbe* might need his reminder, he was told before he could give it that the *rebbe* had reminded himself.

Though the goal is to have continual remembrance of God, there will be times when that is beyond your ability. But if each time after falling from your *d'vekut* you turn again to God with renewed determination, your perseverance in the struggle itself provides an inner continuity—like a stream that, though it occasionally goes underground, is still flowing and unbroken. That is the meaning of the verse, "A *tzaddik* may fall seven times, but after each fall he will get up again" (Proverbs 24:16). Though he stumbles and falls many times, he is still called a *tzaddik*.[15]

There is a lesson in our failure to maintain *d'vekut*, and this is something to be called to mind when we have fallen from our spiritual level—that we cannot stay close to God by our own powers. We need Him to keep us close. We should, then, turn to our Father in Heaven at that moment in prayer, asking Him to have mercy on us and to restore us close to Him.

We should be aware that even our own efforts are dependent on God. The goal is to be conscious that God is acting in everything we do, and have full reliance on Him. When a child walks holding his father's hand he can still slip and, losing his grip, fall; but when his father holds *his* hand, then he can no longer fall.

Rabbi Tzadok ha-Cohen of Lublin:

> It is impossible for a person to remain on one level in *d'vekut*, as by rights he should. About this is it said: "For though he falls, he will not completely fall, because God holds his hand." (Psalm 37:24) (*Tzidkat ha-Tzaddik*, #237)

It also says: "For I am always with You, for You have grasped my right hand" (Psalm 73:23). Thus, we should join our own efforts at *d'vekut* with a recognition that we depend on Him—and pray for His support.

3

Ways in Attainment

ALTERNATE YOUR PRACTICES

To attain continuous God–consciousness, it is a good general principle to alternate your religious practices, engaging in Torah study and prayer, meditation and religious singing, synagogue attendance, the work of charity, and so on. Concentrating on one thing too much will lead to fatigue and boredom. If a person is required to do only one form of work, he becomes tired of it and will have to cease working and take a rest by being idle. But if one kind of work is replaced by another, he can continue working for a much longer time.[1] A good way, then, to keep interest in religious practice is to provide sufficient variety—for that itself constitutes a sort of rest. So you should alternate your religious practices. Sometimes it is best to follow your mood; leave some practices for a while and go to others that appeal to you. At a later time you will return to the ones you left with renewed delight. The purpose of all the traditional practices in all their variety is the same: to remember God and to have God-consciousness.

According to the Baal Shem Tov we will regularly experience periods of expanded and constricted consciousness (*gadlut* and *katnut*). As in what was quoted from Rabbi Tzadok ha-Cohen on p. 49: "It is impossible for a person to remain on one level in *d'vekut*." Another aspect of alternating spiritual practices is to be aware of what your spiritual level is at any particular time and to adjust your divine service appropriately. Choose a practice, then, that fits your mood and spiritual level.[2]

"KNOW HIM IN ALL YOUR WAYS"

This phrase from Proverbs (3:6) is commonly used to express another principle of Hasidism, which is that we should have God-consciousness in all of our doings, even those of a worldly nature, such as eating, working, and the like.

> You should fulfill "Know Him in all your ways" by doing everything for the sake of heaven, even what you do for your bodily needs. (Rabbi Moshe Teitelbaum, *Hanhagot Tzaddikim*, p. 48)

> You should fulfill that which the Sages, their memory for a blessing, said: "What is the smallest section of the Torah from which all its main principles can be derived?—'Know Him in all your ways'" (Proverbs 3:6) [Berachot 63a]. In other words, your eating and drinking, your sleep and sexual intercourse should all be only what is necessary for the service of God, blessed be He—as is explained in the *Shulchan Aruch*, Orach Hayim, section 231. (Rabbi Aaron of Karlin, *Hanhagot Tzaddikim*, p. 3)

> When a person really wants to cleave to God, blessed be He, he has to see that he not cease from his *d'vekut* for even a minute. And if when he takes care of his physical needs, such as eating and drinking, sexual intercourse, etc., he does so without making of them a service of the Creator, blessed be He, then he will not be able to achieve the *d'vekut* that he should [even when performing religious service of Torah, prayer, etc.]. So he should see that he nullifies the physical before the spiritual, and then even his physical body will become on fire to serve Him, and all his bodily doings will all be as service of God, blessed be He. Then he will be able to be attached to God continuously. (*M'vaser Tzedek*, p. 17, quoted in *Avodah u'Moreh Derech*, chap. 17, p. 30)

The great value of hasidic *hanhagot* in the service of God is that they instruct us in how to attain God-consciousness in each area of life, when waking and going to sleep, when eating or having sex, when conversing with other people, or when engaging in work. While there are *hanhagot* appropriate for each time and place and activity, there are also general teachings that can guide us in regard to what we do for our bodily needs.

One principle is that while occupied in worldly activity, while part of our mind is on whatever we are doing, the other and larger part should be fixed on God.

Rabbi Elimelech of Lizensk:

> When a *tzaddik* lowers himself from his *d'vekut* to engage in something material . . . he should not separate himself altogether from his *d'vekut*—just a little bit. Let four fifths of his mind remain in holiness and *d'vekut*, while he uses one fifth for the worldly involvement. And even that one fifth he should elevate again, bringing it back into holiness, by relating to the spiritual aspect of the material involvement, that is, by lifting up the holy spark.[3] (*Noam Elimelech,* Vayigash, p. 22a)

Elsewhere he says:

> When you have some work to do, do not put all your mind to it, but just involve yourself in it by the way, and let the work be done of its own. (*Noam Elimelech,* Emor, p. 56b)

Describing our father Jacob (as a paradigm of the *tzaddik*), he says:

> The essence of our father Jacob's divine service was in his involvement in doing unifications [activities or meditations which join the Upper with the Lower world, the spiritual with the material], and in *d'vekut* . . . and although he had to think about the affairs of his household and his wealth, he would not look into them deeply, with the major part of his mind, but would just give them a superficial attention, to understand the thing and no more. (*Noam Elimelech,* Vayishlach, p. 16a)

To explain what Rabbi Elimelech is suggesting we can consider what a person does when driving a car. He can turn the radio channel with one hand, adjust the speed with his foot, and, at the same time, carry on a conversation with a friend in the front seat; but all the while, his attention is firmly fixed on the road to see that he stays in his lane, and his second hand is on the wheel to steer the car. That is a matter of life and death. So can you do the things you have to do in the world while the greater part of your attention is fastened on God.

If our love for God is strong we will not forget Him even at times when we are not engaged in specifically religious practices. The great hasidic *rebbe*, Rabbi Moshe Leib of Sassov, put it this way:

> A great principle in serving God is expressed well in a concise but valuable parable. If a person is holding a precious stone in his hand, a jewel the size of an egg, and worth so many thousands of dollars that it is almost priceless—if he is occupied for a while with some other work, he certainly will not forget about that jewel or diamond—because whatever work he is doing will not have even a small part of the value of the diamond.
>
> But if he is holding in his hand something of little value like an egg, then, if he begins to do some work for his business, before long he will forget about the egg he is holding, put it down somewhere without thinking, and lose it.
>
> So if a person values the fear of heaven like that precious stone . . . then even if he becomes involved in necessary work, business, or other things not directly religious, he will not forget nor will he ever cease from his fear of God.
>
> Conversely, with someone who hardly values the fear of God at all, even when he is involved in religious practices such as Torah and prayer, thoughts about his business and other doings will enter his mind, because that is what is most important to him. . . . The desires of this world are so dear to him that they are present in his mind always, and do not stop even when he is serving God, or praying. (*Likkutei Rabbi Moshe Leib*, p. 9)

> Rabbi Nachman Kossover, a disciple of the Baal Shem Tov, was speaking to some hasidim who he saw were failing to fulfill "I have placed the Lord before me always" when they were engaged in their livelihood, in commerce, and business dealings. They asked him how it was possible to think of God at that time. He answered that just as they were well able to think of their business dealings while they were supposed to be praying, so could they fulfill "I have placed the Lord before me always" when they were engaged in business. (*Keter Shem Tov*, p. 91)

The way of service during work and worldly activities should be in the manner hinted at in the verse about the building of the Second Temple, where the builders were threatened with enemy attacks. "They who built the wall, and they who bore burdens, loaded themselves in such a way that with one of his hands each labored in the work, and with the other hand he held a weapon."[4] (Nehemiah 4:11) In other words, the lesson here is that while you work, you are to be alert and have your mind directed to God at the same time.

Rabbi Simha Bunim of Pshischa said that you should labor with your hands alone

> but are not to put your thoughts into the work you are doing with your hands. Rather you should think, during the time of your work, good thoughts directed to God. (*Siah Sarfei Kodesh*, I, p. 54, #254)

Where this teaching is recorded, the compiler reports that he once heard something similar in the name of Rabbi Menachem Mendel of Kotzk (the great disciple of Rabbi Simha Bunim), who said:

> The hand should do what it has to do, and the head should be in heaven. . . . A person should work for his livelihood with his hands alone, but his head and mind should be constantly in *d'vekut*, clinging to God, blessed be He. And the greatness of such a person is that by this he ties together and unites this world and the World to Come. (*Siah Sarfei Kodesh*, I, p. 54, #254)

The rabbis say about Hanoch [Enoch] (Genesis 5:24) that:

> Hanoch was a shoemaker who would sew together the uppers and lowers of the shoes. And with each and every stitch he would say, "Blessed is His glorious kingdom forever and ever!"*[5] . . . and he was able to bind together the Upper and Lower Worlds. (*Hedvat Simha*,[6] p. 57)

(Upper and Lower Worlds [as in this quote], the World to Come and this world [as in the preceding quote], heaven and earth, are all essentially parallel expressions, meaning the spiritual and the material.)

Note well that Hanoch, an ideal type of Jewish mystic, repeats this holy sentence (which ordinarily follows the saying of the *Sh'ma*) over and over while working with his hands. Repeating a holy sentence can be an important spiritual practice not only while working, but at other times as well. Rabbi Yaakov Koppel Hasid would say continually, while working, "I have placed the Lord before me always."

According to the *Zohar* (1:18b), the *Sh'ma* represents the "higher unification"; the "Blessed is His glorious kingdom, etc.," repeated by Hanoch, is the "lower unification." In the higher unification, the world's reality is nullified and disappears in God, as the light of the sun in the sun. It is the realization that there is nothing but God: the Lord is One. In the lower unification, the world is seen to be infused with Godliness. The *Zohar* says that this lower unification is represented by the verses: "I saw the Lord" (Isaiah 6:1), "And the glory of the Lord appeared" (Numbers 14:10, 17:7), "So was the appearance of the brightness round about; this was the appearance of the likeness of the glory of the Lord" (Ezekiel 1:28). In other words, Hanoch, while working sewing the shoes, was meditating on the vision of God.

Just as God–vision can be practiced, as we described above, so can you practice having God–consciousness while you are involved in worldly activities. The Baal Shem Tov taught that one way to do this is that at times when you do not need to engage in such things, you do so with the express purpose of practicing maintaining God–consciousness throughout. He said:

> In order to attain to God–consciousness, though the materiality of the body acts as a dividing screen separating you from Him, you should first attach your mind to God, and then get something needed for your house, or do something, or converse with someone about something worldly, all the while you are maintaining that God–consciousness. The point is to practice holding on to God–consciousness by doing this even when there is no real need. Its purpose is to accustom yourself so that when you do need to act or speak in connection with worldly matters you will be able to have God–consciousness at the very same time. This is an important principle. (*Tzavaat ha-Ribash*, pp. 11–12)

It is difficult to achieve a high state of God–consciousness when engaged in worldly activities whose very nature is such that they tend to draw us away from God. But God–consciousness can be maintained during those times, even if on a lower level, and then, when you return to purely religious practices, the continuity you have achieved will help you to return to a high level. The Besht said that:

> When a man is occupied in prayer and Torah study . . . certainly he should have a strong *d'vekut*; but even at other times, and throughout the day, he should fulfill "I have placed the Lord before me always" and should have at least some *d'vekut*. The parable for this is that it is like a candle or some burning coals—as long as there is even a spark present it can still be blown up subsequently into a raging flame as at the first; but if not even a small spark remains, then you have to start all over again and bring new fire. (*Tzavaat ha-Ribash* p. 19; cf. p. 48)

The Baal Shem Tov also taught that the rest we have during times of worldly involvement helps us when we return to purely spiritual activities. He said:

> The spiritual principle that "the life-force ebbs and flows" [that there will always be times of expanded and lowered consciousness] means that when you cease the direct service of God [purely religious practices], while working for a living, eating, and so on, your soul takes a rest and your mind is reinvigorated to return afterwards to the direct service of God. This is the meaning of "the life-force ebbs and flows." (*Tzavaat ha-Ribash*, p. 93)

On the higher rungs of spiritual attainment, though, there is no rest for the *tzaddikim*, even when engaged in worldly activities—or, at most, their rest is only relative. Their service of God is continuous, not only when they work and eat, but for some, even when they sleep. Nevertheless, even they cannot remain on one level, and they, too, will have their ups and downs, times of expanded and lowered consciousness.

The problem inherent in these unavoidable periods of rest or lowered consciousness, from which no one is exempt, is that once one's connection with God and God-consciousness is lessened, the mind will continue naturally to proceed that way through inertia—like a ball falling down the stairs. It is essential, therefore, to be able to stop the slide.

Rabbi Mendel of Ber (a disciple of the Baal Shem Tov) taught that:

> Before you go down into a pit, be sure to have a ladder ready to get out. (*Mishnat Hasidim*, p. 320, #36)

So before you engage in worldly activities that tend to lessen your *d'vekut*, prepare beforehand how to reestablish your spiritual level afterwards.

Rabbi Yehiel Michal of Zlotchov gave a teaching in which he explained that when we reach a certain level of holiness (a "holy place") we must take care that during necessary periods of rest we do not fall back. He said:

> It is written, "Who shall *ascend* into the *mountain* of the Lord? And who shall *stand in His holy place*?" (Psalm 24:3). [This verse is understood as meaning: Who shall ascend in holiness and reach the goal?—the one who can stand in place without slipping back and descending from the level in holiness which he has already

> reached.] This means that when you are in the middle of your ascent up His holy mountain and stop to rest, be careful that you remain in your place in holiness and do not slide back down. It is like a man who rides up a mountain in his carriage. When he is halfway up the horses are tired and he must stop, unharness them, and give them a rest. Now, whoever has no sense, at this point will let the carriage roll back down to where he started. But he who has sense will take a stone and put it under the wheel while the carriage is standing. Then he will be able to reach the top. The man who does not fall when he is forced to interrupt his service, but knows how to pause, will get to the top of the mountain of the Lord. (*Yeshuot Malko*, p. 81)

What shall this "stone" be? It can be that when you begin something which, though innocent enough, threatens to separate you from God and leads to forgetfulness—determine before you begin that at a certain point, or at the end, you will do such-and-such religious act: say a psalm, or whatever. You can also make a vow to this effect.

In another sense the stone can be understood to be the determination to maintain at least some *d'vekut* during times of working for a living, eating, and so on. For example, the Peasetzna Rebbe told his disciples that during the time of work they should occasionally call out something like: "God! I am in a place now dangerous to my remembrance of You. Help me, that I not forget You!" Rabbi Elimelech of Lizensk taught that during eating one should, for similar reasons, call out to God from time to time, "Father, Father!" Of course, there are many other ways to "set a stone under the wheels of the carriage," so if you cannot rise in spirituality, you at least will not fall down.

There are various ways in which our work and our activities concerning our bodily needs can be absorbed into holiness. First, if we work, eat, and sleep, etc. only when we have to, and in order to be able to continue our religious practice, those activities become a part of that practice.

> For if someone eats and sleeps just for the purpose of having strength for Torah study and for the service of God, then it is all considered as preparation [for that service]. (*Ha-Rebbe Reb Tzvi Elimelech mi-Dinov*, vol. 1, p. 212)

Second, we must, in every case, see that these material activities are surrounded, before and after, by holy doings and spiritual practices, and also that when we finish doing something connected with our bodily needs, we *rush* back to some religious activity as soon as possible—for the sign of which side is dominant is shown in how quickly or slowly we move from one to the other. The two spheres of the material and the spiritual are in constant competition. If, then, we limit our material activities to the minimum, only do them when necessary and as a preparation for spiritual things, and if we surround them with spiritual doings, then they will become purified and will be absorbed into the spiritual sphere and into holiness.[9]

TRANSITIONS

A typical and recurring obstacle to *d'vekut* is when we make a transition from one activity to another, or from one place to another. When you are in one place or doing one sort of activity you may have established *d'vekut*, but when you change from one activity or place to another you can easily lose God-consciousness as you make the transition.

For example, with regard to change of place—in your house you may be sitting studying Torah with *d'vekut*, but when you walk out onto the street, you lose it. One function of the *mezuzah* is to regulate this transition from house to street, street to house, or even from room to room. By kissing the *mezuzah* and saying a brief prayer, you are reminded of God as you make the transition. Conversely, there is an additional positive side to this, for if you have become separated from God-consciousness, the reminder of the *mezuzah* as you pass and kiss it can bring you back.

> Every time you go in and out, kiss the *mezuzah* so that you remember God. (*Derech Hayim*, 6–79)

One need not restrict the prayer said when kissing the *mezuzah* to places where there are *mezuzot* (for many houses and gates will have none). Using the suggestion of the tradition and expanding it, you can say the brief prayer at any movement from place to place—bus to street, street to store, and so on. This is one form of such a prayer: "The Lord is my guardian, the Lord is the shade at my right hand. The Lord will guard my going out and my coming in, now and forever." These words of trust will turn your mind to God and also remind you that God is with you and guards you at all times.

Another kind of transition is when going from one activity to another. For that you can develop the habit of saying: "Let me know Him in all my ways" or, "Let all my actions be for the sake of heaven." When you say these words, reflect on what you are about to do (and whether or not to proceed) and how you can maintain your God–consciousness during the activity.

Still another kind of transition that can be used as a reminder for *d'vekut* occurs when you change posture. When getting up, sitting, or lying down say, "You know my sitting down and my rising up." (Psalms 139:2, 3)[10]

PRAY FOR *D'VEKUT*

We should pray to God often that we never forget Him, and that we attain more and more love for Him. "My Father in Heaven, help me to be aware of Your presence and to think of You always, without forgetting You for one minute. Let Your love and fear be always in my heart." Though it is good to say such prayers aloud, according to Rabbi Nachman of Horodenka:

> When you pray to be able to cleave to God . . . it is sufficient that this prayer be made mentally alone. (*Toldot Yaakov Yosef*, Etchanan)

When you feel reluctant to think of God or to do other religious activities, to pray or study Torah, you can reflect on that itself. "My Father in Heaven, I have a most serious disease: I have no taste for doing what will bring me close to You! Before this disease is fatal, help me!" Though there are many spiritual practices that depend on our own efforts, praying for devotion is different and is especially important, because no one can come close to God without being drawn close. In the end, all success depends on His help and goodness.

We are told about Rabbi Nachman of Bratzlav:

> The main way the Rebbe attained what he did was simply through prayer and supplication before God. He was very consistent in this. He would beg and plead in every way possible, asking that God

> have mercy and make him worthy of true devotion and closeness. (*The Praise of Rabbi Nachman*, p. 10, *Shevachey HaRan*, #10)

Rabbi Nachman's great disciple and biographer, Rabbi Natan of Nemirov, draws this lesson from the Rebbe's life:

> The main thing is prayer. Accustom yourself to beg and plead before God. Speak to Him in any language you understand—this is especially important. Beg Him to open your eyes. Ask Him to help you along the path of devotion. Plead that you be worthy of drawing close to Him. (*The Praise of Rabbi Nachman*, p. 30, *Shevachey HaRan* #27)

DO NOT INTERRUPT HOLY ACTIVITY, INTERRUPT WORLDLY ACTIVITY

It is a general principle in the pursuit of continuous *d'vekut* to refrain from interrupting holy activities. For example, religious people will set themselves a rule not to interrupt their fixed session of Torah study once begun. Similarly, prayers should not be interrupted except in cases of urgent necessity.

> Do not interrupt your Torah study or your praying with worldly talk. (*Derech Hayim*, 1-62)

Thus, the holy is set above the worldly and cannot be interrupted by it. This is an assertion of what is central and what is secondary. And most important, the continuity of the holy activity is protected.[11]

Holy activities are then not to be interrupted. Conversely, it is a general principle to interrupt worldly activities, those activities that, in themselves, turn one's attention away from God. Eating is to be interrupted, sleep is to be interrupted, and so on.

> When eating and drinking, between every few swallows, interrupt yourself for at least a moment . . . to compose yourself and bring to awareness the [spiritual] purpose of your action. . . . And you should do similarly for all bodily activities involving enjoyment. (Rabbi Yehezkiyahu Greenwald of Pupa, *Hanhagot Tzaddikim* [III], vol. 2, p. 762, #16)

> The hasidic *rebbe*, [Rabbi Abraham David of Butchatch] said about the holy Rabbi Mendel of Premishlan [a disciple of the Baal

> Shem Tov], that the way he achieved his spiritual perfection was by means of such interruptions. He would interrupt himself in the midst of conversation and stop for a while to break his talk–lust; he would interrupt his vision [by turning away or closing his eyes while looking at something], and so on in many other things. (*Derech Tzaddikim*, p. 4, #21)

Beyond the negative interruption, it is often possible to "fill" that interruption with positive religious activity. For example, eating can be interrupted with Psalms, Torah, holy songs, and prayer.

The "holy interruption" disrupts the continuity and power of the worldly activity, and the successive interruptions of that activity make, as it were, bridges of God–consciousness throughout its duration. Thus, the continuity of *d'vekut* is established in the midst of the worldly activity.

When you do worldly things you do not want your soul to dive down and sink into the activity. As with eating—you do not want your soul to descend into the food. There is a hasidic story about Rabbi Yissachar Ber of Radoshitz, who before he became famous was so poor that he was often extremely hungry. Once when he entered his *sukkah* to eat a meal, a bowl of potatoes was brought in (the first real food he had seen for a while), and he began to eat with appetite and relish. Suddenly he came to himself and stopped eating. He said to himself,

> Berl, you are not sitting in the *sukkah* but in the bowl of potatoes![12] (*Sippurei Hasidim*, vol. 2, #117)

Conversely, in the performance of holy activity you do want single-minded concentration and God–consciousness so that the soul dives into what you are doing. Thus, the hasidic rabbis often speak of how, when you are praying and studying Torah, you should go right "into" the holy letters of what your eyes are on.

Even religious activities can, of course, be performed almost without any *d'vekut*. A person can be very involved in Torah study and forget about God. Learning how to maintain God–consciousness in prayer, Torah study, and so on, will be dealt with in the chapters of this book on each activity. In a sense, even religious activities often have to be interrupted for the purpose of re-establishing *d'vekut*. Thus, the Baal Shem Tov says about Torah study particularly:

> While studying Torah you should remind yourself again and again before Whom you are learning. For occasionally, while learning, you can become separated from God, and it is necessary to recollect yourself again and again. (*Tzavaat ha-Ribash*, p. 8)

Rabbi Shalom Shachna of Probitch:

> During prayers you should interrupt yourself and pause again and again, so as to strengthen yourself and arouse in yourself a burning and pure love and fear of God. . . . And also during Torah study, interrupt yourself and rest this way. (The Seder ha-Yom of R. Shalom Shachna of Probitch, in *D'vir Yaakov*, p. 8)

FOREIGN THOUGHTS

We are to infuse our worldly activities, as much as possible, with holy thoughts. During the time we are engaged in work, household matters, eating, etc., we should turn the greater part of our mind and attention to holiness. But when we are involved in religious practices such as prayer, Torah study, etc., which are in their nature holy and on a higher level, we are to go a step further and make every effort to purify them completely and absolutely, even from the slightest intrusion of any foreign thoughts of outside matters (and from all self-directed motives, too).

So in our preparations before religious practices, we are to separate ourselves from worldliness and outside concerns, and during the time of prayer, Torah, etc., we are to be alert to the entrance of foreign thoughts and stand ready to expel them.[13]

> There is a lower and simple fear of God, as is written about in the *Shulchan Aruch*, Orach Hayim, namely, not to *do* anything wrong, for you *know* that you are standing in the presence of the King of the Universe, the Holy One, blessed be He. However, the higher fear, the fear and awe of God because of His exaltedness, is that during the times of Torah study and prayer and when doing *mitzvot*, you do not even have any foreign *thought*, for you are in a state of intense *d'vekut* [and you do not just "know" that you are standing before God as with the lower fear, but you actually experience the Divine Presence]—as if the Light of the *Shechinah* is all around the personal space [four *amot*] which you have sanctified for yourself for prayer or Torah study. All your limbs will tremble and your

face will burn like a torch because of the greatness of your fear of God and your shame before Him. (*Or ha-Ganuz l'Tzaddikim*, p. 42)

PREPARATION FOR DIVINE SERVICE

In Hasidism the goal is that all spiritual practices be done with an awareness of the presence of God. For that reason there is an emphasis throughout on preparation beforehand, so that *mitzvot* are not done mechanically, but with inwardness, and free of foreign thoughts. Thus, there are periods of preparation for Torah study, for prayer, for *Shabbat*, for meals, and so on.

> The main thing is preparation, whether it is for a *mitzvah*, for Torah study, or for prayer. (Rabbi Yitzhak of Skvira, *Tzror ha-Hayim*, p. 61)
>
> It is an important principle to prepare for every *mitzvah*, for it is by the preparation that one attains to full and complete intentionality in doing the *mitzvah*. (Rabbi Moshe Greenwald of Chust, *Hanhagot Tzaddikim* [III], vol. 2, p. 698, #17)

One of the defining characteristics of early Hasidism was that, due to the great importance ascribed to reaching inwardness in prayer through preparation, many hasidim would delay beginning their prayers beyond the time limit set for them in the *Shulchan Aruch*. This aroused the ire of the *misnagdim* (the opponents of Hasidism) and it was one of their main complaints against the hasidim. The variations of the hasidic response were many, but what it boiled down to was their belief that inwardness was so important that such a delay was justified. The hasidic stories, which revolve around the theme of this argument, are innumerable.

> One of the main innovations of the Holy Jew was his emphasis on inwardness. So, for example, he would sometimes delay praying after the prescribed time until he reached [by his preparations] a state of expanded consciousness, and his mind and soul were truly ready for prayer in an exalted *d'vekut*. (*Ha-Rebbe Reb Tzvi Elimelech mi-Dinov*, vol. 2, p. 476)

Recognition of the high value placed on such preparation will not only give you correct understanding of hasidic practices, but will enable you to develop your own ways spiritually.

A CONTINUOUS STREAM OF HOLY THOUGHTS, MEDITATION

Our spiritual activity operates on the three levels of thought, speech, and action. But whereas sometimes we speak and act and sometimes we do not, activity in the mental sphere is always going on.

An important aspect of religious practice, then, is to maintain in our minds a steady stream of holy thoughts. This will, in fact, be the underpinning of holiness in speech and action.

Traditionally, more often than not, this has meant a concentration on Torah thoughts and continual Torah study (from a book or by repetition of memorized text) at every moment possible. Thus, cessation of Torah learning during any time when you are able to study is considered a transgression in itself: *bitul Torah*, Torah neglect.

This is not, however, emphasized quite this way in Hasidism. Thus, in hasidic circles there can be a story like this:

> The grandson of the Baal Shem Tov, Rabbi Moshe Hayim Ephraim of Sudilkov, was, after his marriage, a great *matmid* [one who studies Torah constantly], and most of his learning was in *Gemara* with Rashi's commentary and *Tosafot*. He had deviated somewhat from the hasidic way [which not only did not emphasize continual Torah learning, but did not concentrate so heavily on *Gemara* and other legal studies].
>
> The Besht liked to take him on excursions every now and then, and this caused his grandson [in a typically *misnagid* way] anguish at having to cease from his Torah study. But once a guest came to them from some town or other, and the Besht asked him about a certain householder from that place. The guest answered with praise, saying that this person was a great *matmid*. The Besht then said, "I am very jealous of his ceaseless learning, but what can I do? I do not have time to learn for I have to serve God, blessed be His name."
>
> When the Besht's grandson heard these words, uttered in holiness and purity, they entered his heart, and he began to conduct himself in the hasidic way from that moment on.[14] (*Siftei Kodesh*, p. 85)

In the hasidic tradition there is not the exclusive concentration on Torah study; rather, the goal is the broader one of *d'vekut* in *all* activities of life. Along with Torah study there is also a frequently mentioned alternative for a continual mental activity in service of God—meditation. Rabbi Eleazar Azikri, a predecessor of this stream in Hasidism that emphasizes meditation, quotes the Ari as saying:

> [A meditation for the sake of achieving *d'vekut* is] seventy times more valuable for the soul than Torah study.[15] (*Sefer Haredim*, chap. 65)

For the Besht and those in his hasidic movement, *d'vekut* and an immediate awareness of the presence of God is what is most important. But while meditation and meditation-in-prayer lead directly to *d'vekut*, the Besht saw that Torah study indeed often produces a lessening of *d'vekut* in someone who has already reached a higher level. This resulted in a change in emphasis from Torah study to *d'vekut* meditation.

> It is a general principle in religious service not to study Torah overmuch. [For] if we will not pay adequate attention to holding onto *d'vekut* with God, blessed be He, and will learn a lot, then fear of God will be forgotten by us, God forbid. And fear of God is the main thing. . . . Therefore, we should decrease our Torah learning and spend much time in meditation on God's greatness, so as to come to love Him and to fear Him, and not to have too many thoughts in our minds, but just one [that all things that exist are filled with the Creator, blessed be He, and that everything that happens is from Divine providence]. (*Darkei Yesharim*, p. 3)

So when the Besht taught, "Happy is the man for whom not thinking of God for a moment is accounted as a sin"—that he is on such a level that he has no other sins but only has to struggle with his occasional, momentary failure to think of God—he was, in a sense, replacing "Torah neglect" with "*d'vekut*-meditation neglect."

We are often told in hasidic works to meditate continually on God and His "greatness."[16] Typically, this means a meditation on how God is the Creator of everything that is, and that all things are kept in existence every moment by His will alone.[17] God's presence is everywhere, for His Glory fills the earth and there is no place where He is not. He fills all worlds and surrounds all worlds.[18] Generally, this meditation on God's greatness is associated with, or includes, a related meditation on His goodness, for everything has been created from love, for the good of His creatures. His greatness arouses, then, our fear and awe, and His goodness arouses our love. The goal of all this is to experience the reality of His Presence, in *d'vekut*.

It is also possible to include in this kind of meditation the thought of God as our true Father, and our eternal relation to Him as His children.[19]

REPETITION OF A HOLY SENTENCE

Meditations for the sake of *d'vekut*, in their varieties, can also be supported by means of the senses, such as by picturing the name YHVH before your eyes, or by repeating a holy sentence (both discussed in Chapter 2). The continuity of the visual or aural support protects the meditation from distraction and keeps it on track.

Aside from its great benefits as a separate and important religious activity with special times devoted to its practice, the repetition of a holy sentence has the additional virtue that it can be done at almost any free moment. Furthermore, it has in this an advantage over continual Torah study, for there are times when one is fatigued or occupied in a way that makes it difficult to concentrate on Torah ideas, but the simple repetition of one sentence, phrase, or word is still relatively easy. A holy sentence can be repeated while you are working with your hands, washing dishes, walking, and so on. Hanoch, when he was sewing shoes, repeated "Blessed is His glorious kingdom for ever and ever," meditating on the reality of God's rule over everything in heaven and earth all the while. Since this simple practice is feasible in many situations where other more demanding religious practices are not, we are able to retain God-consciousness when it would otherwise be very difficult to do so. As a result, it adds greatly to the continuity of our *d'vekut* throughout the day.

Finally, another important aspect of the repeated sentence is that the repetition becomes a habit, and whenever you cease for some reason or other, the mind naturally goes back to it. So if you get diverted from God-consciousness, or are necessarily involved in worldly affairs, at a subsequent moment your mind will of itself turn back to the holy sentence and to God. It is like a compass. You can hold the needle for a while, but when you let go, it once again points to the north.

WITHIN AS WELL AS WITHOUT

The teaching of the Kabbalah and Hasidism is that God is within and without, that "He fills all worlds and surrounds all worlds," that "the whole earth is full of His glory [His *Shechinah*] and there is no place where He is not."

On the higher levels of mystical attainment we are to see God within and without and see His shining presence everywhere. The Peasetzna Rebbe says that:

> You should concentrate your mind fully, and picture how all the world and everything in it is all the Light of Godliness, and His glory fills the world. And I am standing in the midst of His Godliness.
>
> [The goal is to achieve the realization that:] You surround me and also fill my body and my spirit.[20] (*Hovat ha-Talmidim*, pp. 147, 52)

In Hasidism there is the outer meditation, discussed earlier, where we are to perceive that everything outside us is kept in existence by God and that everything that happens to us comes from God; we should attend to the spiritual aspect of every existing thing, the "holy spark" within it. So, too, is there an inner meditation, whereby we are to reflect continually on how our inner being is from God, for the soul, the holy spark within us, is a part of the *Shechinah*, and, as the traditional hasidic expression puts it, is "an actual part of God from Above" (*helek Elohah mima'al mamash*). All our soul powers, then, are also the stuff of hasidic meditation. One form of this is to meditate on our powers of thought, speech, and action. Another form concentrates on our emotion powers. We will discuss these two kinds of hasidic meditation in turn.

OUR LIFE-ENERGY FROM GOD

It is a traditional hasidic practice to engage in an extended inward-looking meditation on our own actions, speech, and thoughts, to attend to how all our life-energy, which is the source of these powers, is flowing to us from God.

The whole universe is moved by the one Divine Power that makes the sun shine and the rain fall, that makes our hearts beat and the blood run through our arteries and veins. God's will and power, the *Shechinah*, is active in nature and in us, and gives us the ability to move, to talk, and to think. When we understand more and more that this is so, we will see God everywhere, and His action in everything that happens—not only outside us, but within us. The more we understand this, the more our ego sense lessens, and we will not so easily think "I am doing this," or "I did that." If we work, for instance, with this ever-present God-consciousness, that it is God's will and power that does everything, our work will be a form of worship. That was the way that Hanoch worked, unifying the Upper and Lower Worlds (the spiritual and the material) as he sewed the shoes. The Rebbe of Moglenitza taught:

> When a man goes to do some business or trading, he piously says that God also should help him. From this it can be seen that he makes himself the main actor, and his thought is just that God should provide some aid. But this is complete foolishness, because the truth is that He is everything, and everything is from Him, blessed be He. Even the thought that you should go to do this or that business or trading or whatever else, is put into your mind by God. Your thinking and decision about whether you should or should not do something, whether you should or should not go someplace, is all from Him . . . for everything is under the direction and guidance of heaven. [*Mazkeret Shem ha-Gedolim*, p. 25n.]

We, of course, usually think that we are doing everything by our own will and desire. But if we are constantly aware that it is God's power that does everything, that consciousness will lead us to holiness in action. It is when we forget God that we also forget to do His will. The rabbis say that even when you are sinning it is God, in His humility and kindness, who gives you the power to do so and to do the opposite of what He wants of you. But when we are aware of how our life and existence comes to us from Above, and of this humility of the Creator of the whole universe, will we not be ashamed before Him? Will we still be able to bring ourselves to act contrary to His divine will? (See *Tomer Devorah*, chap. 1, beginning.)

We must learn to do only the will of God—as the rabbis teach: "Nullify your will before His will" (Avot 2:4)—until finally He alone directs us, as a charioteer his chariot. All the movements and doings of the Patriarchs, of Abraham, Isaac, and Jacob, of Elijah, and of all the holy *tzaddikim*, are directed by the holy spirit (the *Shechinah*)—for they reached the exalted level of being chariots of God.

But how can we imagine that God directs even our voluntary actions? There is a hasidic interpretation of Genesis 6:9, "And Noah walked with God," which helps to explain this.

> The movements of walking, as all others, are performed through the mediation of thought and intention which are a spark of the *Shechinah*, of Godliness—for the soul is a throne for the *Shechinah*. . . . And every movement a person makes is only accomplished through the divine life-energy which God gives. Noah, then, was so completely in a state of elevated God-consciousness that it seemed to him that all his movements were not of his own doing, but were done by God. (*Or ha-Ganuz l'Tzaddikim*, p. 13)

This description of Noah represents a hasidic ideal read back into the life of the biblical hero. Its lesson is that we should understand that God dwells within us and that, as the Rebbe of Moglenitza taught, even our thoughts, desires, and decisions are from Him, for they emanate from our divine soul, which is a part of God.

Hear these deep words of Rabbi Moshe Teitelbaum, words which undoubtedly reflect his own level. He talks about the typical hasidic meditation for *d'vekut*—the meditation on God's "greatness," that He is all, and everything is from Him:

> Through . . . meditating on God's greatness a person will come to see his own lowliness . . . for the more one knows of God the more is he in his own eyes nothing and nil. For he fully understands that there is no true reality other than He, blessed be He. And the one who is closer to God actually sees with his eyes that there is no reality in the world other than His will [which gives existence at every moment to all things]. So he considers himself nothing at all, for he knows that in him also there is nothing but His will that keeps him in existence. When he fully perceives this, that he does not live or feel or move the least bit except through His will, and when through his intense *d'vekut* he does not experience in his own being anything but the Supernal Will that keeps him in existence, then he will not make the least movement except that which is according to the Supernal Will. (*Tefillah l'Moshe*, quoted in *Ha-Gaon ha-Kadosh Baal Yismach Moshe*, p. 189)

It is the continuous flow of God's life-energy to us that allows us to move, speak, and think. Understanding this flow of life and energy from Above as an expression of God's love, we can resolve not only not to sin in the face of His kindness, but to return His love by dedicating that life and energy (in a return flow, so to speak) to Him and to His service.

OUR EMOTIONS

It is a common hasidic practice to pay attention to our feelings and emotions as a continuing meditation, and to raise them up and always direct them to God. For our emotions of love and fear, and so on, come to us from God and are given to us to be used in His service.

Thus, if we feel love for someone, we should connect that love in one way or another to God, to see, for example, that it is God who is the source bringing this beloved person and this joy to us. If we see that we have a desire, a love for something unworthy, for sex or possessions, beyond what is good, we can reflect on how our love should be for God and His service, and turn our love to Him. If we become afraid, we should realize that nothing can happen without God, nothing can harm us against His will, and we should fear only Him. If we are proud, we should understand that everything we are, all our abilities and talents are from God, and all glory belongs to Him. The only pride we should sometimes feel is pride that we are children and servants of God, and if we are, we should be inspired to rise to the high demands of His service. If we become angry, we can either turn that anger on our evil inclination and rebuke it, or we can turn the anger on ourselves with the thought, "How can I be angry and let all holiness flee from me?" Anger can also be pointed more directly to God if done carefully. If we become angry, we can say "God, how can You let me sink in this terrible emotion? Why are You doing this to me? Turn my heart to You and make me calm." The point is that, somehow, we are to always direct our minds and emotions to God.

CONCLUSION

This book includes many *hanhagot*. No one will use all nor will all appeal to everyone. Some are even in essence contradictory, representing different religious attitudes and modes. Others are only possible for people who are almost free from the pressures of earning a livelihood and can devote themselves full-time to spiritual things. So each person should use those practices that appeal to his or her own sense of piety. Once you are familiar with the ways of *hanhagot* and the principles behind them, you can also create others that are particularly suited to you.

Perhaps the best attitude to have about this is that of a craftsman, where the point is first and foremost to get the job done. The "job" in this case, is to somehow get close to God.

The Torah verse that often stands at the head of a list of hasidic *hanhagot* is Leviticus 18:5, or rather, a part of it. The typical expression is: "These are the things that, if a man does them, he will find life therein." The hasidic interpretation of this phrase is that it refers to those spiritual practices that, if done, will make your religiosity come alive. So if you see that, with the help of certain *hanhagot*, your religious life is advancing and becoming more alive, that your love for God is increasing and becoming deeper, then you should know that you are on the right track.

A recently published collection of *hanhagot* in Hebrew (*Yalkut Hanhagot v'Takkanot*) explains in the preface that since service of God must be with the deepest internality and sincerity, it is not proper just to copy the *hanhagot* of the great men of the past. Each age has its own piety and each person has his own uniqueness, which must be expressed in how he serves God. Thus, some of the *hanhagot* of the *tzaddikim* of earlier times will not fit us; still, being aware of the extraordinary way that others served God can inspire us to achieve the same thing in our own way.

Though religious practices can be learned from a book, there are times when it helps immeasurably to see with your own eyes just how a *tzaddik* or a pious person acts—how he or she prays, or greets someone, and so on. It is often something intangible that gives a spiritual practice its grace and sweetness. And it is not only a matter of individual practices, but of seeing how it all fits together, and seeing the beauty of the holiness of a holy man or woman. Every effort should be made to find such people, and to see Jewish spirituality in its living representation. For the same reason, it is very valuable to read hasidic stories, which are the next best thing.

There are many and varied practices spoken about in the tradition that help a person attain holiness and God-consciousness in a particular area of life or activity. But in the final analysis *hanhagot* are not the essence of religious life. That will always depend on something inward, something having to do with the heart. It is a mistake to become too concerned with *hanhagot* if that leads to forgetting their purpose. And the true value of *hanhagot* is that they do help to cultivate the spark of inner devotion when present, and make it grow into a flame.

One should also note that the majority of *hanhagot* deal with the relation of man to God. But the relation of man to man is equally important and essential, and the proper balance must not be lost sight of. There can be no true *d'vekut* and love of God without love of your fellow men.

Many, many *hanhagot* are discussed in this book, and certainly no one will be able to do them all—but even a few, followed with a firm devotion, will add much life to your religious practice. It is also true that many of the *hanhagot* aim at a very high level of spiritual attainment, which not many will reach—but again, everyone should do what he can, and he will see good come from it.

Accomplishing something spiritually requires more than hoping for it, more than just reading or thinking about it—practice, doing, is always the main thing. We need to increase our spiritual practice more and more. A woman can read a cookbook as much as she wants, she can become an expert in learning all the recipes, but if she does not go out, get the ingredients, and cook and eat the food, she will not get the slightest nourishment from it. A word from Rabbi Natan, the great disciple of Rabbi Nachman of Bratzlav, is appropriate here:

> You must have great enthusiasm in serving God. Be eager to do as much as possible every hour and every day. Deeds are the main thing: study much, keep many *mitzvot*, spend much time praying and pouring out your heart before God. You must do as much as possible in every way.
>
> Do not be hurried. You may find many kinds of devotion in the sacred literature and ask, "When will I be able to fulfill even one of these devotions? How can I ever hope to keep them all?" Do not let this frustrate you. Go slowly, step by step. Do not rush and try to grasp everything at once. . . . Proceed slowly, one step at a time. If you cannot do [certain devotions], you should still yearn to fulfill them. The longing itself is a great thing, for God desires the heart. (*Rabbi Nachman's Wisdom*, p. 127, *Shevachey HaRan*, #27)

The other side of this lesson is to not be afraid to aim high. The greatest *tzaddikim* were men and women like ourselves. They reached their awesome levels of holiness through their desire and self-sacrifice. They climbed the ladder into heaven step by step, and the means they used were as simple as can be; there are no tricks involved. Rabbi Nachman of Bratzlav said:

> I have spoken with many great *tzaddikim*. They all said that they attained their high level through absolute simplicity. They would do the simplest things. . . . That is how they attained what they did. Happy are they. (*Rabbi Nachman's Wisdom*, p. 299, *Sichos HaRan*, #15)

People are not ashamed to be ambitious to succeed materially or in their worldly professions. Why should we not be ambitious to achieve the purpose of our existence on this earth and get close to God?

In this time before the coming of the Messiah, when we have been brought back to the Land of Israel, the Jewish people needs heroes, men and women who will reach for the stars. As Hillel said, "In a place where there are no men, try to be a man" (Avot 2:6). We can add also: In a place where there are no women. . . . The rabbis tell us that Israel was redeemed from its first exile in Egypt through the merit of the women. So also must the women help lead us out of the final exile; they must aim for greatness.[21]

In Part Two are separate chapters for various categories of *hanhagot* such as those about prayer, eating, and others. Though the *hanhagot* collected in these chapters are sometimes arranged more or less in a way suggested by the subject itself, it should be understood that the treatment may not be complete because the arrangement is secondary and depends largely on what *hanhagot* were found in the literature. Some of the *hanhagot* included in the arrangement of a chapter may also be according to different approaches and not fully compatible with one another.

The emphasis throughout will be on action and practices—things to do—and this emphasis will necessarily affect the nature of the discussion. We will usually not be dealing with beliefs in Judaism or with ethics (*musar* and *middot*) except insofar as these matters have a connection with specific *hanhagot*. This should be understood, for it will determine the whole perspective of the book, and certain important Jewish priorities and values will not be included. We will also frequently leave out material about *mitzvot* or customs which is generally available and well known. For example, there are many books in English about *Shabbat* and the various *mitzvot* and practices associated with it. We will not be able (nor is it necessary) to discuss many of these things. Thus, there will be gaps of this sort in the treatment of some subjects. The concentration is on those matters less likely to be known to the reader, and on things that go beyond conventional religiosity.

Chapter 30 is about the hasidic practice of men's *mikveh*. Women have their own and different practice of *mikveh*, which, unlike that of the men, is a *mitzvah*-act. Consequently, their use of the *mikveh* has a different character. However, some aspects of the discussion about men's *mikveh* are relevant for women. Published material about women's *mikveh* is readily available.

Finally, it should be noted that Part One of this book is itself full of many important and valuable *hanhagot*, and it should be read not only for the background and overview it provides, but also for the purpose of taking from it those spiritual practices which can be incorporated into your religious life.

PART II

Spiritual Practices

4

Waking and Beginning the Day

4:1 How one wakes up has something to do with how one went to sleep. The best preparation for waking is to go to sleep the right way (see "Sleep and Before Sleep" [29]). If you have holy thoughts before sleep, there is a good chance that something of this will carry over in your mind through the night and be with you when you awake. This is a help, but regardless, when you wake you should begin immediately with religious practice and connect yourself to God. The very first thing to do on awakening and coming to consciousness is to direct your mind to God and to be aware of His presence.

4:2 *MODEH ANI*

The tradition has given us two main practices for the time of waking. The first is the prayer of thankfulness to God, called by its opening words, *Modeh Ani* (I thank You). The text of this can be found in the very beginning of the Siddur. On the previous evening, before sleep, you gave your soul into God's hands for safekeeping. The prayer then said:

"Into Thy hand I commend my spirit." Now you express your gratitude at receiving it back.

What does this mean? The safekeeping has two aspects: first, there is the fact that not everyone who goes to sleep wakes up; and regardless, sleep itself is, the rabbis say, a taste of death. Before sleep we offered ourselves to God as a recognition that He is the Lord of life and death. When we wake, in a similar way, we give recognition that our soul and our life are renewed and are, in fact, a gift from Him. We also recognize and give thanks that God has refreshed us with new energy with which to serve Him—and that this is from His love for us. We then dedicate ourselves to return this love. (A statement to this effect can be added to the *Modeh Ani.*)

> A man should be conscious of the presence of God even while still lying in bed. As soon as he awakes he should acknowledge the loving-kindness of the Lord, blessed be He, inasmuch as the soul, which was committed to God faint and weary, was restored to him renewed and refreshed, thus enabling him to serve God devotedly all day. For this is the true purpose in life of every man. . . . Every morning a man is like a newly created being, and for this he must thank God with all his heart, and while still on his bed he should say the *Modeh Ani.* (*Shulchan Aruch*, 1–2)

Some *tzaddikim* use the opening of the *Modeh Ani* as a cue for a meditation on God's presence. The Apter Rebbe, when asked why he had not yet begun to pray the Morning Prayer, though it was noon:

> I woke up [this morning] and began to praise [God], saying, "I offer my thanks before You" [*Modeh ani lifanecha*]; but immediately I began to consider: "Who is the *I*? And who is the *You* before Whom I am? I'm still pondering this, and haven't yet been able to go onward." (*Ha-Rav mi-Apta*, p. 120)

Another *tzaddik*:

> When I said in the morning [in the *Modeh Ani*] "I offer my thanks before You" I began to make an accounting: "Who is this *I*? And who is the *You* before Whom I am standing?"—until my soul almost left me [for our *I* is as nothing and the *You*, the source of our life and existence, is all]—and I had to pray to God to give me life and energy to continue with the next words [of *Modeh Ani*]: "O living and enduring King," and to return my life to me [that I may continue to exist and endure]. (*Sefer Hayim*, Kochavei Boker, p. 13)

4:3 HAND WASHING

The second of the practices offered by the tradition is the ritual hand washing. *Taamei ha-Minhagim* (p. 1, #1) writes:

> Why was it established that we wash our hands in the morning? Because in the morning we are like a new creation . . . (*Beit Yosef* . . .); and another reason—because an evil spirit rests on our hands (*Zohar* . . .)."

These two reasons need explanation, particularly the latter. During our waking hours we have a greater degree of control and responsibility for our thoughts and actions. When we are asleep, however, our thoughts and dreams pass largely from our conscious control. A person who would be loath to harm someone when awake can do so in his dream; a person who is sexually pure during the day can be unrestrained in his nighttime fantasies.

When we pray before sleep we beg God to protect us during sleep, that our thoughts and dreams not be unworthy. This depends also, however, on what our spiritual level is and how our previous day was spent, what our thoughts, speech, and deeds actually were. Therefore, our thoughts and dreams during the night will often, unfortunately, be low.

Upon waking, the tradition tells us to wash our hands ritually while we are still in bed. The Kabbalah explains this as follows: when we sleep, the holy soul (i.e., the holiest aspect of our soul) departs, and an unclean spirit rests on our body. When we awake, this unclean spirit departs from all the body except the fingers—from which it does not pass away until water is poured on them three times alternately (*Shulchan Aruch*, 2–1).

What is the meaning of this ritual? To translate from the religious psychology of the rabbis: the "unclean spirit" is our uncontrolled mind during sleep, with its lower instincts expressed in dream. When we awake we are in conscious control again, but an impression remains ("on the fingers") from our dreams and thoughts during those hours of sleep. Those lower thoughts have a tendency to continue, from inertia, into the waking state, following the momentum already established in the sleeping and dream state. By ritually washing off this uncleanness we make a separation between what is behind and our new beginning in the morning. This concretizes the potential the rabbis say we have to start anew each morning in our service and devotion to God, to be a "new creation."

This thought should be part of our intention at the time of hand washing. One can make a declaration then, saying, "I separate myself completely from all unworthy thoughts and dreams that I had while I was asleep (and while I was fully waking); let them be completely nullified as I wash them from me."

To help establish in your own mind the efficacy of this water to wash off the ritual uncleanness, one can also say, before the above declaration, "This living water flows from a pure source"* (*Sefer Hayim*, Kochavei Boker, p. 13). That the physical water can effect a spiritual cleansing shows that its spiritual root (or aspect) has a connection with purity. When you utter these words you call to mind this aspect of the water, and this remembrance indeed acts to heighten its potency. Rabbi Shlomo of Karlin, in his list of *hanhagot*, says about ritual hand washing in the morning:

> You should think that in this water also there is the life-power of God, blessed be He and if it were not there the water would pass out of existence. Think of this water as linked to its spiritual root, which is the spiritual water, the pure water that purifies; and that is what this water signifies. (*Shema Shlomo*, I, Hanhagot p. 1)
>
> After pouring the water over your hands, raise them to the level of your face . . . palms inward. Then, slightly cupping your fingers, and with your hands touching, reach out like someone who wants to receive something—this symbolizes the reception of purity. (*Or Tzaddikim*, p. 16a, 4:5–8)

The face and mouth are washed after the hands. The face particularly represents the Divine Image. The mouth is to be washed before we take God's name on our tongue in the holy words of blessings and prayers that are to follow in the morning.

> One must wash his face in honor of the Creator, as it is said (Genesis 9:6): "For in the image of God He made man." One must also rinse the mouth, because we must pronounce the Great Name in purity and cleanliness. (*Shulchan Aruch*, 2–3)

One should have these thoughts as *kavvanot* while performing these actions.

After the declaration about nullifying unworthy sleep and dream thoughts while washing your hands, continue by putting water on your eyes and washing your face. When you do so, say, "Blessed is He who removes sleep from my eyes and slumber from my eyelids"* (*Berachot* 60b).[1] Then say these words of prayer:

> Let all my thoughts, speech, and deeds throughout the day be such as to manifest the Divine Image in which You created me [say this while washing your face], and by which I am Your son/daughter. Let me be a son who serves You in love, and let all my deeds be directed to pleasing You, my Father in Heaven. [Say, then, after washing your mouth:] Let Your holy Name always be in my mouth. (Author)

4:4 MEDITATION—LOVE AND FEAR OF GOD

After the hand washing it is a good practice to direct your mind to God and His service through meditation, and to take upon yourself the love and fear of God.

4:4:1 Rabbi Tzvi Elimelech of Dinov:

> Immediately upon getting out of bed you should arouse yourself to fulfill the *mitzvah* to fear God, and you should meditate on His greatness, blessed be His name, until you are aroused. And so should you do at all times [throughout the day], whenever you remember. . . . And if, due to the coarseness of what you are made of, you do not actually become aroused, you have at least fulfilled the *mitzvah* to fear God in small consciousness. But you should pray to God that He help you so that your soul becomes awakened to His fear in actuality. . . . And it seems to me that you should, as you meditate, picture the name *Havaya* [YHVH) before your eyes . . .
>
> You should go to the bathroom, then wash your hands, and [again] arouse yourself to fulfill the *mitzvah* to fear God, and think of His greatness and how He is Ruler over all, the center and root of all worlds. And He fills all worlds and surrounds all worlds, and before Him everything is accounted as nothing. . . .
>
> And with the *mitzvah* to love God, to fulfill the Torah's *mitzvah* according to your obligation, you have to do everything that was said about fear of God, in all the details just explained. Immediately when you get up you should intend to fulfill the *mitzvah* to love God, and you should think of the goodness of God, blessed be He, and all the good things He does for all His creatures, and especially for His Chosen People. Think of the many good things He does

> each hour and minute and second. Think of how great and wonderful He is and how low we are [and yet He is so good and loving to us], and then your heart will burn with a strong love for Him.
>
> Visualize before you the Name . . . and pray to God that He illuminate your heart and soul, that the love for Him within you come into revelation, so that you will yearn with love of God and His Torah. (*Derech Pikudecha*, Preface)

There is often, in the tradition, an emphasis on recognizing when we awaken God's goodness to us, and this will bring us to a happy frame of mind in which to start the day and begin our service of God with joy. This is the meaning of the *Modeh Ani* and the Blessings of the Morning (See 4:10. See also the quote about this point from Rabbi Aaron of Karlin in Chapter 2, p. 39.)

4:4:2 Rabbi Tzvi Elimelech says elsewhere:

> Immediately after the ritual hand washing [upon awakening] call to remembrance the things that we are commanded to have in our mind and heart every minute without cease:
>
> 1. That there is a God in the world who brings all existent things into being from nothingness and who watches over all things and directs them according to His will.
>
> 2. To believe that He is One and there is no other with Him.
>
> 3. That we are to fear Him with two fears: the fear of punishment for sins and for evildoing, and the fear and awe of His greatness, because He is the Lord of all that is—He fills all worlds and is within all worlds, etc. . . .
>
> 4. To love Him with an intense and devoted love because of all the good He bestows on us every hour and every minute.
>
> 5. Resolve to fulfill the *mitzvah* to cling to Him in *d'vekut*, with an intense love of such power that you are not separated from Him even for one second, even when you are speaking to others.
>
> 6. Remember Him always.[2] (*Hanhagot Adam*, #1)

4:4:3 By the hand washing and the meditation during and after we raise up the lower loves and fears of our sleeping mind to the love and fear of God.

When you get up in the morning, you have to wash your hands immediately because during the night the external forces—external loves and fears—come to rest on you. . . . So you have to wash your hands immediately to remove these external loves and fears from you; you also have to immediately go to the bathroom and clean out your body for the same reason. [Waste within the body influences the mind to lower loves and fears.] (The Seder ha-Yom of Rabbi Shalom Shachna of Probitch, in *D'vir Yaakov*)

4:4:4 Sometimes this meditation on God's greatness, etc., is done after the hand washing upon awakening, other times after the hand washing upon leaving the bathroom. Since the basis for the meditation is about what we should always have in our minds, it applies at both times. When and how you arrange this depends on how you organize your morning activities.

4:4:5 To renew your faith in the morning, when you get out of bed, do not involve yourself in any worldly activity or speech; just go to the bathroom, wash, then meditate, thinking of the Creator of the world with full concentration—that He is One, Single, and Unique. He is the King of the Universe, the Holy One, blessed be He, Ruler and Lord, Root and Source of all worlds. Look [through your window] at the sky and the earth and recall the verse, "Lift up your eyes on high and see—who created all this?" [Isaiah 40:26], and think that He, blessed be He, created it all out of absolute nothingness. And think, "How many are Your works, O Lord, with wisdom have You made them all; the earth is full of Your creations" [Psalm 104:24]. Think of how great His works indeed are, in the creation of the heaven and the earth and all that is in them—inanimate and animate—plants, animals, humans, creatures great and wonderful; He created the ocean and all that is in it, the awesome whales, He formed the mountains and created winds and fire.

And it is all like a tiny mustard seed before the . . . [stars and galaxies, and they are as nothing before the other spiritual worlds of the angels[3]]; for there is no end to His hosts. And they are all as nothing compared to His high and exalted Throne, and the Throne is as nothing compared to His Glory [the *Shechinah*]. And He is the Cause of all causes and the Mover of everything that moves, and there is none but Him.

Then you will become filled with fear [awe] of God, blessed be He. Afterwards arouse love in your heart to cleave to Him. Then, following this meditation, say the blessings after the hand washing [*al netilat yadaim*], after leaving the bathroom [*asher yat-zar*], and

> on the Torah. (*Kitzur Shnei Luchot ha-Brit*, Sh'ar ha-Otiyot, p. 18; cf. Inyanei Netilat Yadaim shel Shaharit, p. 108)

4:4:6 The rabbis instituted the practice of saying, before the Morning Prayers, that we resolve to fulfill the commandment of loving our fellow man. Rabbi Yitzhak of Radevill notes this and says that:

> Immediately after saying *Modeh Ani* you should say: "I want to fulfill the commandment 'and you shall love your neighbor as yourself.'"* (*Eser Orot*, p. 66, #10)

Just as with love of God, love of man can form the basis of a brief waking meditation; and the two can be joined together and integrated.

> **4:4:7** My own holy master and *rebbe*, the Rebbe Reb Zusya [of Hanipol], of blessed memory, taught me the way of God, saying, "My son, as soon as you wake up in the morning, take in your hand the holy *tzitzit* [many men sleep with the small *tallit* on] and direct your mind and heart to meditate on the greatness and majesty of the Creator, blessed be He, and take on yourself the true fear of God—to have awe and fear because of His greatness. This should not be just a matter of rote and habit." (*Or ha-Ner*, #6n.)

4:4:8 In *Seder ha-Yom ha-Katzar*:

> When you wake up, the first thing should be to receive on yourself the yoke of the Kingdom of Heaven. (p. 7)

It goes on to explain how to sanctify the first thoughts, speech, and action upon waking. The first speech is to say *Modeh Ani*, the first action is hand washing, and a suggestion is given for the first thoughts and meditation:

> The first thing to consider when you awake is to make sure not to say one word other than the *Modeh Ani* prayer. . . . Also your first thoughts should be about something holy. . . . and your first action should be something holy—immediately when you awake wash your hands before getting out of bed.

The continuation here explains the teaching of the rabbis, that one *mitzvah* leads to another, and therefore if you start out well you can hope for good. Then it discusses first thoughts:

> The first thing is to think about *tshuvah*. And what is that? To begin with, fix it firmly in your heart and mind that there is a God, and that God, blessed be He, created everything in existence and all the worlds—from nothing He brought into being something. By His power and desire, blessed be He, comes into being everything that is, was, and will be. Every moment and every instant He gives them their being and their life—bringing the something out of nothingness every second. There is nothing at all that comes into being without His will, blessed be He. He watches over everything that exists and over everything that happens.
>
> The greater the effort you make to establish this belief more firmly in your mind, the more you will know your Creator, blessed be He, and be aware of Him. You will actually see that when you strengthen this belief with continued effort, you will every day increase in your knowledge and awareness of the Creator, blessed be He. . . .
>
> Just believe with complete faith that God, blessed be He, fills all worlds and surrounds all worlds, and there is no place where He is not present. . . . Think how God is King and Ruler over all the worlds and how there is no life in anything in existence except what comes from Him, who brings them into being and enlivens them, producing them continually as something out of nothingness. . . .
>
> After you have fixed this faith firmly in your heart, then regret all that you have done against God's will from the day that you were born, in thought, speech, and deed. Resolve with all the determination at your command (though without a vow) that from now on you will do only what is His will, in thought, speech, and deed. (p. 5)

The part of this meditation about God bringing all things into being from nothingness and enlivening them can be personally applied:

> After you wash your hands upon awakening, you should meditate on how you have no existence other than that which comes to you from the Creator, blessed be He. If it would be imagined that, God forbid, the flow of His creative activity stopped, then you would cease to exist. You should think of how the root and source of your life and existence is above, clinging to Him, blessed be He. (Rabbi Shlomo of Karlin, *Shema Shlomo*, I, Hanhagot, p. 1)

We should also realize that it is His energy, renewed within us, that powers us, and we should be alive and vigorous in His service.

> [After saying *Modeh Ani*] say, "The power of the Creator is in His creation,"* for the power of God is within us. If the flow of His life-force would cease for a minute we would disappear altogether, as if

> we never existed. If that is so, why should we be lazy and slow in using this life-energy which He sends into us? (Rabbi Tzvi Elimelech of Dinov, *Hanhagot Adam*, #1)

As in the last words of Rabbi Shlomo of Karlin we are taught that the flow of life to our soul comes to us from God, and that the root of our soul is always attached to God. Another aspect of this is that our soul is, indeed, actually a part of God. Giving recognition to this in our meditation inspires us to fulfill our potential for holiness. The Hasam Sofer, in speaking of a meditation on God's greatness, and our own smallness (to come to humility and *tshuvah*) continues:

> But then be proud that He breathed within you a living Godly soul which is a part of God from Above. (*Yesodot b'Avodat HaShem*, p. 93. See also "Prayer" 5:1:22.)

These things can be part of a waking meditation.

4:4:9 From these examples we see how on awakening we should turn our mind to God through meditation on basic concepts about Him, such as His being the Creator, His transcendence and immanence, and about our relation to Him, our desire to love and remember Him, to repent, to recognize His goodness, and about our fundamental obligations, such as to love our fellow man as ourselves. Another aspect of such a meditation can be to reflect on our relationship to God as His son or daughter, what that means, how we can make it real, and how we can fulfill our purpose by serving our Father in Heaven, giving Him pleasure in us and drawing close to Him.[4]

Everyone can construct such a meditation for himself along these lines, and while engaging in such a meditation (silent or spoken), it is good to do so with a consciousness of His presence with you.

4:4:10 The theme of your meditation should be carried on through the day. The Besht taught:

> It is an important principle that with the thought and meditation with which you begin [your service of God] when you get out of bed, you should go through the whole day with that thought, and not with another. (*Tzavaat ha-Ribash*, Kehot edition #25)

Doing this will increase the effect of your good beginning.

4:5 REPETITION OF A HOLY SENTENCE

There are other possible practices at the time of awakening, to use in place of a meditation or together with it, such as repeating a phrase or line from the Torah, or calling out to God as your Father over and over—perhaps while holding a holy object (as above with the *tzitzit*).

> You should have continuous *d'vekut* with God, blessed be He, and you should not lose it for even one minute, either when you are just waking up or just before you fall asleep. And beginning immediately, when you wake up, it should be a practice of yours to accustom yourself to say continually, "Blessed is the One and Only One,"* and the verse "I have placed the Lord before me always," or at least the word *Shivitti* [I have placed]. (*Rachmei ha-Av, D'vekut*, #16)

These two sentences, if used together, represent the sort of meditation discussed above. The meditation begins with God's greatness, that is the meaning of the "Blessed, etc." (note how the meditation in section 4:4:5 begins); and its end goal is an awareness and experience of His Presence, as indicated by the verse, "I have placed, etc." (See "Repetition of a Holy Sentence" [21] for more about this practice.)

4:6 SERVICE OF THE IMAGINATION

4:6:1 Another practice is to do a service of the imagination. One example of this is to visualize the Name YHVH (see 4:4:1).

4:6:2 *Kav ha-Yashar* (chapter 1) suggests picturing to yourself the scene at Mount Sinai when the Torah was given.

> When you wake up from sleep you should immediately think of how it was when the Jewish people received the Torah at Mount Sinai. You should picture in your mind how pure Israel was at that time, so separated from worldly things—when they stood at the foot of Mount Sinai with trembling and trepidation. And Mount Sinai was smoking because of the fire, when the Holy One, blessed be He, descended upon it with myriads of angels. And there was the sound of the *shofar* . . .

Read Exodus 19:16–20 for the very vivid account of the scene.[5] (See "Service of the Imagination" 19:2 for more about this.)

One can at this time also recite the Ten Commandments:

> so as to remember the scene at Mount Sinai every day, to strengthen our faith in its meaning. (*Kitzur Shnei Luchot ha-Brit*, p. 110)

The rabbis say that the souls of all Jews were present at Mount Sinai, so we were there and have the ability to remember what it was like.

4:6:3 There are, of course, other possibilities for such service of the imagination and visualizations upon waking, depending on your own inclinations and what best inspires you to love and fear of God. (See "Service of the Imagination" [19].)

4:7 EVERYTHING IN GOD'S HANDS

Rabbi Nachman of Bratzlav taught how to give responsibility for your actions into God's hands:

> It is very good to rely on God completely. As each day begins, I place my every movement in God's hands, asking [praying] that I do only His will. This is very good and I have no worries. Whether or not things go right, I am completely dependent on God. If He desires otherwise, I have already asked that I do only His will. . . . [Then I can go through the day] without worrying that I am doing something wrong. I am completely dependent on God and everything I do is in His hands. (*Rabbi Nachman's Wisdom*, p. 106; *Sichos HaRan*, #2)
>
> When the day begins, I surrender my every movement to God. I ask that every motion that I may make be according to God's will. I ask the same for all my children and other dependents. Then, as things occur that day . . . I am not disturbed that my observance might not be proper. (*Rabbi Nachman's Wisdom*, p. 374, *Sichos HaRan*, #238)

Ayin Zochar (a booklet of *hanhagot* from the teachings of Rabbi Nachman, published by the Bratzlaver hasidim) gives this practice for waking (referring to *Sichos HaRan*):

> It is very good, when morning comes, that you cast yourself on God, blessed be He, depending on Him and giving over all your

movements and those of your children and dependents to Him [giving Him the responsibility], that they all be according to His will, blessed be He. And you should say this: "Master of the World! I now give myself over to You, with all my movements and thoughts, and words and actions [throughout the day], and all the movements, thoughts, and words and actions of my children and those dependent on me, that they all be according to Your will as You, in Your goodness towards me, decree."* (1:2, 1:3) (See also "*Shabbat*," 18:1:2:2:9:1.)

Giving God responsibility for your actions is a very deep matter. Instead of relying on yourself you trust in God and rely on Him. You realize that you yourself, by your own efforts, cannot reach the perfection that God wants and that you want. But throughout the day, again and again, you should remind yourself that you are relying on God to direct you—it is His responsibility. This pious attitude, rooted in profound trust rather than self-effort, also frees you to be happy and without anxiety in your service of God.

4:8 YOUR *HANHAGOT*

If you have your own list of *hanhagot* to which you are committed, read it over when you awaken. In the list of *hanhagot* that Rabbi Shmelke of Nikolsburg made for his followers, he suggests reading it over a few times a day, the first time immediately upon awakening. (See "Individual Practices," 39:2 about making such a list for yourself.)

4:9 THE IMPORTANCE OF THE BEGINNING

The basic principle that stands behind most of the attention given practices done upon awakening is the importance of the beginning. If the beginning is good, then what follows will be good too. Thus, it is essential that you start well. Before sleep is a time of potential spirituality because there is a necessary release from our material strivings of the day. In a similar way, the very beginning of the day is a time of potential spirituality because before one has gone out into the world, before the mind is scattered in a multitude of directions toward worldly concerns, it is still relatively unified and separated from material attractions and can be directed wholly to God.

Although in this chapter we are considering practices done more or less immediately upon awakening, in a more general sense the main practice of the morning is the Morning Prayer Service. Because of the particular spiritual significance of the time after waking, it is the most important of the daily prayer services and its function is to establish at the very beginning of the day the strongest direction in the service of God and in God-consciousness.

> All the disciples of the Baal Shem Tov have written that we should be careful when we wake up and get out of bed, that our first thought, our first words, and our first action be devoted to God, in Torah and *mitzvot*. For then all our subsequent thoughts, speech, and deeds throughout the rest of the day will follow in the train of these first. (Rabbi Tzvi Elimelech of Dinov, *Agra d'Pirka*, quoted in *Zichron l'Rishonim*, p. 59)

Following are a series of directives about waking from three different sources quoted in *Derech ha-Tovah v'ha-Yesharah*:

> 1. The very first thing a person should do immediately when he awakens in the morning is to be conscious within himself that the Creator, blessed be His name, has acted lovingly toward him by restoring his soul, and that it [his soul] fills all his body. By this consciousness he sanctifies himself [by devoting his first thoughts to God] . . . before his mind has scattered this way and that.
>
> 2. He should also sanctify the beginning of his use of each of his limbs and senses. His sight, his hearing, and his speech should not be used at all for any ordinary worldly activity until he has first drawn the Creator down onto each limb and sense. As a result, certainly all his actions that day will be imbued with holiness.
>
> 3. The first thing of all is the mind and thought, and speech is a derivative of that, and action is a derivative of speech. Therefore, when a person gets up in the morning he is like a newly created being. . . . If the first speech he engages in is concerned with personal matters (not to mention lies and other such), then even if he will pray and occupy himself with Torah study afterwards,

> everything will spin out from and follow the first speech he began the day with, because just as speech is a derivative of thought and secondary to it, so is the second use of speech [even in prayer or Torah] a derivative of the first. (I, Din Hashkamat ha-Boker)

One should consider the ways to apply the teaching in (2). For instance, let the first thing you look at on awakening be the *tzitzit*, or God's name on a *Shivitti* on your wall. You can also pray that your eyes be sanctified throughout the whole day. Make similar applications for the other senses.

> You should keep your eyes closed when you awake [only opening them to gaze on something holy], so that your first sight will be of holy things, not of the vain things of this world. (Rabbi Yehiel Yehoshuah of Biala, *Seder ha-Yom l'ha Admor mi-Biala*, #1)

> Already in his childhood Rabbi Shlomo Leib of Lentshno began to sanctify and purify his limbs and organs [for God's service] and he accepted on himself *hanhagot* of purity and holiness. One of his practices was to make the parts of his body—his mouth, eyes, and ears—vow that they would be faithful to their true purpose and would do nothing against the will of the Holy One, blessed be He.
>
> The *rebbe* used to tell how all the parts of his body assented and joined in the oath, except for his two eyes. His eyes (and our Sages, of blessed memory, call the eyes the middlemen of sin) were steadfast in their refusal.
>
> One day the young boy Shlomo Leib decided that the next morning he would not open his eyes so as not to stumble into transgression by looking at something forbidden. The next day his mother was astonished to see her son Shlomo Leib, who always got up early and went to the *Beit Midrash*, lying in bed with his eyes closed. His mother asked him if there was something wrong with him, but the child did not answer and continued to lie on the bed in silence. His mother, who did not know what this was about and did not appreciate his behavior, gave him one smack and then another.
>
> Only then did his eyes have mercy on the child, softening their stubborn refusal. They agreed to join in the oath along with the rest of the body, and do nothing that would bring harm to the piety of the child, who was holy from birth. (*Tiferet Avot*, p. 34)

If we understand this story, the likelihood is that the young Shlomo Leib would "make his limbs vow" *every* morning, and would not begin to use them without their agreement to that condition.[6]

4:10 THE MORNING BLESSINGS

The tradition also provides ways for us to link the sequence of our waking actions to God by means of a series of blessings, where a blessing is made for each waking action in turn. These blessings have been put in the Siddur as part of the morning *davvening*, but originally (as can be seen from the Talmud, *Berachot* 60b) they were said during the process of waking. Here are some of them, as they appear in the Talmud:

When you open your eyes, say, "Blessed is He who opens the eyes of the blind";
When you stretch and sit up, say, "Blessed is He who loosens the bound";
When washing your face, say, "Blessed is He who removes sleep from my eyes and slumber from my eyelids";
[Realizing your energy has been renewed, say, "Blessed is He who gives strength to the weary" (In Siddur; not Talmud)]
When you dress, say, "Blessed is He who clothes the naked";
When you stand up, say, "Blessed is He who straightens those who are bent over";
When you put your feet on the ground, say, "Blessed is He who spreads out the solid earth. . . .";
When you begin to walk, say, "Blessed is He who makes firm a man's steps."[7]

Rabbi Hayim Vital writes of the Holy Ari:

> Regarding the eighteen blessings of the morning, which most people say in the synagogue (the prayer-leader says them and everyone answers "amen" after each) I saw how my master, of blessed memory, would not say them in the synagogue, but at home, when he got out of bed and as it is described in the *Gemara*. (*Minhagei ha-Arizal—Petura d'Abba*, p. 4a, #5)

Rabbi Elimelech of Lizensk says that:

> When you dress or otherwise do something to improve your appearance, putting on nice clothes or ornaments, your intention should be holy and for the sake of heaven—to beautify and adorn the Divine Image, as is explained in the *Gemara*. (*Noam Elimelech*, Hayei Sarah, p. 9a)

We saw above how it is good to use one's first thoughts upon awakening to meditate on God's greatness, that He creates everything out of nothingness and were His word removed for a second that thing would immediately disappear and cease to exist. One can have this thought as a *kavvanah* when putting your foot on the "solid ground" as you get out of bed. In a *musar* (inspirational) talk, Rabbi David Blicher said of his master that:

> When he made the blessing "who spreads out the solid earth . . . ," he became full of holy fear—for perhaps in another second the earth under his feet would disappear, since it has no support for its existence other than God's will alone. (*Hayei ha-Musar*, I, p. 7. See also "Sight," 25:11.)

4:11 EXERCISE

Some light movement exercises can be used in the morning to put your body in tune with your spiritual purposes. See "Prayer," 5:1:6 where this is discussed in the context of preparation for the morning *davvening* and suggestions are given for how to elevate these exercises to a spiritual level.

4:12 MINIMIZE NONSPIRITUAL ACTIVITY

On the one hand the tradition helps us to link our first thoughts, speech, and actions to God. On the other hand, we should do everything possible to minimize before the Morning Prayer any thought, speech, or action that is of a personal and practical nature. Rather, everything we do should be for the purpose of directing our minds and hearts fully to God alone, and preparing ourselves spiritually for the Morning Prayer. The Morning Prayer is the high point of our morning spiritual activities, and all that precedes it should largely be seen as its preparation.

> **4:12:1** The first thoughts of the day, from the time you awake, should be considered as preparation for the service of the heart, which is Prayer. And insofar as it is possible to avoid all speech and action before prayer, the better. (Rabbi Aaron of Karlin, *Hanhagot Tzaddikim*, p. 19, #2)

> **4:12:2** From the time you get up in the morning until an hour after the Morning Prayer Service, you should be careful not to do

any kind of work. Neither should you engage in any idle talk during this time, except in cases of absolute necessity, where you are forced to speak. (Rabbi Mordechai of Lechovitz, *Hanhagot Tzaddikim*, p. 41, #2)

4:12:3 You should be careful not to talk at all, from the moment you get up in the morning until an hour after the Morning Prayer, even with your wife and children; and do so also before and after *Minha* [the Afternoon Prayer] and *Maariv* [the Evening Prayer]. (Rabbi Yehiel Michal of Zlotchov, *Hanhagot Tzaddikim*, p. 53, #4)

4:12:4 In a similar instruction, Rabbi Aaron of Karlin says that in the case of absolute necessity you should still seek to minimize conversation to the degree possible (*Hanhagot Tzaddikim*, p. 4, #8).

Do not converse at all before prayer, and if someone asks you something, answer but weakly, in a way that you will not be drawn into an idle conversation or into a low kind of banter and jesting. (Rabbi Asher of Stolin, *Hanhagot Tzaddikim*, p. 6, #4)

4:12:5 From the time we get up out of bed in the morning, until the time we accept on ourselves the yoke of the Kingdom of Heaven during the recital of the "Hear O Israel," we will not speak one word (although we have not made a vow in this), but we will just speak words of Torah and be engaged in the service of God. We will only converse if there is a pressing need or if someone comes to us and we want to conceal our piety from him, for then it is better to speak to him. (*Hanhagot Adam*, #12; the rules of Rabbi Tzvi Elimelech of Dinov, which his disciples committed themselves to follow.)

4:12:6 Always remember that everything should be done according to your level. Even five minutes without conversation right after waking is very good.

4:13 A SOBERING COMMENT

The Seer of Lublin said:

I have received a tradition that any Jew who is not aware of 400 sins he commits from the time he wakes until the time of the Morning Prayer has not even begun the service of God in holiness and purity. (*Ha-Hozeh mi-Lublin*, p. 166; cf. p. 221)

4:14 LIKE A LION

It is the way of many *tzaddikim* to get up and rouse themselves vigorously, with a loud voice and energetic bodily movements, to shake off sleep. This is a very good practice to take on yourself.

> You should arise like a lion to begin the service of your Creator, blessed be He, for if you give your evil inclination any chance to overcome you and lull you into laziness, then, God forbid, you will fall under its control and will not be able to get the better of it. . . . So you should see that you subdue it immediately upon awakening. (*Or ha-Ner*, #2)

4:15 HOW THE *TZADDIKIM* AWOKE

We will conclude our discussion about waking with some descriptions of how the *tzaddikim* awoke. The purpose here is not admiration, but imitation.

> **4:15:1** We saw how our master and teacher and rabbi, the holy and pure Rebbe Reb Elimelech [of Lizensk], of blessed memory, immediately upon awakening from sleep would speak to himself in a thunderous voice and say to his soul, "Woe is you, that you've wasted time in sleep!"[8] (*Maor v'Shemesh* quoted in *Or ha-Ner*, #1, n.)

4:15:2 Here is a description of how the holy brother of Rabbi Elimelech, Rabbi Zusya of Hanipol would awaken:

> Once, the Rebbe Reb Zusya, may his merit protect us, visited the holy *gaon* [Rabbi Mordechai] of Neshkiz, who gave him a room to sleep in. After midnight [at which time Rabbi Zusya rose for *Tikkun Hatzot*, and for devotional service until morning] the Elder of Neshkiz heard how the Rebbe Reb Zusya woke up and jumped out of his bed with holy fervor and ran around the room.
>
> After doing this for a while he called out, "Master of the World, I love You! But what can I do for You? I can't do anything!" Then he ran this way and that as before, and repeated the same thing a number of times. Then he again ran around a number of times until he said, "I know what I can do! I can whistle for You!" He began to whistle with such fervor that the Elder of Neshkiz said to his comrade who was standing there with him, "Let's leave here quickly

> before we get burned up by the breath of his holy mouth." (*Ohel Elimelech*, p. 134, #341)

We are to arouse ourselves to love and fear of God upon awakening. Earlier we cited the teaching of Rabbi Zusya about holding the *tzitzit* and meditating on God's greatness to arouse fear. This story is about Rabbi Zusya's arousal to love.

4:15:3 Of Rabbi Yerahmiel Moshe of Koznitz it is told:

> He got up early in the morning, said the Blessing over the Torah and the *Sh'ma* in a loud voice and said three times, "I am God's and God is mine!" and then, "There is a God in heaven and on earth and over all the worlds—One, Single, and Unique—who was, is, and always will be!" He always said this same thing every day before sleep and again when he awoke.[9] (*Sifran Shel Tzaddikim*, p. 91)

> **4:15:4** It was the way of the holy rabbi, Rabbi David Forkes [a disciple of the Baal Shem Tov] to get up early every morning and call out in a loud voice, "David, David, stand up to serve the Creator!"[10] (*Mishnat Hasidim*, p. 381, #11. See also "Service of the Imagination," 19:13.)

> **4:15:5** [When Rabbi Leibele Eiger of Lublin] woke up in the morning, he got up from the bed with a great clamor and called out loudly, "I am a servant of the Holy One, blessed be He!"* (*Gan Hadasim*, p. 21)

4:15:6 Finally, there is this about how the great hasidic *rebbe*, Rabbi Hayim of Tzanz woke up:

> Our holy rabbi would wake up with a lot of shouting and with an awesome display of fear of God. He washed his hands and then speedily sat on the bed with his holy feet on the floor and began his awesome service of God with all his body and limbs. He hit his hands on his head in a way that simply cannot be described—for fifteen minutes or half an hour—while he shouted out what were usually words of this sort: "There is nothing in the world but one God! Everyone knows this, and we have to serve Him and sacrifice ourselves altogether for His sake!—No thought can grasp You!—And You give a person freedom of choice to follow the Torah.—There is no place where He is not.—And I want nothing at all in

> this world except to exhaust myself in complete devotion to God! . . . I don't want anything except just to serve God!"*—and other words of this sort. (*Darkei Hayim*, p. 6, #2)

Raising your voice, along with vigorous bodily movements, is a good method for shaking off sleep. Presumably, the *rebbe's* hitting himself on the head also served that purpose, as well as being part of his self-encouragement. But the Tzanzer's fiery wake-up certainly also expressed the burning devotion of his heart to serve God.

4:16 LEAVING THE HOUSE

Since it follows naturally in the order of the day, we will discuss here a few matters concerned with leaving the house in the morning (which apply equally to leaving the house at other times of the day).

4:16:1 When you are in your own house you are in a protected environment, where your habits also protect you. But when out on the street, with all its influences and distractions, it is more difficult to be in control of your state of consciousness. This is usually the first big transition of the day. (See chapter 3, p. 58, "Transitions.") When you leave your house it is a good practice to kiss the *mezuzah* and say a brief prayer. The emphasis in such prayers in the tradition is often on being protected from difficulties, both physical and spiritual, which you can meet with in the outside world.

> **4:16:1:1** In the morning when you leave your house, put your hand on the *mezuzah* and say, "Master of the World, have mercy on me and save me from the evil inclination and all its helpers! Amen."* (*Derech Hayim*, 6-80)

4:16:1:2 In the morning be sure to have ritually washed your hands, and then, before leaving your house, put your hands on the *mezuzah* and meditate on how God is the owner of the house and that we are all just transient visitors. Think of the name of God—*Shaddai* ["the Almighty," represented by the letter *shin* on the *mezuzah*] . . . and afterwards say three times "God will guard my going out and my coming in, for life and for peace, from now and for ever." Then say, "Know Him in all your ways."*[11] (*Kav ha-Yashar*, chap. 55)

4:16:1:3 (See "The Synagogue and the Synagogue Service," 6:12, about how Rabbi Eleazar Zev of Kretchnif, when leaving for the synagogue in the morning, would stand by the *mezuzah* of his house for some time in meditation; see also 6:13 about what the Rabbi of Alesk would say in his house before he left for the synagogue, at the *mezuzah* and at all the stages of the way.)

4:16:2 As you leave the house and begin to walk on the street, it is a good practice to say from memory the two prayers found in the Siddur at the beginning of the Morning Service:

> May it be Thy will, O Lord our God and God of our fathers, to make us familiar with Thy Torah, and to make us cleave to Thy commandments. O lead us not into the power of sin, or of transgression or iniquity, or of temptation or of scorn; let not the evil inclination have sway over us; keep us far from a bad man and a bad companion; make us cleave to the good inclination and to good works; subdue our inclination for evil so that it may submit itself unto Thee; and let us obtain this day, and every day, grace, favor, and mercy in Thine eyes and in the eyes of all who behold us; and bestow loving-kindness upon Thy people Israel.[12]
>
> May it be Thy will, O Lord my God and God of my fathers, to deliver me this day and every day, from arrogant men and from arrogance, from a bad man, from a bad companion, and from a bad neighbor, and from any mishap, and from the Adversary that destroyeth. . . .

5

Prayer—The Service of the Heart

The service of prayer is one of the main spiritual practices of Judaism. Involving a direct relation to God, more so than Torah study, it is often for that reason emphasized by Hasidism.

> The Baal Shem Tov learned from his own soul, which told him that he merited to have exalted things revealed to him not because he had learned much Talmud and *halacha*, but because of his prayer. He would always pray with the most intense *kavvanah*, and that was what brought him to his exalted spiritual level.[1] (*Keter Shem Tov*, p. 22b)

> One of the Besht's disciples wrote about his master:

> How well do I know with what great holiness he conducted himself, with such piety and separation from worldliness. But he especially put his efforts and energy into the service of the heart—prayer. He prayed with complete divorcement from the body and from everything material [*hitpashtut ha-gashmiyut*], and with tremendous *d'vekut* with the living God. (Rabbi Meir Margulis, quoted in *Kerem Yisrael*, p. 5, #1)

5:1 PREPARATION

The hasidim have traditionally placed a great emphasis on preparation for prayer, to the extent that the preparation sometimes takes a good deal longer than the prayer itself.[2]

The headquarters for hasidic comment and instruction on preparation for prayer is the famous tradition about how the early hasidim (in the time of the Second Temple) spent an hour before prayer to direct themselves to God, so as to achieve *kavvanah* and *d'vekut.*

> The early hasidim would tarry for an hour before prayer in order to direct their hearts to God. (*Berachot* 5:1)

This tradition is referred to and interpreted again and again by the *tzaddikim* in the hasidic movement of the Baal Shem Tov. For that reason, we will consider it often in our discussion.

In a general sense, its meaning is that the essence of the preparation for prayer is to establish oneself in *d'vekut.*

Rabbi Elimelech of Lizensk states:

> As it says in the *Gemara*—"The early hasidim would spend an hour [before prayer] etc." —They would spend that time binding themselves in *d'vekut* [to God]. (*Noam Elimelech*, Korach, p. 70a)

Sitting in preparation before prayer has a very great influence on its level, and anyone who wants to know what prayer is should take this to heart.

5:1:1 Torah

Some Torah study is often a good preparation for prayer.

> **5:1:1:1** It is an important thing to see that you learn for at least an hour before each and every prayer service. Because it is well known that whoever has the ability to sense it, knows that there is a big difference between prayer that comes after Torah learning and that which does not. (*Seder ha-Yom ha-Katzar*, p. 5)

> **5:1:1:2** When you study Torah and *exert* yourself in studying, that pushes out any extraneous thoughts and purifies your mind, and is the true preparation for *d'vekut* in the time of prayer, and the best way to avoid foreign thoughts during prayer. (The Yehudi, *Siftei Kodesh*, p. 91)

5:1:1:3 The Baal Shem Tov:

> You should exert yourself before prayer so that you will be able to pray with an expanded consciousness, at least without foreign thoughts, and hopefully with *d'vekut.* You can do this by saying psalms or through Torah study, going to prayer right from your involvement in Torah study. But do not overdo it, so that you will not tire yourself out; just enough so that you will have *kavvanah* and an expanded consciousness in prayer. (*Keter Shem Tov*, I, p. 27)

5:1:1:4 When a person learns Torah for the sake of heaven he has a burning desire to sacrifice himself for God, and he yearns to pray. (Rabbi Aaron of Karlin, *Hanhagot Tzaddikim,* vol. 5, p. 28)

5:1:1:5 Torah and prayer support and illuminate each other, so you should engage in both with that end before you. (Rabbi Nachman of Bratzlav, *Likkutei Aytzot ha-Meshulash*, Tefillah, #7)

5:1:1:6 Speaking about Rabbi Elimelech of Lizensk and the great *tzaddikim* and hasidim who gathered around him, a hasid writes:

> Their *kavvanah* in learning Torah was also to purify and cleanse themselves and their minds so that they would be able to pray without any foreign thoughts; and as a result of this their prayer would ascend with the greatest concentration. (*Noam Elimelech*, Igeret ha-Kodesh p. 98a)

This intention can be stated explicitly before learning—that you are learning for this purpose, to purify yourself for prayer.

5:1:2 Fixed Place and Time

It is good, when you pray, whether in synagogue or home, to do so in a fixed place and at a fixed time. The *halacha* gives leeway within general limits for the times of the different prayer services. But there is a value in fixing the time to the degree possible. When the fixed time arrives, and when you go to the fixed place in synagogue (a certain seat there) or home (a certain corner), your mind will, by habit, then take itself to the world of prayer.

5:1:2:1 Be sure to fix for yourself a place for your prayer. (*Derech Hayim*, 3-44; see *Berachot* 6)

5:1:2:2 The author of *Derech Moshe* says that the fixed place in your house should be designated by means of an explicit declaration:

> Choose a fixed place for yourself, a place that is nice and clean, and say out loud in a full voice: "I choose this place for prayer for myself, my family, and for all Israel. May it be Your will that the *Shechinah* rest on this place as it does in all the synagogues of Israel."* If you speak thus, its sanctity is that of a synagogue, and your prayer is accepted when you pray there. (p. 12)

This declaration was intended for those who live where there is no synagogue, isolated, and without a *minyan* to pray with. If you do have access to a synagogue such a place is not its equal. However, such a declaration (minus the final reference to synagogues) can still have a purpose in establishing a fixed place for prayer in a home.

5:1:3 Candles and Incense

There are other ways to prepare the place of prayer in your house so as to make the experience distinctive and heighten your concentration.

5:1:3:1 You can light one or more candles, as was often done in the synagogue.

> **5:1:3:1:1** Be sure to light eternal-light candles during the time of prayer, before the Ark, in the place of prayer. (*DhTvhY*, Tefillah, p. 23b, #29)

> **5:1:3:1:2** Always light a special candle for yourself when you pray [in the synagogue], as it is said, "With lights, glorify God" (Isaiah 24:15). (*Beit Middot*, p. 57)

5:1:3:2 You can burn incense when you pray, or set out pleasant spices. The distinctive scent will suggest to you the specialness of the time.[3] (See also 5:2:9.)

5:1:4 Bathroom

One important physical preparation for prayer that the tradition prescribes is to check yourself, and to go to the bathroom if necessary (see

Shulchan Aruch, 12:3). If not relieved, the internal body messages to the brain during the time of prayer will disturb concentration and also affect the nature of your thought processes and meditation, lowering them to the bodily plane.

> **5:1:4:1** Be careful to keep your body clean of excrement within, and do not transgress the commandment not to make yourself abominable—especially before prayer. Pray with your body cleansed and not when it is abominable and full of wastes, for that influences you so that foreign thoughts come to you during prayer. (Rabbi Nahum of Tchernobil, *Hanhagot Tzaddikim*, p. 37, #20)

> **5:1:4:2** Our holy master, Rabbi Zusya [of Hanipol], may his light shine, said that by delaying going to the bathroom, foreign thoughts came about. (*Darkei Tzedek*, p. 20)

> **5:1:4:3** [Of course, from the same reasoning:] Do not eat close to the time of prayer. (*Derech Hayim*, 2–84)

5:1:5 Hand Washing

A second physical preparation prescribed by the tradition is to wash our hands before praying (*Shulchan Aruch*, 12:5). This gesture of symbolic bodily cleanliness suggests to our mind that the time for prayer has arrived. Through its physical effect it changes our body-feeling and then our mental state. One *kavvanah* for hand washing before prayer can be to "wash off" impure thoughts and separate ourselves from worldly concerns.

Related to the practice of hand washing, some hasidim go to the *mikveh* every morning before prayer, that being the more complete form of this experience of spiritual purity. (See "Men's *Mikveh*" [30] for more about this practice.)

5:1:6 Exercise

Before *davvening* in the morning, it is good to do some light exercises to remove disturbing bodily tensions. There are various intentions that can accompany this. You can, as you move each limb, dedicate it to God and express your resolve that it be used that day in His service. Or you can think of your desire and intention to use your whole body in your prayer, fulfilling the verse, "All my bones shall say, 'O Lord, who is like unto Thee!'" (See also 5:4:1.) Rabbi Nachman of Bratzlav would sometimes talk to his various limbs to "convince" them of the need to serve God. Other accompaniments for such an exercise can be to meditate on how the energy of your movements comes from God, or to express prayer intentions in the gestures of the exercise. You can also repeat a holy sentence.

5:1:7 Special Clothes, *Tallit, Tefillin, Gartel;* Shoeless

5:1:7:1 Special Clothes

> **5:1:7:1:1** It is appropriate to have special clothes which you wear only for prayer. (*Derech Hayim*, 2-61)

> Some people might have one special item of clothing, others more.

5:1:7:1:2 As with the fixed time and place, as soon as you put on special clothes, your mind will, as a result of daily repetition and habit, turn to thoughts of holiness.

To some degree, of course, a *tallit* (prayer shawl) serves the function of special clothing, at least during the daytime. But hasidim, taking this to its fullest extent, have other special clothing as well.

5:1:7:2 *Tallit* and *Tefillin*

5:1:7:2:1 When praying during the daytime, wrap yourself in a *tallit*. Among the kabbalists of Safed it became a widespread custom to don a *tallit* and *tefillin* not just for the Morning Service but for the Afternoon Service as well.

> They put on a *tallit* and *tefillin* for every *Minha*, just as for *Shaharit*, and this custom has spread among all the people. (Rabbi Abraham Galanti of Safed, *Minhagim Tovim v'Kedoshim ha-Nohagim b'Eretz Yisrael*, #3, in *YHvT*, p. 15; cf. p. 11, #17; p. 19, #8)

Traditionally, a *tallit* is not worn at night and you are not allowed to put one on at night with a blessing. However:

> First of all, never pray except when you are wrapped in a *tallit*. Such was the way of my teacher and uncle [Rabbi Tzvi Hirsh of Ziditchov], the memory of a *tzaddik* for a blessing. And for *Maariv*

> [after having it on for *Minha*, putting it on during the daytime with a blessing, and not removing it], he would take it down from covering his head as usual, but prayed with it on his shoulders. (*Yifrach biYamav Tzaddik*, p. 39, #9)

5:1:7:2:2 Both the *tallit* and *tefillin* are helpful in prayer concentration. Learn the traditional way to wrap yourself in a *tallit* when it is first put on. Be aware of the feeling that comes from being clothed and wrapped in a holy garment set aside for prayer.

It is told about Rabbi Nachman of Bratzlav:

> The *rebbe* once gave his old *tallit* to one of his close followers, someone on a high level, and told him, "Be careful to treat this *tallit* with respect and honor. You should know that as many threads as there are in this *tallit*, that is how many tears I shed before God until I understood what a *tallit* is." (*Sichot ha-Ran*, quoted in *Hishtapchut ha-Nefesh*, p. 19)

Regarding this story, hasidim highly value praying in a garment that has been worn by a great *tzaddik*, for having been in contact with his holy body, it gives rise to holy associations.

5:1:7:2:3 Siddurs often have a meditation to be said after putting on the *tallit* [said while it is fully over the head and eyes and before it is put on the shoulders—see *Shulchan Aruch* 9:8]. The following example suggests something of the significance of the *tallit*:

> How precious is Thy loving-kindness, O God! And under the shadow of Thy wings do the children of men take shelter. They shall be satisfied with the best food of Thy house, and of the river of Thy pleasures shalt Thou give them drink. For with Thee is the fountain of life; in Thy light shall we see light. Draw down Thy loving-kindness to them that know Thee and Thy goodness to the upright in heart. (Psalm 36:8-11)

We can see from this that when we are surrounded and covered by the *tallit*, there is the consciousness of being in the shadow of the wings of the Divine Presence, along with an awareness of the spiritual pleasure and bliss which comes from closeness to God.

> When you put on a *tallit* you should think that the Light of the Infinite One is hidden within this *tallit* that you wrap yourself in . . .

> and that when the wings of the *tallit* cover you, you are covered in the wings of the Light of the Infinite One. (*Or ha-Ganuz l'Tzaddikim*, p. 36)

We can intend when putting on the *tallit* that it separate us and shield us from outside distractions and from foreign thoughts. The large prayer-*tallit* surrounds one and this symbolizes protection.

> The meaning of the *tallit* is that of something which covers and surrounds—the secret of a great surrounding light—for the surrounding light [of God] protects a person from every evil . . . and he is saved from the wayward influence of the Shells [negative forces]. (*Kitzur Shnei Luchot ha-Brit*, Mesechet holin, inyanei tzitzit, p. 81)

For a meditation before putting on the *tallit*:

> . . . and through the *mitzvah* of *tzitzit* may my soul and my prayer be saved from the external forces and influences, and may the *tallit* spread its wings over them and save them. (*Kitzur Shnei Luchot ha-Brit*, p. 84. See also 5:2:3 for more about *tallit* and *tefillin*.)

5:1:7:3 *Gartel*

It is traditional among hasidic men to wear a special cloth (twined silk) prayer belt called a *gartel*, whose purpose is to make a symbolic separation between the lower body with its organs of sex and excretion, and the heart and brain. Rabbi Tzvi of Stretin:

> The *gartel* with which a man of Israel girds himself—what is its purpose? To make a separation between the upper part of his body and the lower part. (*Midor Dor*, vol. 2, #1336)

Following a parallel symbolism, hasidic men do not wear ties during prayer.

> The Master [Rabbi Menahem Mendel of Kotzk] would never wear a scarf or anything else around his neck while praying, so as not to make a separation between the brain and the heart. (*Emet v'Emunah*, p. 120)

In one case, the heart and brain are not to be affected during prayer by lower influences; in the other, the path from the heart to the brain is to be without hindrance.

Rabbi Eleazar Zev of Kretchnif considered the *gartel* as special clothing for prayer.

> [In the morning, after going to the *mikveh*, he] began his preparations for prayer by putting on a special garment for prayer, and he also put on a white *gartel* which was only for prayer and which he didn't wear the rest of the day. [Usually the *gartel* is black.] (*Raza d'Uvda*, p. 10)

It would be appropriate before prayer for men to say, when putting on the *gartel*, "Blessed are You, who girds Israel with strength," and to feel yourself strengthened with God's strength to serve Him. Remind yourself also of the *kippah* by touching it and saying: "Blessed are You, who crowns Israel with glory," thinking of the glory of God above you.[4] (Both these blessings come from the series of blessings said in the morning.)

There is a lovely story about the *gartel*:

> It was the custom of the holy rabbi, Rabbi Elimelech of Lizensk, every day after *Minha*, to speak words of Torah in his sweet way with his close disciples. Afterwards he would go into a special room where he prayed *Maariv* by himself, in holiness and purity. His disciple, the holy Rabbi Naftali of Ropshitz, whenever he was with his *rebbe*, always wanted very much to get into that room somehow so he could see what the *rebbe* was doing there. One time he went in without anyone knowing it and hid himself under the bed. The holy *rebbe*, the memory of a *tzaddik* for a blessing, went into the room, as was his holy custom, and closed the door after him. He then took his *gartel* to gird himself. When he wound it around his loins once, the room became filled with a great and wonderful light—something not of this world. When he wound it around him a second time, the light increased until the Ropshitzer could not bear it any longer, and beginning to faint, he cried out. Rabbi Elimelech, hearing him and becoming aware of his presence, said to him, "Naftali, my son, are you here? If you are here when I wind the *gartel* around me the third time, certainly your soul will leave your body from the excess of light. So depart from here at once." (*Ohel Elimelech*, p. 96, #248)

5:1:7:4 Shoeless

When you pray in your house, you can sometimes pray without shoes, for being without shoes tends to give us a feeling of humility. Rabbi

Hirsh of Tchortkov, the father of Rabbi Shmelke of Nikolsburg, prayed in a *minyan* where:

> All of them wore white. And during the time of prayer they covered the windows with a sheet of cloth so no one could look in. And all of them were shoeless.[5] (*Shemen ha-Tov*, p. 108, #110)

5:1:8 Pipe Smoking

Although this would not be a good idea today because of health reasons, it is interesting to know that at the beginning of the hasidic movement it was fairly common practice to smoke a pipe as a preparation for prayer. Pipe smoking encourages a meditative mood and the rising of the smoke has an inherent symbolic effect as the smoke goes up into "heaven" . . . like the smoke of the incense in the Temple.

> **5:1:8:1** It is written in various holy books from the disciples of the Besht, that smoking a pipe is, for the *tzaddikim*, like the burning of the incense in the Temple.[6] (*Avodah u'Moreh Derech*)

> **5:1:8:2** The secret of the smoke is that of the binding together of the worlds to God, blessed be He, as is explained with regard to the secret of the burning of incense in the Temple.[7] (*Darkei Tzedek*, p. 19)

5:1:8:3 The burning of incense in the place where you pray at home (see 5:1:3) can be used then with a somewhat similar intention as pipe smoking. One can look at the burning incense and its smoke, and think: "May I have great fervor in my prayer, and may it rise Above, and be pleasing to my Father in Heaven."

> **5:1:8:4** The Besht, the memory of a *tzaddik* for the life of the World to Come, said in regard to how well our prayers ascend [to heaven], that certainly the prayer does not "go up" in a material way when the words leave a person's mouth; but it is like the going up of smoke [which is due to the fire], and is just [symbolically] the desire of the person [expressed in his prayer], with arousal and with fervor [fire].[8] (*Or ha-Meir*, quoted in notes to *Tzavaat ha-Ribash*, Kehot edition, p. 109)

5:1:9 Breathing Meditation

It is possible to use a breathing meditation as part of a preparation for prayer. Our breath leads us to think of God, for it is connected with Him and is good evidence of our direct dependence on Him at every moment for our life. The rabbis were led from this thought to the obligation to praise God always.

The Torah says that God, when He created Adam, "breathed into his nostrils the breath of life" (Genesis 2:7). God does so for each of us now, too. And as the rabbis say: "You should praise God with each and every breath that you take" (*Bereshit Rabba* 14, end).

This thought of the rabbis is reflected in the prayer found right at the beginning of the Morning Service, a prayer that can be integrated into a breathing meditation:

> O my God, the soul that You have given me is pure—You created it, You formed it, You breathed it into me and You keep it within me. . . . And so, as long as my soul is within me, I will thank You and praise You, O Lord my God and the God of my fathers, Master of all actions, Lord of all souls.

Breathing exercises, such as taking long, regular breaths for a period of time, can be used to calm the mind before prayer and to dedicate the breath that comes from God, to be used now in His praise. Various holy words can be repeated mentally during such a breathing meditation. A few things can be noted from the tradition.

> **5:1:9:1** Our Sages said, "Let every soul [*neshamah*] praise God [Psalm 150). This means praise Him with every breath [*neshimah*]." So you can say at all times, "Blessed is the Merciful One, King of the Universe, Master of this time," or "of this moment."* (*Or ha-Ganuz l'Tzaddikim* p. 45) [We could ask: Why not "Master of this breath"?]

> **5:1:9:2** Once, the son of a certain *tzaddik* praised his [departed] father in the presence of Rabbi Tzvi Hirsh of Ziditchov, saying that his father did not cease from his *d'vekut* for even one twentieth of every twenty-four-hour period. But Rabbi Tzvi Hirsh [who thought this was small praise for that *tzaddik*] said to him in his pure language, "What are you saying? Young man, I tell you that with each and every breath that he took, when he breathed in it was with the name *Elohim*, and when he breathed out it was with the name

YHVH, blessed be He and blessed be His name." (*Eser Orot*, p. 151, #5)

This story might provide a suggestion for a breathing meditation, so we can just mention that the name of God, *Elohim*, is a plural word that alludes to the manifold powers of the Creator in nature. It is an aspect of kabbalistic/hasidic spiritual practice to work to identify all the active powers in the world with their source, the one God, whose name is YHVH.

5:1:9:3 As we see from Genesis, the breath represents the soul in a special way. Speech, which is a function of breath, also "has soul within it," and carries and communicates our personality and essence in a unique way. If you purify your thoughts in preparation for prayer, and keep your speech pure by not speaking improperly, the soul within your speech and breath will join and merge with the Speech and Breath of God, which breathes the soul (and life) into you, and they become as one. Since your soul is the part of the *Shechinah* within you, this is the part joining with the whole.

> [After purifying your thought and speech] if your prayer is clear and pure, certainly the holy breath which exits from your mouth will attach and join to the Upper Breath which is attached to you and continually enters you. As the rabbis, of blessed memory, said on the verse, "Let every thing that breathes praise God—with each and every exhalation of a man the breath goes from Below to Above, and then returns to him from Above to Below [when he inhales]. Certainly [if you have kept yourself pure] the Divine part within you can easily unite with its source." (*Likkutim Yekarim*, p. 15b)

Thus, in a breathing meditation you can meditate in exhalation on your soul going out to God, yearning for Him and praising Him for the life and goodness He continually gives you; with the inhalation, meditate on the *Shechinah*, the life and soul from God entering within you. Or simpler: for inhalation, meditate on God's love coming to you, and for exhalation, on your love going out to Him.

5:1:10 Avoid Conversation

Be silent for some time before and after prayer.

5:1:10:1 You should not talk for an hour before and an hour after

> prayer. (Rabbi Yehiel Michal of Zlotchov, *Hanhagot Tzaddikim*, p. 55, #9)

(Certainly this practice comes from reflecting on the tradition about the early hasidim mentioned in 5:1; see also 5:5:1.)

5:1:10:2 Silence before and after prayer sanctifies the words spoken to God; conversation devalues them.

> Rabbi Menahem Mendel of Rimanov used to say that when you engage in worldly talk before the Morning Prayers, you are pushing away the fear of God with both hands. (*Ateret Menahem*, p. 18, #37)

5:1:10:3 Of Rabbi Shlomo Leib of Lentshno it is told that:

> Before prayer he would not speak, even for something urgent; he would not even communicate with someone through his personal attendants, let alone speak directly. When he studied Torah through the night, even if his windows were closed and shuttered, he knew when the sun rose and he would stop speaking [with those who were with him] before dawn. (*Mazkeret Shem ha-Gedolim*, p. 167. See also "Waking and Beginning the Day," 4:12.)

The point here is not to converse. One can still greet others to show them honor.

5:1:11 Going Inward—Concentration of Vision

In the list of *hanhagot* of Rabbi Aaron the Great of Karlin, after instructing silence before and after prayer, he continues:

> Similarly, you should not look outside your personal space [four *amot*] before and after prayer, and at least on your return trip from the synagogue, and all the more so on your way there. (*Zichron l'Rishonim*, p. 38, #8. See also 5:2:2.)

5:1:12 Longing to Pray

A good preparation for prayer, before you open your mouth in speech, is to sit silently, meditating on your deep longing to pray. Think to yourself: "My Father in Heaven, I so much want to pray to You, for I know that if I am separated from You I am separated from life itself. I can picture in my mind how the holy people are so close to You and can talk with You freely. I long to be able to pray that way. I beg You to open my heart and my mouth now in sincere prayer."

(For more about this practice, see "Talking to God and Being Alone with God—*Hitbodedut*" [33]; and for an explanation of its efficacy, see "*Mitzvot,*" 11:4:1–4.)

5:1:13 *Tshuvah* (Repentance)

Do *tshuvah* before you *davven* (see "Repentance—*Tshuvah,*" 14:1:1 and 14:1:2). Our sins are a barrier separating us from our Father in Heaven. Before we come close we have to do all we can to remove that barrier.

> **5:1:13:1** Confess before you pray, and remember your lowliness. Also pray a short prayer of repentance. (Rabbi Shmuel Valtzis, *Midrash Pinhas,* p. 45a, #7)

You can say the Prayer of Repentance of Rabbeinu Yonah (quoted in "Repentance—*Tshuvah,*" 14:2) which speaks specifically of prayer. It is a good idea to copy it over, for this purpose, on the inside of your Siddur.

5:1:13:2 Doing *tshuvah,* as well as many of the things that follow in our discussion of preparation for prayer, can, it should be noted, be done verbally.

5:1:14 Open Your Heart to Love and Fear of God

5:1:14:1 Rabbi Moshe Teitelbaum:

> Before you pray and before Torah study, enwrap yourself as fully as you can with the love and fear of God. (*Hanhagot Tzaddikim,* p. 50, #33)

5:1:14:2 Rabbi Tzvi Elimelech of Dinov:

> Before prayer and before Torah study, after first meditating on *tshuvah,* arouse your heart to fear of God based on your love of Him. For without fear and love your service will not ascend to heaven. This

> self-arousal is to be done through meditation on God's greatness and exaltedness, and on all the overflowing good things that He continually showers upon us. And after all this, perhaps He will help us to reach this holy level for the sake of the honor of His name so that we will be inspired with a true fear and love of Him and our hearts will be opened. At the least our efforts will arouse the merit of Abraham, Isaac, and Jacob, for we have as an inheritance from them the potential for fear and love of God and for truth. You should also continually pause during your Torah study [and prayer] to meditate on this. (*Hanhagot Adam*, #10) (See also 5:2:8.)

When God's greatness is spoken of in Hasidism, what is usually meant is a meditation on how God is the Creator of all and the Ruler of all, how everything in existence is created by His will, and were His Will removed it would all disappear in an instant. Moreover, everything that happens is directed by God and nothing happens without His will. Awareness of His greatness leads to awe and fear of the Lord of the universe. But continuing this meditation to God's goodness arouses love for Him, because the purpose of the creation is God's will to do good to His creatures, and His benevolence is flowing to us at all times.

The fear based on love which the *rebbe* speaks of is the higher fear of God, where our "fear" is that we are afraid of not pleasing Him whom we love—and so we seek to do His will.

Doing such a meditation on God's greatness and goodness to arouse fear and love means to go over these ideas in our minds, silently or verbally. (See "Meditation," 17:2 for more about this typical hasidic meditation and how it leads into a meditation on being in the presence of God, which is the goal of prayer.)

5:1:14:3 Here is a slight adaptation of this idea, where the emphasis is on using something worldly to open your heart and arouse love.

> I heard from our master, Rabbi Zusya [of Hanipol], that when he wanted to have love in his heart for God, for prayer, etc., he would remind himself of some worldly love. So for anyone—when you are reminded of what you love, your children, or your money, when you have aroused happiness in your heart by this thought, and brought the love hidden within you into revelation—then, afterward, when you reflect on God's wondrous doings and kindnesses, great love for God will be aroused within you. For all loves and good things are rooted in Him who is their source. I saw this holy

> way used by the Rabbi, the Maggid of Rovno [the Maggid of Mezritch]. For when you want to burn some wood and it will not take fire, you bring some straw and light it first, and then the wood begins to burn. . . . And so sometimes it is good to light your inner fire first with "straw"—the joys of this world . . . and afterwards use this fire to light a fire in your soul. (*Menorat Zahav*, p. 119)

5:1:15 *Tzedaka*

5:1:15:1 Before you pray, give some money to charity, for this opens the heart. If you are in the synagogue there should be a receptacle for *tzedaka*; if you are praying in your house you should have a special jar, etc. available in which to collect it.

> **5:1:15:2** Give as much charity as you can, and give every day and before you pray. (Rabbi Aaron of Karlin, in *Hanhagot Tzaddikim*, p. 4, #4)
>
> Rabbi Yehiel Michal of Zlotchov says the same thing, and adds:
>
> And on *Shabbat* and *Yom Tov* [when you cannot touch money], state verbally what you will give, and give it after the day. (*Hanhagot Tzaddikim*, p. 52, #7)
>
> **5:1:15:3** [The Talmud says that] Rabbi Eleazar would give a coin to a poor man and afterward say his prayers; as it is written, "And I, with *tzedek* [righteousness—understood here to mean *tzedaka*, charity] will see Your face" [Baba Batra 10]. . . . And you should say this verse [Psalm 17:15] when you give *tzedaka* before prayer. (Rabbi Hayim Liberzohn, *Megaleh Amukot*, p. 9)

5:1:15:4 Some hasidic *rebbes* suggest making a connection particularly with the Land of Israel.

> Before every prayer give something to the poor of the Land of Israel. (Rabbi Mordechai of Lechovitz, *Hanhagot Tzaddikim*, p. 41, #6)
>
> By giving *tzedaka* to the poor of the Land of Israel before prayer you are included in the air of the Land of Israel and are saved from foreign thoughts. (Rabbi Nachman of Bratzlav, *Likkutei Aytzot*, *Tefillah*, #41)

5:1:16 Love and Forgiveness

As a preparation for prayer put yourself at peace with your fellow men.

> Before you begin your prayers in the synagogue you should receive on yourself to fulfill the commandment "you shall love your neighbor as yourself" (The Ari Hakodesh, *Minhagei ha-Arizal—Petura d'Abba*, p. 3b)

This is often done by means of an explicit declaration. (See 5:1:17 and 5:1:18:3:1 about this.)

A good time to meditate on your desire and commitment to love others is when you are giving some *tzedaka* before prayer. You should forgive anyone who has offended you and pray that God forgive him. And if you sin against someone, resolve that you will appease him that day.

If you are separated from your fellow men (except where the Torah dictates) you are thereby separated from God. So before you approach God in prayer you must first remove the barriers in your heart between you and other people.

We know from the teaching of the rabbis that a sin against another person is also a sin against God, and that before Yom Kippur, before you pray to God to forgive you your sins against your fellow men, you have to go and ask forgiveness of the people you have sinned against. But this teaching about Yom Kippur (like most of the lessons of the holidays) is to be applied always and throughout the year.[9] Thus, it is a good practice that every day before you pray and before you ask forgiveness of God for your sins, you first ask forgiveness of anyone you have offended, or at least resolve to go to him as soon as possible. Similarly, you should forgive others their sins.

> Do everything possible to enlarge your capacity for forgiveness, and forgive everyone who harms you in deed or word—even if he does not ask you to forgive him. (*Alpha Beta* of Rabbi Tzvi Hirsh [of Nadborna], Mehilah in *YHvT*, p. 65)

5:1:17 Join with All Israel and with the *Tzaddikim*

Many *rebbes* teach that before prayer you should link yourself in a spiritual bond with all of Israel.

Rabbi Yehiel Michal of Zlotchov said that:

> Before every prayer I join myself with all Israel. (*Mazkeret Shem ha-Gedolim*, p. 14)

It is usually taught that you are to link yourself particularly to the high spiritual people of your generation (see the prayer of Rabbi Abraham Hayim of Zlotchov, 5:1:20:4).

You can say: "I join myself and my prayers with the prayers of all the Community of Israel throughout the world, that our prayers should rise together before our Father in Heaven. I also join myself and my prayers with the prayers of all the *tzaddikim* of the generation."

If you know any *tzaddikim*, picture their faces and images before you at this time. One version of this declaration has the following:

> I accept on myself the commandment "and you shall love your neighbor as yourself"—and after saying this, join in complete love with the holy souls of the *tzaddikim* of the generation whose visages you know, and picture them before you in your imagination at this time. (*Yosher Divrei Emet*, #33)

(See "Individual Practices," 39:26 for more about this.)

> This is the accepted version among our [Bratzlaver] fellowship [according to the teachings of Rabbi Nachman of Bratzlav] for what to say before prayer: "I bind myself in my prayer to all the true *tzaddikim* of our generation and to all the true *tzaddikim* who sleep in the earth. . . ." (Rabbi Aaron Leib Tzigelman, *Hanhagot Tzaddikim* [III], vol. 2, p. 736)

You can mention the names of *tzaddikim* from our generation or former times with whom you have a soul connection: "I join myself with the holy Baal Shem Tov, with the holy Rabbi Levi Yitzhak of Berditchev, with the holy Rabbi Zusya of Hanipol," and so on. According to hasidic tradition the mere mention of the names of the *rebbes* has a holy power.

5:1:18 Meditation for *Kavvanah* and *D'vekut*—to Separate from this World and to be Before God

There are various things that can be included in a meditation of preparation for prayer. Much of what we have already discussed can be part of such a sitting meditation. But the essence of meditation for prayer is to attain *kavvanah* and *d'vekut*.

5:1:18:1 Separate Yourself from This World

> Let your prayer be with the *kavvanah* of your heart, and before praying, empty your mind of all your worldly concerns. (*Derech Hayim*, 3-3)

The wheels of the mind roll on with thoughts of worldly things and have to be brought to a stop before you pray. When you are preparing for prayer, separate yourself from this world and its concerns. Remind yourself of the links with this world that can hold you back spiritually and can disturb your prayer, and separate yourself from them one by one. Assert your determination, based on faith and trust in God, that job, money, family problems, health, and all other worries of this world will not keep you back. When you separate yourself from the troubles of this world, you can then pray with a joyful heart.

Rabbi Abraham of Slonim told this story about himself:

> Once, before prayer, a great bitterness came over me, such that I could not even begin to pray. But I thought to myself, "Maybe this is not a holy bitterness, due to sadness over my sins and faults, but connected with things of this world. So I began to compose myself and to disassociate myself from all concerns of this world, from worrying over making a living and such things. And indeed this worked. It helped me to dissipate the bitterness, until I was actually able to pray with great joy."
>
> [The text continues:] His grandson related in the name of Rabbi Abraham that once he was so immersed in deep sadness that none of the various traditional counsels for arousing joy worked. So he decided, and made his heart follow his decision, that all the things of this world that are able to cause a person depression would not have any place at all in his heart. But even this did not help until he decided that even matters of the World to Come, even spiritual hopes and desires would not have any hold on him whatsoever. Because what is the World to Come to him if it causes anxiety, which is against the will of the Holy One, blessed be He? . . . For the Holy One, blessed be He, desires that we serve Him with joy. And this firm resolve of the *rebbe* was enough to arouse joy in his heart. (*Torat Avot*, p. 171)

The culmination of separating oneself from this world is reached during prayer in the state of *hitpashtut ha-gashmiyut* (removing the soul from materiality and from the body as if taking off a garment). For more about this, see 5:3:15.

5:1:18:2 Separating yourself from worldly concerns (as well as many of the other preparations already discussed) will empty your mind of thought and make it calm. But that is only the first, and negative, aspect of *kavvanah*. The positive side is that through focusing more and more on God, you will come to experience His presence. The goal, then, is that the intense and directed attention of *kavvanah* lead to *d'vekut*.

> What is the definition of *kavvanah*? It means that a person should empty his mind of all thought and see himself as if he is standing in the presence of the *Shechinah*. (The Rambam, *Yad*, Tefillah 4:16)

We have just discussed the negative aspect of the preparation for prayer; now we pass to the positive aspect.

5:1:18:3 In the Presence

5:1:18:3:1 *Light Meditation; God as "The Place"*

> The early hasidim would spend an hour before prayer in order to direct their minds to God [literally, The Place]. [*Berachot* 5:1] They would empty their minds of the things of this world and bind themselves to the Lord of all with awe and love. Imagining that the Light of the Divine Presence that was above their heads was flowing down and spreading around them, they would sit in the Light and tremble and shake from their awe. And they would also rejoice at this awe that came on them, as it says, "Serve God with fear and rejoice in trembling." (*Maabar Yabok*, quoted in *Avodah u'Moreh Derech*, chap. 25, p. 42)

In the tradition of the mishnah (*Berachot* 5:1), the hasidim are said to have directed their minds to God, who is called by one of His names: The Place. (As the rabbis teach: He is the Place of the world.) The "place," therefore, where you sat and prayed was related to the reference of the mishnah. God is understood as being The Place which surrounds you, and His Light and Presence are revealed all around you in that place where you pray. This version of the ancient tradition (using the name,

The Place) led the hasidim of the era of the Besht to a light meditation. The light of the Divine Presence is imagined as above the head (according to the traditional conception, the halo) and flowing down and surrounding the person.[10]

The Peasetzna Rebbe suggests such a meditation, but without the idea of the light above the head:

> When a Jew is about to pray, he should concentrate fully, and picture how all the world and everything in it, everything, is God's light, and His glory fills the world. And I am standing in the midst of His Godliness. (*Hovat ha-Talmidim*, p. 147)

Elsewhere a suggestion is made: Before prayer or during prayer, you are to close your eyes occasionally and concentrate on your surroundings as manifesting the light of the *Shechinah*, relating to their spiritual essence rather than their material forms.

> When you are praying, you should close your eyes so that you do not see material things, rather you will see more subtle things, and you will be connected to the spiritual side, which is the subtle life-energy residing within the coarser material objects that appear before your eyes. (*Avodah u'Moreh Derech*, chap. 25, p. 43)

> [Rabbi Shneur Zalman of Ladi] once asked his son (the Middle Rebbe) what meditation he was using to direct his prayers. He answered, "With the lesson about 'Whatsoever is lofty shall bow down before Thee.'" Afterward, he asked his father the same question in return, "With what are you praying?" He answered him, "With the floor and the bench." (*Beit Rabbi*, I, chap. 28, p. 178)

The note in the text here explains that "This is a meditation on how even the wood and stone are kept in existence by the Divine life-energy, and if it were removed for a second the material thing would immediately return to nothingness." (See "Sight," 25:11.)

Other texts speak not of being in the midst of the Light of the *Shechinah*, but of visualizing it before you. The following instruction somewhat combines the two:

> During the time of your prayer [or in the preparation before] think that His glory [the *Shechinah*] fills the world. Be in awe and fear. Stand in holy shame and cast down your glance, and think that a great light is in front of you; and stand before the God of glory who is the source of light without limit." (*Derech Hayim*, 1–58)

This fits with the traditional practice in the *Shemoneh Esreh* when you take three steps forward to symbolize the intention of entering into the very presence of the King who is before you. On the other hand, the *Sh'ma* connects with the other aspect (the surrounding light), as we are told that when you say *echad* (one) in the *Sh'ma*:

> You should extend the *chet* sound until you have recognized God's kingship over heaven and earth . . . and extend the *dalet* until you have meditated on how He is one in His universe, and rules over all four directions of the world. . . . There are those who nod their heads at this time to above and below and in the four directions. (*Orach Hayim*, Hilchot Kriyat Sh'ma, 61:6)

The Baal Shem Tov says:

> "Hear O Israel, the Lord our God, the Lord is one." The meaning of "one" is the unification which is involved in the recitation of the *Sh'ma*, to intend that there is nothing in the world except the Holy One, blessed be He, for His glory fills the earth. The essence of the *kavvanah* is that a person consider himself as nothing and nullified, and that his essence is only the soul within him, which is a part of God from Above. So there is nothing in the world except the One, the Holy One, blessed be He, and the main part of the meditation for saying this "one" is that His glory fills the earth and there is no place where He, blessed be He, is not present. (*Sefer Baal Shem Tov*, vol. 2 p. 163)

Whether all around you or before you, the *Sh'ma* and the *Shemoneh Esreh* are good times to concentrate on being in the presence of God this way; the meditation before the prayer prepares for that. It would seem that such variations about picturing the light of the *Shechinah* around you or before you, can be used according to preference, even though, undoubtedly, they represent different aspects and sometimes different levels of spiritual realization. (See also "Torah," 15:18 for more about light meditation.)

The typical hasidic meditation on God's greatness and goodness (described earlier) often leads into a meditation on being in the presence of God. (See the entire chapter on "Meditation"; note the quote there of Rabbi Tzvi Elimelech of Dinov who explains the meditation and suggests its use before prayer.)

The light meditation is often spoken of as imagining oneself in the Garden of Eden, where the light of the *Shechinah* is revealed. See the quote in "Torah," 15:18:4:2 from the Maggid of Mezritch where he says: "We know that when a person learns Torah or prays he should think of himself as being in the Garden of Eden, where there is no jealousy, or lustful desire, or pride, and he will thereby be saved from having such thoughts while he studies or prays."

The Talmud teaching on which this is based is about how the *tzaddikim* will enjoy the radiance of the *Shechinah* in the World to Come (the Garden of Eden), where there is no eating, drinking, or other worldly activities.

The Maggid of Mezritch had his son Abraham (who was known as the Angel because of his complete separation from worldliness) study together with Rabbi Shneur Zalman of Ladi. Here is a story about them:

> Once, the holy Rabbi Abraham and Rabbi Shneur Zalman were praying, and when the latter finished first he brought over some food and began to eat. After this incident, Rabbi Abraham refused to study Torah with him for three days. Rabbi Shneur Zalman informed Rabbi Abraham's father, the holy Maggid, about this, and he asked his son why he was so angry and why he refused to learn with Shneur Zalman. Rabbi Abraham answered him, "How did he dare to bring something so material [food] into my Garden of Eden!" But under order of his holy father, the Maggid, he began again to learn with him as before. (*Beit Rabbi*, I, chap. 25, p. 123, n. 2)

5:1:18:3:2 *Our Father in Heaven*

Along with the version of the early hasidim's preparation for prayer which refers to God as The Place, there is another version (some versions of the Mishnah [*Berachot* 5:1] and also the Talmud version):

> The early hasidim would spend an hour [before prayer] to direct their hearts to their Father in Heaven. (*Berachot* 30)

One possible meditation, or prayer before prayer, is to strengthen the belief in our minds and hearts that God is indeed our Father and we are His children.

Rabbi Samson Rafael Hirsch, on the very purpose of our prayers:

> The prayers should raise man in the purest perfection to be as a child towards his Father in heaven, perceiving the Father everywhere, allowing everything to be permeated by the thought of the Father, resolving the whole world, and the whole of life, in the single relationship of Father and child. (*Horeb*, #688, vol. 2, p. 544)

> During prayers, one of the hasidim of the Kotzker Rebbe was crying out to God, "Father, Father!" But another hasid, making a joke of this, called out, "Maybe He's not his Father" [meaning his behavior was not on that spiritual level]. The *rebbe*, hearing this, answered him, "If you cry out often enough, "Father, Father!" He actually becomes your Father in truth." (*Siah Sarfei Kodesh*, IV, p. 29, #68)

The following personal story is told by a contemporary Bratzlaver hasid, the late Rabbi Hirsz Wasilski of Brooklyn:

> Some years ago his little son, who was just learning to talk, had come to him in the living room of their house and said, "*Tatteh*" [Father]. "What do you want, my child?" Wasilski had asked, but the child did not say what he wanted. He had only repeated the word *tatteh* in a tone [Rabbi Wasilski said] "which almost made me cry—as if he was trying to say something. I kept on asking, 'What is it, *mein kind*?' till I suddenly realized that he was not asking. He was saying something. He was saying, '*Tatteh*, I know you are there if I need you; I know you will take care of me if I'm hungry, if I'm sad.' He was telling me that he trusted me, that he was glad I was there.
>
> "I forgot all about it until Rosh Hashanah, when I was praying here. I pray in a corner in the synagogue and the prayers of the congregation are nice. They were nice and yet something was wrong—with my own prayers. I thought to myself, here I am after so many years trying to pray and learn but my prayers are on a lower level than they were when I was a child in the yeshivah. I felt worse and worse, and my prayers grew more and more weak until suddenly I thought of my son. I turned to the corner and started saying over and over again, '*Tatteh, Tatteh*.' Just that, over and over again. I don't remember what happened except that when I looked down the floor was wet with tears, and I knew that I had been praying." (*9 1/2 Mystics*, p. 201)

There is a remarkable parallel to this story in the teaching of the Peasetzna Rebbe quoted in "Song and Dance," 24:7.

Calling out to God as our Father, aloud or silently, can be done as a prayer/meditation in preparation for prayer; it can be done again and again during the prayers and at other times as well. (See 5:2:4.) It can also be accompanied by other words that express our recognition of God as our Father and His kindness to us, along with prayers about our desire to feel our relation to Him more strongly, to have trust in Him as a child, etc.

5:1:18:3:3 *Face to Face*

Sefer Haredim understands the tradition about the early hasidim spending an hour before prayer to direct their hearts to mean a silent meditation where you come face to face with God:

> Lift your eyes upward to the Only King, the Cause of all causes, as if He were the target for an arrow. Then, "As water reflects a face, so does the heart of a man reflect what is in the heart of his fellow." So when you come and turn your face and eyes to God, He, blessed be His name, will turn His face to you, and you will cling to each other in *d'vekut*. (chap. 73; cf. chap. 65 end, where the connection is made with the tradition of the early hasidim)

It is notable that *Sefer Haredim* speaks of this kind of meditation as a practice in its own right, not just in connection with prayer. (A practical point: I assume that one can have one's eyes open or closed for this meditation.)

5:1:19 Determination to Overcome Obstacles

Resolve while preparing to pray that you will not be distracted by obstacles, but will go straight to your destination, which is to be in the presence of God and to stand before Him. Resolve to go deeper and deeper as you pray. You can express your intention in this as a declaration.

> There is a screen of separation between God, blessed be He, and man [caused by sin]. And during the time of prayer you have to exert all the energy of your mind, making the words that you say shatter and break through that separating barrier until you are able to cling to Him, blessed be He, in *d'vekut*. (*Darkei Yesharim*, p. 7)

The Besht told a parable about this:

> There was once a king who was very wise, and by magic which deceived the eyes of the beholder, he made imaginary walls and towers and gates to surround his palace. He also gave a command that those who wanted to see him must enter through the gates and towers. He further ordered that at each gate riches from his treasuries be given away.
>
> Now there were those who came to the first gate, received money and, being satisfied, went back home. There were those who [were deterred by the imposing walls and barriers, or who lost their way in all the various gates and walls]. No one was able to enter and see the

> king, until the king's beloved son came—and he was determined to exert all his efforts to see his father, the king, without being deterred by good or bad. And [due to this firm determination and unrelenting desire] he saw that there was no barrier at all between himself and his father, for it was all just a magical illusion.
>
> The application of this parable is easily understood: that the Holy One, blessed be He, hides within various garments and barriers. But when you know that God, blessed be He, fills all the earth and there is no place where He is not present, that every movement and thought of yours is from Him, blessed be He, that all the angels and heavenly palaces were all created and made, so to speak, from His own essence, blessed be He, like the snail whose garment is part of its own body, that there is no barrier between a man and God, blessed be He—with this knowledge all the workers of iniquity [the Shells that seem to separate man and God] are scattered. (*Keter Shem Tov*, p. 13)

Note that it is the *son* who is not deterred by fear or bought off by slight rewards, but spurred forward by love and trust and his intense desire to be in the presence of his Father. (See 5:2:10:5 for suggestions of the Peasetzna Rebbe on how to force your way forward in prayer.)

5:1:20 In the Land of Israel

Another meditation before prayer can be to imagine that you are in Israel.

> **5:1:20:1** [Rabbi Yitzhak Isaac of Ziditchov] said once that every day, before praying the Morning Service, he takes a walk to the Holy Land. (*Pe'er Yitzhak*, p. 94, #5)

5:1:20:2 Of course, if you have been in the Land of Israel, in Jerusalem, and at the Western Wall, it is easier to picture yourself as being there. It is told of Rabbi Pinhas of Koretz that:

> He said to someone who had been in the Land of Israel, that he should picture before himself, during the time of prayer, its views and scenes, with their seas, lakes, and rivers, and its [Jewish] inhabitants—and he will see how great is the power of these scenes to help his prayer. (*Tosefta l'Midrash Pinhas*, #27)

(This probably means during all the service, not only the *Shemoneh Esreh*.)

5:1:20:3 Photographs or paintings of Israel, Jerusalem, or the Western Wall on your wall can also be used to this end when praying at home.

5:1:20:4 Related to all this, Rabbi Abraham Hayim of Zlotchov said:

> I received a tradition that before every prayer, in the evening and in the morning, one should say: "I am sending my prayer from here to the Land of Israel, and from there to Jerusalem, and from Jerusalem to the Temple Mount, and from the Temple Mount to the Temple Court, and from there to the Hall leading to the Holy Place, and from there to the Holy Place, and from there to the Holy of Holies (and from there to the Heavenly Temple), the place where my fathers, Abraham, Isaac, and Jacob prayed. And together with all the prayers of all the synagogues and houses of Torah study, and in unity with all Israel, and especially those of Your children who know the profound intentions of the prayers and all their holy secrets—according to this intention I pray to You, with both love and fear, in the name of all Israel."* (*P'ri Hayim*, quoted in *DhTvhY*, Tefillah, #21)

5:1:20:5 This imagination-meditation about being in Israel will then lead into the meditation done at the time of the *Shemoneh Esreh*, the high point of the prayer service, where you are to imagine that you are standing in the Holy of Holies, in the Temple. (See also 5:3:13:3.)

5:1:21 In Heaven/The Garden of Eden

Another meditation that can be used for prayer (and at other times) is to imagine that you are in heaven or, what often amounts to the same thing, the Garden of Eden.

> **5:1:21:1** It is very good for a person, when praying or studying Torah, to think that he is not now in this world, but in the Garden of Eden in the presence of the *Shechinah*—for by doing this he will purify his thoughts. (*Reshit Hochmah*, Sh'ar ha-Kedushah, chap. 4, #23)

> **5:1:21:2** When you are praying, think to yourself that you are going around in the Upper Worlds; as it says in *Reshit Hochmah*, you should think of yourself as being in the Upper Garden of Eden. And then you certainly will not have any shame or self-conscious-

> ness before other people. So, too, should you think when you are studying Torah. (*Darkei Tzedek*, p. 10, #81)

5:1:21:3 Rabbi Abraham the Angel spoke of the personal space where he prayed as being his Garden of Eden (see 5:1:18:3:1).

5:1:21:4 This meditation can be used as a preparation for prayer and for all of the prayer, but there are those who particularly use it for the *Shemoneh Esreh* (see 5:3:14 and 5:3:15).

5:1:22 God's Greatness and Your Smallness; Your Soul and God

The Hasam Sofer taught that it is due to the influence of the body that foreign thoughts come to a man, so that during prayer his heart turns this way and that to the vanities of this world. To counter this intrusion of foreign thoughts, one should, before prayer, do a preparatory meditation that exalts the soul over the body.

> Before prayer you should meditate on the greatness of the Creator, blessed be He, and the smallness of the man who stands opposite Him [yourself]. But then be proud that He breathed within you a living Godly soul which is a part of God from Above whose upper portion is bound Above and whose lower portion is bound within the miserable body. Realize also that all the life-energy of the soul comes from Him in this time of prayer, when you bind it in *d'vekut* to the Most High God, as it is written, "And you that cleave [to God are alive all of you this day]." Then all foreign thoughts of the vanities of this world will be nullified. (*Yesodot b'Avodat HaShem*, p. 93)

Such a meditation on God's greatness and your smallness, mentioned in this teaching of the Hasam Sofer is typical. A hasidic story begins:

> The *gaon* and *tzaddik* Rabbi Levi Yitzhak of Berditchev, of blessed memory, once . . . got up in the morning and, wanting to prepare himself for prayer, meditated on the exaltedness of God, blessed be He, and his own lowliness, until he felt that there was no one in the world worse than he—and his heart broke within him. (*Derech Tzaddikim*, p. 53)

The story continues about how he then "went too far" and fell into sadness, and since we must pray and serve God with joy, he had to find a way to make himself happy. He finally succeeded when he thought of how happy he was that he was a Jew. This has a general lesson for us regarding meditations in preparation for prayer that involve repentance and thinking about our lowliness. Note that the teaching of the Hasam Sofer has the same pattern. He solved this problem by teaching that we should rejoice in our innate Godly nature (our soul).

5:1:23 A Declaration Nullifying Foreign Thoughts

As discussed above, you must separate yourself from the concerns of this world and place yourself in the spiritual world. For prayer to be pure it must not have foreign thoughts of worldly matters mixed in with it. Your mind and heart should be on God alone. Expressing a determination to avoid foreign thoughts, and nullifying them if they occur, can be a part of a preparation for prayer. It is possible to make an explicit declaration to this effect, saying: "God, my sincere desire is to pray to You without any foreign thoughts whatsoever. But since, because of my lowliness, I am not in complete control of this, I hereby declare before You that I nullify altogether and absolutely any thoughts other than thoughts of holiness that come to my mind during the time of prayer—because I don't want them at all. If such is Your will. Amen."

This declaration can also be repeated during prayers. (For related declarations dealing with unwanted thoughts, motives, etc., see "The Synagogue and the Synagogue Service," 6:24, "Torah," 15:7, and "Individual Practices," 39:12. In 5:2:10:1 we will discuss other methods of dealing with foreign thoughts.

5:1:24 Pray to be Able to Pray in the Right Way

You may feel that you are inadequate to achieve the kind of prayer you know you should pray (and this is a proper way to feel). Pray, then, for God's help. You may even lack the desire to pray. You can pray to God, then, that He give you the love of prayer, and He will fulfill your request. If this is your situation, pray from the depths of your heart, "My God, I'm in a bad way; my condition is mortal. I have a serious disease—I have no desire to pray. I beg You, before I die from this disease, give me a love for prayer!" Make other petitions also that express your wish that your prayers be pure, that they be sincere, and not mechanical, etc.

Praying to be able to pray is a widespread hasidic teaching. It is also typically connected with the tradition of the prayer preparations of the early hasidim.

> **5:1:24:1** The holy Rabbi Yosef of Neishtadt once asked his master, the Tzanzer Rebbe, "What does the *rebbe* do before prayer?" He answered, "I *davven* to be able to *davven*." (*Mekor Hayim*, p. 111, #372)

5:1:24:2 Rabbi Yehiel Michal of Zlotchov said about the tradition of the early hasidim and their lengthy preparations before prayer, that:

> The hour that they were waiting, they were praying that they would be able to direct their hearts in their prayer . . . and that God would help them pray aright. (*Mazkeret Shem ha-Gedolim*, p. 24; the same thing is said in the name of Rabbi Yitzhak of Vorki in *Ohel Yitzhak*, p. 17, #32)

5:1:24:3 Rabbi Shmuel of Slonim said that there were many preparations for prayer, various meditations, etc., that involved our own effort, but that ultimately it all depends on God, and we should pray to Him:

> The Sages, of blessed memory, said that "The early hasidim would wait an hour and then pray" (*Berachot* 30). Sometimes a person does make much preparation for prayer. . . . But the main thing is to know that whatever you do and prepare amounts to nothing, and that everything is from Him . . . and that you should pray to God, supplicating and begging for His mercy, that He put light into your heart that you be able to pray. . . . This was the level of the early hasidim, for though on the one hand they waited for an hour, engaged in their great preparation for prayer, together with this they would pray and pour out their hearts before prayer, that God, blessed be He, give them light. (*Divrei Shmuel*, p. 199, #5)

5:1:25 The Intentions Beforehand

One practice used in preparing for prayer is to go over the *intentions* of all the different prayers (meditating on them or praying silently) before beginning.

> The Rabbi of Barniv told how the first time he visited the Tzanzer Rebbe after he was married, when he was still very young, about 15

or 16 years old, he came into the *rebbe's* holy house in the morning to receive his greeting of peace. But when he entered the room, the *rebbe*, may his merit protect us, did not even look at him or pay him any heed or greet him. He just sat there, smoking his pipe as was his holy way.

After an hour or more, though, the *rebbe* stopped smoking and greeted him, and asked him who he was. . . . [After a brief conversation] the *rebbe* said to him, "Let me tell you why I didn't greet you as soon as you came in. I was then in the middle of the *kavvanot* for the prayer of the Song at the Sea [in the Morning Service which the *rebbe* had not yet said], so I was not permitted to interrupt to greet you. But now that I've completed the preparation for the prayer I am able to greet you." (*Otzar ha-Sippurim*, II, p. 16)

Note the pipe. (See 5:3:12 about silently going over beforehand the intentions of individual prayers during the service.)

5:1:26 Song and Dance

Though it is not typical, some hasidim prepare for prayer through song and even dance.

5:1:26:1 About Rabbi Abraham Kalisker and his hasidic followers:

In order to set for themselves the proper mood for the daily prayers, they felt the need of a lengthy period of inspirational preparation through dancing and singing. (Rabbi N. Mindel, *Wellsprings*, p. 7)

5:1:26:2 A hasid once complained to the Tzaddik of Rizhin [Rabbi Israel] about his son-in-law, that he wasted his time before the Morning Prayers—he did not study Torah or go to the *mikveh* as all the hasidim do. The *rebbe* asked him, "Nevertheless, what *does* he do then?" The hasid answered, "He walks around singing to himself your *niggunim* [melodies]." "If so," the *rebbe* said, "you should know that my melodies purify as does the *mikveh*." (*Beit Rizhin*, p. 120)

5:1:27 Concluding Notes about Preparation for Prayer

5:1:27:1 It is worth knowing that some of the preparations described above are more commonly practiced (and generally considered more essential) than others. The ones that are most widely used are: Torah study, *mikveh* (before the Morning Prayer), *tshuvah*, *tzedaka*, accepting love of neighbor on yourself, joining with all of Israel, meditation for love and fear of God, meditation for *d'vekut*, and praying to be able to pray.

5:1:27:2 A book about the Tzanzer Rebbe that has a chapter on his *hanhagot* gives his preparations for the Morning Prayers, which included: Torah study, pipe smoking, *mikveh*, *tzedaka*, prayer to be able to pray, and meditation on God's greatness and glory (*Rabbeinu ha-Kodesh mi Tzanz*, pp. 212–214).

5:1:27:3 Many of the things involved in the preparation for prayer can be done verbally, or accompanied verbally. This is true of the meditations also, though whether they or other preparations are done mentally or aloud depends on the individual.

Much of the preparation can also be done as an extended prayer–meditation spoken to God, declaring how you commit yourself to repentance, to loving Him and your fellow men, etc.

5:1:27:4 Certainly anyone who wants to take prayer seriously should set a preparation period before prayer for a specific amount of time—five, ten, fifteen, thirty minutes or more (start with five)—where a general outline of the various elements mentioned above is followed. Use those that help you. Many can be done one after the other. The value of this practice will be shown in experience.

5:1:27:5 It is a good idea to write a brief outline of an order for your prayer-preparation somewhere in your Siddur, noting just the headings of various topics mentioned above, so that you have it ready at hand.

5:1:27:6 *Mishnah Berurah* (Orach Hayim, Siman 94:1) about the early hasidim meditating for an hour before prayer:

> However, this is for the hasidim and the most pious; for the rest of the people, some small amount of time is sufficient.

5:1:27:7 Much of what follows in this chapter about how to pray is also relevant for the period of preparation, for that is an appropriate time to remind yourself of various things you want to do when praying, and to resolve to do them. For example, you might remind yourself to raise your voice, move your body, control your glance, all of which will be dealt with in the following pages.

(A further brief discussion of preparation for prayer is found in *hanhagot* connected with the synagogue. See "The Synagogue and the Synagogue Service," 6:17.)

5:2 CONCENTRATION AND *KAVVANAH*

Prayer, to achieve its purpose, must be with directed attention (*kavvanah*), with burning intensity (*hitlahavut*), and with love and fear of God. Without these qualities, as the kabbalists say, it does not rise up into the heavens.

5:2:1 Continuity, Not Interruption; Dive Deep

Your concentration in prayer, your ability to dive deep, will be increased by the continuity you achieve in your praying. The tradition about the early hasidim in the mishnah of *Berachot* 5:1 has this added note:

> The early hasidim would spend an hour directing their hearts to their Father in Heaven. Even if the king speaks to him in greeting while he is praying, he should not answer, and even if a snake is wound around his heel ready to strike, he should not interrupt.

Thus, you should make every effort not to interrupt your prayers in any way.[12] The less you interrupt and the fewer times you need to come to the surface, the deeper you will be able to dive. The hasidic *rebbes* often speak in terms of letting yourself dive into the letters of the prayers in the Siddur before you, to picture that the Divine Presence resides in the letters, and you want to join yourself with Him there. This is used as a meditation technique to achieve concentration. But the kabbalistic emphasis on the actual letters is not necessary for the basic idea.

This practice actually solves a problem that comes with praying from a book. If a person has to look into the book, the Siddur, to read the prayers, it can distract him from directing himself to God, who is (he imagines) "elsewhere." (See 5:3:3.) But if God is manifested in the Siddur, however in a special way, and if you concentrate on the thought that God is "in the book," you can look into it for the prayers and pray to God at the same time.

According to the *halacha*, the time most to be protected from interruption is, in the Morning Prayers, from *Baruch sh'amar* (Blessed is He who spoke) to the end of the *Amidah*, which is the high point and culmination of the service.

> Do not converse from when you begin *Baruch sh'amar* until you finish the Whispered Prayer [the *Amidah*], nor during the time when the prayer leader repeats the *Amidah*—except for words of Torah or for something connected with the performance of a *mitzvah*, or to offer or answer a greeting of *Shalom*. (*Orchot Hayim*, 1-4) (See the *Shulchan Aruch* for more information about permitted interruptions, as even the exceptions mentioned here do not apply for certain parts of the service.)

5:2:2 God's Name before Your Eyes; Your Glance

To concentrate and focus your mind, you must avoid the distractions that come from wandering eyes. When you pray at home have a card with God's name YHVH (יהוה) written on it, before you on a table as you pray. Look at it from time to time, or steadily for a period of time, to direct your attention. (See also "Torah," 15:20, pp. 28–29.) Or have such a card or a *Shivitti* on the wall. A *Shivitti* is a traditional wall card, poster, or plaque with the phrase from Psalms 16:8— "I have placed YHVH before me always"—on it. You can also work to achieve the ability of seeing the Name before you without external visual aids.

> A wonderfully effective way to keep concentration in prayer and avoid foreign thoughts is to picture before your eyes the name Havaya [YHVH], blessed be He, for the whole time of the prayer service. (Rabbi Arele Roth, *Noam ha-Levavot*, p. 41n.)
>
> The Sages of the Kabbalah have written in their books that to purify your mind during prayer you should continuously imagine the name יהוה before you as if written in black ink on white paper. . . . Many people write the name יהוה on a piece of parchment . . . and keep it in front of them while they pray, according to the way of "I have placed the Lord before me always." And this brings awe of God into the heart and clarifies your soul to

> purity. (*Kitzur Shnei Luchot ha-Brit*, Hilchot beit ha-knesset, p. 145)

Some have used a small card or *Shivitti* of this sort placed in their Siddur. (This, of course, would be appropriate for *davvening* in the synagogue.)

> There are those who write on a piece of parchment or paper the name *Havaya*, blessed be He, along with the words of Psalm 67 all formed into the shape of a *menorah*, and place it within their Siddur, above, so as to look at it continually, to fulfill "I have placed the Lord before me always . . ." (*Kaf ha-Hayim*, 12:13, p. 170)

It is not clear how this actually should be arranged, though of course there are various possibilities. Hebrew bookstores often have small paper *Shivittis* which can be used for this purpose.

Do not let your eyes wander when praying. Look in the Siddur, at a card, a *Shivitti*, or at the *tzitzit* on your *tallit*. Look at the sky through the window, or at the wall. In the synagogue you can also look at the Ark. Control of your glance will aid you greatly to control your mind and focus it on God. This is why in the synagogue, before the stand from which the prayer leader prays, there is usually a *Shivitti* on the wall facing him. The rabbis also said that you should try to pray in a room with windows (referring to Daniel 6:11) so that you can look out at the sky, for the sky reminds you of heaven and inspires religious feeling (*Berachot* 31). (See also "Sight," 25:10.) Praying with the *tallit* over your head can also be useful in controlling your glance.

> Be very careful not to look around. . . . The way to do this is that you should not take your eyes off the Siddur in your hands, or if you do not have a Siddur [and are praying from memory], close your eyes or look at the *tzitzit* or at the name *Havaya*, blessed be He, which is before you. (*Kaf ha-Hayim*, 14:33, p. 194)

5:2:3 *Tefillin, Tzitzit*

5:2:3:1 When you have *tefillin* on it is a traditional practice (and one that increases prayer concentration) to frequently touch them (first arm, then head) and kiss your fingers (although not during the *Shemoneh Esreh*). This is so you do not forget for a moment that you have on these holy devices. When you do this, direct your attention to God, for the *tefillin's* purpose is to keep His remembrance before us. (See also Chapter 1, p. 26.)

5:2:3:2 The *tzitzit* can also be used this way during prayer.

5:2:3:2:1 Be careful to look at the *tzitzit* often, to remind yourself continually of the love and fear of God, of the need for *d'vekut*, and of all the other holy intentions related to the *tzitzit*. (Rabbi Nahum of Tchernobil, *Hanhagot Tzaddikim*, p. 36, #16)

5:2:3:2:2 Always look at the *tzitzit*; it is even better if you kiss them frequently. (*Derech Hayim*, 5-42)

Kissing holy objects is a typical way to cultivate and express our devotion. (See "Individual Practices," 39:21.)

When you kiss the *tzitzit* and the *tefillin* or the *sefer* Torah say, "Let Him kiss me with the kisses of His mouth [for His love is better than wine]" (Songs 1:2), and have as your intention that just as you kiss the *tzitzit*, etc., so does the Light of the Infinite One and the Supernal Will that is clothed within this *mitzvah* [-object] kiss you—the attachment [*d'vekut*] of spirit to spirit. (*Or ha-Ganuz l'Tzaddikim*, p. 59)

5:2:4 Call Out to Your Father in Heaven

[It is a hasidic practice to] call out loudly again and again during the prayers "Sweet Father!" and other such addresses to God.[13] (*DhTvhY*, I, Hosafot, p. 41b. See also 5:1:18:3:2 for the stories of the Kotzker Rebbe's hasid and of Rabbi Wasilski.)

5:2:5 All Our Energy

5:2:5:1 Let your prayers be said with a loud voice and with all your energy. (Rabbi David ha-Levi of Steppin, *Hanhagot Tzaddikim*, p. 55, #8)

5:2:5:2 The rabbis say that:

Voice arouses feeling (*kavvanah*). (*Kitzur Shnei Luchot ha-Brit*, Inyan birkat ha-mazon, p. 56)

5:2:5:3 Rabbi Moshe of Kobrin taught:

> When a Jew says the word *Baruch* [Blessed], he should say it with all his energy, until he does not even have the energy left to say the next word *ata* [are You]. Then the Holy One, blessed be He, will give him new energy to say *ata*. So should it be for each and every word, that he gives up all his energy [to God] in saying it, and God will bestow on him new energy to say the next word. (*Mazkeret Shem ha-Gedolim*, p. 192)

This is to pray with complete *mesirat nefesh* (self-sacrifice), giving yourself wholly to God.

5:2:5:4 In Hasidism, counsel is often given that we put all our energy, physical, mental, and emotional, into the prayers. This is why many of the early great hasidic *rebbes* prayed with exaggerated movements such as swaying etc., and with a loud voice like the roar of a lion.

Of the Maggid of Koznitz it is said:

> During prayer he burned like a flaming torch with great fervor, dancing and leaping, and roaring like a lion.

Of Rabbi Mordechai of Lechovitz:

> In prayer he roared like a lion until the hearts of all who heard him would break and melt like water. (*Mazkeret Shem ha-Gedolim*, pp. 119, 103)

There are similar statements about many other *rebbes*.

However, not all the hasidic *rebbes* prayed this way, and the thing depends somewhat on individual personality and other factors. When *d'vekut* reaches a higher level it may be better (or it may even happen involuntarily) that the voice lowers, even to a whisper. Certainly many of the *rebbes* often reached a state of *d'vekut* where they could no longer even say the words. And of course the *Amidah*, when we are in greatest intimacy with God, is also called the "Whispered Prayer."

5:2:5:5 To some degree a substitute for actually raising the voice is the method of the whispered shout. Thus, the Baal Shem Tov said:

> You should learn Torah and pray even the psalm-verses of song [*P'sukei d'zimra*] in a low voice, and you should accustom yourself

> to shout in a whisper. You should say the words, whether the *zemirot* [songs] or the Torah, with all your strength, as it says, "All my bones will say, O Lord, who is like unto Thee!" (Psalm 35:10). For the shout and the crying out that comes from *d'vekut* is in a whisper. (*Tzavaat ha-Ribash*, p. 5)

(Note: The Jewish way is that the fixed prayers, even if said in the merest of whispers, are always to be said with moving lips. "One who prays should move his lips" [*Berachot* 31]. This is an absolutely essential part of prayer.)

Rabbi Nachman of Bratzlav (the Besht's great-grandson) taught the related practice of the "silent shout" for optional prayer. But he said that the formal prayer had to be with a loud voice. (See also "Individual Practices," pp. 23–26, 39:23.)

5:2:5:6 The Maggid of Mezritch said that:

> without fervor, even if you pray with *kavvanah*, it is nothing. (*Or ha-Emet*, p. 23)

The Peasetzna Rebbe explains how service of God with feeling, and beyond that, with fervor, is the basis for hasidic piety, and they are the necessary preparation for your becoming a chariot for the Divine Light. Although there are various ways to arouse yourself, the most basic way, and the one over which you have the easiest control, is the most external one—the exertion of energy through raising your voice and moving your body.

The Peasetzna Rebbe:

> When you act completely without enthusiasm it is not possible that much Light from Above will come to rest on you, since for that inspiration from Above a revealed soul is needed, as a chariot into which it can descend. . . . But when you do your holy service with fervor, since your soul is coming into revelation and your senses are somewhat nullified, then you are able to receive a greater influx from Above.
>
> When a person wants to arouse himself, it is easier if he also then performs some service of God with all his energy. . . . This you can do even when you are otherwise feeling unenthused. You can force yourself to do it. . . . Through this service with energy and exertion, it is as if you grabbed your soul by its neck, and even against its will dragged it out of its hiding place. It would be very unlikely

> that by this some feeling would not be produced—of love, or fear, or longing for God. . . . And though by praying with moving lips alone you did not succeed in arousing yourself, yet by doing so with a loud voice and with vigorous bodily movement, you will awaken your feelings. As the holy books say, "Voice arouses *kavvanah*." (*Hachsharat ha-Abrechim*, p. 7b)

5:2:5:7 Although you pray with great energy and concentration, remind yourself that the matter is not basically "muscular," and that you should be *sincere* in talking and praying to God from your heart.

5:2:6 Chanting and Swaying

Rhythmic swaying (when standing or sitting) can be an aid in concentration. Much the same is true for chanting and singing of prayers when possible. (It is easier to chant the prayers spontaneously once you are already in the spirit of the praying.) Chanting and swaying are alike in their function. Both are rhythmical movements (of voice and body), and reflect the movement of the Spirit; they are inherently "spiritual."

Rabbi Pinhas of Koretz:

> The world is filled with God's Light, but [because of our sins] . . . there is a separating screen that prevents us from seeing it—like clouds that obscure the light of the sun. . . . And during prayer, it is through our words of prayer, which are called wind/spirit, as it says, "the *ruach* [wind/spirit] of God spoke through him"—that the "clouds" are dispersed. And this is also the reason for our swaying in prayer. (*Nofit Tzufim*, p. 8b, #132)

(See 5:4:1:4 for more about swaying.)

5:2:7 Heart Not Head

Be aware before and during prayer that the prayers are mainly from the heart, not the head.

> A hasid once came to Rabbi Simha Bunim of Pshischa and told him of the trouble he was having, that whenever he prayed he always got a headache from his concentration. "What has prayer to do with the head?" the *rebbe* answered in surprise. "Prayer is service of the heart, not a labor of the head." (*Midor Dor*, vol. 1, p. 212)

5:2:8 Reconnect Again and Again

Although you are not to interrupt your prayer for anything else, you can and should interrupt your speaking and recitation in order to reestablish and increase your *d'vekut* and *hitlahavut* (fervor).

> During prayer you should interrupt yourself and pause again and again, so as to strengthen yourself and arouse in yourself a burning and pure love and fear of God; then your prayers will soar aloft into heaven and bring joy and pleasure to your Maker. (The Seder ha-Yom of Rabbi Shalom Shachna of Probitch, in *D'vir Yaakov*, p. 8)

5:2:9 Scent

The rabbis have said that scents have a special spiritual efficacy, delighting the soul while the body remains unaffected. The Baal Shem Tov, and other of his followers in the hasidic movement, used snuff during prayer, particularly when having trouble attaining *d'vekut*, or in order to reestablish it when their concentration had been disturbed.[14] Although not connected with prayer, the following about Rabbi Yitzhak Isaac of Ziditchov, will help us to understand this use of snuff:

> Once, one of his grandsons entered his chamber after the hour of noon on Friday, when the holiness of *Shabbat* was already on the *rebbe*. The *rebbe* opened his box of snuff and let him smell the scent; then he asked him if he had smelled the scent of the Garden of Eden. When he said he did not, the *rebbe* said, his voice resonating with holiness, "In the future you will smell it!" Not everyone merited to smell from the *rebbe's* snuff box. When once he let an important rabbi sniff from it, he said to him the verse, "And his delight shall be in the fear of the Lord" (Isaiah 11:3)—as if to say that his intention was to infuse him with the fear of God. (*Pe'er Yitzhak*, p. 124, #6)

Although snuff is not used much today, there is the possibility of using incense, a spice box, or other pleasant scents for this purpose during prayer (particularly, of course, in your own home. See 5:1:3:2). When smelling the scent one should think of the sweet fragrance of the Garden of Eden. (See 5:1:18:3:1 about imagining oneself in the Garden of Eden during prayers and "Torah," 15:17 for the use of spices during Torah study.)

5:2:10 No Foreign Thoughts

Pray with complete attention and concentration on the meaning of the prayers, and be alert not to let your thoughts wander.

5:2:10:1 Make every effort not to let thoughts of your worldly concerns enter your mind, but make your prayers pure, without any deviation of self-awareness and interest, and without any foreign thoughts, God forbid. (Rabbi Nahum of Tchernobil, *Hanhagot Tzaddikim*, p. 35, #6)

5:2:10:2 I have heard from a great master of Kabbalah a way to remove foreign thoughts during prayer. Before you pray, pass your right hand over your brow three times, and each time say the verse from Psalms [51:12], "Create in me, O God, a pure heart, and renew within me an upright spirit." If a foreign thought comes to you during a prayer when you are not permitted by *halacha* to interrupt [verbally], be quiet for a minute, pass your hand over your brow, and say this verse mentally. Then immediately you will be able to pray with *kavvanah*. (*Kitzur Shnei Luchot ha-Brit*, Inyanei tefillah, p. 134)

5:2:10:3 A declaration nullifying foreign thoughts can be said in the preparation for prayer and repeated during the time of prayer. (See also 5:1:23.)

5:2:10:4 The Peasetzna Rebbe:

If you are having trouble directing your mind in prayer, and it is difficult for you to overcome the many confusing thoughts and direct yourself to God, then picture yourself pushing forward through a great crowd of people to get to where God is. And actually do this, that is, tense your body and make the bodily motions of someone trying to push forward this way; actually contort your face and think, "I am going to get through them all and get to God. I am going to force my way to God." But *do not* involve your mind in the tension and strained effort of your body. Just let your body strengthen itself where it will, but let your mind strengthen itself in the thought of "to God." Doing this, you should experience that you have drawn close in your mind and concentration to Holiness.

But if you have exerted yourself against your profane thoughts and did not succeed in overcoming them, and if you have tried with fierce determination to have your mind dive deep into Holiness, but failed, try this:

> Picture to yourself that at this moment, the part of your soul that is Above [for the most exalted part of the soul is not in the body but attached Above, in heaven] is running from menacing animals to the Gates of Paradise. She is running and they are pursuing her. This one is biting her and that one is breaking a bone; this one is casting her down and the other is blocking her way. From this terrible fear and agony your soul is crying out bitterly, "Please, God, save me and draw me to You!" Then picture how heaven and earth tremble, and how the Gates of Paradise tremble and shake at this cry, as do the wild creatures pursuing—and how they are terror-stricken and stop in their places, while she, the soul, escapes into the Garden of Eden.
>
> And like that part of your soul that is above, so that part that is in you should fear those predatory thoughts. Let your soul cry out with a great and hidden cry within the confines of your heart, and they will be stopped in their tracks, and you will enter into a holy prayer space. (*Hovat ha-Talmidim*, p. 101)

5:2:11 Pause After Every Few Words

There are times when it is possible to *davven* fast, but for most people and at most times, *davvening* slowly aids *kavvanah*. Rabbi Alexander Ziskind taught the method of pausing after every few words:

> What will establish your *kavvanah* in prayer is letting the words out of your mouth as if you were counting out money. Pause to take a breath after every two or three words. You should not say more than three words in one breath. (*Yesod v'Shoresh ha-Avodah*, Gate 5, chap. 1, p. 83)

In the examples Rabbi Ziskind gives we can see that he sometimes paused after a single word. He also taught that you can translate the words of prayer into your own language during each pause.

> It is very good if you mentally translate each word, or two together, or sometimes three words together when the matter is extended. But you should not take four words together even if it seems to you that they naturally go together—stick to three words at a time and no more. There are many benefits in this method. The first is that you will be protected from foreign thoughts because your mind will be fully occupied with the holy thoughts of translating the words. (*Yesod v'Shoresh ha-Avodah*, Gate 5, chap. 3, p. 86)

5:2:12 Repeat Things

Sometimes it is good to repeat things many times to be able to grasp the meaning of what you are saying and to get deep into it. (This is why some verses are repeated in the Siddur itself, sometimes two or three times.)

5:2:12:1 It is said of a hasidic *tzaddik*, Rabbi Naftali Hayim Horowitz:

> His way in prayer was to repeat a few words or verses many, many times, an innumerable number of times, over and over. (*Otzar ha-Sippurim*, Helek 11, p. 12)

5:2:12:2 Sometimes you might say a prayer in Hebrew and then in English.

> When [Rabbi Moshe Teitelbaum] finished the prayer *Emet v' Emunah* [*Shaharit* and *Maariv* after the *Sh'ma*] he would repeat it in Yiddish. And he did the same with *Hashkiveinu* [*Maariv*]. (*Ha-Admor mi Ohel*, p. 75)

5:2:13 Less with More Intention

Sometimes it is better to say fewer things in the prayer service in the Siddur and to say them more slowly and with fuller and deeper intention, than to say everything quickly but without true intention.

In the *Shulchan Aruch* of Rabbi Eleazar ha-Katan, he says about prayer:

> Say the whole prayer service in order, but, as the rabbis say: "Whether you do more or less, it is all the same, as long as your heart is turned to God" [*Berachot* 5], and: "A little prayer with your heart directed . . . is better than much without it" [Tur]. (Dinim of synagogue and prayer, #5, 6)

This also contains a lesson on the preparation for prayer: It is better to say a little less of the prayer itself in order to have some time to spend in preparation, where you will direct yourself to God.

5:2:14 Stay in a Good Place

To a large degree the purpose of prayer is to reach a state of *d'vekut*, to get to a certain spiritual place. Therefore, be aware of your own moods. If you see that you have reached a good place and are getting somewhere, one possibility is to stop for a while and take advantage of that. Do not just move on if that will uproot you. Stay there for a while and go deep. Sometimes this may mean continuing with what you are doing. For example, it seems that too often people begin to sing a *niggun*, a religious melody, and just when they reach a point where they can begin to "take off," they unthinkingly stop, feeling guilty about not saying more words of the prayers. Other times, when you have gotten somewhere by *davvening*, it is a good idea to stop and engage in a silent meditation—looking at God, as it were. (See also 5:1:18:3:3.)

5:2:15 Disturbances

The Besht taught how we can maintain our *d'vekut* in the face of disturbances to our concentration. The essence of his counsel is that we are to see that this too has come to us from God—so even the disturbance will remind us of Him, and once it does it is overcome.

> So if you are being disturbed when praying or studying Torah, by a person or any other way, take it as being for your good—that you were not concentrating properly, and so heaven sent you this disturbance to make you aware that you should strengthen your *kavvanah*. (*Keter Shem Tov*, p. 66)

Elsewhere he says:

> If, when you are praying, you hear someone talking [and disturbing you], you should think to yourself, "Why did God bring him to me to talk while I'm praying?—for certainly this is also a part of Divine Providence. But [the answer is that] speech is a manifestation of the *Shechinah* and the *Shechinah* has enclothed Herself in the speech of this person so that I will strengthen myself in my divine service. And how much must I strengthen myself in my service—my prayer!" (*Tzavaat ha-Ribash*, Kehot edition, #120)

Rabbi Shneur Zalman of Ladi discusses this saying of the Baal Shem Tov at length in his *Tanya* (Igeret ha-Kodesh, chap. 25) and points out that your reaction to such a disturbance should be that you are:

> aroused to pray with greater devotion, from the depths of your heart, until you will no longer hear his words.

Why has God sent this disturbance to you? To *tell* you that if your prayer was deeper you would not hear this at all. So work to reach that deeper level! And the way to do this is to meditate on the reality that "The whole earth is full of His glory [the *Shechinah*]," and how the *Shechinah* has enclothed Herself in the speech of this person, etc.

5:2:16 Hebrew and English

If you do not understand Hebrew, feel free, as you are learning it, to pray part of the service in English—to help your *kavvanah*. One of the interpretations of the rabbis on the *Sh'ma Yisrael* (Hear O Israel, the Lord is our God, the Lord is one) is that "Hear O Israel" means that you can say this in any language that you can "hear" (understand) (*Midrash ha-Gadol* on Deuteronomy 6:5). The *Orach Hayim* (101:4) says about the *Shemoneh Esreh*: "You can pray it in any language that you want."

> It is better for a person to pray in his own language, which he understands, than in the holy tongue without understanding what he is saying. How can he have *kavvanah* when he does not even know what he is saying and is just making noises that are nothing more than the chirping of a bird?[15] (*Shulchan Aruch* of Rabbi Eleazar ha-Katan, p. 7, #14)

Only because of the threat to the primacy of Hebrew in modern times did the rabbis (and the standard *Shulchan Aruch*) decide that we should avoid praying in other languages. But while learning Hebrew, people are sometimes encouraged to pray most or part of the service in English, depending on their level.

Certainly, there is an obvious value in knowing clearly what you are praying. On the other hand, the holiness of Hebrew is very important, even if you say the Hebrew without understanding its meaning (or from a general familiarity with the translation)—because the sound of the holy tongue, with the knowledge that you are speaking to God, will direct your mind to holy thoughts and intentions. The psychology of the association of ideas is such that if the mind knows that these Hebrew words, even if not understood, relate to God and are vehicles to carry your innermost thoughts and deepest spiritual longings to God—that is enough.

Be aware, then, as you pray, that this is what is happening, that the Hebrew sounds you utter are vehicles carrying your soul to God. It is also a good idea, if your understanding of Hebrew is limited, that you call out from time to time to God, particularly at the beginning of sections: "Father in Heaven!" "Master of the World!" and other such terms of address to direct your attention again and again.

If you are praying in Hebrew and your understanding of the language is poor, you can also make it a point to include English in the service in some other way. For example, you can pray the intentions of the prayers beforehand silently in thought, in English (see 5:1:25 and 5:3:12), or you can have a regular practice of speaking to God in personal prayer in English in the *Shemoneh Esreh* or at the conclusion of the prayer service. (See also 5:3:16.) If you include English in this way, then, when you pray the fixed prayers in Hebrew you will not feel that you have not been able to express yourself as you want to.

Regardless, there is no question but that advancement in mastery of Hebrew is the greatest aid to appreciation of the prayer service.

> You should be completely familiar with the meaning of the Hebrew of the prayers. (*Derech Hayim*, 1-4)

5:3 THE SIDDUR AND THE PRAYER SERVICE

5:3:1 There are three basic prayer services, although actually four—*Shaharit*, *Minha*, *Maariv* (the services for morning, afternoon, and evening), and the service before bed. The Morning Service is the longest by far and very important, because at the beginning of the day it sets the tone for the whole day and for everything that follows. *Shaharit* and *Maariv* serve to link the two great natural daily events of sunrise and sunset, day and night, to the Creator. The psychology of day and night is so different that there are these two prayer services to direct us in each. Ideally, they should be said at the beginning of each time period, at sunrise and sunset. From a slightly different perspective, there is prayer associated with the personal events of waking and sleep—again, *Shaharit* (which is connected with both day and waking) and the prayer service at bedside. In the middle of the day, ideally coming as a break in the work or activity of the day, is *Minha*. This prayer service helps to remind us, in the midst of the bustle and confusion of our daily activity, that there is a God, and also serves as an interruption of our worldly doings, with all of the significance that such interruptions have (as explained in Part One).

5:3:2 Memorize the Prayers; Praying with Closed Eyes or from the Siddur

> Whenever you are not involved in Torah study or prayer, use your time to memorize different prayers. (Rabbi Elimelech of Lizensk, *Tzetl Katan*, #17)

When you have (individual) prayers memorized you can close your eyes when you pray and direct yourself more easily to God, reaching a higher level of *kavvanah.*[16] The prayers can be memorized in Hebrew or English depending on your level and development in learning Hebrew. It is best to concentrate on memorizing the more important prayers, one at a time. Each day focus on memorizing that one prayer. When you have accomplished that, do another.

However, many great *tzaddikim* made it a point always to pray from the Siddur (though they certainly knew all the prayers by heart).

> The writing [of the printed words] arouses *kavvanah.* And, regarding the prayers, it is even good, if possible, to say them from beginning to end out of the Siddur. And so did my own master [Rabbi Moshe Cordovero] do. (*Totzaot Hayim*, p. 15)

The Besht said:

> If at a particular moment during prayer you are on a low level spiritually and in a state of small consciousness, it is better to pray from the Siddur, because seeing the letters has the power to help you to have more *kavvanah.* But when you are on a higher level, in a state of expanded consciousness, and are attached to the Upper World, then it is better to close your eyes [and say the prayers by heart], so that you will not be distracted by what you see from your attachment to the Upper World. (*Tzavaat ha-Ribash*, p. 5)

5:3:3 Do Not Let the Siddur Get between You and God

It is important when you are using the Siddur, to say your prayers *to* God—and not as if you are reading a book to yourself. One way to do this is, from time to time, to read *out*, not *in*. Look at the line in the Siddur which is to be said. Then, do not pray into the Siddur. Pick a phrase, close your eyes or look away from the book, focus towards the Presence of God and repeat it.

The point here is not to let the book, the Siddur, somehow get between you and God. Previously (5:2:1) we discussed another method of overcoming the same problem—where you do pray *in* to the Siddur, but only after focusing on God's Presence *within* the words and letters of the Siddur. Again, this problem is also resolved by "removing" the Siddur by memorizing prayers.

5:3:4 Make the Siddur a Starting Point

Make the Siddur a starting point for your own prayers. This is especially appropriate in the *Shemoneh Esreh*, but it applies to other prayers as well.

> Although it has been taught [traditionally] that you should pray for your [personal] needs in the [*Shemoneh Esreh*] blessing of "He who hears prayers," at the end of each individual blessing you can also say the things that relate to that blessing . . . if someone in your house is sick, pray for him in the blessing about the sick; if you have a problem in earning your living, pray for that in the blessing of the years. (*Avodah Zarah* 7, quoted in *Menorat ha-Maor*, p. 214)

This kind of spontaneous prayer based on the fixed prayers does not have to be about personal requests alone—whatever the prayer is about, you can add something of your own.

5:3:5 Write in the Siddur

When appropriate, make a note in your Siddur of something to remember or pray about, or whom to remember.

5:3:5:1 The Besht said to two brothers who were his disciples, when he wanted to show them favor:

> "My children, you are very precious to me and I love you both very much. What special thing do you choose that I do for you?" They

answered, "Our master, do what you think is good." He said, "I have a handwritten Siddur that I use every day. Write your names and the name of your mother in it, next to any blessing in the *Shemoneh Esreh* that you want." They chose "He who hears prayer." (*Emunat Tzaddikim*, p. 7)

5:3:5:2 You can write for yourself other instructions or encouragements in the margins.

You should write on the top of every page of the Siddur the word *tefillin* so you will not forget for even a minute that you have the *tefillin* on you. (*Kaf ha-Hayim* 10:26, p. 142)

5:3:5:3 So that you can remember to have special *kavvanah* at the end of all the blessings in prayer, when you say the name of God ("Blessed are You, O Lord [*Havaya*]"), *Shnei Luchot ha-Brit* suggests writing on every page where such a blessing appears:

Hebrew	*Translation*
יהוה	YHVH
ארון הכל	Lord of all
היה הוה יהיה	[Who] was, is, and [always] will be

(Hanhagat ha-tefillah, p. 126)

5:3:5:4 You can put on the top of the page or in the margin "Father in Heaven!" etc. to remind yourself to call out to God that way (as suggested in 5:2:16).

5:3:6 Be In Tune with What You are Saying

When you are saying parts of the service that are about joy, be joyful, clap your hands, etc.

The whole *kavvanah* of the praying is to serve Him according to the verse you are saying at the moment. When the verse is about love, serve Him with love; when the verse is about fear, serve Him with fear; and so, too, with joy. Although you should have love and fear of God throughout the service, still, when you say a verse, for example, about love, you should have more love than joy or fear, and so on for all the others. (*Darkei Tzedek*, p. 9, #65)

As an example: There are many times when joy and happiness are mentioned in *Shaharit*; since we are to pray and serve God with joy, use those references to arouse yourself to joy.

5:3:7 Make the Words Real

The Peasetzna Rebbe explains how the words recited from the Siddur are not to remain just intellectual, but are to become real for us as we say them.

> When you draw out the powers of your mind, your imagination and your feeling, and strengthen them, then when you serve God in prayer it will be from inside you, not just your brain. It will be made real, so that you will *see* what you express with your lips. And when you say "To You every knee will bend"—even if you have aroused your feelings only a little, you will already see that you and all the world are bowing before God and nullifying yourselves before Him, blessed be He. And when you say "Praise the Lord from the heavens, etc." [in the continuation of this verse of Psalm 148 in the Morning Service, the angels, sun, moon, and stars, trees, animals, and all people are called to praise God] with feeling, then you are standing before all the world—all the creatures of the Upper and Lower Worlds are actually before you—and you are telling them: "Stand up and praise God! Let us together sing to Him!" (*Hachsharat ha-Abrechim*, p. 29b)

5:3:8 Use Your Imagination

When appropriate, use your imagination. Identify with what you read in the Siddur.

> **5:3:8:1:1** Have great intention when you say the Song at the Sea [in the Morning Prayer Service], saying it with a loud voice and joyfully—as if you have just come out of Egypt and are standing on the shore after having gone through the split Sea, having been saved from the Egyptians. (Rabbi Moshe Teitelbaum, *Hanhagot Tzaddikim*, p. 47, #4)

> **5:3:8:1:2** You should say the Song at the Sea with great joy and sweetly, and picture yourself standing on the dry land in the middle of the Red Sea and the Egyptians are drowning and you are saved. And as is known, this has a special effect for the forgiveness of sins.

(Rabbi Hayim Yosef David Azulai, *Avodat ha-Kodesh*, Tziporen shamir, 2–24)

5:3:8:1:3 [Once, Rabbi Shmelke of Nikolsburg said the Song at the Sea as prayer leader with such holy power that] when they [the congregation] recited with him the verses about the crossing of the Red Sea they all lifted up the hems of their kaftans to keep them from getting wet, for it actually seemed to them that they had gone down into the Sea which had split before them. (*Ohel Yitzhak*, p. 74; see the whole story in "Sleep and Before Sleep" [29].)

In a fascinating parallel to this, the following scene of childhood recollection is recorded in a recently published book by Rabbi Abraham Twerski (of the famous hasidic dynastic family), whose father was a hasidic *rebbe* in Milwaukee:

> The seventh night of Passover was a special event. Inasmuch as the seventh day of Passover commemorated the miracle of the Israelites crossing the Red Sea, people would gather at our home after the evening meal to join in the Song of Triumph which had been composed by Moses. . . .
>
> After completion of the [responsive] reading of the Song of Moses, the group joined hands and danced in a circle, to the lively melody of "When You Divided The Red Sea, Your Nation Saw Your Might And Glory."
>
> The identification with our ancestors who had participated in the miraculous crossing of the sea once grew so intense that one of the group ran off and brought a bucket of water and poured it on the floor where we were dancing. Mother was not at all pleased with this attempt to simulate the historic experience. (*Generation to Generation*, p. 100)

5:3:8:2 When you say the part in the Siddur in the Morning Service that tells of Abraham going to sacrifice Isaac, picture in your mind that you are allowing yourself to be bound [on the altar and sacrificing yourself] for the sake of God, blessed be He.[17] (Rabbi Nahum of Tchernobil, *Hanhagot Tzaddikim*, p. 36, #17)

5:3:8:3 When you recite the line in *Maariv*, the Evening Service, recalling the reaction of the people to Elijah's miracle and his call for faith on Mount Carmel, picture yourself there with them in their answer, "And all the people, when they saw it, fell on their faces and they said, 'The Lord—*He* is God! The Lord—*He* is God!'" (*Maariv*, taken from 1 Kings 18:39).

Imagine yourself now prostrating and call out this declaration of faith on your own behalf, against your own doubts and in unity with other Jews who affirm their belief in the God of Israel.

There are many other things in the *davvening* like this where you can use your imagination.

5:3:9 Song and Melody

If you know melodies for certain verses of the *davvening*, use them when you are praying alone. Or if you know a wordless melody that comes to mind when you are *davvening*, sing it. Feel free to sing for some time, because if you do so with a holy intention it will lift your prayer higher than almost anything else, for song is a movement of the holy spirit and is on a higher level. Just remember to sing before the Holy One, blessed be He.

5:3:9:1 Rabbi Shalom Ber of Lubavitch:

> Song and melody during prayer have special power to bring out the animal soul of a person so that it can be purified, and what is good in it can be elevated. Song also has special power to awaken the inner meaning of prayer. (*Sippurei Hasidim*, vol. 1, p. 459)

> **5:3:9:2** In one of his talks, Rabbi Shalom Ber of Lubavitch dwelt on the custom of the hasidim to sing during prayer, and he divided the melodies of prayer into their categories: the *niggun* of joy, the *niggin* of [holy] bitterness [at your spiritual lowliness], the *niggun* of "running" [*r'tzo*—movement into the world to do God's will] and the *niggun* of "returning" [*shov*—movement back to God], the *niggun* of yearning and the *niggun* of love with delights. And all the *niggunim* are with *Chabad* fervor, with *d'vekut* and yearning for God. (*Sippurei Hasidim*, vol. 1, p. 459)

5:3:10 Dance

5:3:10:1 If you feel inspired, jump up and dance.

The Besht taught that:

> The dances of the Jew before his Creator are prayers.[18] (*Encyclopedia Judaica*, Dance, vol. 5, p. 1267)

5:3:10:2 But one must dance before God. It was said of Rabbi Tzvi Hirsh, the "Servant" of Rimanov, that:

> All his Divine service in prayer was with great joy, as if accompanied by the joyous sound of the flute. The deepest chords within him would vibrate with happiness during prayer, when he prayed, as one should, with dancing and awesome fervor. (*M'vaser Tov*, p. 9)

> **5:3:10:3** An old man who knew the Tzanzer Rebbe in his youth said that every day when he put on *tefillin*, he would grab the bench and hold on to it during prayer, and he would dance in awe and fear before the awesome majesty of God, blessed be He. And all the people in the synagogue would watch his unbelievable fervor with amazement. (*Mekor Hayim*, p. 104, #344)

(Note that the Tzanzer always danced at a particular part of the service.)

5:3:10:4 About Rabbi Yehudah Pesah of Lipsk:

> His praying was with great *d'vekut* and a thunderous voice, like the roar of a lion, with great fervor and singing *and dancing*, with shaking and trembling, with bowing and prostrating—such that the hair on the bodies of all who were present when he prayed would stand up, when they would see and be overwhelmed, and be aroused to repent." (*Shema Shlomo*, II, p. 44, Yesharaish Yaakov #4) (Italics mine.)

5:3:10:5 It is told about the Morning Prayers of the Koznitzer Maggid:

> In the morning, when the holy rabbi came to the synagogue to pray, he walked through two rows of men. He was wearing *tallit* and *tefillin* and was accompanied on both sides by his attendants who carried large burning candles in their hands. The maggid entered with holy emotion and joy, with a sefer Torah in his arms, and he danced one dance before the holy Ark; then he placed the sefer Torah therein. Then he danced another dance before the stand for the prayer leader, on which candelabra were placed; and they put the candles in it. That was where he sat and stood and prayed. And also during the *Shemoneh Esreh* he jumped up on his pure table (which was next to the stand) and walked back and forth on it. Then after the *Shemoneh Esreh* he danced from the table down to the ground. (*Ohalei Shem*, p. 30, #9)

5:3:10:6 When it is impossible to dance during public prayer in the synagogue, one can still "dance" in imagination. See "Service of the Imagination," 19:14 about this practice.

5:3:11 Rest

Be careful about straining yourself. Take a break from continuous speaking of the words of the Siddur to remember before Whom you are praying (see 5:2:8). Take this rest by humming a *niggun* to yourself or swaying or repeating a holy verse or sentence, or by just picturing yourself sitting before God in His Presence, directing yourself to Him, and letting love flow out of your chest and heart to Him. Say (whispered or mentally): "*HaShem*, all these prayers are to You. My love is for You. Let me feel Your loving Presence." Of course, there are many other ways to rest from continuous recitation.

5:3:12 Intend Before

In order to properly intend the meaning of the prayers, your method should be to precede the intentions to the saying of the words. For example, before you say "*Adon Olam asher malach*" [Lord of the World, who ruled], you should go over in your mind the meaning of these words. Then as you are thinking about that, say the words. This method is very effective and valuable, not like those who do the opposite and say the words first and afterwards reflect on their meaning. It seems to me that they accomplish nothing by this, for what is done is done, and they have already said the words without intending the meaning. (Rabbi Meir Margulis *Sod Yachin u'Voaz*, p. 36. See also 5:1:25.)

5:3:13 Standing in the Temple in Jerusalem

The Morning Service reaches its high point in the *Shemoneh Esreh* when you are to make your greatest effort to stand before God and be in His presence. As a preparation for this you should put yourself in the presence of God through imagining yourself in His holy place, in the Temple in Jerusalem.

5:3:13:1 You should imagine that you are standing in the Temple in Jerusalem, in the Holy of Holies. (*Mishnah Berurah*, 94:1)

5:3:13:2 Rabbi Elimelech of Lizensk:

> It says in the *Gemara* [*Berachot* 30a] that he who stands praying the *Shemoneh Esreh* should direct his heart to Israel, and he who is in Israel should face towards Jerusalem. [If he is in Jerusalem he should turn toward the Temple, and if he is in the Temple, to the Holy of Holies.]
>
> But another aspect of this is that a person who wants his prayer to be accepted should picture to himself that he is in Israel, and that the Temple is built, and that the altar is established on its base in the Holy Place. . . . Through this a person will achieve clearness and complete *d'vekut*, and he can pray with complete *kavvanah*, with love and fear of God, as if he were standing in the Holy of Holies itself. . . .
>
> So should you imagine to yourself: Make a picture in your mind when you are praying that you are really standing in Israel and in the Holy Temple and that you are actually seeing everything with your eyes. . . . And when you imagine this is so, that you are standing in Israel, you will achieve great clarity in your prayer. (*Noam Elimelech*, Lech Lecha, p. 6a)
>
> **5:3:13:3** Before beginning the *Shemoneh Esreh* you should visualize that you are actually standing in the Temple and want to pray there before the Creator, blessed is He. And how good if you call this intention to mind a number of times during the prayer." *Yesod v'Shoresh ha-Avodah*, Gate 5, chap. 1, p. 82)

5:3:13:4 The Peasetzna Rebbe:

> And even when you are not praying, and have time, you should also imagine this [the scenes in the Temple], that when you pray you are in the Temple, etc. Then, when you do come to pray, it will be easier for you to arouse yourself. (*Hachsharat ha-Abrechim*, p. 32b)

5:3:13:5 Even if you do not do a full meditation on being in the Temple, when you direct yourself towards Jerusalem for the *Shemoneh Esreh* you should be aware of the underlying intention, and so too particularly when Jerusalem or Israel is mentioned in the *Shemoneh Esreh*.

Rabbi Moshe of Prague said it was a good practice to

> direct your prayer and the breath of your mouth towards Jerusalem, even when you are not praying the *Shemoneh Esreh*, because there is the Gate to Heaven. (*Tzavaat Rabbi Moshe mi Prague*, #18 *Tzavaot v'Derech Tovim*, p. 31)

5:3:14 In Heaven

5:3:14:1 *Orach Hayim* 95:2 says about the *Shemoneh Esreh*:

> A person should imagine he is standing in the Temple, and he should direct his heart above to heaven.

Another practice for the *Shemoneh Esreh* is to think of yourself as being in heaven. (One could first imagine oneself in the Temple and then in heaven; see 5:1:20:4.)

5:3:14:2 Rabbeinu Yonah (on *Berachot* 25):

> You should imagine that you are standing Above, in heaven, and should remove from your heart any thoughts of this world's pleasures or of bodily enjoyments—as those of earlier times said: "If you want to have *kavvanah*, strip your body from your soul as a garment." And after you reach this consciousness (that you are in heaven), then also think that you are standing here Below in the synagogue. Doing this will make your prayer more acceptable to God. (*Shema Shlomo*, I, p. 3, Yesharaish Yaakov **)

How can one imagine that he is above and below at the same time? Remember that Above and Below as designations for the spiritual realms, heaven and earth, are in essence symbolic. The point is then (I presume) that we are to imagine ourselves in heaven before God so that this world is removed altogether from our consciousness as if it did not exist. Then, we are to imagine that we are again below. We are to still remain before God, but the world "reappears" and exists, but this time "before God"—everything in our surroundings being one, manifesting His presence. We are also to consider ourselves then as heavenly beings and not part of this Lower World. (See the quotes to this effect from *Reshit Hochmah* in Chapter 1 of this book, p. 11.)

5:3:15 Markers on the Way; Slipping Out of the Body as a Garment; Soul-Ascent

There is a hasidic/kabbalistic understanding of the order of the Service in which the thought is that you go in stages from the lowest to the highest of the four worlds (Action, Formation, Creation, Emanation [or Nearness]), the latter, and the one closest to God, being reached in the

Shemoneh Esreh. Without entering into the kabbalistic discussion, and without praying in this kabbalistic fashion, the divisions of the Service can still be used as markers, so that at each transition point you make an effort to go even deeper in your *kavvanah.*

Earlier, quotes were cited which taught that before prayer you should arouse your heart to love and fear of God, and that during prayer also you should pause to do the same (see 5:1:14:2). In *Derech Pikudecha,* Rabbi Tzvi Elimelech of Dinov teaches that this should certainly be done at the transitions from one spiritual world to the next.

> You should arouse fear and love in the transition to each higher spiritual world, that is, before *Baruch Sh'amar* [Blessed be He who spoke and the world came into being] when the world of Action [*Asiyah*] is elevated to the world of Formation [*Yetzirah*]; also before the blessing of *Yotzair Or* [He who forms light] when there is the elevation to the world of Creation [*Briah*]; and before the *Shemoneh Esreh* when there is the elevation to the world of Nearness [*Atzilut*]. For all these elevations are by means of the two wings by which the bird of prayer can fly upwards—fear and love. (*Derech Pikudecha,* quoted in *Kulam Ahuvim,* p. 40)

According to Rabbi Hayim Vital:

> [The rabbis] established in the prayers a *Kaddish* at the transition from each world to the next. (*Minhagai ha-Arizal,* p. 10)

So we can, at each *Kaddish,* when we say the *Y'hai Shmai Rabba* with all our energy and *kavvanah,* remind ourselves of our love and fear of God and go deeper into our meditative prayer state. (See "The Synagogue and the Synagogue Service" 6:30.) Of course, when we enter the *Shemoneh Esreh* we intend the same, and in the most complete way.

Rabbi Yaakov Yosef of Polnoye reports in the name of his master, the Besht:

> I heard from my master regarding the daily prayer service that . . . you should exert yourself gradually and in stages: first, from the beginning of the service until *Baruch Sh'amar,* that being coordinate with the world of Action [*Asiyah*], which is below, and the place of many Shells [negative and contrary forces]; then increase your concentration and *kavvanah* from *Baruch Sh'amar* until *Yishtabach* [Praised be Thy Name], which is coordinate with the world of Formation [*Yetzirah*], where there are fewer Shells than in the world of Action; then from *Yishtabach* until the *Amidah* [the

> *Shemoneh Esreh*, which is coordinate with the world of Creation, *Briah*]; and then in the *Amidah* [which is coordinate with the world of Nearness or Emanation, *Atzilut*]. . . . you should strip yourself of materiality altogether, as is written in *Orach Hayim*, section 98; see there. (*Toldot Yaakov Yosef*, Aharei, p. 97d)

The Besht explains the pinnacle of prayer, the "stripping yourself of materiality" this way:

> *Hitpashtut ha-gashmiyut* means that you remove the soul from the body as a garment is stripped off; and your soul should be clothed rather in the thoughts that you speak, and then you will see various higher worlds. (*Keter Shem Tov*, II, p. 62)

Elsewhere the Besht says:

> In *hitpashtut ha-gashmiyut* one no longer has any awareness of the body, nor any consciousness [*tziyur*] of this world, only of the Upper Worlds. (*Keter Shem Tov*, I, p. 44)

In *hitpashtut ha-gashmiyut* a person is completely and fully focused on what he is doing, on the spirituality of prayer, and he has blocked out any awareness of the outer world or of any materiality, even his own body.

Orach Hayim, in the place referred to in the above quote from Rabbi Yaakov Yosef (reporting the Besht's teaching), says:

> When you pray, you should direct your mind and heart to understand the meaning of the words that your lips are saying, and meditate on the Divine Presence being before you. Remove all other disturbing thoughts so that your mind is clear in prayer. This is what the hasidim and men of deeds would do, for they separated themselves from others, and would direct themselves in prayer until they reached the state of stripping off the body from the soul like a garment . . . until they came close to the level of prophecy.

Rabbi Tzadok ha-Cohen, in his comment on this passage, says that this means that in prayer you can reach *hitpashtut ha-gashmiyut*

> through *d'vekut* with God and intense awareness of His presence before you. (*Tzidkat ha-Tzaddik*, #210)

Rabbi Pinhas of Koretz said:

> The essence of prayer is *d'vekut* with the Creator of the world; and the essence of *d'vekut* is *hitpashtut ha-gashmiyut*, which is similar to the exit of the soul from the body. (*Sippurei Hasidim*, vol. 1 p. 454)

Of course, this high level of separating the soul from the body cannot be just a matter of prayer. It depends on your removing yourself, in your daily life, from materiality and the matters of the body to spirituality and the primacy of the soul.

Rabbi Mendel of Premishlan:

> If a person . . . is actually separated from materiality *always*, even though he still *feels* it, when he prays the holiness will assert itself within his soul through the *mitzvot*[19] [done previously] and the prayers [at the moment] said with love and fear . . . and he will become stripped of the body completely. (*Darkei Yesharim*, Likkutim Hadashim, #14)

As we noted earlier (see 5:1:18:2), there are two sides to prayer: one side is the separation from this world, from materiality and body consciousness—becoming "unattached"; the other side is rising to awareness of the spiritual world and to God-consciousness, and "attaching" oneself cleaving to God in *d'vekut*.

The four worlds represent different levels of reality and of consciousness, and even without concerning ourselves with the matters of kabbalistic theory, they can be used as a framework for the progression of our prayer. As Rabbi Levi Yitzhak of Berditchev explains, the world of Action (*Asiyah*) is the world of bodily action, Formation (*Yetzirah*) is speech, Creation (*Briah*) is thought, and Nearness (*Atzilut*) is awe, beyond even thought, when one is nullified before God (*Kedushat Levi*, Emor, p. 54).

So can we go in the order of the prayers from concentration on involvement in bodily movement to putting our consciousness within our speech, then into our thoughts, and finally to that God-consciousness in nearness to God which is beyond thought.

The Besht:

> At the beginning [of prayer] you have to arouse yourself by exerting yourself bodily with all your energy. . . . Later you will be able to serve with thought alone, without any bodily movement. (*Tzavaat ha-Ribash*, Kehot edition, #58)

Elsewhere he says:

> In prayer you must put all your energy into the words . . . until you forget your body and material reality . . . and this is the world of Formation; afterward you will become enveloped in your thought and you will not hear what you speak—and this is the world of

> Creation; after this you come to complete self-nullification, where all your bodily powers and senses cease to operate—this is the world of Nearness. (*Keter Shem Tov*, p. 48a–b)

When a person prays he first exerts himself bodily, with movement and forceful expression of the words, putting his very self into the prayer. This is the beginning of losing himself to Godly reality. This is the world of Action. Then he concentrates on speech alone, until he forgets his body and the material world. Then he advances to the thoughts alone and his senses begin to detach from materiality, until he can not hear his speech and what he prays. Finally, all his senses detach and he loses his awareness of the outer world and his body altogether. He is no longer conscious of materiality, but only of spirituality. He goes beyond thought and completely enters the spiritual world.[20]

A hasidic story about Rabbi Tzvi Hirsh, the "Servant" of Rimanov, gives a good characterization of this high state of *davvening.*

> He stood up to pray *Shaharit* in his awesome, holy way. And while he was standing before God and praying with great fervor his soul cleaved in *d'vekut* to the Supernal Light, until he was no longer aware of this world. For his soul yearned for the heights, and he soared to the heavens and was altogether separated from materiality; his thoughts were roaming in the Upper Heavens. He had no consciousness at all of his surroundings . . . he heard nothing of what was said [by those near him], and he himself was calling out loudly, in the fullest voice, his prayers. (*Otzar ha-Sippurim*, XIV, story 1)

Although "sound and movement" are good for prayer, they are hardly the essence. The disciple of Rabbi Levi Yitzhak of Berditchev (who prayed with the fervor of a seraph, a fiery angel), Rabbi Aaron of Zhitomir, said that:

> My master did not like it when someone raised his voice in prayer more than what was appropriate to the words and what his true intensity warranted.

And Rabbi Aaron commented that:

> There are people who chant and sing energetically while praying, and thinking that this itself is holy service, they become enthused and imagine that they are giving pleasure to God. But it is all false and counterfeit and they have not even taken a first step to truth, because the true path is that when you pray, you are to remove

> yourself from the materiality of this world—like removing a garment —until you feel that you are not in this world. (*Tiferet Beit Levi*, p. 8)

There are innumerable stories about the hasidic *rebbes* who reached this level of freeing the soul from the garment of the body and were in a trance (as the inadequate English translation might put it).

When Rabbi Levi Yitzhak of Berditchev prayed the *Shemoneh Esreh* he was in another spiritual world, and his physical senses were turned off. One story tells of how he himself said that he prayed the *Shemoneh Esreh* with his eyes open (contrary to the *halacha*) because, though his eyes were open, he did not see anything (*Sippurei Hasidim*, vol. 1, p. 45). Not that the Berditchever would do anything against the *halacha*, but in the state he was in his eyes remained open by themselves, and as he could not see, the *halacha* was not really violated.

Here is another story that shows his prayer with *hitpashtut ha-gashmiyut*:

> Once, during a war in Russia, a regiment of troops came to Berditchev, and as is the custom, they were given a few hours to go through the town pillaging and looting. When some soldiers came to the Berditchever's synagogue while the congregation was praying, everyone fled. But the *rebbe* was in the middle of the *Shemoneh Esreh* and he alone remained, for he heard nothing of what was happening around him.
>
> The soldiers, seeing that he alone was there, began to talk to him, and when he did not answer, they beat him cruelly with a stick, hitting him again and again. But when they saw that he did not scream out or say a word they realized that this was not natural, that a man of flesh and blood should receive such blows without making a sound. So they left him, saying, "This is not a man!" and went away.
>
> Afterwards, when the *rebbe's* people came back to the shul and found the *rebbe* still there, they finished their prayers, but the Berditchever still said nothing. When he went home, he said to his family that he felt some pain in his shoulder. Taking off his coat and shirt they immediately saw the terrible bruises and wounds. But the holy rabbi had had such great *d'vekut* that he felt nothing at all when he was praying. (*Kulam Ahuvim*, p. 30b, Tikkun ha-Nefesh, chap. 15)

This story, like that of his praying the *Shemoneh Esreh* with his eyes open, shows how Rabbi Levi Yitzhak prayed with *hitpashtut ha-gashmiyut*.

As many hasidic stories and teachings inform us, many hasidic *rebbes*, and others also, not only shut out the outside world and physical reality to be completely focused on their praying, but went another step and made soul-ascents (*aliyot neshamah*) to heaven.

> In the writings of the Ari it is said that before the *Shemoneh Esreh* . . . you should imagine that you are standing Above, in the heavens among the angels; and you should not allow any thought of this world to enter your mind. (*Kaf ha-Hayim*, p. 232)

We discussed earlier the practice of imagining oneself in heaven for prayer, particularly during the time of the *Shemoneh Esreh* (5:1:21 and 5:3:14). But there is a further imaginative step involved in the soul-ascent. With eyes closed one imagines oneself leaving the body, ascending to heaven, and praying there.

The Besht taught that you are to first establish strong *d'vekut* in small consciousness in the Lower World by meditating on God's greatness, that His glory [the *Shechinah*] fills the whole world and that you are in His presence; then you enter the state of expanded consciousness by ascending to the Upper Worlds. He taught that where a man thinks, there he is himself; and that such a meditation is not just imagination, but reality.[21]

(For the preparatory meditation see 5:1:14:2 and 5:1:18:1–2.)

> At first you should attach yourself in *d'vekut* to God, blessed be He, here Below, in the proper way, and afterward you can ascend upward. . . . You should think that you are above the sky, and then exert yourself to go farther and farther up . . . [When you reach the highest heavenly place you can attain] you can speak to God there in that world.
>
> You should [then, first] meditate on God and how His glory fills the earth, and how you are always in the presence of the *Shechinah*. . . . Meditate on how just as you are looking at material things, so are you looking at the *Shechinah*, in whose presence you are. This is the service for the state of small consciousness. . . . When you serve in a state of expanded consciousness, however, you can exert yourself with great energy and ascend, in your mind, and split through all the heavens at once, and ascend above even the angels and the *ofanim* and the *serafim* and the thrones—and this is perfect divine service. (The Besht, *Tzavaat ha-Ribash*, p. 23)

> You can be in a state of small consciousness, but yet in great *d'vekut* with the *Shechinah*. Then immediately, in one moment, when you think of the Upper Worlds, you are there; for as a man thinks, that is where he is (for if you were not in the Upper World, you would

not be thinking [about it] at all.[22] (The Besht, *Tzavaat ha-Ribash*, p. 10)

5:3:16 Talk to God

5:3:16:1 More so than the fixed prayers, the essence of prayer is the personal conversation that you have with your Father in Heaven. It is a good practice to set some time at each prayer service when you can talk to God in your own words. This should not be seen as something secondary and "stuck in," but as a high point of the service. (See "Talking to God and Being Alone with God—*Hitbodedut*" [33] for thoughts about the content of such communication.)

There are various times traditionally used for the purpose of talking to God. One is during the blessing in the *Shemoneh Esreh* which ends "Blessed are You, O Lord, who hears prayer" (that is, the personal things go right before these words). Another place is after the *Shemoneh Esreh* is completed, but before the last words ("Do if for the sake of Thy name etc.") and before taking the three steps back—while you are still standing in His presence.[23] In this case the rabbis say that, if you want to, you can extend this time of personal conversation to the length of the whole *Yom Kippur* service! (*Avodah Zarah* 8a)

Various hasidic *rebbes* would stand in the *Amidah* for hours at a time. Certainly, part of what they were doing was engaging in personal prayer.

> It was the practice of our holy master, the Baal Shem Tov, may his soul rest in the heavenly Garden, to say the *Shemoneh Esreh* a very long time, and he would stand in the *Shemoneh Esreh* for a number of hours. (*Hitgalut ha-Tzaddikim*, p. 29)

About the Seer of Lublin:

> The *rebbe's* custom was to stand in the whispered *Shemoneh Esreh* for a long time. (*Niflaot ha-Rebbe*, p. 29, #45)

Also about the Lubliner:

> His way was to stand in the *Shemoneh Esreh* for so long that everyone else would be finished and leave the synagogue, and he was still there. [He said that the reason he prayed the *Shemoneh Esreh* for several hours was that] he did not do this intentionally. It just happened because he had so many requests to make of God for necessary things. (*Niflaot ha-Rebbe*, p. 77, #21; p. 84, #266)

> It was known that Rabbi Yechezkel Abramsky (1886–1966), the noted Slutzker Rav and the Av Beis Din (head of the rabbinical court) of London, spoke to Hashem during his *Shemoneh Esrei* as a son might talk to his father. He would make his requests and plead for them like a devoted son, addressing Hashem as *Tatte* (Father). (*The Maggid Speaks*, p. 175)

You may not be able to stand this way for hours, or have the time to do so, but you can determine to stand in the *Amidah* beyond the prescribed prayers at least for a few minutes, communicating with God personally. You can make it a part of your regular service of God to accept on yourself always to talk to Him this way for a set minimum time at each prayer service.

Although formal prayer must be said out loud, it is not necessary to do so with personal prayer. One option is to pray in thought alone. Rabbi Menahem Mendel of Vorki said that such *silent prayer* is on a higher level than spoken prayer (*Beit Yitzhak*, p. 157).

Another time for personal talk with God can be after completing the whole prayer service.

> See to it that after the Morning Prayer Service each one of you prays specifically in German [i.e., the language you are most familiar with], from the depth of your heart, for all the things that you need [both spiritual and material]. (Tzavaat Rabbi Yonah Landsofer z"l, #2, in *YHvT*, p. 23)

Regardless of when during the service you engage in personal prayer, it is a good idea during the preparation for prayer to consider what you want and need to pray about (and, in fact, it should be noted that the preparation is itself a time for personal communication with God).

You should use this time of personal prayer foremost for your spiritual needs. Pray that God help you attain religious and ethical qualities.

> Within the prayer service, pray that God, blessed be He, save you from anger and pride, and that He lead you to humility. (*Derech Hayim*, 3–28)

It would be useful to compose a short prayer of this sort for yourself and copy it into an empty page of your Siddur. See *Berachot* 16 and 17 for many examples of such prayers composed by different rabbis for themselves. Each report begins: "After he finished his daily prayers, he prayed. . . ." The prayer at the end of the *Shemoneh Esreh*, which begins

"O my God, guard my tongue . . ." is based on the personal prayer of Mar, the son of Rav Huna. You can change this personal prayer from time to time, as you feel the need, and also use it as the basis for spontaneous conversation with your Father in Heaven.

5:3:16:2 It is taught that it is a good practice, whenever you make supplications to God, to join a *confession* with it. This is because our sins act as accusers against mercy being shown to us—since we are unworthy—and repentance and confession change that. Sometimes it is suggested that the confession be before the supplication, sometimes after. So when we talk with God and ask Him for things, we should include a confession.

> Be sure to make confession before any prayer of supplication and say, "I have sinned, etc." and only afterwards pray for what you need. (*Derech Hayim,* 3–22)

When you confess Below, before you pray, your prayer is not accused Above:

> The value of confession is that it removes the accusation. (*Totzaot Hayim*, p. 47)
>
> If you make confession before prayer, it is like confessing in court and agreeing to the fine or punishment *before* the witnesses come. And when you do this you are released. If the Satan comes afterwards and begins to accuse you, the Holy One, blessed be He, says to him, "He already confessed before you came to make your accusations against him." And then the Satan is forced to speak in your favor. (*Derech Moshe*, Day 10)

For many people it is helpful to understand these things by first translating them, so to speak, into psychological language. Here we can say that when you pray, asking God for something, your prayer cannot be completely sincere and wholehearted because your own subconscious accuses you, saying, "How do you expect your prayer to be answered when you have done this and that against God's will?" But when you confess and ask for forgiveness, and bring everything into consciousness, this "accuser" is silenced.

Since personal requests are often made in the "who hears prayer" blessing of the *Shemoneh Esreh*, that is where many say a confession also.

In the blessing "who hears prayer," before saying the words "for You" [*ki Ata*], say: "O God! I have sinned, I have done wrong, I have transgressed before You. Forgive my transgression and pardon my sin, and let my wrongdoing be atoned for, in all that I have sinned and done wrong and transgressed before You since I was born until this day."* (And if you committed some new sin that day, mention it in the next prayer, whether *Shaharit* or *Minha*). (*Kitzur Shnei Luchot ha-Brit*, Dinei Tefillat Shemoneh Esreh, p. 121)

It was said of the great *tzaddik*, Rabbi Menahem of Horodna, that:

More so than all the other prayers and supplications with which he was always and continually moving his lips, he was constantly saying the confession—because before he would say any prayer or supplication, and before he prayed for a sick person, he confessed before his prayer, while a flood of tears rolled down his cheeks.

Once, a great Torah sage asked him about this practice of his . . . and the *tzaddik* answered him, saying, "I learned this practice from the Torah of Moshe, and it is a wonderful way to make your prayers acceptable to God, blessed be He. . . . For those people who pray, 'Master of the World, God merciful and gracious, patient and full of kindness!'—and they make many prayers and supplications—by doing this they arouse Above on themselves the Attribute of Judgment, to investigate them and their deeds, to see if they are worthy of mercy being shown them or not. But what you should do is this: If you want to pray for anything, before praying make confession at the very beginning, saying, 'I have sinned, etc.,' with great humility, and with tears in your eyes—and afterward say all your prayers and supplications. Then you will call and God will answer." (*Toldot Menahem*, p. 103)

Rabbi Shalom Shachna of Probitch:

You should make your requests to God, but before you finish and say "who hears prayer," you should make at least something of a general confession (not specifics). For when you have confessed and abandoned your wrongdoing, you will receive mercy from Above [and your requests will be fulfilled]. [The *rebbe* continues that after you end the *Shemoneh Esreh* and bow:] the Shells [negative forces] see that you have come before the King of all kings, the Holy One, blessed be He, and have exited from His presence, and they begin to make many accusations. So at that point you should make a full confession out loud . . . and by that you cut off all accusers, since "He who confesses and accepts the punishment is released." (Seder ha-Yom of Rabbi Shalom Schachna of Probitch, in *D'vir Yaakov*, p. 6)

5:4 GESTURES, POSTURES, ETC.

Our concentration and intention in our prayers can be greatly affected by our gestures and postures. For the body affects the mind. Certain things are ordained in the tradition, certain prayers are said standing, there are the three steps forward and back in the *Amidah*, the bowing, etc. The point is, first, to make these gestures meaningful and not just automatic. If you take three steps into the *Amidah*, which is understood as entering the presence of God, have this as your conscious intention; if in bowing you are humbling yourself in reverence before God, have that as your intention—when you bow let it be real and not perfunctory. Rabbeinu Yonah notes the teaching of the rabbis with regard to bowing, that when you do so it should be done until

> all the vertebrae in your spine separate one from the other, [and] . . . you can see the smallest coin on the ground underneath where your heart is. (*Sefer ha-Yirah*, p. 191)

We should perform the movements referred to in the prayers as we say them:

> In all the prayers and hymns we have to bow and bend our heads when that is in the prayer, for example, when we say "Come let us bow down" [Sabbath evening prayers] or "I will bow down towards His holy Temple" [said when entering the synagogue]. (*Kitzur Shnei Luchot ha-Brit*, Inyanei tefillah, p. 133)

(His understanding is that we can perform *hishtahaviyah* [translated as to prostrate or bow down] simply by bowing our heads.)

Posture is also important:

> When you are praying sitting down, do not lean back for support, nor to the side, and do not stretch your legs out in a prideful way. (*Shulchan Aruch* of Rabbi Eleazar ha-Katan, p. 76, #17)

We can add that you should not cross your legs when you pray seated. We are innately aware of the meaning of our postures, and our postures during prayer should be attended to, to see that they reflect a reverential and devotional attitude.

5:4:1 Swaying

Swaying when standing or sitting helps concentration. See how others do this in a Jewish way.

> **5:4:1:1** I found it written in a *midrash* that a person should sway when praying, for it is said (Psalm 35:10), "All my bones shall say: O Lord, who is like unto Thee!"—and doing such is the practice of the hasidim. (*Menorat ha-Maor*, section 103, p. 208)

> **5:4:1:2** You should learn the required Hebrew prayers and their translation well, and have the translation so firmly in your memory that you will then be able to pray with your heart and with all the limbs[24] of your body, in the way of the verse "All my bones shall say [O Lord, who is like unto Thee!"] . . . [for] the movement of the limbs arouses *kavvanah*. (*Tzavaat Rabbi Moshe mi-Prague*, Kuntres 3, #12)

5:4:1:3 In describing in detail the ways of Rabbi Eleazar Zev of Kretchnif, we are told that:

> Even when he prayed sitting on his chair he would sway very much. (*Raza d'Uvda*, p. 36)

> **5:4:1:4** Insofar as prayer is called "service" [*avodah*], as in the service of work, and since Israel are called "servants" of God, it is fitting that a person exert himself by lifting up his voice in prayer and by swaying all his limbs—in addition to directing his heart and mind and listening to what he is saying—until he actually tires himself out . . . through the exertion of his service. And so too with Torah study should you "labor" and exert yourself . . . and so too with the *mitzvot*. . . . When you "serve" God you should do so with movement of all your limbs as well as involving your powers of sight and hearing. (*Sefer Haredim*, chap. 66, #30)

5:4:2 Looking Up

Looking up (at the ceiling or sky) directs our mind to God "Above." Of course, God is everywhere, but the gestures have their own inherent meaning which works. The Talmud:

> Abaye and Rava, when children, were sitting before Rabba. "To whom do you pray?" Rabba asked them. "To God," both answered. "But where is God?", he asked. Rava lifted up his hand and pointed toward the ceiling, and Abaye went outside and pointed toward the sky. "Both of you," he said "will certainly become rabbis."[25] (*Berachot* 48a)

We can look up occasionally during prayer, but one particular time when we are to look up at God and think of Him also looking at us, is the *Kedushah* (where we lift ourselves up to God on our toes).

> It is said about the *Kedushah* (when you are to lift your eyes up) that God says, "I have no greater pleasure in the world than at that time when their eyes are lifted up to Me and My eyes are on them." (*Sefer Hechalot*, quoted in *Yesod v'Shoresh ha-Avodah*, Gate 5, chap. 6, p. 97)

5:4:3 Use Your Hands

Make appropriate gestures with your hands to fit the prayer. Have your hands clasped or outstretched, for example. It is often suggested that in the *Amidah* you are to have your hands outstretched for those parts that are requests; in the other parts you should have your hands on your chest, the right hand over the left.[26]

5:4:3:1 Clapping

Clapping helps bring alertness and joy. Hasidim often clap their hands and snap their fingers during prayer to arouse themselves and to express their inspiration and happiness.

5:4:3:1:1 Rabbi Nachman of Bratzlav:

> We clap our hands during prayer, for by this the air of the place where a man of Israel prays is purified, and the air of holiness is drawn there, as in the Land of Israel itself. And so when you pray, it is the air of the Land of Israel, which is a remedy for foreign thoughts in prayer. (*Likkutei Aytzot*, Tefillah, #41)

5:4:3:1:2 Rabbi Mordechai of Neshkiz:

> Sometimes a person works to inspire himself while praying and claps his hands and makes other movements so as to push away foreign thoughts. (*Mazkeret Shem ha-Gedolim*, p. 157)

5:4:3:1:3 When you clap your hands, picture all foreign thoughts flying away as a flock of blackbirds at the clap of thunder.

5:4:3:1:4 Generally, Rabbi Nachman also talks about the value of making "holy noise," as opposed to the noise of the Other Side.

If people who revel in base things are not ashamed to make all kinds of noise and to blare out raucous music, why should we be ashamed to make holy noise and to express our joy in God?

5:4:3:2 Many gestures can be used to express the words of the *davvening*. For example, when you say in the *Sh'ma* "and you shall talk of them [words of Torah] when you are sitting in your house," touch your lips; in the *Aleinu*, when you say "and you shall know this day and take it to heart, that the Lord, He is God in heaven above and upon the earth beneath," point to your heart and then to heaven and earth; and so on in many other places.

Rabbi Eleazar Zev of Kretchnif himself served as prayer leader on *Shabbat*. The following is told of his saying the *Kedushah* in the repetition of the *Shemoneh Esreh*:

> Often, when he said "and let our eyes see the revelation of Your kingdom," he cried with copious tears and was greatly aroused. And in his holy talks to us he explained a few times how this meant that we should see with these very eyes the salvation and consolation of the Congregation of Israel. . . . And sometimes when he said these words in prayer, he passed his holy hand over his pure eyes, with this *kavvanah*. (*Raza d'Uvda*, p. 38)

5:4:3:3 Raising Your Hands

> It is very precious to God that you raise your hands with spread fingers when you are praying from the depth of your heart . . . also when you wash your hands [before prayers or eating], say the blessing over the washing as you dry them, and raise them up to receive the holiness. . . . The Torah tells us about Abraham, who said, "I have raised my hands to God the Most High" (Genesis 14:22). And the ancient Aramaic paraphrase, the *Targum*, has: "I have lifted my hands in prayer". . . . And so also about Moses it is written how when he prayed for the defeat of Amalek, "and when Moses raised his hands, Israel would be victorious in the battle" (Exodus 17:11). And so, when you are praying or making blessings or saying praises of God, it is even obligatory to lift up your hands and fingers. (*Kav ha-Yashar*, chap. 63)

Different hand movements influence the mind differently. Rabbi Nachman of Bratzlav explained that lifting one's hands above the head has a special influence relating to prayer as "going beyond [above] the intellect."

Another beautiful and very meaningful gesture (especially when singing or listening to a song) is to wave with one hand held fully aloft, as if waving to someone leaving on a ship.

5:4:4 Pacing

You can pace back and forth or walk around while praying. In some hasidic groups people even run around during prayer. One author, describing his own experience on the night of *Shabbat* in the synagogue of Rabbi Yissachar Ber, the *rebbe* of Belz, tells how the hasidim ran about the *shul* as they *davvened* in ecstasy with loud voices—unconcerned when they sometimes banged into each other (*Hasidic Prayer*, p. 65).

Of Rabbi Hayim of Tzanz it is told:

> Once, in his youth, he ran around in his room for a number of hours, back and forth, with awesome fervor, whispering with his lips moving. Rabbi Shalom of Kaminka went up behind him quietly (Rabbi Hayim, due to his great *d'vekut* did not see the Kaminker Rabbi), and he heard that the holy Tzanzer was saying over and over, "I mean nothing but You, nothing but You alone." (*Mekor Hayim*, p. 88, #135)

> [When Rabbi Yehudah Pesah of Lipsk served God during the night hours, his manner of prayer was] to run from wall to wall back and forth, bent over as if swimming; and he would sing songs and praises of God with tears and shouting, with joyful melody and song, all in an astonishing way. And when he had sweat through his shirt, his personal attendant would give him another from the dresser, and there were many times when he went through many shirts in one night. (*Shema Shlomo*, II, Yesharaish Yaakov, p. 44, #9)

5:4:5 Full Prostration

Full prostration before God is conducive to thoughts of complete submission to His will and to self-sacrifice in His service.

> The exile communities are to be gathered only in the merit of prostration in prayer. . . . Israel is only redeemed in the merit of prostration. . . . The Holy Temple was only built in the merit of prostration. (*Yalkut Shimoni* on 1 Samuel 1:28)

We are told in the Talmud how Rabbi Akiba prayed with such abandon and fervor that:

> When praying alone [without a *minyan*—though other people may have been present] he engaged in so much kneeling and prostrating that if someone was with him and saw him in one corner of the

room, when he walked out and came back he would find him in the opposite corner. (*Berachot* 31)[27]

This about Rabbi Akiba is the model and there are numbers of hasidic *rebbes* who are compared to him and who *davvened* in just this way. (See 5:3:10:3 which is typical.)

Prostration means lying flat on the ground with arms and legs outstretched. Although today we only prostrate in public worship on *Rosh HaShanah* and *Yom Kippur*, there are innumerable stories of hasidic *rebbes* who prostrated in prayer; sometimes this was in public, but more often they were discovered when they were praying alone or communing with their Maker, and were found in full prostration.

Here are some typical stories:

5:4:5:1 Of Rabbi Moshe Teitelbaum we are told that during *Shaharit*:

> When he recited the *Sh'ma* he prostrated himself fully on the ground, with outstretched arms and legs for several hours, and he uttered groans, and all his limbs shook so that his *tallit* would slide off him—though he wasn't aware of that at all.[28] (*Ha-Admor mi-Ohel*, p. 74)

5:4:5:2 About Rabbi Meir of Premishlan:

> Of his holy ways, we know that he prayed with such energy and so loudly that the pillars of the building would shake. When he recited the *Sh'ma* he did so with complete self-sacrifice. And in the morning *davvening* on *Shabbat*, he would prostrate himself completely on the floor and would lie there in total *d'vekut* for hours at a time, until most of the other worshipers finished their prayers and went home to eat; and then, after their meal, when they returned, they would find him first standing and saying the *Shemoneh Esreh* or maybe just finishing the *Sh'ma*. (*Or ha-Meir*, p. 16)

5:4:5:3 It was said about Rabbi Avigdor Yehudah ha-Levi, the Rabbi of Koyl:

> When he was still a rabbi in the city of Bloshky, his holy custom after the Morning Prayer Service was to remain the whole day, until night fell, in the synagogue, with the doors locked, covered in his *tallit* and crowned with *tefillin*. It happened once that for one reason or another some people looked in through the windows that were in the women's section, and they saw an amazing sight. He was lying on the floor in *tallit* and *tefillin*, stretched out, arms and legs

extended in full prostration before the holy Ark, which was open, and surrounding his holy body were many white doves. And so was he pouring out his heart in prayer before his Creator, blessed be He. (*Abir ha-Ro'im*, #141)

5:4:5:4 About Rabbi Nachman of Bratzlav:

The Rebbe had his own apartment in Uman, but his landlord had the right to enter at will. Once the landlord entered the Rebbe's room without warning and found him lying prostrate on the floor, stretched out in prayer. (*Rabbi Nachman's Wisdom*, p. 307; *Sichos HaRan*, #164)

5:4:5:5 It is told of Rabbi Menahem Mendel of Kossov that:

His holy way was to lead the congregation in prayer himself. In the synagogue there was a screen between him and the people, who would hear his clear and sweet voice, and they too would direct their hearts to pray with love and fear of God in a sweet way. And no one would ever dare to look over the screen into the holy place during the time of prayer.

But once someone lifted himself up on the wall of the screen to look over, and was startled and jumped back, falling on the ground. He lay there like a stone in a faint, and only with difficulty did they bring him to. Upon regaining consciousness, he told them that he saw the holy rabbi fully prostrate on the ground and a fire was blazing all around him as if he were an angel of God; and that was why when he looked he was stricken and fainted. (*Even Shtiya*, p. 22, #1)

Certainly then, this practice of prostration is valuable in private prayer. In the synagogue, during public prayer when this would be impossible in most cases, prostration can be done in imagination. (See "Service of the Imagination," 19:14.)

Practically, it is a good idea to have a special sheet, to be used only for this purpose, to be laid down on the floor, so as not to dirty yourself when you prostrate at home.

Of Rabbi David Biderman of Jerusalem (a *tzaddik* and *rebbe* in the House of Lelov) we are told:

He frequently locked himself in his room and there were those who were curious to know what Rabbi David'l was doing there. They looked through the crack in the door and saw how he spread a sheet on the floor and lay down on the ground in full prostration with

> arms and legs outstretched. He then beat on his breast forcefully, repenting before God and crying like a child as he confessed, saying, "David Tzvi Shlomo, son of Motil Feiga—what did you do in such and such a place, and in that other place what did you do?" So did he cry and sob and beg that God forgive him and show him a little light. (*Tiferet Beit David*, p. 93)

(See "*Tikkun Hatzot*," 31:16–18 for more about prostration.)

5:4:6 Weeping

Many of the rabbis tell us to accustom ourselves to weep tears of devotion. Learn to open your heart to God without shame. Such tears are very holy; they are numbered by God and kept by Him in a special jar. As the rabbis say, though the gates of prayer may at times be closed, the gates of tears are never closed.

How can we learn to cry though? Rabbi Moshe Hasid of Prague said:

> If you cannot cry, then at least pray in a crying voice, for God wants the heart.[29] (*Tzavaat Rabbi Moshe mi Prague*, #10)

Anyone who has heard a *Chazan* pray has heard this.

> When the rabbis said you should make your prayers a request for mercy [*tahanunim*—Avot 2:18] . . . they meant that you should make sad expressions with your face and lips as you pray, just like a child pleads before his father, when he puts his soul into it with his facial expressions, to arouse his father's compassion. And so should you do. . . . These facial expressions, which are of course bodily actions, ignite your emotions and will help you to cry when you make requests in your prayers. (*Yesod v'Shoresh ha-Avodah*, Gate 5, chap. 1, p. 83)

There is a story of some hasidim who, in the presence of their *rebbe*, were dancing and singing before God, all in great *d'vekut*, and they were all crying holy tears. There was one among them, though, who could not cry, and he felt so terrible about this that he ran and got some onions, which he held to his eyes so that he too could cry. The *rebbe*, seeing this, praised him, saying it was very precious to God that he wanted to cry.

5:4:7 Groaning and Sighing

Rabbi Nachman of Bratzlav taught about the use of groaning and sighing in prayer as well as at other times.

The Rebbe once spoke to a man who was very far from God. He told him that he could help himself by sighing and groaning. (*Rabbi Nachman's Wisdom*, p. 265, *Sichos HaRan* #135)

Elsewhere he says:

A holy sigh is very precious, for when a man sighs because of how far he is from holiness, through this he cuts himself loose from the rope of impurity binding him, and attaches himself to the rope of holiness. . . . A man's sighing [from the depth of his heart] over his sins and over his deficiency in holy awareness, is more valuable than many self-afflictions and fasts. (*Likkutei Aytzot*, Anacha, #3, 4)

Of a disciple of the Besht, Rabbi Nachman of Kossov, it is told that:

When Rabbi Nachman would groan while praying, it would break the heart of anyone who heard it, and it would seem to him as if he had been cut in half. (*Mishnat Hasidim*, p. 302, #28)

Rabbi Nachman of Bratzlav also taught the silent shout, and he in fact often used a wordless silent shout. One could also sigh or groan this way (silently) during public prayer, without problems. (See "Individual Practices" 39:23 for more about the silent shout.)

5:5 AFTER THE SERVICE

5:5:1 One should not talk or enter into conversation for some time after prayer. (See 5:1:10:1–2.)
5:5:2 The Talmud tells us that:

The early hasidim would spend one hour in preparation for prayer, one hour in prayer, and one hour after prayer [in meditation]. (*Berachot* 32).

And the rabbis teach here in association with this that: "When you pray, you should tarry an hour after prayer [in meditation]"—where the Maharsha's view is that this means "looking at God's face without prayer."[30] (See also 5:1:18:3:3.)

Another use for the meditation after prayer can be to gather the inspiration received during prayer, direct it, and apply it to our worldly endeavors.

5:5:3 At the end of the service it is common to feel, "Oh, now I'm finished and can relax." But as we explained in Part One, our goal must be to achieve continuous *d'vekut.* So although it is natural to be somewhat fatigued after prayer, we should work to turn our religious awareness to our next activities. It is a good idea, therefore, when you reach the last words of the service, to do something to bring yourself to a calm state of mind, until you are able to see how to direct the religious energy and inspiration set in motion during the *davvening* to your daily involvements.

5:5:3:1 Rabbi Elimelech of Lizensk outlines the problem:

> When a person is engaged in Torah study or prayer or another holy activity, he is in a state of expanded consciousness [*mohin d'gadlut*]. The way of the *tzaddikim* is that *before* prayer [for example] they compose themselves and settle their minds in meditating on before Whom they are praying. And the holy activity itself [prayer] lifts up their consciousness *during* the time of their involvement in it. But *after* the prayer or other holy activity many people descend again to a state of constricted consciousness [*mohin d'katnut*], as they go their way in the vain pursuits of this world.
>
> But this is not the purpose of a perfect service of God. A person should always be in a holy and pure state of mind without a moment's cessation. And for this you have to bind yourself to God, blessed is He, so strongly during the time of expanded consciousness, that even when you leave it you will remain attached to Him. (*Noam Elimelech*, Emor, p. 56a)

The way to accomplish this purpose of binding yourself to God so strongly that you will carry the *d'vekut* into your daily activities is by means of a special meditation after prayer—as with the early hadisim mentioned above.

> **5:5:3:2** The early hasidim would remain meditating for an hour after their prayer—in order to see that the life and the God-consciousness [*yirah*] of the prayer would stay with them for the whole day. (Rabbi Aaron of Karlin, *Hanhagot Tzaddikim*, p. 21, #18)

What is intended here is that this meditation be used to fasten the impression received during the *davvening* into your consciousness so that it stays with you for as long as possible throughout the day.

5:5:3:3 *Kaf ha-Hayim*, speaking about the flow of Divine light from the Upper World, which can be brought down during prayer:

> After the prayer, that flow leaves and returns to go back up from whence it came—and no impression of it remains. So the early hasidim would wait for an hour after prayer [and meditate], in order to muster spiritual force so that the light would not remove. (11:23, p. 161)

5:5:4 Rabbi Yerahmiel Yisrael Yitzhak of Alexander said about the tradition that the early hasidim would meditate for an hour after prayer:

> They would reflect on whether their prayer had been altogether sincere and truthful, without any self-consideration or falsity, God forbid. (*Eser Z'chuyout*, p. 94)

5:5:5 Another good practice is, after prayer, having talked with God, for you to sit silently for a while listening for a response—to hear what He is saying to you. Perhaps He wants to direct you in one way or another. Thus, you will be leaving some space in your time of prayer to hear as well as to speak.

> When you give over all your thoughts to God, blessed be He, so that He will form them and send you, in your thoughts, what you need to do (as it says "Cast your burden on God" [Psalm 55:23]), and then you feel a strong desire to do some pious thing—it is certain that you need to do that, so God, blessed be He, has sent you that thought. And our master, the Besht, said that when you are in *d'vekut* with God, blessed be He, and some thought falls into your mind, it is certainly true, and this is a little of the holy spirit. (*Likkutei Yekarim*, p. 3a)

So after prayer, sit in *d'vekut*—where the test for this will be if you see that you have no foreign thoughts at all. Then dedicate your thoughts to God and recognize that He is the source of all that is, even your thoughts. Pray that He send you thoughts of His will—and attend to what comes to your mind.

This can also be done during the personal prayer of the *Shemoneh Esreh*—that in a state of *d'vekut* you ask God to speak to you and send you thoughts of His will. Otherwise, whenever you are praying and in a higher and purer state of consciousness and a thought falls into your mind, it should be attended to as a message from God.

> When you are speaking [in prayer] in the Upper World, and have no foreign thought, and a thought comes to you, like prophecy, certainly it will be so, and it will come to pass. And this thought came

> due to the heavenly proclamations, which are always being announced Above about everything. And sometimes you will hear, what sounds like a voice speaking. (*Likkutei Yekarim*, p. 3c)

Now most of us are not on the level to hear actual prophecy, but according to the Baal Shem Tov this process applies to humbler manifestations of the holy spirit and receiving direction from God. (See " Individual Practices" 39:29 for more about this practice.)

5:5:6 Just as some Torah study is a good preparation for prayer, so is it a good practice to study some Torah after prayer.

> **5:5:6:1** Be sure after the Morning Prayer Service to study some Torah, everyone according to his own ability and intelligence, and according to the time available. Even if you do have to eat or go to work, study at least something, so that you will not be casting off the yoke of Torah immediately after prayer. (Rabbi Aaron of Karlin, *Hanhagot Tzaddikim*, p. 8, #10)

> **5:5:6:2** Immediately after the Morning Prayers learn something, even one verse if that is all you have time for. (*Derech Hayim*, 2-63)

5:5:6:3 It is especially good to learn Torah with the *tefillin* still on:

> After the Morning Prayer Service, be very sure to learn Torah in *tefillin*. . . . And it is good to learn in one of the *musar* books [books of ethics and character development]. The holy master Rabbi Moshe of Lelov, may his merit protect us, used to learn *Pirke Avot* every day in *tefillin*. (*Or ha-Ner*, #18)

After *Shaharit* it is appropriate to learn *musar* or *Avot* so as to carry the inspiration of prayer into these lessons about our behavior, and then from there into our day-to-day activities.

6

The Synagogue and the Synagogue Service

6:1 The synagogue is a place of holiness, and cultivating this awareness is a worthy practice. The more you develop and increase your feeling for the holiness of the synagogue, the more you will be influenced for good when you go there.

6:2 The synagogue should inspire us with both love and fear (awe) of God. On the one hand, it is the house of our Father in Heaven, for we are the children of God and should develop our own love of His house and feel comfortable there. On the other hand, it is the dwelling on earth of the King of the Universe, the Holy One, blessed be He, and we should feel the awe of this place from which a ladder goes up to heaven.[1]

6:3 Frequent attendance at His house is a sign of devotion to God and brings His blessing. The rabbis applied to this the proverb, "To the place that my heart loves, there do my feet lead me." When God sees that we come again and again to His house He knows that this shows the devotion in our heart, and when we come to the synagogue He comes too and we receive His blessing, as it says, "In every place where I cause My name to be mentioned, I will come to you there and bless you." (Exodus 20:21)

6:4 The Peasetzna Rebbe's description of how his hasidim should think of their meetinghouse (where they studied and prayed) fits a synagogue as well:

> The meetinghouse for our fellowship should be for each of you a sanctified place, a place where God dwells, and, so to speak, a [spiritual] bathhouse wherein to bathe and purify your souls—the place where your souls enter the camp of the *Shechinah*, which is found there. When you are on your way you should consider it as if you are then leaving the domain of this world and going to a region of the Lower Garden of Eden which God has brought down to your meetinghouse. Your heart should rejoice with holy trepidation at your great happiness, that even in this world you have merited to hide under the wings of the *Shechinah*.
>
> And even more so when you are in the meetinghouse should you rejoice, and think, "The holy *Shechinah* is among us; O God, my soul is lovesick for You; please, please bring her healing by showing her the beauty of Your radiance."[2] Yearning should be aroused within you that God should reveal to your heart at least a spark of the beauty of His radiance and the glory of His majesty which are found there. (*B'nai Machshavah Tovah*, Nusach ha-Kabbalah, #8)

It is appropriate occasionally to express verbally our longing to go to the synagogue, and also, when we are there, that its holiness be revealed to us, that we should experience it and feel it.

6:5 You should cultivate your own emotional reaction to the synagogue and one way to do this is, when you go there—walk quickly.

> **6:5:1** It is a *mitzvah* to walk quickly when you go to the synagogue. (*Berachot* 6b)
>
> **6:5:2** When you leave your house in the morning [for the synagogue], kiss the *mezuzah* . . . and say the verse "The name of God is a tower of strength; a righteous person will run there and be safe, he will be lifted up above all harm [Proverbs 18:10]." (*Or Tzaddikim*, p. 20)
>
> **6:5:3** Walk briskly to the synagogue and have in your mind this intention: "I am going to the synagogue to serve my Creator." Have

> this as your intention, in great joy, all the time you are walking there. (*Yesod v'Shoresh ha-Avodah*, Gate 2, chap. 8, p. 36)

Elsewhere (*Kitzur Shnei Luchot ha-Brit*, Inyanei Tefillah, p. 111) it is suggested that we say this aloud as a stated intention.

> **6:5:4** And you should walk quickly when you go to the synagogue . . . and as you go say the verse, "So let us know, and let us run to seek knowledge of God; for His going forth is as sure as the sun in the morning, and He shall come to us as certainly as the showers, the spring rains that water the earth" (Hosea 6:3). (*Or Tzaddikim*, p. 5, #21)

> **6:5:5** When you go to the synagogue, as you get close, hurry your steps, as it says, "To the House of God we will go with heightened emotion" (Psalm 55:15). (*Sefer ha-Yirah* of Rabbeinu Yonah, p. 188)

6:6 As you walk along, do not look this way and that, but keep your glance controlled and wrap yourself in religious thoughts and meditations.

Rabbi Yehiel Michal of Zlotchov instructed his disciples that they were to limit their vision:

> at least when you are walking to the synagogue and when you leave it (*Hanhagot Tzaddikim*, p. 54, #5; see the full quote in 6:23).

But when you get within sight of the synagogue, lift up your eyes and say, "How holy and full of awe is this place! This is none other than the House of God, and this is the gate of heaven!" (Genesis 28:17)

6:7 Rabbi Arye Levin, the *tzaddik* of Jerusalem (who passed away in 1969) would rise every day before dawn to join a minyan that prayed at the rising of the sun:

> On his way to the synagogue he made it a point to greet everyone he met on the street; and he was especially careful to wish a good morning to the street cleaners, who also rose early to work. (*A Tzaddik in Our Time*, p. 101)

Greeting others first, and in a warm way, is a part of love for our fellow man, and is good preparation for serving God in prayer with love. (See "Loving and Honoring Our Fellow Men," 9:5.)

> **6:8** When you arrive at the synagogue, before you enter, bow toward it and say, "As for me, in the abundance of Thy loving-kindness will I come into Thy house [I will worship (prostrate/bow) toward Thy holy Temple in the fear of Thee]. (*Kitzur Shnei Luchot ha-Brit*, Inyanei Tefillah, p. 111)

(It is a good custom, when seeing any synagogue, to bow your head slightly as you pass by and say, "How goodly are thy tents O Jacob, thy tabernacles, O Israel! As for me . . . I will bow toward Thy holy Temple in the fear of Thee" [See 6:11:5].)

> **6:9** Rabbi Israel of Koznitz was in poor health from his childhood on. He was always in a bed since he was so sick and so very thin. But when he prayed he would burn with love of God like a flaming fire. . . . He was so thin that the doctors were amazed how he could be alive, for his thighs had no flesh on them at all—something whose like is not found in any creature in the world. And his legs were as thin as those of a deer. So weak was he that they had to carry him around on a litter. But when they brought him to the door of the synagogue he called out in a thunderous voice, "How full of awe is this place!" and he put his feet on the ground and almost flew to the prayer-leader's stand. (*Eser Orot*, p. 69, #10)

> **6:10** It was a holy practice of the holy Rabbi Meir'l of Tiktin, every *Shabbat*, to circle the synagogue seven times [before entering for prayer]. (*Shemen ha-Tov*, II, #122)

By this act he expressed his reverence for the Divine Presence within the synagogue. (See also 6:15.)

6:11 As with other acts of Divine service, before entering the synagogue you should spiritually prepare yourself.

> **6:11:1** Certainly it is right that a person feel a holy shame and awe when he comes to the synagogue or to the House of Torah study, for they are called "a holy Temple in miniature" (Ezekiel 11:16). And he should see that he is infused with awe of the holy place before he enters, as it is written, "and you shall have awe for My holy places" (Leviticus 19:30)—and only afterwards should he enter within, and therein feel awe and reverence due to his devotion to the King of the Universe, the Holy One, blessed be He. (Rabbi Mordechai of Tchernobil, *Likkutei Torah*, quoted in *DhTvhY*, Hilchot Beit ha-Knesset, #1, p. 26b)

6:11:2 Before you enter a synagogue you should be careful to stop for a minute at the door and show that you fear and tremble and quake in entering the Palace of the King. (*Minhagei ha-Arizal*, p. 5b, #11)

6:11:3 Rabbi Yerahmiel Moshe of Koznitz (a descendant of Rabbi Israel of Koznitz) compared the entrance of the synagogue to a border between two countries, where you have to check your luggage beforehand for contraband, and if you have any you have to throw it away. And he said that:

> Before you enter a synagogue you should remove and cast away all thoughts about the vanities of this world, so that they will not interfere with your prayer. (*Sifran Shel Tzaddikim*, p. 79, #23. See also "Prayer," 5:1:18:1 about how to do this.)

6:11:4 Before you enter a synagogue you should pray this short prayer: "God, please accept the offering of my prayers and teach me Your ways. And may it be Your will, my God and God of my fathers and mothers, that my prayer be clear and pure and untainted by any admixture of such thoughts as would blemish my sincere intentions."* (*Kav ha-Yashar*, chap. 63)

6:11:5 It is often suggested that we say Psalm 5:8 before or on entering the synagogue (as in 6:8 above). But many Siddurs have a fuller prayer to say on entering, formed from a selection of verses:

> How goodly are thy tents O Jacob, thy tabernacles
> O Israel!
> As for me, in the abundance of Thy lovingkindness
> will I come into Thy house:
> I will worship [prostrate] toward Thy holy Temple
> in the fear of Thee.
> Lord, I love the habitation of Thy house,
> and the place where Thy glory dwelleth.
> As for me, I will worship [prostrate] and bow down:
> I will bend the knee before the Lord my Maker.
> And as for me, may my prayer unto Thee, O Lord,
> be in an acceptable time:
> O God, in the abundance of Thy lovingkindness,
> answer me in the truth of Thy salvation.

(The verses here are Numbers 24:5, Psalms 5:8, 26:8, source unknown, and Psalm 69:14.)

These words, in the Siddur at the beginning of the Morning Service, are said by some before and by some after entering the synagogue. Some sources also have certain of these lines said at different stages when entering. Consider them well, and assimilating their meaning, say them from the heart. As with other things of this kind, it is a good idea to write the words down on a piece of paper and keep it with you to read from as you enter the synagogue, until you have it memorized.

6:11:6 In the book *Avodat ha-Kodesh* we hear of:

> The *mitzvah* to tarry outside the door of the synagogue before entering, and getting permission [from God] to enter by reciting the verse "And as for me, in the abundance, . . ." (*Tzavaot v'Derech Tovim*, p. 80, #10)

6:11:7 Before entering the synagogue, says Rabbi Yaakov Hagiz:

> "Know before Whom you are going to pray," and think beforehand of His greatness, and see that your mind is fastened on awe of Him. Note the conditions that King David mentioned in the psalm for those who are worthy of entering the Temple: "Who shall ascend the Mount of the Lord, and who shall stand in His holy place? He who has clean hands and a pure heart etc." [Psalm 24:3]. If you have these qualities, enter; but if not, at all events feel regret at your unworthiness. And think to yourself of the great kindness that God does in receiving you within His house when you are covered with sins. These thoughts should be in your mind when reciting "And as for me, in the abundance of Thy loving-kindness will I come into Thy house"—even though I am not worthy of it. (Zichron l'Vnai Yisrael, #19, in *YHvT,* p. 42)

6:11:8 Rabbi Elijah deVidas explains the verse said on entering the synagogue this way:

> You should realize that the synagogue is the house of the King. And not all the servants of a king of flesh and blood merit to serve him in his house and in his presence, but only those who win his favor and are worthy. How much more is this true then of someone serving before the King of the Universe, the Holy One, blessed be He, and having the opportunity to stand in the presence of His *Shechinah*, even though he is not worthy of the honor.

> This is the meaning of "And as for me, in the abundance of Thy loving-kindness will I come into Thy house"—that is, You have shown me great love in accepting me among those who can enter Your house, the place where the *Shechinah* dwells. And by this you should draw on yourself awe of God, when you bring to mind that the synagogue is the house of the King, that He dwells there and He comes there. Then the verse continues: "I will worship [prostrate] toward Thy holy Temple in the fear of Thee." This means that now that through His loving-kindness I have been allowed to be among those who enter the King's presence even though I am unworthy, I should bow towards the holy sanctuary [the Ark] which is especially holy. For although the whole synagogue is the place of the *Shechinah*, the Ark is where He actually is, and that is where I go to pray before Him. (*Totzaot Hayim*, pp. 69–70)

Regarding our unworthiness to enter the synagogue, Rabbi Elijah deVidas adds to his meditation before entering the thought from the *Zohar*: "You enter the synagogue with the help of the three Patriarchs." One can think and imagine when entering the synagogue that you do so in the holy company of Abraham, Isaac, and Jacob, Sarah, Rebecca, Rachel, and Leah, and with their support.

> It was the custom of the holy rabbi, Rabbi Yitzhak of Ziditchov, of blessed memory, on the holy Sabbath, before the morning prayers, to sit not on his chair but on his bed [while he was preparing to leave for the synagogue]. And he said that this was the custom of our holy master, the Rebbe of Lublin, the memory of a *tzaddik* for a blessing. His reason for this was that his holy ancestors, Abraham, Isaac, and Jacob would come to him before prayers, so he would leave the chair empty for them. And you, my dear reader, look at the Preface to the *Zohar*, p. 11a, where it says "A person should not go to the synagogue to pray until he first takes counsel with Abraham, Isaac, and Jacob . . . and you should first join yourself together with them, and then enter the synagogue and pray." And this is the source of the custom of the Lubliner, who merited having this visitation of the Patriarchs actually revealed to him. (*Niflaot ha-Rebbe*, p. 111, #346)

6:12 Kiss the *mezuzah* of the synagogue as you enter. About Rabbi Eleazar Zev of Kretchnif:

> In the morning, on his way to the synagogue, he would stand by the *mezuzah* of his house for some time in meditation, and so also at the *mezuzah* of the *Beit Midrash*. (*Raza d'Uvda*, p. 10)

6:13 It is written of the Rebbe of Alesk how every morning he recited particular verses and prayers at each stage of his journey from his house to the synagogue:

1. When he was ready to go to the synagogue to pray, but still in his house, he said the verse, "I have considered my ways, and I will turn my feet back to Your testimonies" [Psalm 119:59]; and then he also said Psalm 122 [A Song of Ascents, of David: "I rejoiced when they said unto me, Let us go unto the House of the Lord etc."]
2. When he was going out the door, he kissed the *mezuzah* and said the verse *Sh'ma Yisrael* [Deuteronomy 6:4] and "Salvation is of the Lord etc." [Psalm 3:9], "Lord of hosts etc." [Psalm 84:13], "Lord, save! etc." [Psalm 20:10], "Please, O Lord, please save! O Lord, bring success!" [Psalm 118:25], and another prayer.
3. When he reached the courtyard of the synagogue he said, "To the House of God we will go with heightened emotion" [Psalm 55:15].
4. Before he entered the synagogue, he said, "How holy and awesome is this place! etc." [Genesis 28:17].
5. When he was standing on the threshhold of the entrance he said, "As for me, in the abundance of Thy loving-kindness etc," and another prayer of the form "May it be Your will."
6. Having entered he said, "Our feet are standing within they gates, O Jerusalem etc." until "I will seek thy good" [Psalm 122], and other supplications and petitions. And afterwards he would say seven times the verse, "How beautiful and how sweet love is, with its delights" [Song of Songs 7:7], then a number of times the verse, "A continual fire shall burn on the altar; it shall not be put out" [Leviticus 6:6], and other prayers and supplications. (*Lev Sameah ha-Hadash, Or Hadash,* p. 138)

All the verses the *rebbe* used served to heighten the emotions of love and fear of God; the latter two (about the delights of love and the "continual fire") are the culmination, so that he should experience great love and holy fire in the synagogue. One can also see in this practice of the *rebbe* the potential elsewhere for linking appropriate verses and prayers with our actions and movements.

It should be noted that although certain verses are typically associated with various stages on the way to the synagogue, one source uses one verse at one point, and another source will have it at another point.[3]

6:14 After having said the "And as for me, in the abundance etc." on the threshhold of the synagogue:

> When you come in and are facing the Ark, say, "I will bow toward Thy holy Temple in the fear of Thee" and you should bow deeply and think that you are bowing to the Creator, blessed be He, from reverence for Him. (*Yesod v'Shoresh ha-Avodah,* Gate 2, chap. 10, p. 39)

> **6:15** After entering the synagogue [and bowing toward the Ark] say Psalm 67, which has seven verses, and with each verse circle the *bimah*; but on *Shabbat* circle just once. (*Or Tzaddikim*, 12:2, p. 19b)
>
> When the holy Rabbi Hayim of Tzanz came to the *Beit Midrash* on *Shabbat* night to make the *kiddush*, he would circle the *bimah* seven times, following the practice of Rabbi Meir'l of Tiktin on the evening of the holy *Shabbat*.[4] (*Mekor Hayim*, p. 155)

The *bimah* in the synagogue is in place of the altar in the Temple courtyard[5]—so the *bimah* is circled to fulfill "I will circle Your altar." (Psalm 25:6)

> **6:16** You should have a fixed place to sit in the synagogue for whenever you go to pray . . . and do not change it if you can help it . . . because a person can concentrate better in a familiar place. (*Menorat ha-Maor*, p. 204)

> **6:17:1** After coming into the synagogue, sit for a little while and say, "Happy are they that sit in Thy house, they shall be ever praising Thee. *Selah*." [Psalm 84:5] (*Kitzur Shnei Luchot ha-Brit*, Inyanei Tefillah, p. 111).

(One can also add the following line: "Happy is the people that is in such a case; happy is the people whose God is the Lord!" These two lines are the words with which the *Minha* service begins and the Hebrew can be easily found in the Siddur.)

6:17:2 When you enter the synagogue, do not immediately open the Siddur and begin saying prayers, but sit down and compose yourself and put yourself in the right spiritual mood. Prepare yourself for prayer.

Rabbi Shmelke of Nikolsburg:

> Remember that before prayer you should go within yourself and picture that the King of the Universe is standing before you, and afterward, when you pray you will know before Whom you are speaking. But when you come to a synagogue to pray, and immediately upon coming in begin to say the prayers without any preparation beforehand, then you are committing the error of preceding the mouth to the ear. (*DhTvhY*, Hilchot Tefillah, #8, p. 18b)

6:17:3 After entering the synagogue:

> Sit in your place, then cover yourself with a *tallit* and make the blessing, and then sit without opening your mouth—wait for a while in meditation and put your heart to consider before Whom you are standing and speaking and Who is listening to your words. (Rabbeinu Yonah, *Sefer ha-Yirah*)

6:17:4 As indicated by these quotes, after sitting down is a good time for a meditation on being in the presence of God, and particularly on the presence of God in the sanctified place of the synagogue. (See "Meditation" [17] and "Prayer," 5:1:18 for more about this kind of meditation.)

> **6:17:5** When you enter the synagogue, sit or stand for a while to compose yourself, and then say, "I receive on myself the yoke of the Kingdom of Heaven and the commandment 'You shall love your neighbor as yourself.'"* (*Derech Hayim*, 7–13)

This would be an appropriate time to look around at your fellow congregants and think of them with love—for they also have come to worship their Father in Heaven. Think of how they, like you, are made in the image of God and are His children, and that in loving them you can express your love for Him. Have compassion on them, even with their faults, and know that they too, in their hearts yearn to serve God.

You can think that God is happy to see all these, His children, in His house. For just as we are happy to sit in His house praising Him, so is He made happy. As the rabbis say:

> Three times a day when Israelites enter synagogues or Houses of Torah Study and answer: "May His great Name be praised!" [*Y'hai shmai rabba m'vorach*], the Holy One, blessed be He, nods His head in satisfaction and approval and says, "Happy is the king thus praised in his own house!" (*Berachot* 3a)

Although usually the commandment to love one's neighbor is called to mind and accepted on oneself before praying, there are other times for this during the Service. For instance:

> [During the *Kedushah* in the *Shemoneh Esreh*] you should accept on yourself the positive commandment "and you shall love your neighbor as yourself." For we say in the *Kedushah* that: "Just as the ministering angels in the high heavens sanctify God," we of Israel here below are to imitate them; just as they relate to each other in love and complete unity, so are we to be that way to each other. And you should commit yourself to this sincerely, not just say it and have in your heart, God forbid, hatred for any Jew.
>
> And my custom when I was in any Jewish gathering was always, a number of times, to lift up my eyes to look from one end of the group to the other, to see if I had love for each and every one there, and to see if my acceptance of the commandment to love was real and true. And, blessed be God, so did I find it. Even if I did find someone who had done something to me, I would immediately forgive him then and there, and I accepted on myself love for him. If my heart forced me not to love him, then I would actually utter great blessings on that person until I succeeded in removing any hatred or dislike from my heart.[6] (*Imrei Kodesh*, The Testament of Rabbi Yoel Frumkin of Amtzislav, #9, p. 23)

Before prayer is a good time to join yourself with all of Israel, as is often suggested, and to say: "I join myself and my prayer, in love, with all the congregations of Your people Israel throughout the world."[7] (See "Prayer," 5:1:17 for quotes about this declaration.)

Rabbi Arye Levin in praising the value of prayer with a congregation:

> Is it not a higher level of spirituality, when a man stands in entreaty not for himself alone but for the whole group with him? When an entire people stands in prayer not for itself alone, but for every human created in the Divine image, indeed for the entire world? (*A Tzaddik in Our Time*, p. 422)

(See Chapter 5, "Prayer," for more about preparation for prayer.)

> **6:18** A person should turn his head to the wall of the synagogue and pray with humility and reverence—because the walls of a synagogue are very holy and the light of the Divine Presence covers them always. For that reason it is a good custom to kiss the walls of the synagogue because of their holiness. (*Kav ha-Yashar*, chap. 50, end)

It is for this reason we kiss the Western Wall in Jerusalem.

> **6:19:1** Make it a point not to engage in any secular, worldly conversation in a synagogue or *Beit Midrash*. (Rabbi Moshe Teitelabum, *Hanhagot Tzaddikim*, p. 48, #8)

> **6:19:2** You should not engage in any idle conversation from the time you enter the synagogue until you leave. . . . So we should be careful not to engage in any idle talk whatsoever in the synagogue, but only the words of prayer should be in our mouth. And when a person does engage in idle conversation he is like someone who while speaking with the king turns his face away and says, "My lord king, I don't want to speak with you now for I have some private matter to take care of." And by doing this it is as if he is shoving aside the feet of the Divine Presence,[8] God forbid. (Rabbi Mordechai of Tchernobil, *Likkutei Torah*, quoted in *DhTvhY*, Hilchot Beit ha-Knesset, #1 and 2, p. 26b)

6:19:3 Worldly conversation interrupts the continuity of the service and detracts from its holiness. In essence, from one point of view, what we are offering to God with our prayers is our speech, our words; when we use them for another purpose then, this aspect of their being set aside and sanctified is weakened and devalued.

> **6:19:4** And so, my dear children, be very, very careful not to engage in idle conversation in the synagogue . . . and the counsel to follow here is that before you walk to the synagogue spend a little time reflecting on this, accept on yourself this practice, and set for yourself some penalty if you fail to uphold it. Also fix your place in the synagogue among those who are known to you as fearing God and wholehearted [and away from those who like to talk during Services]. (*Nahalat Avot*, p. 14a)

6:20 A very effective practice during the synagogue service is to repeat a holy sentence. (See "Repetition of a Holy Sentence" [21].) Repeat a verse from Psalms or call out to God, "Master of the World!" or "My Father in Heaven!"* over and over during any and all breaks in the Service, or even when you are turning pages in the Siddur ("Prayer" 5:2:4). You can do this silently and moving your lips slightly, closing your eyes from time to time. This practice prevents your attention from being diverted and helps to make your God-consciousness continuous throughout the service, increasing its intensity greatly. There is probably no more effective aid to devotional intensity than this.

A Polish hasid once told a parable to explain why the hasidim from Poland, though they prayed with fervor, prayed quickly:

> It is like the case of a man who built a fence around his garden to prevent the pigs from getting in. If he makes the fence of boards set one after the other, without any space between them, he will accomplish his purpose. But if he leaves open spaces between the boards, the fence is no help, for the pigs will slip in through the holes. (*Sippurei Hasidim*, vol. 1, p. 454, #465)

Rather than praying quickly to keep out foreign thoughts, one can accomplish this end by filling in any "spaces between the boards" by a repeated holy sentence or phrase or name of God.

6:21 The *tzitzit* could be used for the same purpose as the repeated sentence):

> Always keep looking at your *tzitzit*. (*Hanhagot Adam* [Y. L. Lipshitz], p. 10)
>
> Always be looking at your *tzitzit*; and it is even better when you kiss them continually. (*Derech Hayim*, 5–42)

Have in mind, when you do this, the thought: "Let me remember You always, with love, and do Your will."

6:22 Every part of the service should be participated in fully, even those things that others treat lightly. By complete concentration throughout, without interruption, you build up intensity and go higher and higher. If you see members of the congregation acting with disrespect for the sanctity of the synagogue, conversing during the Torah reading, and so on, ignore them, knowing that they do not understand their own loss.

6:23 Also helpful during synagogue services to increase concentration and *d'vekut* is to avoid looking at people (with the exception of a holy person if one is present; it is good to look at him from time to time). Look in the Siddur, look at the Ark, look out the windows at the sky, look up "through" the ceiling to God, look at the floor, the walls, or close your eyes. Most of these things have a special manifestation of holiness. But, as said, you can even look at the floor—for in everything you see there is Godliness, for there is no reality at all other than God.

> The holy *tzaddik*, Rabbi Mendel of Ber, a disciple of the Besht, said that the reason he always kept his eyes lowered when praying was to find a very low place, because God's Presence is there also, for there is no place where He is not. (*Mavo ha-Shaarim*, chap. 7, p. 38b; see also "Sight," 25:11.)

> Make it a practice not to look beyond your immediate personal space, your four *amot* [cubits], at the least as you are walking to the synagogue and when you leave it, and certainly when you are in the synagogue—except when there is a pressing need.—Pray out of the Siddur [that is, with your eyes fastened on the book], standing by the wall, with full concentration. (Rabbi Yehiel Michal of Zlotchov, *Hanhagot Tzaddikim*, p. 54, #5 and p. 55, #24)

When praying in a synagogue there is always the possibility of being distracted through an unhelpful awareness of other people—such that while we are praying we are self-conscious and thinking how we look in their eyes. It is usually best to ignore others during prayer and to avoid their glance.

> A tried and tested method of avoiding self-conscious posing [*p'niot*] during prayer and at other times is to control your glance at all times; especially during the time of prayer, you should face the wall and close your eyes so that you do not see the other people present. In this way you will cease to think of them and you will not be adversely affected by an awareness of them. (*Derech Tzaddikim*, p. 17, note 2)

The author of *Erech Apayim* writes there, in his own list of personal *hanhagot*:

> During prayer I will be as careful as possible not to look at another person, from the beginning of the service to the end, and not to look at or listen to anything else that will distract me and prevent concentration. (3:18, p. 76, Vayosaif Avraham, #22)

Another way to control our glance and lessen our awareness of others is to pray with the *tallit* over our head (which limits vision to what is before us, the Siddur, etc.). A recent newspaper article about a *shtibel*[10] in Brooklyn tells how it is a custom there that all the men pray the Morning Service with their *tallises* over their heads. The rabbi said (quoting a commentary of the *Shulchan Aruch*) that "covering the head with the *tallit* humbles a person's heart and brings him to the fear of heaven."

Why do we wrap ourselves with a *tallit*? "Because that covering humbles the heart of a man and brings him to the fear of heaven." "You should cover your head so that you will pray with fear of God." (*Taamei ha-Minhagim*, p. 6, #11, quoting two commentators)

6:24 Rabbi Tzvi Elimelech of Dinov:

We have a tradition from our rabbis that the practice which works effectively against being distracted by self-consciousness and the tendency to pose [*p'niot*] during prayers and Torah study, is to make a declaration, even just to yourself, each time you remember to do so, that you nullify any and all thoughts of making yourself look good before others [*p'niot*] and any false worship, and that your innermost desire and will and intention is truly to serve God sincerely. (*Derech Pikudecha* quoted in *Derech Tzaddikim*, p. 17, note 2; see also "Individual Practices," 39:12.)

These are the words from that declaration in *Derech Pikudecha*:

Master of the World! It is known and revealed before You that my will is to do *Your* will. But it is possible that in the middle of the prayer my *yetzer ha-ra* will distract me and some other thought will fall into my mind, to serve You in prayer with some ulterior self-motive. So I declare now that whatever that thought or musing or desire is, I hereby nullify it completely, because in truth it's locked in my bones and fixed in my mind to serve You perfectly, for the sake of God alone.* (See also "Prayer, 5:1:23.)

6:25:1 During the time of prayer your mind should be so fastened on God in such great God-consciousness that it seems as if there is no one else present in the room and that you are alone with God. (*Hovot ha-Levavot*, quoted in *Ohel Elimelech*, p. 20, #81)

6:25:2 When you stand in prayer let it seem to you as if you were standing alone before Him, blessed be He, without anyone else present. Then you will escape from self-consciousness and posing. (Rabbi Nachman Horodenker, *Milei d'Avot*, p. 85, #5)

6:25:3 When you stand in the service of prayer, picture in your mind that you are in a forest all by yourself and far away from any men—and then pray to God alone, without the slightest consciousness of other people around you. (Rabbi Kalonymus Kalmish of Peasetzna, *Hachsharat ha-Abrechim*, p. 66)

Perhaps the thought of Rabbi Simha Bunim of Pshischa will help for this:

> He used to say: "It seems to me that all the world is a forest, and all the men and the creatures in it are trees. And the Holy One, blessed be He, has none in His world but me; and I have none in my world but the Holy One, blessed be He, alone." (*Midor Dor*, vol. 2, #1329)

6:26 Of course, even keeping in mind all of the above there are times when it is good to relate to those around you in the synagogue, and everyone should use his own intelligence about this. For a spirit of love and unity with the other congregants is essential to prayer and should be cultivated. As noted earlier, before prayer you must accept on yourself the commandment of loving your neighbor. Level one of this is friendliness. One of the few exceptions to the rule of not talking in the synagogue or during the Services is that we are permitted to greet someone and give him the blessing of peace (*Tzavaat Rabbi Moshe Hasid mi-Prague*, #14, in *Tzavaot v'Derech Tovim*, p. 42).

6:27 It is important when you are in the synagogue and involved in the service not to allow shame before others to influence you or inhibit you from acting out of piety. You cannot experience the presence of God when you are ashamed of what people will think.

> When a person has *d'vekut* he is not ashamed in front of those who would make fun of him; but if he falls from his rung [on the ladder of holiness] and loses his *d'vekut* he becomes ashamed; this then is a sure sign to know about your *d'vekut*. (*Darkei Tzedek*, p. 14, #62)

If you are praying with religious fervor, if you sing with a full voice, chant the prayers with vigor, clap your hands, perhaps some people will say, "Look at him, who does he think he is? Is he crazy?" Forget them and forget all such considerations. Picture yourself alone before the Holy One, blessed be He.

And as the rabbis said: It is better to be called a fool your whole life than to be out of God's favor for one moment. In the famous story in 2 Samuel 6:14–22, King David danced uninhibitedly in joy before the Ark of the Lord as it was led in procession to Jerusalem. When his highborn wife, Michal, Saul's daughter, despised him for it and ridiculed him, he answered that to give honor to God he would hold himself even lower than what he had already done. Certainly one is not to be wild, and some attention to decorum is necessary, but today all the weight is on the side of inhibition—and that is poison for true worship.

> It is a principle in the service of prayer not to be ashamed in front of those who would make fun of you, God forbid. For you should know, my dear children, and consider, how all the worlds and the angels wait for each word that you speak to the Creator with love and yearning. So why should you care about some fool or idiot who does not know his right hand from his left?
>
> Nevertheless, when you are among people who are not familiar with real praying, do all you can to keep yourself within limits, so as not to give them an opportunity to mock. And certainly you shouldn't make strange and crazy movements in prayer, for everyone of our group knows well that I do not approve of this, and it is not our way. Just exert yourself with all your effort, with self-sacrifice, with all your limbs and with the full effort of your mind . . . and what you cannot control, do not pay any attention to what the whole rest of the world thinks, God forbid, and do not keep back at all from giving pleasure to your Creator.
>
> And this is what I have seen in the holy writings of one from the King's Palace, one of the disciples of the Besht, may his merit protect us and all Israel. (Rabbi Arele Roth, *Shomer Emunim*, Maamar Pitchu Shaarim, p. 291a)

Rabbi Elimelech of Lizensk wrote in his *Tzetl Katan* about the value for shy people of acquiring the ability for the holy kind of *chutzpah*:

> If you are naturally shy, that is, the bad kind of shyness (not the religious kind), force yourself for forty consecutive days to pray in a loud voice, with vigorous movement of your whole body, to fulfill "All my bones shall say [O Lord, who is like unto You!"] . . . until help comes to you from heaven and they remove the bad shyness from you. . . . For in everything, habit is king . . . [and] you will receive help from heaven. (*Tzetl Katan*, #16)

(See "Individual Practices," 39:7 for the full quote and for more about the method of breaking your nature by going to the opposite extreme.)

6:28 The synagogue service can be very beautiful and spiritually uplifting; but, to our sorrow, there are synagogues that mitigate against this, where piety is so foreign that it is not even understood and is disapproved of. One way to counteract this is that when you go to the synagogue, have it clear in your own mind that your purpose in going is not for your own enjoyment, but to *serve* God (see 6:5:3). The way to do this is to participate actively in all aspects of the synagogue service with the intention of giving pleasure to your Father in Heaven.

Another helpful thought is to realize that by your own sincere devotion you can add something to the service, and lift the level of worship.

One aspect of this is that when you join with the other members of the congregation in love (see 6:17:5) you can help them by praying that they be lifted up. At the same time, help yourself by joining with those who are on a higher level than your own and also with all the great *tzaddikim* of the generation, who can lift you up and support you. From the Vorker Rebbe:

> Before prayer everyone should bind himself to his brothers who are on a lower level than he, and pray for mercy for them; and also join himself to a Torah sage and *tzaddik* who is greater than he, so that his prayer will be included in the prayer of the *tzaddik* which will lift it up. . . . And for this reason every Jew is obligated before prayer to receive on himself the positive *mitzvah* "You shall love your neighbor as yourself." (*Ohel Yitzhak*, p. 20, #46)

But even with a congregation that might work to depress rather than inspire you, you can still benefit greatly from the service if you yourself are wrapped in your own devotions as described above. For in a sense you can isolate yourself through your own devotion from negative influences and yet still be open to the good and positive things that will always be present.

However, ultimately there is an out, if necessary:

> Pray with a congregation if your mind is at ease with them; but if not, pray alone. (*Or ha-Ner*, #12)
>
> If the congregation prays quickly so that you cannot stay together with them, then go ahead of them [by starting before they do] in the order of the prayers, so that you will not have to cut things out. Do the same for the *Shemoneh Esreh* and begin before they do. . . . Then you will be able to finish together with them and you will be able to hear the repetition of the prayer leader and respond. (*Or ha-Ner*, #13)

The radical hasidic attitude of Rabbi Menahem Mendel of Kotzk is expressed by his biographer in these words:

> "Certainly . . . the best way to fulfill the *mitzvah* of prayer is with a congregation . . . but if prayer in seclusion allows you to deepen your *kavvanah*, the innermost rooms are preferable to congregational prayer. And if by shortening your prayers you have greater concentration and *kavvanah*, it is preferable to shorten them, for a little with *kavvanah* is better than much without." (*Sneh Boar b'Kotzk*, p. 63)

6:29 There is a greater manifestation of God's presence in the synagogue because having been designated as a synagogue, the place itself is holy. God's presence is also specially revealed there because there are (usually) present in a synagogue one or more Torahs, and within its walls many prayers have been offered to God. Not only is the place holy, but it is there that you can pray with a *minyan*; and there is a greater manifestation of God's presence in a gathering of ten or more.

> [Pray] in a congregation whenever possible, because . . . all prayers said with a *minyan* of ten, where the *Shechinah* is present, accomplish things as if they were said by great *tzaddikim*. (Rabbi Aaron of Karlin, *Hanhagot Tzaddikim*, p. 19, #5)

When we pray alone there are various obstacles and distractions that are not present in the synagogue and in group prayer. The presence of others gives us a certain protection and support.

In the language of the Kabbalah:

> In group prayer there is no fear of the external forces [*hitzonim*]. (The Holy Jew, *Tiferet ha-Yehudi*, p. 34, #67)

Praying in a synagogue with a *minyan* is like swimming with the current. You are carried along by the water; and when you also make your own effort by swimming, you go even faster.

The book *Avodah u'Moreh Derech* notes another aspect of this, that it is good to pray with others because:

> In heaven they are strict in judging someone who prays alone [but not when he prays with others]. (p. 46)

The thought (translated) is that when you pray alone, your own sins and faults are very much present as the background of your prayer, and work to disqualify it (if only in your own unconscious, affecting the sincerity you can muster in praying, and your belief in the value of your prayers). But when you are together with others, your own failings are covered up by the stronger presence and spiritual strength of the group.

6:30 The congregational responses in the synagogue have as two of their purposes to keep up the continuity of congregational participation, and also to keep the prayers of the individuals basically coordinated. You are regularly and periodically kept in touch with the congregation. Learn what to say and when (this is all fairly simple) and participate fully.

Traditionally, great stress is put on saying "Amens" and "*Y'hai Sh'mai Rabba*s" (in the *Kaddish*) loudly and with vigor, with all your energy.

> **6:30:1** Be sure to say "Amen" with all your concentration and energy, and so, too, with every congregational response. (Rabbi Nahum of Tchernobil, *Hanhagot Tzaddikim*, p. 36, #17)

6:30:2 Among the various things that effect the atonement of sins, Rabbi Moshe Teitelbaum lists, first:

> To answer "Amen, *Y'hai shmai rabba*" [May His great Name . . .] with all your energy, until all your limbs are astir; and in a loud, strong voice answer "Amen" after every blessing that you hear. (*Hanhagot Tzaddikim*, p. 47, #4)

> **6:30:3** In the city of Plunsk, the old men tell stories of the tremendous holy service of prayer they saw from the Tzanzer Rebbe when he was there . . . and how when he said, "Amen, May His great Name . . . ," his voice was a roar and like a thunderclap in a storm, with awesome holiness. (*Mekor Hayim*, p. 142, #487)

6:30:4 Each time the congregation together says, "*Y'hai shmai rabba* . . ." think of how our Father in Heaven is getting great pleasure by seeing His children in His house. (See p. 186.)

6:31 We mentioned previously about bowing toward the Ark when entering the synagogue. The Ark, the special residence of holiness, should also be the focus of your concentration during the service. You should think of the *Shechinah* as present there, and particularly when it is opened you can send prayers (those of the Siddur or your own) in that direction.

6:32 When the Torah is taken out of the Ark and carried in procession around the synagogue, it is a sign of devotion, and a practice that cultivates devotion, to kiss it. Do not let this be just a rote act, but direct all the love of your heart to God's Torah, which is your life and the life of the world. When you kiss the Torah, say in quiet prayer, "God, please help me to fulfill all that is written here," or any other appropriate prayer.

> When you kiss the . . . *sefer* Torah say, "Let Him kiss me with the kisses of His mouth [for Thy love is better than wine]" (Song of Songs 1:2), and have as your intention that just as you kiss . . . [the *sefer* Torah], so does the Light of the Infinite One and the Supernal Will that is clothed within this *mitzvah* [the Torah] kiss you—the attachment [*d'vekut*] of spirit to spirit. (*Or ha-Ganuz l'Tzaddikim*, p. 59)

It is also a mark of devotion that when the Torah is in procession, you do not wait until it reaches you, but rush to it when it comes near.

6:33 During the Torah reading your full attention should be concentrated on what you hear. The *Zohar*:

> When the *sefer* Torah is removed from the Ark and placed on the *bimah* everyone should take on himself awe and fear of God with trembling and quaking, and should think that he is now standing at Mount Sinai to receive the Torah. He should bend his ears to hear and listen closely, and no one has permission to open his mouth in conversation. (Vayakel, p. 206a, quoted in *Derech Moshe*, p. 40a)

The scene at Sinai could be used for a visualization at this time.

> You should listen to each and every word with fear and awe, and picture yourself standing on Mount Sinai and hearing it from the Holy One, blessed be He. . . . And you will find amazing things said about this in the *Zohar*, Vayakel. (*Imrei Kodesh*, #15, p. 28)

There is a story of how a simple Jew, a wagon driver, was in the synagogue, standing as he listened with the congregation to the reading of the holy Torah, and tears were streaming down his cheeks. Afterwards, an insensitive Torah scholar came over to him and said, "Why were you crying so? Not only don't you understand a word of the Hebrew, but you're illiterate altogether." The man answered, "That's true. But all the time that the Torah reader was chanting the holy words I saw before me all of Mount Sinai on fire and heard the sound of a *shofar* louder and louder. And I realized that the Holy One Himself, blessed be He, had come down to us to give the Torah to His children."

During the Torah reading keep yourself open to hear something that will speak particularly to you and be relevant to you and your life and service of God. And what you do hear, remember, and meditate on it after the service.

6:34 When you listen to the sermon you are not to sit passively. The pious attitude is first of all to pray to God before and during the sermon that He send down light to the rabbi and open his mouth for holy words. Pray also that He open your heart and the hearts of others present to receive those words. Regardless of the level of the teacher, you are to see him as an agent of the Holy One, blessed be He, and God will send you teaching through him if you listen with an open heart and mind. (See also "Torah," 15:38.)

6:35 After the service do not rush out, but sit quietly for a while and compose yourself, preparing yourself for the transition you have to make as you leave the synagogue. (See "Prayer," 5:5 about what spiritual practices and meditations are good for this time.)

> **6:36:1** When you get up from your seat in the synagogue to leave, as you go keep your face toward the holy Ark. (*Derech Hayim*, 6–73)
>
> **6:36:2** Upon leaving the synagogue it is proper to take care not to exit with one's back turned toward the Ark in which the Torah scroll is contained. Rather, one should face the Ark while leaving. The same holds true when one steps down from before the Ark [as after having been called up for an *aliyah*]. (*Reshit Hochmah*, Sh'ar ha-Yirah, chap. 15, #43)
>
> **6:37** When you exit the synagogue, do so calmly and bowing [toward the synagogue] as you leave, and say (Psalm 5:9), "Lead me, O Lord, in Thy righteousness, protecting me from those who would hinder me;[11] make Thy way straight before me." [This verse of the Psalm follows the one you say before you enter the synagogue: "And as for me, in the abundance of Thy loving-kindness etc." (Psalm 5:8)]. (*Sefer ha-Yirah* of Rabbeinu Yonah, p. 192)

6:38 Earlier (6:11:3) we quoted the parable, in the name of Rabbi Yerahmiel Moshe of Koznitz, about the door of the synagogue being like the border between two countries, and how when you entered you had to examine your thoughts. The same parable is found in the name of a disciple of the Besht, Rabbi Lippa of Hemelmik, and he uses it not only for entering but for leaving the synagogue, when, he says:

> As you leave the synagogue to go to work [on weekdays], you should, at the door as you exit, examine what thoughts you are taking with you to work. (*Mishnat Hasidim*, p. 410)

Remember how Rabbi Yehiel Michal of Zlotchov said that when leaving the synagogue we should hold on to our spiritual concentration and direction, achieved during prayer, by keeping our glance contained (see 6:23).

7

Work

7:1 Before you leave the *Beit Midrash* after Morning Prayers and Torah study, if you are going to work, pray that God sees that you will be able to earn your livelihood. (Seder ha-Yom of Rabbi Shalom Shachna of Probitch, in *D'vir Yaakov*, p. 7)

7:2 The next teaching is somewhat confusing because of its redundancy and lack of organization, but it offers good suggestions for stated intentions and prayers to say before and after work. The connection is made particularly with business and commerce, but that, of course, can be adapted.

If you are about to go to some business, say, "I trust in God"; and if you profit, say, "[I did this] with the help of God" . . . and when you go to some business, say, "I am going to do this with God's permission." And say, "Master of the World! In Your holy scriptures it is written, 'Kindness will surround him who trusts in God' [Psalm 32:10], and it is written, 'You enliven them all' [Nehemiah 9:6]—so bestow Your kindness on me, and send a blessing in the work of my hands so that I will be able to earn a living." And say, "I am doing this for the sake of the unification of the Holy One, blessed be He, and His *Shechinah*" . . . and you should learn Torah before you go out to engage in business, and say, "I am going to engage in business with honesty and with faithfulness to God and His Torah, for the sake of the unification of the Holy One, blessed be He, and His *Shechinah.* And I trust in God that He will prosper my way and give me my livelihood, and I will profit from this business." And when you do succeed, remember God and give Him thanks. Also, say before you go to engage in business, "O Lord, God of truth, bestow Your blessing on me and give me success in all the work of my hands. And I trust in You, that through this work of mine You will send me a blessing, and the verse will be fulfilled in me that says, 'Cast on God your burden, and He will care for you and support you.'" [Psalm 53:23] And if, God forbid, you had an adverse outcome, say, "This was from God,"* and consider your actions to see if perhaps this happened to you because of your transgressions. Nevertheless, give *tzedaka* [in other words, do not decrease your charity because of a loss]. (*Hanhagot Adam*, Y. L. Lipshitz, p. 18)

Much of the material in this quote is found in *Kitzur Shnei Luchot ha-Brit* (Sh'ar ha-Otiyot—Emet v'Emunah, p. 19). There the text says: "I am going to do this with God's permission, *for the sake of His Name.*"* This addition makes the meaning somewhat clearer. Work is not a *mitzvah* per se but a matter of choice. Presumably, then, the point is that you have considered at some time the religious motive for work, and you are working so that you can live to serve God. Put another way, you are working for a religious purpose and for the sake of God. Consequently, you go with His permission, after having turned to Him with some of the suggested prayers, etc., as above. Also, that you are going with His permission suggests you are putting yourself and your success in His hands.

Based on the various suggestions in this quote, you can compose some appropriate words of stated intention and prayer to say when setting out for work or on the way; so, too, for when you are working and when you have finished.

7:3:1 Be careful regarding everything the Torah gives caution about . . . and conduct your business dealings in faithfulness to the Torah's teachings. (*Or ha-Ner*, #22)

7:3:2 Let your "yes" be true and let your "no" be true, and let all your business dealings be honest. Stay far away from theft and robbery, even from stealing one cent from a non-Jew. (Rabbi David ha-Levi of Steppin, in *Hanhagot Tzaddikim*, p. 56, #11 and #14)

> **7:4** Rabbi Israel of Salant was once sitting with his close followers and discussing with them the ways of life, and speaking words of *musar*. They began to consider the question of who is higher—someone who sits in the *Beit Midrash*, turning his nights into days and occupying himself full-time with Torah study and prayer and other Divine service, or someone who sits in his store and conducts his business dealings in faithfulness to the Torah's teachings? "It is known," said Rabbi Israel, "that there is nothing higher than doing business in faithfulness. But that being so, how sad when someone in business spends his time thinking he should have his attention on the kerosene or the salt or the salted fish [rather than the spiritual tasks involved]!" (*Midor Dor*, vol. 2, #1366)

> **7:5** Before you go to work, have a time of preparation to make yourself ready to be careful about all forbidden things and ready to fulfill God's warning, and not transgress, God forbid, such things as theft and robbery, fraud, lying, cheating, false weights and measures.
>
> After eating your midday meal, and before you go back to work, prepare yourself again as you did in the morning, going over in your mind the various things to avoid. And happy are you if you fulfill all this. (Rabbi Hayim Yosef David Azulai, *Avodat ha-Kodesh*, Moreh b'Etza 3-97 and 3-122)

In the morning you can vow that you will devote two or five minutes to such a preparation for work, perhaps doing this on your way there.

7:6 Our intention during work can be to serve God by adhering to everything in the Torah connected with work.

> Rabbi Yitzhak of Vorki, his memory for a blessing, told of how once he was together with his master, Rabbi David of Lelov at sunrise. The *rebbe* was enrobed in his *tallit* and crowned in *tefillin*, ready to pray the Morning Prayer, when a gentile came in, pounded on the table and asked that he sell him a quantity of liquor. [It seems that in the *rebbe*'s house—this was before he became famous—there was a store where liquor was sold.] There was no one else in the house then to sell it to him, so the *rebbe* himself went with alacrity, measured it out himself, and put it before the man. [When asked about this by Rabbi Yitzhak, who was amazed at how the *rebbe* would leave off his preparation for prayer to do some business], the *rebbe* explained to him softly, "Listen to me, my sweet friend. My path in the service of God is 'Know Him in all your ways'. . . So when I went to measure out the liquor, my whole

intention was to fulfill the Torah's *mitzvah* about honest measures and to give pleasure to God by this; and that is why I happily ran to do it with such haste." (*Kodesh Hillulim*, pp. 150–151)

"Know Him in all your ways" is the Torah phrase which represents the hasidic ideal to serve God in all areas of life and activities—in eating, sleeping, work, etc.—as well as in religious pursuits such as prayer. So to the *rebbe* it was all one, serving God in prayer or serving Him in faithful and honest business dealings.

7:7 The holy *rebbe*, Rabbi David of Lelov, had meditated on work and the true *kavvanah* in work. He taught that if your work involves serving others and supplying their needs, you should have as your intention while working to show love to your fellow man. Here is another story reported by his great disciple, Rabbi Yitzhak of Vorki, where again he teaches about work:

> Rabbi Yitzhak of Vorki was once traveling with the holy rabbi, Reb David'l of Lelov, the memory of a *tzaddik* for a blessing, and they came to the town of Elkish at night, at 1 A.M. The Rebbe Reb David did not want to wake anyone to ask for a place to sleep, for (as is famous) his love for all Jews was so great [he did not want to wake anyone for his own benefit]. "So," the Vorker said, "we went to Reb Berish's bakery [for he would be awake and at work]. When we arrived there we found him at work, by the oven, and Reb Berish [who was a devout hasid and a disciple of Rabbi David] was embarrassed at being found this way [in the midst of such lowly manual labor]. But the holy Lelover said to him, 'Oh, if only God would let me earn my living by the work of my hands! For the truth is that every man of Israel in his innermost heart, which even he himself doesn't know, wants to do good to his fellow man. So everyone who works—as a shoemaker or tailor or baker, or whatever, who serves others' needs for money—on the inside he doesn't do this work in order to make money, but in order to do good to his fellow man—even though he does receive money for his trouble; but this is just secondary and unimportant, because it is obvious that he has to accept money in order to live. But the inner meaning of his work is that he wants to do good and show kindness to his fellow man.' And," Rabbi Yitzhak of Vorki said, "from the words of Rebbe David'l we can understand that everyone who works to serve others is fulfilling the *mitzvah* of showing kindness, even if his intention is just to receive money in return for his work." (*GMvGhTz*, Helek 2, p. 14)

Although many who work at a job might not understand this inner desire of their heart, certainly anyone who strives to live in the light of God should have this as a conscious intention at work, and should express this intention with his lips during work—to serve his fellow man as an act of love and kindness.

The following story shows how Rabbi Yitzhak of Vorki learned the Lelover's lesson:

> Rabbi Yitzhak of Vorki was once at an inn, and seeing how the innkeeper took care of all the guests' needs, praised him, saying, "How wonderful are the deeds of this man in fulfilling the *mitzvah* of hospitality!" One of the *rebbe's* people asked him, "But isn't he just doing this for the money, to earn a living?" The *rebbe* answered him, "The money he takes is so that he can continue to fulfill the *mitzvah*, for if he wouldn't take the money how would he be able to go on doing the *mitzvah*?" (*Derech Tzaddikim*, p. 55)

Again, these stories teach us how we are to think about work, and during work we should occasionally express these thoughts with our lips: "God! Let my work be a service to my fellow men, who are Your children and made in Your image, and so let it be a service to You."

7:8 During work our attention should be focused on God as much as possible.

Religious storekeepers study holy books or recite psalms while they sit waiting for customers; one can also recite Torah or psalms from memory. What religious practice fits all depends on the nature of your work. About Rabbi Moshe Leib Gentzler, a disciple of Rabbi Moshe Teitelbaum:

> Rabbi Moshe Leib was known throughout the city for his piety. . . . He would sit in his store studying Torah. (*Ha-Gaon ha-Kadosh Baal Yismach Moshe*, p. 353)

A story telling how the father and father-in-law of Rabbi Yitzhak of Vorki, both merchants, met and arranged his marriage begins:

> At one of the fairs the booths of Rabbi Shimon of Zloshin [his father] and Rabbi Meir of Zhorik were adjacent. In free moments between sales Rabbi Shimon stood alone at his booth reciting psalms, and Rabbi Meir also stood by himself at his booth reciting psalms. [Not surprisingly, they became friends.] (*Sneh Boar b'Kotzk*, p. 247)

See the section "Know Him in All Your Ways" (in Chapter 3) that if you work with your hands, you can have your mind attached to God. You can use a repeated holy sentence as Hanoch did or a Torah meditation, etc. See also the quote in Chapter 2, pp. 36–37 from *Rachmei ha-Av*, which teaches frequent repetition of holy phrases and words. He says there, "You should accustom yourself to say continually 'Blessed is the One and Only One,'* and the verse 'I have placed the Lord before me always' [*Shivitti HaShem l'negdi tamid*]—or at least the word '*Shivitti*' [I have placed]."

This is told about Rabbi Yaakov Koppel the Hasid of Kolomaya, who was a disciple of the Besht:

> He was known among the gentiles of the town as the *Shivittinik*—because his holy way was that all the time, even during work (he had a small store), he would pass his hand over his eyes and say the verse "I have placed the Lord before me always." And they considered him a holy man. (*Even Shtiya*, p. 17, #1)

Another kind of meditation, during physical work, is to meditate on how it is God's will and power, His life-energy, that moves us. Working with this God-consciousness makes our work a form of worship. (See Chapter 3, p. 52.)

If your work is intellectual work and it is more difficult to meditate or think Torah thoughts, accustom yourself, as soon as you do have some free time, even seconds or minutes, to turn your mind to some holy practice.

The previous Lubavitcher *rebbe*, Rabbi Yosef Yitzchak Schneersohn said:

> Whether he is standing in his shop or in the marketplace, every businessman should have a book in his pocket—such as a *Chumash*, *Tanya*, *Mishnayos* or *Tehillim*—so that whenever he has a free moment he can read a verse of *Chumash*, or a few lines of *Tanya*, or a *mishnah*, or a passage of *Tehillim*. (*Likkutei Dibburim*, p. 158)

Rabbi Hayim Yosef David Azulai says that if a businessman

> is going over his account books, let him not remove the fear of God from on him; and it is good if he says between sections: "I have placed the Lord before me always," "Happy is the man who never forgets You [and happy is he who strengthens his faith in You" (*Rosh HaShanah Musaf*)]. (*Avodat ha-Kodesh*, Moreh b'Etzbah 1–38)

Another possibility is that as you do mental work you can have your hands attached to God, so to speak, by holding something that will remind you of Him, if only with part of your consciousness. For example, you might hold a *mezuzah* in your hand; or you can just have it on the table near you, as was the custom of Rabbi Shneur Zalman of Ladi (Chapter 2, p. 35).

7:9 During work you can have a continual conversation with God by praying for all your needs at work, both great and small, and thanking God for their fulfillment, or justifying His judgment for reversals or mishaps. (See Chapter 2, pp. 41.)

7:10 See the *midrash* quote in Chapter 2, p. 41 about how Joseph, when he came into his master Potiphar's presence, would whisper a prayer that it was only in God that he trusted. You also can do this at work when you come into the presence of your superior or employer. (Of course, if you are the superior, there are equally appropriate prayers to make to help you remember humility and to treat your subordinates with dignity, since they are created in God's image.) The *midrash* also mentions that Potiphar saw that God's name was always in Joseph's mouth, in other words, as in 7:8 and 7:9.

> **7:11** Let every one of our group, if he is occupied during the whole day with running after his livelihood, consider it an obligation to say a number of times during the day, in the middle of his exertions: "Master of the World! I am now in places dangerous to my soul and to my holiness; O Lord, do not abandon me! Support and watch over me, O Guardian of Israel!"* This does not have to be said in this exact language, but something like it, in whatever words you find fitting and comfortable. (The Peasetzna Rebbe, in *Hachsharat ha-Abrechim*, p. 62b)

> **7:12** Every man of Israel, when he is in the synagogue or the *Beit Midrash* and involved in Torah study or prayer, is closer to God. But a person also has to be involved with matters of this world, and sometimes he is distracted by them. He should try to exert himself so that he not be deceived then, God forbid, by the false advice of his evil inclination. And when God, blessed be He, helps him, so that even when he is occupied with the matters of this world he remembers God and has longing and yearning for Him, he should

> then pray to God that He always help him to be on that level, and that he should not fall from it. (Rabbi Yehoshuah of Belz, *Sefer ha-Hasidut mi-Torat Belz*, vol. 2, p. 322)

7:13 You can make a vow that during work, at more or less specific times, like during a break, you will have one or two periods of *heshbon ha-nefesh*, spiritual stock-taking—for just a few minutes—to see where you are. Reflect, then, on the time that is past, and prepare for what is ahead. You can also vow to say a psalm or two.

> I heard that a merchant who had gone to be with a certain *tzaddik* explained to him apologetically that he was so involved in his business that he did not have any time to compose himself [and think of religious things]. He was told that whenever he went to the basement to get some wine [to sell] he should stand there for a few minutes in meditation [on why he had come to this world, and how he was spending his time].[1] (*Likkutim Hadashim*, p. 4a)

7:14 *Minha* is very important because it breaks into the hectic work part of the day, and it is good to pray *Minha* at a time when it does interrupt your workday routine.

The Besht (although speaking about the simple man, not the one striving for perfection) taught:

> When someone is altogether preoccupied with his work he can run around the whole day in the markets and on the streets, such that he almost forgets there is a God who created the world; but when the time for *Minha* arrives he remembers that he should pray. Then, thinking of how the whole day has passed in these empty pursuits, he lets out a groan and sighs within his heart, and he runs to a little side street and prays *Minha*. And though he does not even know what he is saying, for he does not know Hebrew, this prayer is greatly valued and very precious to God, and his sigh splits the heavens. (*Zichron l'Rishonim*, p. 70)

7:15 If you have *d'vekut* during work, your prayers and other solely religious activities will be purer; but if you give worldly thinking free rein during the time of work, without spiritualizing it ("separating off the bad from the good"), then these thoughts will come to you as foreign thoughts intruding on your prayers and disturbing them—since you did not deal with them when you should have.

When someone engages in business and fulfills "Know Him in all your ways," and unites the Holy One, blessed be He, and His *Shechinah* during work . . . [by that] he is purifying the good part and removing the bad. Then, when he goes to pray, this earlier activity [during work] adds to his illumination and holiness during prayer.

But if, God forbid, during work he forgets that there is a Creator who directs the world, and he goes around in the World of Confusion, then it is impossible for him to remove the bad part. As a result, later, when he is praying, the bad part [all the bad and inappropriate thoughts that can be associated with work] come to him and confuse his praying, because the bad part is still clinging to him, not having been removed earlier. (*Tikkun ha-Nefesh,*[2] chap. 15, p. 31b)

8

Trust in God

8:1 The holy Rabbi Moshe of Kobrin said that you should always strengthen yourself in your faith, and have trust in God and not let your heart fall from the vagaries of time and events. Through this nothing evil will be able to overcome you. The main principle of trust in God is to believe with complete faith that everything happens with His Divine providence and therefore is certainly good. Whatever is not within the grasp of our understanding, there the goodness is just hidden, and is, without a doubt, good on an even deeper level. (*Or ha-Ner* #30)

8:2 Psalm 84:13 says, "Lord of hosts, happy is the man who trusts in You!" When Rabbi Mordechai of Neshkiz felt the need to strengthen his trust in God, he would repeat this verse over and over, so many times, until he became filled with trust in God, blessed be He. And the source of this practice of his is in the Jerusalem Talmud, *Berachot*, chap. 5, halacha 1, which says: "Let this verse never cease from your lips—Lord of hosts, happy is the man who trusts in You!" (*Admorei Neshkiz, Lechovitz, Kaidenov, Novominsk*, p. 34)

8:3:1 Rabbi Tzvi Elimelech of Dinov:

Pray every day for your livelihood . . . so that you will have faith that all your food and other needs come to you from Divine

> providence and not ultimately from the work you do. (*Hanhagot Adam*, #30)

8:3:2 Before going to work pray for your livelihood, and before your first meal of the day pray for your food. (See "Work," 7:1 and 7:2, "Eating," 10:10, and the quote from Rabbi Nachman of Bratzlav in Chapter 2, p. 42).

8:4 If you trust in God fully you will pray to Him about everything you need, big and small, and you will give thanks to Him for everything that happens to you. See the quote in Chapter 2, p. 41 from Rabbi Arele Roth; note particularly there the practice of Rabbi Alexander Ziskind who would give thanks to God for even the smallest things, as when a glass dropped and did not break. (See also "The Service of Praise" [34].)

8:5 You should see God's hand in the bad (as well as the good) that befalls you. Recognize the justice of the affliction, repent, and pray that it be an atonement for your sins. (See "Afflictions" [35] about this.)

> **8:6** Whenever you see and recognize the workings of God's providence in your life, stop and give praise and thanks to Him, blessed be He, who has bestowed on you, as a gift, this precious vision. (Rabbi Abraham of Slonim, *Torat Avot*, p. 154, in the writings of Rabbi Moshe Minder)

8:7 Let these phrases always be in your mouth:

This also is for good.

Everything that the Merciful One does, He does for good.

If this is good in His eyes, how much more so in mine.

Blessed is God (*Baruch HaShem*).

Praise God.

God-willing.

Such was God's will.

With God's help.

May this [affliction] be an atonement for me.

(See "Pious Phrases" [26] for more about these and others.)

8:8 When something bad happens and you lose things that you value, say, in the words of Job (1:21): "The Lord gave and the Lord has taken away; blessed be the Name of the Lord."

> **8:9** Be careful that whenever something good comes to you from people, you have the awareness it was God who put it in their hearts to do it, and they are just His messengers and agents. And though you should be grateful to them, yet because of your trust in God you should realize that it is from Him, and that they are just doing His will. (*Darkei Tzedek*, p. 10, #77)

8:10:1 Rabbi Tzvi Hirsh of Nadborna:

> When you have need of anything, great or small, as soon as it comes to mind that you need something from people, ask God that He put it in their hearts to help you; and then afterwards ask them. For everything is from His hand. (*Alpha Beta* of Rabbi Tzvi Hirsh, in Tzorech *YHvT*, p. 65)

8:10:2 Rabbi Tzvi Elimelech of Dinov:

> It is permitted to seek help from someone if you have the need in some matter, but you should, at the same time, put your trust in God to save you through this particular person, who serves, so to speak, to make it all look as if it is a natural thing in the regular course of events. (*Agra d'Pirka*, Sh'lach, in *DhTvhY*, p. 20, Bitachon #7)

> **8:10:3** Accustom yourself when you ask a favor from people that your intention should be that you are asking it from God (and the person is just His agent); for this was the level of the first *tzaddikim*, and this is a high level and involves much practice to attain it. (*DhTvhY*, p. 20, Bitachon, #8)

The point here is that when you ask the person for help, you should consider yourself as actually talking before and to God. (see "Speech," 23:2:2.)

8:11 We saw in Chapter 2, p. 41 a practice (ascribed by the Midrash to Joseph in his behavior before Potiphar) that when a man enters the presence of his superior or employer he can whisper a prayer saying that he trusts in God, not in flesh and blood.

> When he entered his master's presence to serve him [Joseph coming before Potiphar], he would whisper a prayer: "Master of the World! You are the one whom I put my trust in. You are the only one on whom I rely. Let me find grace and favor in the eyes of all who see me and in the eyes of my master Potiphar."

8:12 If worries and anxieties beset you, and if it looks as if something bad is about to happen to you or yours, stand firm in your trust in God, and say aloud: "I trust in God and am certain that this will not happen to me."

> Our Rabbis taught that Hillel the Elder was once on the road approaching the city when he heard a loud outcry. He said to his disciples and those with him, "I am certain that this is not coming from my house." About Hillel and such as he does the verse say, "He will not be afraid of threatening news, his heart is firm, trusting in the Lord" (Psalm 112:7). [*Berachot* 60a]

And if, may God spare us, something bad does befall you, then too, you are to be firm in your trust that everything God does is for good. (See "Afflictions" [35] for more about this.)

8:13 Another aspect of trust in God is the attribute of equanimity. If everything is from God and is surely for our good, what difference does it make whether we receive one thing or another? One way to develop this quality is by praying again and again that God give you what He knows is for your good.

This does not mean, however, that you do not also pray for what you perceive are your needs; you do pray—but at the end, add each time that He answer according to His wisdom. That way, whether your prayer for your need is fulfilled or not, your prayer that He answer according to what He knows is good for you is always fulfilled, and then you can more easily accept whatever might happen.

The Baal Shem Tov:

> Whatever happens it should be all the same to you—whether people praise you or condemn you, and for all other things—in food,

> whether you eat delicacies or not—it should all be equal in your eyes, since the *yetzer ha-ra* is removed from you completely.
>
> So for everything that happens to you say, "Is this not from Him, blessed be He? And if it is good in His eyes etc.* [it should certainly be so in mine]." And all your intention should be just for the sake of heaven—but for yourself it should not make any difference [whether you receive one thing or the other]. This is a very high spiritual level. (*Tzavaat ha-Ribash*, p. 2)

> It is an important principle to: "Commit your deeds to the Lord, and then your thoughts and plans will be established" [Proverbs 16:3]—that with everything that comes to you, you think that it is from Him, blessed be He.
>
> And you should see that you pray to God, blessed be He, that He always bring to you what He, blessed be He, knows is for your good, and not what seems so to men according to their understanding. For it is possible that what is good in your eyes is really bad for you. So cast everything, all your affairs and needs, on Him, blessed be He. (*Tzavaat ha-Ribash*, p. 2)

When you make this prayer often, as the Besht teaches, you will be prepared to say for everything that happens, "This also is for good" or, "Is this not from Him, blessed be He? And if it is good in His eyes etc."

In the circumstance of making a prayer for your needs, after your request you can add at the end: "And what is good in Your eyes, do" (והטוב בעיניך עשה).[1]

The Hafetz Hayim:

> When a person puts his prayer and request before God, he should not say, "Master of the World, give me this!" For a person cannot know [for certain] what is for his good. . . . He should pray: "Master of the World, if this is good for me, give it to me, but if it is not, do not." (*Michtivei Ha-Hafetz Hayim Ha-Hadash*, vol. 2, II, no. 5, p. 52)

9

Loving and Honoring Our Fellow Men

9:1 LOVE AND HONOR

The rabbis understood the command to love our fellow men as including both love and honor (*Avot d'Rabbi Natan*, chap. 26).

9:1:1 Be careful of the honor of all men and honor them as they should be, with the thought that you are thereby giving honor to God Himself, blessed be He, because they are the work of His hands and His creatures. (*Derech Hayim*, 7–7)

9:1:2 Honor every man, whether poor or rich, and let your thought be that you are honoring them because they are created in the image of God, and when you honor them you are honoring the Craftsman who made them. (*Derech Hayim*, 6–48)

9:2 FOR REMEMBRANCE

When you see a fellow man you should immediately call to mind the commandment "and you shall love your neighbor as yourself." (*Or ha-Ganuz l'Tzaddikim*, p. 43)

9:3 NOW

When you are with a fellow man, say to yourself, "I am going to fulfill the commandment of 'love your neighbor as yourself' with this very person now." For the Baal Shem Tov taught that love your neighbor meant that you are to love the person you are with at the moment. (Heard from a great rabbi and *tzaddik*.)

9:4 HONORING HIS IMAGE

When seeing any man we should remember that he is made in the image of God and should give him our love and honor. By doing so we remember God and offer our love and honor to Him.

The rabbis say: He who receives his fellow man is as if receiving the Divine Presence (*Yerushalmi Erubin* 5–1). So when you greet anyone or speak with him, bow the least bit (or, in imagination), and say to yourself: "My Father in Heaven, I bow before this Your image. Let me serve You through love and service to my fellow man."

We can show love and honor even to the wicked, though of course we are not to act toward them in a way contrary to Torah wisdom. Rabbi Natan Netta of Chelm said about Jacob's bowing before Esau (Genesis 33:3):

> It is known that Esau represents the Other Side [Evil]—but in truth, our father Jacob did not bow before Esau but before the holy power, the spark that was within him, and which is a part of God from Above. And by bowing before this holy spark in Esau, Jacob added holiness to it, and gave the holy spark power to overcome the evil in Esau.[1] (*Netta Sha'ashuim*, p. 25)

What Rabbi Natan Netta is calling the "holy spark" is the soul, which the rabbis say is actually a part of God from Above, and is equivalent to the "image of God" in Genesis.

When a good person acts humbly and shows love and honor for someone who has gone astray, he encourages that person to repent. So, we are told, Aaron the High Priest warmly greeted everyone, even the wicked and the sinful, until they would say:

> How can I continue in my sinning? For how will I be able to look in Aaron's face when he greets me on the street?" (*Avot d'Rabbi Natan*, chap. 12)

9:5 GREETINGS

Greet everyone warmly, and greet them first. Do not ignore others or pretend that you do not see them.

The rabbis teach:

> Receive everyone warmly and with joy. (*Avot* 1:15, 3:16)
>
> Always be first in greeting all men with the blessing of peace. (*Avot* 4:22)
>
> It was said of Rabbi Yohanan ben Zakkai that no one had ever greeted him with the blessing of peace before he had himself greeted the other first—not even a gentile in the marketplace. (*Berachot* 17)

The lesson of this last story is that you are to greet everyone, even someone you might be inclined to ignore; moreover, you are to do so even in the busiest place where you might be inclined to overlook people.[2]

Greeting is the first step and a symbolic one in our relation to others. And sometimes the first step can be the most important one.

Rabbi Arye Levin of Jerusalem, the *tzaddik* and lover of mankind (who passed away in 1969), wrote in his ethical will to his children, to teach them the way of God:

> I was very careful to receive everyone cheerfully, until this became second nature to me. I was careful, too, to take the initiative in greeting everyone. (*A Tzaddik in Our Time*, p. 464)

When he greeted someone, Reb Arye would take that person's hands in his own and hold them in a loving, caressing way that would be electric with holiness, sending God's energy directly into his heart. There are many other *tzaddikim* who have taught by their example too, how in a greeting, we should focus lovingly on the person we are with.

9:6 BROTHERLINESS IN SPEECH

> You should always try to join yourself to your fellow man and to show love for him in your speech. Although, of course, the essence of brotherly feeling is in the heart, nevertheless, see that this brotherliness is also revealed in your speech, such that you call him "My brother" when you speak to him. And when you do this,

> certainly such speech is on the level of actual deed. (Rabbi Menachem Mendel of Kossov, *Ahavat Shalom*, parshat Kedoshim, quoted in *DhTvhY*, II, p. 4, Ahavat Yisrael #10)
>
> About Rabbi David of Lelov:
>
> He called everyone "My brother."[3] (*Tiferet Banim Avotam*, p. 238)

This teaching and practice comes from the *midrash*, where we learn a lesson from the way that our father Jacob spoke to men of Haran, whom he came across at a well outside that city.

> And Jacob said to them, "My brothers, where are you from?" [Genesis 29:4]—From this source it was taught that a man should always be at one with others, and address them as "Brothers" and "Friends." And he should greet them first with the greeting of peace, so that angels of mercy from Above will so greet him. (*Midrash ha-Gadol* on Genesis 29:4)

Related to this teaching, it is well known that when you know someone's name, you honor him by using it.

9:7 BE KIND

> Fulfill the commandment "and you shall love your neighbor as yourself," and, as much as you can, do kindnesses with everyone. (*Derech Hayim*, 1–2)

Of course, doing good and helping even those who hate us is taught by the Torah in Exodus 23:5, "If you see the ass of him that hates you lying under its burden, and you might think not to help unload it—you shall surely unload it with him." For though someone hates us and is our enemy, he is still our brother (cf. Deuteronomy 22:4).

9:8 STATED INTENTIONS

Doing favors for others is one of the essentials of true religiosity. The holy rabbi, Reb Kalonymus Kalman of Peasetzna, who, in the Warsaw Ghetto was the *rebbe* of hundreds of children, many of them orphans, would always teach them this, saying: "Children, precious children, just remember—the greatest thing in the world is to do somebody else a favor." (Heard from a great rabbi and *tzaddik*.)

It is a good practice to say, before doing a favor or an act of kindness for people, "I am doing this to fulfill 'and you shall love your neighbor as yourself.'" That way you elevate what might be a normal good tendency of yours by seeing it in its inner meaning.

Rabbi Alexander Ziskind:

> If you have heard of some harm that may come to someone if he does not take some precaution, it is an important obligation of the commandment "and you shall love etc." to tell him, and to encourage him to be careful and protect himself. And before you go and do this, and speak to him, say [as a stated intention] with great joy: "I am prepared and ready to fulfill the commandment of the Torah 'and you shall love etc.'"
>
> And the positive *mitzvah* of returning a lost object is also rooted in this. For all these *mitzvot*—such as helping another to load and unload [a pack animal] and others like that are of one sort. . . .
>
> And also in the category of the positive *mitzvah* of loving your neighbor is if you see the clothing of your fellow man lying on the ground and you pick it up; and you should say aloud, "I am prepared and ready to fulfill the positive *mitzvot* of 'and you shall love your neighbor as yourself' and returning a lost object—as my Maker and Creator, blessed be He, commanded me." For certainly, if it was your own piece of clothing on the ground you would pick it up so it would not be damaged. (*Yesod v'Shoresh ha-Avodah*, Gate 1, chap. 8, p. 16)

So when you warn someone that his tire is flat, or his car door is open, or help him push his car, or tell him that he dropped a glove—turn your inner glance to God and say, "God, I am doing this to fulfill 'and you shall love your neighbor as yourself.'" When you put your (perhaps small) deed in its holy context, its true significance will be revealed. In this way you will get the beneficial influence of your own act, according to its enlarged meaning, your heart will open and you will be led to more good deeds; for, as the rabbis say, "According to the intentions of the heart are things judged."[4]

See "Work," 7:3:2 for the teaching of Rabbi David of Lelov, that everyone, in his innermost heart, wants to do loving service for his fellow men. And if we provide such service in the work we do for our livelihood, we should *intend* this inner meaning, and it will *have* that meaning, even though, of course, we receive payment for our efforts.

9:9 DOING WHAT OTHERS WANT

Of course, we show our love for our fellow men by doing them good, and the ways to do good and serve others cannot be numbered. But a practice that shows love and also humility, and has many other ramifications, is to do what others want, rather than what we want. We are to nullify our will, not only before God, but before the will of our fellow man. And, in truth, from this very high level one can often see the expressed will of his fellow man as being the will of God.[5]

> Love all men and honor them. And nullify your will before the will of your fellow men. (*Derech Eretz Zutta*, chap. 1)
>
> [As it is said,] Doing a man's will is the way we show him honor. (*Beit Shlomo*, p. 56)
>
> About Rabbi Judah the Prince:
>
> Our Rabbi was very humble. And he used to say, "Anything that anyone tells me to do, I do." (*Genesis Rabba* 33–3)
>
> Rabbi Tzvi Hirsh of Nadborna:
>
> Make your will cleave to the will of the Creator, blessed be He, and have no preference other than what God, blessed be He, decrees for you. Be satisfied with that—since you were not created other than to do His will, blessed be He. And let there be no difference for you whether your will is done or not done—for in either case it is God's will that is accomplished. And as part of this, accustom yourself to always fulfill the will of your fellow men. (*Alpha Beta* of Rabbi Tzvi Hirsh, Ratzon, in *YHvT*, p. 65)

9:10 DO NOT JUDGE

The rabbis have always taught that one of the main ways we show our love for others is by not judging them harshly.

Rabbi Alexander Ziskind:

> But it is clear and simple that a person can never fulfill the positive commandment of "and you shall love your neighbor as yourself" truly and perfectly and consistently if he is not on the level where he truly and perfectly and consistently fulfills the positive commandment of "Justly shall you judge your neighbor." [This verse was used to teach that we are to judge others favorably, and even when it appears otherwise, to see them as being "just"], for they are dependent and united with each other.
>
> [Rabbi Ziskind continues, explaining how if you have a bad view of someone] you certainly will not make an effort to the limit of your abilities to do him a favor when he has some need—and then you will transgress [not only the commandment to judge others favorably, but] also the positive commandment "and you shall love etc." (*Yesod v'Shoresh ha-Avodah*, Gate 1, chap. 8)

How can we learn to judge others favorably? The Besht taught that when you see someone else do something wrong (or hear about it), realize that God brought this before you because you have done something similar, and so *you* will repent. Do not judge him, judge yourself. Since you have done something of the same sort, you will not be arrogant in judging him, but will be busy correcting your own faults, not his. (See "Repentance," 14:7, for this quote.)

> **9:11** Whenever I came across anyone whom I had an inclination to dislike, I would utter many blessings for his welfare, so as to turn my heart to love him and to desire his good. (Rabbi Yoel Frumkin, *Imrei Kodesh*, #9, p. 23)

9:12 RETURNING GOOD FOR EVIL; TAKING NO REVENGE AND BEARING NO GRUDGE

Most people are familiar with the Golden Rule, which according to the tradition is the rule of thumb for the practical application of the commandment of loving your neighbor as yourself. The idea is that your neighbor is "as yourself," so if you want to know how to act toward him, consider how you would feel in the situation he is in, and how you would want to be treated.

Fewer people, however, are familiar with the rabbis' equally important rule about the application of the commandment not to take revenge or bear a grudge. As a matter of fact, though, the commandments not to take vengeance or bear a grudge, and to love, are in the very same verse (Leviticus 19:18) and they are intimately related. The verse reads: "Thou shalt not take vengeance, nor bear any grudge against the children of thy people, but thou shalt love thy neighbor as thyself; I am the Lord."

Here is the rule:

> The rabbis said: What is considered "revenge" and what is "bearing a grudge?"
>
> If you say to your neighbor, "Lend me your scythe," and he refuses, and the next day he comes to you and says, "Lend me your spade," if you answer, "I won't lend it to you, just like you wouldn't lend your tool to me"—that's revenge. Therefore the Torah says, "You shall not take revenge."
>
> And what is considered bearing a grudge? If you say to your neighbor, "Lend me your scythe" and he won't lend it to you, and the next day he comes and says, "Lend me your spade," if you answer, "Here, take it. I'm not like you, who wouldn't lend your tool to me"—that's bearing a grudge. And therefore the Torah says, "You shall not bear a grudge." (*Yalkut Shimoni* on Leviticus 19:18)

What this means is that you should return good for evil. When someone treats you badly, you should not only be ready to do him good, but you should not even remind him of what he did. You should neither take revenge nor bear a grudge, but love your neighbor as yourself.

Certainly this rule explaining how not to take revenge or bear a grudge has many real and important applications in daily life.

The great teacher of *musar*, Rabbi Israel Salanter, had a practice of returning good for evil, but he went beyond doing so just when the other person approached him; he went and sought him out.

> It is known that one of the foundations of the way of humility is to negate any anger and irritation at others, and to forego one's "rights." . . . And our master and teacher and rabbi, the memory of a holy *tzaddik* for a blessing, in his great humility, also excelled in this matter of negating any irritation at others and "passing over his measures." For we know about a number of incidents where people abused him—and the extraordinary way he dealt with them. But not only did he negate any anger against others and not stand on his honor, but his holy way reached even higher, for if someone sinned against him, and did him some evil or caused him trouble, he would immediately make an effort to find some way to do some good or a favor for that person, and to do him some act of kindness—to repay

> him with good in return for evil. He would say that this was a positive commandment of the Torah, part of the *mitzvah* to cleave to God's own ways. . . . And when we reflect on God's ways we will see that in the very moment when a person sins against God, He does good to him, and bestows on him the gift of life—for without the continuous Divine flow, which gives reality to all things, it is impossible to remain in existence for a single moment. So too should a man act with someone who bothers and troubles him. Our master and teacher and rabbi acted this way in practice. So should all those who are upright learn from his way. (*Or Yisrael*, p. 115)

One of the incidents mentioned in this quote is found in a beautiful story in *Midor Dor* (vol. 1, #782). After being treated contemptuously by an obnoxious young Torah scholar in a train carriage traveling to Vilna, Rabbi Israel of Salant not only forgave him when the young man found out who he had insulted and apologized, but did everything to help him achieve the purpose of his journey to Vilna: to become a *shochet* (ritual slaughterer). Rabbi Israel not only helped him to get his education (he was deficient) so he could be certified, but actually got him a good job. When asked by the young man why he had troubled himself so much to do such favors for him, he answered:

> When you first came to me and apologized I said that I forgave you completely and had no resentment at all against you. And I sincerely meant what I said. But a person cannot completely control his emotions, and I was concerned that maybe I did have a trace of bad feeling in me. And it is an important principle that "Deed erases thought." So I decided to do you a favor, to remove any possible trace of resentment from my heart and so that I would truly be your friend. For it is human nature that when you do a kindness for someone you come to love him and feel yourself his friend.

A somewhat similar story is told about Rabbi Yissachar Dov, the *rebbe* of Belz. A rabbi who had opposed and insulted the ways of the Belzer hasidim and their *rebbe* visited him and (after some discussion clarifying matters in contention) apologized. The *rebbe* forgave him, but when some fruit that the *rebbe* had asked for was brought in, he himself peeled and cut it and offered it to his erstwhile critic. When the latter asked him why he had made a point of going out of his way to serve him, the *rebbe* also referred to the Talmudic teaching that "Deed erases thought," and explained that only after this deed was his foregiveness complete (*Admorei Belz*, I, p. 306).

9:13 PRAYER AS AN EXPRESSION OF LOVE

9:13:1 When you are outside, on the street, pray for people you see who are in need, or could use a prayer and blessing to succeed.

9:13:2 When you come to know of someone sick, pray for him or her in your prayer [in the blessing for the sick of the *Shemoneh Esreh*], even if you are not asked to do so. By this you fulfill the positive commandment of "you shall love your neighbor as yourself." (*Peninei Yam* #7, *YHvT*, p. 97)

9:13:3 Always remember to pray for others, especially your loved ones. Consider what they need (in things beyond the scope of your help and aid), and pray for them in the *Shemoneh Esreh* as well as at other times.

9:13:4 When out of nowhere you suddenly feel tenderness for your father or mother or other relatives who are far away from you, this is sometimes a sign that you are being aroused [from heaven] so you should pray for them, for they, at that moment, have some need for God's mercy and for prayer. So you should pray for their welfare and give *tzedaka* for them [on their behalf] according to your ability—since you had no thought of them and suddenly it came to your mind. (*Darkei Tzedek*, p. 19)

9:14 INCREASING LOVE

Love of your fellow man can be cultivated. One way to do this is to pray that God open your heart to others. When you do feel love and compassion, and merit to do an act of compassion, turn to God and thank Him, and pray for the future, telling Him that this is what you so much desire.

If your heart is hard as iron when it comes to the poor, arise and call out to the Lord your God. Pray that the King of Mercy give you a soft heart, a Jewish heart that hears the cry of the lowly and yearns to do kindness to the poor. (*Yesod Yosef*, p. 59)

9:15 THINKING ABOUT LOVE OF OTHERS

For meditations on love of neighbor and doing good to others, upon awakening, before sleep, and in the bathroom, see "Waking and Beginning the Day," 4:46, "Sleep and Before Sleep," 29:1:18:2, and "Bathroom," 27:4:8.

10

Eating and the Holy Meal

Religious people always know that religious practices are to be performed in holiness, and sanctified. But the addition of the hasidic way is to sanctify all aspects of life. Since eating is a fairly large part of our this-worldly reality, much attention is paid in Hasidism to the way to eat in holiness and how to have holy meals.

One common traditional theme which expresses the goal of sanctifying the meal is to say that a man's table is to become like an altar of sacrifice, and it has the high dignity of purifying him and atoning for his sins.

> As long as the Temple was in existence, the altar was the means of atonement for Israel; but now it is every man's table that atones for him. (*Berachot* 55)

The altar in the Temple was the "table" in God's house, on which His "house-servants" (the priests) offered His "food" (the sacrifices). In his vision, the prophet Ezekiel was shown the heavenly Temple of the future, and he was shown the altar. And the angel said to him: "This is the table that is before the Lord." (41:22,23) Now that the Temple is no longer in existence, the table at which each of us eats must become an altar, a table at which God is present.

Various aspects of the meal—all of which go to sanctify it—are connected to this thought of the table being an altar. The meal is made holy by blessings before and after, through Torah and song, through charity and through meditation.

On the higher levels of spiritual attainment, the motive in eating should not be to satisfy our personal need or pleasure, but should be connected to God and be a service of God. Eating is to be a devotional act.

> The main service of God is through eating—so have I heard from my masters; and it is similar to prayer. . . . And the *tzaddikim* meditate as they eat, in love and fear of God, as with prayer (*Darkei Tzedek*, p. 18)

> The holy rabbi, Rabbi Hirsh the "Servant" [of Rimanov], said . . . that service of God through eating is greater, and a higher level of service, than that of prayer. (*Divrei Shmuel*, p. 211, #9)

> It was said of Rabbi Abraham Yaakov of Sadigura that

> it was visible to the eye how his service of God while eating was as great as that of prayer. (*Eser Orot*, p. 139, #4)

> Rabbi Elimelech of Lizensk said:

> Most people exert all their energy in the time of prayer, to direct their heart and to ward off foreign thoughts. But when they eat they make no effort or exertion, since they eat only for their own pleasure—so where is there a place for effort or exertion? But as for the *tzaddikim*, the Sages, of blessed memory, have already said: "The time of eating is a time of war." The *tzaddikim* have no need to exert themselves when they pray; then, their minds are always pure and clear. But during the time of eating, that is when they have to use their energy and exert themselves. (*Mazkeret Shem ha-Gedolim*, p. 43)

The desire for food must be mastered. We are not to simply give in to our hunger. The *rebbes* taught this important lesson even to their children.

> Once, one of the hasidim of Rabbi Israel of Rizhin saw one of the *rebbe's* children, who was just a little boy, holding a bagel in his hand and crying. The hasid asked him why he was crying, and the boy answered that he was hungry. "But don't you have food in your hand?" replied the hasid. "Why don't you eat it?" Hearing this, the

> boy burst out in tears, saying, "But didn't Daddy say that when you're hungry, you're not allowed to eat?" (*Raza d'Uvda*, Sh'ar ha-otiyot, p. 29, #3)

The lesson the *rebbe* intended to teach his son was that when your desire to eat is greatest, that is just the time to assert your spiritual will and control over yourself. A practice is sometimes recommended to delay eating, even if only for a little while, to conquer your hunger.

10:1 PREPARATION FOR THE MEAL

If a meal is to be made holy and a service of God, you cannot just sit down and eat. You have to prepare.

10:1:1 Even during the *preparation of the food* it is not too early to begin spiritual preparation for the meal by stating your intention and praying: "I am cooking this food so that it be for a holy meal and a service of God. My Father in Heaven, let me taste in this food the pleasure of the radiance of the *Shechinah.*"

In a hasidic story (told about both Rabbi Elimelech of Lizensk and Rabbi David of Lelov) the *rebbe* praised the humble meal of a poor woman very highly, saying that it tasted of Paradise. The reason for this was that the woman who prepared it had, while cooking, prayed that God put the taste of the Garden of Eden in her food[1] (*Niflaot ha-Rebbe*, p. 28, #42; *Kodesh Hillulim*, p. 139). (See 10:14 about the taste coming from the *Shechinah*, and 10:4:8 about thinking of yourself as being in the Garden of Eden, before the *Shechinah*, when you eat.)

10:1:2 *Set the table nicely* so that it is worthy of being called a table before God; have this as your intention when you prepare the table, and state it aloud. These holy intentions regarding the food and the table will make it easier to have holy thoughts during the meal.

Rabbi Levi Yitzhak of Berditchev told how Queen Esther made a meal

> with such holiness and purity, that holiness rested on each and every dish of food, and on the table and all its utensils. (*Ohalei Shem*, p. 26, #45)

Of Rabbi Shlomo Leib of Lentshno:

> His way in holiness was to be very clean in everything—so much so that it cannot be imagined or described. There was no one like him when it came to cleanliness. All the utensils that he ate with, for example, the knife, spoon, and fork, were always kept in a locked drawer so no one else would use them. If it happened that someone else did use them even once, he considered them unfit and would never eat with them again. This was also the case with the cup he used for drinking on weekdays, not to speak of the one he used for *kiddush* on *Shabbat.* And he made sure that the tablecloth was always white, fresh, and clean. (*Eser Atarot*, p. 21, #6)

The rabbis teach that cleanliness leads to holiness, and also that physical cleanliness induces a feeling of spiritual cleanliness. If the table is an altar, and if the dishes and utensils are used in the holy act of eating, they must be treated as holy vessels, at least according to Rabbi Shlomo Leib. As Zechariah prophesied about the Day of the Lord, at that time it would not be the pots of the Temple alone that would be holy: "And every pot in Jerusalem and Judah shall be holy to the Lord; and all they that sacrifice shall come and take of them, and cook in them." (14:21)

> **10:1:3** The Side of Uncleanness gets power through the holding in of excrement and wastes unnecessarily, and this can lead to foreign thoughts. . . . So you should not eat unless you have first cleaned out your insides from your previous meal. (*Darkei Tzedek*, p. 20. See also "Bathroom," 27:5:1.)

10:1:4 Connected with the theme of the table as an altar:

> Putting food on the table is a great service of God; even more so is removing the dishes from the table after the meal. (Rabbi Asher of Stolin, *Beit Aharon*, p. 286)
>
> The Baal Shem Tov once traveled to be with Rabbi Yitzhak of Drobitch, may his merit protect us, to offer him personal service—for it is a great act of devotion to God and purifies the soul to offer personal service to the holy sages. And so the Besht himself brought to Rabbi Yitzhak his coffee in a pot and served him. After he drank the coffee, the Besht himself removed the coffee pot and the cup and the spoon from the table, and brought them into the kitchen. Rabbi Yitzhak's son, the holy Rabbi Yehiel Michal of Zlotchov said to the Besht, "Holy Rabbi, I can understand why you want to offer personal service to my holy father. But why did you also trouble yourself to

carry out the empty dishes?" The Besht answered him by explaining that carrying the spoon out from the Holy of Holies [in the Temple] was also part of the service of the high priest on the Day of Atonement.[2] (*Mishnat Hasidim*, p. 420, #21)

10:1:5 Repentance and Confession

10:1:5:1 Meditate on repentance before prayer, before Torah study, and before eating. (Rabbi Moshe Teitelbaum, *Hanhagot Tzaddikim*, p. 50, #34)

10:1:5:2 Before washing your hands for the meal, say the prayer of repentance of Rabbeinu Yonah. (Rabbi Elimelech of Lizensk in his *Tzetl Katan*, #15. See also "Repentance," 14:2 for this prayer.)

10:1:5:3 You should confess before a meal in order to silence the "accusers." (*Derech Hayim*, 1–26)

When we eat we are close to acting not for God, but for our lower desires. Confession, which is part of repentance, silences heavenly accusations against our sincerity (echoes of our unconscious) by bringing our faults out into the open (and into consciousness).

10:1:5:4 If someone is a *baal tshuvah*, a repentant sinner, he should confess before he eats, for by this too he "sacrifices" his *yetzer* [evil inclination]. So did Rabbeinu Yonah write—that a *baal tshuvah* should confess beforehand, and that he should go over in his mind the deeds he had done until then. By doing this he will keep himself from being a glutton, for he will think of how many are his sins, and how he is not worthy because of this, to receive the food. It only comes from God's great mercy, for He gives sustenance to both the wicked and the good. . . . And by this meditation he sacrifices his *yetzer*, and his table becomes an altar of forgiveness for him. (Rabbi Elijah deVidas, *Reshit Hochmah*, Sh'ar ha-kedushah, chap. 15, #72)

It seems to me that everyone ought to confess, not only the *baal tshuvah* . . . because eating is in the place of a sacrifice, and with every sacrifice the person who brought it had to confess, to atone for his sins. . . . So you should say the confession, "We've done wrong etc., we've done wickedly etc.," until, "He who is great in forgiveness." And on *Shabbat* and *Yom Tov*, when the confession is not to be said, say instead the verse (Deuteronomy 30:6), "And the Lord your God will circumcise your heart and the heart of your off-

> spring, so that you will love the Lord your God with all your heart and with all your soul, that you may live"—and meditate on repentance [from love] within your heart. (*Shnei Luchot ha-Brit*,[3] in *Reshit Hochmah*, Sh'ar ha-kedushah, chap. 15, #72, n. 171)

10:1:6 *Tzedaka*

10:1:6:1 Before eating, give something for *tzedaka*. (Rabbi David ha-Levi of Steppin, *Hanhagot Tzaddikim*, p. 56, #19)

10:1:6:2 A main aspect of the rabbinic saying about your table being an altar is understood to be that it becomes so when you share your meal with a poor person who eats with you. For like the priests (who as God's representatives often shared in the eating of the sacrifices), the poor are considered to be, in a special way, God's people.

But it is hardly possible today in most cases to share every meal with a poor person. There is, however, something to do as a substitute. *Reshit Hochmah* teaches that:

> In a place where poor people are not to be found, what can a man do such that his table will be an altar? It is possible to say that he should estimate what the cost of the meal for a poor man would have been, and put that amount aside for charity before he himself eats. (Sh'ar ha-Kedushah, chap. 15, #64)

However, do note that any *tzedaka* before eating sanctifies the meal; giving what *Reshit Hochmah* suggests is an added measure of piety.[4]

10:1:7 The hasidic *rebbe*, Rabbi Abraham of Slonim said:

> When I was a boy of eight I used to eat because I wanted to eat, and my father would rebuke me . . . saying, "Why are you stuffing yourself?" I didn't know what he wanted from me. But later, when I had grown up a bit, I understood him. And I made myself a "fence": to decide before a meal how much to eat, and no more. Because once you start eating and your stomach expands, you can be dragged into overeating. (*Torat Avot*, Maasei avot, #167)

10:1:8 Aspects of a Meditation Before Eating (YOUR HUNGER IS FROM GOD; EATING FROM DESIRE GIVES ENERGY TO THE OTHER SIDE)

10:1:8:1:1 When you become hungry or thirsty, you should realize that just as food and the satisfaction of your hunger is from God, so is the hunger itself. This is suggested in the blessing made after food: "Blessed are You, O Lord our God, King of the Universe, who has created many living things and also their needs, for all that You created to enliven every living thing [and to satisfy these needs]. Blessed are You, the life of all the worlds." As in the blessing, God creates both the need (the hunger), and also the food that satisfies it.

So Rabbi Zusya of Hanipol taught that before or when you eat, you should meditate on how God could have created things differently; but He created man so that he should live by eating. He said:

> The will of the Creator, blessed be He, then, is to "enliven every living thing" by means of eating. So I have to eat in holiness and purity, for I am doing His will by eating. And when you think this way, then you can accomplish the spiritual purpose of eating by lifting up the holy sparks to their source. . . . And you should realize that it is He who has brought you to this hunger and thirst. For the hunger is from Him.[5] (*Mazkeret Shem ha-Gedolim*, p. 79)

When we meditate on how our hunger is from God, it is spiritualized and lifted up out of the realm of our ego and bodily desires. God has given us the hunger because there is a spiritual goal to be accomplished in eating.

> **10:1:8:1:2** The *tzaddikim* of Israel do not desire enjoyment from the material things of this world [but only from what is spiritual] . . . and you should know that if you feel a desire for food it is really your soul that desires to lift up the holy sparks within the food . . . and that it is God who has sent this desire to you. (The Hasam Sofer, *Yesodot b'Avodat HaShem*, p. 12n.)

(The concept of the spiritual task of lifting up the holy sparks while eating will be discussed later. We can just say here generally, that the essential thought is that by eating in holiness and concentrating on the spiritual aspect of the food, we incorporate it into the spiritual world.)

10:1:8:1:3 Rabbi Tzadok ha-Cohen of Lublin:

> [You should realize that] God, blessed be He, created the food that is before you, and He gives it its existence and puts within it its taste and nourishing qualities. And He gives to a man the desire to eat

and also his sense of taste, whereby the food tastes good.[6] (*Menorat Zahav*, quoting and summarizing from *P'ri Tzaddik*, Kuntres Ayt ha-Ochel)

10:1:8:2 Part of a meditation before eating can be based on an awareness that eating more than necessary, just for your desire, by giving in to your desire, adds energy to that side of yourself that works against your attaining holiness, and counters and frustrates your own hopes for good.

10:1:8:2:1 In all weekday meals, whatever you eat more than is necessary for your health goes to the Other Side. So a spiritual person . . . should lessen his pleasure in food during weekdays [*Shabbat*, note, is different], for such enjoyments, as it were, are like building a dwelling place for the Other Side. (*Avodat ha-Kodesh*, Moreh b'Etzba 3–105)

10:1:8:2:2 The kabbalists have written that anything you eat on weekdays that is more than what is necessary for satisfaction adds more power to the Other Side and strengthens your *yetzer ha-ra* so that it will gain control over you. [Contrarily, eating just for the necessary satisfaction of the body and no more, and eating primarily for the satisfaction of the soul, adds to the power of holiness within you.] (*Pele Yoatz*, quoted in *Kedushat ha-Shulchan*, p. 146)

10:1:9 Pray for God's Help

10:1:9:1 [The Holy Yehudi] used to teach that we should be careful not to eat with lust, and that we should pray before eating that we have the merit of the fathers to support us, that we not fall into our desires for the food, and we not become coarsened as a result of the meal. (*Derech Emunah u'Maaseh Rav*, p. 63)

10:1:9:2 Always confess before you eat and say, "Master of the World! Help me that my eating be in holiness, and that my intention in eating be for the sake of heaven. Save me from falling into overeating."*[7] (Rabbi Shmuel Valtzis, in *Midrash Pinhas*, p. 45a, #17)

10:1:10 Pray for Your Food

10:1:10:1 Pray for your food before you eat. (*Derech Hayim*, 6–63)

10:1:10:2 It is a higher level of closeness to God to draw all of your needs, including food, to you through prayer—even though God would give them to you anyway. (See the quote from Rabbi Nachman of Bratzlav in Chapter 2, p. 42 about this.)

> **10:1:10:3** Every day, after the Morning Prayers and before you eat, pray for your food—so that you can be called a child of God. . . . And let everyone pray according to his ability. The men of deeds make it their custom to say before washing their hands: "You, O God, sustain and feed, through Your kindness, all Your creatures, from the mighty wild ox with its gigantic horns to the tiny eggs of the smallest insects. [Give me, I pray, my daily bread, and let all those of my household have the food they need before it is needed—easily and not with difficulty, by permissible ways and not forbidden, for life and peace from the Divine abundance of blessing and good, from the flow of heavenly blessing from above—so that we can do Your will and study Your Torah and fulfill Your *mitzvot.* Let me not be in need of the gifts of flesh and blood, or of their loans, but only of Your helping hand, which is full, open, holy, and ample.] "The eyes of all wait upon Thee, and Thou givest them their food in due season. Thou openest Thine hand and satisfiest every living thing with favor" [Psalm 145:15–16*] (*Totzaot Hayim*, p. 18; the addition in brackets is from a version of this prayer [with identical beginning and end] in *Kitzur Shnei Luchot ha-Brit*, Inyanei tefillat yud-chet, p. 121.)

> **10:1:10:4** You should pray for your sustenance before eating. . . . If you are not able to memorize this prayer, then have a copy of what to say on the table where you eat, so it will be at hand and easy to say. (*Kaf ha-Hayim*, chap. 23, #1)

10:1:10:5 The holy *Zohar* praises Rabbi Yissa the Elder, who, although he had food, would not eat before he first prayed to the King for his sustenance.

> He always said, "We're not going to set the table until our food is given to us from the King's palace." (*Reshit Hochmah*, Sh'ar ha-Kedushah, chap. 15, #85)

> **10:1:10:6** The holy way of the holy Rebbe Reb Zusya was that after the Morning Prayers he would not tell his servant to bring him something to eat; he would just say aloud, "Master of the World, Zusya is very hungry; please see that his meal is brought to him!"

> And when the servant heard this he knew to bring in the food. [The beautiful story (too long to give in full) tells how once the servants decided that they would not bring him anything to eat until he asked them explicitly. But that morning, on his way to the *mikveh* before prayers on a rainy day, the rabbi had had an encounter with a crude visitor from out of town. This person, not knowing the rabbi (who was always dressed poorly), and thinking him to be just an old beggar, had, for a joke, pushed him off the sidewalk and into the mud. When he found out later that this was the holy rabbi, he immediately went to beg forgiveness—and took with him some liquor and cake as a token for the rabbi to taste after his prayers. Of course, he entered just when the rabbi called out, as always, for God to give him his food—and the servants saw that God watched over him, and approved of his practice.] (*Butzina Kadisha,* p. 31, #74)

We see from this story that although Rabbi Zusya received his meals from the servant, he was completely dependent on God; he was like a child before his Father in Heaven. So he prayed for his food before eating, and knew from whom it really came.

10:1:11 Stated Intention

Before eating say aloud what your intentions are in the meal. For example, say "I am eating so that my body will be strong for the service of God."

The *Shulchan Aruch*:

> For everything from which you derive benefit or enjoyment in this world, your intention should be not your own pleasure but to serve God, blessed be He, as is written, "Know Him in all your ways." Our Sages said, "Let all your deeds be for the sake of heaven." Even things of personal choice, such as eating and drinking, walking, sitting and standing, sexual intercourse, conversation, and everything connected with the needs of your body—all should be for the service of God, or for something that leads to the service of God. So even if you are hungry and thirsty, if you ate and drank for your own pleasure it is not praiseworthy; you should intend that you are eating and drinking to keep yourself alive for the service of God. (31:1,2)

Mishna Berurach (*Orach Hayim* 231:1) notes here, in the name of another commentator:

> I have seen that those who are men of deeds, before eating, say, "I want to eat and drink so that I'll be healthy and strong for the service of God."* (*Orach Hayim*, Siman 231)

A higher and more hasidic level of intention can be added to this first one. *Reshit Hochmah* speaks of two levels of holiness, one higher than the other, which he calls this world and the World to Come, or the Lower Garden of Eden and the Upper Garden of Eden:

> In the lower holiness the person sanctifies himself and separates himself from the things of this world, as if he is not of this world. But the higher level of holiness depends on the sanctification of his mind and thoughts in *d'vekut* to the Upper [spiritual] World. For example, with regard to eating—the first level of holiness means that he separates himself from enjoying the physical sense pleasures of the food. Rather, his intention in eating is that his body be healthy and strong for the service of God. But in the second and higher level of holiness his intention is that he is eating from the Upper table that is before God, and his food is coming to him from God's hand. . . . Such a person, although he is in this [physical] world, his mind is not here, but in the World to Come [the spiritual world]. (*Reshit Hochmah* Sh'ar ha-Kedushah, chap. 4, #21)

In line with this, one can say as a stated intention: "I am eating so that I can be in the presence of my Father in Heaven, sitting at the table before Him and receiving life from His hand. And my intention is to serve Him now while I eat." (Serving God now, while you eat, will be explained later.)

Various other, more specific stated intentions can be added here, as will be seen from our full discussion of eating and the holy meal, which follows. For example: "I want to eat so that my eating itself will be a service of God by lifting up what is material into the spiritual realm," or "so that my eating will be a sacrifice before God, from which rises a sweet scent, and which atones for my sins." (These concepts will become clearer as our discussion proceeds.)

Your stated intention can also be repeated throughout the course of the meal.

10:1:12 A Declaration Nullifying Unwanted Thoughts, Motives, and Desires

One can make a declaration before eating (and also repeat it during the meal) that your eating is not for your own desire but for the service of

God alone. For example: "Master of the World! I intend my eating as a service of worship and devotion, with all my thoughts of mind and heart dedicated to You alone. Due to my low state it is possible that motives of desire for the food, and foreign thoughts of other things, will enter my mind while I eat. But You know that my true will is to do Your will and come close to You. So I declare now that if any extraneous thoughts or low desires come to me while eating, I consider them empty and worthless and null, for I do not want them at all."

(For more about nullifying bad thoughts, etc., by means of a declaration, see "Individual Practices," 39:12, and "The Synagogue and the Synagogue Service," 6:24.)

10:1:13 Further Aspects of a Meditation Before Eating (MEDITATION ON GOD'S GREATNESS AND GOODNESS; BEING IN THE PRESENCE; LOVE AND FEAR)

> The *tzaddikim* meditate as they eat, in love and fear of God, as with prayer. (*Darkei Tzedek*, p. 18)

In the chapter on Meditation you will find teachings on how to awaken your love and fear of God through meditation on His greatness and goodness. The basic points are that through meditating on God's all-encompassing nature and creative power, one is aroused to awe (fear), and that through meditating on His overflowing goodness, one is aroused to love. In addition to the discussion there, we can say that in the context of a preparation for eating, such a meditation can particularly include a focus on God's greatness and goodness in the creation of all living things and their needs, as well as the foods to satisfy them, and also on the spiritual aspect of food.

The typical hasidic meditation of this sort is, moreover, generally carried into a reflection on the immediacy and personal application of the concepts, such that one becomes aware of God's presence in the place where you are at that moment, in love and fear. This meditation should be done at the table, and one should meditate on being at the table before God. (See 10:4. See also "Meditation" [17] and "Prayer," 5:1:18.)

10:1:14 The final part of a preparation for eating, before washing the hands, can be to prepare for the blessing. With the bread or food on the table before you, you can meditate on the spiritual aspect of the food. It is probably best to do this standing, as that asserts the intention that the food be lifted up into the spiritual realm rather than your descending to the material. See the discussion that follows for more about the blessing and about the meditation on the spiritual aspect of the food. (See also "*Shabbat*," 18:2:4:5:8:2 for the lovely story involving the Baal Shem Tov and Rabbi Yaakov Koppel Hasid about the preparation for a holy meal, and a meditation of this sort, done standing before the table. This story is also discussed in 10:14, p. 258.)

10:1:15 Just as with prayer, the devotional service of eating requires preparation. So if you would sanctify your meal, to begin with, set a minimal period of five minutes, during which time, sitting at the table, you can prepare yourself according to the general order of what has been outlined above. (Of course, you can decide for yourself which individual practices to include, or you can use all of them.) In the discussion that follows you will find many more things that can be included in such a preparation—intentions, meditations, etc. Practices done during the meal can also be included prospectively in the preparation when you give thought to what you intend to do while eating. (See "Individual Practices," 39:35 for a wonderful example of considering your actions beforehand.)

10:1:16 Washing the Hands

Before eating a meal with bread we ritually wash our hands (*Shulchan Aruch*, chap. 40). As the water pours over our hands, we are to think about the removal of lower self-concerns and desires in eating. And when we lift up our hands afterward, we take on the holy intentions for the meal.

> **10:1:16:1** The intention of washing the hands before meals is to remove the self-direction of hunger and the desire for the food. (Rabbi Mordechai Yosef of Ishbitz, in *Ha-Admorim mi-Ishbitz*, p. 44)
>
> **10:1:16:2** Before you make the blessing on the washing of the hands [before drying them], lift up your hands—this is a hint of the reception at this time of purity. (*Derech Hayim*, 1–12)

10:1:16:3 [Slightly different:] Lift up your hands after washing, as you make the blessing; and hold your arms together as one. (*Zohar Hadash*, Ruth, 866, quoted in *Reshit Hochmah*, Sh'ar ha-kedushah, chap. 15, #103)

10:1:16:4 Before you dry your hands, raise them upward, with your fingers outstretched as if you want to receive something. And you should meditate on the greatness of the Creator, for He is One, Single, and Unique, the Holy One, blessed be He, the King of the Universe. (*Kitzur Shnei Luchot ha-Brit*, Inyanei netillat yadaim shaharit, p. 108)

10:1:16:5 Raise your hands high and say, "Lift up your hands to the Holy Place and bless God!" [Psalm 134:2] (*Hanhagot Adam*, Y. L. Lipshitz, p. 14; *Shulchan Aruch* 40:5)

10:1:16:6 It was the custom of the Baal Shem Tov, when he washed his hands for the meal, to be in an intense state of *d'vekut*.[8] (*Mishnat Hasidim*, p. 379, #6)

10:2 THE BLESSING

In itself, eating and other physical enjoyments tend to deaden our spiritual consciousness. Rabbi Yehiel Michal of Zlotchov said:

> Be careful to say all blessings with fear and love of God as much as possible—especially those blessings on worldly enjoyments. Because when you do not make the blessings with the appropriate consciousness, the food deadens your heart and makes you forget the service of God, and you will fall into sin, God forbid. (*Yeshuot Malko*, p. 138)

10:2:2 The tradition has provided the practice of blessings before and after the meal, which surround it and sanctify it. The after-blessing for a meal with bread or a full meal (even without) "expands" to become the long Grace after Meals.

The simplest and main blessings said for any food that does not require a special and specific blessing for itself, have the basic ideas that teach the intention behind all the blessings over food.

The before-blessing is: "Blessed are You, O Lord our God, King of the Universe, by whose word everything comes into being." In this before-blessing we give recognition that God is not only the ultimate, but also the immediate source of the food. Without His word, which keeps it (like all created things) in existence, this food would revert to nothingness in a second.

The after-blessing is: "Blessed are You, O Lord our God, King of the Universe, who has created many living beings and also their needs, for all that You created with which to enliven every living thing. Blessed are You, the life of all the worlds." Having eaten, and feeling enlivened from the food, we give our recognition in this after-blessing, that it is God who enlivens us through the food.

When we focus our attention on the food as we make the before-blessing, it is the appropriate time to think of the spiritual aspect of the food and how it is coming to us from God. According to the S'fas Emes the food has a physical reality and also a spiritual reality. And the more we see the spiritual reality with our mind's eye, the less we see the physical aspect with our physical eye (*Kedushat ha-Shulchan*, p. 27). Later we will see how, while eating, we can also attend to the spiritual reality and tune in to the life from God that flows into us as we eat.

> **10:2:3** The blessing you make at the table should be with greater *kavvanah* than other blessings, because food and drink usually lead to a coarsening of your nature and to pride—and from this you will forget God. . . . To counteract this you should devote yourself to a more intense meditation at this time, so that your table will be a table before God. You should see that your heart is drawn to a desire for God when you sit down at the table, rather than to a desire for the food and drink. You should remember what is important, particularly when there is a possibility that you will forget it. . . . When you are eating, your heart should cleave to God more so than at any other time during the day.
>
> The headquarters for this concept is that which is said [about the seventy elders at Mount Sinai], that "They saw God, and they ate and drank." In other words, while they were eating and drinking they were meditating on and seeing the Glory [the *Shechinah*].
>
> So you should sanctify yourself at table during a meal. The rabbis said about the words of the Torah, "You shall be sanctified to Me," that you should sanctify yourself in what is permitted to you, and you should eat before God. This means, while you are eating, think of

> how you are eating before God and how there is no screen of separation between you and Him, blessed be He. (*Shnei Luchot ha-Brit*, Parshat Ki Tavo, quoted in *Kedushat ha-Shulchan*, pp. 30–31)

(See Chapter 20, "Blessings," for more on how to make a blessing.)

10:3 SALT

> **10:3:1** It is required to have salt set on the table before breaking bread, and to dip the piece of bread over which *Hamotzi* is said into the salt—because the table represents the altar and the food symbolizes the offerings. As it is said (Leviticus 2:13): "With all thine offerings thou shalt offer salt." (*Shulchan Aruch*, 41:6)

We can remind ourselves of this verse and its significance, repeating it mentally, when using the salt.

10:3:2 The meaning of the salt has to be understood in the larger context of the altar. The food offered on the altar was, so to speak, God's food. The model is that of a man eating, and the priests who make the offering in the Temple are His servants bringing Him His food in His House. Men eat food seasoned with salt, therefore that is the way to bring an offering on God's table (the altar).

But what is the symbolic meaning? One aspect of this is that salt is a seasoning that makes food palatable and pleasant-tasting. Dipping the bread in the salt symbolizes that our service to God (at the table and always) must be true and sincere—with *kavvanah*, with love and fear of God, and with adherence to His laws—the moral laws included. Only then will it be acceptable to Him. Our intention when we dip the bread in the salt is that our service be pleasing to Him and acceptable.[9]

Another aspect of the salt relates to the fact that:

> Salt prevents putrefaction. . . . Salt is a preservative, and typifies that which is abiding. (*Hertz Chumash* on Leviticus 2:13)

Leviticus 2:13 says: "Nor shall you suffer the salt of the covenant of your God to be lacking [from your offering]." The salt, then, symbolizes the abiding covenant between the Jewish people and God. We can call to mind our covenant and our relation with God, and this supports us if our divine service is poor—for if we are unworthy now, we have faith that God still wants His children at His table.

This covenant of salt also protects us from negative forces and influences:

> You should dip the bread of the *Motzi* three times in the salt, and intend to remove the Other Side from the table. (*Seder ha-Yom l'ha-Admor mi-Biala*, #123)

10:4 SITTING BEFORE THE PRESENCE OF GOD

10:4:1 When you eat it is good to have before you on the table a card (with a support like that for a picture frame so it can stand) on which is written יהוה YHVH—to look at during the meal so as to remember God. (See "Torah," 15:20.)

10:4:2 As you sit down at the table, look at the card if you have one and say, "This is the table that is before the Lord." (Ezekiel 41:22. See also *Avot* 3:4.)

> **10:4:3** The principle is that when you eat, even if you eat alone, you should consider yourself as if eating in the presence of a king—for the whole earth is full of His glory—and it is in His presence that you eat and say the blessings.[10] (*Totzaot Hayim*, p. 36)

> **10:4:4** When you eat you should meditate on how it is as if you are eating before the King, and what you eat is from the flow of Divine beneficence from the Supernal Table at which you have been privileged to sit. About this is it said, "And you shall eat before God." (*Derech Hayim*, 6–64)

10:4:5 Rabbi Israel, the Maggid of Koznitz, said that:

> When a *tzaddik* eats, he always has God-consciousness, and eats before God. (*Mazkeret Shem ha-Gedolim*, p. 128)

> **10:4:6** While you are eating, think of how you are eating before God, and how there is no screen of separation between you and

> Him, blessed be He. (*Shnei Luchot ha-Brit*, quoted in *Kedushat ha-Shulchan*, p. 31)

10:4:7 There is a story about the first meeting of Rabbi Yitzhak of Drobitch (the father of Rabbi Yehiel Michal of Zlotchov) and the Baal Shem Tov. In the story, Rabbi Yitzhak eats at the Besht's house on *Shabbat*. And at the table:

> Immediately after the *kiddush*, our master and rabbi, Rabbi Yitzhak, placed before himself a small silver plate on which the name YHVH was engraved, and he rested it against his thumb. For it was his holy practice to have this little plate before him when he ate; and whenever he took food into his mouth he looked at the Name, and would he do so throughout the whole course of the meal.[11] (*Mazkeret Shem ha-Gedolim*, p. 4)

Elsewhere we hear how, in his journey to the Besht, Rabbi Yitzhak was served some bread at an inn, and as always, as he ate he looked at the Name of God on the silver plate. When he was finished with the bread he was served, he asked for some more.

> The female innkeeper gave him more bread, and seeing he was hungry, kept on giving him more each time he ate what was put before him. And all the while he was looking at the Name of God. Finally, he had eaten so much she had nothing left. After some time the holy rabbi from Drobitch lifted his head slowly, as if waking up, and inquired of her where was the bread he had ordered—because he was so immersed in his holy meditations on the Name of God engraved on the plate that he was not at all aware that he had already eaten much more bread than what he had asked for. (*Raza d'Uvda*, Sh'ar ha-otiyot, p. 25, #2)

(See 10:1:4 for another story of Rabbi Yitzhak of Drobitch and the Besht.)

10:4:8 When you sit at table you should meditate on being in the presence of God, and think of yourself as being in the Garden of Eden before the *Shechinah* (*Reshit Hochmah*, Sh'ar ha-kedushah, chap. 4, #21, #23; cf. chap. 15, #61, #62). (See also "Prayer," 5:1:18; "Torah," 15:18; and "Meditation" for suggestions about this.)

10:4:9 When you are at table eating, be aware that you are before God, and see that all your manners are refined and appropriate.

> Propriety [*derech eretz*] is always a prior condition before the higher goals of Torah can be approached. This is especially true with regard to meals, where you should be careful to conduct yourself properly. For if you do not have decent manners you are contemptible in the eyes of God as well as in the eyes of men. (*Kaf ha-Hayim*, p. 332, #63)

10:5 Rabbi Yehiel Michal of Zlotchov said that it was a practice of his

> never to lean down to the food, but to sit upright, and . . . bring the food to his mouth. (*Mazkeret Shem ha-Gedolim*, p. 26)

In *Seder ha-Dorot ha-Hadash*, where this word about the custom of the Zlotchover also appears, the author adds the note:

> It was so that he should not be drawn into the physical lust, that he did not lean toward the food. For someone who has a strong desire to eat bends down to the plate. (p. 55)

We hear the same thing about Rabbi Israel of Rizhin:

> He never moved his mouth toward the utensil with which he ate. (*Beit Rizhin*, p. 232)

10:6 INTERRUPTIONS

As we explained in Chapter 3, p. 60, activities such as eating should be interrupted to break the strength of our desires which increase at this time; thus, we will not fall during the meal. This is, as we said, just the opposite of what we do during purely religious activities such as prayer or Torah study (in which we directly serve God), where the goal is continuity and avoidance of interruption.

If you pay attention to what happens to your consciousness during the course of a meal (particularly after having prayed or studied Torah), you can actually become aware of how it is lowered and sinks into the food. We mentioned in Chapter 3, p. 61 about the *rebbe* who realized he was not sitting in the *sukkah*, but in the bowl of potatoes. If you see to it that you not only interrupt the eating, but further, do so with holy activities such as Torah and meditation, you can feel yourself ascend out of the food and up. In fact, if you just close your eyes during the meal and turn your internal gaze to God, and direct yourself to "fly upward," you can feel your consciousness rising from below to above. We noted how Rabbi Yehiel Michal of Zlotchov and Rabbi Israel of Rizhin would not bend down to the food, but would lift it to their mouths. This practice counters the natural tendency to sink down into the materiality of food, and helps us instead to raise the food into our spiritual realm.

There is this teaching in *Emunat Tzaddikim*:

> The essential advice on how to deal with food lust is that when you eat you should be aware of what you are doing; then it ceases to be just an animal action. The lust for food is intact if you allow your mind and all your senses to be immersed in eating until you forget what you are doing. Then eating is like an animal's action.
>
> But if you think over what you are doing, and act with consciousness, then you clothe that part of *your* life-energy within this elevated consciousness, and join it with the holy spark within the food [*its* life-energy], and you are removed from the lust. (p. 78)

To switch to a more modern idiom, what this teaching is referring to as animal action, we also call automatic—when what you do goes on without conscious thought or control (although it is particularly "animal" in that it is from our lower self).

The goal here is to raise your activity to a conscious/spiritual level when eating the food, which is considered in terms of its spiritual reality.

A related comment from Rabbi Tzadok ha-Cohen of Lublin regarding a general counsel for dealing with lusts, and which he applies to eating:

> Be deliberate—because one of the fundamental bases of lust is haste. For when a man acts out of lust he wants to swallow up and fulfill the object of his lust quickly. (*P'ri Tzaddik*, quoted in *Menorat Zahav*, p. 33)

> **10:6:1** As we know from books on spiritual character development (*musar*), if you interrupt yourself in the middle of eating, for the sake of His name, and when your desire is at its strength, it is counted as if you had brought a sacrifice before God, blessed be He. (*Derech Emunah u'Maaseh Rav*, Mochlim, p. 62)

10:6:2 The words of the holy Seer of Lublin:

> The Sages said that "During a meal, when you see that you are starting to indulge your food lust, draw back your hand from it." You should be careful that your intention is only for God in everything that you do. If you see that your sense-enjoyment in a

meal is overcoming you, and your holy direction to God is weakening, "draw back your hands" and stop eating until you break your lust for the food; then go back to eating. (*Or Yesharim*, Eshil Avraham, p. 184)

10:6:3 After eating with *kavvanah* . . . you should also see that you fulfill the saying that "You should draw back from a meal from which you are deriving physical pleasure." It is written in the book *Derech Eretz* that the meaning of this is not that you should stop eating altogether, but that you should stop until the force of your lust is broken, and afterwards continue to eat. As I heard from my grandfather, the holy Rabbi Hershele of Eptchena, the memory of a *tzaddik* for a blessing, that between each and every swallow you should pause somewhat to compose yourself. (*Seder ha-Yom ha-Katzar*, p. 6)

10:6:4 Do not take your mind off the service of God for even a minute, and decrease your enjoyment of worldly things to the greatest extent possible. And while you are eating, when you feel the greatest desire, pull back your hand. If you do this at every meal it will be as if you were offering a sacrifice at every meal, and your table will be an actual altar on which to sacrifice your evil inclination. (Rabbi Joseph Karo, in his Azharot v'Tikkunim v'Sayagim in *YHvT*, #14, p. 9)

One way that a man's table becomes an altar is by his breaking his food lust. This is a self-sacrifice before God. And just as with the sacrifices on the altar in the Temple, when they were accompanied by an attitude of repentance and a sincere desire to come close to God, so too does this sacrifice at a man's table bring with it the atonement of sins.

For a man's table should be pure [the hasidic *rebbes'* table is always called their "pure table"], that is, he should not be drawn to the pleasures of the body which come from the *yetzer ha-ra*. A man's table is called an altar of atonement for him; and when he is not drawn after the pleasures of his *yetzer*, it is then that he subdues his *yetzer*, and his table becomes an altar of atonement to purify his sins. (*Reshit Hochmah*, Sh'ar ha-Ahavah, chap. 11, #47)

What is spoken about in this quote is not just a metaphor, because when you do not eat for your own pleasure and enjoyment, but as a service of God, you are truly giving up and sacrificing your *yetzer ha-ra*; and this real sacrifice for the sake of God brings with it the forgiveness of many sins.

> **10:6:5** Our teacher and rabbi, Rabbi Yitzhak of Neshkiz, told of how when he was a child he sat at table with his father, Rabbi Mordechai, and wanted to drink some water after he had eaten some fish. His father told him to wait a little. But when his father turned away, he took the water and drank. When his father saw this, he reproached him sternly and said, "Now you are little and you lust for this; what will happen when you grow up and lust for something else?" The rabbi said, "I began to cry, and I cried and cried. But I put those words on my heart so as to remember them always. And since then they are in my heart and I've never forgotten them." (*Mazkeret Shem ha-Gedolim*, p. 100)

Rabbi Mordechai wanted his son to pause and delay giving in to his desire. The allusion in the *rebbe's* words "lust for something else" is to sex.

Rabbi Tzadok ha-Cohen of Lublin:

> The lusts for eating and sex are sisters . . . and the fixing of eating precedes, because it is easier to deal with. And that will lead to the fixing of the second lust [sex]. (As summarized in the commentary of *Menorat Zahav*, p. 33)

10:6:6 It is possible to interrupt a meal many times, but everyone should try to do so at least once in the middle of the meal. It is a custom to say the Twenty-third Psalm (which should be memorized if possible) during such an interruption (either after the *Motzi* [*Shulchan Aruch* 62:5] or later on [see 10:10:12]). This is a beautiful practice, and the words of the psalm fit the purpose well. For while eating you give recognition that "The Lord is my shepherd, I shall not want [lack food or anything I need]. He makes me to lie down in green pastures. He leads me beside the still waters. [He provides me with food and drink.] He restores my soul [through the life coming through the food]. . . . for You are with me. [I am sitting in Your presence.] . . . You prepare a table before me in the presence of my enemies [the negative influences of food lust, foreign thoughts]. . . . My cup overflows. . . ."[12]

10:6:7 If the strength of our involvement in our desires and in the physical side of the meal is broken by interruptions, and if the interruptions are, moreover, those where we do holy things—Torah, meditation, psalms, holy songs (as on *Shabbat*)—the holy segments of the meal are strong enough to link to one another, "bridging over" the eating segments, and the continuity of the holiness overwhelms the continuity of the eating segments. We will see a little further on how even while we are actually doing the physical actions involved in eating—chewing, swallowing, then the eating is altogether absorbed in the holiness, the material in the spiritual, and the meal becomes a holy meal, etc.—various kinds of meditation (Torah and otherwise) done at the same time also serve to decrease the physical side of the experience and turn it into something spiritual.

I had read about holy meals in hasidic books, but the first time I experienced one was in the holy city of Tiberias in the Land of Israel, where I was invited to a meal on *Sukkot* in the *sukkah* of an elder Bratzlaver hasid who, it seems to me, is one of the hidden *tzaddikim*. There were many courses in the festive meal, but this *tzaddik*, during each course and between courses, was completely immersed in reciting out of his kabbalistic Siddur the "Seder of the Holy Guests," singing holy songs and dancing in the *sukkah*. The aura of holiness completely absorbed the eating/material side of the meal, which became all holiness, a holy meal indeed.

> **10:6:8** Interrupt yourself when eating and drinking two or three times during a meal to look in a holy book or to think over what you have heard [taught about eating]. And each time you should pray mentally, "Master of the World, teach me how to do Your will; and save me from the evil inclination!" (*Midrash Pinhas*, p. 45a, #18)

10:6:9 When the meal becomes a holy meal, you are not to interrupt it with idle conversation (the same way you are not to interrupt prayer). The following story is told of Rabbi Zev of Z'bariz:

> An important rabbi once came into his house to visit him while he was at the table eating. But Rabbi Zev did not greet him or say anything to him at all. The visitor was greatly surprised by this as were all the others who were standing in the room.
>
> But the moment the *rebbe* finished eating he turned to his guest with a face shining with love and affection, and greeted him with the blessing of peace, and asked him to be seated. Rabbi Zev's glowing face left no question about his affection for this guest, and how happy he was that he had merited the honor of serving him during his visit. He also did not neglect to apologize to him, and said, "My dear friend, please forgive me for not greeting or speak-

ing to you when you entered, since I wasn't able to interrupt in the middle of my meal. For it's a halachic decree that one is not permitted to talk during a meal." (*Toafot Ha-Rim*, p. 258)

Halachic authorities differ as to whether conversation is allowed at meals (see *Shulchan Aruch* 42:5 and commentaries), and not everyone would go as far as Rabbi Zev did. Indeed, as the rabbis teach, Abraham himself interrupted his communion with the *Shechinah* to greet the three visitors. Regardless, the point is made that when one eats as a service of God, interruptions are not to be taken lightly.

At the Sabbath tables of many *rebbes* an awesome silence would reign, except for the singing of *zemirot* (table hymns), the Torah teaching of the *rebbe*, etc. The *rebbes* themselves would often go for periods of time into withdrawn meditative states of *d'vekut*. (See the story and note the condition of Rabbi Abraham the Angel in "*Shabbat*," 18:2:4:5:6. See also "Song and Dance," 24:11.)

10:6:10 Rabbeinu Yonah (in *Yesod Tshuva*) discusses, in the name of Rabbi Abraham ben David, another practice during meals that checks lust:

> The greatest and most wonderful fence is to leave food uneaten on the plate. . . . When you are eating and still have an appetite for the food, leave some of it uneaten and forget your desire, for the honor of your Creator; do not eat just according to the demands of your appetite. Doing this will keep you from sin, and remind you of the love of God more than if you were to fast once a week; because this is something you do every day, whenever you eat or drink—leave your desire unsatisfied, for the honor of your Creator.

10:7 CALL OUT TO YOUR FATHER IN HEAVEN

Some of the hasidic *rebbes* would call out softly to God while they ate, "Father, Father!"

> The holy rabbi, Rebbe Reb Elimelech [of Lizensk], may his merit protect us, once said that knowing the holy *tzaddik* Rabbi Pinhas of Koretz, may his merit protect us, helps bring a man to have fear of heaven. Hearing this, the *rebbe's* son, Rabbi Eleazar, immediately traveled to Koretz to make the acquaintance of Rabbi

> Pinhas. While he was sitting at the table of the holy Rabbi Pinhas, he said again and again, "Father, Father!"* The holy rabbi Pinhas said to him, "Perhaps he's not your father" [Perhaps Rabbi Eleazar is not yet on the high spiritual level to be worthy of being called a son of God]. Rabbi Eleazar did not answer, but when he returned home and told his father, the holy rabbi, Rebbe Reb Elimelech, what had happened, his holy father told him, "You should have answered him, 'Isn't it written, "Ask your father, etc." [Deuteronomy 32:7]? If you call out to Him and ask Him to be your father, He becomes so in truth.'" (*Eser Tzachtzcahot*, p. 28, #52; cf. *Ohel Elimelech*, p. 14, #50; and *Sichot Hayim*, p. 14)

(See the similar story about a hasid of the Kotzker Rebbe in 5:1:18:3:2. It is a hasidic practice to call out to God during prayer, "Sweet Father!" etc. See "Prayer," 5:2:4.)

Rabbi Elimelech says elsewhere that he heard from his own *rebbe*, the Maggid of Mezritch, that:

> A man should call out and cry out to the Holy One, blessed be He, "Father!" until He becomes his father. (*Eser Orot*, p. 28, #21)

> It was a practice of Rabbi David Moshe of Tchortkov, while sitting at his pure table before God, together with his disciples, to call out again and again, "Holy Father!, Holy Master of the World!"[13] (*Eser Orot*, p. 147, #8; cf. *Tiferet Adam*, p. 16)

(See "Sleep and Before Sleep," 29:2 for the full quote of this story.)

Rabbi Elimelech taught his son Rabbi Eleazar this practice of calling out to God, "Father!"[14] He also had a parable to explain it (reported by Rabbi Shmelke of Nikolsburg in his name). In summary, the parable is that a father and son are traveling a long distance in a carriage, and when they pass a forest with sweet fruit growing in it, the child makes his father let him get out and pick them. Although they had a long distance to travel, his father could not get him away from the fruit, because the son was unable to control his desire. The son went farther and farther into the forest. Finally his father told him that:

> he should continuously call out "Father, Father!" and he would answer him, "My son, my son!" As long as he heard his father's answering voice he would know that his father heard him and that he was safe. But if he did not hear his father's answer, he would know that he was lost in the forest, and should run until he found his father again. (*Eser Tzachtzachot*, p. 34, #87; also *Ohel Elimelech*, p. 26, #98. The original source is *Divrei Shmuel* [Nikolsburg], Behukotai.)

The parable teaches about worldly desires in general, but applied specifically to eating, the "sweet fruit" is the food, and going deeper and deeper into the forest until you get lost is sinking into the forgetfulness of bodily pleasure. By calling out to our Father in Heaven, we prevent this from happening.

The meaning of the parable is perhaps clarified from elsewhere, where we are told:

> If you are eating or drinking . . . you should picture someone calling to you, "Why are you sleeping? Arise and call out to your God!" [cf. Jonah 1:6] (Rabbi Moshe Leib of Sassov,[15] *Likkutei Rabbi Moshe Leib*, Likkutei Tehillim, p. 15)

This practice should be considered in its own right, but note the possible relation it has to the son hearing his father's answering voice in the parable. In other words, it may be that in the practice which Rabbi Elimelech taught his son, when you call out to God, "Father!" you are to imagine His answer. The ability to do so is a sign that you have not lost your *d'vekut* while eating. On the other hand, if you cannot "hear" that response, stop eating and do what is necessary to reestablish your *d'vekut*.[16] Regardless of whether or not this understanding is correct, it should not be thought that calling out to God while eating must have this accompaniment.

10:8 REPEAT YOUR STATED INTENTION(S)

It is also a good practice to state your holy intentions for the meal many times while eating. For instance: "I am eating this meal for the sake of heaven," or "I am making myself a chariot for the *Shechinah*."* Compare this to how traditionally on *Shabbat* we say, "I am eating for the honor of *Shabbat*" many times during the meal (see "*Shabbat*," 18:2:4:5:5:1).

10:9 PRAYER

We saw (in 10:1:10) that in preparing for a meal you should pray not to fall into food lust and be coarsened by eating. This kind of prayer can be repeated throughout the meal.

> I found a counsel about how to avoid being coarsened by eating. . . . Between each and every swallow, pray in a whisper, "May God guard me and save me from my *yetzer ha-ra*, so that I will not be coarsened by my eating."* (*Likkutim Hadashim*, p. 3b)

10:10 TORAH

It is an important practice to study some Torah at the table. As it says in *Avot* 3:4 about those who study Torah at the table, it is "as if they had eaten at the table of God, as in the verse that says, 'And he said unto me, This is the table that is before the Lord [Ezekiel 41:22].'"

> **10:10:1** Before you eat, make it a regular practice to learn at least something of Torah, and in a fixed order. (*Derech Hayim*, 5–73)

Presumably, this would be before hand washing and at the table. The thought in putting the Torah first is explained by Rabbi Hayim Yosef David Azulai:

> Torah study is food for the soul and should be given priority over physical food which is sustenance for the body. (*Avodat ha-Kodesh*, Tziporen shamir, beginning of section 5, #59)

It is written of Rabbi Yaakov Yosef of Polnoye, the great disciple of the Besht, that:

> Before eating, he studied seven pages of the Talmud, and even during the meal, between dishes, he did not stop reciting his studies. (*In Praise of the Baal Shem Tov*, #52)

But it is more common to find the suggestion that Torah be studied after the meal, before the Grace after Meals.

> **10:10:2** Set yourself a fixed lesson of Torah learning before the Grace After Meals. This is an important obligation, as can be seen from the holy *Zohar*, parshat Terumah. (Rabbi Yonatan Valliner, Marganita Taba, #41, in *YHvT*, p. 94)

> **10:10:3** When you are eating, think over some *mishnah*; and when you finish eating, say aloud one chapter of *mishnah* before the Grace after Meals. (Rabbi Joseph Karo, Azharot v'Tikkunim v'Sayagim, #12, in *YHvT*, p. 8; cf., #3, p. 101)

10:10:4 It is best to set aside a particular book to learn from at the table during a meal and to go through it in order, from beginning to end—not randomly one time in this part and one time in another part. (Rabbi Yosef Yuzpa, in *Yosef Ometz*, 130, quoted in *Reshit Hochmah* vol. 2, p. 436, n. 248)

10:10:5 We hear of Rabbi Yaakov Yehudah of Nadzrin (the son-in-law of Rabbi Menahem Mendel of Vorki) that:

> During the meal he had many different set study-sessions for himself in different areas of Torah. (*Ha-Tzaddik ha-Shotek*, p. 126)

10:10:6 If you think over words of Torah with each and every chew, then the food you eat will be like a sacrifice, and the water and the wine you drink like a libation poured out on the altar. (Rabbi Moshe Cordovero, Hanhagot Rabbi Moshe Cordovero, #32, in *YHvT*, p. 12)

10:10:7 Aside from the Torah that you should recite at table [as before the Grace after Meals], even while you are chewing the food, your mind should be meditating on words of Torah. (*Reshit Hochmah*, Sh'ar ha-Kedushah, chap. 15, #110)

10:10:8 Let learning of Torah at the table be an obligation to you just like the three daily prayers—*Maariv*, *Shaharit*, and *Minha*—and make it a point to learn a *musar* book then [of ethics and character development]. (Rabbi Alexander Ziskind, *Tzva'a Yekara*, #3)

Rabbi Ziskind also says to learn a book in order, a minimum of one page at a meal, and when you finish one *musar* book, start on the next.

10:10:9 Our rabbis, of blessed memory, say that "He who would be a hasid—let him fulfill the teachings of *Avot*." . . . Before the Grace after Meals recite a chapter of *Avot* each day until you know the whole thing by heart. (*Tzavaat Rabbi Yehudah ben Asher*)

10:10:10 The teachings of *Avot*, chapter 6 are particularly good to say at the table. They speak in praise of the Torah and how to acquire it and advance spiritually. When there is time, it is also possible to say one teaching (*mishnah*) between each bite. The value of this is that according to the dictates of our desire for the food before us, one bite ordinarily follows the other essentially automatically. Pay attention and you will see that this is the case. By saying a teaching aloud after each bite you will see that this continuity can be effectively broken.

> **10:10:11** It is good and appropriate that at each meal you learn something concerning the sacrifices; study the *Shas* [the Mishnah or Talmud], order of *Kodashim*, or any other similar matter. Then your eating will be as if you had offered a sacrifice. (*Derech Hayim*, 3–66)

Rabbi Naftali of Ropshitz had his disciples study a *mishnah* in the first tractate of *Kodashim*: *Zevachim.*

> Rabbi Naftali of Ropshitz instructed his disciples to say the *mishnah* in *Zevachim* (4:6) when eating: "Six matters must be borne in mind when a sacrifice is slaughtered etc." This is done because the table takes the place of the altar, as is known. (*Eser Tzaĉhtzaĉhot*, p. 88, #24)
>
> [The *mishnah*:] Six matters must be borne in mind when a sacrifice is slaughtered: that it is being done as a sacrifice; that it is being done on behalf of this person offering it; that it is being offered to God; that it is being offered as an offering made by fire [into the fires of the altar]; that it is being offered for its scent before God; that it be pleasing before God.[17]

This *mishnah* can be said to remind one that the table is in place of the altar and can also provide material for meditation when its six categories are considered closely. Some brief thoughts about it: In the context of a meal, the "offering made by fire" means that what delights God is the fervor of the one who eats as a divine service; "that it is being offered for its scent" means that one realizes that God's "eating" has nothing to do with physical food, but is something spiritual (the "scent"); and what makes the offering "pleasing" is that the one eating as a service does God's will, both generally and in this service itself. (For more about this, see the teaching of the Maggid of Mezritch, 10:14, p. 259.)

> **10:10:12** Learn Torah during the meal. If you are not able to learn Torah, then say psalms. (*Hanhagot Adam*, Y. L. Lipshitz, p. 16)

The psalms he suggests are: 23; the psalm of the day (see the end of the Morning Prayers); on weekdays, 37; 79 to remember the destruction of the Temple; 67; and 121.

10:11 Rabbi Elimelech of Lizensk had another practice that he recommended for interruptions during a meal.

> When you are experiencing enjoyment from something material . . . like food, accustom yourself to think of how you are ready to give up your life for the sake of God . . . for this is of great benefit on the soul level. And when you are worthy of it, you will feel that the honor of sacrificing yourself for the sanctification of God's name would give you more enjoyment than eating. And even if they take you away to be martyred and thrown into the fire in the middle of the meal, you would enjoy it more. But think this only if it is the truth, otherwise not. (*Darkei Tzedek*, p. 3, #10)

Now this teaching of Rabbi Elimelech's is severe, and there are very few of us who are on such a level that we could, in truth, contemplate such a thing or could prefer martyrdom to the food. But certainly the purpose of this practice, and its intensity, is to burn up the fire of our desire for the food in the flame of holy dedication. So even if you do not use this thought about martyrdom (which had reality in the time of Rabbi Elimelech), you can think while eating that you are ready to interrupt your meal for any other *mitzvah* that should suddenly present itself, and that you would prefer to do that *mitzvah* and serve God, and would get more enjoyment from it than you would from the food. Pause from eating when contemplating this. This repeated internal readiness to jump up and leave the meal will break the force of the desire for the food. An appropriate time for this thought would be when you are raising the food to your mouth, to pause then for a split second and so meditate. Or this could be done right before you swallow the food, as in the story (10:13) about Rabbi Elimelech himself.

There is a story about Rabbi Shlomo of Karlin that is related to the practice of repentance before the meal and also to Rabbi Elimelech's teaching just discussed.

> The holy Rabbi Shlomo of Karlin once passed through the city of Yorivitch where there lived a certain Rabbi Elijah Katz, who was a close disciple of Rabbi Nahum of Tchernobil. When Rabbi Elijah heard that the holy Rabbi Shlomo of Karlin was coming, he went out to meet and welcome him, and he requested him to stay at his house while he was in the city. Rabbi Shlomo acceded to his wish and went home with him. Rabbi Elijah gave him a room of his own,

and Rabbi Shlomo went in, locked the door, and prayed the Evening Service, allowing no one to be with him while he prayed.

This pained Rabbi Elijah, who was accustomed with his own holy *rebbe* to be permitted always to enter into his holy presence whenever he wanted—and here, in his own home, Rabbi Shlomo would not admit him even when he prayed. After finishing his prayers, Rabbi Shlomo asked that his dinner be brought to his room, and when they did so he again shut the door behind him and would not let anyone be in his presence.

This went on for a number of days. Rabbi Elijah, who very much wanted to know what Rabbi Shlomo was doing in his room, had a small hole made in the door, to peek through when the time came. In the evening, when he looked through it, he saw that the food was on the table, and, in the middle of the meal, Rabbi Shlomo was lying prostrate on the floor with his arms and legs outstretched. Afterward, he got up, tasted a little more of the food, and then went to sleep. . . .

A number of weeks later, Rabbi Elijah traveled to Tchernobil to be with his own *rebbe*, Rabbi Nahum, and when his *rebbe* asked him what he had to tell him of Rabbi Shlomo when he was at his house, Rabbi Elijah said that Rabbi Shlomo was a very holy *tzaddik*, and told him what he had seen. Rabbi Nahum answered, "Yes, it is true that Rabbi Shlomo received the secret of falling on the face [*nefillat apayim*] from the Rebbe, his memory for a blessing." [Rabbi Nahum and Rabbi Shlomo were both disciples of the Maggid of Mezritch.] (*Admorei Tchernobil*, p. 80)

Totzaot Hayim says about falling on your face in prayer (*nefillat apayim b'tahanun*) that:

> You should intend that you have died for your sins, and you are as if nullified altogether and departed from this world. Then the cloud of judgment will be removed from over you, since death atones for all sins. (p. 101)

This story about the Karliner relates on the one hand to the repentance and confession before the meal that silences the accusers (see 10:1:5), and also to Rabbi Elimelech's practice of interrupting yourself while eating and meditating on readiness to give up your life for God.

Rabbi Shlomo of Karlin was known for being ready to offer up his life in the service of prayer. He would say his "last" good-bye to his family each time before prayer. From this story we can see that, in the hasidic way, he ate as a devotional service—similar to prayer—and that he was also ready to give up his life in the service of eating; he put his whole self into his devotions. When he did not let his host see him praying or eating, certainly he was prostrating and offering himself up in both divine services.

Even if you do not fully prostrate before or during a meal (hardly a common practice), the "lesser" form of this is to bow slightly to nullify yourself in repentance before God. Or you could put your head down on your hand and arm, resting on the table, as in the *Tahanun* prayer. There are other prayer movements and gestures that are appropriate while eating (see 10:12).

10:12 SWAYING AND OTHER BODILY MOVEMENTS

Just as swaying and other movements are used to help concentration in *davvening*, at least some *rebbes* also use them when eating. In the words of their contemporary, Rabbi Moshe Leib of Sassov:

> The holy Rabbi [Shmelke] of Nikolsburg makes strange movements when praying, and the holy Rabbi Levi Yitzhak of Berditchev even more so when eating. (*Zichron l'Rishonim*, p. 95)

10:13 There is a story about Rabbi Elimelech of Lizensk teaching a disciple, by example, about eating, where the point is that one should not eat with lust for the food, but just to satisfy your hunger so that you can keep yourself alive to serve God. During the meal Rabbi Elimelech made a series of interruptions with self-conversations reflecting on his own motives.

> One of Rabbi Elimelech's hasidim, who was with him, was engaged in the service of God, in Torah study and prayer and Hasidism, but his *rebbe* felt that he had not yet broken his lust for food. So the *rebbe* invited him to eat the morning meal with him. The hasid went to the meal full of joy that he had merited to eat with his holy *rebbe*. The table was set, but all that was on it was the poorest kind of rye bread together with some salt and a knife.
>
> They ritually washed their hands and made the blessing over the bread. But when Rabbi Elimelech took a piece of the bread used for

the blessing into his holy mouth and had almost swallowed it, he began to be overcome with holy bitterness and to speak to himself, saying, "Melech, Melech, look at how you're eating! Look at the low lust you are filled with as you're chewing the bread, until you want to swallow it in one swallow, and already your eyes are big and you're lusting to chew and swallow the whole loaf at once. Your lust is greater than that of an animal!" He said other things of this kind. Then he answered himself and defended himself saying, "No! I'm not eating because of food lust, but just to satisfy my hunger. If I don't eat I won't be able afterwards to study Torah and serve God, blessed be He. I'm only eating to keep myself alive!"

Then he cut himself another small piece of bread, the size of an olive, and put it into his mouth. But when he was just about to finish swallowing it, he again said the same things as before. Then he said "Melech, Melech, who are you fooling and who are you deceiving in saying that your intention in this eating is just to keep yourself alive so that you can serve God, blessed be He? Isn't that all lies and falsehood? How can you deceive yourself by saying such lies in complete self-delusion? Don't your own eyes see that all your limbs and your whole body are full of animal lusts, and that you really want to swallow everything immediately?"

He kept on speaking this way, "How can you dare say that you're eating for the sake of heaven!" And he again answered himself, "No, no! Truthfully, I'm not eating because of lust for the food! But what can I do? For after all, I'm created from clay, and I'm only flesh and blood, so I have to give my body its share. For if not, it won't want, and won't be able, to serve me. I can't live without this bread. The truth is as I'm saying, that I'm not eating for the sake of any lust, but because of the necessity to keep myself alive." Then he put another small piece of bread the size of an olive into his mouth.

Of course, it is understood that when the hasid, the *rebbe's* guest, heard these kinds of words from the holy *rebbe*, his heart broke within him, and it melted until it was like water. For if the *rebbe* had to war like this with his *yetzer*, what was his own lowly situation? And so he sat silent and still as a stone from his great bitterness at his own lowliness, and from the brokenness of his spirit, until he could not move from his place the least bit.

The *rebbe*, seeing that he had received enough "treatment," stopped and said the Grace After Meals. Nevertheless, the hasid fainted due to his bitterness of soul; only after great efforts were they able to revive him. But from then on he became a hasid on a very high spiritual level, who all his days ate just for the sake of heaven, in truth. (*Ohel Elimelech*, p. 73, #173)

Here Rabbi Elimelech spoke aloud for the sake of the hasid. Such a running meditation can be verbalized, and can serve also to interrupt the eating. (Note that the *rebbe* interrupts himself before each swallow.)[18] It is also possible to have a continuous meditation and/or conversation with God silently and mentally (which can be done even while chewing and swallowing) about all the various kinds of thoughts relevant to the service of eating.

Note that in essence Rabbi Elimelech was stating out loud the questions of the "accusers" (10:1:5) and answering them. And this back-and-forth battle was the "time of war" during mealtime that he spoke about in the quote at the beginning of this chapter. Here he was teaching the hasid how to fight that war.[19]

10:14 MEDITATION (MEDITATION DURING EATING AND ON EATING; THE SPIRITUAL SIDE OF THE FOOD AND THE HOLY SPARKS)

In order to explain the subject of eating as a meditation as clearly and fluently as possible, we will leave some of the relevant quotes to a later point in our discussion.

The hasidic view of food and eating is based on the Kabbalah. But an appreciation of its essential aspects does not require a familiarity with the broader kabbalistic framework.

As we said earlier, on the higher levels of spiritual attainment the motive in eating should not be to satisfy our personal need and pleasure. Of course, it is a necessity that we eat, but the consciousness we have connected with eating will determine its spiritual meaning and effect.

One level is that you eat so that your body will be healthy and strong and fit for the service of God. Thus, in many places there is the recommendation that we make it a practice to say before eating: "I am not eating now to give myself pleasure, but so that I will be healthy and strong for the service of God." Another level, more hasidic in intent, understands the pleasure of eating also in relation to God. For it is through meditating on the source of the pleasure that we can come to *d'vekut* with God. This kind of meditation is part of what is called "lifting up the holy sparks in the food."

The Besht said:

> It is an important principle in everything that you do for the sake of heaven that you see that there be some service of God immediately within the act itself. For example, in eating, do not just say that your intention in eating for the sake of heaven is so that you should have energy afterwards to serve God—although that is certainly *also* a good intention. Nevertheless, the essence of spiritual perfection will be when the deed done for the sake of heaven has an immediate connection to the service of God—such as lifting up the holy sparks within the food.[20] (*Keter Shem Tov*, p. 25)
>
> The holy Maggid of Mezritch, his memory for a blessing for the World to Come, said, "Give me credit that in this I was greater than all the other disciples of the Baal Shem Tov, of blessed memory —for I saw that everything that the Baal Shem Tov put into his mouth—food or drink—he lifted up [spiritually]. And I was the only one of his disciples who saw this. (*Emunat Tzaddikim*, p. 7)

Thus, in the more hasidic view, the intention in eating is not only that you should thereby strengthen yourself to do something "religious" like Torah study or prayer at a later time, but in the act of eating itself you are to serve God.

Reshit Hochmah (quoting Rabbeinu Bahai in *Shulchan Aruch Arba*) says that when you eat with holy thoughts, and meditate on the *Shechinah*:

> The eating itself is a bodily matter and a natural action, but it is transformed into an exalted service of the mind . . . And eating this way is accounted as a full service of God as all others, and as a *mitzvah* as all others. (Sh'ar ha-Kedushah, chap. 15, #91)

One important thing to know about eating from this hasidic perspective is that food, like every other thing in the world, gets its existence from the life, the vitality, that God puts into it. This aspect of the food is the "holy spark" that gives a thing existence and "life" (vitality on whatever level, such that even inanimate things are included). If God withdrew His will from this or that thing for even a moment, it would immediately cease to exist. It is this holy spark, which is a spark of the *Shechinah*, that gives each thing, not only its existence, but also all its attributes and qualities. So too with food. All its qualities—its appearance, its pleasurable taste, etc.—come from the holy spark within it.

The main thing to understand about this "spark" is that it means the spiritual side of the thing (here, the food), as opposed to its material side and existence. Thus, the way to eat with God-consciousness is by relating to the spiritual side of the food. This can be done in a number of ways. Some aspects of this were spoken about earlier when we discussed the thought behind the blessings over the food. The basic ideas there were, first, our recognition that God created this food with His word, and second, that being aware that life and pleasure are coming to us from the food as we eat it, we perceive that this is coming to us from God.

During a meal, when you are hungry and therefore weakened, if you attend to what is happening to you as you eat, you will see that you are being enlivened, feeling better and stronger, and you feel enjoyment from the taste of the food. When this happens, as you chew or drink you can turn your attention to God who is the source of this good coming to you—and think, moreover, how He is doing this because of His love for you, for you are His son or daughter.

This realization that our life and existence is not within our own control, that it comes to us from outside, is very clear in the act of eating, where food, which is necessary for our continued life, is seen as coming to us from outside. What is important here is to recognize what this means. As the Torah says, "Not by bread alone does a man live, but by every word that proceeds out of the mouth of the Lord" (Deuteronomy 8:3).

The only other such dependence on external things for our life is our dependence on the air we breathe—and each of these, eating and breathing, is worthy of a meditation on the fact that God is the source of our life. Hasidism concentrates on the former; but as for the latter, the Torah says that God, when He created Adam, "breathed into his nostrils the breath of life" (Genesis 2:7). God does so for each of us now too. And as the rabbis say:

> You should praise God with each and every breath that you take. (*Bereshit Rabba*, 14, end)

This then can also be the basis for a meditation similar to the meditation on eating. This very comparison and practice is suggested in the hasidic book *Or ha-Ganuz l'Tzaddikim*:

> It is appropriate when you eat to praise God on every swallow of food (and certainly at least when a new dish is brought out) . . . and

> to say, "Blessed is the Merciful One, King of the Universe, Lord of this food" or on drink, "Lord of this drink." And our Sages said, "'Let every soul [*neshamah*] praise God' (Psalm 150:6)—this means praise Him with every breath [*neshimah*]." So you can say at all times, "Blessed is the Merciful One, King of the Universe, Lord of this time" or "of this moment*" [why not "of this breath?"].

Similarly, *Reshit Hochmah* says (quoting Rabbeinu Bahai):

> When you eat, you should clear your mind of all else and meditate on the Holy One, blessed be He . . . with each and every swallow, as is written about the seventy elders on Mount Sinai that "They saw God while they ate and drank." And this is similar to what our Sages said on the verse, "Let every soul praise God" (Psalm 150:6)—with each and every breath give Him praise. (Sh'ar ha-Kedushah, chap. 15, #90)

To return to eating (about which we said that life comes to you from outside, through the food, from God)—as you chew the food or drink, turn your attention to God as described, and resolve, in recognition and gratitude, that you will return the energy and life that you feel coursing into you, and which He is giving you through the food, in His service. And you will return the love and the pleasure He is giving to you, by loving Him and seeking to give Him pleasure and satisfaction. You can close your eyes and, looking at Him with your inner eye, promise Him this mentally.

All pleasure, according to the Kabbalah and Hasidism, is one, but it can be experienced on lower or higher levels. Thus, rather than experience the taste and goodness of the physical food, you are to enjoy the radiance of the *Shechinah*. It is taught that when we eat we should think that the taste of the food is the holy spark within it (for it is the holy spark of the *Shechinah* that gives a thing all its characteristics and qualities. The taste of the food, therefore, "is" the spark). Although this thought is not necessary for the meditation described above, its purpose is to make the link between the taste and God (as its source), and to absorb the physical sensation in the larger awareness of the spiritual reality.

Before you make the blessing you should think, "When I eat, I will experience pleasure in the taste of the food—and this taste comes from the radiance of the *Shechinah* and from God." If you think of this beforehand (shortly before the blessing, in the preparation for the meal), it will help you to ward off food lust. And you should repeat this same thought during the course of the meal.

Realizing that the taste and pleasure and life from the food is coming to us from God leads us to direct our love to Him even as we eat. Rabbi Tzvi Hirsh of Ziditchov said that:

> The root of the *kavvanah* in eating is to prepare yourself to receive love from Him who delights in kindness; for this is the will of the Master of kindness. (*Yifrach biYamav Tzaddik*, p. 45b)

Moreover, you should recognize that this good is coming to you from God because of His love for you, and because you are His son or daughter. So accompany the thought of your returning the love with the consciousness that He is your own Father in Heaven, whom you want to please and give satisfaction to. (This meditation can, if desired, be joined with the practice of calling out "Father, Father!"—which can be done mentally also. See 10:7.)

While eating, you can close your eyes, turn your mental gaze to Him, and look at the face of God while you meditate on thoughts of receiving from Him and giving back, all in love. You can also intend (and fulfill) that some of the energy you are receiving from the food, you will return now, in fervent Torah study and other spiritual practices at the table, and in saying the Grace After Meals at the table (see the quote from the Besht in "*Shabbat*," 18:2:4:5:5:4). Referring to what was suggested earlier about Torah during the meal, it is possible to use this food meditation while chewing with eyes closed, and in between swallows to recite words of Torah. For example, utter one saying of *Avot* 6 each time, reading from a book before you on the table.

The pleasure of the food is merely a small channel to achieve the higher spiritual joy of *d'vekut*. For as the Torah says, "There is joy in His place." (1 Chronicles 16:27)

Yesod v'Shoresh ha-Avodah writes that after meditating on how the taste of the food comes from the holy spark, you should think to yourself:

> If from the one little holy spark from the Upper World which is in this food, there comes to me such pleasure, how much more pleasure is there in the Upper World itself, which is of the nature of pleasure? Why should I attach myself to the minute pleasure of this one holy spark, rather should I cleave to the holy Upper World itself. (Condensed from two parallel sections in Gate 7, chaps. 2 and 3)

Rabbi Elimelech of Lizensk, speaking of the way the *tzaddik* eats, puts it this way:

> If he ate something that tasted good, he would think, "This food is created. Who then put this good taste in it? Is it not the Creator, blessed be He? And if this food is so pleasurable, is it not certain that all pleasure, but in an unlimited measure, is in the Creator?" (*Noam Elimelech*, Beshallach, p. 34a)

The pleasure of the food is an entrance and an opening into the world of God's light.

> Is not all the body like a small hole that opens to the Divine life-energy which hovers over us, whose greatness and value is unlimited? And they [the worldly] exchange this great light for an insignificant enjoyment for their worthless body. (*L'Yesharim Tehillah*, p. 119, #9)

It is like a person sitting in a very dark room. He sees a small beam of light entering through the crack under the door. If he is foolish he enjoys the little he can see of his surroundings with the help of that little light. But if he is intelligent, he uses that small beam of light to find the door, open it, and go out into the bright world of day.

Or, it is like a person who receives a gift from someone whom he loves and who loves him. The gift pleases him, but its deeper purpose is to re-awaken the love of the relationship. The true joy is when he turns his mind to that love and embraces the one who gave him the gift.

So should that be our attitude to the enjoyment of eating and the pleasure that comes from the food. Although you enjoy the taste of the food, you are to derive even greater joy from the knowledge of who is giving it to you—your Father in Heaven. Then, who the gift is from is more important than the gift itself.

We are to use the pleasure of the food and the natural happiness that comes from eating to rise into God awareness. "This pleasure of the food is coming to me from my own Father in Heaven who loves me. 'Father, I know that sitting here at the table I am in Your presence!'"

(See on pp. 265–266 stories of how the hasidic *rebbes* would enter into states of great *d'vekut* during the meal, stripping themselves of all materiality and ascending altogether into the Upper World, the world of spirituality.)

Every religious person can know from his own experience the meaning of the metaphor that during lustful eating your soul "sinks down" into the food, into materiality. But the spiritual service of eating is that you should, rather, reverse this and "lift up" the material food to spirituality. Man, of course, has a body and a soul; so too does the food. There is its material aspect, and also its spiritual aspect, the holy spark within it. When you eat in a holy way you "raise up" that spark by asserting the spirituality of the food—that food becomes part of the spiritual world and reality through your action and eating.

On the one hand, you lift the food to spirituality by recognizing its source; on the other hand, whenever you use the energy and life-force of the food for serving God, whether during or after the meal, you are also raising up that energy, that aspect of the holy spark, through turning it to a spiritual purpose.[21]

As we saw, the Besht said that there should be service of God during the meal itself, such as "lifting up the holy sparks within the food." Through interruptions, meditations during the meal, and so on, the meal is spiritualized and made holy. As we have seen, these meditations can be varied: it can be a running conversation with God, a meditation on Torah, looking at God, who is the source of the goodness coming to you through the food, or the more kabbalistic "lifting up of the sparks." (We will not discuss this latter concept in detail as it requires as background the whole kabbalistic viewpoint.) While you are eating, your mind is to be completely engaged in holiness. When you eat like this, all your eating is like a sacrifice before God.

> One day three *tzaddikim* came together at the house of the holy *maggid*, Rabbi Israel of Koznitz—the Holy Jew of Pshischa, the Rebbe Reb Fishel of Strikov, and the Rebbe Reb David of Lelov. The Maggid received them all warmly and joyfully, and gave order to set the table, whereupon he sat down for a meal with the three *tzaddikim*. He sat the Holy Jew down together with himself at the head of the table, and put the Rebbe Reb Fishel and the Rebbe Reb David'l at the sides of the table to the right and left.
>
> Now the holy Maggid was sitting and talking with the Holy Jew in the most intimate way from mouth to ear. The Rebbe Reb Fishel very much wanted to listen to what they were saying, so he bent over to pick up their conversation. Meanwhile, the Rebbe Reb David'l was occupied in eating his bread and butter.
>
> The Maggid then turned to the Rebbe Reb Fishel, and pointing to the Rebbe Reb David'l, said to him, "Why don't you learn from this young man who knows what to do? He eats one piece of bread spread with butter and offers a sacrifice in eating it. . . . He eats

another piece of buttered bread—another sacrifice." (*P'ri Kodesh Hillulim*, p. 18)

When they eat, the *tzaddikim* are absorbed in God-consciousness, either through their minds being engrossed in Torah thoughts or through an eating-meditation where they look at the beauty of God and enjoy the radiance of the *Shechinah*.

It is told of Rabbi Arye Leib Lipshitz of Vishnitz, that:

> He never ate except at a *mitzvah* meal [such as a Sabbath meal or a feast celebrating a *bris*]. Once, the holy rabbi, our teacher Rabbi Meir, the son of the *tzaddik* Rabbi Eleazar of Dzikov, the memory of a *tzaddik* for a blessing, came to him and stayed with him for *Shabbat*. When he returned home and came before his father, he asked him what he saw when he was with the holy *gaon*. His son told him, "Father, I saw that he didn't eat his soup with a spoon but with a fork, due to his *d'vekut*. His *d'vekut* was so intense that he didn't notice it and wasn't aware of it at all." (*Dor Deah*, vol. 1, Rabbi Moshe Teitelbaum of Ohel, end)

A similar story is told about Rabbi Leibele Eiger of Lublin:

> Once, at the third meal on *Shabbat*, when he made the *Motzi* [the blessing on the bread], he cut his finger. And because of his great fervor and *d'vekut* he did not feel it. So the blood was flowing until others at the table saw it [and came to his aid]. (*Gan Hadasim*, p. 21)

This is similar to the story above (10:4:7) about Rabbi Yitzhak of Drobitch being so immersed in God-consciousness during a meal that he did not realize the large amount of bread he was eating—as the female innkeeper kept bringing him more and more.

A hasidic story tells how Rabbi Abraham Joshua Heshel, the Apter Rebbe, ate a tremendous amount of food at a *Shabbat* meal:

> Then he made an awesome-sounding groan, and stripping off the materiality from his soul as if it were a garment, elevated himself completely into the pure spiritual realm. (*Raza d'Uvda*, Sh'ar ha-otiyot, p. 26, #4)

Our goal in eating, then, should be to reach the exalted state of the stripping off of physicality, just as in prayer (see "Prayer," 5:3:15).

Sometimes the *rebbes* would also make soul-ascents (*aliyot neshamah*) to the Upper Worlds[22] when at the table, as was probably the case in this story about the Apter Rebbe.

Not uncommonly, hasidic *rebbes* would go into states of intense *d'vekut* for long periods of time while at the Sabbath table with their hasidim. About Rabbi Hayim of Tzanz it was told:

> Once, on the evening of the holy Sabbath, the dessert was brought to the table, but the *rebbe*, as was his custom, was immersed deeply in *d'vekut*. This time it continued for a number of hours through the night, and by the time he came back to normal consciousness the day had already dawned. The *rebbe* then called out, "The sun has come up, but for the honor of the holy Sabbath we'll rely on the opinion of the holy Belzer Rebbe that it's still considered night [and we are permitted to finish the meal]!" (*Rabbeinu ha-Kodesh mi-Tzanz*, p. 80)

A similar story is told about Rabbi Nachman of Bratzlav:

> Once, on the evening of the holy *Shabbat*, Rabbi Nachman washed his hands before the meal and made the blessing over the bread; so too did all those who were at his table. Then they all ate the piece of bread they had made the blessing over. But as soon as Rabbi Nachman ate his *Motzi*, his mind ascended to where it ascended, and he cleaved to God, blessed be He, with great *d'vekut*. With tremendous awe he sat there silently, with his eyes open, in a powerful and wondrous *d'vekut* the whole night. No one else at the table dared to put out a hand to take any of the food that was on the table, for they were completely astonished at his state, and were afraid that they would disturb him. Finally, dawn came and the first rays of the sun appeared; then they all said the Grace after Meals, left the table [without eating more than the one bite of bread] and went home. (*Shivhei Moharan*, p. 7)

> Once when Rabbi Naftali of Ropshitz was with his master, the Rebbe Reb Elimelech of Lizensk, during the third *Shabbat* meal, he realized that Rebbe Elimelech was so high in *d'vekut* that he was close to removing his soul from his body altogether and, God forbid, leaving this world. So he quickly began to pound on the table to disturb him and bring him down. [When the *rebbe* complained to him and asked him how he dared to disturb his *d'vekut*, the Ropshitzer explained to his holy master, satisfactorily we are told, that he was still needed in the world.] (*Ohel Naftali*, p. 45, #125)

These hasidic rebbes so burned with love of God that they would think of Him at all times and at every moment, even while eating. Remember the words of the Rambam (Chapter 1, p. 5) about how we should love God: he compared it to "one who is love-sick and cannot take his mind off the woman he loves, but always thinks of her—when lying down or rising up, when eating or drinking."

There are two sides to a meal, one relating to the body, the material side, and one relating to the soul, the spiritual side. What the body gets from the meal is the physical food itself, but what the soul enjoys are the spiritual elements of the meal. There are a number of aspects to this, but in the larger sense, the soul derives joy when the meal itself becomes, through the service of God connected with it, a *mitzvah meal.*

Thus, *Reshit Hochmah* interprets:

> "A *tzaddik* eats for the satisfaction of his soul" (Proverbs 13:25)—when he eats and his intention is that the meal become a *mitzvah*, so that his soul will derive satisfaction from the *mitzvah.* (Sh'ar ha-Kedushah, chap. 15, #63)

How does a meal become a *mitzvah meal*? It is made so through all the spiritual practices associated with the meal: repentance and confession, *tzedaka*, the blessings, Torah, meditation, and so on. But aside from these added spiritual practices, it is made a *mitzvah meal* by the spiritual nature of the actual eating. Particularly with regard to the physical act of eating, the soul derives pleasure from the spiritual aspects of the food.

First, kosher food has a spirit of holiness that rests on it, and this holiness pleases the soul.

> When someone eats for the sake of heaven . . . and from those things that the Torah permits, and on which rests a spirit from the side of holiness and purity, the soul gets enjoyment from that eating, from its aspect of holiness. (*Reshit Hochmah*, Sh'ar ha-Kedushah, chap. 15, #2)

Second, there is the spiritual aspect of the food in regard to its holy spark or "soul," whereby its existence and qualities come directly from God. When you meditate on this while eating, your soul finds its enjoyment.

> Every piece of food has a body and a soul. The physically observable food is its body, the holy life-force from Above that gives it its being and qualities . . . its soul. When a person eats it, then . . . his soul derives enjoyment and sustenance from the soul of the food, and his body from the body of the food.[23] (*Kitzur Shnei

> *Luchot ha-Brit*, Sh'ar ha-Otiyot, ha-Kedushah, p. 41, quoting the Arizal)

There is a beautiful story about the Baal Shem Tov which casts light on our subject. In the story (given in full in the "*Shabbat*," 18:2:4:5:8:2) the Besht happened to come upon a hasid who, in his home, was dancing and singing in ecstatic joy at his prepared Sabbath table before eating. When he was finished, and was asked by the Besht for the meaning of his custom, he explained that he does this

> so that first he delights in the spiritual aspect of the food, the holy vitality and life within it, and only afterward does he eat [the physical food]. (*Kol Sippurei Baal Shem Tov*, vol. 4, p. 170)

From an interpretation this hasid gives, in the story, on a verse in the Grace after Meals, we can see that his main thought was the awareness that the food is indeed from the hand of God. What this hasid did was a preparation for eating, carried out standing at the table before sitting down to eat (see 10:1:14). But in his holy joy he began dancing, and singing too. From his meditation in preparation we see how for him the real meal was the spiritual one, the physical one an afterthought. In this story the hasid enjoyed the food first through contemplation alone, and what his eyes saw.

It was said of Rabbi Yehiel Michal of Zlotchov that:

> Though his meal every day was like that of a king, the pleasure he derived from it was only from what his eyes took in. (*N'tiv Mitzvotecha*, Hakdama)

How could this be? The answer is that his "eyes" were on the spiritual side of the food, and through it he was looking at God. (See also 10:20:7.)

There are other possible directions for this kind of eating meditation we have been discussing. The meditation can be personalized, so to speak, by thinking as you eat, either of how God is feeding you, or of how you are feeding Him.

The meditation described above, that is, focusing as you eat on how the life-energy, as well as the taste of the food, is coming to you from God, can be put in the more personal context of "being fed" by God. Close your eyes and imagine that it is God Himself who is feeding you. The other practice about "feeding God" can be understood as follows: the sacrifices in the Temple (God's "house") were taken to be His "food"—meals provided for Him by His devoted servants (the priests). Of course,

God does not eat; but what was offered to the altar in the fire, or eaten by the priests, was taken to be as if God Himself were eating. So if a person is, like the priests were, truly dedicated to God, and if he is eating not for his own bodily enjoyment but for the sake of heaven, then, like with the priests, it is considered a sacrifice and as if God Himself were eating.

> The purpose of the creation of man, who is made in the image and likeness of God, is to see that the creature becomes like its Creator, so to speak. You should be like Him in all your ways, as it says, "You are gods" [Psalm 82:6]. And so your eating should be according to the secret of the sacrifices, and you should be sanctified in all your eating. The principle is that when a man is a *tzaddik* and eats only what the Torah permits, then his eating takes the place of a sacrifice. For a *tzaddik* indeed makes the creature like the Creator, so to speak, and therefore his eating is sanctified just like the "eating" of the altar [whose fire "eats" the food]; he eats only for the sake of his soul [which is a part of God], so that it will remain in his body and he will be able to serve God.[24] (*Shnei Luchot ha-Brit*, quoted in *Kedushat ha-Shulchan*, p. 30)

> The goal of mankind is to become similar to the Most High [that our eating be purely spiritual like His]. . . . When a man sanctifies himself in his eating and drinking, then, his food is in accord with the secret of the sacrifice and his drink is in accord with the secret of the wine libation on the altar. With the Holy One, blessed be He, His "eating" and "drinking" are mentioned in relation to the secret of the sacrifice. . . . The secret of eating is the spiritual arousal during the meal of men who serve God, which rises from below to Above, as a pleasing scent before God. [It is then that our eating becomes His eating.] (*Shnei Luchot ha-Brit*, quoted in *Kedushat ha-Shulchan*, p. 29)

The pleasure that God derives from the food or the eating is not physical. His pleasure comes from the service that is offered to Him in the eating, and the holy way it is done. As Rashi (on Leviticus 1:9) explains the meaning of how the sacrifice is a "sweet scent" to God: God says—"It is satisfying to Me that I have told you what to do, and you have done it according to My will [more literally: that I spoke and My will was done]."

The Maggid of Mezritch:

> What gives God pleasure is that a man intends to give Him, blessed be He, pleasure by his actions, and acts with fervor. The main thing is the man's desire to do His will, and not what the particular action

> is. The pleasure He gets from the doing of the *mitzvah* [His "food," so to speak, and the essence of His "eating"] is from the fire of the person's fervor, as it says, "An offering made by fire for a sweet scent before God" [Leviticus 1:9]. And our rabbis interpreted this "sweet scent" to mean that God's pleasure came from: "I spoke and My will was done." But the fervor itself is without a vessel and has to be clothed in the doing of actual deeds. (*Maggid Devarav l'Yaakov*, #97, p. 169)

(Note that this teaching is not applied particularly to eating, but that is nevertheless a very natural and appropriate application as can be seen from the previous quote, and since eating is compared to the sacrifice and the table to the altar.)

> While eating, intend the secret of "an offering made by fire, for a sweet scent before God." (*Hanhagot Adam*, Y. L. Lipshitz, p. 15; cf. *Reshit Hochmah*, Sh'ar ha-Kedushah, chap. 15, #96)

Another insight into the meaning of eating as a sacrifice comes from Rabbi Tzadok ha-Cohen of Lublin:

> A clear spiritual perception of the meaning of eating comes from the power of a man's better side, his soul, which is a part of God. When that side dominates during eating, then the enjoyment of your soul during the meal is nothing less than the pleasure above [God's pleasure] from a sacrifice—because the part is equivalent to the whole. (*P'ri Tzaddik* quoted in *Menorat Zahav*, p. 33)

So when you eat with a full awareness of the spiritual meaning of eating, that God in His love and humility is "serving" you and feeding you, giving you life and pleasure, you can go from being the receiver to being the giver. You can serve Him with everything you do during the meal. When you do this, and eat in holiness, it is as if you were "feeding" God.

As the rabbis say about the people of Israel's service of God: "Israel is providing food for their Father in Heaven." Usually the father provides for the son, but sometimes this is reversed and the son provides for his father (usually when he is older). "Feeding God," then, reflects how God allows Himself to be the one receiving rather than the giver.[25] Thus, you can make it a practice during the meal to picture yourself feeding God by your holy service as you eat. (See the story about Rabbi David of Lelov eating as a sacrifice [p. 264], and about the *mishnah* Rabbi Naftali of

Ropshitz would say to call to mind the idea of the sacrifice while eating [10:10:11].)

10:15 HAND WASHING AFTER EATING

Before the Grace after Meals we clean our fingers and lips with water (*Shulchan Aruch*, chap. 44) so as not to say words of prayer with an unclean film of food on us. The kabbalists say that this water, once washed off, is an "offering" to the Other Side.

> After a person has eaten and enjoyed himself, he should give this remnant of a portion to the Other Side.
>
> [Since the Shell should get nothing from the food itself which is holy,] and so that it will not make accusations, it was ordained that it [the Other Side] be given this after-eating water as its portion. (*Zohar*, quoted in *Reshit Hochmah*, Sh'ar ha-Kedushah, chap. 15, #49)

How can we translate this kabbalistic explanation into more understandable modern terminology? Probably the point is that doubt about one's motive in eating will always remain on some level, and it is best to recognize that doubt in order to put it to rest. But the "recognition" given to the power of our lower side is one of contempt: the minute and filthy remains that we wash off.

10:16 A REMINDER OF THE DESTRUCTION OF THE TEMPLE

The happy state of mind usually produced by eating should be tempered by our awareness of the unredeemed state of the world.

10:16:1 Before the Grace after Meals on weekdays we say Psalm 137, which serves to remind us of the destruction of the Temple, may it be rebuilt speedily in our days.

> **10:16:2** The *Zohar* (II, 157) says: Someone who enjoys himself at a meal should remember with concern the desecrated sanctity of the Holy Land, and the King's Palace, which is in ruins. And for this sadness that he feels at his table, the Holy One, blessed be He, ac-

> counts it as if he had actually rebuilt His House and restored all the ruins of the Holy Temple. Happy is his lot. (*Sefer Haredim*, chap. 35, #3)

10:10:3 It is good to preface this Psalm (137) with a stated intention, that: "I am now going to call to mind our Holy Temple, which is in ruins."

> **10:16:4** Everyone with sense can understand that you certainly do not fulfill your obligation by saying the Psalm [137] with your mouth and lips alone, while your heart is elsewhere. The main thing is that you should bring your heart and mind to feel grief at the destruction of the Temple. (*Yesod v'Shoresh ha-Avodah*, Gate 7, chap. 6, p. 142)

10:16:5 When a hasid of Rabbi Eleazar Zev, the Kretchnifer Rebbe, ate at the home of the very wealthy Rabbi Yitzhak Reich, he reported that:

> His table was like a king's table, with the best food and dishes and silverware; there were even musicians playing during the meal to add to its pleasure. . . . And before the Grace after Meals they played a melody for the psalm "By the rivers of Babylon." [Psalm 137] Rabbi Yitzhak himself had a small drum that he tapped on as part of the accompaniment. And while he sang, streams of tears flowed down his face, all the way to the lapels of his coat—as he mourned the destruction of our Holy Temple. And all this after a king's meal, at which it seemed that he had enjoyed all the delicacies that could be had, like one of the great nobles. (*Raza d'Uvda*, Sh'ar ha-otiyot, p. 27, #8)

10:17 THE GRACE AFTER MEALS

The Grace after Meals is very beautiful and also important, its length being a good indication of that. It is altogether worthy of the fullest concentration and attention.

> It is well known how our master, Rabbi Dov Ber [the Maggid of Mezritch], may his merit protect us, taught the importance of having full intention when saying the Grace after Meals, even more so than during the daily prayer services. (*Hanhagot Tzaddikim* [III], vol. 2, p. 748)

The tradition takes the feeling of satisfaction after a meal and, connecting it with God, turns it into thankfulness. Thus, the natural feeling is lifted up into the realm of spirituality. (See also 10:20:2 and 10:20:8.) This happiness, now religious and spiritual, can be lifted up even further and carried into singing (see 10:18).

> **10:17:1** Be careful with the washing of hands after meals, and do not make any interruption between it and the Grace after Meals, which you should say in a loud voice. (Rabbi David ha-Levi of Steppin, *Hanhagot Tzaddikim*, p. 56, #17)

> **10:17:2** Before you say the Grace after Meals, have the *kavvanah* that God has been very kind to you in having given you this food to enliven you, and through this you will come to a joyful state of mind and to love of God. (*Derech Hayim*, 6–18)

10:17:3 While saying the Grace after Meals it is good to sway sometimes, as when *davvening*, as this helps greatly in attaining *kavvanah.*

> **10:17:4** Have great *kavvanah* when you say the Grace after Meals . . . and place your hands, right on top of left, over your chest as you say it. (*Hanhagot Adam*, Y. L. Lipshitz, p. 16)

10:17:5 You can also add words of your own after the Grace after Meals, in English.

> [Rabbi Nachman of Bratzlav] once told how, when he was a boy, after his meals, he would give praise and thanks to God in Yiddish, and he was not satisfied with just the Grace after Meals. But he offered his own praise and thanks to God in Yiddish for every food that was given to him that day, for example, if they first gave him a little liquor and a piece of honeycake, and afterwards some radish before the meal, etc. Thus, he gave thanks for each and every thing he was given to eat in the various courses of the meal. (*Shivhei Moharan*, p. 6, #8)

(See "Blessings," 20:13 about this practice.)

> **10:18** There are some who sing religious songs and hymns after the meal; and this is a good custom. (*Reshit Hochmah*, Sh'ar ha-Kedushah, chap. 15, #109)

Of course, on *Shabbat*, singing of *zemirot* at the table is the common practice.

10:19 Rabbi Elimelech of Lizensk says that:

> [Part of the *kavvanah* while eating is] to accept on yourself that after the meal, as soon as you feel that you have to go to the bathroom, you won't delay and leave the waste inside you to make your mind and heart unclean, God forbid, for even a minute. (*Tzetl Katan*, #15)

It would seem that a good time to remind yourself of this would be following the Grace after Meals.

10:20 With the above as a background and explanation, we can quote here some representative sayings and teachings about eating and the holy meal. Although they are not all completely understandable without a knowledge of the kabbalistic framework, the essential points will come through.

10:20:1 The Baal Shem Tov:

> When you eat and drink you should set your mind to be strong for the service of God while eating. And you must, to that end, strengthen the spiritual pleasure you have in eating until it is greater than the physical enjoyment. As a result of this you will derive more spiritual energy from the food. (*Keter Shem Tov*, p. 67)

10:20:2 The Baal Shem Tov:

> A person benefits from the life-energy in every piece of food that he eats. But when he eats, even from bodily necessity, and afterward serves God with the life-energy his body received, he thereby fixes and repairs the sparks [in the food]. (*Keter Shem Tov*, p. 48)

A parallel quote elsewhere makes this somewhat clearer:

> Since a person is strengthened to serve God from the energy in the food he eats, and afterward he does serve God with the life-energy that was in the food, there is an elevation for [that life-energy]. (*Derech Emunah u'Maaseh Rav*, p. 63)

> By eating the food, the holy sparks in it enter within him and by means of this energy he says the Grace after Meals, and says Torah at the table—and thereby elevates those sparks. . . . When a person eats, this brings him to a happy state of mind, and with that happiness he says words of Torah and serves God. (Rabbi Israel of Koznitz, *Avodat Yisrael*, Likkutim, p. 12, on Avot 3:4)

10:20:3 When you make the blessing over the food, particularly when you say God's name, you can tune in to the spiritual side of the food. The

Ari Hakodesh says that this spark of the food, its spiritual side, is what provides the food for the soul (while the physical side of the food provides nourishment for the body).

The Baal Shem Tov:

> When a man takes a fruit or other piece of food and makes a blessing over it with focused attention, and says, "Blessed are You, O Lord," and mentions the Name of God [Lord/*Adonai*], he, at that moment, arouses the life-energy that created the fruit and resides within it . . . and this life-energy is the food of the soul . . . for the soul is nourished by the spiritual side of the food. (*Keter Shem Tov*, p. 43; cf. p. 100)
>
> [Making the blessing with *kavvanah*] causes the holiness of God's name to rest on the bread and draws the life energy of the bread close to the source from whence it was taken. (*DhTvhY*, Seudah, p. 30b)
>
> **10:20:4** You should accustom yourself when you sit down to eat, or when you take in your hand something to drink, to think that within this food or drink there are spiritual holy sparks, and it is from them that the pleasurable taste and the enjoyment of the food and drink comes. And certainly, when you think about this before eating and drinking, you will not be coarsened by the pleasure (which is from the holy sparks) that you experience when you are eating and drinking. (*Kedushat ha-Shulchan*, p. 25)
>
> When you eat and drink you will certainly experience enjoyment and pleasure from the food and drink. So you should be careful to arouse yourself every moment to ask yourself in wonder, "What is this enjoyment and pleasure, and where is it coming from?" And answer yourself, "This is nothing but the holy sparks from the Upper holy worlds that are within the food and drink." (*Kedushat ha-Shulchan*, p. 24)
>
> **10:20:5** Concerning the blessings of enjoyment (over food, etc.)—at first sight one would have thought that we are to get enjoyment only from spiritual things and not from the things of this world. As the rabbis say: "During a meal, when you see that you are starting to indulge your food lust, draw back your hand from it." But yet we see that the rabbis ordained that we make blessings for enjoyment over material things like food, such as "Blessed are You . . . who creates many living things and their needs etc."
>
> The resolution of this seeming problem is that certainly we are permitted to get a spiritual pleasure, but not a physical sense pleasure.

And, regarding the pleasure and enjoyment we derive from food, the Besht said that this is from the World of Pleasure. His meaning is that the pleasure in the Upper [spiritual] World is from the radiance of the *Shechinah*; as the rabbis said, "In the future world the *tzaddikim* will sit with their crowns on their heads and enjoy the radiance of the *Shechinah*." . . . And so the taste in the food and the pleasure within it is from the pleasure of the radiance of the *Shechinah*, which is enclothed in this lower world in the taste of the food. This is the matter of raising up the holy sparks. . . . When you make blessings of enjoyment you should arouse that higher pleasure and the light of the radiance of the *Shechinah*, which is in that food. This is what is said, "Taste and see that the Lord is good" (Psalms 35)—which means that the goodness and pleasure in every thing is from God. . . . The life-energy and the spiritual aspect is contracted within that fruit. But when you make the blessing of enjoyment over it, you can raise it up from the state of contraction to that of love. For through the life-energy that comes to you from the food you can cling to God. . . . And this food which you eat gives you the strength and energy to say holy words of Torah and prayer. The holy people say that it is like a bee that transforms the food it eats into honey. So can a person lift up the food from a physical pleasure to an experience of the light of the radiance of the *Shechinah* and a spiritual pleasure. (*Or ha-Ganuz l'Tzaddikim*, p. 83)

10:20:6 The Baal Shem Tov:

When you eat, your thought should be that the taste and the sweetness of the food you are eating are coming from God's enlivening power and from the Supernal sweetness which is the life of the food. (*Tzavaat ha-Ribash*, p. 14)

When you are eating or drinking something, have it in your mind that the taste you feel in your mouth when you are chewing or swallowing is the innermost holiness of the food, the holy spark that is in the food or drink. (*DhTvhY*, Seudah, p. 27b)

When you eat something pleasurable, you should think that all of the pleasure is coming to you from God. (*Darkei Tzedek*, p. 6, #36)

If you eat something from which you derive pleasure, have in your mind that with this pleasure you are enjoying the radiance of the *Shechinah*. (*Or ha-Ganuz l'Tzaddikim*, p. 34)

10:20:7 Rabbi Abraham Yaakov of Sadigura said:

You should . . . believe with complete faith that God, blessed be He, gives life and existence to every thing that is, and that in every thing there is found some of God's enlivening power to enliven it and give it its existence and cause it to flourish. When you think about this while you eat, and join yourself with that life and that spark within the food, you are not benefiting from *this* world one bit. As with Rabbi Judah the Prince, who, although his table was always blessed with the very best food at all times, yet said, "I have not derived the least enjoyment from this world." [*Ketubot* 104a] And as it says about the seventy elders who ate on Mount Sinai, "They saw God, and they ate and drank." [Exodus 24:11] Because, I tell you, through their eating and drinking they attached themselves to God, and were looking at the beauty of God. [Psalm 27:4] (*Beit Yisrael*, p. 76)

10:20:8 Rabbi Abraham of Slonim said:

Contrary to what one might think, it is possible sometimes to come closer to God when you are involved in material things like eating and drinking, than when you are involved with "religious" activities like Torah and prayer. Because when the heart opens up due to the sense pleasure, and there is a feeling of satisfaction and happiness, then is the fit time to come close to holiness. (*Torat Avot*, p. 195)

As Rabbi Abraham explains elsewhere in *Torat Avot* (p. 264), the thought is that this lower sense delight should be used to turn yourself to holy things. Use it as an opening to the much greater splendor of delight that comes from the realm of holiness.

10:20:9 Rabbi Mendel of Ber taught how our purpose in eating should be to lift up the holy sparks. Now his personal attendant heard this and he began to eat large quantities of food. When Rabbi Mendel asked him why he was eating so much, he said, "I heard from you that by eating we separate out the holy sparks." But Rabbi Mendel said, "Let me tell you a parable. It is like a man who is drowning in the river. If another man comes to rescue him and pull him out, he has to grab him by something delicate, like his hair; then he will succeed. But if he grabs him by a big limb, an arm or leg, then the one drowning will pull down the one trying to save him. So here too: you have to take hold of something delicate." (*Mishnat Hasidim*, p. 319, #32)

If you want to lift up the "spark," the spirituality of the food, you have to eat delicately. For if you eat a lot, the materiality of the food will rather overcome and pull you down.

10:21 WHAT TO EAT

It is important that the body be kept healthy, because, as the Besht taught, only a healthy body can be fully fit for spiritual activities:

> When your body is sick, your soul is also weakened, and you cannot pray as you should, even though you are free of sins. So be very careful about the health of your body. (*Keter Shem Tov*, p. 25b)
>
> Eat nothing that does harm to the body. (*Derech Hayim*, 2–18)

Beyond this, it is necessary that the food we eat should have a positive, not a negative influence on our spiritual practice. Of course, kosher food has on it a spirit of holiness. But if you eat too much you will become heavy and lazy and will not be able to concentrate on God; prayer and Torah study will be affected.

It is not only a matter of how much food, however, but what food. Since the goal is to have God–consciousness, we should pay attention to how different foods affect us personally. Watch what you eat and see how it affects your spirituality; and adjust your diet accordingly. When we eat to serve God, we will not choose our food to suit our taste and lust, but according to its health qualities and how it affects us spiritually.

> A person should direct his heart and all his deeds to one end alone: to know God, blessed be He . . . and he should do all these [physical] things just to the degree necessary for the body. . . . And whatever he eats or drinks . . . he will not have enjoyment as his purpose, so that he ends up eating only what is pleasurable to his palate . . . but his intention will be to keep his body and limbs healthy. So he will not be thinking of his pleasure in choosing what he eats . . . but he will eat what is healthy, whether it is bitter or sweet. His practice will be to have his intention that his body be healthy and strong so his soul will be fit and able to know God. For it is not possible to understand and become wise in Torah and *mitzvot* when you are hungry or sickly or when one of your limbs hurts. (*Orchot Tzaddikim*, Gate 5, p. 39)

10:22 CONCLUSION

The practices discussed in this chapter are, in their full performance, beyond most people's attainment for every meal. But meals on the

Sabbath can be on a higher level, or some practices can be done at one meal during the day, or one meal on the Sabbath, or just at the beginning of a meal—each one according to his own level. It is good to make the first meal you eat in the day holy and dedicated to the service of God. Go right from the Morning Prayers (or the Torah study after that) to a sanctified meal.

The main point is that you should not let your inability to do everything inhibit you from doing what you can.

> Through eating one dish and one meal a week (or a *Shabbat* meal) with true *kavvanah* for the sake of heaven, and to lift up the animal powers of your soul to God, blessed be He, you raise up spiritually all the food and meals you ate that week. (Rabbi Tzadok ha-Cohen of Lublin, *P'ri Tzaddik*, quoted in *Menorat Zahav*, p. 33)

11

Mitzvot

11:1 Rabbi Abraham of Slonim:

> There are three stages and levels in the service of God with both love and fear. First, you have to firmly root the love and fear of God, blessed be He, in your mind and thought. Next, you have to infuse this love and fear of Him into the feelings of your heart. Finally, you must bring this love and fear into the different ways you actually relate to the world, and this is done through the way you do *mitzvot* that require action.
>
> Because the body is physical, if you do not put love and fear of God into something physical, into something involving action, you are in danger of losing everything you have already attained on the levels of your mind and of your heart. As a result of doing a *mitzvah*, acting in this physical world, with love and fear of God, you cause . . . the separation of the holy from the profane, etc. (*Torat Avot*, p. 68)

Thus, we are to do every *mitzvah* with *kavvanah* and *hitlahavut* (concentration and fervor), with love and fear. Of course, this will usually require some preparation before the *mitzvah* is done.

11:2 Rabbi Levi Yitzhak of Berditchev was famous for the fervor with which he did the *mitzvot*.

> His Divine service in doing the *mitzvot* of God was with the most powerful love and the most intense longing, as a fire burning in his bones.
>
> The night after a *Yom Tov* he could not sleep; he had such longing to put on *tefillin* the next morning [*tefillin* are not used on *Yom Tov*] that he would remain awake the whole night in expectation, anxiously looking for when dawn would come and he could don the holy *tefillin*.
>
> The first night of *Sukkot* he also would stay awake the whole night waiting for the moment that the first light would arrive so that he could fulfill the *mitzvah* of the four species [*etrog*, *lulav*, *aravot*, *hadassim*]. When the time did come and he took them in his hands, his joy knew no bounds, as if he had just found the greatest treasure. He would kiss them with all his heart, with the greatest love.
>
> That was his way with all objects used for *mitzvot*, to kiss them with all his heart. When he did any *mitzvah*, all his limbs would be on fire, in the most wondrous and awesome *d'vekut*, so that he was entirely separated from this world. (*Toldot Kedushat Levi*, p. 16)

(See also "Individual Practices," 39:21.)

There are many stories of how Rabbi Levi Yitzhak's ecstasy when doing *mitzvot* was so great that sometimes he would even reel and fall.

> When he sat at the seder table on *Pesach* he would get so excited when you hold up the matzah and say, "This matzah . . ." that he would roll on the floor under the table in ecstasy. The table would overturn with all the seder plates and matzahs and everything on it. By the time he came to himself they would have another all prepared, with matzahs and wine cups, and they would have another clean white *kittel* for him to wear. And he would say, again, "This matzah . . ." like someone who was giving life to himself with something, and he would say, "Ah, ah, this matzah!"
>
> Once he went to the well to do the *mitzvah* of drawing water for the making of the matzahs, and his *d'vekut* was so great that he fell into the well. Fortunately, the water was not deep so there was no disaster.
>
> When he made the blessing before the reading of the Scroll of Esther on *Purim* he would dance right on top of the stand and almost on the *megillah* scroll itself. (*Eser Orot*, p. 46, #6, 7, 8)

11:3 The *mitzvot* are to be done with all our energy, with *kavvanah* and *hitlahavut*; we are to immerse ourselves entirely in the holy fire of God-directed activity. It is often taught that we are to exert ourselves in doing a *mitzvah* until we sweat.

The holy Seer of Lublin once told his holy disciple Rabbi Moshe Teitelbaum, that when he did not have access to a *mikveh*, he could immerse himself in the River of Fire—in the fire of *d'vekut*. (See "Men's *Mikveh*," 30:11.)

The River of Fire (*Nahar diNur*)[1] is said to come from the sweat of the holy animals that bear the Throne of Glory (the Divine Chariot). The ministering angels are said to immerse in this stream (*Bereshit Rabba* 79-1; *Beit ha-Midrash*, vol. 2, V, pp. 165, 183). The "wheels" of the Divine Throne or Chariot, as well as the "holy animals" that bear it and pull or transport it, so to speak, represent different kinds of angels (*ofanim* and *hayot ha-kodesh*) and also different levels or aspects of human spiritual service. Religious practice with such fervor and devotion that you sweat is the level where you have harnessed the animal energy of the body in Divine service; this fervor is the River of Fire, which is the sweat of the holy animals. Such service has an effect on the body, and works to transform the body feeling and set, "breaking the Shells" (to use kabbalistic language) that surround and constrict, so to speak, the freedom of the soul (See "Torah," 15:13:3 and 15:30:3).

We often hear how we are to study Torah and pray until we sweat with the effort; this is also relevant for other spiritual activities. The Holy Jew of Pshischa was among the greatest of the disciples of the Seer of Lublin and followed this teaching of his master about immersing in the fire of *d'vekut*.

> The Holy Jew strove for a supernal purity, he burned with a yearning for purity, and he established it as a practical *halacha* (one followed by all those who belonged to the School he founded) that the beads of sweat a man draws out of his body through his exertions in Torah study purify like the waters of a *mikveh*. (*Ha-Admor Rabbi Hanoch mi-Alexander*, p. 26)

> The holy rabbi, the Maggid of Trisk, the memory of a holy *tzaddik* for a blessing, said . . . that you can draw yourself close to the Holy One, blessed be He, through songs and melodies . . . and that when you sing until you sweat it is as if you had immersed in the *mikveh*. (*Sifran Shel Tzaddikim*, p. 51, #5)

> About Rabbi Nissan Hayim of Brodshin:

> After his dancing [on *Shabbat* evening after the meal] his *payot* and beard would be altogether dripping with sweat from the greatness of his service of God in dancing, and the holiness of *Shabbat* that burned within him. This happened even though he did not dance

with exertion, but softly and quietly. The fire that burned within him brought out much water [*mayim rabbim*], as if he had just stepped out of the *mikveh.* (Toldot Rabbi Nissan Hayim mi-Brodshin, *Raza d'Uvda*, p. 144)

There is a story of Rabbi Yosef of Yampoli who was once very sick and in bed. His soul ascended to heaven, and he was praying there with great *kavvanah.* He was immersed in the River of Fire, and below on earth his body began to sweat and he got well (*Kahal Hasidim ha-Hadash*, p. 45, #85).

One of the hasidim of Rabbi Shalom Yosef [a son of the Rizhiner] was outside the *rebbe's* room when he was praying. Though he was standing close to the door he did not hear any sound of the *rebbe's* voice or any movements he was making in prayer; he just heard the soft tread of his feet as he paced about the room. After a few hours the *rebbe's* attendant went in, and when he came out he had in his hand the *rebbe's* shirt, which was soaking wet. . . . The hasid was astonished at this sight, and he became even more astonished when the attendant told him that this happened every day.

This hasid also used to spend time with the *tzaddik*, Rabbi Arye Leibush, the head of the religious court of Tomashov. At the first opportunity he told the rabbi, with great excitement, what he had seen and heard. The Rabbi of Tomashov said to him, "This is the level mentioned in *Kedushat* '*Keter*' [the prayer] of *Rosh Ha-Shanah*: "Sweating without cease from fear of the Throne [of God]." (*Beit Rizhin*, p. 287)

There is, of course, a difference between sweating from outright physical exertion in Divine service, and sweating caused by intense inward spiritual activity with little outer bodily movement.

Rabbi Tzadok ha-Cohen of Lublin discusses four levels of increasing depth in the fear of heaven in Divine service (speaking particularly of prayer, but with broader application): first, when you speak loudly; then, when you are hardly able to speak, as you feel yourself in God's presence; then, the trembling of the body; and last, when you sweat from fear of God.

It is said about this latter level (in Hagigah 13) that "from the sweat of the *hayot* [holy animals] a River of Fire goes out and falls on the heads of the wicked in hell" . . . for when you reach the level of fear where you sweat, then a River of Fire of your fear of God burns up all the root of the physical lusts in your heart. (This is called "the heads of the wicked in hell." ["The heads of the wicked, etc." is interpreted to mean the roots of your own wicked lusts]). . . . The powers of lust and desire . . . are burned up through the sweat that results from the holy vitality [*hiyut ha-kedushah* equals *hayot ha-kodesh*, the holy animals] that is in a man. When the sweat comes to a man from his fear of heaven, there is nothing higher than that . . . just that this level is rare and hard to attain; but, in any case, it is easy to achieve the same effect through the vigorous activity of a man in doing the *mitzvot* with his limbs. (*Tzidkat ha-Tzaddik*, #194)

11:4 There is great value, according to hasidic teaching, in preparation before the doing of *mitzvot*. One aspect of this can be spending time meditating on the longing of our heart to do the *mitzvah* and on our determination to do it in the best way, going over in our minds the different aspects of what we intend to do and how.

Following are three teachings about this from Rabbi Shalom of Belz, from his grandson, Rabbi Yissachar Dov of Belz, and from Rabbi Shalom's son, Rabbi Yehoshuah of Belz. (The quotes are all from *Sefer ha-Hasidut mi-Torat Belz*.)

11:4:1 When a Jew wants to do some service of God, he first has to connect his mind to it, and think that his will is to do this particular service. It is known that the Power of Evil does not have the ability to steal away energy for itself from something that is just being thought about [while it can do so from a physical act whose motivation is not pure]. Thus, this practice of thinking about the particular service of God beforehand, being protected, is an aid in seeing that the act is done with holiness and purity. (p. 143)

11:4:2 It is written in the name of the Ropshitzer Rebbe, his memory for a blessing, that: "We sometimes see that a man is aroused to do a *mitzvah* and has a great desire to do it, but when it comes to the actual doing, his fervor is dissipated and he can not fulfill the *mitzvah* with the same great desire he had at the beginning. This is because the original arousal came from the soul, while for the actual doing of the *mitzvah* the services of the body were necessary. From that side there is opposition and resistance." . . . Now the way to weaken this opposition of the body is to begin every *mitzvah* in thought . . . for since the mind is in the spiritual realm there is no opposition to what goes on there from the side of the body. And since "God will take a good thought and intention and link an action to it," this thought is accounted as the beginning of the doing of the *mitzvah*. Then, when there is no opposition to the beginning of the *mitzvah*, it will be easy to proceed further with the actual *mitzvah* itself. (p. 144)

11:4:3 You should prepare yourself before the doing of every *mitzvah*. The reason is simple: when a person wants to do a *mitzvah* there are always things that hinder and work against it, and, "All beginnings are difficult." But as a result of the preparation, whereby he burns with desire and longing to fulfill His *mitzvot*, may He be blessed, and as for these longings, the hindrances to them are not so many, then God will link the action to the good thought and consequently, when he reaches the stage of actually doing the *mitzvah*, it is not accounted as the "beginning" and it will be easy to accomplish his thought and desire. (p. 146)

11:5 The author of *Niflaot ha-Rebbe*, speaking about the hasidic *rebbes*, says:

In the preparation of a *tzaddik* to do a *mitzvah*, he often shakes and trembles and sways . . . but the essence is still not this but the inner aspect of his service of God. . . . Once I went on *Sukkot* to the holy congregation of Lublin, to be with the man of God, the holy Seer of Lublin, of blessed memory. Before saying the *Hallel* [a group of psalms of praise recited in the prayer service at certain festivals], the *rebbe* went to the *sukkah* to make the blessing on the *lulav* and the four species, and everyone followed him there, myself included. Before saying the blessing, the holy *tzaddik* was shaking and trembling with amazing and awesome exertions and making all sorts of movements [this is the external aspect], for about an hour. . . . When he finally made the blessing [which is the essence of the *mitzvah* and its inner aspect] the level he was on cannot be described. (p. 94, #325)

11:6 There are various intentions that a person can choose to think of or say before each *mitzvah*. Here are some examples:

11:6:1 With everything that he does [not only *mitzvot* in the narrow sense] he should think, "I am doing this because this is what God commanded." (Rabbi Moshe of Kobrin, *Torat Avot*, p. 161, #32; see the full quote in "Leading Thoughts," 13:1)

11:6:2 Before doing a *mitzvah*, say "I am doing this *mitzvah* for the glory of God."* (*Derech Hayim*, 2–5)

11:6:3 Before every *mitzvah*, say "I am doing this to fulfill the command of my Creator, who created me for His glory."* (*Beit Midot*, p. 52)

> **11:6:4** In everything you do, whether Torah, prayer, or *mitzvot* that require action, accustom yourself to say beforehand, "I am doing this for the sake of the unification of the Holy One, blessed be He, and His *Shechinah*, and to give pleasure to the Creator, blessed be He."* And after a while, when you have regularly said this with concentration and complete sincerity, you will feel a great divine glow in its utterance. (Rabbi Elimelech of Lizensk, *Tzetl Katan*, #4)

These words include the kabbalistic intention about unification, and another common intention about giving pleasure to God; these two are independent and can be said separately. The idea of giving pleasure to God, *nahas*, goes well with awareness of Him as our Father in Heaven.

11:6:5 Since all our actions and service of God are to be done with love and fear (see 11:1), general stated intentions frequently include a reminder of that. To say, for example, "For the sake of the unification of the Holy One, blessed be He, and His *Shechinah*, with love and fear"; or one might say: "I am doing this because this is what God commanded, with love and fear"; or, "I am doing this to give pleasure to my Father in Heaven, with love and fear."* Of course, the main thing is not just the words but a preparatory meditation on things like the presence of God, how He is our Father in Heaven, love for Him, that we want to give Him pleasure in us, and so on.

11:7 Since every action of ours is to be done for the sake of God, and is to be a *mitzvah*, there are those who say such general stated intentions before everything they do, from drinking a glass of water, to sitting down or rising up.

Rabbi Yitzhak Isaac of Komarna said about his *rebbe*, Rabbi Tzvi Hirsh of Ziditchov:

> I saw how my teacher, my holy uncle, our master Tzvi Hirsh, used to say out loud on everything that he did, great or small, "For the sake of the unification of the Holy One, blessed be He, and His *Shechinah*"*—even when he drank a little water. (*Ateret Tiferet*, p. 7, #27)

11:8 One hasidic approach is to do every *mitzvah* with thought, speech, and deed. After a preparatory meditation (that is, *thought*), some hasidim will, before every action, *say* a stated intention, sometimes a general one together with a specific one directly related to what they are *doing*. For suggestions about the content of a preparatory meditation, see 11:1, 11:4, 11:6, 11:9, and 11:10. For general stated intentions, see 11:6 above. Some examples of specific stated intentions can be found in the *Seder ha-Yom* of Rabbi Shalom Shachna of Probitch (*D'vir Yaakov*, p. 7). He gives a common stated intention before eating: "I am eating in order that I have energy to do God's commandments"; and he says "You should say this aloud before eating." He also has that when you put on nice clothes (as for *Shabbat* or a holiday) you are not to have motives of pride, but are to say: "I am putting on these nice clothes to fulfill the verse, 'Prepare to meet your God, O Israel.'" (This verse was connected by the rabbis with preparing oneself, particularly with regard to clothing, for special times of "meeting" with God, such as prayer and *Shabbat*.) When you put on warm clothing on a cold day, according to Rabbi Shalom Shachna you are to say the stated intention: "I am putting on these warm clothes so that my body will be healthy for the service of God."*

> **11:9** Before every *mitzvah*-act and before Torah study and prayer you should consider well if your intention is really just for His name, or if, God forbid, you have some selfish motive in your heart. So you should make a verbal declaration beforehand that your intention is just to serve God alone. (Rabbi Tzvi Elimelech of Dinov, *Hanhagot Adam*, #11)

(This can also be part of a preparatory meditation.)

11:10 One can have as a meditation before and during a *mitzvah* (such as when putting on *tefillin* or lighting *Shabbos* candles) that it is the *Shechinah* that is moving your limbs and making you act. Before the blessing on the *mitzvah*, think: "God, my will is to do Your will. I know that without Your life-energy I cannot think or speak or move. Let me now do this *mitzvah*, as is Your will." Then say: "I am making myself a chariot for the *Shechinah*."*

This *kavvanah* can also be accompanied as you do the *mitzvah* by a visualization, where you picture God's life-energy flowing into your soul and body—into your brain and nerves and limbs and senses—and moving you to action. And as you act, feel yourself moving to do the *mitzvah* by God's will and life-energy. (See Chapter 3, "Our Life-Energy From God," p. 67.)

11:11 We are allowed to make a vow to fulfill the *mitzvot*. (*Midrash ha-Gadol* on Deuteronomy 6:13)

It can be a great help to your determination and resolve to make vows to do *mitzvot*, either ordained *mitzvot* or those done in the way of "In all your ways know Him." With the use of vows, when you are aroused to do something, you can guard against your enthusiasm failing, or against your laziness. For instance, you can vow: "I vow to You God that today I will spend two hours studying Torah," or "I will not go to sleep tonight until I do this favor for so-and-so." There are some precautions to take in this, because it is very bad to make a promise to God through a vow and then not perform. So you should not make a vow that binds you far in the future; do not vow, "This month I will do such and such," but, "Today I will do this." And do not vow things far above your ability and level or not within your control.

> If someone sees that he cannot put himself on the right path in some matter, or that he cannot overcome his laziness to fulfill the *mitzvot*, it is a good practice for him to make a vow to fulfill them in order to make a fence for himself. And this is what is taught in the Talmud in the first chapter of *Nedarim*, p. 5, that: "According to Rav Gidel, Rav said: 'From where in the Torah do we know that it is permitted to swear to fulfill the *mitzvot*? Because it says in Psalm 119 "I have sworn and I will fulfill, etc."' But is there not a standing vow already from Mount Sinai to do all the *mitzvot*? [All Jews, according to the tradition, were at Sinai "in soul," and there vowed to fulfill all the Torah.] There is, but we hold that a man is permitted anyway to vow, in order to inspire himself. And according to Rav Gidel, Rav said: 'When someone makes a vow and says, "I will get up early and study this chapter of Mishnah, or this one mishnah, or this tractate of Talmud"—this is a great vow, a vow to the God of Israel.'" (*Menorat ha-Maor* p. 102)

(See Chapter 12, "Vows," for more about this.)

11:12 Choose for yourself at least one *mitzvah* to perform in the absolutely fullest sense, with all of its many details and ramifications. (*Derech Hayim*, 6–11; this is also recommended by Rabbi Abraham of Slonim, *Hanhagot Tzaddikim* [II], 6–20.)

This traditional practice, whose source is in the Talmud, ensures that you have at least one channel through which you will receive the full flow from heaven. As the Besht taught: He who has grasped a part has grasped the whole. This one *mitzvah* will provide you with one very strong connection, and it will also be a standard to pull up the rest of your observance.

> **11:13** Run when you are going to do a *mitzvah*, either when you are going to the synagogue or to the *Beit ha-Midrash*, or when you are going to try to make peace between two people or to do someone a kindness . . . but do not do this in a way that will arouse mockery; be subtle, do not exactly run, but move quickly, etc. (*Hanhagot Tzaddikim*, p. 78, #15)

Of course, in *Avot* (5:23), we are told to "run like a gazelle" to do the will of our Father in Heaven.

> The holy way of the holy Rabbi David of Amshinov was to always walk quickly as if almost running . . . for he was always either running to do a *mitzvah* or running away from a transgression. (*Siah Sarfei Kodesh*, II, p. 121, #467)

Some years ago, when living in Jerusalem, I was told by a friend who had spent *Shabbat* in the presence of a young hasidic *rebbe* in the holy city how all his movements were quick, as if racing for each thing. Perhaps this practice was behind it. (See "Individual Practices," 39:7:2 about how to acquire this trait.)

12

Vows

A vow is a promise to God to do something specific for His sake, and it is a very effective way to lift yourself up spiritually and to insert discipline into your religious life. God has given us the power, by our spoken vow, to obligate ourselves like at Mount Sinai. For when you make a vow, a solemn promise to God that you will do something, you are obligated equally as with the commandments given on Mount Sinai.

> When you make a vow it has the same sanctity as something that God Himself commanded us to do or not to do. For when a word goes out from the mouth of the Holy One, blessed be He, certainly it has a great and holy power and a foundation in all the worlds; but in just the same way does your vow have such great and awesome power. (*Siftei Kodesh*, p. 48)

The vow is indeed a key and a great secret in how to advance spiritually, going from strength to strength.

12:1 To make a vow just say "God, I vow that . . ." or, "I promise You that . . ." For example: "that this week I will study Torah for an hour each day."

12:2 When you are in a state of low consciousness, make a vow to study Torah for an hour, or to say Psalms—for example, vow to say ten psalms that day—and then fulfill your vow immediately, or as soon as possible. The force of the vow and its fulfillment will pull you back to a higher level.

12:3 The hasidic *rebbe*, Rabbi Tzvi Elimelech of Dinov:

> I have received it as a tradition, that when your evil inclination is getting stronger and threatens to overcome you, you should make a vow to give something for *tzedaka*, and you will be saved. (*Agra d'Pirka*, quoted in *Derech Emunah u'Maaseh Rav*, p. 54)

12:4 On the one hand, you can use vows to strengthen yourself when you are in a low state and in danger. On the other hand, you can also use them when you are in a higher state of consciousness, to prepare yourself for the temptations you will face later.

For example, in the morning *davvening*, during the *Shemoneh Esreh*, when you feel close to God, you can make a vow or vows. Or after the *davvening*, when you are inspired, and it is time to draw the power of your *davvening* into your daily life, you can use vows to set yourself goals for the day. Or before the Sabbath, you can make vows to lift up the level of your observance and devotion on *Shabbat*. Similarly, at the end of *Shabbat*, when it is time to draw the power of *Shabbat* into the weekdays, you can make vows which set high goals for the week.

12:5 From *Erech Apayim* (p. 70):

> [Another way to improve yourself] is to strengthen yourself through the use of vows and oaths, so as to establish both the essence of the character trait you are working on, as well as the fences [you have made for yourself] surrounding it.
>
> The main reason things remain in such a low state with regard to character traits is that a person is apt to treat such matters lightly, and his transgressions come to seem to him as if they were actually permitted. So when a person's evil inclination incites him to transgress, he does not fight with all his might to hold himself back. Even less does he guard himself in the various fences that he made for himself, because he is not inclined to take it very seriously, and it almost becomes in his eyes as if it were something permitted. As a

result of this, he is finally drawn, not only to transgress regarding the fences, but even with regard to what is actually forbidden.

But if he makes a vow or an oath he is forced to fight with all his strength to uphold it. So too even with the fences, because of the great seriousness of violating a vow or an oath.

We have already come across this way in the service of God in many holy books, and with many true servants of God. In Psalm 119:106, King David, peace be upon him, says, "I have sworn an oath and I will fulfill it, to keep Your righteous judgments," and in Psalm 132:1–5, "Lord remember unto David . . . how he swore unto the Lord, and vowed unto the Mighty One of Jacob: Surely I will not come into my house, etc." Also in Ruth 3:13 where Boaz swears, "As the Lord lives!—lie down until the morning," and our Sages interpreted this to mean that he swore for the purpose of restraining his evil inclination, so that he would not commit a sin with Ruth. In *Temurah* 3 it says that part of the commandment "and to swear in His name" (Deuteronomy 6:13) is the commandment to swear to fulfill the *mitzvot.* So too in *Nedarim* 67 and *Avot* 3 it says that "Vows are a fence to separation from lust and from sin." In Rabbeinu Tam's *Sefer ha-Yashar* and in *Reshit Hochmah* it says explicitly that a good way to avoid anger is to swear with a severe oath . . . and it is written about the holy Rabbi Nachman of Bratzlav, of blessed memory, that his way in fixing his character traits involved much use of vows and oaths. . . .

And there are all kinds of categories of oaths. . . . There are oaths just about your soul or your body, like "By my life in the World to Come!" or "By the life of my body!" and others like that. And according to the situation and the need of the hour you should use sometimes lighter and sometimes more severe oaths. [The point here about oaths is that you say that if you do not fulfill what you have vowed and committed yourself to, then let your life be forfeit and may God let you die, etc.]

And it seems to me that it is a good idea to be careful about vows and oaths and taking things on yourself [*kabbalot*, sing., *kabbalah*—you can obligate yourself to a religious practice without going so far as to use a vow or an oath] . . . in two ways:

1) Whenever you see that something is difficult to do, you only take it on yourself for a short time—and the more difficult it is, the shorter the time you obligate yourself for. For it is possible to bear even something very difficult if it is only for a short period of time, not for an extended period. This way you will be able to stand up under the obligations that you take on, and you will not end up acting loosely with them and treating them lightly, and

you will not be forced to have them annulled for you by the rabbis. And when the time you committed yourself for expires, then you can again take the obligation on yourself. . . .

2) It is good to make a condition for every vow and oath and *kabbalah*, that you are obligated only when you remember that you took this on yourself. But when you forget, or when you have a situation where in your opinion, you did not intend to obligate yourself for this kind of thing [unforeseen circumstances, etc.], you have no vow or oath or *kabbalah*.

12:6 The quote below from *The Praise of Rabbi Nachman* [of Bratzlav] is a good illustration of the principle behind the first of these two conditions and its usefulness.

The following is told about Rabbi Nachman's youth:

12:6:1 No religious experience came easily for the Rebbe. Whenever he served God he experienced every possible hardship.

For example, he initially found it very difficult to sit alone in a special room for several hours, devoting himself to God. At first this was next to impossible for him. But instead of merely giving up, he forced himself, overcoming his basic nature by spending many hours meditating in his special room.

The same was true of his daily religious obligations. They burdened him like a heavy yoke, and he often felt that it would crush him. His difficulties were unimaginable.

But the *Rebbe* discovered a way that enabled him to bear even the heavy yoke of his devotion. Each day he would say to himself, "I have only this one day. I will ignore tomorrow and all future days. I only have this one day alone."

In this manner, the *Rebbe* was able to bear the yoke of his devotion for that day. It was only for one day, and for just a single day one can accept all sorts of burdens. It was only when one day's devotions were finished that the *Rebbe* accepted the next day's responsibilities.

This was the *Rebbe*'s way. He would only consider one day at a time. In this manner, he was able to bear an extremely heavy yoke of devotion, a burden he could otherwise not endure at all.

For even the *Rebbe* served God with all sorts of devotions requiring great exertion and effort. His routine was so difficult that it would have been absolutely impossible had he not considered each day as the only day. (*The Praise of Rabbi Nachman*, p. 14, *Shevachey HaRan*, #14)

It should be understood that it was this heavy yoke of devotions which Rabbi Nachman took on himself that enabled him to reach his goal; indeed, as a result of his self-sacrifice Rabbi Nachman attained the pinnacle of spirituality and freedom in God–consciousness.

12:6:2 Rabbi Nachman used vows extensively in his religious practice:

> The *Rebbe* used to make frequent use of vows. He would plan out an order of devotion for each day, and often at the beginning of the day make a vow to fulfill it. Then, because of the vow, he would be obliged to complete his plan regardless of how difficult it was. This was a very frequent practice.
>
> The *Rebbe* would use all sorts of safeguards to keep him from particular temptations or bad traits. Among his many devices was his use of vows. Often he would make an inviolable oath, holding a sacred object in his hand [grasping a Torah or *tefillin*], just to strengthen his resolve and keep him from something he wished to avoid. (*The Praise of Rabbi Nachman*, p. 15, *Shevachey HaRan*, #15)

12:7 To a plan for a daily order of devotion in the morning, reinforced by vows, one can join a recital of Psalm 61.

> **12:8** Regarding the teaching that "Vows are a fence for separation from lust and sin" [*Avot* 3:13], an intelligent person will not make vows that he will have to have annulled by rabbis. But you should make a vow for a day, or for half a day, like those we find about Rabbi Yohanan, who used to say, "I declare that I am fasting until I reach my house." [*Taanit* 12a; *Makkot* 24a] (*Reshit Hochmah*, Sh'ar ha-Kedushah, chap. 14, #21)

12:9 One can also swear for the purpose of resisting a temptation that suddenly presents itself. For example, when Boaz found himself sleeping in the same place as Ruth for the night, he made a vow with an oath to restrain himself, so that he would not commit a sin with Ruth (see 12:5).

12:10 One can also use a vow to restrain oneself from anger or from answering back with angry words. (See 12:5; see also "Anger," 37:5.)

12:11 In the Midrash, the rabbis give a practice in the use of vows, citing King David as an example. The practice is to make vows before performing all the *mitzvot*. (One could do this also for all dedicated actions.)

> "I have sworn and I will fulfill my oath, to keep Your righteous ordinances" (Psalm 119:106). David would get two rewards: one for fulfilling the oath he swore and another for doing the *mitzvah*. He swore to take and wave the *lulav*, and did it; he swore that he would build a *sukkah*, and built it—and he got a reward for the oath and also for the *mitzvah* of the *sukkah* and the *lulav*, and of the *tzitzit* and of the *tefillin* and of performing a circumcision.

One can surmise that the real point of this practice is not only to reinforce our performance of the *mitzvot*, but to "build up" our vowing power by use—for then, when we most need it, it will be ready.

12:12 In order to remember your vows (particularly when you make a number of them) it is imperative that you write them down—preferably on a piece of paper you can carry with you and look at from time to time.

> Have a little book in which to write down vows you have made, to be with you at all times so you will not forget them. (*Reshit Hochmah*, Sh'ar ha-Kedushah, chap. 14, #22)

It is further suggested that this book also be used for recording your transgressions throughout the day—so that at the time of repentance they will be remembered. (See "Individual Practices," 39:4; "*Mitzvot*," 11:11; and "Tiredness," 28:5.)

13

Leading Thoughts

It can be helpful to use a leading thought to guide yourself through the day in your Divine service.

The Baal Shem Tov:

> You should have just one thought in the service of God, blessed be He . . . for it is from the multiplicity of thoughts that confusion comes. (*Tzavaat ha-Ribash*, p. 12)

Most often the leading thoughts suggested in the tradition are direct motives for action; the most common ones are doing the will of God and giving pleasure or satisfaction (*nahat ruah*) to God. Another motive, very popular in Hasidism, is the kabbalistic motive of uniting the Holy One and His *Shechinah.*

> **13:1** When you get up in the morning and say the blessing after morning hand washing [the first *mitzvah*-action of the day], have the intention that your will is to do His will, blessed be He, because He commanded us to wash and to make the blessing. So, too, in everything that you do, before anything else, see that you have this simple intention when you are about to pray or when you eat and drink, when you are occupied in Torah study—in everything, think:

"I'm doing this because God commanded it." (Rabbi Moshe Leib of Kobrin, *Torat Avot*, p. 161, #32)

13:2 The main thing is to be thinking at every moment what God's will is, and not to think many thoughts in the service of God: just one—about where you are at that very minute. In other words, think only of what you are able to do to fulfill God's will now, in deed, speech, or thought. You should be doing this every minute. (*Seder ha-Yom ha-Katzar*, in *Niflaot Hadashot*, p. 5)

13:3 Purify all your ideas and thoughts, and do not think many thoughts, but one alone: to serve your Creator with joy. And let all the thoughts that come to you be included in that one thought. (Rabbi Shneur Zalman of Ladi, in *Kitvei Kodesh*, p. 23)

13:4 Whenever you do anything, do it with the thought that you want to give pleasure to God, and not for your own benefit, God forbid, or your own pleasure. (*Darkei Yesharim*, p. 2)

13:5 A general *kavvanah* in the doing of all *mitzvot* and in prayer, should be to give pleasure to God. If you pray and cannot concentrate properly, do not be upset that you have no pleasure in praying, but that you are not giving God any pleasure with such prayer. (*Darkei Tzedek*, p. 2, #4)

13:6 The kinds of leading thoughts mentioned above fit very naturally with the development of an intense and felt relationship to God as a servant, or a son or daughter. In fact, the relationship itself can be the leading thought: "I am a servant of God," or "I am His son (or daughter)—and should act that way." For example, a servant acts to give satisfaction to his master, or because that is what his master commanded him to do. A son should act to give pleasure (*nahas*) to his father, and to do what his father tells him to do. The ideal mentioned in the prophets (Malachi 3:17) is to be a son who serves his Father.

13:7 [The holy Seer of Lublin] had a firm practice from his youth that he would not think, speak, or do anything except what gave some satisfaction or pleasure to God. (*Seder ha-Yom ha-Katzar*, p. 12)

The Rebbe of Lublin, when he was a young man, once went to be with his master, the holy rabbi, Rebbe Reb Elimelech of Lizensk, of blessed memory. One day as he traveled along there was a very heavy rain and it was extremely cold. At night he lost his way and was drifting in the forest. Seeing a house with lit windows he went to it and entered. It was very warm and nice inside and he felt much better after having suffered so much from the rain and the cold.

Inside the one room there was only a single woman who was young and pretty, and the *rebbe* did not know what to do about the prohibition of being alone with a woman. And she, it became clear, wanted to talk him into sinning. She started telling him how she was unmarried and ritually clean, and the *rebbe* became very distressed by her enticements and her attempted seduction. But though he felt he was losing his mooring, he at least remembered the fence he had made for himself and answered her, saying, "I have accepted on myself not to do anything, not even something permitted, except what gives some pleasure to my Creator. But what satisfaction will God derive from this?"

As soon as he uttered these words he saw that the whole scene before him was imaginary—there was no forest, no house, and no woman; it was all just to test him. And he found himself alone, by the side of the road he had to go on. (*Eser Orot*, p. 89, #23)

13:8 A leading thought can be as simple as doing everything for the sake of God. And *Kitzur Shnei Luchot ha-Brit* says that you should say aloud before everything you do, that you are doing it for God:

> [Not only for spiritual things should you say that you are acting for the sake of God] but even before all worldly activities you should say aloud, "For the sake of God" [*L'shem HaShem*] . . . or "I am doing this for God."* (Sh'ar ha-Otiyot, Ot Aleph, Emet v'Emunah, p. 20)

13:9 Very common among the hasidim is the kabbalistic intention, stated before every act, "For the sake of the unification of the Holy One, blessed be He, and His *Shechinah*."*

13:9:1 The essential meaning of this is that the *Shechinah*, which is God's presence in this world, strives to reach out and join with the Holy One, God as apart from this world (that is, the immanent and transcendant aspects of God); the Holy One also seeks to come together with the *Shechinah*, so that the two will become one. The unification sought is the Supernal union of the "female" *Shechinah* and the "male" Holy One.

When people do Divine service to reach out to God it is the *Shechinah* within them that impels them, for their souls are indeed a part of the *Shechinah.* So when you do a holy act, you do it consciously with this intention, and in order to accomplish this unification of the Holy One and His *Shechinah,* and so that ultimately all reality will become one in God.

> **13:9:2** "For the sake of the unification of the Holy One, blessed be He, and His *Shechinah*"—God, blessed be He, put holiness and Divine life-energy into everything . . . also within man; and that is the "part of God from Above" [the soul] within him; for life-energy has flowed into him from the Creator, blessed is He and blessed is His name. When a person believes that the whole earth is full of His glory and that there is no place where He is not, then, when he does any *mitzvah,* for example, praying, with all his intention, energy, and fervor, he clings in *d'vekut* to the Creator—in prayer, through his speech. [For the words of prayer, those on the page and also the sounds you utter, are holy, and the Holy One, blessed be He, is in them; so as the *Shechinah* prays through him he joins with the Holy One, blessed be He, in the words of prayer.] And when he does the *mitzvah* or prays with vigor the part of the *Shechinah* that dwells within him clings to the Holy One, blessed be He (for *Shechinah* means "indwelling"). And this is what is called the "unification" [or "union"], which is an expression of sexual union. All such acts are the heavenly matings where he mates the life-energy in his speech or the *mitzvot* he does, and all the life-energy that dwells within him, with the Creator, blessed be He. (Rabbi Nahum of Tchernobil, *Maor Ainayim* quoted in *Shaarei Tefillah,* in *Yesod ha-Avodah,* p. 4)

13:9:3 Rabbi Meir of Premishlan told a parable to explain one aspect of the use of this kabbalistic stated intention:

> There was a certain man who was bringing a gift to the king, and he was afraid of the highwaymen who might waylay him on the road, for they were known to wait in hiding to rob travelers. So he hit upon the device that, as he went along for the whole length of his journey, he cried out loudly that he was carrying a gift to the king. Then the highwaymen were afraid to bother him, for they knew that anyone who dared harass someone who was carrying something of the king's was sure to meet a dire fate at the hands of the army.
>
> So is it when you are engaged in doing some holy deed. For then the forces of the Other Side are always ready to snatch and steal what you are doing and bring it under its power [by leading you

> into wrong motives]. But if you say, "I am doing this for the sake of the unification of the Holy One, blessed be He, and His *Shechinah*"—I am carrying a gift to the King of the Universe—who will dare to steal what belongs to the King? (*Zichron l'Rishonim*, p. 38, n. 26)

13:10 The teaching of the Premishlaner just quoted applies to other stated intentions also, not only the kabbalistic one. As we mentioned previously, in Part One, the early hasidim expressed their *kavvanah* verbally. So the various leading thoughts can be said out loud before each act. To put things into the language of the Premishlaner, let us say that you are praying; you might be inclined to show off your piety before others or have some other false motive sneak into your subconscious. If that happens, much of the energy you are putting into the prayer flows to the Other Side. It goes to support your ego, not your good side. But if before praying you declare what your true motive is, you nullify the ulterior motives, the "robbers" waiting to grab your "gift." (See "The Synagogue and the Synagogue Service," 6:24, and "Individual Practices," 39:12.)

> **13:11** Be careful always to say before every action you do: To unify the name of the Holy One, blessed be He, and His *Shechinah*, with fear and love, in the name of all Israel. (Rabbi Rafael Abulafia, *Hanhagot Tzaddikim* [III], vol. 2, p. 590, #1)

To the kabbalistic motive of unification of the Holy One and His *Shechinah* two other clauses are often appended, as in this quote: "with fear and love, in the name of all Israel."* The first part is to remind yourself that all your actions should be motivated by love and fear of God, and, minimally, to arouse these emotions through their mention. The second clause links your action to the task and mission of the whole people of Israel. Either of these clauses could as well be joined to other leading thoughts or motives, for example: "I am doing this to give pleasure to God, with love and fear."*

13:12 As noted above regarding the relationships of being a son or servant of God, a leading thought does not have to have a direct reference to action. The Baal Shem Tov had a leading thought regarding the presence of God. A hasidic story tells how from his childhood the Besht had a leading thought given to him by his father, who said: "My son, always remember that God is with you; never let this thought out of your mind. Go deeper and deeper with it, every hour and every minute, wherever you are." (See the full quote in Chapter 1, p. 18.) In Hasidism, such a leading thought about God's presence is typically joined, secondarily at least, with the effect it is to have on our behavior—for if God is actually with us always, certainly we must act so as to please Him.

The leading thought of the Baal Shem Tov was to be aware of God's presence and to be in *d'vekut* always. The Lubavitcher Rebbe, Rabbi Menachem Mendel Schneerson, quotes, in a letter, from a teaching of the Besht about this (part of which was used at the beginning of this chapter). Two additional parts of the Besht's teaching appear in the first two bracketed statements:

> The interpretation of the Besht in this is well known [and these are his words]: "It is an important principle that a person should always and continously have just one thought in the service of God, blessed be He . . ." [For it is from the multiplicity of thoughts that confusion comes] "and he should think of how everything in the world is all filled with God, blessed be He . . . and he should cleave in *d'vekut* to His Glory, blessed be He, with complete love . . ." [thinking, "I want to give Him pleasure always and serve Him always"] "Let his mind be continuously in *d'vekut*. . . . And this is the meaning (on the level of 'hint') of the verse, 'And from the holy place let him not go out' [Leviticus 21:12]—that when you speak about [or otherwise involve yourself in] worldly matters, it should be like a man who has gone out of his house with the intention of returning immediately, and while he is walking outside he is thinking continually about when he will return home. For your main 'house' and dwelling is to be God, blessed be He." (*Tzavaat ha-Ribash*, Kehot edition, Hosafot, p. 88)

13:13 Being aware of God's presence and getting close to Him through *d'vekut* can, then, also be a leading thought. The following quote, discussed in Part 1, is one variation on that theme:

> The main effort and work is to see in everything you are considering doing, whether it is a good counsel for achieving *d'vekut*. If so, do it; but if it does not bring you to *d'vekut*, refrain. (*Or ha-Ganuz l'Tzaddikim*, p. 73)

(See Chapter 1, p. 7 for more about this.)

14

Repentance—*Tshuvah*

14:1 SET TIMES FOR REPENTANCE

It is a custom of many hasidim to have a fixed practice of doing *tshuvah* before Torah, and/or prayer, eating, or sleep.

14:1:1 Before learning Torah or before prayer, do *tshuvah*. Confess your sins or at least give thought to repentance, in order to attach yourself to God, blessed be He. (Rabbi Nahum of Tchernobil, *Hanhagot Tzaddikim*, p. 35, #6)

14:1:2 You should turn your mind to repent before you pray, before you study Torah, and before eating. (Rabbi Moshe Teitelbaum, *Hanhagot Tzaddikim*, p. 50, #34)

14:1:3 To merit doing a sincere and real *tshuvah* . . . pray the Prayer of the Repentant with all your energy three times a day at mealtime—in the morning, in the afternoon and in the evening, as Rabbeinu Yonah established. . . . [The prayer is quoted below.] You should make the recitation of this prayer a regular practice. (*Totzaot Hayim*, p. 30)

14:1:4 Before sleep you should be like a shopkeeper checking his books at the end of the day. You should consider everything you did for good or for bad. You should then make confession for anything you did wrong and turn back to God. (Rabbi Moshe Teitelbaum, *Hanhagot Tzaddikim*, p. 50, #35)

14:1:5 Before *Shabbat* is a special time for repentance, so too *Rosh Hodesh*, and of course the High Holidays. See also "A Full Day Set Aside" [36] for the practice of devoting a whole day to repentance. For more about *tshuvah* done at these various times, see the section about *tshuvah* in "Torah," "Prayer," "Eating and the Holy Meal," "Sleep," and "*Shabbat*."

14:2 RABBEINU YONAH'S PRAYER OF THE REPENTANT

(From his *Yesod ha-Tshuvah*; also found in *Totzaot Hayim*, p. 30 and in many other places.)

God! I've sinned, I've done wrong, I've transgressed (I've done this and this) since my earliest days on this earth till today. But now my heart has lifted me up, and my spirit has carried me to turn to You in truth and in complete sincerity, with all my heart, with all my soul, and with all my strength, so that I'll be one who confesses his sins and then abandons them altogether; so that I'll cast my transgressions away from me and make for myself a new heart and a new spirit, so that I'll be zealous in the fear of You.

And now, O Lord my God, who open Your arms to receive those who repent, helping them to come and purify themselves—open Your arms to receive me and receive my complete repentance before You. And help me to be strengthened in the fear of You, and support me in the face of the Adversary who battles against me with all manner of stratagems and devious tactics to put me to death so that he won't conquer me. And remove him from all my limbs and organs and cast him into the depths of the sea. Rebuke him, that he not stand at my side to fight against me and incite me. And by Your doing, see that I walk in Your statutes; remove the heart of stone from within me and give me a heart of flesh.

My God! Hear the prayer of Your servant and his pleas! Receive my repentance, and let no sin or iniquity of mine hinder my prayer and my repentance from coming before You. Let there be before the Throne of Your Glory angel-advocates to speak on my behalf, and to gain entrance for my prayer into Your presence. But if, because of my sins, which are many and great, there is no angel to defend me—then do You Yourself see that a hole is dug under the wall of Your heavenly palace, for me to squeeze through and come into Your presence . . . so that You receive my repentance, and I not return empty-handed. For You, O Lord, hear the prayer of those who pray to You.*

Rabbeinu Yonah continues:

Accustom yourself to say this prayer regularly at mealtime before you eat, and in it confess all your sins. Anything you did wrong, confess. And if mealtime comes and you search for your sins and find none, then thank and praise your Creator that He helped you to escape your enemies and made you worthy to be at least one hour of your life in repentance in this world.

Rabbi Elimelech of Lizensk instructed his disciples to memorize Rabbeinu Yonah's Prayer of the Repentant (*Tzetl Katan*, #17).

14:3 We should pray to God to help us come to *tshuvah*.

Meditate continuously on *tshuvah* and accustom yourself to say again and again: "Create for me, O God, a pure heart, and renew within me an upright spirit" [Psalm 51:12]. (Rabbi David Lida, *Hanhagot Tzaddikim* [III], vol. 1, p. 113, #30)

A great disciple of the Seer of Lublin writes about the way of his *rebbe*, who taught:

When you pray about *tshuvah* and you express your hopes, you should say that you want to repent out of joy and expansiveness and amidst bounty, and not from sadness and stress and in need and poverty. And I heard from his own holy mouth how he rejoiced so much at this gift he received from heaven, to have this understanding and illumination, to know to pray for this explicitly. (*Menorat Zahav*, p. 117, n. 63)

14:4 Rabbi Elijah deVidas:

I heard from my master [Rabbi Moshe Cordovero] that in order to remember to do *tshuvah* every day, it is a good idea to make some sort of alteration in your food and drink and in your clothing. For example, one week do not eat fruit, another week do not eat meat or drink wine, or do not eat hot food. (*Totzaot Hayim*, p. 34)

14:5 SEE LESSONS FOR YOURSELF IN OTHERS' FAULTS

One of the practices of the Baal Shem Tov is that whenever you see another person commit some wrongdoing, you should reflect on your own comparable faults, and thus not only will you learn to judge yourself and not others, but you will have continual reminders for your repentance.

14:5:1 *Darkei Tzedek* summarizes this well:

> If you happen to see someone committing some sin, it is so you yourself will think of repentance for what you have done similar to that sin or to some aspect of it. (p. 10, #1)
>
> **14:5:2** The Besht was once pained to see one of the common people desecrating the Sabbath, and he became very despondent about this, asking himself what desecration he had committed such that [heaven] made him see this. And [from heaven] it was revealed to him that he had transgressed by having made servile use of a Torah sage [by having him do something for him]—thereby desecrating his holiness.[1] (*Zichron l'Rishonim*, p. 70)

14:5:3 *Seder ha-Dorot ha-Hadash*:

> [The] great root teaching which the Besht, his memory for a blessing, planted for us, [is that] if you see another person doing something ugly, meditate on the presence of that same ugliness in yourself. And know that it is one of God's mercies that He brought this sight before your eyes in order to remind you of that fault in you, so as to bring you back in repentance, and to save you from hell. For if you saw someone desecrating the Sabbath, or desecrating God's name some other way, you should examine your own deeds and you will certainly find among them desecration of the Sabbath and *hillul ha-Shem*. Or if you heard some profanity or obscene language, you should consider your own impudence, and when you failed to conduct yourself modestly. If you heard some skeptical or atheistic talk from someone, then you should work to strengthen your faith and trust in God.
>
> Without a doubt, anyone who follows this path and behaves in this way will not judge his fellow man unfavorably and in the scale of guilt, for he will see with his own eyes that he is no better than the other person and has the same fault and blemish in

himself. And he will repent completely for all the things that he has done wrong since coming of age. He will also appreciate the mercies of his Creator, blessed be He, with him, in so reminding him of sins long forgotten.

For the truth is that there is nothing that happens in this world without a purpose, and everything that happens before your eyes was sent to you from heaven for you to see. And for someone who fears God there is not even a word spoken in his presence in which he cannot hear some hint from heaven to remind him of some forgotten sin. [This is particularly true when he hears about another person's wrongdoing (teaching from the Besht in *Milei d'Avot*, p. 63, #14.)]

So too are all the wayward and evil thoughts that drift into your mind for your good, and to remind you to repent for something that you forgot about. Whether it is a thought of lust, or some bad trait like anger or pride, you should not be so foolish as to neglect to pay attention to what is coming into your brain; but be alert and understand what is being hinted at to you from Above, and do a complete repentance. Then without a doubt everything that is evil will be ameliorated, and the bitter will be turned to sweet.

And everyone who conducts himself this way will certainly be among those of whom the Psalmist says, "My sin is always before me," and he will be contrite in the face of his many faults and will trouble himself to correct them, and he will repent continuously. (*Seder ha-Dorot ha-Hadash*, p. 59f.)

14:6 DIVINE HINTS TO REPENT

The previous quote said, "for someone who fears God there is not even a word spoken in his presence in which he cannot hear some hint from heaven to remind him of some forgotten sin." Here are two examples where it is not "some forgotten sin," but a general "hint" to repent:

14:6:1 Once on *Rosh Hodesh Elul*, the New Moon of the month of *Elul*, [which leads into *Rosh HaShanah* and *Yom Kippur*] the rabbi and *tzaddik*, Rabbi Levi Yitzhak of Berditchev, was standing in his house looking out the window at the street, when a shoe repairman passed along and asked him, "Don't you have something to fix?" Immediately the *tzaddik* sat down on the floor and began to cry and wail, saying, "Woe is me, and alas for my soul! For the Day of Judgment is fast approaching and I still haven't fixed myself!" (*Zichron l'Rishonim*, p. 96)

14:6:2 The holy Rabbi Simha Bunim of Pshischa was a merchant before he became a *rebbe.* Once he went to the market to purchase produce, and he wanted to buy what a particular farmer was selling, but the farmer wanted more money than he was willing to offer. The farmer said to the holy rabbi in Polish, "Do better"—meaning that he should make a better offer on the price. But when Rabbi Bunim, his memory for a blessing, returned home he took these words to heart and thought that if even the farmer was trying to arouse him to better himself and his deeds, the time had come that he should do *tshuvah.* (*Siah Sarfei Kodesh*, I, p. 33, #160)

(For similar stories see "Speech," 23:2:5:4.)

14:7 PSALMS AS AN INSPIRATION TO REPENTANCE

How does one merit to have the inspiration to repent? Rabbi Nachman of Bratzlav taught that one should say Psalms:

If you want to become worthy of doing *tshuvah*, you should accustom yourself to saying Psalms, for the Psalms have a special power in bringing one to *tshuvah.* There are many things that prevent one from coming to repentance. Sometimes a person has no inspiration at all to *tshuvah.* And even someone who is aroused to do *tshuvah* will have a number of obstacles in his way. There are some for whom the gate of repentance is closed before them. Others do not know how to reach the particular gate that is for them—the gate through which they have to go to return to God. And there are other such hindrances keeping a person from *tshuvah*, until, God forbid, someone can pass all his days and die without repentance.

For this, the saying of Psalms has a special power. Even if you have no inspiration to repent, you can become aroused to repentance through Psalms. For each and every person, according to who he is, can find himself [and his gate] through saying Psalms; through this he will merit to become aroused and do *tshuvah*, find the gate of repentance that is right for his soul, and open that gate until he comes to do a complete repentance.

As a result of this, God will also return to him and show him compassion—happy is he. For this reason, during the month of *Elul* and the Ten Days of Repentance [which include the High Holidays] all Jews occupy themselves with saying Psalms. For the saying of Psalms has a special power for repentance. But you should occupy yourself all the year with saying Psalms with *kavvanah* so as to merit coming to repentance. (*Likkutei Aytzot*, Tshuvah, #32)

15

Torah

15:1 TORAH AS DEVOTION

To learn Torah as it should be done it has to be understood that Torah study, in addition to its virtue for attaining religious wisdom, is a devotional exercise, similar to *davvening* (praying).

We are told that Rabbi Zusya of Hanipol

> would pray the Morning Service until noon, calling out with cries so awesome that they were really beyond human nature; and after praying he learned Torah . . . with the same amazing devotional intensity as in his prayer. (*Mazkeret Shem ha-Gedolim*, p. 64)

When Rabbi Meir of Kretchnif

> learned *Gemara* tears flowed from his eyes without cease, until sometimes the book that he was learning from would be altogether wet and waterlogged from the tears that fell down from his holy eyes. (*Raza d'Uvda*, p. 4)

This devotional nature of Torah study means that it is quite different from the Western way of "reading a book." The holy Torah is the revealed light of the One Who Spoke and the World Came into Being. Instead of being neutral or skeptical, you should read with an open heart and with a devotional attitude.

When one learns this way, Torah study purifies the soul and leads to a greater love of God. That this is so can be seen very clearly from the fact that it has this effect even if a person "studies" Torah without understanding. Thus, in a hasidic book it is reported that:

> I heard about a simple man who studied the *Gemara* without understanding what the words meant. His practice was just to recite the words. Yet, through this he reached the level where he had mystical revelations of Elijah. (*Derech Tzaddikim*, p. 49, #10)

15:2 SET TIMES

Make set times for your Torah study, and for the different branches of Torah. Be sure to study sometime during both day and night to fulfill "and you shall meditate in it day and night" (Joshua 1:8). As a sign of devotion and commitment it is traditional that these various daily sessions are fixed and are not skipped or changed except in very pressing circumstances. Similarly, they are not to be interrupted (see 15:14). Your own practice in this matter should be established by a *kabbalah*, your own predetermined commitment to accept upon yourself certain rules.

15:3 A SET PLACE

> **15:3:1** Have a special room for yourself dedicated just to Torah study that will have the sanctity of an actual *Beit Midrash* (House of Torah Study). But if that is impossible, then at least dedicate one corner of your room to this purpose, and set times to study Torah there. (*Kav ha-Yashar*, chap. 53)

15:3:2 The mind works by habit. If you set fixed times for Torah study in a fixed place, after a while, when that time arrives and you go to that place, you will feel a desire for Torah and your mind will turn to God.

> **15:3:3** It is helpful that at the time of Torah study you make some sort of change in your doings that will affect your body, for example, a change of place. If at all possible try to study elsewhere than

in your home. If you do not have anywhere else to go, or if there are people in that place who will disturb you—then at least have in your home a special room or at least a special place in a room dedicated to Torah study.

There is a purpose in all this, because, first, the place that is set aside and dedicated to Torah study is sanctified and is, as a result, more conducive to Torah study. But it is also the case that the movement you make and the change you make then with your body when you go to study will work to change all your thoughts and concepts and to break the web in which they have you chained to the things of this world. Your soul as well as your body will wake up from their slumber or from their involvement in this world in which they had been sunk until now and will say to themselves, "Enough, let us strengthen ourselves from now on to engage in Torah study." (*Hovat ha-Talmidim*, chap. 2, end)

15:3:4 See what is said about the initial difficulty that Rabbi Nachman of Bratzlav had in getting used to spending hours in his special room—"Vows," 12:6:1.

15:3:5 Rabbi Alexander Ziskind always expressed heartfelt gratitude to God for having provided him with a special room for Divine service. See "The Service of Praise," 34:2.

15:4 CONFESSION AND *TSHUVAH*

Before learning Torah, do *tshuvah* and repent, confessing your sins.

15:4:1 When the Seer of Lublin would open up a holy book [*Gemara*] to learn, he would say first, "Master of the World, perhaps of me it is written, 'But to the wicked, God says: "What have you to do with speaking of My statutes or taking the words of My covenant in your mouth?"' [Psalm 50:16]. So I declare before You that I accept on myself to do *tshuvah* and to repent from now on."* And so did he do every time he sat down to learn Torah.[1] (*Tiferet Mordechai*, p. 13a)

15:4:2 There is a sweet prayer for repentance and confession before Torah study from Rabbi Moshe Teitelbaum, the great disciple of the Seer of Lublin. Due to its length, the prayer is given at the end of this chapter.

15:4:3 Rabbi Eleazar Mendel of Jerusalem, of the Lelover line of hasidic *rebbes*, hired a Torah teacher for his young son.

> He was greatly surprised when his son told him how every day before he began the Torah lesson his teacher would stand completely still at the window staring out into space, and his eyes would stream tears nonstop, like rainwater gutters. That same day the *rebbe* called the teacher to his house and pressed him to explain his strange behavior. [The teacher agreed and told how, many years earlier, he had seen a miracle, a revelation of the holy spirit by the Holy Grandfather of Radoshitz. Aroused and excited, that very night he hid in the *rebbe's* room to see what his devotions were in the hours when others slept. He was discovered, however, and started to run away in great fear.] "But the *rebbe* turned to me and asked, 'Young man, what were you seeking?' 'The fear of heaven!' I answered. 'May it be His will,' said the *rebbe*, 'that whenever you begin to learn Torah, thoughts of *tshuvah* sparkle within you!' So did the Holy Grandfather bless me. Since then," said the teacher concluding his story, "tens of years have already passed, but the *rebbe's* blessing is still in force, and a day never passes that I don't do *tshuvah*. For the moment I get ready to begin to learn Torah, feelings of *tshuvah* are awakened in my heart, and my eyes stream with tears." (*Tiferet Beit David*, p. 18)

15:4:4 The main purpose of learning and involvement in Torah study is to make yourself into a throne for the Divine Presence. When you are dirty with all kinds of sins and transgressions then the *Shechinah* can't come to rest on you because each and every sin is like a thorn that hurts Her. To remove this obstacle, confess your sins before you begin to learn Torah. (*Kav ha-Yashar*, chap. 53)

15:4:5 Men of deeds make it a regular practice to confess their sins before they begin to learn, in order to remove the Shells which darken the mind and prevent them from understanding what they are learning. (*Totzaot Hayim*, p. 33)

15:4:6 A man should know that it is his sins that have darkened the light of his soul so that the light of Torah and of Wisdom do not illuminate it. As it is said, "Your sins have made a screen of separation between you and your God" [Isaiah]. So you have to repent in order to break the screen of surrounding Shells. And the proof of this is what is said in the *Tikkunim* [Kabbalah], that when a person is studying *halacha*, and he has questions and difficulties in understanding, he can remedy this by giving some *tzedaka* or performing some *mitzvah*, and immediately the truth will be revealed to him. Because the difficulties in comprehension are Shells which darken the light of his intellect, and when he repents and gives *tzedaka* he breaks the Shells. (*Totzaot Hayim*, p. 32)

15:4:7 As a young man, the holy *gaon*, Rabbi Mordechai of Neshkiz, was a disciple of the Zlotchover Maggid, Rebbe Reb Michli [Yehiel Michal], his memory for a blessing, and Rabbi Michli himself traveled to the Great Maggid of Mezritch. On one such trip his young disciple Rabbi Mordechai went with him. While he was there it happened that one day Rabbi Mordechai was looking for his master, and one of the great and famous disciples of the Mezritcher Maggid asked him who he was looking for. He answered, "My master." When asked again who his master was, he said, "The Maggid of Zlotchov." The other then said to him, "Your master himself needs a master." The Neshkizer looked at him with disgust and put his hand on the other's shoulder, as if to say, "You have said something important."

Now the Maggid of Mezritch used to learn with this great disciple of his every day after midnight the hidden wisdom [Kabbalah], and on that night the Maggid saw that he was not able to grasp what was being taught. He said to him, "Why is tonight special? I see that you are not understanding a thing. Have you sinned somehow, God forbid?" The disciple answered, "I am not aware of anything." The Maggid said to him, "Think. Maybe you have sinned against one of our group here." The hasid said, "I am not aware of any sin—except for what happened with that Rabbi Mordechai," and he told him the story. The Maggid of Mezritch told him to go immediately and appease him, for if not, there was no cure for his sickness. He did so [and the story continues further]. (*Kahal Hasidim ha-Hadash*, p. 47, #90)

Because of his sin against the younger hasid, the disciple's ability to understand the teaching of the Kabbalah disappeared. For this reason repentance before learning is necessary.

15:5 MEDITATION; FEAR AND LOVE OF GOD

Before prayer and before Torah study, after having meditated on *tshuvah*, arouse your heart to fear of God based on your love for Him, because without such fear and love the prayer or Torah will not ascend to heaven [will not attain to a high and effective spiritual

> level]. This arousal should be done by means of meditating on God's greatness and exaltedness [to arouse fear and awe], and on all the overflowing goodness that He bestows on us [to arouse love]. . . . You should also continually pause during your Torah learning to meditate on this. (Rabbi Tzvi Elimelech of Dinov, *Hanhagot Adam*, #10)

(See "Meditation" [17] for more about this typical hasidic meditation, and 17:3 for a related quote of Rabbi Tzvi Elimelech from his book *Derech Pikudecha*.)

15:6 STATED INTENTION

Before you begin Torah study you can go over your intention mentally or say it out loud as a stated intention. The general intention might be simply: "I am going to study Torah now to serve God, with love and fear." There are also various more specific intentions, some of which will be discussed in what follows. For example, one might say: "I intend to see in what I study ways to serve God so I can learn how to serve Him and give Him pleasure; and I intend to do what I learn is His will, blessed be He." The specific intention can also be varied depending upon what you learn, for different branches of Torah study (*halacha*, *musar*, *midrash*, etc.) have somewhat different purposes.[2]

The stated intention you say at the beginning of Torah study can be repeated throughout the time of learning.

> It is appropriate for a person to arouse himself during the time of learning almost every minute, to think this *kavvanah* even mentally, and in a shortened form. (*Yesod v'Shoresh ha-Avodah*, Gate 6, chap. 5, p. 125)

One can always add a short prayer for God's help such as "God, open my heart and mind to receive the light of the holy Torah."

15:7 A DECLARATION TO NULLIFY FOREIGN THOUGHTS

You can make a declaration beforehand that any bad or foreign thoughts that come to you during Divine service are nullified—for such service should be pure, without intrusion. The following, by Rabbi Tzvi Elimelech of Dinov, includes not only a declaration, but stated intentions and a prayer for Divine assistance.

> I am declaring now that any bad thought or musing or desire that comes to my mind and heart, especially during the time of prayer or Torah study, in any way whatsoever that is not according to the honor and will of God, blessed be He, I hereby nullify those bad thoughts or musings or desires that are against the will of the Holy One, blessed be He, completely, like a broken clay shard; and all the more so if I say any bad or forbidden speech—from this moment let them all be nullified altogether and completely. And now I reveal my intention and will, with all my heart, that my desire and hope and intention is to serve our God, the God of Abraham, the God of Isaac and Israel, with a perfect and pure service, in thought, speech, and deed, with fear and love and joy, in the proper way, and that all thought, speech, and deed which are against His will, blessed be He, are from now on completely nullified, for they are from the side of the evil inclination and are all empty and worthless. All my service to God, blessed be His name—in thought, speech, and deed—is just to give pleasure and satisfaction to Him alone, without any other motive at all. And the main thing: let my study now be for the unification of all existence in God, with fear and love . . . in the name of all Israel. . . . May the Lord, in His mercy, help us in this, for the sake of the honor of His name, from now and forever. May the words of my mouth and the meditations of my heart be acceptable before Thee, my Rock and my Redeemer.*[3] (*Derech Pikudecha*, Mitzvah 26, quoted in *Seder ha-Yom l'ha-Admor mi-Biala*, p. 26)

15:8 PRAY FOR GOD'S HELP

> The main thing is that as you study Torah you should be in fear and awe, in humility and lowliness, and should seclude yourself completely during the time of learning. You should confess your sins and *pray that God help you to come to the inner meaning of the Torah and to* d'vekut *with God, blessed be He* [italics mine]. And I know that this works from my own experience with the help of God. Certainly you also will have heavenly assistance. (Rabbi Mordechai of Kremenitz, Shtar Tza'a, in *Ha-Hasidut ha-Litait*, p. 68)

15:9 To open your heart in devotion and reverence for the Torah:

> When you open a book to learn and when you close it, kiss the book. (*Derech Hayim*, 5-61)

This is parallel to what we do in the synagogue when called up for an *aliyah*, or when the *sefer* Torah is carried around through the congregation.

15:10 THE BLESSING OVER THE TORAH

According to the *halacha*, the blessing on the Torah said in the morning applies for the whole day, and it does not have to be said again each time you study (and should not be said in Hebrew). Such words may be said in English, however, and there is good reason to do so.

So that you learn Torah with the proper intention, make a blessing in English each time you learn, at start and finish. The purpose of Torah study is to connect yourself with God, and when making the blessings you can focus on the divinity of the Torah, how it comes to us from God, on how our study is to be a devotional service of God, and so on.

One may use a long and a short form for blessings at the beginning and close of Torah study, both of them taken from the Siddur. The long form may be said in Hebrew in the morning the first time you study Torah that day (or as part of the Morning Service), and the short form in English every subsequent time.

Long

Beginning

> Blessed art Thou O Lord our God, King of the Universe, who hast sanctified us by Thy commandments and commanded us to occupy ourselves with the words of Torah. Make pleasant, therefore, we beseech Thee, O Lord our God, the words of Thy Torah in our mouth and in the mouth of Thy people, the House of Israel, so that we, with our offspring and the offspring of Thy people the House of Israel, may all know Thy name and learn thy Torah. Blessed art Thou, O Lord, who teachest the Torah to Thy people Israel. Blessed art Thou, O Lord our God, King of the Universe, who hast chosen

us from all nations and given us Thy Torah. Blessed art Thou, O Lord, who givest the Torah.

Close

Blessed is our God, who hath created us for His glory, and hath separated us from them that go astray, and hath given us the Torah of truth and planted everlasting life in our midst. May He open our heart unto His Torah, and place His love and fear within our hearts, that we may do His will and serve Him with a pure heart, so that we not labor in vain and not give birth to confusion. May it be Thy will, O Lord our God and God of our fathers and mothers, that we keep Your statutes in this world and that we may be worthy to live to witness and inherit happiness and blessing in the days of the Messiah and in the life of the World to Come.

The first of these blessings is in the early part of *Shaharit*, the second in the later part.

Short

Beginning

Blessed art Thou, O Lord our God, King of the Universe, who hast sanctified us by Thy commandments and commanded us to occupy ourselves with the words of Torah.

Close

Blessed art Thou, O Lord our God, King of the Universe, who hast given us Thy Torah of truth, and hast planted everlasting life in our midst. Blessed art Thou, O Lord, who givest the Torah.

The first of these blessings is the beginning of the longer one above and is the blessing over the Torah said each morning, which halachically covers Torah studied throughout the day. The second blessing is the one made after a section of the Torah is read in the synagogue.

The hasidic book *Or ha-Ganuz l'Tzaddikim* also suggests making a blessing over the Torah each time you study:

> When you occupy yourself in Torah study, even though according to *halacha* you do not have to make the blessing over Torah study each time—since when you make the blessing in the Morning Prayer Service it applies for the whole day—nevertheless, so that you remember to have God-consciousness, say each time before you study Torah, and again and again while studying: "For the sake of the unification of the Holy One, blessed be He, and His *Shechinah*. Blessed is the Merciful One, the King of the Universe, who is the Lord of this Torah."* (p. 45)

(The first [kabbalistic] part of this, about the unification of God and His *Shechinah*, may be omitted by someone who does not use this motive and intention, or it can be replaced by another intention. See "Leading Thoughts" [13] about the meaning of the kabbalistic motive and about alternatives.)

This blessing is halachically permitted because it is not in Hebrew but Aramaic. It can, then, also be said in English. Note the suggestion that it should be said again and again while studying.

15:11 *TALLIT* AND *TEFILLIN*; *GARTEL*

It is a good practice when you study Torah to wrap yourself in a sacred shawl, a *tallit*, and if possible, both a *tallit* and *tefillin*. During the night, however, *tallit* and *tefillin* are not to be worn unless they were put on while it was still day and not removed.

15:11:1 *Reshit Hochmah* refers to the *Tikkunim* (Kabbalah):

> He who engages in Torah while wrapped in *tallit* and *tefillin* will attain spiritual elevation [literally: to a *nefesh*, *ruah* and *neshamah*, the three soul levels]. (Sh'ar ha-Kedushah, chap. 6, #58)
>
> **15:11:2** You should learn Torah every day, at least something, while you still have *tefillin* on [that is, after the Morning Prayers]. (*Derech Hayim*, 4–31)

15:11:3 Some hasidim also wear a *gartel* (a twined silk belt usually worn by men for prayer) during Torah study. The *gartel*'s purpose is to make a symbolic separation between the lower body with its organs of sex and excretion, and the upper body, the heart and brain, so that they will not be affected by any lower influences. (See also 5:1:7:3.)

15:12 POSTURE

Pay attention to your posture when you study Torah, and how it affects your attitude. It is traditional to study at a table, but other ways are acceptable. What is important is to be aware of the effect of your posture and to choose what is suitable. For example, it may be acceptable to study hasidic stories in a relaxed posture in an easy chair, but studying *musar* (character improvement) that way is probably less appropriate. Of course, this depends on the individual too.

> **15:12:1** Let your learning be with awe and fear and do not sit leaning or relaxing, but as if you were in the presence of the king, as it says, "Prepare to meet your God, O Israel". . . . And so should your clothes be appropriate too. (*Totzaot Hayim*, p. 13)

15:12:2 For the sake of the awe of the holy Torah, some study standing up. But as the rabbis recognized (*Megilla* 21), this is difficult to do. One of the comments in the Talmud discussion where this practice is mentioned is that one should stand when learning easy, straightforward things, while sitting for difficult subjects where more thought is required.

> **15:12:2:1** Learn standing up. (*Derech Hayim*, 5–24)

For this you would probably need a stand on which to place the book.

> **15:12:2:2** It is told that the Kotzker Rebbe, in his younger days, was a *misnagid* and against the hasidim. He was so assiduous in continual Torah study that he learned standing up the whole day, holding in his hands a large, heavy copy of the Amsterdam edition of the Talmud, with its wooden covers and heavy clasps of burnished brass. (*Shivhei Tzaddikim*, p. 42)

15:12:2:3 It is told of Rabbi Zusya of Hanipol that:

> It was his holy way . . . that after praying the Evening Service he would study Torah through the whole night standing up, and he slept just two hours. (*Mazkeret Shem ha-Gedolim*, p. 64)

15:13 COMPLETE DEVOTIONAL INVOLVEMENT

When you learn, do so with complete devotional involvement. Sway as you study, forward and back or from side to side as you sit. Read out loud with a melody if possible; if you read silently, at least move your lips.

> Raise your voice in learning, for this will cause what you learn to stay with you. (*Derech Hayim*, 5–28)

However, the degree of activity of this sort depends on what and when; there are times when it is appropriate to read without movement and quietly, when concentration requires it.

15:13:1 The Baal Shem Tov:

> You should learn Torah . . . in a low voice, and should shout in a whisper, and say the words . . . with all your strength, as it says, "All my bones shall say: O Lord, who is like unto You!" [Psalm 35:10] For the shouting which is from *d'vekut* should be in a whisper. (*Tzavaat ha-Ribash*, p. 5)

> **15:13:2** Since Torah study is to be a "service" of God whose servants we are, and the rabbis speak of "laboring" in the Torah, we are to exert ourselves when we study, moving our whole body, directing our vision and hearing, until we are actually fatigued in the effort of our service. (*Sefer Haredim*, chap. 66, #30)

> **15:13:3** You should learn putting all your strength into it, until you sweat. By doing this you break the evil Shells that surround your soul. (*Kav ha-Yashar*, chap. 53)

Torah study with such *d'vekut* and fervor has a deep effect, reaching even to the body-feeling, breaking the ingrained body-set (the "Shells") which constrains the freedom of the soul. (For more about this important matter, see "Men's *Mikveh*," 30:10 and "*Mitzvot*," 11:3.)

> **15:13:4** Your eyes, heart, and ears should be directed fully to the words of Torah. (*Yalkut Shimoni*, Haazinu, 947)

Your eyes should be fastened on the page, your ears directed to hearing the words of Torah that your mouth is saying, your heart open. If possible, do not take your eyes off the words of Torah, do not let your glance go where it will. But you can also look out the window at the sky (this inspires fear of God and *d'vekut* [See "Sight," 25:10]), or at God's name on a *Shivitti* or a card (see 15:20).

15:13:5 Do not look away in the middle of Torah study so that your *kavvanah* is disturbed; just look at what you are learning. (*Marganita Taba*, #26, in *YHvT*, p. 92)

15:13:6 You should make it a point to study Torah in a room with windows, and look out frequently at the sky, as this helps in comprehension. (*Kav ha-Yashar*, chap. 53)

15:14 WITHOUT INTERRUPTION

As with other holy activities you should avoid interrupting your Torah study.

15:14:1 Do not interrupt your Torah learning in the middle for the sake of a conversation about worldly matters. (Rabbi Moshe Teitelbaum, *Hanhagot Tzaddikim*, p. 48, #10)

15:14:2 During Torah study, all the while the book is open before me, I will not interrupt for any conversation or for looking and listening to anything else. (From the personal *hanhagot* of the author of *Erech Apayim*, p. 77)

15:14:3 Rabbi Shlomo Leib of Lentshno starts a story about something that happened to him this way:

> Once when I was studying the *Zohar* at night as usual, an old man came over and sat next to me. But I did not want to interrupt my Torah study to see who it was. When I finished studying I turned to see who it was, but he had gone. (*Emunat Tzaddikim*, p. 89, #193)

15:14:4 A person can make rules for himself or herself about what to do if the phone rings, of if someone begins a conversation when he is studying Torah in a fixed session.

15:14:5 Every man of Israel, whether poor or rich, healthy or sick, should have a fixed time in the day and another at night when he will learn Torah—each one according to his own ability and understanding. Whether much or little, it is all one thing as long as his heart is directed to heaven. Moreover, he should *fix* the time so that it is not skipped for any reason in the world, even if he has a chance to earn a great deal of money. Let him give up all the money but not give up his set time for Torah.

This is the whole point of fixing a time—that it is actually fixed and an obligation, not something haphazard that can be forgotten or neglected if something else comes up. In that case its being fixed has no significance; it seems that he is just learning Torah because he has nothing else to do, and when something comes up he leaves the Torah and does that. And this is nothing other than belittling the Torah, God forbid. So when you study Torah, fixing the time, you should not interrupt your learning for the sake of anything else . . . but learn for the set amount of time uninterruptedly, finish, and only afterwards attend to your other concerns. (*Seder ha-Yom*, p. 22b)

15:15 FOREIGN THOUGHTS

It is not only conversation and dealings with others that should not be allowed to interrupt Torah study during fixed sessions, but "conversations" with oneself, too. As with prayer, foreign thoughts of any outside matters should be recognized if they appear, and dropped.

15:15:1 Rabbi Elimelech of Lizensk:

You should concentrate fully and see that you make no interruption at all, not even by thinking a thought that has nothing to do with the learning. (*Tzetl Katan*, #10)

15:15:2 If you have a bad thought or just a vain thought that disturbs your prayer or Torah study, look upward to heaven, or close your eyes, and think, "*Adonai*, *Adonai*, God merciful and gracious" (say this mentally, not aloud)—and the thought will certainly pass away, with the help of God. (*B'nai Machshavah Tovah*, Seder Hadracha v'Klalim, #6)

15:16 GOD AND HIS LIGHT WITHIN THE TORAH

When learning Torah be aware that God has manifested Himself through the holy book you have before you, through these holy letters. Tune in to the revelation, and to the light that is coming through to you.

15:16:1 The Baal Shem Tov:

> As you learn you should think . . . [and] say to yourself, "Has not God contracted Himself, so to speak, and descended into this Torah that I am studying?" Realizing this [that you are now with Him and close to Him], you should learn with joy, and with fear and love of God. (*Tzavaat ha-Ribash*, p. 19)
>
> **15:16:2** When you are learning Torah and praying from the Siddur, realize that the holy letters are like chambers of a palace in which the king dwells. And if you intend wholeheartedly to attach your soul to the king who is there, you will be able to say the words with great fear and love of God. (Rabbi Mordechai of Tchernobil, *Hanhagot Tzaddikim*, p. 63, #3)

15:16:3 This kabbalistic view of the letters of the Torah as vessels into which God's light has descended serves as an aid to concentration. The desired response is that you pour your own soul into those same letters as you read them with burning intensity, for it is within them that there is the meeting of your soul and God.

15:16:4 The kabbalistic interest in the letters is not necessary for this *kavvanah*.

> The Torah is a great light emanating from the radiance of God, blessed be He. So when you serve Him by Torah study, have as your intention that He should shine His light, blessed be He, on you and then you will delight and rejoice in Him, blessed be He. (*Sefer Haredim*, chap. 66, #144)

15:16:5 The Besht said:

> The purpose of Torah study for its own sake is to cleave in *d'vekut* to the One who is hidden within it, and to become a chariot for Him. (*Avodah u'Moreh Derech*, chap. 8, p. 16)

15:16:6 When you are doing worldly things such as eating, you want to interrupt yourself so that your soul will *not* descend into the food; with Torah, however, you want to avoid interruption and *dive* into it.

15:17 SCENT; THE FRAGRANCE OF THE GARDEN OF EDEN

Any and all aids to concentration should be used for Torah study. For example, spices or incense, with their sweet smell, can be helpful. Thus, the hasidic *rebbe*, Rabbi Shmelke of Nikolsburg, would have spices on the table where he studied.

> Our holy master, the Rabbi of Lublin, said that when, as a young man, he studied Torah in the *yeshivah* of the holy *gaon*, Rabbi Shmelke of Nikolsburg, . . . he would smell the sweet fragrance of the Garden of Eden while he learned from the *rebbe*. But the Rebbe Reb Shmelke would try to hide this, and whenever he learned with the *talmidim* [student disciples] he had on the table different kinds of spices so that if one of them would detect something he would think it was just the spices. (*Ohel Elimelech*, p. 135, #343)

The Baal Shem Tov would sniff tobacco during Torah study (as well as during prayer) because of its spiritual influence in expanding the mind. He would experience in the pleasant scent the sweet fragrance of the Garden of Eden (*Kol Sippurei Baal Shem Tov*, vol. 4, p. 20, story 5). This practice of the Besht in using the scent of tobacco during Torah study was certainly part of what is said about his imagining himself in Paradise (the Garden of Eden) before and during Torah study (see directly below).

15:18 MEDITATION: IN PARADISE; THE LIGHT OF THE *SHECHINAH*

15:18:1 Before studying Torah the Baal Shem Tov would say to God: *HaShem*, I'd like to be in Paradise with You for a few minutes. So before studying Torah, surround yourself with the pure air of Paradise. (Heard from a great rabbi and *tzaddik*.)

15:18:2 It is the practice among some hasidim to meditate before Torah study and prayer. They imagine the light of the Divine Presence above their heads and then around them:

> [He is] to imagine the light of the *Shechinah* . . . above his head and as if the light is flowing down around him. He is in the midst of the light, sitting in the pure air, and he trembles with joy. . . . Through this he can come to the state of the separation of the soul from body and senses, taking off materiality as one removes a garment. . . . So he should sanctify his little space of prayer and his little space of Torah study, and imagine that the light is glowing around him.[4] (*Or ha-Ganuz l'Tzaddikim*, pp. 10; cf. pp. 11 and 22)

Note what is said here about this preparatory meditation producing a state of separation of the soul from the body and senses. This is called *hitpashtut ha-gashmiyut*, "taking off materiality as a garment." In intense *d'vekut* and attachment to God one separates from the body and the material world. This state is also a goal for Torah study itself. (See 15:19.)

15:18:3 The Parables of the Fish in the Sea, of the Drop of Water in the Ocean, of Diving for Pearls

In the above quote and elsewhere, *d'vekut* is understood as being aware of the light of the *Shechinah*. Before Torah study or prayer one is to meditate to achieve this consciousness with regard to one's immediate surroundings. But the larger goal is to have this awareness always and vis-à-vis the whole world.

> Why does the Torah say, "Today you are standing before God" [Deuteronomy 29:9]; does not God's glory fill the earth? If so, a man is always standing before God. So what does this verse tell us about how to serve God? The explanation, according to the Baal Shem Tov, is that a person should be in such a state of God–consciousness that he should not have to make a special effort at the times of prayer and Torah, etc. to realize that he is in the presence of the King of the Universe, the Holy One, blessed be He. He should always see God in his mind's eye, and it should appear to him as if the Light of the Infinite One surrounds him and as if he is completely immersed in the Light of the Infinite One and the Light of the *Shechinah*. (*Or ha-Ganuz l'Tzaddikim*, p. 92)

Speaking of how we are to imitate the attainments of Abraham, Isaac, and Jacob, who were "continuously in a state of God-consciousness" and who were "chariots" of God, he continues:

> Just as fish are immersed in the sea and surrounded by water, so should you attain to such an awareness of God's light. From a state of great God-consciousness you should understand yourself to be completely immersed within the Light of Godliness, that great sea, which fills all worlds and surrounds all worlds.
>
> And in this state of consciousness you become like a drop of water that falls in the ocean and your separate existence is altogether nullified. . . . For just as the Light of Godliness fills the upper worlds, so does it fill the lower worlds, as it says, "Holy, holy, holy is the Lord of hosts, the whole earth is full of His glory." [Isaiah 6:3]
>
> The Holy One, blessed be He, fills all worlds and surrounds all worlds, and there is no place where He is not. The Baal Shem Tov taught us that when a person wants Godliness to rest on him the main thing is to know and understand that there is nothing in him but Godliness; and consciousness of that truth is a preparation that Godliness come to rest on him, when he realizes that he is nothing.
>
> The parable for this is of someone who dives down into the depths of the ocean to gather pearls. He has, first of all, to be careful that he holds his breath and does not suffocate from taking in water. And second, he should be very quick to search and gather whatever pearls he can. For if not, all his trouble will go for nothing. (p. 31)

He goes on to explain that when you are about to study Torah or pray, you should imagine yourself surrounded by the Light of Godliness, and that it is within you also. When you realize that you are nothing, and that God's light and life animate everything and move you too, you will become aware that you are not speaking the words of Torah, but it is the life-energy of the Godliness within you that is speaking. Words emerging from this holy consciousness are the "pearls."

The parable of the fish in the ocean indicates that we are to see ourselves as immersed in Godliness. The parable of the drop in the ocean illustrates a higher stage, that the individual is nothing, and that Godliness is everywhere, within and without. The parable of diving for the pearls teaches that we should dive into our Torah meditation and not "take in water," that is, allow distracting thoughts from our environment to reach us. While entering this consciousness we should use it well to speak holy words (there, pp. 79–80).

(For more about the light meditation, see "Prayer," 5:1:18:3:1.)

15:18:4 The light meditation described above is imagining oneself in Paradise, the Garden of Eden, where God's light is revealed.[5]

The Tree of Life in the middle of the Garden is the Torah, which you sit down to study.

> **15:18:4:1** It is as if a man sits in the Garden of Eden with the Light of the Holy One and His *Shechinah* . . . and he occupies himself with the Torah, which is called the Tree of Life. (*Or ha-Ganuz l'Tzaddikim*, p. 12)

15:18:4:2 The Maggid of Mezritch:

> "The Tree of Life in the middle of the Garden" [Genesis]—We know that when a person learns Torah or prays, he should think of himself as being in the Garden of Eden, where there is no jealousy, lustful desire, or pride, and he will thereby be saved from having such thoughts while he studies or prays. But we have to ask: How is it possible for a person to think of himself as being in the Garden of Eden when he indeed knows that he is in this world?
>
> This is the way to understand this matter: when a person studies or prays with love and fear of God and cleaves to God, he attaches his mind to his Creator and considers that His glory fills the whole earth and there is no place where He is not. He realizes that everything that exists is full of the Divine life-energy that has been drawn down into it. By way of example, if he sees another person, he sees his appearance and he hears his voice and what he is saying and is aware of the other person's intelligence, yet he knows that all this comes from the Divine life-energy that is in him. And with everything he sees and hears he has this perception. For everything has its appearance and its purpose, or its scent, or whatever other qualities it possesses—but whatever it is is from the Divine life-energy which is in everything. For everything is from Him; it is just that He is clothed, so to speak, in different garments.
>
> So when a person learns Torah with love and fear, since he is attached to God he does not see or hear anything but the Divine life-energy and vitality in everything. In such a case how is it possible for him then to have any personal desires or lusts relating to this world, when all that he sees before him is the life-energy of the Creator in everything?[6] (*Maggid Devarav l'Yaakov*, #200, p. 325)

The suggestion here seems to be that before and (at least occasionally) during Torah study (and prayer), you meditate on your surroundings, so that you see them as manifesting the Light of the *Shechinah*, and you see their spiritual essence rather than just their material form.[7]

One way to do this is to look at what is before you and then close your eyes to connect with the spiritual essence that resides in the things you see; then open your eyes again and try to retain that perception.[8] (See the quote from *Avodah u'Moreh Derech* in "Prayer," 5:1:18:3:1.)

This suggestion of the Maggid of Mezritch can be related not only to sight and hearing, but to scent (which he refers to). This is what the Besht, his master, was doing with his tobacco, and what Rabbi Shmelke, the Maggid's disciple, was doing with his spices (see 15:17). You can have pleasant spices on the table when you study Torah to "remind" you of the Garden of Eden. Traditionally, the Garden of Eden is said to have a most delightful fragrance; and according to the rabbis, pleasant scents are inherently spiritual, giving delight to the soul and opening the mind. So by having spices on the table as you study Torah, you can use your sporadic awareness of them to turn your mind to the Garden of Eden, thinking of how this lovely fragrance comes from the *Shechinah*, and thereby encouraging your own consciousness of being in the Garden of Eden where everything reveals God's presence. (This parallels the meditation during eating where the pleasurable taste of food is taken to be the taste of the Garden of Eden, the pleasure from the radiance of the *Shechinah*. See "Eating and the Holy Meal," 10:1:1, 10:4:1, and 10:14.)

15:18:5 As we have seen, one meditation to accompany Torah study is that of being surrounded by the Light of the *Shechinah*/Garden of Eden. Another meditation, perhaps more full of awe and designed to impart even greater intensity, is:

> When you are learning Torah, you should picture yourself standing in the midst of a great fire and surrounded by fire. (Rabbi Abraham of Slonim, *Torat Avot*, p. 166)

Rabbi Abraham intended this to be somewhat like the scene of the awesome fire at Sinai when the Torah was given. (See "Service of the Imagination," 19:1 for the full quote.)

15:18:6 There is a meditation before Torah study based on imagining the actual scene at Mount Sinai when the Torah was given. (See "Service of the Imagination," 19:2.)

15:19 LEAVING THE REALM OF MATERIALITY

The goal of devotional Torah study is very similar in one regard to that of prayer: there is to be complete immersion in the Light of holiness, until there is *hitpashtut ha-gashmiyut*, the stripping off of materiality and bodily awareness. As the Maggid of Mezritch said (see 15:18:4:2), one will cease to have thoughts related to the body and based in the lower emotions—of lustful desire, pride, etc. Finally, the soul is entirely in the spiritual world and even the senses are largely "shut off."

> You should find delight in Torah study such that the desire of your soul increases until your bodily senses cease to operate. Your soul should cleave in intense concentration to the Torah until you cease to be aware of the things of this world. . . . I have heard of many sages who had such great *d'vekut* with the Torah that they lost awareness of this world altogether. For just as intense desire for a woman nullifies all other thoughts and his heart burns with the fire of his love for her even when he eats, drinks, and sleeps, and all his thoughts are on what he desires, such should be our love for the Holy One, blessed be He. (*Reshit Hochmah*, Sh'ar ha-Ahavah, chap. 4, #30)

> Baruch, the personal attendant of Rabbi Hayim of Tzanz told this story. He used to sleep in the room adjoining that of the holy rabbi, and once he woke up and saw that the house was full of smoke. He jumped up and ran to the room where the rabbi was awake, at the table studying Torah. He peeked in through a crack in the locked door—and the table was on fire! The rabbi was standing there, one foot on the chair and the other on the floor, immersed in his thoughts, looking in some Torah book as if nothing was happening!
>
> Baruch began to bang on the door, and when the rabbi did not open it, he slammed his shoulder into it, breaking it open, the lock flying off. Immediately the rabbi ran toward him to hit him with the pipe that was in his hand, for disturbing him from his concentration and interrupting his Torah study. But the attendant cried out, "*Rebbe*, don't you see the table is on fire!" Then the *rebbe* looked and did see that the table was in flames, for until that moment he had not noticed anything. (*Mekor Hayim*, p. 35, #122)

This story is extraordinary because of the fire (certainly from the *rebbe's* pipe). Otherwise, it is somewhat typical in showing the *d'vekut* that can be achieved by holy rabbis in Torah study.

15:20 GOD'S NAME BEFORE YOUR EYES

15:20:1 The Baal Shem Tov once gave another *tzaddik* a card on which he had written the name of God, so that he would look at it while studying Torah and remember God. There is a story of how a rabbi (who inherited this card) brought it and another similar gift to the Seer of Lublin when he went to appease him over what he feared was an unintentional slight on his part.

> [And as he went] he carried in his hand two pieces of parchment. On one, which he had made, there was written [in Hebrew] "I have placed the Lord before me always." He used to hold this card in front of him whenever he learned Torah. The other card was from the Baal Shem Tov, on which the Besht himself had written in his own handwriting the four-letter name of God. This card had been given as a present to the rabbi's father, who had been a disciple of the Besht.
>
> When he came before the Lubliner . . . [and] showed him the card which he had written, the Seer gazed at it carefully and said, "Ah! Light! Light!" Then the rabbi showed him the other card from the Baal Shem Tov with its black letters on the white parchment, and immediately the *rebbe* leaped up from his chair and called out with emotion, "Black fire on white fire!" and with an expression of deep gratitude he eagerly took from him these precious and invaluable gifts. (*Kol Sippurei Baal Shem Tov*, vol. 1, p. 242, story 4)

15:20:2 Rabbi Tzvi Hirsh of Ziditchov notes:

> The practice has become widespread to write the name *Havaya* [YHVH] on a piece of paper or parchment and to look at it.[9] The Ari instructed those who are knowledgeable to write the name *Havaya*, blessed be He, [that way]. (*Yifrach biYamav Tzaddik*, pp. 38b–39)

15:20:3 It is an excellent practice to make a card such as this, with God's name on it, to stand on the table before you when you study Torah (also when you eat) and to look at it frequently. You can make the card with a prop on the back to hold it up, such as is used for photo frames. This card can be made of paper, or better and nicer material such as parchment. It is also possible to make a small plaque or plate of hard material, even silver. (See also "Eating and the Holy Meal," 10:4.)

15:21 Even without a full-blown meditation as described above:

Think while you are learning that you are not in this world, but are in the presence of the *Shechinah*. (*Derech Hayim*, 5–59)

15:22 REMIND YOURSELF AGAIN AND AGAIN

15:22:1 The Baal Shem Tov:

You should continually remind yourself before Whom you are learning, because it happens that even while you are learning Torah you can easily lose your awareness of God. So you should bring yourself back to that awareness again and again, every minute. (*Tzavaat ha-Ribash*, p. 19)

The card with God's name on it that the Besht gave to his disciple was for this very purpose.

15:22:2 When you learn you should pause periodically to return your mind to a state of God-consciousness, even though during the actual time of Torah learning it is impossible to achieve the highest levels of *d'vekut*. But Torah learning purifies the soul and it is a Tree of Life to those who hold on to it and if you do not learn, your God-consciousness will disappear. Even though compared to meditation your God-consciousness is somewhat lessened during the time of Torah learning, we pay no attention to that. Just be sure to collect yourself again and again in God-consciousness as said above. (*Darkei Yesharim*, p. 3)

15:22:3 Even while learning Torah you must remember to maintain your God-consciousness. Only someone who does not understand says that the Torah study itself is the *d'vekut*. (*Rachmei ha-Av*, #16)

15:22:4 Rabbi Tzvi Elimelech of Dinov taught that we are to continually reconnect ourselves in *d'vekut* throughout the time of Torah study. We are to do *tshuvah* and meditate on God's greatness and goodness to awaken our hearts to fear and love. (See 15:5 for the quote.)

15:22:5 When the Seer of Lublin was a young man and a disciple of Rabbi Shmelke of Nikolsburg, Rabbi Shmelke asked him to sit by him when he was learning *halacha* and *Tosafot*—for these subjects require such intense mental concentration that he might be distracted from his *d'vekut*. So Rabbi Shmelke told him that if it seemed to him that this was happening, he should pull his sleeve a little to remind him.

And the Lubliner said that it never did happen that Rabbi Shmelke needed his reminder, for he saw that he was never without *d'vekut*, even while learning the most complicated things. Once, however, the Lubliner had seen that Rabbi Shmelke was very deep in his concentration, and he was concerned that perhaps he had become separated from his *d'vekut*, and he wanted to tug gently at his *rebbe's* sleeve, as he had been told to do. But before he could do so, Rabbi Shmelke turned to him and said, "My son, my son, I remembered on my own." (*Mazkeret Shem ha-Gedolim*, p. 60)

15:23 A CHARIOT FOR THE DIVINE PRESENCE

While you are learning Torah frequently repeat words to this effect: "I am making myself a chariot for the Divine Presence. *HaShem*, cause Your *Shechinah* to rest on me!"*

> My teacher [Rabbi Elimelech of Lizensk] told me that while learning Torah one should think again and again, "I am making myself a chariot for the *Shechinah*"* . . . even a thousand times a day. He said that the body is much sanctified by this, and that when one becomes accustomed to it the mind is purified and thoughts of sin disappear, and one is able to pray with holy thoughts. (*Darkei Tzedek*, p. 5, #26)

(Note that this is a stated intention and can be used this way in your preparation before Torah study.)

When learning, you make yourself a chariot for the *Shechinah*, or, in other words, a vehicle for God and His will, in two ways: by fulfilling His command to study the Torah, and by filling yourself with the light of His presence communicated through the holy Torah. At the same time you pray that God increase His presence and direction in your life.

This kind of declaration and prayer can be said at all times when you are doing the will of God, not just when studying Torah.

The *Kav ha-Yashar* says that when you sanctify your body you become a dwelling place for the *Shechinah*.

> You should have this short prayer always in your mouth: "Master of the World, help me to be a throne for the *Shechinah*!"* For when the body is made holy it becomes a throne for the *Shechinah*. (chap. 52)

The "throne" on which the king sits is a parallel expression to the "chariot" into which the charioteer enters to hold the reins.[10]

15:24 YOUR TEACHER BEFORE YOU

One practice for Torah study recommended by various hasidic *rebbes*, and whose origin is in the Talmud, is to imagine that the teacher whose words you are reading is present and speaking to you personally.

15:24:1 Rabbi Elimelech of Lizensk describing the ways of the *tzaddikim*:

> When in studying the Torah you mention the name of a *Tanna* [an authority quoted in the Mishnah] or someone who reported a tradition, you should imagine that he is alive and standing in front of you . . . as is explained in the Jerusalem Talmud. (*Noam Elimelech*, p. 98a, Igeret ha-Kodesh, second letter)

> **15:24:2** Rabbi Simha Bunim of Pshischa once told this story to his *talmidim*: Once he came to his *rebbe*, the Holy Jew, his memory for a blessing, and his *rebbe* was surprised to see how terribly depressed he looked, as if he were sick, God forbid. He asked him what had happened. Rabbi Simha Bunim told him that someone had just humiliated him in the worst way, so that he was deeply hurt. His *rebbe* was again surprised and asked who would dare to do this. "But," Rabbi Bunim continued, "I wouldn't tell him. He urged me very strongly to tell, because he wanted to punish whoever it was. When I continued to refuse he became angry. He asked me what I answered back after I was humiliated so, and I told him that I kissed the one who did it on the mouth. At this the *rebbe* was still more surprised and finally ordered me, as my *rebbe*, to tell him who it was. So I was forced to tell him, and I said to him that in the Jerusalem Talmud (*Shabbat*, perek 1, halacha 32) it says that when you are learning you should consider the master of the tradition as if he were standing before you. So that was my thought as I was studying in the book of character development, *Shevet Musar* [*The Rod of Musar/Reproof*]. And the holy author was shaming and humiliating me greatly, until I saw that I hadn't even begun to serve God, and that I hadn't the slightest bit of the fear of God or holy

> shame or any one of the many virtues that a son of Abraham, Isaac, and Jacob should have. When I saw that what he said was true I was overcome with shame and almost fainted. But afterwards I took the book in my hands, kissed it with all my heart, and then put it in the bookcase with all the other books."
>
> When the Holy Jew heard his disciple "explain" what had happened to him he became very happy and joyful at his wisdom. (*Simhat Yisrael* p. 27, #65)

From this story we can see that the point for Rabbi Simha Bunim was not to visualize the author of the book before him (athough elsewhere something like that is often indicated), but to call up his presence in the most vivid way so that as he read he took what was said as if spoken to him personally at that moment, as if the author were there, speaking directly to him.

This practice is particularly valuable when learning from a *musar* book, as in this case.

15:25 PSALM 119

Memorize various lines of Psalm 119 and say them throughout the time of learning Torah. Many of these verses are basically separate and independent and seem to have been intended for such a purpose. Verse 18 is an example.

> "Open my eyes, that I may behold wondrous things out of Thy Torah!" [Psalm 119:18]. You should continually pray this verse, that God enlighten your eyes in His Torah, that you merit to understand the Torah's secrets, which are its inside meaning. (Rabbi Natan Netta of Shinovi, *Hanhagot Tzaddikim* [III], vol. 1, p. 273, #13)

You might keep Psalm 119 open beside you as you study, and read out of it periodically, or use the verses of the psalm for suggestions about what to say in your own words.

15:26 MOUNT SINAI

Rabbi Levi Yitzhak of Berditchev suggests that at the time of Torah study you recite a prayer containing a description of the scene of the giving of the Torah at Mount Sinai (see "Service of the Imagination," 19:2).

15:27 IF YOU DO NOT UNDERSTAND

15:27:1 Pray

When you do not understand something as you study Torah it is appropriate to pray for comprehension and understanding. A hasidic story begins this way:

> The holy Rabbi Aaron of Karlin, of blessed memory, was once studying the *Gemara* and he had a difficult time understanding a certain matter. This made him so unhappy that he started to become depressed. So he turned to God in prayer and prayed mentally to Him, blessed be He, that He lighten his eyes. Then he applied himself in total concentration to try again to understand. (*Zichron l'Rishonim*, p. 27)

Note how this practice leads us to a devotional attitude to Torah. It keeps us from pride over our Torah knowledge and makes us realize that our ability to understand, our intelligence, and wisdom, comes from God.

15:27:2 Repent

We saw that you are to repent as a preparation for learning (15:4). During Torah study, also, if you do not understand something, repent and make confession.

> **15:27:2:1** If a person finds something in the Torah hard to understand, it is because of some sin or transgression he has committed. [In the words of Rabbi Tzvi Elimelech of Dinov:] "So the remedy for this, according to the kabbalists, is that whenever you do not understand something in the Torah: do *tshuvah* and shed tears." (*Ha-Rebbe Reb Tzvi Elimelech mi-Dinov*, vol. 1, p. 208)

> **15:27:2:2** If you do not understand something, make a confession of sins, cry, and give some *tzedaka*—this is a proven method—and your eyes will be enlightened. (*Or Tzaddikim*, p. 16b, #17)

15:27:2:3 If you do not understand something in your learning, shed tears about it and give something to *tzedaka*, and say *Ahavah Rabbah* [*Shaharit*, before the *Sh'ma*] with *kavvanah*, as explained in *Shnei Luchot ha-Brit*. (*Derech Hayim*, 5–27)

15:27:2:4 The way of Rabbi Zusya's Torah learning is known to all. His holy way was to attain to an understanding of all the difficult things in the Torah just through crying and prayer. Once he was teaching a very intelligent young man who asked deep questions the *rebbe* could not answer. So he would go into his room for a little while—and when he came out he would give an amazing answer, as if from one of the *gaonim* [Torah geniuses; Rabbi Zusya of Hanipol was not great in Torah compared to others]. After this went on for a while, the astonished young man wondered how the rabbi came up with these answers, which were way above his level of Torah expertise. So he looked through a hole in the door to see what Rabbi Zusya was doing in the room, and saw that he was crying profusely and hitting his head against the wall, and praying to the Holy One, blessed be He—"Why don't You reveal to me the wisdom of Your holy Torah?" (*Mazkeret Shem ha-Gedolim*, p. 68)

15:28 THANKS AND PRAISE FOR UNDERSTANDING

When you are learning and have an insight, turn to God in praise; or if you have trouble understanding something and finally come to understanding, give Him thanks.

15:28:1 When you have some new insight in your Torah learning immediately give praise and thanks to God. (*Derech Hayim*, 3–23)

15:28:2 When you are learning a Torah book and there is something hard to understand, where you cannot comprehend the intention of the author—but after hard study you do reach the true meaning, you should give praise and thanks to God, blessed be He, mentally and even verbally, and say with great joy, "Master of all the worlds, I give praise and thanks to Your Great Name that You gave me the intelligence and ability to understand Your holy and pure Torah!" (*Yesod v'Shoresh ha-Avodah*, Gate 1, chap. 6, p. 13)

15:29 *NIGGUN*

A beautiful practice among hasidim is to stop sometimes during Torah study to sing a *niggun*, a hasidic melody. Such a melody can express your devotion to the Master of the Torah that you are learning. It is the hasidic way that you do not have to wait for a cue—just stop, without reason or cause (other than the joy that comes from Torah learning), and sing before your Creator.

The *niggun* can also open up the mind to God's wisdom. Once, Rabbi Shneur Zalman of Ladi, the first Lubavitcher *rebbe*, was in Shklov, and he was asked by the Torah scholars there a number of difficult questions before he went to give a talk in the *Beit Midrash.*

> When he entered the *Beit Midrash* he went up on the *bimah* and said, "Instead of speaking words of Torah and answering your questions, I will sing a melody for you—because souls are elevated and brought to God by means of melody and song." And he began to sing with great *d'vekut.* A hush descended on the *Beit Midrash* and there was complete silence; all became deeply immersed in thought. Each one was lost in his own world. Suddenly, in the middle of the *rebbe*'s *niggun*, the Torah sages of Shklov felt that all their questions and difficulties were resolved and answered; the *rebbe*, with his *niggun* of *d'vekut* had opened up for them channels from the fountains of wisdom, and their minds were opened. [And one of them said that when his questions were answered] "I felt like I was a small child." (*Sippurei Hasidim*, vol. 1, #446)

15:30 TO DO WHAT IS TAUGHT

One of the strongest perspectives from which to learn Torah is that you are learning to *do* what is taught. You have to prepare yourself for this intention, as the Jewish people said at Sinai: "*Naaseh v'nishmah,*" "We are ready to do whatever You tell us." This attitude requires a shift in consciousness, and is held by the rabbis to be the secret by which the angels serve God.

> **15:30:1** The main thing is to do and fulfill what you learn because Torah is so great—when it leads to action. (Rabbi Mordechai of Tchernobil, *Hanhagot Tzaddikim*, p. 64, #12)

15:30:2 When you involve yourself in learning about the commandments of God, when you study the Prophets, the Writings, the words of the Sages of the Talmud, and when you see the warnings and punishments spoken of, and the sweet lessons on how to act, let your heart be awakened and say to yourself, "How can I study the holy Torah as if it were just a book of stories? No! I will commit myself to keep and do everything that I read!" (*Orchot Tzaddikim*, Gate 22 p. 122)

15:30:3 When you open a holy book to learn . . . you should say, "I want to learn Torah so that my learning will lead to doing and to good character traits, and to a correct understanding of the Torah." Again and again while you are learning you should say, "Let the light that is in the Torah bring me back to the good path!"*

And whenever the evil inclination tries to get you to stop and to shorten your time of learning because of fatigue or because you do not understand what you are trying to learn or because there are distractions such as the noise of the children, rebuke the evil inclination and overcome it and overcome your natural tendency, learning more than your habit and with all your strength, until you are sweating. By doing this you break the Shells and the evil forces and you cause atonement for your sins. Because when Torah learning . . . is with all your strength and effort and with a loud voice and a pleasant melody [in chanting], without any foreign or distracting thoughts, and with the swaying of your body, it purifies you and makes your soul shine, and sharpens your intellect and breaks the Shells. (*Shemen ha-Tov*, the *hanhagot* of Rabbi Shmelke of Nikolsburg, #51, 52, p. 52)

15:30:4 It was said of the Zlotchover Maggid that:

> Whether he was learning in a book of the revealed or the hidden Torah [Kabbalah], he never saw anything except what he needed to serve God. (*Yeshuot Malko*, p. 132)

This is a perspective related to the readiness to do: that everything you see in the Torah should be to teach you how to serve God. A common hasidic teaching is along these lines: if you read a Torah story about someone who lived long ago—what is in it to teach *you* how to serve God? Or if it is, let's say, something in the *Chumash* about a law that relates to doings in the Temple, which today does not exist—how can *you* learn from it how to serve God? Since the Torah is eternal there will always be a lesson for today and for you personally.[11]

Rabbi Uri of Strelisk said of himself that he never left what he was studying without taking from it something for the service of God; and after he found the hidden pearl he did not leave it until he took it into the inner recesses of his heart, to serve the Holy One, blessed be He. (*Mazkeret Shem ha-Gedolim*, p. 138)

15:31 AFTER TORAH: A SELF-ACCOUNTING; NOT PRIDE BUT LOWLINESS

Before learning Torah you should make a self-accounting and see that you know before Whom you are learning, before the King of the Universe, the Holy One, blessed be He; and dedicate your learning to The One Who Spoke and the World Came Into Being. And after learning Torah, again make a self-accounting. Look at your character traits and be heartbroken over your failings and your lowliness, and how far you are from what the Torah says you should be. About this King David said, "A broken and contrite heart, God will not despise."

There are those who sit down with a full belly and learn without any accounting of where they are, and after the learning they are proud of themselves and think, "How well I learn," and their hearts' thought is, "Who could the king desire more than me?" . . . What is such learning worth in God's eyes?—for the purpose in giving us the Torah was that we learn it and do it. (Rabbi Aaron of Karlin, *Hanhagot Tzaddikim*, pp. 28, 29)

15:32 TO APPLY AND DO WHAT YOU LEARN

Always be diligent with regard to your Torah study such that you try to apply what you learn. When you get up from studying, see if there is something in what you learned that you can apply and do. (The Ramban's letter to his son, in *Reshit Hochmah*, Sh'ar ha-Ahavah, chap. 6, #74)

It can be made a regular practice to devote a few minutes after Torah study to *tshuvah* and to considering how what you have learned can be applied.

15:33 TORAH INTO PRAYERS

To connect Torah study with doing, Rabbi Nachman of Bratzlav told his disciples to transform his Torah lessons into prayers, and to pray that they attain what was taught.

> It is very beneficial to make prayers out of Torah, either out of what you learn from a book or what you hear from a true *tzaddik*. Beg and plead before God concerning everything in that teaching and ask: "When will I merit to come to all this?" Speak about how far away you are from it now. . . . And if you are sincere, God will lead you along the true path so that you will know how to work out these kinds of prayers in the right way. (*Likkutei Moharan*, II, section 25)

Some of Rabbi Nachman's disciples composed written prayers of this sort. One could also spontaneously create such prayers as part of a brief period of self-accounting after Torah learning.

15:34 PRAYER DURING TORAH

Another practice, related to that suggested by Rabbi Nachman (15:33), is to merge prayers spontaneously into your Torah study. If you are studying something about how to control your anger, turn to God and pray that He help you to accomplish this; if you are studying something about having trust in God, pray to Him that you attain such trust, and so forth.

15:35 FROM TORAH TO PRAYER AND BACK

Torah and prayer are complementary; it is good to go from one to the other. Study Torah as a preparation for the prayer service; and after prayer go to the Torah.

> **15:35:1** Immediately after the [Morning] Prayers see that you learn Torah, and "go from strength to strength." (Rabbi Mordechai of Kremenitz, *Tzavaot v'Hanhagot*, p. 138)

15:35:2 Make it a fixed practice for yourself that immediately after the Morning Prayers you learn some Torah, whether much or little. (Darka Shel Torah, #6, in *YHvT*, p. 101)

15:35:3 Rabbi Uri of Strelisk said:

Through Torah study you attain to true prayer to God, blessed be He; and afterwards the prayer brings you to the study of Torah for its own sake in truth. (*Mazkeret Shem ha-Gedolim*, p. 138)

15:35:4 Rabbi Shlomo of Karlin said:

When a person learns the Torah for its own sake his heart burns to give himself in complete self-sacrifice for God and he yearns to pray. (*Hanhagot Tzaddikim*, p. 28)

15:36 MEDITATIONS ON TORAH

It is possible to do meditations on Torah, according to your needs and interests. Do not just read about what you are learning in Torah, but set aside time to meditate on a story or a topic. Sit down, close your eyes perhaps, and spend time with the Torah in intimate communion. Engage your mind in Torah, submerge it fully in the dye of holiness.

The main thing is that you do not just think Torah thoughts when you are learning from the book, but that you continue afterwards to think and meditate about what you read there. This is not just so that you can remember to do what is written, but also for the purpose of purifying and strengthening your mind. . . . Is it not to your benefit in this and the coming world that instead of letting your thoughts drift about uncontrolled in whatever comes to mind, that you think of holy things? And if it is too difficult when you have some free time to bend your mind to think about complicated matters like those of the *Gemara*, then why not think things from the *Aggadah* which are so attractive, and Hasidism . . . when you have a free hour or even fifteen minutes, and when you are walking outside on the street?

If at first this is difficult, then you should know that it is always easier to do what you want and to wallow in whatever, rather than holding yourself to some standard, to the way of goodness and to piety. But when you have accustomed yourself to this kind of Torah

> meditation . . . and have done it for some time, then you will not even be able to go around without holy thoughts.
>
> If it happens on an occasion that you were walking on the street and not meditating on Torah thoughts and on holy things as you went along, you will feel inside as if, God forbid, you had actually committed the transgression of neglecting a time that you had set aside and devoted to Torah study. (Rabbi Kalonymus Kalmish Shapiro, the Rebbe of Peasetzna, *Hachsharat ha-Abrechim*, p. 32)

What the *rebbe* discusses here is how to fulfill that part of the first paragraph of the *Sh'ma* we say each day: "And these words shall be upon thine heart . . . and thou shalt talk of them when thou sittest in thine house, and when thou walkest by the way, and when thou liest down, and when thou risest up."

Rabbi Kalonymus Kalmish, in the book quoted here, gives good advice on how to expand Torah thoughts into extended meditations. One example he gives relates to stories in the *Tanach*. He says that when you learn these stories and/or the *midrashim* of the rabbis which discuss and add to them, you should personally identify with the events and characters in the story.

> When you learn *Tanach* try to identify with all the happenings as if you yourself were there at the time. Go with Abraham and Isaac to the binding of Isaac on the altar; involve yourself in the anguish and fear of Jacob when he prayed to God to save him from the wrath of his brother Esau. And so too when you learn *Midrash*, for there are many *midrashim* on verses from the *Tanach* that reveal many additional things about the events. (*Hachsharat ha-Abrechim*, chap. 7, p. 33)

The Peasetzna Rebbe says to take all you know of a story (from both the *Tanach* and the *Midrash*), for instance, the story of the binding of Isaac by Abraham, and meditating on it, go over each detail in your mind, with personal involvement.

First, do this based on your knowledge of the sources. Later, when you are more accustomed to this kind of meditation, you can add your own innovations and interpretive thoughts. Imagine the scene as God told Abraham to sacrifice Isaac, how Abraham chopped the wood for the burnt offering and how he saddled the ass; imagine the conversation he had with Isaac on the way, and what they both were thinking about as they walked along—about what Sarah was thinking and doing then at home, and so forth.[12]

A second kind of Torah meditation is on a religious thought or concept. Start by considering everything you know about the idea, and go over it thoroughly in your mind. After doing that, apply the concept or idea personally and to your own real-life situation. If you are meditating on God's omnipresence, for example, after meditating in depth about the concept, focus then and there on His presence with you, etc. The same approach can be used for any Torah concept. (See "Individual Practices," 39:32 for another example of a meditation on a Torah concept, and "Meditation," 17:6 about the *ada-ata d'nafshey* ["until it reaches you"] aspect of meditation.)

15:37 TORAH GROUPS AND TWOSOMES

It is valuable to study Torah in groups, for such study has a special spiritual aspect and power similar to group prayer. It is also traditional and helpful to study with a steady partner, a *havrusa.* Try to arrange for yourself both these forms of study if possible.

15:38 LISTENING TO TORAH

When you are present at a Torah talk or class or listening to a sermon you are not to sit passively. The pious attitude is first of all to pray to God before and during the talk that He send down light to the teacher and open his mouth for holy words. Pray also that He open your heart and the hearts of others present to receive those words.

Regardless of the particular spiritual level of the teacher or his intellectual abilities, you are to see him as an agent of the Holy One, blessed be He. Ignore any personal deficiencies he might have and focus on the part he is playing now in your life. God will send you teaching through him if you listen with an open heart and mind.

> The more that the people desire to hear the preacher, to that degree does he receive the flow of Light from Above with which to speak the Word to them. (*Milei d'Avot*, p. 114, #5)

The kind of receptive and devotional attitude you are to assume is essentially like that which you should have in your own individual Torah study.

15:39 CONTINUOUS TORAH STUDY

The traditional goal of a main stream of the religious community is to attain to a continuous connection with God through *continuous* Torah learning, *hatmada*, Torah learning without cease (except of course for other necessities, material and spiritual). Any cessation of Torah study for the least amount of time is accounted a transgression (*bitul Torah*).

The hasidic tradition does not emphasize Torah study quite this way (see Chapter 3, p. 64). However, understanding of the ideal is beneficial. Even if you are not one who studies Torah continuously or strives in that direction, this can be at least a part of your spiritual practice—to turn regularly to Torah study. Thus, even when you have only a few minutes you can learn Torah. It is a sign of your love for God and His Torah that when you are only free for the briefest time, for just one minute, you turn to the holy Torah.

It is also good to learn by heart some piece of Torah that appeals to you, so that you can learn by repeating it to yourself when you cannot have a book with you, such as when you are walking on the street. The Mishnah of *Pirke Avot* is appropriate for this kind of use (see 15:39:5).

15:39:1 Let it not seem trivial in your eyes to learn Torah even for just five minutes if it happens that you have no more free time than that. (Darka Shel Torah, #4, in *YHvT*, p. 101)

15:39:2 [Someone who truly loves the Torah and appreciates how precious it is] will not rest or relax from meditating on it whenever he has a chance, even for one minute. Instead of wasting that minute in worthless things or talk, God save us, he will grab whatever holy book is near at hand, whatever it is, and look in it to learn, even a few lines or words, for that minute—because of his deep love for the Torah. (*Tzva'a Yekara* of Rabbi Alexander Ziskind, #35)

15:39:3 It is important for any Torah scholar to know some *mesechet* [tractate] of the Torah by heart and at least some chapters of the Mishnah—for often you are in a situation where you cannot learn from a book, especially when you are traveling. (Darka Shel Torah, #2, in *YHvT*, p. 101)

15:39:4 Reb Arele Roth:

Happy is he who knows words of Torah by heart, which he can continually go over [when walking outside, etc.], for they will certainly save him from undesirable and low thoughts. (*Noam ha-Levavot*, p. 40)

15:39:5 This piece of Torah that you learn by heart can also be used for study during meals.

> It is also good to learn a tractate by heart and to recite it frequently; it is good, too, to recite it every day and also to use it when eating, and by this the meal becomes a *mitzvah meal.* (*Darkei Tzedek*, p. 19, #20)

By reciting the Torah of your choice at meals, with the book before you, you can then memorize it and have it for recitation at other times.

> Before the Grace after Meals recite a chapter of *Avot* each day until you know the whole thing by heart. (*Tzavaat Rabbi Yehudah ben Asher*)

(For the practice of Torah study at meals, see "Eating and the Holy Meal," 10:10.)

A PRAYER TO SAY BEFORE TORAH STUDY

This prayer from Rabbi Moshe Teitelbaum, which is quite long, has been edited and shortened slightly.*

> I am afraid, as I open my mouth, to approach the holy Torah, for I know that my sins have reached even above my head, and as a heavy load, are too weighty for me to bear. So I make my confession, with bowed head and with bowed stature, of all the sins and transgressions and iniquities I've committed.
>
> I've spoken slander, and been a gossiper and tale bearer, I've lied and talked scornfully, I've conversed [during prayer and Torah study and other times] when it is forbidden to interrupt; I've had profane conversations in holy places, the synagogue and the *Beit Midrash*—even during the Torah reading, and even when I had *tefillin* on, and I took my mind off them. I've profaned the Glorious Name, I've profaned, in speech and deeds, Sabbaths and holidays, I've looked at what should not be looked at; I've listened to what it's forbidden to listen to, I've caused spiritual blemishes in all my senses, I've caused blemishes in not keeping the covenant of the

tongue, and the covenant of the sexual organ, the holy seal. I've spoken words of empty conversation, words with no holy purpose, I've wasted my time, time that could have been devoted to Torah; I've given others bad advice, I've allowed myself to be raised up at the expense of lowering others, and rejoiced at their humiliation; I've embarrassed my brother, and I've referred to others in disparaging terms, even in public; I've hated others of Israel, even without cause, I've hated those whom I should have loved, and I loved those who should have been hated; I've been jealous of others, I've sinned by being proud, I've sinned by being angry, I've walked proudly erect, without any humility; I've sworn and made oaths and not fulfilled them. I've shaken hands and attested to falsehood, I've revealed my friend's secret, I've spoken one way with my mouth, but had something else in my heart; I've deceived others, eaten and drunk forbidden things, filled my mouth with laughter, though the world is yet unredeemed and drowning in sadness, failed to make blessings of enjoyment and to say the Grace After Meals as was fit, prayed without *kavvanah*, was thinking of my private affairs during the time of prayer—even of worthless things, and worse, even bad thoughts; I've stumbled unintentionally. On *Shabbat* I've carried things from a private domain to a place neither public nor private, I've studied Torah with impure motives, done *mitzvot* and good deeds so that others would praise me, I've sinned through hypocrisy.

And for all the other evil sins that I've committed, those I know I did and those I'm not aware of—for them all, I confess, and ask, with lowly supplication and brokenness of heart, for forgiveness and pardon and atonement, from the forgiving and pardoning King.

I've sinned through speech, action, and thought, with all the limbs of my body and all the parts of my soul. I've caused blemishes in all the worlds, I've chopped down the saplings,[13] I've destroyed the channels of the heavenly flow, and have led that flow from its Supernal Source down to a place of filth, a trap of lewdness.

Woe is me! Woe is me! Alas for me and alas for my soul! My sin is beyond bearing, my transgressions are too great to be atoned for! I regret them all, with all my heart, and after I've repented, I am in deep sorrow, and after I understood, I clapped my hands in grief.

I declare now that I regret all the sins I've done, and that I'm ashamed, for I've shamed myself. Woe is me for the shame! Woe is me for the humiliation! How can I any longer lift my face to the King of the Universe, the Holy One, blessed be He, and stand before Him and study His holy Torah? What will I do when God shall arise and come to judge—what can I answer Him? Woe is me for the Day of Judgment! Woe is me for the Day of Rebuke! I declare now that I lament all my sins and wrongdoings and transgressions, that I've sinned and done wrong, and transgressed against the Lord of the Universe, my Creator and Maker, who has done so much good to me, in everything and every way. But I've done evil. Woe is me, what have I done? How have I rebelled against the King of the Universe, the Holy One, blessed be He, and against His holy Torah? How have I blemished my own soul, choosing an ephemeral world over one that is eternal? What will I do on the Day of Visitation, when I descend to the place of punishment? Oh! My heart is weak, for that I've rebelled against the King of the Universe, the Holy One, blessed be He, the Cause of all causes, the Mover of all that moves. He is pure and His ministers, they who do His will, are pure; while I am disgusting, a lowly dog, a corrupt sinner and contemptible, so much have I made myself unclean.

I regret completely what I've done, and if I've done wrong in any way I'll not continue so, and I'll never do so again all the days of my life. And I'll add fences and barriers, that I'll not even come near to transgressing in my former ways, but will keep myself from even approaching the realms of sin.

And now, my heart has lifted me up to return to You, O God; and I've come to confess my sins and abandon them for good. [And so] May it be Your will, O my God and the God of my ancestors, that my prayer come before You; don't hide from my supplication. For I'm not brazen and stiff-necked, saying, "O God and God of my ancestors, I'm righteous and haven't sinned"—but I have sinned. I've been guilty and acted deceitfully. What can I say before You, who sit in the eternal heights, my Maker and Redeemer? May it be Your will, my God and God of my ancestors, that You atone for all my sins, and forgive me for all my transgressions, and pardon me for all my iniquities—

for the sin that I sinned before You by my eating and drinking,

for the sin that I sinned before You with regard to the Grace after Meals,

for the sin that I sinned before You by pride,

for the sin that I sinned before You in swearing and making oaths,

for the sin that I sinned before You in thinking sinful thoughts,

for the sin that I sinned before You by joining in a gathering to advance a dispute, for the sin that I sinned before You through fornication and sexual licentiousness,

for the sin that I sinned before You through violating a ban and by doing that which is punished by a period of excommunication,

for the sin that I sinned before You in *treif* and forbidden foods,

for the sin that I sinned before You in forbidden wine,

for the sin that I sinned before You in failing to give honor to Torah sages,

for the sin that I sinned before You in slander, tale-bearing and gossip,

for the sin that I sinned before You in not giving tithes,

for the sin that I sinned before You in matters of the ritual washing of hands,

for the sin that I sinned before You in public and in secret,

for the sin that I sinned before You in oppression and in robbery,

for the sin that I sinned before You in sexual matters and in nocturnal emissions of semen,

for the sin that I sinned before You in regard to *tzitzit*, *tefillin* and *mezuzah*,

for the sin that I sinned before You in *kiddush ha-Shem* and in *hillul ha-Shem*,

for the sin that I sinned before You by my anger and rage,

for the sin that I sinned before You by falsehood, etc., against the Torah of Moshe,

—for I've transgressed in *mitzvot* of doing and *mitzvot* of not-doing, in things for which there is the punishment of being spiritually cut off, and the punishment of the four death penalties of the *Beit Din*; I've transgressed against the written Torah and the oral Torah. I've forgotten Your Great Name, I've held in contempt Your kingdom and Your fear. And You are justified in all that You've brought upon me, because You've acted truthfully, and it's I who have acted wickedly.

And so, I'm afraid, and tremble to begin studying the holy Torah, for how can a mouth blemished with all kinds of blemishes give utterance to the holy Torah? A mouth that's spoken lewdness, how can it utter the words of the holy Torah? How can blemished eyes look on the words of the holy Torah? How can ears blemished by listening to slander, and with other faults and blemishes, listen to the sound of the words of the holy Torah? How can a mind and an imagination made unclean by bad thoughts meditate on the holy Torah? And I fear that it is said of me, God forbid, "And to the wicked has God said, How can you mouth My statutes or take the words of My covenant on your lips?"—for "the sacrifice of the wicked is an abomination"; and perhaps, God forbid, my hope and my expectation from God is lost. But yet, my heart says to me, "How can you sleep? Rise and call out to your God! For He desires mercy, and has no pleasure in the death of the sinful man, but that he turn from his sins and live."

Not on my righteousness do I rely, in making supplication before You, O Lord, but on Your abundant mercies—for You are a King who forgives and pardons, and Your hand is stretched out to receive those who return to You.

So, may it be Your will, my God and God of my ancestors, that You dig a tunnel under Your Throne of Glory, so that my repentance and prayer reach You, in the face of all obstacles, and You accept them; and that You forgive and pardon me for all the transgressions and sins that I've committed from my beginnings until today, whether in this life or a previous one. Turn me not away from Your presence emptyhanded; hear my prayer, in Your abundant mercy; for You hear the prayer of every mouth. Store away my tears in Your bottle. May the words of my mouth and the meditation of my heart be acceptable before You, my Rock and my Redeemer.

And so, from now, I want to learn in His Torah, for the sake of His name, blessed be He, to fulfill His commandment—for He, blessed be He, commanded us, His people Israel, to meditate in His holy Torah—and in order that this study lead me to action and to good character traits and to correct understanding of the Torah—and in order to teach and to keep and to do. May it be Your will, O Lord my God and the God of my ancestors, that with this Torah learning all the blemishes that I've caused in the Upper Worlds or in my soul, throughout my life, or in previous lives, be repaired.

Make me worthy to learn and to teach, to keep and to do, so that I'll be one of those who know Your name, and one of the Children of the King's Palace, and one of those who are lifted Above. Lead me in the path of truth that I not stumble in the ways of the misguided; open for me the fountains and treasuries of wisdom; enlighten my eyes with the light of Your Torah, the revealed Torah and the hidden Torah, that I become like an ever-stronger-flowing spring, and like a plastered cistern that loses not a drop—that I forget nothing of what I learn. Unite my heart in love and fear of Your name, and purify my thoughts and my heart, to understand, comprehend, to learn and teach, to keep and do, and to fulfill all the words of Your Torah in love. Lead me in the path of Your commandments, open my eyes that I see the wonders of Your Torah, make my heart cleave to Your *mitzvot*, and make my heart brave and strong in Torah and *mitzvot*, to stand firmly against my evil inclination, the leaven in the dough. Make me worthy to do many, many *mitzvot*, fulfilling them in their full depths, according to all their rules and ramifications, in all their details, and according to all their true intentions.

And save me from every evil sin, and from even the merest trace of sin, and from the least stumbling block of sin there is, and from *hillul ha-Shem*. And give me a heart courageous and bold to pursue the commandments with all my strength and energy and ability, with vigor and life. Make me worthy to fulfill all the *mitzvot* that I should fulfill, with fear and love, and with great joy which is unbounded, unlimited.

And may we merit to see the consolation of Zion and Jerusalem.

May the words of my mouth and the meditation of my heart be acceptable before You, my Rock and my Redeemer.

For the sake of the unification [of the Holy One, blessed be He, and His *Shechinah*, with love and fear, in the name of all Israel]. (*Pe'er v'Kavod*, p. 49)

Note that the prayer includes at two points stated intentions ("And so, from now . . ." on p. 349, and the final words, "For the sake . . ."). Note also where the *rebbe* says "Store away my tears, . . ." (p. 349); he certainly felt that a person should attempt to cry, if possible.

There is no reason that this prayer cannot be adapted, with parts added or removed, to suit your own heart.

16

Psalms

16:1 Reciting psalms is a traditional pious practice. Very often people know many psalms by heart, which they can recite while engaging in work or other daily activities. People can also carry with them a small Book of Psalms, and at any free moment take it out and recite a psalm or two, or whatever is possible. It is not considered necessary to understand Hebrew for the recitation to be spiritually effective (as is also the case for *davvening* in general). However, small psalm books are available in English, and one can recite the psalms in English, too.

> **16:2** Accustom yourself to say psalms. (Rabbi Moshe Teitelbaum, *Hanhagot Tzaddikim*, p. 50, #32)
>
> **16:3** Be sure, without fail, to say a number of psalms every day. (Rabbi Menahem Mendel of Vitebsk, *Hanhagot Tzaddikim* [II], chap. 3, #21)
>
> **16:4** Say some psalms every day; and if you can complete the whole book every week, how good. (Rabbi Yehiel Michal of Zlotchov's Hanhagot, #3, in *Zichron l'Rishonim*, p. 81)

(In many Hebrew Books of Psalms the psalms are divided up according to a portion for each of the seven days of the week and also according to a portion for each of the thirty days of the month. Thus, you can say the psalms so as to finish the whole book each week or each month.)

> **16:5** Study the Book of Psalms a number of times, so that the words and their translation will be thoroughly familiar to you, as well as Rashi's interpretation. Then you will understand well what you are saying when you say Psalms. (Tzavaat Rabbi Yaakov mi-Lisa, #4, *YHvT,* p. 68)

> **16:6** He should keep a Book of Psalms with him always, and whenever he has a free moment, he should say a psalm. This recitation does not require *kavvanah,* and he will receive the same reward as for studying the most difficult parts of the Talmud.[1] (Tzavaat Rabbi Moshe mi-Prague, p. 20b, #8, in *Tzavaot v'Derech Tovim,* p. 40)

When a person takes out his Book of Psalms in a free moment of a busy day, and says a few psalms quickly, it is hard to have deep *kavvanah.* But the recitation is still spiritually effective, and is even more precious coming at such a time in the midst of worldly activity. The recitation of psalms is, then, a spiritual practice that can be done during almost any free time. As mentioned, you may have favorite psalms memorized and say them under your breath while working, walking along the road, and during other activities.

16:7 The Baal Shem Tov, whose hasidism had a place for the simple people, valued their piety very highly. There are many stories where the Besht praises their recitation of Psalms and compares it favorably with the Torah study of those who are learned. In this he was supported by the Talmud tradition (mentioned at the end of the previous quote) that said the recitation of Psalms was of equal spiritual worth as the study of even the most difficult parts of the Talmud.

> **16:7:1** [The Neshkizer Rebbe once] saw two men who had been with the Baal Shem Tov, the memory of a *tzaddik* for a blessing, may his merit protect us. The holy Baal Shem had told them how they had reached their high spiritual level. To one he said it was through his recitation of Psalms. And to the other he said that he had reached his high level through Torah study, of *Gemara* with the commentary of Rashi, and *Tosafot.* (*Rishpei Aish,* ha-Shalem, #135)

16:7:2 The Baal Shem Tov praised the uncomplicated piety of

> a Jewish wagon driver who was illiterate, but whose practice was to complete the whole Book of Psalms five times every day. He would say the Psalms all the while he was traveling in his wagon.[2] (*Sippurim Niflaim*, #38)

16:7:3 Another story in which the Besht appears tells of the greatness of

> a simple and righteous man, who was called by the people "the psalm-sayer" because the Book of Psalms was never out of his mouth—for he was accustomed to say Psalms from memory in the midst of whatever work he was doing. (*Kol Sippurei Baal Shem Tov*, II, chap. 13, story 14)

16:7:4 One story tells how the Baal Shem Tov approved of how the simple people would chant psalms in his *Beit Midrash* on the afternoon of *Shabbat*. He taught his disciples that even though they did not understand the meaning of the words, their worship was valued in heaven, even more than their (the disciples') own, because these simple people directed all their chanting to their Father in Heaven with the greatest humility and with an outpouring of the soul. In the midst of their saying the Psalms they would call out such things as "Oy, Father, help us!" "Compassionate God, have mercy on us!" and "Master of the World, how long must we stay in this bitter exile? Let us go out!" And the Besht said to his disciples about them:

> [These] simple people . . . are saying psalms in the synagogue, and since they do not know the meaning of the words they are just saying them with a pure and simple piety, and calling out to God from the depth of their heart in the middle of the Psalms [as above]. And God, blessed be He, who searches the hearts of men and hears their cry, hears them now, for their voices are splitting the firmament. (*Sippurim Niflaim*, #37; cf. *Kol Sippurei Baal Shem Tov*, vol. 1, chap. 7, story 1)

If you are reciting Psalms, with or without understanding the words, it is possible to call out to God as in this story.

16:8 Traditionally, chanting Psalms was a practice to which simple people, especially, were devoted (although not they alone!). This was because Torah learning was not available to them without Hebrew, and the chanting of Psalms did not even require understanding the words.

The high level they could attain through this practice can be seen from the opening of the following hasidic story about the Seer of Lublin and a heavenly message that came to him through a "simple" Jew.

> The Rebbe of Lublin first lived in the city of Lanzhut in the province of Galitzia. In that city there was a certain man, one of the simple people, who, through the power of his recitation of Psalms with great and pure *kavvanah*, merited having an angelic preacher from heaven [a *maggid*] who would appear to him from time to time and teach him. (*Hitgalut ha-Tzaddikim*, p. 21)

16:9 Many great rabbis also loved to chant Psalms.

16:9:1 About Rabbi Abraham Moshe of Pshischa (the son of Rabbi Simha Bunim):

> His holy way in service of God was with Psalms, and for a number of hours a day he was occupied with saying Psalms with a holy and awesome fervor. (*Eser Z'chuyot*, p. 12)

16:9:2 Rabbi Yitzhak of Neshkiz said about the Shpola Zeyde (Grandfather):

> The Holy Grandfather of Shpola was a man of wonders. No one ever heard him give Torah talks, no one heard him when he prayed. But at all times and at every free moment, he would always be saying Psalms from memory, and in a whisper, such that those who were near him did not hear the words but just a humming, moaning sound: zim, zim, zim. (*Ish ha-Pele*, p. 151)

The Shpola Zeyde himself told of how when he was in "exile" and lived (as a hidden *tzaddik*) in a small town:

> All the days of the week I sat in the *Beit Midrash* and said chapters of Psalms. They used to call me "Leib the psalm-sayer." (*Ish ha-Pele*, p. 235)

> **16:9:3** When Rabbi Elimelech of Lizensk went into "exile" to share the suffering and exile of the *Shechinah*, he once came to Pshevorsk, arriving after midnight. Seeing that light was coming from the window of one of the houses, he went there. That was the home of the holy rabbi, Rabbi Moshe of Pshevorsk, the memory of a holy *tzaddik* for a blessing, and he asked him if he would let him lodge

there for the night. Rabbi Moshe answered him saying, "I just now got up [this was to perform the midnight vigil], so you can lie down in my bed." Rabbi Elimelech asked if there was something to eat. He gave him something, and he ate, and then he lay down in the bed.

When Rabbi Moshe thought that his guest was asleep, he began to say Psalms softly, but when Rabbi Elimelech heard him, he got up from the bed and stood next to Rabbi Moshe. When Rabbi Moshe noticed him, he motioned him to go back to sleep; and he lay down again. But when he started to say Psalms again, Rabbi Elimelech jumped up again and stood next to the table at which Rabbi Moshe was sitting. Again he motioned him to go to sleep [he did not want to interrupt his recitation with profane speech].

This happened still a third time, until finally Rabbi Moshe rebuked him for disrupting his recitation. "How can I sleep" replied Rabbi Elimelech, "when I see King David standing next to you!" Hearing this, and realizing this was no ordinary person, Rabbi Moshe said to him, "Are you Melech?" [Although he did not know him, Rabbi Elimelech's fame had reached Pshevorsk]. And they excitedly began to make each other's acquaintance. (*Sifran Shel Tzaddikim*, p. 19, #3)

16:10 Psalms—You should find yourself and everything that happens to you in the psalms that you say. And all the thanksgivings in the Psalms you should say about yourself, for the kindnesses that God has done with you all your life. (*The Bratzlaver Seder ha-Yom*, #14)

16:11 Rabbi Nachman of Bratzlav:

The essence of the recital of psalms is to say all the psalms about yourself, and to find yourself in each and every psalm. For the Psalms were made for all the people of Israel in general and for each one in particular. The wars that every person has with his evil inclination and everything that takes place in his life, are all present in the Psalms and are explained there. Indeed, the whole Book of Psalms was said and established only with regard to the war with the evil inclination and its minions, which are the chief enemies and adversaries of a man.

This is what David prayed to God about: that He would save him from them. So everyone should interpret all the Psalms as being about himself, even the verses where King David praises himself, such as "Guard my soul, for I am pious!" You should also interpret this verse and others of this sort about yourself. In truth, you should judge yourself for good, and find in yourself good

> qualities so as to strengthen and encourage yourself in the service of God. (*Likkutei Aytzot ha-Meshulash*, vol. 5, Tefillah, #15)

This teaching of Rabbi Nachman gives good counsel for the recitation of Psalms. Many psalms are about the anguish caused by enemies. Certainly they were written for a personal situation of hostility and great stress. It may seem that such psalms have nothing to do with your situation. (On the other hand, anyone who has been under serious threat or harassment and persecution knows how relevant these psalms then become.) The rabbis took the Hebrew word for psalm, *mizmor*, from the root *zamar*, "to make music," and related it to another form of that root (*zmr*), *zimair*, which means "to cut off" or "prune." Thus, the Psalms were said to be very effective in cutting off and fighting negative spiritual forces, pictured often as trees or briars and thorns.[3]

This is what Rabbi Nachman intends when he says that the evil inclination and its minions are the chief enemies of a man. When you read the many psalms where David talks about his enemies, if you are fortunate enough that the psalm is not literally relevant to your personal situation—understand it the other way.

16:12 Rabbi Nachman of Bratzlav:

> Whoever wants to merit becoming worthy of doing *tshuvah*, should accustom himself to saying psalms, for the Psalms have a special power to inspire repentance. (*Likkutei Aytzot*, Tshuvah, #32)

(See "Repentance—*Tshuvah*," 17:7 for the full quote.)

16:13 As a boy, Rabbi Nachman of Bratzlav himself did much reciting of Psalms.

> His father's house had a small garret, partitioned off as a storehouse for hay and feed. Here the young Rabbi Nachman would hide himself, chanting the Psalms, and . . . begging God that he be worthy of drawing close to Him. . . . He also had the practice of chanting only the verses in the Psalms speaking of prayer and the cry to God. He would go through the entire Book of Psalms in one stretch, saying only those verses and leaving out the rest. (*Rabbi Nachman's Wisdom*, p. 10, *Shevachay HaRan*, #10)

This latter practice is also adaptable to other kinds of selections from the Psalms. The Psalms were a main part of Rabbi Nachman's spiritual practice as a youth, and they helped bring him to his awesome levels in holiness.

Rabbi Natan, Rabbi Nachman's great disciple, reports:

> I heard that the Rebbe once said, "My achievements came mainly through simplicity. I spent much time simply conversing with God and reciting the Psalms." (*Rabbi Nachman's Wisdom*, p. 299, *Sichos HaRan*, #154)

16:14 Psalms are used as a way to make supplication for God's help. When you are in need or in trouble, along with making your request to God in prayer, you recite Psalms as an offering and as another form of prayer to arouse God's mercy.

Rabbi Yaakov Yosef of Polnoye, the great disciple of the Besht, said once to a simple Jew:

> If a person has a need and a request to make of God, he should say Psalms with *kavvanah* and with all his heart, and God, blessed be He, will help him. (*Maasiyot u'Maamarim Yekarim*, p. 25)

Psalms are also used as a way to pray for others. We can pray for those in need by saying more or fewer psalms on their behalf. Very often psalms are said for those who are sick. Of course, depending upon the need involved, it is more appropriate to say certain psalms than others. So, for example, one book suggests to say Psalms 38, 41, 86, 90, 108, and 118 for a sick person.[4]

A story tells how when Rabbi Yechezkel Abramsky, the Slutzker Rav, was in his younger years arrested and exiled to Siberia by the Bolsheviks, the Hafetz Hayim "prayed frequently for his release, saying four chapters of *Tehillim* (Psalms) on his behalf every day" (*The Maggid Speaks*, pp. 175–178).

> **16:15** The saying of Psalms is a *tikkun* [a means of spiritual repair] for sin. (*Or ha-Ner*, note on #7)

In other words, when you have done something wrong, as part of your repentance and to set aright in your soul whatever you have damaged, you can say Psalms. This can even be systemized, so that you can have a rule, for example, that if you get angry, you will say so many psalms, etc. (See 16:16:5 and 16:16:6.)

16:16 It is a traditional practice to say the whole Book of Psalms through without a break. (Remember what was explained in Part One about the significance of not interrupting.)

> **16:16:1** In regard to a number of a person's needs, such as his livelihood, or to various difficulties that a person might be in, the Rebbe [Rabbi Pinhas of Koretz] would instruct him to say the whole Book of Psalms, from beginning to end, without a break. (*Midrash Pinhas*, p. 13, #28)

> **16:16:2** It is written of Rabbi Pinhas' great disciple, Rabbi Rafael of Bershad that he said: "It was an important obligation in the eyes of the Rebbe, his memory for a blessing, to complete the recitation of the Book of Psalms twice each week, once without a break, and once with. He himself would say one of the five books of the Book of Psalms each day. In my youth I used to finish the Book of Psalms once each month, but the Rebbe told me to say more than that, without setting an exact amount, but just according to the heart. And he told me to say all the Book of Psalms, without interruption, once each month." (*Pe'er l'Yesharim*, p. 10b, #107)

16:16:3 Some people use the unbroken recital of the whole Book of Psalms on *Erev Shabbat* to prepare for the Sabbath (see "*Shabbat*," 18:1:2:2:6). Some say the whole Book of Psalms without interruption on *Shabbat* itself—either in the evening, or in the morning (see "*Shabbat*," 18:2:5).

16:16:4 Some say the Psalms this way on *Erev Rosh Hodesh* (the eve of the new month). Rabbi Shalom Shachna of Probitch said that on every *Erev Rosh Hodesh*, which is a special time for *tshuvah*:

> You should say the Book of Psalms until the end without a break. (Seder ha-Yom, in *D'vir Yaakov*)

> **16:16:5** It is written in many holy books . . . that a wonderfully effective method to "sweeten the judgments" is to recite the whole Book of Psalms at one time. (*Erech Apayim*, p. 107)

The phrase to "sweeten the judgments" has a kabbalistic meaning, but translated into modern idiom carries the thought that the cloud that hangs over a person who has somehow transgressed (and which calls down bad things on him) is dissipated. Since anger calls down judgments on a person, it is suggested in *Erech Apayim* that you make it a set practice, when you become angry, as a self-fixing as well as a penalty, to recite the whole Book of Psalms to free yourself from that "cloud."

16:16:6 Another *rebbe* suggests recitation of the whole Book of Psalms as a way to use speech to fix a previous sin of speech:

> When you have committed a sin in your speech, repent by staying up all Thursday night learning Torah. Or if it is impossible for you to stay up the whole night, then, on the holy Sabbath recite the whole Book of Psalms through without an interruption. (Rabbi Mordechai of Tchernobil, *Hanhagot Tzaddikim*, p. 68, #19)

From another source we know that Rabbi Mordechai would have his hasidim recite the whole Book of Psalms this way on the morning of the Sabbath (*Admorei Tchernobil*, p. 150).

A story tells how Rabbi Yaakov Yosef of Polnoye used the Psalms as a *tikkun* (self-fixing) to repair a sin of speech.

Once he said an unnecessary blessing and was very distraught. (It is slighting God's name to utter it without purpose.) Moreover, in a dream he was shown that, as a result of his transgression, he had planted, so to speak, a garden of trees in the realm of uncleanness. To repair his sin and to uproot those trees:

> He took the Book of Psalms in his hand and said in a thunderous voice the first book [of the five], and at the sound the whole heavenly host trembled. One of them came to him and said, "Know that the fruits of the trees have fallen off." And he said the second book of Psalms with a loud voice, and another angel came to him and said, "Know that the leaves have fallen off." And he said the third book, and one came and said, "The small branches have fallen off." He said the fourth book in a loud voice and was told, "The big branches have fallen off." And he said the fifth book and one came and said, "Know that the trees themselves have fallen."[5] (*L'Yesharim Tehillah*, p. 10)

As mentioned, the negative spiritual forces activated by sin are often pictured as trees or thorns and briars, which the recitation of Psalms effectively cuts down.

> **16:17** It has been received as a tradition from Rabbi Elimelech of Lizensk, may his merit protect us, that for one who says all the

> Book of Psalms three times in one day, it is accounted as if he had fasted from one Sabbath to the next [an ascetic practice of the time]. And I have also heard it said in the name of his disciple, our master and rabbi, Rabbi Mendel of Rimanov, that saying the whole Book of Psalms three times in one day is like a sword and spear against the evil inclination. But it is well to remember the principle that "A little with *kavvanah* is better than a lot without." (*Ateret Menahem*, p. 18, #42)

Note that nothing is said here about reciting the Book without interruption. As to the latter point in the quote, compare:

> It is better to get used to saying two or three psalms with intense *kavvanah* than to be one of those who says all the psalms, but quickly and without *kavvanah*. (Tzavaat Rabbeinu Yonah, #3, in *Tzavaot v'Derech Tovim*)

16:18 The way of Rabbi Kalonymos Kalmish of Peasetzna, as expressed in his teaching, involved taking advantage of any occasion of emotional arousal regardless of its source, in order to turn it in a holy direction. In parts of this practice he taught how the Book of Psalms could be used to that end.

For example, here are his instructions for the situation where you have passed into a mood of one sort or another without any obvious cause, and without knowing why.

> When your feelings have been aroused with this as the background, first of all, do not rush to seek some physical satisfaction. For example, if you feel slightly anxious, do not think you are hungry and run to find something to eat. Just attend to the feeling and see what it is. If it is some depression that you feel, then look within and consider: "Perhaps I committed some sin recently, or did something low, or said or thought something improper. But the reason I do not know what has produced this sadness is because I am doing everything in a hurry, and all the years of my life are passing quickly and in confusion. Due to this sin, whatever it is, my soul is smitten and has become sick. She is groaning now from her deep pain and causing me to be depressed."
>
> And sometimes, after a little investigation, you will find something you did. "Yes. I did this bad thing, or I said or thought something improper." There is a good sign, moreover, that will tell you when you do find the true cause of your feeling, because *as soon as you hit upon it, the depressed feeling will lift from your*

heart. But do not be satisfied with this discovery alone. You have to accept the obligation not to do this bad thing again. Even a *kabbalah* like this is not enough, because when you accept something on yourself without making fences to protect yourself [from future transgressions], and without considering stratagems to overcome the problem, it means little.

Whether you find the source of your depression or not—or whether it is a feeling of depression or one of happiness—whether it is a feeling that came to you from within or was aroused by something outside you—have concern for yourself; do not just ignore this feeling and pass on. Your soul has revealed itself somewhat in this feeling. Be quick to strengthen it. Take hold of it and do not let go. Expand the feeling and say some psalms that fit the mood so that it will expand in breadth and depth, so that it will be sharper, and will abide and not disappear in a flash.

If the mood is one of depression, say psalms that will clarify the mood, such as 3, 6, 10, 13, 16, 17, 22, 25, 31, 38, 42, and especially 51, which you should say frequently. . . . Or if it is a happy mood, say psalms that increase the feeling of happiness, such as 1, 8, 9, 19, 23, 24, 27, 29, 30, 33, 34, and other songs and praises of God.

But whatever psalms you recite, do not say them as if they were a report of what King David said thousands of years ago. Rather, say them as if this is what David purposefully arranged just for you. When you say, for example, "My God, my God, why have You forsaken me?" imagine that you are standing before the Throne of Glory and pouring out your heart and soul, "My God, my God, why have You forsaken me and my family and all Israel? Why have You hidden Your face, and made everything so dark for us?"

If it is impossible for you to say psalms or to learn Torah at that moment, then speak to God in your own words, pouring out your soul to Him, with a broken spirit, or with an exalted soul, or with joy, according to whatever mood is aroused at the time. Say, for example, "Master of the World! My Father and King! How far I am from You and from Your holiness. What will be the end of me? Again and again I want to come close to You, but after all my attempts I am still sunk in the mire. Master of the World, have mercy on me so that finally I will draw myself close to You! Lift me up and help me and all Israel in spiritual and material things, with revealed kindness—and we will serve You in truth, in joy, in holiness, and in purity."

After all this, and when you have become inspired, as the Ramban, his memory for a blessing . . . advised, try to invest your spiritual arousal in deed and action, by doing some *mitzvah* or studying Torah. (*Hachsharat ha-Abrechim*, p. 46)

In this teaching we see how the Psalms are used to draw out an emotion or mood and raise it up to God.

The Peasetzna Rebbe teaches the use of Psalms in another kind of situation:

> A feeling of happiness or weariness that comes to you from something that has happened to you, without any connection with a *mitzvah*, or contrarily, with a bodily desire [leading to transgression], just a feeling from some happening in your life, . . . such inner feelings of happiness or worry about worldly matters will, of themselves, when you expand them and speak of them to God, become fixed and repaired. Your soul will rise up of itself and turn the feeling into something holy. Because with any mood that a Jew experiences, even connected with business or other bodily matters, whether of sadness or of happiness, there is an aspect of a revelation of the soul, except that it is covered up in a clothing of the needs of this world, and you have to take advantage of the moment. So when you feel some depression, even in something related to bodily needs, turn aside and stand by a wall and say a number of psalms that fit what has happened to you and that reflect your anxiety. For example, if you are disturbed because of those who hate you, pray Psalm 3, "Lord, how many have my enemies become! etc." And with a different anxiety, pray, "I have sunk deep into the mire" [Psalm 69:3], or "I lift up my eyes to the mountains; from where will my help come?" [Psalm 121:1]
>
> The idea is not that you should just come in from the marketplace or your place of work and start saying words without your heart or mind being involved in them. You should first reflect on those anxieties that hold you back and trouble you so much. And consider: who can you go to, or who will save you, if not the Holy One, blessed be He, He for whom everything is possible—our Merciful Father.
>
> Imagine yourself approaching now before His glorious throne, and picture the Glory of God before whom, blessed be He, you are now standing and supplicating, saying, "How many have my enemies become! etc." [Psalm 3:1], "Many say to my soul, God cannot save him" [3:3]—so they say, "But You, O God, are a shield surrounding me, etc." [3:4]
>
> After you say a number of psalms, then pray with your own words, in whatever language you understand. Say whatever comes to mind. And from word to word, from sentence to sentence, you will feel your spirit and mind becoming stronger, rising up little by little, until your bodily needs are forgotten, and a cry breaks forth from the depths of your heart, "Master of the World, draw me close to You, cleanse me!

> Lift me up from all these worries so that I can be close to You, with a pure heart and soul." At the end of your prayer, it is good to say one verse of encouragement and strengthening, such as "The Lord is my shepherd, I shall not want, etc." [Psalm 23:1], or "I will fear no evil, for, Master of the World, You are with me" [23:4]. Then you can be happy, for God is with you. For in truth He is with you, and especially in this moment when you poured out your heart to Him, in a moment of elevation and closeness.
>
> And the whole day after such a prayer you will feel a kind of spiritual pleasure, a pure kind of pleasure, for your soul was in the Garden of Eden today, and what can compare to her and her happiness." (*Hachsharat ha-Abrechim*, p. 47b)

Note how the *rebbe* suggests the use of Psalms to help us be able to open our mouths in personal prayer.

16:19 When saying more than a few psalms, there are traditional prayers that can be said before and after; there are also three verses said immediately before and three others said immediately after the recitation.

16:19:1 Here is a slightly shortened version of the prayer said before psalms:

> May it be Thy will, O Lord our God and God of our fathers and mothers, who has chosen David His servant, and his seed after him, and who has chosen these songs and praises, to turn with compassion to hear these psalms that I will recite, as if it were King David himself, peace be upon him, who is saying them.
>
> And may the merit of these psalms serve to atone for our sins and transgressions and wrongdoing, and to cut off the forces of negation and evil, to chop down the briars and thorns that surround the beautiful Rose on High, the *Shechinah*, and join the Wife of Youth, the Congregation of Israel, with her Lover, in love and affection. And may the recitation of these psalms bring down from on High a flow of spirit into our souls to purify us from our sins, so that our transgressions be forgiven and our wrongdoing atoned for; as You forgave David, who said these psalms before You, as it is written, "So has God removed your sin; you shall not die."
>
> O God, do not take me from this world before my time; let me live out a full span of years, and let me live to fix what I have damaged. And may the merit of King David, peace be upon him, protect us and surround us, so that You will be patient with us until we have returned to You in a complete and full *tshuvah*. May You

be gracious to us, though we are not worthy of it, from Your treasury of causeless compassion, as it is written, "And I will be gracious to whom I will be gracious, and I will have mercy on whom I will have mercy."

And as we say before You these songs in this world, so may we merit to say songs and praises before You in the coming world. And through the saying of these psalms may the Congregation of Israel, the Lily of Sharon, be awakened from her sleep of exile, to sing with a sweet and joyful voice before You, when the Holy Temple, the Glory of Lebanon, is returned to her, and there will be majesty and holy beauty in the House of our God, soon and in our days. Amen. *Selah.*

16:19:2 After this prayer and right before beginning, say these three verses:

"O come, let us sing before the Lord, let us call out in joy to the Rock of our salvation. Let us come before His presence with thanksgiving, let us shout for joy unto Him with psalms. For the Lord is a great God, and a great King above all the gods." [Psalm 95:1–3]

16:19:3 Immediately after concluding, say these three verses:

"O that the salvation of Israel would come out of Zion! When the Lord returns the captivity of His people, then Jacob will rejoice, Israel will be glad." "The salvation of the righteous is from the Lord; He is their stronghold in a time of trouble." "The Lord will come to their aid; he will take them and remove them from the grasp of the wicked to save them, because they took refuge in Him." [Psalms 14:7, 37:39, 37:40]

16:19:4 After completing a full book (one of the five) of the Psalms, this prayer can be said (shortened and adapted from the original):

May it be Thy will, O Lord our God and God of our fathers and mothers, in the merit of this [first, second, etc.] book of the Psalms, that You atone for all our sins and forgive us for all our transgressions, that You turn us back to You in a complete and full *tshuvah*, and lead us to Your service, and open our hearts to learn Your Torah.

Send a full healing to the sick of Your people [particularly this person]. Declare freedom for those unjustly held captive, and for those in prison without right, let their barred doors be opened; and for all those of Your people Israel who are traveling, by land, sea, or air, keep them safe from trouble and harm and bring them to their destinations alive and well.

Give children to those who have none, and they will grow up to serve You with love and fear. May all the pregnant women be spared from miscarriages, and may they be kept from all harm when giving birth, in Your great mercy. Keep all the children of Your people the House of Israel from all sickness and harm; let them grow up healthy and happy to serve You in truth.

Annul any and all evil decrees anywhere in the world by which Your people the House of Israel are persecuted, and may Your people who live in our Holy Land, the Land of Israel, be safe and prosper and flourish.

Send a blessing of success in all the work of our hands, and give us our livelihood from Your open and generous hand, fulfilling the needs of each and every one. Hurry our redemption and build our House of Holiness and Glory. And in Your overflowing mercy, help us, O God of our salvation, for the sake of the honor of Your Name; and pardon us for our sins, for the sake of Your Name. Blessed is the Lord forever. Amen and amen.

16:19:5 On Sabbaths and holidays the three verses before and after are said, but not the prayers. Instead, just this shorter prayer is said afterwards:

May it be Thy will, O Lord our God and God of our fathers and mothers, in the merit of this [first, second, etc.] book of the Psalms we have recited before You, and in the merit of King David, peace be upon him, may his merit protect us and be our support, that we be found worthy of saying before You songs in the World to Come, and of singing with sweet voices, joyful and exulting, in the Holy Temple, the Glory of Lebanon, soon and in our days. Amen. *Selah.*

(These prayers are from *Kitzur Shnei Luchot ha-Brit*, Hanhagat Tehillim, pp. 142–143, with some shortening and adaptation. The Hebrew can be found in almost all separately published Books of Psalms.)

16:20 As a final, practical note, if you are buying a Book of Psalms that has English, be aware that the Israeli translations are usually very poor.

16:21 WHICH PSALMS TO TURN TO

Many psalms have more than one message, and mean different things to different people. But the following list should at least help in suggesting which psalms to turn to according to your mood and situation.

1. When studying Torah—1, 19, 119
2. In the synagogue—5, 26, 27, 63, 65, 73, 84, 96, 122, 135
3. In nature—19, 104, 148
4. Desire to repent—40, 51, 90
5. After committing sin—25, 32, 51, 130
6. Sad, depressed—30, 42, 43
7. Cannot sleep—4
8. Lonely—25
9. Disruptive changes in your life; disaster—46, 57
10. Frustration at wickedness of people—36, 52, 53, 58
11. Anxiety from enemies—3, 5, 6, 7, 9, 17, 22, 25, 31, 35, 38, 43, 54, 55, 56, 57, 59, 71, 140, 142
12. Anxious concern about livelihood—23, 62, 68
13. Suffering, afflicted—38, 102
14. Want to pray, say psalms, speak to God—51
15. Need to increase your trust in God—22, 23, 56, 62, 84, 123, 125, 128, 131, 146
16. Single, hoping to find soulmate—68
17. Uplifted feeling—8, 19, 24, 47, 48
18. Need God's help, protection—70, 91, 121, 130
19. Confused by success of wicked, envious of rich—1, 37, 49, 73
20. Beset by old age—71
21. Perplexed by injustice and God's distance—10
22. Doubts about faith—1, 2, 19, 37

23. Feeling confused religiously—25, 143
24. Israel, Jews, Judaism pressed, abused, threatened—53, 74, 83, 124
25. Betrayed, hurt by others, someone close—35, 41, 55
26. Feel abandoned—27, 88, 142
27. Feeling of thankfulness to God—9, 18, 65, 66, 116
28. Grateful to God for success, prosperity—65, 144, 147
29. Feel threatened, anxious, or afraid—4, 22, 23, 56
30. Slandered, abused verbally, victim of wrongdoing—39, 64, 120
31. Great troubles and distress—6, 31, 34, 55, 69, 77, 86, 88, 107, 121, 138, 142
32. Feel humiliated by people—22

This list can be copied onto the inside cover of your Book of Psalms.

17

Meditation

17:1 More so than in other streams of Judaism, meditation has a special place among the spiritual practices of the kabbalists and the hasidim.

In formal terms, meditation may be considered as directed thought for the purpose of concentration. It can be divided into two categories that we will call vacuum meditation and pressure meditation. *Vacuum meditation* works by emptying the mind of its contents; *pressure meditation*, conversely, seeks to fill the mind so completely with particular thoughts and feelings that what is meditated on is realized in experience. The meditations discussed in this chapter are pressure meditations; whether they involve concentration on one thing or many (and are based on extended trains of directed thought), they all have the goal of achieving *d'vekut*, and an immediate experience of the presence of God.

> There is service of God that involves movement, such as all the *mitzvot* which involve action and doing, and also Torah study and prayer [which involve speech, movement of the lips, etc.]. . . . But there is also service of God through stillness and complete absence of movement, when a person sits alone and in silence, and meditates on God's exaltedness, blessed be He. For he enters the world of thought, which is the world of absolute rest and stillness, and he draws this on himself.[1] And so should you, when you want to cleave

to God through God–consciousness, sit in absolute stillness with holy thoughts and awe and *d'vekut.* (*Or ha-Ganuz l'Tzaddikim*, p. 72)

17:2 Hasidic sources regularly speak of meditating on two aspects of God: His greatness and His goodness. (The quote above, for example, speaks of His "exaltedness" [*romemut*], this being an expression parallel to "greatness" [*gedulah*].)

Greatness, in English, although literal, is not the ideal translation, and even somewhat misleading. What is intended usually is that God is the Source and Creator of everything in existence. Typically it is emphasized that He brought the whole creation into being out of nothingness (*yesh mai'ayin*). He made the universe and everything in it, from the greatest galaxies down to the smallest atoms. He created all worlds, including those in other spiritual dimensions, and He created our world and everything in it. Everything physical and everything nonphysical; everything perceived by the senses—the shapes of objects, their colors and qualities—is all from Him. Everything mental—the world of thought, our thoughts, our emotions—is likewise from Him. So, too, everything that happens is from the hand of God.

Not only has He created and formed everything, but His creative power is continuously at work as the support behind every existing thing. Were He to remove His will for an instant, it would immediately revert to nothingness. This creative power of God, ever-active, which is within everything and gives all things their existence and life, is His Presence, called the *Shechinah*. This presence of God in the world is also sometimes called His Glory; thus, it is said again and again that "His Glory fills the earth, and there is no place where He is not."

His Presence, the *Shechinah*, is within everything and also beyond it. (For though there is nothing in this world but God, He is not identical with it. As the rabbis say: "God is the place of the world, but the world is not His place.") So it is always said that "He fills all worlds and surrounds all worlds."

Such concepts as these are usually what is indicated by meditation on God's greatness, though sometimes other related ideas are present, as, for instance, the recognition of God's great miracles.[2] In any case, the essence of the notion of God's greatness is the awesome awareness that God is all in all, that He is all and does all.

Here is a typical expression of this concept, in the words of Rabbi Mordechai of Tchernobil:

> First, you must know and believe with complete clarity that there is a God who was before everything else; and He brought into being all created things and creatures, those of the Upper Worlds and those of the Lower Worlds, in infinite diversity and without end, from a lone original point. He is One, Single, and Unique, the Infinite One, blessed be He, the Cause of all causes, the Mover of all that moves; He created the Upper and Lower Worlds, in infinite diversity and without end.
>
> He fills all worlds and surrounds all worlds . . . and you must believe with strong and perfect faith that the whole earth is full of His Glory and there is no place where He is not; His Glory, blessed be His name, is in each and every thing that exists and His Kingdom rules over all. . . . It is His flow of life-giving power that supports and sustains everything, and were it to cease and be removed for even a minute from anything, it would revert back to *tohu* and *bohu*, the emptiness and void before creation. (*Likkutei Torah*, Hadrachah 2)

The second typical aspect of hasidic meditation is on God's goodness. And a meditation on His goodness naturally follows one on His greatness, because it was for the good of His creatures, and for their sakes, that He created everything that is. Everything that happens is for good, and God's goodness and love are imprinted in every thing and in every event. We are to perceive this goodness generally and also more specifically: His goodness to all living things, to all men, to His people Israel—and to you yourself. Your existence and everything you are and have, material and spiritual, are from God. He is the Source of everything good—of goodness and love itself. Everything beautiful and noble, everything that inspires you, everything that you love and revere, has its root in Him.

17:3 But Jewish meditation is not just mind meditation; it is emotion meditation as well. It is not only the head that must be directed and focused, but the heart also.

We are to use our meditation on God's greatness to arouse our fear of God. What this means is that an awareness of His great and wondrous power, of His all-encompassing nature, of His overwhelming distance from us as well as His immediacy, can and should inspire us with awe.

Similarly, our meditation on God's goodness is to be used to arouse our love of God. For realizing all the good He does to all, and to us, and His love for us, our hearts open in an answering love.

In each case, the mind meditation on God's greatness and goodness is to awaken the emotions of our heart—to fear and love of God.

The following three quotes (which are not, however, particularly about sitting meditation) are fairly representative, and merit close study:

Rabbi Tzvi Elimelech of Dinov, in the preface of *Derech Pikudecha*, says that someone who has purified himself is always in God's presence, and always sees His greatness. But someone who is not purified has to remind himself of God's greatness and goodness continually, to arouse love and fear in his heart. (Note in what follows the use of the visualized Name of God to support the meditation.)

> You should intend to fulfill the *mitzvah* of fearing God. And to arouse fear of God in yourself think of His greatness, and how He is Ruler over all, the Center and Root of all worlds, and you should picture before you the name *Havaya* [YHVH].
>
> . . . And similarly fulfill the *mitzvah* to love God. To attain this you should think of all the good things He does for all His creatures, and especially for His Chosen People, and think of the many good things he does each hour and each minute. Think of how great and wonderful He is, and how low is our state [yet He is so good and loving to us]; then your heart will burn with a strong love for Him. Visualize before you the Name . . . and pray to God that He illuminate your heart and soul, that the love for Him within you come into revelation, so that you will yearn for God and His Torah, in love.
>
> You should meditate this way before all Torah study and prayer, and before doing any *mitzvah*, and any time during the day when you remember to so meditate.

Compare the words of this same *rebbe* in his small list of *hanhagot* (where the expression is more concise):

> Arouse your heart to fear of God based on your love for Him. For without fear and love, your service will not ascend to heaven. This self-arousal is to be done through meditation on God's greatness and exaltedness, and on all the overflowing good things that He continuously showers upon us. (*Hanhagot Adam*, #10)

> You should accustom yourself to think continually of the greatness of God, and the full extent of His freely given goodness to His

> creatures and to us—all due to His mercy. For according to our many sins, we do not deserve His wonderful goodness. He is the Root of all, and He is our true Father . . . who loves us and is always giving us good things, who has compassion on us and saves us in our time of trouble.
>
> When you think about this more and more, and about God's great goodness to you, love for Him will become fixed in your heart. You will long for Him, and your soul will become aroused to give pleasure to Him by doing His will. . . . And the remembrance of His name, blessed be He, should not cease from your lips, and the remembrance of His greatness should not depart from your thoughts. . . .
>
> If a person's heart and mind were always aroused to think thoughts of God's wonderful lovingkindness and His great power, continually—and if he were to place God always before him, as if God were actually before him, then would his love for God be what it is supposed to be. (*Beit Middot*, p. 24)

17:4 Meditation on God's greatness and goodness can also be easily joined to concepts of our relation to Him. Both His greatness and goodness can be contained within the thought of His being the Creator and the King of the Universe, whose servants we are, who creates all and is good to all—us included. Or, as in the quote above from *Beit Middot*, He is our heavenly Father, who has created us and given us life; His love and goodness embrace us at all times and He protects us from all harm, if we put our trust in Him.

We have to somehow know God as our very own—and through this awareness of an eternal relation to Him as our Father, for example, our love for Him will grow and become stronger, and our feelings of devotion and reverence for Him will draw us to hold up our side of the relationship, in deeds.

It is by meditating on our relation to God, as servant to master, or as son or daughter to father, that we can bring that relation from being just a concept of understanding to something experienced.

17:5 Regardless of the matter of the relationship (which is not always, or necessarily, emphasized), the point is that we must see that the fear and love of God aroused by our meditation on His greatness and goodness finally touches the springs of our behavior. What goes from mind to heart must also end up leading to action.[3]

17:6 An important aspect of hasidic meditation is what is called "*ada-ata d'nafshey*" thinking, that is, "until it reaches you" thinking. After having meditated on something in sequence, abstractly, you turn that meditation to give it an in-the-present dimension. Going from a meditation on God's greatness and goodness, to an arousal of fear and love is the beginning, but there is a further step. Because according to our meditation on God's greatness, and our realization that His *Shechinah* is everywhere, He is here now; in His goodness He is now giving us existence and life, and His love is now directed to us. We are now (and at every moment) standing before Him and in His presence.

To give an illustration of such *ada-ata d'nafshey* thinking we can, for example, study the problems of space travel and of the exploration of the moon. One can consider in detail all the many aspects of the spacecraft and of the conditions on the moon. But then you can switch from this objective viewpoint to a subjective, personal one—you imagine that *you* have just made a space flight to the moon, that *you* are an astronaut and are walking around, viewing the moonscape, looking back at earth. Now the meditation touches your emotions—you are thrilled and in awe. This is *ada-ata d'nafshey* thinking.

Or, another example: one can study the conditions of life in a prison, the harsh and spartan surroundings, the lack of freedom, and the fear of both guards and fellow prisoners. But then you go to the mode of *ada-ata d'nafshey* thinking, *you* are (for some reason) in prison—trapped; and your emotions will be in turmoil in response to this personal disaster that has overtaken you.

This matter of *ada-ata d'nafshey* is an important aspect of hasidic meditation for *d'vekut*. The goal of our meditation is not, after all, intellectual but existential—to be directly aware of the presence of God and in loving *d'vekut* with the *Shechinah*. So after going over in your mind, in order and in detail, thoughts about God's immanence, on how His Presence fills the worlds and there is no place where He is not, you transfer to *ada-ata d'nafshey* thinking: God's life-energy and light fill everything in your surroundings, everything you see, hear, and touch. His Divine vitality fills you, your body, even your thoughts and feelings are of Him—for there is nothing besides Him; you are in His presence.

When you reach this stage your emotions will respond, but what is more important is that you focus not on that but on Him: turn to Him fully and be with Him face to face. Remain in this *d'vekut* then, looking at the shining Face of your loving Father in Heaven.

17:7 Three quotes from *Sefer Haredim* discuss a meditation where we put ourselves face to face with God:

17:7:1 It is God's glance that gives life, and when we turn our eyes to Him we receive most fully.

> It is written, "I have placed the Lord before me always." Since life-energy and existence come to all things from God's looking down at them, and if He were to turn away for a minute they would disappear as if they never existed, is it possible that one who receives this life-energy should hide himself and not look to God and seek His glory? This is what is written, "God, from heaven looks down on the children of men, to see if there is one who is wise."
>
> It is when the moon is facing the sun that she receives its full light; so is it fitting for a man to do. And on this is it said, "From the light of the king's face comes life." So should you not turn away the eyes of your mind from Him for even a minute, and then will you receive the light of His face, as is written, "May the Lord shine His face on you." For His light, blessed be He, fills the world, and He gives life to all things each and every minute. And if His light is not visible to you, then be ashamed before Him, and be silent, with bowed head and lowered eyes." (*Sefer Haredim*, chap. 66, #37)

17:7:2 Turning the eyes of your mind to God is itself a spiritual practice that has an effect, and causes God to look at you. And God's mere glance brings with it everything good.

> O son of man, see your Creator always, with the eyes of your mind. For God looks down from heaven on the sons of men to see if there is someone who is wise and seeks God, who, with the eyes of his mind, seeks the sight of God. By your looking itself you have an effect—like the female ostrich who, by looking intently at her egg, causes the baby bird within to form and develop and then to split the egg open. [And when you turn your eyes to God, the "effect" is that God turns His face to you.] So too, when God looks down on you is there an effect, and there comes to you a flow of all good and blessing.
>
> About this is it written (Deuteronomy 16:16), "Every male among you shall appear [*yira'eh*]"—where the rabbis, of blessed

> memory, interpreted this (Hagigah 2) as *yireh* and *yira'eh*, "to see" and also "to be seen [appear]." Just as he came [to the Temple] to see [God], so does he also come to be seen [by God]. For the majority of people this will mean—at the three pilgrimage festivals when the Temple was standing. But to those who are wise it means every day and always, at every moment and in every place [that they want to see God and have His gaze on them]. When you look upward with the longing of your heart, you arouse above a corresponding longing from the Will of all wills, blessed is His name forever and ever. (*Sefer Haredim*, chap. 66, #137)

17:7:3 The previous two quotes spoke of a continuous meditation to be done at all times. In the following quote *Sefer Haredim* gives instruction for a specific meditation which strives to advance in this practice. In it he teaches the connection of *d'vekut* with seeing God, and emphasizes the mutuality between yourself and God in this meditation for *d'vekut*.

> At special times you should go to a special place where you will not be under the gaze of other people, and you should lift your eyes on high to the Only King, the Cause of all causes and the Mover behind all that moves. Turn your eyes to Him as an arrow to its target, and as it says, "As water reflects a face, so does the heart of a man reflect what is in the heart of another." When you turn your face and eyes to God, He, blessed be He, will turn His face to you, and you will cling to each other in *d'vekut*. (chap. 73, Segulah 5)

(See Chapter 1, p. 17 for the Baal Shem Tov's teaching about seeing God and being seen.)

The Talmud (*Berachot* 32) tells us that the early hasidim meditated after prayer. The Maharsha, in his commentary, explains this meditation as "looking at God's face without prayer." So the worded prayer that the hasidim directed to their Father in Heaven was followed by a silent and wordless contemplation of His "face" and Presence.[4]

17:8 It is important to realize that the goal of the kind of meditation we are discussing is to be in the presence of God. Not every source will suggest a full sequence of directed thought and feeling (that is, meditation on God's greatness and goodness, an arousal of love and fear, etc.). Some will rely (as in this last quote from *Sefer Haredim*) on something like just turning your inner gaze to Him. The more a person is immersed in holiness, the shorter the sequence of preparation need be; one can put oneself before God simply by thinking of Him. Finally, as the Besht taught, one no longer requires an effort of this nature, because one is always in this exalted state of being in the presence of God.

17:9 A lesson about the meditation for *d'vekut* comes from a hasidic story. The Rebbe of Pshischa, Rabbi Simha Bunim, once encountered his future disciple who later became the Rebbe of Kotzk.

> "Young man," the *Rebbe* asked, "where can one find God?" "Everywhere!" the young man responded. "His Glory fills the world." "Young man," the Pshischer repeated, "I asked you—Where can one find God?" "There is no place where He is not present," the Kotzker answered. "Young man, haven't you heard me?" the Pshischer asked. "Tell me, where can one find God?" The Kotzker was stymied. "Well, if I don't know, then please tell me," he said.
>
> The Pshischer answered, "Listen to me, young man. God can only be found where He is welcomed and invited to enter." (Adapted from *Generation to Generation*, pp. 40–41; cf. *Siah Sarfei Kodesh*, I, p. 71, #357)

When you meditate for *d'vekut*, you must also have humility and a welcoming attitude to your Father in Heaven. He is everywhere, but you cannot force yourself into His presence; rather, you have to open yourself to Him and invite Him into your heart and into your being.

17:10 It is a higher level of mystic awareness when a person perceives that the *Shechinah* is within as well as without. And one comes to this realization when the "typical hasidic meditation" is applied not only to the outer world, but to you yourself, to your own body, and to your own mental and emotional processes.

The Peasetzna Rebbe taught that the goal is to have the realization (in actual experience and perception) that

> You surround me and also fill my body and spirit. (*Hovat ha-Talmidim*, p. 52)

The difference in the two levels of consciousness, seeing God only without versus seeing the *Shechinah* within and without, is expressed in *Or ha-Ganuz l'Tzaddikim* by two metaphors: a fish in the ocean versus a drop of water in the ocean (see "Torah," 15:18:3). In the latter case, when the Divine Presence is seen both within and without, there is only "water."

There is another good metaphor for the level that stops short of complete self-nullification: it is like a glass jar placed under water—there is water inside and outside, and clear glass between. This shows how the clarified ego divides between "within" and "without," and illustrates how a person can be in this high level of consciousness and still retain an awareness of their individuality and separate existence.

When someone is on this exalted level so that they actually perceive that there is nothing but God, that their own existence and being is created every moment, that their movements, emotions, and thoughts are coming to them from God, then all their actions and doings will be God-directed and done with God-consciousness. (For discussion and quotes about this important subject, see Chapter 3, "Within As Well As Without"; "Waking and Beginning the Day," 4:4:8; "Prayer," 5:5:5; "Individual Practices," 39:29; and "Sex," 32:1:8:6.)

The point is that in our own practice we are to make this self-application, and (turning the direction of our meditation inward) strive to attain this holy perception and realization that the *Shechinah* is within as well as without.

17:11 Meditations on God's presence can be supported by visual and aural means. A traditional hasidic practice is to have before your eyes the name YHVH, to literally fulfill the verse (Psalm 16:8). "I have placed the Lord before me always." By having His Name before your eyes in this way your mind is continually brought back to God as you meditate on Him. The Name can either be on a *Shivitti* or card, or just be visualized (See the quote from *Derech Pikudecha* at the beginning of this chapter.)

In a similar way, there are various sentences, phrases, or words that can be repeated over and over during a meditation for this same purpose of remembrance. You can call out to God, "Father, Father!" or "Master of the World!" You can use the Psalm verse just mentioned, repeating it again and again. Thus, with this Psalm verse, you can employ both the visual and aural together, in support of a meditation on God's presence. You can meditate on God's presence, with God's name before your eyes and the words of the verse filling your ears.

There is also a light visualization often suggested to facilitate meditation on God's presence. The traditional phrases tell us that the *Shechinah* fills the earth and there is no place where He is not, that He fills all worlds and surrounds all worlds, and that He is, and there is none else. God's

Glory/*Shechinah* is, then, pictured as light, and you are to imagine yourself surrounded by light and filled with light. Sometimes this kind of meditation starts with visualizing the light above your head, and then flowing all around you.[5]

Keter Shem Tov says that *d'vekut* is when

> the soul becomes a throne for the light of the *Shechinah* above the head. And it is as if the light spreads around him and he is within the light, sitting and trembling with joy. This is also why the heavens are in every place a half sphere. (p. 42)

17:12 We began with a quote from *Or ha-Ganuz l'Tzaddikim* about a silent, sitting meditation on God's exaltedness to achieve *d'vekut.* That same book explains how to carry such a meditation into activity.

> When you are sitting alone in silence, you should imagine that you are a vessel for the world of thought, for you draw this on yourself,[6] and you should greatly sanctify your mind and thought. As soon as you come out of meditation, however, and go from stillness to movement, see that everything be done as a unification, joining your movement, speech, and walking [all together as one, in God-consciousness], that they all be done in holiness, just as your thought was sanctified when you were meditating. You should also move and speak and walk so as to receive the yoke of the Kingdom of Heaven, which keeps you in existence from nothingness, and so as to do the will of the Kingdom of Heaven—and by this you accomplish a unification. (p. 46)

The first sentence of this quote also teaches us something else of importance about meditation: that when you are meditating on God's greatness you should understand your thoughts as coming from God ("the world of thought"). This will help even more to turn your mind from your own self to God.

17:13 In most Jewish and hasidic sources, meditation is usually found in close association with other spiritual practices. For example, it is regularly joined in various ways with prayer.

Typically, meditation is used as a preparation for prayer, to direct one's mind and heart to God, and to put oneself in His presence. But there are meditations done in the midst of prayer or after prayer (as 17:11 or at the end of 17:7).

Meditations of various kinds are similarly used frequently in association with Torah study. So too, the essence of the hasidic way of eating is as a meditation; blessings on enjoyments and on *mitzvot* are really short meditations. Altogether there are many aspects of hasidic spiritual practice that involve meditation or are meditations. One can even say that hasidic spirituality is ideally one continuous meditation on God by diverse means.

Since so much of the hasidic material about meditation is found intimately linked to other spiritual practices, I have left it in those other contexts and discussed it there. See particularly: Chapter 1, "In the Presence of God" p. 17; Chapter 2, p. 45; Chapter 3, "A Continuous Stream of Holy Thoughts," p. 64; "Prayer," 5:1:18; "Torah," 15:18; "Waking and Beginning the Day," 4:4.

For visual and aural supports to a meditation for *d'vekut*, see: for both, Chapter 2, "Aids to Remembrance," p. 36; for the former, "Service of the Imagination," 19:10; for the latter, "Repetition of a Holy Sentence" (21).

17:14 As mentioned in Chapter 3, "A Continuous Stream of Holy Thoughts," the traditional path of the sages has been that of continuous Torah study. Those who favored meditation (or prayer) had to struggle somewhat to make some room for their way. *Sefer Haredim* quotes the Ari as saying that a meditation for achieving *d'vekut* is "seventy times more valuable for the soul than Torah study" (chap. 65). There were and are those who say that Torah study is itself *d'vekut*. But *Darkei Yesharim* (p. 3) takes the position that during Torah study our God-awareness is inevitably lessened compared to direct meditation for *d'vekut*. And *Rachmei ha-Av* makes light of those who think that learning itself is *d'vekut*; rather, while learning, you must make a special effort to keep an awareness of the presence of God. (See "Torah," 15:22:1 for this quote.)

In this context it is interesting to compare some seemingly divergent views about the relation of the *mitzvot* to *d'vekut*. For example, Rabbi Yehiel Michal of Zlotchov said that:

> When a person commands his fellow to do something and he does his will, through this there is a connection with him. And so with us, when we do God's will and commandments, we are clinging to Him in *d'vekut*. (*Nofit Tzufim*, p. 24b, #31)

And yet, Rabbi Elimelech of Lizensk can say something like this:

> A *tzaddik* is allowed to interrupt his *d'vekut* with God, blessed be He, in order to go and do His *mitzvot*. (*Noam Elimelech*, Likkutei Shoshanah, p. 86b)

But of course Rabbi Elimelech also believed that by doing the *mitzvot* one is in *d'vekut* (as he indeed indicates elsewhere). For the matter is really one of degree.

Certainly Torah study and doing *mitzvot* involve *d'vekut*; but it is less than that *d'vekut* directly achieved by meditation. If we would express it metaphorically, we could say that it is the difference between reading a letter from a friend (Torah), or going to do something he asked you to do (*mitzvot*), and actually being in his presence and together with him (meditation).

However, this comparison should not be pressed too hard or taken too literally. From another perspective, we can also understand that there are different ways in Judaism, and that depending on someone's personality, one will experience God's closeness and presence more in prayer, another in meditation, another in Torah study, etc. The particular virtue of meditation for *d'vekut*, however, is that the experience of the presence of God is its immediate goal; it is most direct. As a result, for those who seek this spiritual experience of *d'vekut* before anything else, it has much to offer.

18

Shabbat

The Sabbath is one of the most important spiritual practices in Judaism, so important that it is an essential part of the creation story itself, and our own observance of the Sabbath is said to be modeled on God's Sabbath rest.

On its simplest level the Sabbath is a day set aside once a week entirely for spiritual practice. By completely eliminating all the distractions of work and labor, full concentration can be devoted to the service of God. And attaining a higher level of spirituality on that one special day can act, over time, to lift the other six days to its height; then the process begins again.

There is another practice of individual piety of setting aside one day each week for spiritual activity (see "A Full Day Set Aside" [36]). But one thing that differentiates the Sabbath, aside from its God-given sanctity, is that it is not the time for repentance from fear, from sadness over transgressions, or even for spiritual "work"; it is the time for repentance from love of God and for joy in God.

As Rabbi Tzvi Hirsh of Ziditchov said:

> The Sabbath day, the Day of the Soul, is made for love. (*Yifrach biYamav Tzaddik*, p. 56a)

Rabbi Moshe Leib of Sassov said:

> During the days of the week fear of God is ascendant, while on the Sabbath day love is ascendant. (*Eser Tzachtzachot*, p. 54, #37)

Rabbi Meir of Parisov once said:

> On the Sabbath you should not involve yourself in things requiring much effort, even in the labor of the service of God. (*Derech Tzaddikim*, p. 15)

A rabbi reports how his father told him that once when the *rebbe*,

> Rabbi Moshe of Koznitz, heard him sigh on *Shabbat*, he said to him that "Even sighing and being troubled over spiritual things is forbidden on *Shabbat*." (*Derech Emunah u'Maaseh Rav*, p. 91)

On the one hand, the rule is that the spiritual level of our Sabbath will reflect the level of our spiritual activity during the preceding week, which prepares for the Sabbath. Conversely, the level of spiritual activity during the following week will be influenced by what kind of Sabbath we have.

Rabbi Moshe Leib of Sassov:

> The six workdays are a preparation for the holiness of *Shabbat*. The situation can be compared to a man who was sitting in the dark for many days and suddenly went out into the light. As is well known, he will not be able to stand the light for it will harm him. So it is that someone whose actions are dark during the weekdays will not be able to receive the light of the holiness of *Shabbat*. (*Eser Tzachtzachot*, p. 55, #44)

In every way you should add holiness to everything you do on *Shabbat*; whatever level you are at, take things up a notch: in the way you pray, eat, talk, etc.

Rabbi Tzvi Hirsh of Nadborna:

> On *Shabbat* let all your holy thoughts be more humble, and see that your eating and drinking as well as your sexual intercourse be in holiness, and that all your actions be for the sake of heaven, more so than on weekdays. And after *Shabbat* draw from this holiness into the weekdays. (*Alpha Beta* of Rabbi Tzvi Hirsh, Shabbat, in *YHvT*, p. 66)

The various rules and practices that define the shape of *Shabbat* have as their purpose and goal to spiritualize the day and the one who keeps it.

Observance of the restrictions in the material sphere results in the build up of spiritual power, so that we are able to receive the special flow of Divine energy which comes down from Above on *Shabbat*. This increase of soul power, this access to higher levels of spirituality, is what the rabbis called receiving an "extra soul" on *Shabbat*.

> By keeping the Sabbath according to the *halacha* you will feel an additional spiritual power within your soul. (*Reshit Hochmah*, Sh'ar ha-Kedushah, chap. 2, #22)

The ideal for the Sabbath is that, using this higher level of spirituality, we attain to one whole day of unbroken God–consciousness, filled with love for the Holy One, blessed be He.

Through keeping the Sabbath we separate ourselves from materiality and attest that we are spiritual beings.

> The Sabbath is of the nature of the World to Come [the spiritual world to be fully revealed in the future]; and the Divine intention in giving us the sanctity of *Shabbat* was to make us aware that our true dwelling is not in this world, wherein we are merely sojourners, but in the soul world, the world of spirituality, which is the World to Come. So we rest from labor which is characteristic of this world, and we sanctify the Sabbath, thereby showing that we are ourselves sanctified and that we are not involved with the things of this world. For, as is known, the essence of holiness is separation [from worldly things and bodily desires]. (*Reshit Hochmah*, Sh'ar ha-Kedushah, chap. 2, #24)

On *Shabbat* we accustom ourselves to living in the spiritual world.

Another aspect of the Sabbath rest is its inherent teaching that God created the world and is its master. When we refrain from all creative physical work on the Sabbath we give recognition that all action in this world depends ultimately on God's doing. This consciousness, moreover, should be carried into the weekdays when we do work, and we should work and act with a Sabbath–consciousness that God's energy and will is the source of all that happens in the world, even that which comes from our own doing. On the one hand, we are to act, but at the same time we are to have the Divine peace in action that comes from the realization that the *Shechinah* is acting through us.

The Sabbath is so great, there are so many facets to its diamond spirituality, that our discussion of its practices necessarily must be incomplete and limited. There are a number of excellent books on *Shabbat* and its ways available in English. See them for further material.

18:1 PREPARATIONS FOR THE SABBATH

In Hasidism the emphasis is always on preparation in spiritual practices, for preparation is the secret of inwardness, of *kavvanah* (God-directed intention), and *hitlahavut* (fervor). If you truly want to see the glory of the holy Sabbath and be aware of the special manifestation of the *Shechinah* on that day, you must prepare beforehand.

18:1:1 Preparations throughout the Week

> **18:1:1:1** We should always be looking forward to the coming of *Shabbat* the whole week, thinking "When will *Shabbat* come?" (Rabbi Asher of Stolin, *Beit Aharon*, Likkutim, p. 286)

It is good to express this kind of longing verbally. The more this is done the higher the Sabbath will be, for it is sanctified by such words of longing.

18:1:1:2 The tradition provides us with a device we can use to remember the Sabbath every day—the psalm of the day. Each day of the week there is a particular psalm said during *Shaharit*—there are seven in all (see the Siddur). The introduction to its recitation is: "Today is the [first, second, etc.] day of the week [in Hebrew, "the *Shabbat*"], on which the Levites sang in the Temple: [the particular psalm of the day, which follows in the text]."

In Hebrew the days of the week do not have separate names, but are all simply numbered and put in relation to *Shabbat*: Sunday is the "first day" (of the week that ends with this *Shabbat*), Monday is the "second day," and so on. The rabbis say that the purpose of this scheme of naming the days of the week is to remember the Sabbath. When saying the psalm of the day each day in the morning we can then use this introductory line as a remembrance of the Sabbath, and perhaps (after the psalm) add some expression of longing for its coming and briefly consider some way, that day, to prepare for its coming.

> **18:1:1:2:1** Every day say the psalm of the Levites and before it, "Today is the first day of the week [which ends with this Sabbath]" and so on for each day. By doing this you fulfill the *mitzvah* "Remember the Sabbath day," because we have to remember the Sabbath each day. (*Derech Hayim*, 5–55)

18:1:1:2:2 This continual remembrance of the Sabbath on weekdays not only prepares spiritually for the Sabbath but also draws the sanctity of the Sabbath into the weekdays.

> The Sages established that every day we say in the psalm of the day, "This is the first day of the Sabbath," "This is the second day of the Sabbath," etc., so that through these words we draw the holiness of the Sabbath into that day. (Rabbi Kalman Kalonymus of Cracow in *Maor v'Shemesh*, quoted in *Or ha-Shabbat*, p. 20)

18:1:1:3 In Hebrew, of course, the continual mention of the days of the week in everyday conversation has an indirect reference to *Shabbat*: the first day, the second day, etc. But what can we do in English with its Monday, Tuesday, etc.? One possibility is to accustom yourself, whenever you mention a day of the week in English, to mentally translate for yourself. For example: Monday—the second day of the week which ends with *Shabbat*. Through repetition you can train yourself to make this association.

18:1:1:4 By speaking about *Shabbat* often, in Torah conversation and otherwise, we not only remember and sanctify the Sabbath day, but draw its holiness into the weekdays.

Hear this story that Rabbi Yuda Tzvi (a grandson of Rabbi Yitzhak Isaac of Ziditchov) told about his father-in-law, Rabbi Hayim of Tzanz:

> Once the holy *gaon* sat at table on Wednesday at some *mitzvah* meal and was speaking about the holiness of the Sabbath. He became so excited and full of fervor that when he finished the meal and turned to go he called out to all those sitting there, "*Shabbat Shalom* to you!" It seemed to Rabbi Yuda Tzvi that that day was *Erev Shabbat* and that the holy *Shabbat* was quickly approaching, so he went home, got his good white shirt out of his dresser, put it under his arm and went to the *mikveh* in honor of the holy Sabbath. On the way there he met another young man who had heard the holy Tzanzer and he too had his shirt under his arm and was going to wash himself in hot water in honor of the holy Sabbath.

> But when they arrived at the *mikveh*, and saw that no one was there, they realized their mistake, and understood that the fervor of the Tzanzer had affected them so that they thought *Shabbat* was already on them! (*Pe'er Yitzhak*, p. 125, #10)

Whenever and however we use the name *Shabbat* we draw its holiness to ourselves (see 18:2:11:2:2–3).

18:1:1:5 Rabbi Moshe Teitelbaum:

> All the days of the week receive strength from *Shabbat*, so it is good to draw the holiness of *Shabbat* into the weekdays, through remembrance of it, as is known. And an effective way of doing this is through studying the laws of *Shabbat* every day. (*Ha-Gaon ha-Kadosh Baal Yismach Moshe*, p. 228; cf. p. 232)

18:1:1:6 Although most of the preparations for *Shabbat* are done on *Erev Shabbat*:

18:1:1:6:1 Every weekday prepare something for the needs of *Shabbat*. (*Derech Hayim*, 7–1)

18:1:1:6:2 Every day remember the holy *Shabbat* by preparing, if possible, something for the honor of *Shabbat*. (*Derech Hayim*, 7–42)

18:1:1:7 A lesson about *Shabbat* can be learned from the way of the Rebbe of Ropshitz with *Sukkot*. He was so deeply attached to the festival of *Sukkot* and to the *mitzvah* of the *sukkah*, that:

> The *tzaddikim* of Rabbi Naftali of Ropshitz's generation said that his soul was from the *mitzvah* of *sukkah* in the Torah. The truth is that the whole year he was involved with the *mitzvah* of *sukkah*. Every day he did something connected with his *sukkah*, one day banging in a peg, another day studying the Talmud tractate *Sukkah*. And this was his custom all his life. In addition to all this, every day of the year he found a way to mention the name *sukkah* in conversation, and always found a way to turn the conversation around until he could say something about the *sukkah*. (*Ohel Naftali*, p. 5, #3)

In our remembrance of *Shabbat* during the week, then, one day we can prepare something for *Shabbat*, another day we can study a little about *Shabbat*—its laws and customs, the prayers or the Song of Songs. A person can also seek to bring *Shabbat* into his conversation every day.

18:1:2 *Erev Shabbat*

18:1:2:1 Physical Preparations

18:1:2:1:1 For everything done in preparation (washing clothes, shopping, cooking, etc.) say as a stated intention:

> I am doing this for the honor of the holy Sabbath.* (*Or ha-Shabbat*, p. 34)
>
> **18:1:2:1:2** Whenever buying or cooking anything for the Sabbath, say out loud, "I am doing this," or "I am cooking this in honor of the Sabbath."* (*Hanhagot Adam*, Y. L. Lipshitz, p. 42)
>
> **18:1:2:1:3** Once on *Erev Shabbat* the shadows were already getting longer, and in the house of Rabbi Menahem Mendel of Rimanov there was still no fish [as traditional] in honor of the holy Sabbath. But the *rebbe* instructed his holy servant, the rabbi and *tzaddik*, Rabbi Tzvi Hirsh, to put a number of empty frying pans on the fire on the stove; and each time he did so he was to say "In honor of the holy Sabbath."*
>
> Rabbi Tzvi Hirsh did as he was told, and while he was thus engaged someone came from afar to visit the *rebbe* and, as a gift, he brought with him some fish in honor of the holy Sabbath. Everyone in the household was amazed when this happened.
>
> On the day of the holy Sabbath the *rebbe* explained, saying, "When the holiness of the Sabbath descends from heaven there comes with it a flow of supernal beneficence. Someone who wants to receive this supernal flow of goodness has to bring his desire to do so into speech, and to say 'In honor of the holy Sabbath'; then the flow will come down of itself from Above . . . for the thing depends on speech. So do not be amazed that I was so sure that there would be fish in honor of the holy Sabbath." (*Ateret Menahem*, p. 19, #46)

18:1:2:1:4 A special holiness rests on things set aside in advance for *Shabbat* use.

> Every item of food that you mentally set aside for the sake of heaven for *Shabbat*, you thereby cause holiness to enter it. When you eat the food on *Shabbat* (and when the evening of *Shabbat* arrives with its heavenly flow of holiness from Above, it enters within that food also, and when it enters the body, provided that you eat it in holiness, you receive an illumination and holiness from Above. (*Siddur Olat ha-Tamid*, quoted in *Or ha-Shabbat*, p. 234)

(See also "Individual Practices," 39:20 for the teaching of the Yehudi about a holy purchase.)

When you set something aside for *Shabbat* it is best to express this verbally:

> The *mitzvah* of remembering *Shabbat* is done with both the heart and the mouth . . . and it applies to food, dishes, utensils and other objects, clothes, etc. So if you come across something nice, set it aside for *Shabbat* by saying out loud, "This is for *Shabbat.*"* (*Sefer Haredim*, Be'urim v'Hiddushim, p. 326, #8)

18:1:2:2 Spiritual Preparations

As *Shabbat* approaches, and once the physical preparations are readied, we should prepare ourselves spiritually.

18:1:2:2:1 *Torah*

It is traditional before the Sabbath, as part of the spiritual preparation, to study the Torah portion (*Sedrah*) for that week along with the Haftorah. The Torah portion is read three times: twice in Hebrew and once in the Aramaic Targum (paraphrase). Since the whole purpose of the Targum was to translate the text from Hebrew into the language people could understand, you can (as is halachically permitted) read the Torah portion today in English rather than the Aramaic—that is, twice in Hebrew, once in English.

> **18:1:2:2:1:1** Do not interrupt your reading of twice Torah/once Targum at all, even for conversation. ([Ladier] Rav's *Shulchan Aruch*, 285–6, quoted in *Or ha-Shabbat*, p. 37)

The significance of avoiding interruptions was discussed in Chapter 3, p. 60.

18:1:2:2:1:2 The Torah reading is part of the spiritual preparation for *Shabbat*, when you reach a higher spiritual level, the "extra soul" of the rabbis. For easier understanding we will refer to this as "extra soul-power."

> Through reading twice Torah/once Targum extra soul-power comes to a person. (*Yalkut Reuveni* quoted in *Or ha-Shabbat*, p. 38)

18:1:2:2:1:3 Interrupting this reading would spoil its purpose of building up spiritual power so that you are able to receive the special Divine flow at the onset of the Sabbath.

> You should be careful not to interrupt your reading of twice Torah/once Targum for any conversation, even of Torah, so that you do not slacken the taut rope working to sanctify and to empower your soul. . . . After the reading of twice Torah/once Targum you should meditate on repentance, because if you are still in your impurity, how can you attain to the light of the Sabbath's holiness? (*Or ha-Shabbat*, p. 37)

18:1:2:2:1:4 A hasidic story that takes place on *Erev Shabbat* tells:

> The Seer of Lublin was sitting in *tallit* and *tefillin*, going over the *Sedrah*, reading the portion of the day with the traditional chant, when his daughter came in, sent by her mother. She told him that it was already noon and she had no money with which to buy wine for *kiddush*. But the *rebbe* could not answer her because he did not want to interrupt in the middle of reading twice Torah/once Targum. So he gestured to her to follow him to the *Beit ha-Midrash* where there would be many hasidim. And once there he signaled to the hasidim that they listen to what his daughter had to say, and take care of the matter. (*Kodesh Hillulim*, p. 134)

18:1:2:2:1:5 Rabbi Zev Wolf of Zhitomir told:

> Once on Friday the Great Maggid [of Mezritch] sat in his room, which was next to his *Beit Midrash*, and recited the Torah portion of the week, twice Torah/once Targum. A number of us students were sitting in the *Beit Midrash* [studying] when suddenly a great light shone on us. Immediately the door of the Maggid's room opened and his flaming countenance was revealed to our eyes. This rare vision almost caused us to lose our minds. Rabbi Pinhas of Frankfort and his brother Rabbi Shmelke of Nikolsburg, and Rabbi Elimelech of Lizensk and his brother Rabbi Zusya of Hanipol, all fled outside. Rabbi Levi Yitzhak of Berditchev went into a state of ecstasy and rolled on the floor under the table. Even I [who am so unused to any emotionalism] clapped my hands in uncontrollable excitement. (*Ha-Maggid mi-Mezritch*, p. 69)
>
> **18:1:2:2:1:6** Be careful not to go to the *mikveh* until after you have read the Torah portion of the week, twice Torah/once Targum. Otherwise, you will not have the ability to receive the illumination of the *Shabbat* [part of which comes at the *mikveh*]. You should also

be careful to go over the Torah portion while you still have your *tefillin* on [after *Shaharit*, which is the time often suggested for the practice of twice Torah/once Targum]. (*Or Tzaddikim*, quoted in *Or ha-Shabbat*, p. 36)

18:1:2:2:2 Tshuvah, *Forgiveness, and Peacemaking*

Before *Shabbat* you should repent as you do before Yom Kippur: confess your sins before God and return to Him with all your heart; and also return to a state of peace with everyone around you by asking forgiveness for your sins, and by forgiving others for their sins against you.

18:1:2:2:2:1 Every holy *Erev Shabbat* you should meditate on repentance with a broken and contrite heart. You should feel regret for all the sins you committed that past week so that you can enter the holy *Shabbat* in a state of holiness and receive the illumination of the extra soul-power. (*Avodah u'Moreh Derech*, p. 49)

18:1:2:2:2:2 Rabbi Elimelech of Lizensk taught:

Erev Shabbat is in the same category as *Erev Yom Kippur*. (*Eser Tzachtzachot*, p. 31, #65)

18:1:2:2:2:3 Every *Erev Shabbat* you should think over your deeds as on *Erev Yom Kippur*. Just as *Yom Kippur* is the end of the year, so is *Erev Shabbat* the end of the six workdays of the week. And so you should make confession and receive on yourself a great holiness and purity so that you will enter the Sabbath the right way and with an expanded God-consciousness [*l'dabaik et atzmo b'yirah ilai*]. (*Toldot Aharon*, quoted in *DhTvhY*, Hilchot Shabbat, p. 2, #2)

18:1:2:2:2:4 I heard it from my master and teacher and rabbi, the Rabbi of Barniv, the memory of a *tzaddik* and a holy man for a blessing, and he heard it from an old man who was a servant in the court and house of the *rebbe*, Rabbi Elimelech of Lizensk. The old man said that "*Erev Shabbat* even the men and women who were servants in the *rebbe's* house, myself included, would ask forgiveness from one another, just like on *Erev Yom Kippur*. They would all be trembling and crying and their knees would be knocking against each other until the candles of the holy Sabbath were lit. And when the candles were lit a great joy fell upon each and every one—and we all tasted the joy of *Shabbat*, experiencing a very great and elevated joy." (*Or Zarua l'Tzaddik*, quoted in *Or ha-Shabbat*, p. 48 n.)

It was a true and deep repentance, and a holy grief, that gave birth to this great Sabbath joy. One clears out, as it were, an empty space into which the light of the Sabbath can enter.

An old woman in Lizensk told Rabbi Shlomo of Radomsk about Rabbi Elimelech:

> Every *Erev Shabbat* was like *Erev Yom Kippur*. The whole town gathered in the synagogue to say Psalms and they cried their hearts out; and Rabbi Elimelech would preach *musar* [inspirational words of repentance]. (*Ohel Elimelech*, p. 82, #198)

So before *Shabbat*, one can lead oneself to *tshuvah* through Psalms and a *musar* book.

> **18:1:2:2:2:5** It is good to meditate on *tshuvah* and to confess your sins on *Erev Shabbat*. You should empty your heart of all bad thoughts, and remove all anger and argument from your house. (*Totzaot Hayim*, p. 42)

18:1:2:2:2:6 It is important to understand that the pressure of preparing for *Shabbat*, plus the added energy coming into the world then, can easily be channeled into anger and argument. Knowing this should help you to see that this new energy is turned to good, and that it is translated, as it was intended, into extra soul-power. One essential way to accomplish this is by acting to foster peace and forgiveness.

> The afternoon before *Shabbat* is a dangerous time for arguments between husband and wife and between servants, for the Other Side exerts much effort to incite a dispute. But someone who fears God should subdue his evil inclination and see that no argument or annoyance is aroused. On the contrary, he should seek peace and be peaceful in everything. (Rabbi Hayim Yosef David Azulai, *Avodat ha-Kodesh*, Moreh b'Etzba, 4–140.)

18:1:2:2:2:7 When you repent before the Sabbath, asking forgiveness from those you have offended, and forgiving those who have offended you (even if they do not ask forgiveness), you can then also ask God to likewise forgive you your sins against Him.

> **18:1:2:2:2:8** You should be careful on the holy Sabbath to cleave to your fellow man in love and brotherhood, peace and friendship—

> even more is this true between husband and wife. . . . So if two people had some dispute they should each one approach the other with words of reconciliation and love before the entrance of *Shabbat*. And a person should always be quick to reestablish peace and ask forgiveness—with men and with God, and especially with his wife. (*Yesod v'Shoresh ha-Avodah*, Gate 8, chap. 5, p. 168)

If you have some dispute during the week, resolve it before *Shabbat*; but if you have not had any dispute, then go a step further and raise the peace and love to a higher level.

> If you had a dispute with someone during the week, or with your wife, make peace for *Shabbat*. *Shabbat* should be different [higher] than the weekdays in every way. If you were at peace with everyone all six weekdays, then on *Shabbat* have additional closeness and reconciliation with one another, with increased love. . . . And so should a man be more gracious and loving to his wife on *Shabbat*, with loving words. (*Tikkunim*, quoted in *Yesod v'Shoresh ha-Avodah*, Gate 8, chap. 5, p. 169)

18:1:2:2:3 *Washing in Hot Water and* Mikveh

18:1:2:2:3:1 Hot Water

It is a traditional practice to wash in hot water before *Shabbat*. The hot water will change your body-feeling, removing any negativity and the weekday "set," and ready you for the renewal that comes with *Shabbat*. Bodily cleanliness also has a spiritual effect. It is hard to feel spiritually pure when you are physically unclean; conversely, being clean in body naturally conduces to a feeling of spiritual cleanliness.

> Cleaning the body restores purity to the soul; and when the body is unclean some blemish will certainly reach the soul. (Rabbeinu Yonah, in *Sefer ha-Yirah*, quoted in *Reshit Hochmah*, Sh'ar ha-Ahavah, chap. 11, #23)

> **18:1:2:2:3:1:1** It is a *mitzvah* on *Erev Shabbat* to wash your whole body with hot water; but if it is not possible, then at least wash your face, hands, and feet. It is also a *mitzvah* to shampoo. (*Shulchan Aruch*, 360–1)

> **18:1:2:2:3:1** It was the custom of Rabbi Yehudah bar Ilai to have a basin full of hot water brought to him every *Erev Shabbat*. He would

wash his face, hands, and feet, and then he would wrap himself in a linen garment having *tzitzit*, and sitting there he looked like an angel of the Lord of hosts. (*Shabbat* 25a)

18:1:2:2:3:1:3 Why do we wash with hot water *Erev Shabbat*? This is parallel to the immersion of the soul in the River of Fire to remove the stains of its sins. So when you bathe in hot water *Erev Shabbat* the stains of your sins are removed. (*Taamei ha-Minhagim*; p. 119)

18:1:2:2:3:1:4 When going to the bath or shower to wash in hot water:

You should have as your intention that you are doing this to wash away and cleanse yourself of the stains of all your sins and of the filthiness of the unclean spirit [which your sins have caused to rest on you]. Afterwards, go to the *mikveh*. (*Minhat Shabbat*, quoted in *Or ha-Shabbat*, p. 53)

Some sources tell you to wash in hot water before the *mikveh*, others after.

18:1:2:2:3:1:5 Close to the onset of *Shabbat* wash your face, hands, and feet with hot water; if you can also immerse yourself in the *mikveh*, how good. (*Shulchan Aruch* of Rabbi Eleazar ha-Katan, p. 12, #6)

18:1:2:2:3:2 ***Mikveh***

Many hasidim go to the *mikveh* before *Shabbat*.

18:1:2:2:3:2:1 The closer to the onset of *Shabbat* you go to the *mikveh*, the better. (*Kaf ha-Hayim*, p. 369, #16)

18:1:2:2:3:2:2 On the eve of the holy *Shabbat* one immersion in the *mikveh* is needed to remove all of the Other Side from you, and a second one to draw on you the holiness of the Sabbath. . . . But it will do no good to imitate the real thing, like a monkey, and to think about casting off your sins and not doing so at all, so that your iniquity and filthiness stay fixed in your heart. . . . In that case there is certainly no value whatsoever to the *mikveh* by just the physical act. If you do not cast off the bad, you will certainly not take on any holiness. (*Sidduro Shel Shabbat*, quoted in *DhTvhY*, Hilchot Shabbat, p. 3, #6)

The point here is that before you enter the *mikveh* and while you are in the *mikveh* you are to repent sincerely and then to take on holiness.

> **18:1:2:2:3:2:3** When you are in the *mikveh* [on *Erev Shabbat*], confess all you did wrong that week. (*Imrei Kodesh*, #14, p. 27)

> **18:1:2:2:3:2:4** The reason why we go to bathe in the *mikveh Erev Shabbat* is that it is a matter of spiritually taking off one soul-garment and putting on another. We have to have a different spiritual aspect altogether on *Shabbat*, a different soul-garment. So we go to the *mikveh*, remove our weekday clothes, go through the transforming experience of the bath and put on our Sabbath clothes—all this being duplicated with our spiritual garments. (*Pe'er l'Yesharim*, p. 22a #248)

This thought can be our intention when removing our clothes, bathing, and dressing in preparation for *Shabbat*.

18:1:2:2:3:2:5 Some sources speak of the two immersions as the time for this meditation on spiritual garments; others relate it to the removal of weekday clothes and the donning of Sabbath clothes.

> [The former:] You have to immerse yourself twice, one after the other; the first is to strip off the weekday soul-garment and the second is to take on the garment of extra soul-power for the honor of the Sabbath. (*Minhagei ha-Arizal*, p. 31b)

Kaf ha-Hayim, who follows this scheme of the two immersions representing the taking off and putting on of soul-garments, writes:

> When you immerse for the first time, say, "In immersing I am removing the weekday soul-garment"; immerse a second time and say, "I am immersing so as to receive the soul-illumination of *Shabbat*" . . . and then bow and continue, "and to receive the extra soul-power of Shabbat."[1*] (p. 371)

The second scheme connects the taking off and putting on of soul-garments with the changing of real garments, taking off your weekday clothes before entering the *mikveh* and putting on Sabbath clothes after.

> When you divest yourself of your weekday garments, intend to divest yourself of all vices—do *tshuvah* and examine your deeds—and intend to cast from you the Other Side that rests on you. When

> you put on your Sabbath clothes, intend to draw an additional holiness on yourself and accept on yourself all virtue and good conduct. (*Hok l'Yisrael*)

Of course, both these schemes can be used for the meditation, separately or together.

> **18:1:2:2:3:2:6** A person can investigate and try for himself, that when he directs himself to have the fear of God in his heart in truth and makes his deeds acceptable before God, that after he goes in the *mikveh* on *Erev Shabbat* with the right *kavvanah* to receive the holiness of *Shabbat*, he will indeed see that he has extra soul-power. He will feel within himself that exalted fear of God's majesty that has come to him, until he burns with the love and fear of God. This is tried and tested by the experience of many people, immeasurable times, without any doubt. But if your soul is not purified, you will not feel the holiness of *Shabbat*. (*Zichron Torat Moshe*, quoted in *Derech Emunah u'Maaseh Rav*, p. 83)

18:1:2:2:3:2:7 In a book he wrote, a hasid reports how he asked his father, who was a hasid of Rabbi Hayim of Tchernovitz, about the *rebbe*:

> I asked my father if there was truth to what they say about Rabbi Hayim, that from *Erev Shabbat*, after he was in the *mikveh*, until the holy *Shabbat* ended, he was a full head taller than he was on weekdays. He answered me, "Son, you know that it's not my way to exaggerate, and of course I didn't measure his height. But this I can tell you, with clear testimony, that I saw him every *Erev Shabbat* when he walked to the *mikveh* and as he came back—and I can tell you that the man who came back was not the same man. He looked like a completely different person: his face, his height, and everything about the look of his holy body was changed from what it had been." (*Shaarei Orah*, p. 9)

18:1:2:2:3:2:8 If you do not have access to a *mikveh* before *Shabbat* you can attempt to achieve the transformed soul/body state which is its goal by intense *d'vekut*. The Seer of Lublin told a disciple that when you do not have access to a *mikveh*:

> "You can immerse yourself in the Supernal River of Fire"; then he whispered into his ear, "in the fire of *d'vekut*." (*Eser Orot*, p. 98, #66)

If, in your preparation for *Shabbat* your devotion is with such fervor that you sweat, the effect on your body-feeling is considered equivalent to going to the *mikveh.* That is part of the meaning of the Lubliner's remark, as we learn from related teachings. The fiery devotion spoken about can come actually from any religious practice used in preparation for *Shabbat*: meditation, Torah study, prayer, song, etc. (For an example, see 18:1:2:2:7:6.) Those who are on a high level can come to a state of bodily sweating through their fiery inner devotion; but others can achieve this through intense religious activity with the body.

(For more about immersion in the Supernal River of Fire, see "*Mitzvot,*" 11:3; and for a story about a hasid "immersing spiritually" by meditation when he could not get to a *mikveh* before *Shabbat*, see "Men's *Mikveh,*" 30:11.)

18:1:2:2:3:3 Comparison of Hot Water Washing and *Mikveh*

Although the Talmud speaks specifically of washing with hot water before *Shabbat*, the *mikveh* immersion before *Shabbat* also became a regular hasidic practice.

If we consider the relation between these two things, the hot water is a physical washing and cleansing, where you honor God by taking care of your body because you are made in the image of God. Furthermore, the water as well as its heat has a bodily effect, changing our body-feeling.

The *mikveh*, contrarily, has nothing to do with bodily cleansing—you are to wash and clean yourself thoroughly before you even enter the *mikveh.* Although its water also changes our body-feeling, the significant thing is not that the *mikveh's* water is hot (it usually is not) but that it is water which has a natural sanctity, if we can say such a thing, never having passed through man-made ducts, etc. Either it is collected rain-water or is a natural body of water, such as a river, lake, or ocean. The *mikveh* is also deep enough to allow full immersion. That is another important difference from hot water washing, because in using the *mikveh*, full immersion, not washing, is the essence. Perhaps for that reason the sources seem to speak about hot water washing in terms of removing negativity, while with *mikveh* there is that, but in addition they also speak of receiving holiness.

18:1:2:2:4 Shabbat *Clothes*

You should try to have special Sabbath clothes, worn only on the Sabbath. It is desirable to wear white on *Shabbat*, all white if possible.

> **18:1:2:2:4:1** Try to wear different clothes on *Shabbat*; remove your weekday clothes and put on good Sabbath clothes. Happy is he who has special clothes from top to bottom for *Shabbat*. You should not wear a single thing that is from the weekday. For everything you do on the sixth day in preparation for *Shabbat*, washing yourself, dressing, and so on, say out loud that you are doing it for the honor of *Shabbat*. (Rabbi Hayim Yosef David Azulai, *Avodat ha-Kodesh*, Moreh b'Etzba, 4–139)

18:1:2:2:4:2 Rabbi Hayim Vital said about his teacher, the great master of the Kabbalah, Rabbi Yitzhak Luria:

> My teacher, of blessed memory, cautioned me . . . that it is improper for a person to wear any of the clothes he wore during the week on the Sabbath. Conversely, it is wrong to wear any of your Sabbath clothes, even your Sabbath shirt, during the rest of the week. . . . Moreover, on the Sabbath a person must wear white garments. (*Minhagei ha-Arizal*, p. 33, #15, 16)

The different garments symbolize the different soul state, and the white a more pure one. The clothes actually not only symbolize these things, but suggest them and induce them in the person who wears them. Having on special Sabbath clothes also helps us to remember throughout the day that it is *Shabbat*.

18:1:2:2:4:3:1 It is good to have [at least] four white garments for the honor of the Sabbath. (*Derech Hayim*, 1–37)

18:1:2:2:4:3:2 The Ari told his disciples that when you put on the Sabbath shirt on *Erev Shabbat*.

> [Have a special *kavvanah*]: to draw holiness on yourself. You should also wear white clothes and not those of any other color, or black. And you should not have fewer than four white garments, the upper garment and the one below, the girdle that is on the lower one, and the shirt that is against your skin [that is, coat, pants, belt or *gartel*, and shirt]. (*Minhagei ha-Arizal*, p. 33)

Which garments the four are is not fixed; elsewhere, for example, the hat replaces the coat (*Hanhagot Adam*, Y. L. Lipshitz, p. 43).

> **18:1:2:2:4:3:3** The *tzaddik* Rabbi Moshe the Great from Pshevorsk said that when a man wears four white Sabbath garments, he is forgiven all his sins. (*Zohar Hai*, quoted in *DhTvhY*, Hilchot Shabbat, p. 7, #13)

> **18:1:2:2:5** It was the custom of the holy Rabbi Yehiel Michal of Zlotchov on *Erev Shabbat* immediately after noon to go to the *mikveh* to immerse in honor of *Shabbat*. Then he would lock himself in his room for a while to spiritually prepare himself for *Shabbat*. (*Toafot ha-Rim*, p. 162)

18:1:2:2:6 *Psalms*

Some hasidim prepare for *Shabbat* with the recitation of Psalms. Some do this before the morning prayers on Friday, before or at dawn, others after prayers.

> **18:1:2:2:6:1** Hasidim are accustomed to saying the whole Book of Psalms on *Erev Shabbat*, before prayer. (Rabbi Moshe Teitelbaum, *Ha-Gaon ha-Kadosh Baal Yismach Moshe*, p. 191)

18:1:2:2:6:2 A hasidic story tells of someone going to visit Rabbi Hershele of Nadborna:

> Upon my arrival there on Thursday evening, I asked the young hasidim what preparations need I make in order to properly experience *Shabbos* here? I was told to rise early in the morning and immerse myself in the *mikveh*, then pray [*Shaharit*] and later recite the complete Book of Psalms without interruption. (*Connections/ Hakrev Ushma*, 1:2:9)

(See "Psalms," 16:16 for this practice of reciting the whole Book of Psalms without interruption.)

A hasidic story about Rabbi Zusya of Hanipol begins:

> **18:1:2:2:6:3** When Rabbi Zusya was doing personal service as a disciple for his holy master, the Great Maggid of Mezritch, he was once, close to the onset of *Shabbat*, saying Psalms with great fervor. (*Ha-Maggid mi-Mezritch*, p. 172)

18:1:2:2:7 *Song of Songs*

It is a hasidic tradition to recite the Song of Songs right before *Shabbat* (after *mikveh* and before the candle-lighting) or at its inception (after the candle-lighting, either at home or in the synagogue). As a preparation or as a beginning, the Song sets the mood of love that reigns on *Shabbat*.

> On *Erev Shabbat*, from the time of *Minha* on, be sure to recite the Song of Songs while wearing your Sabbath clothes, to arouse the love between lovers [between each Jew/the Congregation of Israel/the *Shechinah*—and the Holy One, blessed be He]. (*Or Tzaddikim*, p. 22, #9)

> **18:1:2:2:7:1** After the *mikveh*, put on your Sabbath clothes, go home, and say the Song of Songs at an easy pace and with a sweet voice. . . . And do not interrupt your recital. If you do not have time to recite it on *Erev Shabbat*, do so on *Shabbat* whenever you can.[2] (*Yesod v'Shoresh ha-Avodah,* quoted in *Or ha-Shabbat*, p. 56)

18:1:2:2:7:2 Of Rabbi Eleazar Zev of Kretchnif:

> Before he went to say *Minha* on *Erev Shabbat*, he recited, in his room, the Song of Songs slowly and with great *d'vekut*. (*Raza d'Uvda*, p. 24)

18:1:2:2:7:3 According to tradition, the love poetry of the Song of Songs is symbolic of the love between God and Israel and between God and every Jew. Usually the relation of love for God is spoken of in terms of the love between a son and his father. This is a great love. But an even deeper love, one more mature and equal, is that between man and woman, between two lovers.[3] How can we understand this greater equality? The Congregation of Israel represents the *Shechinah* (God's Presence on earth), and each Jew is a part of God from above, for his or her soul is a spark of the *Shechinah*. So both Israel and God are within God, and "equal" in that sense, one the "woman," the other "man."

At the special time of the entrance of the Sabbath we may be able to get a taste of this very high level, even if we are not otherwise worthy of it. So when you read or chant the Song, let your mind be open and fluid to its allusions and spiritual meanings. Of course, study of the text and its commentaries will familiarize you with the Song and will offer suggestions of meanings. But as a further aid, it may be helpful to know that some of the hasidic *rebbes* would take gentile love songs and change the words to their "true" meaning—the love of the soul for God, etc.[4] (This is permitted by *halacha.*) They sometimes said that the song was one the Levites had sung in the Temple or that David had sung with his harp accompaniment when he was a young shepherd on the hills of Judea, but that it had been lost from Israel and "gone into exile" among the gentiles in distorted form, changed to the lower rather than the higher love. But as for the Song of Songs, the holy of holies of the writings (*K'tuvim*), all this is only a suggestion of how we can hear the higher, in words that may seem to be about the lower, love.

18:1:2:2:7:4 This practice of reciting the Song of Songs must be done with great *kavvanah*. The reason is that it represents such a high level of spirituality, and reciting the Song when you might be inclined to react to the lower level of the literal sense of the words would be the height of profanity.

18:1:2:2:7:5 If you do not have time to say all of the Song of Songs before welcoming the Sabbath, say these four verses:

Let Him kiss me with the kisses of His mouth;
for Thy love is better than wine [1:2]
Awake, O north wind! And come, O south wind!
Send a breeze over my garden, that the fragrance of its spices will waft abroad.
Let my Beloved come into His garden
and eat its delightful fruits. [4:16]
The sound of my Beloved approaching! He is coming!
—leaping over the mountains, rushing to me over the hills! [2:8]
I have come into My garden, My sweet sister, My precious bride;
I have gathered My myrrh with My spices,
I have eaten My honeycomb with My honey;
I have drunk My wine with My milk.
Eat O dear ones, and drink deeply till drunkenness,
O beloved companions. [5:1]
(*Siddur Shirah Hadashah*; also cf. *Kitzur Shnei Luchot ha-Brit*, Mesechet Shabbat, p. 152)

Although these four verses are traditional, others can be used if they help bring you into the mood of the Song.

18:1:2:2:7:6 The holy rabbi, our rabbi and master, Rabbi Tzvi of Ziditchov, his memory for a blessing, told how once when he was in Medzibuz he hid himself [in the *rebbe's* room] with another hasid to hear the recital of the Song of Songs from the holy mouth of the Rebbe Reb Baruch, the memory of a *tzaddik* and holy man for life. When Rabbi Baruch began the Song with fervor and longing the other hasid turned to Rabbi Tzvi and said to him that his mind was becoming confused due to the great fire that was burning within him. And when Rabbi Baruch said the words "His banner above me is Love; support me with the trunks of the thickest trees, let me lean against the apple trees, for I am reeling with love" it actually looked as if fire was burning around the *rebbe*, and the hasid who was with Rabbi Tzvi fled because he could not bear the great and awesome fire.

Rabbi Tzvi said that he saw the sounds and the tongues of flame, and the house was altogether on fire. He strengthened himself and gathered his courage to hear the voice of that angel of God—until he came to the verse "I am my Beloved's and all His desire is for me"—then he almost lost his mind. But our holy master, Rabbi Tzvi, said to himself, "Whatever happens, I am ready to give my life to God with love to hear these words of the Living God as they were spoken at Sinai. If, God forbid, my soul leaves my body, I am prepared for whatever is the will of my Creator, blessed be He." Then there came on him a new spirit from on high, and he saw the fire of God flaming in the house in a way that cannot be described. He stood there until the *rebbe* said the words of the verse "For love is as strong as death, jealousy as cruel as hell; her coals are coals of fire, her flame is a mighty flame of God"—and then, because of the greatness of the fervor and longing, he almost passed out of existence, God forbid; but God was his aid until the whole of the Song of Songs was completed.

The holy rabbi, Rabbi Tzvi always said that when it sometimes happens, God forbid, that he falls in his service of God, from mental dimness or for other reasons, he remembers those precious moments when he heard the Song of Songs from the holy mouth of the Rebbe of Medzibuz, and light returns to his eyes, because the words were like a flaming fire within his holy and pure heart. (*Yifrach biYamav Tzaddik*, p. 55, #8)

18:1:2:2:8 Tzedaka

18:1:2:2:8:1 Give a lot of *tzedaka Erev Shabbat.* (Rabbi Nahum of Tchernobil, *Hanhagot Tzaddikim*, p. 36, #14)

18:1:2:2:8:2 The main time for the giving of *tzedaka* is *Erev Shabbat* and *Erev Yom Tov*. (*Derech Hayim*, 3–4)

18:1:2:2:8:3 As always, *tzedaka* opens our heart and prepares it for love. And as the rabbis say: In the merit of *tzedaka* you can see God's face.

18:1:2:2:8:4 It is also customary to give some *tzedaka* right before lighting the *Shabbat* candles (*Or ha-Shabbat*, p. 63).

18:1:2:2:8:5 A hasidic story tells how two hasidim, one of the Kotzker Rebbe and one of the Tchernobiler (Rabbi Mordechai) were comparing the ways of their *rebbes*:

> The Kotzker hasid asked his friend, "What is the way the Tchernobiler Rebbe teaches his hasidim?" His comrade answered, "Our *rebbe* instructs us to stay awake all of Thursday night studying Torah until the sun rises; and in the morning on *Erev Shabbat* we go to the *mikveh*, and then distribute *tzedaka*, everyone according to his ability and means. On the morning of *Shabbat* we chant the whole Book of Psalms through, without an interruption." (*Admorei Tchernobil*, p. 150)

Obviously the Tchernobiler Rebbe emphasized *Shabbat* and the preparation for *Shabbat* with his hasidim. Note how the Torah vigil on Thursday night leads into the other preparations of *Erev Shabbat.*

18:1:2:2:9 We see then that the Torah portion, repentance, forgiveness and peacemaking, hot water washing and the *mikveh*, special clothes, Psalms, the Song of Songs, and *tzedaka* are all preparations for reaching a higher level of spirituality, for receiving the extra soul-power that comes with the Sabbath.

There are other possibilities for *Shabbat* preparation depending on each person's individual needs.

18:1:2:2:9:1 *Hok l'Yisrael* suggests a time of *solitude* for an hour or two, perhaps going to a solitary place. (Some of the *rebbes* would lock themselves in their room; for example, see 18:1:2:2:5.)

18:1:2:2:9:2 It is often suggested that we have a *spiritual friend* with whom we can talk over matters in the service of God (see "Individual Practices," 39:7). Rabbi Moshe Cordovero advises this, and adds:

> Discuss with this friend, every *Erev Shabbat*, what you did the past week and with that as spiritual preparation, go to welcome the

Sabbath Queen.[5] (The Hanhagot of Rabbi Moshe Cordovero, #15, in *YHvT*, p. 11)

18:1:2:2:9:3 There are those who take a *nap*.

18:1:2:2:9:3:1 Rabbi Mordechai of Lechovitz, may his merit protect us, was always careful to take a nap *Erev Shabbat*, for this is also part of the honor of *Shabbat*, to receive *Shabbat* with a clear mind and fully awake. (*Or ha-Ner*, p. 11, #1)

18:1:2:2:9:3:2 According to kabbalistic tradition, on Friday you go to the *mikveh*—pure rainwater—or you go to a lake, and after that you have to sleep also, to receive your super-soul before *Shabbat*. (*Connections/Hakrev Ushma*, 1:5:25)

18:1:2:2:9:3:3 A rabbi told this story:

Once I was with our holy master and teacher and rabbi, the Rabbi of all the Children of the Exile, Rabbi Elimelech [of Lizensk], when he came back from the *mikveh* on *Erev Shabbat*. He lay down on his bed, saying, "Who can bear the sweetness of these fragrances [of *Shabbat*/the Garden of Eden]?"[6] (*Taamei ha-Minhagim*, p. 120)

Perhaps Rabbi Elimelech took a nap to receive a new ability to bear the great Sabbath holiness and light coming into the world. See the words of his nephew, the son of his holy brother Rabbi Zusya of Hanipol, below.

18:1:2:2:9:3:4 The *tzaddikim* are always advancing higher and higher in their service of God, going from chamber to chamber, ever higher in the heavenly Palace, and ascending from World to World. But before they can advance, each time they must first cast from them the life-spirit that they have now, so as to be able to receive another and greater one. Then they will receive a new consciousness and a new illumination will shine on them at every elevation. And this is the secret of sleep. (Rabbi Tzvi Mendel, the son of Rabbi Zusya of Hanipol, *Menorat Zahav*, p. 98)

18:1:2:2:9:4 Place Your Observance in God's Hands and Pray for His Help

The Sabbath is the day of love and of joy. So if you concern yourself too much with its restrictions (whose purpose is to free you spiritually) and with the fear of God, you lose the very essence of the day.

The Holy Jew said:

> "There is no way to avoid some minor desecration of the holy Sabbath, God forbid—except by being bound hand and foot." And after pausing, he continued, "And even that would not help, because by doing so you would prevent the delight of the Sabbath [*oneg Shabbat*, which is also part of the *mitzvah* of keeping the Sabbath]. Understand this." (*Niflaot ha-Yehudi*, p. 62)

Rabbi Nachman of Bratzlav had a practice for *Shabbat* which helps to remove anxiety and increase joy:

> Before each Sabbath or festival I always place my observance in God's hands, and ask [pray] that it all be according to His will. I can then celebrate it without worrying that I am doing something wrong. I am completely dependent on God and everything I do is in His hands. (*Rabbi Nachman's Wisdom*, p. 106, *Sichos HaRan*, #2; see also p. 374, #238)

This practice is for those hasidim who, in a radical way, put their complete trust in God for everything, even for their service of God. After expressing their own desire and choice for good, they make it His responsibility, so to speak.

For the truth is that no matter how much you prepare for *Shabbat*, it all depends ultimately on God how things go; and you should pray to Him that He let you experience the illumination of *Shabbat*.

You can, then, make a declaration of putting your Sabbath observance in God's hands, and follow it with a prayer that your desire is that everything be according to His will. (See "Waking and Beginning the Day," 4:7 for a related practice of Rabbi Nachman's at the start of every day; also note the kind of declaration one can make.)

18:1:2:2:9:5 In a *musar* book, among the things suggested that you accept upon yourself to do regularly:

> [Write down] everything you have to do on the sixth day, whether great—or small, such as cleaning your hat for the honor of *Shabbat* and other similar things. (*Hayei ha-Musar*, III, p. 89)

18:1:2:2:10 To fully experience the Sabbath you must prepare. You can easily see from this discussion that to do this properly requires early cessation of work on Friday. But everything depends on your level in the service of God. Do not look at the wonderful preparations of the *tzaddikim* and hasidim and say, "How can I ever reach this?" But, as with all spiritual practices, start small if you are beginning, and set aside at least a short period of time to prepare spiritually for the holy Sabbath. Do not despise even the smallest amount of time, for every minute of preparation has its effect and reward. As your religiosity develops and your delight in *Shabbat* increases, you can slowly add new practices and devote more time and effort to *Shabbat* preparation.

18:2 THE SABBATH

18:2:1 Candle-Lighting

The Sabbath is sanctified and brought in at the candle-lighting and at the *kiddush* over the wine. The *kiddush* will be discussed later, in its place.

18:2:1:1 Before lighting the candles:

> Burn some incense before the arrival of *Shabbat* and give your room a pleasant scent for the honor of *Shabbat*. (*Derech Hayim*, 6–42)

The scent will help to expand your spiritual consciousness; as the rabbis say:

> What is it that the soul enjoys yet does nothing for the body? a pleasant scent.[7] (*Berachot* 43)

As mentioned in 18:1:2:2:8:4, give some *tzedaka* right before lighting the candles.

18:2:1:2 It is a good custom to light many candles in the room where you eat and to light at least one in each room of your house. The increased light represents the increased spiritual light of *Shabbat*.

> **18:2:1:2:1** Light many candles on *Shabbat*. (Hanhagot Tovot from Rabbi Meir Paparish, #14, in *YHvT*, p. 22)
>
> **18:2:1:2:2** The more candles, the more praiseworthy it is. (*Shomer Shabbat,* quoted in *Or ha-Shabbat*, p. 61)
>
> **18:2:1:2:3** On the holy Sabbath, whose inner meaning is the spiritual elevation of all the worlds . . . the Sabbath candle serves to

symbolize the elevation of the soul and of holiness. (*Divrei Hayim* quoted in *Or ha-Shabbat*, p. 65)

18:2:1:2:4 You should light *Shabbat* candles in all the rooms you use. (*Be'er Hativ*, quoted in *Or ha-Shabbat*, p. 61)

18:2:1:2:5:1 Of course, two candles on the table where you eat are most traditional, but there is a practice of having a candle for each member of the family (the first two for husband and wife and an additional one for each child).

There are holy books which say that a woman should add another candle at the birth of each son or daughter. (*Or ha-Shabbat*, p. 62)

18:2:1:2:5:2 There are those whose custom is to light seven candles for the seven days of the week; others light ten, for the Ten Commandments. (*Or ha-Shabbat*, p. 61)

18:2:1:2:5:3 Some of our masters of former times were very careful always to light thirty-six candles, symbolizing the thirty-six hours that Adam had the benefit of the Divine Light before it was hidden away. (*B'nai Yissachar* quoted in *Or ha-Shabbat*, p. 65)

Adam was created on the sixth day. On that day, *Erev Shabbat*, he had use of this light for twelve hours; together with the twenty-four hours of *Shabbat* that equals thirty-six hours.

18:2:2 Outside, at Sunset

18:2:2:1 It is a beautiful custom, initiated by the kabbalists of Safed, to receive the holy Sabbath out in an open field. In describing the order to follow, based on the *hanhagot* of his master, Rabbi Yitzhak Luria (the Ari), Rabbi Moshe Cordovero says:

This is the order of receiving the Sabbath: Go out into an open field and recite: "Come and let us go into the Field of Holy Apple Trees; [a hymn composed by the Ari] in order to welcome the Sabbath Queen. Stand in one place in a field or open area; it is preferable if you are able to do so on a high mountain [remember that they were in Safed!] and even better if it is one from which you have a clear view for as far as the eye can see, and if it is also clear for at least a small distance [four cubits] behind you. Turn your face toward the West where the sun sets, and at the very moment it sets close your

> eyes and place your left hand upon your chest and your right hand upon your left. Direct your concentration—while in a state of awe and trembling as one who stands in the presence of the king—so as to receive the special holiness of the Sabbath. [The hymn *Lecha Dodi*, Come My Beloved, was sung at this time.] (*Minhagei ha-Arizal*, p. 33, #17)

In the Kabbalah, the Field of Holy Apple Trees, or the Holy Apple Orchard, refers to the *Shechinah*, and to a state of holiness as exalted as that of the Garden of Eden before Adam's sin.[8]

18:2:2:2 A hasidic story about the Baal Shem Tov begins:

> Once the Besht went with his holy disciples to welcome the Sabbath—and his way was to always go out to a field to do so, in the early part of the afternoon, about two or three o'clock in the summer, and he would receive the Sabbath there. (*Adat Tzaddikim*, p. 28)

18:2:2:3 It is told of the Baal Shem Tov that:

> Once when he welcomed the Sabbath out in a field and was praying, the many sheep that were there lifted up their front feet to heaven, and stood that way on their hind feet like men, all the while. (*Beit Aharon*, quoted in *Or ha-Shabbat*, p. 66)

18:2:2:4 Although it is beautiful to welcome *Shabbat* in a field, there are of course other possibilities for being outside, such as in a courtyard, backyard, or on a roof.

18:2:2:5 There is a remnant of this practice of the kabbalists in the synagogue service. When we sing *Lecha Dodi*, and end with *Bo'i Kallah* (Come O Bride), we turn west towards the door and bow as we receive *Shabbat* and the *Shechinah* into our midst. At this time it is also good to receive the holiness of *Shabbat* into your heart as well and you can picture how the *Shechinah* enters you and fills you.

18:2:3 The Synagogue

18:2:3:1 It was a holy practice of the holy Rabbi Meir'l of Tiktin, every *Shabbat* to circle the synagogue [before entering] seven times. (*Shemen ha-Tov*, II, #122)

This circumambulation expresses one's reverence for the Divine Presence within the synagogue.

18:2:3:2 Another version says that Rabbi Meir'l circled the *bimah*:

> When the holy Rabbi Hayim of Tzanz, came to the *Beit ha-Midrash* on *Shabbat* night to make the *kiddush,* he would circle the *bimah* seven times, following the practice of Rabbi Meir'l of Tiktin on the evening of the holy *Shabbat.* (*Mekor Hayim*, p. 155)

18:2:3:3 Some *tzaddikim* and hasidim wear the *tallit* for the evening *Shabbat* service (*Pe'er Yitzhak*, p. 40, #2). That is, they wear the *tallit* at *Minha* and do not take it off.

> Many of the *tzaddikim* prayed even the night of *Shabbat* in their *tallises* . . . though this was not required and "The night is not the time for *tzitzit.*" Nevertheless, they followed in the ways of the Ari and his disciples who urged this practice in their Siddurs. (*Halachot v'Halichot b'Hasidut*, p. 149)
>
> I saw how the holy rabbi [Rabbi Shalom] of Belz, of blessed memory, and also the holy rabbi, Rebbe Eleazar Tzvi Safrin of Komarna, of blessed memory, had a custom on *Erev Shabbat* and *Erev Yom Tov* to put on a *tallit* before *Minha,* even when they did not pray before the Ark [as prayer-leader], and they kept the *tallit* on until after *Maariv* and even during *kiddush.* (*Derech Tzaddikim*, p. 39, #4)

18:2:4 Home

18:2:4:1 When you come home from the synagogue, that is the time to turn your thoughts to peace with your loved ones (recall how before *Shabbat* you sought forgiveness and made peace). When you walk in the door, greet anyone in the family who remained at home with a warm and loving greeting of peace, "*Shabbat Shalom.*"

18:2:4:2 When you sing "*Shalom Aleichem*" open yourself to the thoughts and feelings of peace that God is sending to your heart and mind on *Shabbat*. The song is directed to the "angels of peace." Angels are messengers or agents of God, and can be natural forces or thoughts. (See Maimonides's *Guide for the Perplexed*, Part II, chap. 6 about this.)

The "angels of peace" of the Sabbath are the thoughts and feelings of peace that come with the Sabbath; and the song expresses our openness to receive these feelings into us.

Commenting on the custom of singing *Shalom Aleichem*, the book *Or ha-Shabbat* notes:

> It is well known that when *Shabbat* enters each Jew receives extra soul-power during the time of the Evening Prayer Service. . . . With this there enters into the heart of every Jew, each according to his own spiritual level, new love and fear of God and a new desire to serve Him, and there come into being new soul-powers which can then be manifested. These good powers are in the category of angels, for they are sent from God as are the angels. (p. 80, #15)

It is nice to accompany your singing of *Shalom Aleichem* with gestures expressing and fitting the verses of the song, about greeting and welcoming the angels of peace, asking for their blessing, and blessing them on their departure.

It is told of Rabbi Shlomo Mordechai (the son-in-law of Rabbi David, the son of Rabbi Shmuel of Koriv), who went to live in the land of Israel, in Safed:

> Every *Shabbat* night after *Kabbalat Shabbat*, when he left the Synagogue of the Ari, he would walk through the ancient, narrow, and winding pathways, his hands lifted up to heaven, and with his voice raised, chant the hymn "*Shalom Aleichem*, ministering angels, angels of the Most High," and finish the *Tikkunei Shabbat* [kabbalistic recitations for *Shabbat*] by the time he reached the door of his house. (*Ha-Shvil v'ha-Derech*, p. 51)

18:2:4:3 After receiving the heavenly flow of peace associated with the angels it is good to renew and reaffirm the peace within your family by hugging and kissing one another. Then, this peace is given a verbal expression—first, with the blessing of the children by the parents, and second, between husband and wife, with the recital of the "Woman of Valor" (Proverbs 31:10–31). There is no reason why the wife should not also offer a parallel praise of her husband. And though the tradition usually speaks of the father blessing the children, the mother, too, should bless them.

> **18:2:4:3:1** It is a custom in Israel to bless sons and daughters on the evening of the holy Sabbath after prayer or after you return

> home from synagogue. Adult children also receive a blessing from their fathers. Those who bless put their hands on the [head of the] one to be blessed and say, "May God make you like Ephraim and like Menashe" [see Genesis 48:14–16, 20]. And for daughters, "May God make you like Sarah and Rebecca and Rachel and Leah." Then say, "And may the Lord bless you and keep you; and may the Lord make His face shine upon you and be gracious to you; the Lord turn His face unto you and give you peace" [Numbers 6:24–26]. And then everyone adds a blessing of his own, according to the ability he has to express himself. Afterwards he should say, "And may there rest upon you a spirit of wisdom and understanding, a spirit of counsel and might, a spirit of knowledge and of the fear of the Lord." (*Or ha-Shabbat*, p. 72)

It is very sweet to see that this latter blessing is taken from Isaiah 11:2, which describes the spirit of God that will rest on the Messiah. For every Jewish child should be to his or her parents a potential Messiah, a saviour of the Jewish people.

The child should, before the blessings, kiss the back of his parent's hands before they are placed on his head (*Or ha-Shabbat*, p. 72). It is a beautiful custom that before one person blesses another, such as a father his child, he should bless God first. So he should put his hands on the child's head and say, "May the Holy One, blessed be He, be blessed." (*Yitborach Sh'mo shel ha-Kodosh Baruch Hu.*) (*Or ha-Shabbat*, p. 72)

18:2:4:3:2 The recital of *Eshet Hayil* ("Woman of Valor") has a mystical meaning also, in that the "woman" is taken by the kabbalists to be the *Shechinah.*[9] This intention can be combined with the one directing the hymn to the wife, for according to the Kabbalah she is the "representative" of the *Shechinah.* All women, particularly the wife and mother, represent and remind one of the "feminine" side of God's nature, while men represent His "masculine" side.

> Now I would like to tell of what I heard from my grandfather, of blessed memory, about the greatness of his *rebbe*, the holy and godly master, Rabbi Yitzhak of Vorki, the memory of a holy *tzaddik* for a blessing—for he said to me that when he heard him chanting *Shalom Aleichem* and *Eshet Hayil* with the melodies he used, he could not at all imagine what could have been more when the Torah was received at Sinai, when they heard from the mouth of the Holy One, blessed be He, "I am [the Lord thy God]" and "Thou shalt not have [any other gods before Me]," etc. and there was

> thundering and lightning, etc. So was it when the Vorker Rebbe said and chanted *Shalom Aleichem* and *Eshet Hayil*—for every one there was crying, out of their great joy and *d'vekut* in fear and love of God. (*GMvGhTz*, p. 30)

18:2:4:4 *Kiddush*

18:2:4:4:1 The *kiddush* is recited over a full and overflowing cup of wine, as it says in Psalm 23: "My cup runneth over," as a symbol of God's overflowing goodness to us in everything, blessings both material and spiritual.

> **18:2:4:4:2** Make the *kiddush* with joy, and have the intention that you are giving witness that God created the world in six days and rested on the Sabbath. (*Derech Hayim*, 1–41)

18:2:4:4:3 The wine gives joy and symbolizes joy. When drinking the wine of the *kiddush*, think, "May I experience the holy joy of the Divine Presence and the holy joy of *Shabbat*."

18:2:4:4:4 The Talmud (*Yoma* 76) says: "Wine and fragrant scents open the mind." We saw above how some associate the burning of fragrant incense with the candle-lighting. The *kiddush* also brings in the Sabbath, and it, too, opens the mind and the heart.

18:2:4:4:5 "Wine gives joy to the heart of men and to God" (Judges 9:13).

> The rabbis said: Certainly wine gives joy to men, but how does it give joy to God? They answered: From this verse we learn that wine is to make men sing before God, and that is what gives Him joy. (*Berachot* 35; *Yalkut Shimoni*)

When you drink the wine of the *kiddush*, pray to God that He open your heart, and that when the wine goes in, the secret of your heart will go out, in song, of your love for Him, and that you will be inspired to sing *zemirot* with fervor during the meal. (See also 18:2:4:5:5:4 for the quote of the Besht about the intention in eating.)

18:2:4:5 The Meal

18:2:4:5:1 It is a kabbalistic and hasidic custom to circle the Sabbath table; some do this twice, once to the right and once to the left (*Or ha-*

Shabbat, p. 76, from *Siddur ha-Arizal*). Walking around the table sets it off as a holy space and shows our awareness of its sanctity. The table is to be an altar of forgiveness (see "Eating and the Holy Meal" [10]) and the altar in the Temple was circumambulated (Psalm 26:6). Compare this to the practices of circling the synagogue and the *bimah*. Circling the table before the meal can, of course, be done together with others, the family, for instance.

18:2:4:5:2 The Sabbath is the best time to sanctify your eating and raise it to a spiritual experience and a devotional service of God. See "Eating and the Holy Meal" for all aspects of the holy meal; particularly note, with regard to *Shabbat*, the quote from Rabbi Tzadok ha-Cohen of Lublin (10:22).

18:2:4:5:3 *Shabbat* is not the time for repentance from fear but from love, so we do not say the confession before eating. Instead, we recite Deuteronomy 30:6, "And may the Lord circumcise your heart and the heart of your generations, that you may love the Lord your God with all your heart and with all your soul, in order that you live"—and then we are to meditate on repentance from love. (See "Eating and the Holy Meal," 10:1:5:4.)

18:2:4:5:4 On *Shabbat* we make the blessing over two loaves of bread in remembrance of the double portion of manna which came down on the sixth day, for that day and for the Sabbath, so no work in gathering would have to be done on the seventh day (Exodus 16). As we say God's Name in the blessing, we raise up the loaves, and looking at them, reflect on our trust in God, who will always provide for us.

> **18:2:4:5:5:1** It is a custom in Israel, on the holy Sabbath, to say while eating, again and again, "I am eating in honor of the Sabbath."* (*Or ha-Shabbat*, p. 120)

18:2:4:5:5:2 About Rabbi Eleazar Zev of Kretchnif:

> With every bite that the holy rabbi ate on the holy Sabbath, he would say, "For the honor of the holy Sabbath."* (*Raza d'Uvda*, p. 42)

18:2:4:5:5:3 Some people say this before partaking of each course.

18:2:4:5:5:4 The Besht taught that you should also have the intention that

> you are eating so as to rejoice the body in order that your soul be able to rejoice God by singing songs and praises during the meal and by praying the prayers of the holy Sabbath—all with fiery enthusiasm. (*Or ha-Shabbat*, p. 120)

18:2:4:5:6 At the Sabbath tables of some hasidic *rebbes* there is a holy silence without any conversation whatsoever, to encourage *d'vekut* during the meal.

> The way of the holy Rizhiner [Rabbi Israel] was to sit at the [*Shabbat*] table in great *d'vekut*, and no sound was heard in the *Beit Midrash* [where the meals were], and there was no conversation, so as not to disturb him. (*Eser Z'chuyot*, p. 22)

(Of course this silence does not necessarily exclude Torah or *zemirot* at the table.)

18:2:4:5:7 It is traditional to sing Sabbath songs, *zemirot*, between courses during the meal, and again after the meal. These holy songs help sanctify the meal and raise it up from a physical to a spiritual experience. And this singing is a great service of God when you sing before Him with love and devotion.

> **18:2:4:5:7:1** It is a *mitzvah* to sit at the Sabbath table and sing praises of God, as it says (Psalm 92), "A psalm, a song for the Sabbath day. It is good to give thanks to God, and to sing praises to Your name, O Most High." (*Sefer Hasidim*, #271)
>
> **18:2:4:5:7:2** [The Rebbe, Rabbi Nachman of Bratzlav] would always tell us and urge us to sing *zemirot* on *Shabbat* . . . and he himself, all his life, used to sing many *zemirot* every *Shabbat* and also on *Motzai Shabbat*. (*Likkutei Moharan* Tinyana, siman 104)
>
> **18:2:4:5:7:3** The Rebbe [Rabbi Nachman of Bratzlav] also told us to sing many *Zemiros* and other Sabbath songs. He said, "Do not

> pay attention to any obstacles. Others may be sitting at the table and not seem to have any desire to sing. Strengthen yourself and sing with joy. Conduct the Sabbath table in a happy mood. The main thing is Sabbath joy. (*Rabbi Nachman's Wisdom*, p. 301, *Sichos HaRan*, #155)

18:2:4:5:7:4 A hasidic story tells how a disciple of the Besht, the *Chazan* of Zoslav, was once a guest on *Shabbat* of the Besht's grandson, Rabbi Baruch of Medzibuz. Each prayer service and each meal he expected to be honored by being asked to lead the prayers or to sing the table *zemirot* he loved so much; but it seemed that with Rabbi Baruch they did not sing at all, neither in the prayers nor at the table! As with some of the other *rebbes* also, a holy silence reigned throughout the Sabbath meal, as all sat in meditative awe.

During the second meal on the day of *Shabbat*, the *Chazan* said, "*Rebbe*, let's sing *zemirot*!" But Rabbi Baruch answered, "I don't need to sing." So what could he do? By the time the third meal arrived though:

> They all washed their hands and began to eat, but the voice of his Lover was knocking on the door of the heart of the holy *Chazan* and he could no longer restrain himself from singing and from meditating on all the *kavvanot* and unifications of the whole Sabbath. He did not wait until they were close to saying the Grace After Meals, but as soon as they had eaten a little bread and the fish he shouted out, "Let's sing for the honor of *Shabbat*!" And he began to sing with great *d'vekut*. The hasidim who were around the table wanted to run over and shut him up, for they were not used to this. But the Rebbe Reb Baruch signaled to them that they should not dare to interrupt him, for they were putting themselves at risk, and God forbid that they should disturb such a holy man.
>
> So the *Chazan*, who was in another world altogether, chanted and sang with his sweet voice for a few hours, until he had gone through all the *kavvanot* of all the prayers and songs and *zemirot* of the holy Sabbath. And the holy rabbi, Rabbi Baruch, and all the others sat silently and listened as he sang. After he finished, Rabbi Baruch said to him, "You should have sung yesterday also. I only said that I don't have to sing; but for the honor of *Shabbat* you should have sung yesterday too." (*Sichot Yekarim*, #47)

> **18:2:4:5:7:5** Everyone should sing at his Sabbath table . . . and this is a great and important service of God, and one in which all

the supernal angels engage, for that is their service. (*Pele Yoatz*, quoted in *Or ha-Shabbat*, p. 130, #6)

18:2:4:5:7:6 Once, on the night of *Shabbat*, before the Grace After Meals, the holy Seer of Lublin was immersed in an awesome *d'vekut*—actually almost until expiration. When he returned to normal consciousness after a number of hours he began to sing the hymn *L'El asher shavat* [To the God who rested] with a completely new melody that the hasidim had never heard before. The Seer told them afterward that he had learned this *niggun* while he was deep in *d'vekut* [and in the Upper Worlds, having made a soul-ascent], from the angels who were singing before the Holy One, blessed be He. (*Otzar Hayim*, quoted in *Or ha-Shabbat*, p. 155)

18:2:4:5:8 *Dancing*

Hasidim often serve God by dancing during *Shabbat*, and after the meal on Friday night is a special time for dancing.

18:2:4:5:8:1 It was the custom of the holy Rabbi Hayim of Kosov, every holy *Shabbat* night, to lead dancing among those who sat as guests at his pure table, for about an hour. (*Even Shtiya*, p. 48, #11)

18:2:4:5:8:2 Most of the time the dancing is after the meal, but there is a beautiful story of dancing before the meal:

The Rabbi Reb [Yaakov] Koppel Hasid, who in his youth lived in Kolomaya, made his living from a small store he had, and he was very hidden in his ways, such that no one knew of his great piety. When the Baal Shem Tov once spent a *Shabbat* in Kolomaya, on the evening of the holy *Shabbat* he felt a great light glowing within the city. So he went out to walk around the city to find where this great light was located—until he came near a small house. When he approached it he felt that the great light was within this house.

He entered, and he found there a beautiful pearl, namely Rabbi Koppel, who was singing and dancing for the glory and honor of the holy Sabbath, with blazing devotion and without any weariness. He danced for one hour and then two, while the Sabbath table was there laden with all sorts of good things. The Besht waited, not moving, beholding this sight for a long time.

> When Rabbi Koppel finished singing and dancing, he saw the Baal Shem Tov standing there and he greeted him warmly and full of joy, with the blessing of peace, and the Besht returned the greeting with the same warmth. Then the Besht asked him, "What is the meaning of this that you sing and dance so before you eat?" Rabbi Koppel answered him saying that he does this at all three Sabbath meals, standing before the table and even singing and dancing, so that first he delights in the spiritual aspect of the food, the holy vitality and life within it, and only afterwards does he eat.[10] (*Kol Sippurei Baal Shem Tov*, vol. 4, p. 170)

(To understand this answer fully, see "Eating and the Holy Meal," p. 268) Also note that the story says that Reb Koppel, who was singing and dancing alone, was doing so for the glory and honor of the holy Sabbath.

18:2:4:5:8:3 It is told of one of the descendants of Rabbi Naftali of Ropshitz, Rabbi Reuven Horowitz of Dembitz, that:

> From the age of 12 he never slept on *Shabbat*, but throughout the night would dance before Queen Sabbath. And the townsfolk organized themselves into four groups, to sing and dance with him during each of the four watches of the night. (*Ohel Naftali*, p. 31, #75)

18:2:4:5:8:4 In hasidic dancing you do not need an invitation—when you feel inspired, or even when you do not, just jump up, draw in family or guests if present, and dance.

See "Song and Dance," 24:11 for beautiful stories of the *Shabbat* dancing of the Shpola Zeyde and Rabbi Moshe Leib of Sassov.

18:2:5 Psalms

> **18:2:5:1** It was the custom of the Rebbetzin, the *tzaddeket* Feigele [whose husband was Rabbi David Moshe of Tchortkov] to say the whole Book of Psalms the night of *Shabbat*. (*Tiferet Adam*, p. 11)

18:2:5:2 Rabbi Yitzhak Isaac of Ziditchov would, during the course of *Erev Shabbat* and *Shabbat* together, complete all five books of the Psalms (*Pe'er Yitzhak*, p. 78, #2).

18:2:5:3 The Tchernobiler hasidim would say the whole Book of Psalms without interruption on the morning of *Shabbat* (see 18:1:2:2:8:5).

18:2:6 Songs at Night

The Rebbe of Tzanz said:

> It is a great *tikkun* [fixing] for the soul on the night of *Shabbat* when you [stay up late into the night and] sing songs and praises to God, blessed be He. (*Rabbeinu ha-Kodesh mi-Tzanz*, p. 221)

(See 18:2:7:2 for the full quote.)

18:2:7 Sleep

Various great *tzaddikim* and hasidim did not want to sleep on *Shabbat* and miss out on these precious hours of exalted God-consciousness. Perhaps that was the thought of Rabbi Reuven Horowitz of Dembitz just mentioned (18:2:4:5:8:3).

18:2:7:1 Of the *rebbe* Rabbi Meir Shalom of Kolishin (the grandson of the Holy Jew of Pshischa):

> His way was to stay awake all the night of *Shabbat* and occupy himself with Torah and the service of God. (*Tiferet Banim Avotam*, p. 223)

> **18:2:7:2** The Tzanzer Rebbe used to say: "It is a pity to sleep on the night of the holy *Shabbat*—for you lose the special illumination of *Shabbat*. And it is a great *tikkun* for the soul on the night of *Shabbat* when you sing songs and praises to God, blessed be He. . . ." And he would explain the practice of sleeping the minimum on *Shabbat* with a parable of a wise king who slept little, saying, "It is a pity to lose his kingship—for when he is asleep, he is not a king." But for all that, the Tzanzer did sleep some on the night of *Shabbat*, so that he could pray with a clear head in the morning. (*Rabbeinu ha-Kodesh mi-Tzanz*, p. 221)

18:2:8 *Mikveh* in the Morning

> Be sure to immerse in the *mikveh* before *Shaharit* on the morning of the holy Sabbath day, even when there is no necessity [for sexual reasons]. And even those who do not go every morning to the *mikveh* should accustom themselves to do so at least on the holy Sabbath, for the holiness of the night of *Shabbat* cannot be compared to the [greater] holiness of [the day of] *Shabbat*, and one requires an immersion to separate one holiness from another [and

higher one and to receive the greater holiness]. [R. Aaron of Karlin] wrote: To go to the *mikveh* on the morning of *Shabbat*, it would be worth walking three miles to get there. (The Bialer Rebbe, *Seder ha-Yom l'ha-Admor mi-Biala*, p. 49a, Inyanei Shabbat Kodesh, #7)

18:2:9 Charity before Prayers

Rabbi Yehiel Michal of Zlotchov said:

On *Shabbat* and *Yom Tov* [when you cannot touch money] state verbally [before prayers] what charity you will give, and give it after the day. (*Hanhagot Tzaddikim*, p. 52, #7)

18:2:10 Torah

Torah study on *Shabbat* should be different—deeper and more creative.

18:2:10:1 On *Shabbat* learn Kabbalah. (*Derech Hayim*, 3–11) (The point is not that everyone must learn Kabbalah, but that in some way you deepen and renew your Torah learning.)

18:2:10:2 See that you innovate something in your Torah learning every *Shabbat*, and immediately when *Shabbat* ends, write it down. (*Derech Hayim*, 7–26)

18:2:10:3 Rabbi Alexander Ziskind:

Happy is he who is worthy to have revealed to him some new truth in the Torah, and happy is he who labors in Torah study and exerts himself to discover the truth and to draw something new out of the holy Torah. For by this new thing he creates a new heaven and a new earth, as the holy *Zohar* explains. [And he says this is particularly true on *Shabbat*, the day of "more," for the renewal of the spiritual world—"creating a new heaven and earth"—is particularly appropriate on *Shabbat*.]

And certainly the Holy One, blessed be He, is not demanding what is beyond a person's capabilities, to innovate something extraordinary—but just according to his intelligence . . . [for example] to come up with an original interpretation of some verse in the *Tanach*.

Another possibility in this for the holy *Shabbat* is to innovate some good *hanhaga* in the service of our Maker and Creator, blessed be He, by which you will conduct yourself all the days of the week, to give pleasure to your Maker, blessed is He and blessed is His name—either a spiritual practice related to purifying your mind and thoughts, or a *hanhaga* related to speech, which helps you speak as little as possible, or something by which you increase your Torah study more than in days past, or add new *kavvanot* to your prayer or blessings of enjoyment, etc. The spiritual practice you innovate can even relate to how you eat and drink or be something connected to your work, to determine some way to be more religious in how you conduct yourself at work. It is clear to me that such an intellectual effort to innovate for yourself a new spiritual practice is considered as Torah study, and that the Creator, blessed be He, will delight in it with His heavenly host, and will be crowned with it, Him and all His angelic host, together with the souls of the *tzaddikim* in the Garden of Eden. (*Yesod v'Shoresh ha-Avodah*, Gate 8, chap. 12, p. 185)

18:2:11 Remembering That It Is *Shabbat*

18:2:11:1 To fully experience *Shabbat*, the ideal is that you

never cease to be aware that it is *Shabbat*. (Rabbi Nahum of Tchernobil, *Hanhagot Tzaddikim*, p. 36, #14)

18:2:11:2 Throughout *Shabbat* many people keep their minds on *Shabbat*, and add sweetness and holiness to the day, by saying again and again phrases such as: "Holy Sabbath," "Sweet Sabbath," "Peaceful Sabbath,"* all in a sweet and pleasant voice.

18:2:11:2:1 About Rabbi Eleazar Zev of Kretchnif:

On *Shabbat* he would say many times, softly but with great feeling . . . "Holy *Shabbos*, Holy *Shabbos*,"* over and over. (*Raza d'Uvda*, p. 28)

18:2:11:2:2 The Admor [Rebbe] of Parisov, the memory of a *tzaddik* for the life of the World to Come, would go around all the night of the holy Sabbath, saying again and again without cease, "Holy *Shabbat*, His precious day" [*Shabbat kodesh, yom hemdato*]. (*Vayakel Shlomo*, p. 16)

18:2:11:2:3 It is good to mention often on the holy Sabbath the name "*Shabbat*," because *Shabbat* is one of the names of God, and He and His name are one. (*Ahavat Shalom*, quoted in *DhTvhY*, Hilchot Shabbat, p. 10, #22)

When God's name is mentioned, He Himself is present; this is something to be aware of when uttering the name "*Shabbat.*"

18:2:11:2:4 Rabbi David of Zablitov said:

> "When you wake someone up from sleep you call him by his name and then he awakens, because, as we know, the living soul of the man is the same as his name. So too with *Shabbat*: when you call out the name '*Shabbat*' you draw to yourself the life-energy of the Sabbath and also to all the days of the week" [when you utter "*Shabbat*" during the week]. (*Eser Atarot*, p. 62, #12)

In *Ahavat Shalom* the same is explained at greater length and it says:

> We, the Children of Israel, have to arouse and draw down to us the light of the holiness of the Sabbath, and bring it within us, through calling out the name "*Shabbat.*" So for all the actions we do for the sake of *Shabbat* [eating, singing, etc.], we should say, "For the honor of *Shabbat.*"* (Quoted in *Milei d'Avot*, p. 169, #8)

18:2:11:3 When you meet a friend on *Shabbat*, do not say "Good morning" etc. as on weekdays, but "Good *Shabbos*" . . . so as to remember the Sabbath. (*Kitzur Shnei Luchot ha-Brit*, Hanhagat Shabbat, p. 162)

18:2:11:4 Whenever you mention *Shabbos* you should always say "Holy *Shabbos.*" (*Hagahot Mahartza*, Yitro, quoted in *DhTvhY*, Hilchot Shabbat, p. 10, #22)

This of course applies whether you are mentioning *Shabbat* on weekdays or the Sabbath.

18:2:11:5 On *Shabbat*, when you kiss the *mezuzah* [as you go in and out] do not say, as on weekdays, "May God guard my going out, etc." but say, "Remember the Sabbath day [*Z'chor et yom ha-Shabbat*]." This is because the Sabbath itself guards us. (*Kitzur Shnei Luchot ha-Brit*, Hanhagat Shabbat, p. 162)

18:2:12 Keeping the Sabbath Holy, Free from Profane Talk

18:2:12:1 You should not involve yourself in any secular conversation about profane matters, as this profanes the sanctity of the Sabbath. (*Totzaot Hayim*, p. 51)

18:2:12:2 On the holy Sabbath you should not speak of anything connected with the workaday world or of anything that arouses sadness or worry, nor should you speak of anything having to do with the time following the Sabbath, such as making plans for after its conclusion.

> **18:2:12:3** [Rabbi Mordechai of Neshkiz] was very careful about not speaking any profane words on *Shabbat*, and would strongly caution others about this. (*Zichron l'Rishonim*, p. 105)

18:2:12:4 It is a good practice to try to converse in Hebrew on *Shabbat*, if you are able, even if only for a while.

> *Shnei Luchot ha-Brit*, in speaking about how your speech on *Shabbat* should be different from that on weekdays, says that a Jew should, on *Shabbat*, speak exclusively in the holy tongue. (*Torat ha-Naum v'ha-Drasha*, p. 64)
>
> About the Maggid of Mezritch:
>
> His custom was, on Sabbaths and holidays, to speak [only] in the holy tongue. (*Imrei Pinhas*, p. 14)
>
> On *Shabbat* the Seer [of Lublin] spoke only Hebrew. (*Ha-Rebbe Reb Tzvi Elimelech mi-Dinov*, p. 51)

18:3 CONSIDERING YOUR SHABBAT

It is good to set some time before the end of *Shabbat*, or right after, to consider what kind of *Shabbat* you had and how well you prepared for it and kept it. Then do *tshuvah*, feeling regret that your service of God was not adequate to receive all the holy light, and arouse your determination to do better for the coming *Shabbat*. You can also make plans and resolutions for the next *Shabbat*. But to fully experience *Shabbat*, our *tshuvah* must be general, not only about matters concerning *Shabbat*, and we have to commit ourselves with all our hearts to doing God's will.

> The Holy Jew [Rabbi Yaakov Yitzhak of Pshischa] said that the Third Meal [of *Shabbat*] is a time for everyone together to do *tshuvah*. And I [the author of *Niflaot ha-Yehudi*] heard a parable about this:

A great king sent a message to a city in his realm telling them that he was coming to visit them at an appropriate time, and they should prepare fit quarters for his stay. The wise people in the city did so; they exerted all their energy to prepare rooms for the king and only devoted the minimum time for their own livelihood, just enough to keep themselves alive. The foolish people, however, spent all their time on their livelihood, and therefore were not able to prepare nice quarters for the king.

When the king came at the appointed time, he was delighted at the efforts of the wise, but was angry with the fools. When he was about to leave the city, the foolish people threw themselves at the king's feet and pleaded that he forgive them for the past and promised him that from now on, and for his future visits, they would do everything in their power to prepare.

The application is that the wise person prepares himself the whole week and removes from his heart everything bad, so that when *Shabbat* comes its holiness will find a place to rest within him. But those who are foolish do not do this. Rather, they devote most of their time to material things, and when *Shabbat* comes their heart is not emptied and prepared, so they cannot receive the holiness. During the Third Meal and *Motzai Shabbat* [the time right after *Shabbat*] is the time to do *tshuvah* and to appease God, blessed be He, that from now on we will do His will, so that when *Shabbat* comes our hearts will be cleared of everything bad and ready to receive the holiness. (*Niflaot ha-Yehudi*, p. 44)

19

Service of the Imagination

Using your imagination to serve God is not ordinarily spoken about as a separate category on its own terms, but suggestions about it are made here and there.

19:1 STUDYING TORAH IN THE MIDST OF FIRE

The Torah was given with fear and it was given with joy, for those who received it at Sinai were made to experience awe and joy at its giving. And it was also given with fire, for God descended on Sinai in fire and the whole mountain was smoking like a furnace. And a person who learns Torah should do so as when it was originally given, for as he learns it now it is being given anew. He should, therefore, not only learn with fear and joy together, but he should picture to himself that he is standing in the midst of fire. And then, when he learns with fear and joy, and surrounded by fire, he will advance and rise in spirituality each day. (Rabbi Abraham of Slonim, in the Writings of Rabbi Moshe Minder in *Torat Avot*, p. 166)

19:2 SINAI AT THE TIME OF WAKING

19:2:1 When a person wakes up from sleep he should immediately think of the scene when the Jewish people received the Torah at Mount Sinai. He should picture in his mind how Israel was so pure at that time and so separated from lower things—when they stood there at the foot of Mount Sinai in awe and fear, with trembling and quaking [from the tremendous spiritual experience they were undergoing]. And Mount Sinai was smoking because of the fire when the Holy One, blessed be He, descended upon it with myriads of angels. And there was the sound of the *shofar*. (*Kav ha-Yashar*, chap. 1)

19:2:2 In 19:1 about Torah study, though Sinai is brought in, the actual thing to be imagined is that you are surrounded by fire. In 19:2 on the other hand, where the practice is recommended for waking up, we are to experience in imagination the actual scene at Sinai, seeing the people at the mount, the fire, smoke, and lightning, and hearing the thunder and the *shofar*. (Note that Deuteronomy 4:9 tells us about the gathering at Sinai, not to forget "what your eyes saw.") Of course, this imagining of the scene at Sinai could be used at other times too, such as before Torah study or at the time of the Torah reading in the synagogue. In that context we can mention the following from Rabbi Levi Yitzhak of Berditchev:

> I have heard that it is good to remind oneself, while studying Torah and doing the *mitzvot*, of the words of the prayer said during *Rosh HaShanah Musaf*: "You revealed Your glory in a cloud, to speak to Your holy people. You caused them to hear Your heavenly voice and You manifested Yourself to them in a mist of purity. The entire world trembled before You, all the creation was in awe of You, when You, our King, manifested Your presence at Mount Sinai to teach Your people the Torah and the commandments. You made them hear Your glorious voice and Your divine precepts from the midst of the flames of fire. Amidst thunder and lightning You made Yourself known to them, amidst the sound of the *shofar* You revealed Your presence to them. As it is written in Your Torah: And it came to pass on the third day, when it was morning, that there was thunder and lightning, and a thick cloud upon the mountain, and the mighty sound of a *shofar*; and all the people that were there in the camp trembled. And it is also written: All the people perceived the thundering and the lightning and the sound of the *shofar* and the mountain in smoke; and when the people saw it they trembled and stood afar off.* (*Divrei Torah*, p. 58)

To make use of this suggestion of Rabbi Levi Yitzhak of Berditchev it would be necessary to write these words on a piece of paper to have by you when studying Torah for example. Memorizing it would make the visualization and audibilization[1] (imagined sound) easier, as you could picture the scene to yourself as you repeated the words. Alternatively, one could memorize the Torah verses which describe the scene (Exodus 19:16ff.). (See "The Synagogue and the Synagogue Service," 6:33 for a lovely story about such a service of the imagination.)

19:3 A VISUALIZATION OF MARTYRDOM

Kav ha-Yashar (chap. 63) speaks about those prayers where (it is often taught) we are to meditate on our readiness for martyrdom, as for example, during the first paragraph of the *Sh'ma* where we say "and you shall love the Lord your God with all your heart and with all your soul and with all your might." The rabbis understood "with all your soul" to mean "even if He takes your life" and puts you in a situation where you have to give yourself in martyrdom for your love of God.

And *Kav ha-Yashar* says:

> You should picture there is a great fire before you—and they are demanding that you give up your Judaism or be martyred. Then visualize throwing yourself into the fire with love and joy [for the sake of God].

In the time this book was written there were severe persecutions and pogroms, and this was not just an idle exercise, although even in our own time such things, and worse, have happened.

Rabbi Alexander Ziskind also strongly emphasized this practice of martyrdom in imagination. In his book *Yesod v'Shoresh ha-Avodah*, he devotes a chapter to it (Gate 1, chap. 11) and throughout the book gives instructions for its use at many points during the prayer services. He explains how you are to picture persecutors demanding that you renounce Judaism—if not they will murder you. You refuse and they carry out their threats. He gives various suggestions for visualizing different kinds of scenes of such martyrdom and says that you are also to imagine and "feel" the pain and suffering you would experience as you are put to death. In the light of recent history, you can picture yourself in some sort of confrontation with the beasts in human form where you sanctify God's name in the face of torture and death.

This practice of imagining one's martyrdom was very important to the great hasidic *rebbe*, Rabbi Elimelech of Lizensk, and in his famous and widely published *Tzetl Katan* (The Little Note), the list of *hanhagot* for his disciples, he begins:

> Any time you are not learning Torah, and especially when you are sitting by yourself, unoccupied, in your room or lying on your bed without being able to sleep, you should meditate in fulfillment of the positive *mitzvah* of: "And I [God] will be sanctified among the Children of Israel" [understood as the sanctification of God's name by martyrdom]. You should visualize a great and awesome fire burning in front of you, up to the heart of the heavens, and that you, to sanctify the name of God, overcome your lower nature and throw yourself into the fire as a martyr. And as we know, the Holy One, blessed be He, takes a good thought that is unfulfilled in action and counts it as if it was; thus, it is as if you actually did martyr yourself, because you were truly willing to do so. As a result, instead of sitting or lying down doing nothing, you have fulfilled a *mitzvah* of the Torah.
>
> When saying the first verse of the *Sh'ma* and the first blessing of the *Shemoneh Esreh*, you should also imagine the above . . . [In saying the verse *Sh'ma Yisrael* you are to meditate on your belief in God's oneness and your acceptance of His kingship and rule. After that accept on yourself self-sacrifice for God, using the visualization of martyrdom (*Yesod v'Shoresh ha-Avodah*, Gate 3, chap. 5, p. 70)].
>
> But you should be careful that you are completely sincere about your intention in this, and that when you are imagining all this it should be determined with certainty in the innermost recesses of your heart, in absolute truth, that you are willing to give up your life for God; and you should not, God forbid, be in a position of deceiving Him.

Persecution was also something very real in the time of Rabbi Elimelech. His own way in holiness leaned to the side of *gevurah* (strength).

It should be emphasized that the ways that you serve God in imagination do not have to be just by visualizing martyrdom, although that practice is certainly a good one.

19:4 GIVING UP POSSESSIONS

Here is a suggestion for an adaptation of the visualization of martyrdom: Just as "with all your soul" of the *Sh'ma* was understood by the rabbis to mean "even if He takes your life," so the "with all your might" was interpreted to mean that you were willing, if necessary, to give up all your possessions, particularly those most dear to you, to serve God out of love. In our desire to offer everything to God and to keep our possessions from entrapping us, we can picture in our imagination all of our various possessions and how we are ready and willing to give them up if necessary to serve God with love.

Rabbi Alexander Ziskind suggests one way of doing this, and after a visualization on "with all your soul" about martyrdom, he continues with a visualization for "with all your might" (also linking it to the thought of persecution):

> "And with all your soul"—as the Sages, their memory for a blessing, said: "Even if He takes your life." So you should not be false when you say these words, God forbid, you should accept this with self-sacrifice and visualize one of the four kinds of death penalties the court can decree. "And with all your might"—as the Sages, their memory for a blessing, said: "With all your money." So you should not be false when you say this, you should picture in your mind that persecutors are saying to you: "Bow down to these idols—or we will take all your money and everything you own." And you answer: "Take all my money; I will not bow down or prostrate myself." And you should picture to yourself that they take all your money, a chest full of gold coins, and go, and you are left with nothing, and destitute because of your love for God, may He be praised and exalted. (*Yesod v'Shoresh ha-Avodah*, Gate 4, chap. 5, p. 73)

One does not have to link the imagining of readiness to give up our possessions for God to persecution.

19:5 IN THE HOLY TEMPLE; IN THE LAND OF ISRAEL

Rabbi Elimelech, as we have seen, taught a visualization of martyrdom. But he made other uses of this service of the imagination. For example, he described in detail a traditional visualization for prayer, about picturing yourself in the Holy Temple in Jerusalem. See the chapter on "Prayer," 5:3:13. There too you will find the related suggestion of Rabbi Pinhas of Koretz to someone who had been in Israel, to imagine, before and during prayer, the scenes and views of the Land of Israel (5:1:20:2).

19:6 THE SACRIFICE OF ISAAC

In another prayer visualization related to the idea of martyrdom, Rabbi Elimelech says:

> When anyone recites the *Akedah* [the Binding of Isaac on the altar] in *Shaharit*, and his intention is as if he is letting himself be bound on the altar to be sacrificed, the Holy One, blessed be He, considers this intention and thought as if he actually did this. (*Noam Elimelech*, Vayetze, p. 13b)

From the comparison with the language and content of the visualization suggested in the *Tzetl Katan* (19:3:1) it is clear that the intention here is also that you are to use your imagination to picture the scene, and, it seems, identify yourself with Isaac. A parallel quote from Rabbi Nahum of Tchernobil makes this a little more explicit. (See "Prayer," 5:3:8:2 for that quote.)

19:7 CROSSING THE RED SEA

There is a traditional visualization used during the daily Morning Prayers, when reciting the Song at the Sea, of picturing yourself crossing the Red Sea. See "Prayer," 5:3:8:1 for this.

19:8 There are hasidic meditations which are service of the imagination where before (and during) Torah study and prayer you are to picture yourself surrounded by the light of the Divine Presence, or (and this is related) in the Garden of Eden (Paradise). Note that in 19:1 the visualization is of fire rather than light. Another imagination-meditation for prayer is to picture yourself ascending above the sky and then up through the different heavens until you are in a heavenly world close to God, and then praying there. See "Prayer," 5:1:18:3:1 and 5:3:14; and "Torah," 15:18.

19:9 YOU ARE A *TZADDIK*: CHASED INTO PARADISE

The Peasetzna Rebbe:

> If you have already tried everything else and had no success, and if you have tried in every possible way to arouse and inspire yourself religiously and could not, and you were careful in all things requiring care, and you yearned, in word and thought, for everything that you should long for—and nothing helped, then do this. Picture that you are a *tzaddik*, one fully righteous, and see in your imagination the greatness of your soul in its root in heaven, and its glory in the hour when God, and all His holy ones with Him, comes to share delights with your soul and to stroll with it in the Garden of God in Eden.
>
> Become immersed in this thought-picture for some time, having it before your eyes; it is then impossible not to be aroused to zealous care for your own holy soul, to not sully its majestic beauty when it is resting in the arms of the King of the Universe; and an overwhelming longing will be awakened in your breast to merit all this. (*Tzav v'Zairuz*, #24)

Compare this visualization with the suggestion of the Peasetzna Rebbe in "Prayer," 5:2:10:5 where he says that when you cannot otherwise fight off mental distractions during prayer you can picture your soul as being chased by vicious wild animals (representing evil and negative spiritual forces), and then escaping through the Gates of Paradise to safety and peace. Just as with Rabbi Elimelech of Lizensk, it seems that the Peasetzna Rebbe was particularly interested in service of the imagination and visualizations.

19:10 THE NAME BEFORE YOUR EYES

It is a hasidic practice to imagine always before your eyes the four-letter Name of God יהוה. The ability to do this requires some practice, and a way to develop it is to use a card with the Name written on it, meditating on that for a period of time. After a while you can begin to switch to visualizing the Name with your eyes closed, and having attained that, practice seeing it with the eyes open.

19:10:1 Rabbi Elimelech of Lizensk:

> You should always have the name *Havaya* [YHVH], blessed be He, before your eyes, as is written, "I have placed the Lord [YHVH] before me always." (*Noam Elimelech*, Devarim, p. 78a)

19:10:2 Of Rabbi Nachman of Bratzlav we hear that:

> As a young child the Rebbe wanted to literally fulfill the verse (Psalm 16:8), "I have set God before me constantly." He continually tried to depict God's ineffable Name before his eyes even while studying with his tutor. His thoughts were so occupied with this that he often did not know his lessons, making his teacher very angry. (*Rabbi Nachman's Wisdom*, p. 5, *Shevachay HaRan*, #2)

19:10:3 We know of many other *rebbes* who also did this. This practice is discussed in Chapter 2, p. 36, "Sleep and Before Sleep" 29:1:13, "Sight," 25:6, and "Repetition of a Holy Sentence," 21:12.

19:10:4 Once you have achieved the ability to have the Name before you, and it sometimes disappears:

> Do not push to picture the letters of the name *Havaya* before you when it does not come up of itself, for that is called "taking the king's daughter by force into the ruins." Just have God always in your thoughts, at one time with one verse, at another time with a different one; and so occupy yourself until the letters of the Name appear before you by themselves. Do not force it then, just remember God one time with love, another time with fear. (*Darkei Tzedek*, p. 10, #6)

(See, however, the story in Chapter 2, p. 36, where Rabbi Yitzhak of Drobitch was ready to die if the Name would not reappear before his eyes.)

19:10:5 The Peasetzna Rebbe:

> It is known from the holy books how great and holy it is to visualize the name Havaya before your eyes, in the way of "I have placed the Lord before me always." And it is considered a bad sign for someone if he cannot visualize this.
>
> But what should the unfortunate person do, who wants to picture the Name, but cannot? And as if to provoke him to frustration,

the more he wants to do it and exerts himself, the harder it becomes; he cannot even visualize one letter!

[The *rebbe* goes on to explain a psychological law connected with visualization, that whenever you have visualized even the most familiar and easiest thing, such as the face of a loved one, if you then look at it as an observer, to see what you have done, or if you think of your will or desire to visualize it, it immediately fades; because when your self-consciousness increases, your power of imagination and visualization decreases.]

[So, he continues:] The more you want to overcome the difficulty you are having, and do this visualization, and the more your self-consciousness is strengthened, your ability to visualize is to that very degree weakened, and it becomes harder to picture the Holy Name.

[The *rebbe* gives one suggestion (he says there are many others) for dealing with this problem:]

Forget your desire to visualize the Holy Name; instead, begin to think of something unconnected with it. And since you have no particular desire for that other thing you will not have any trouble thinking about it.

For example, think of [picture] the Torah reader who chants the Torah in the synagogue, and how you are standing or sitting, and listening to him. Suddenly they call you for an *aliyah* (and you should immerse yourself in picturing all the details of this scene). At first you are slightly confused . . . you think which way you should go up to the *bimah,* from this side . . . or that. When you are on the *bimah* the Torah reader opens the *sefer* Torah and you look at it and see the verse which begins "And God spoke to Moshe saying." Then you should concentrate on remembering if you saw there, "And Elohim spoke" (וידבר אלהים), or "and Havaya spoke" (וידבר יהוה). And that way, you will be able to visualize the whole verse, together with the name Havaya, without your *yetzer* interfering. [He continues that this suggestion works best if you always make it a point when you actually do get an *aliyah* to look at the Divine names with concentration.] (*Mavo ha-Shaarim,* chap. 10, p. 57)

19:10:6 However, there are deeper obstacles to having the Name of God always before your eyes. Thus, Rabbi Elimelech of Lizensk says that:

It is a sign of a complete *baal-tshuvah* that he will have the name Havaya, blessed be He, before his eyes. And this is a sign that with his fear of God he has fixed all his sins. (*Noam Elimelech,* Noah, p. 3a)

> After a *tzaddik* has completely purified his body, God bestows on him the ability to see the great Name, the name Havaya, blessed be He, go before him always. (*Noam Elimelech*, Vayishlach, p. 14a)

19:10:7 We mentioned the particular interest of Rabbi Elimelech and of the Peasetzna Rebbe in visualization and service of the imagination. The Peasetzna Rebbe was explicit in his attention to this subject and was also aware of the emphasis Rabbi Elimelech put on it. In the same discussion (see 19:10:5) about visualizing the holy Name, he continues:

> You also have to learn how to strengthen your power of imagination itself. For how can you visualize the Holy Name and other things suggested in the holy books, particularly in *Noam Elimelech* [by Rabbi Elimelech, which says many times:] "*You should visualize this as if you were actually seeing it with your own eyes*"—if your ability to visualize is itself weak? (*Mavo ha-Shaarim*, chap. 10, p. 57)

The Peasetzna Rebbe is, to my knowledge at least, almost unique in his discussion of service of the imagination as a category in its own right.

19:11 TRUTH BEFORE YOUR EYES

There are various hasidic practices that involve visualizing words before your eyes. Here is one example, from Rabbi Tzvi Elimelech of Dinov:

> Speak truth and never falsehood. . . . You should also frequently picture the letters אמת [Truth] before your eyes, and with your mouth too bring this to remembrance, saying "Truth, truth . . ." (*Hanhagot Adam*, #26)

19:12 SOMEONE EXHORTING YOU

A practice recommended by various hasidic *rebbes* is to always picture someone at your side exhorting you to serve God. This involves not only imagining a person's presence beside you, but also imagining a voice.

19:12:1 Rabbi Elimelech of Lizensk:

> Always picture in your mind, and especially when reading this *Tzetl Katan* [a list of *hanhagot* he prepared for his followers], that

someone is standing by you and encouraging you with a thunderous voice to do all these spiritual practices, such that you ignore not the smallest detail. And when you accustom yourself to doing this, after a period of time you will develop the power of this arousal from within your own soul, with coals of fire and flames from the source of holiness. (*Tzetl Katan* #12)

There is a story about Rabbi Elimelech that may relate to this practice. It is said that:

Immediately upon awakening from sleep [he] would speak to himself in a thunderous voice and say to his soul, "Woe is you, that you have wasted time in sleep!" (*Or ha-Ner*, #1. a.)

This suggests that Rabbi Elimelech was calling out to himself with the voice of the imagined spiritual guardian. The language of a quote about the similar practice of the Besht's disciple, Rabbi David Forkes, also supports this understanding of what Rabbi Elimelech was doing (see "Waking and Beginning the Day," 4:14:4).

19:12:2 A disciple of Rabbi Elimelech reports:

I have heard about a *hanhaga* where you imagine that someone is standing next to you and always exhorting you to love God, blessed be He, and fear Him, and not to sin, and to do *tshuvah* and *mitzvot* (of doing and refraining). And as a result of this you will come to have this arousal from your own soul, such that although you might forget these things in the midst of your worldly concerns, an arousal will come to you so that you remember them. (*Darkei Tzedek*, pp. 16–17, #3)

19:12:3 In still another version of this:

An essential for achieving perfection is that you always imagine that someone is calling to you, "Serve God!" And if you are eating or drinking or doing other things of personal discretion, you should picture that someone is calling you, "Why are you sleeping? Arise and call out to your God!" And when someone is a complete *tzaddik*, then, after much practice in serving the Creator this becomes his very nature and he feels the holiness. (Rabbi Moshe Leib of Sassov, *Likkutei Rabbi Moshe Leib*, Likkutei tehillim, p. 15)

19:12:4 Some holy people would actually hire someone to stay by their side, or they had a disciple perform this service for them, to see that they did not forget God. (See "Torah," 15:22:5 for an example.)

19:13 OTHER POSSIBILITIES

There are many possibilities for Divine service through imagination. The particular ones described above should be considered not only in their own right but for the suggestions they provide for others of a similar sort. Thus, just as with the scene of the Giving of the Torah at Mount Sinai, other Torah scenes can be used as sources of inspiration, and to set particular spiritual moods. Similarly, just as Rabbi Elimelech's imagining of martyrdom, either by fire, or by identifying with the *Akedah* (the Binding of Isaac), we can also serve God with imagining of other kinds of Divine service.

For example, let us consider going to the *mikveh* and immersing. Of course, there are many times when we should go to the *mikveh*. But there are occasions when it is not practicable or possible, and one can do a service of the imagination for this. Once the Rebbe of Rizhin said to another *tzaddik* he was with, "A Jew must learn how to immerse in the River of Fire" and immediately, he bent himself over three times as if immersing. (See "Men's *Mikveh*," 30:11 about this.)

Another example of Divine service through imagination is that you can close your eyes and picture yourself prostrating fully before God. (See "Prayer," 5:4:5 about the value and significance of prostration.) Rabbi Nachman of Bratzlav spoke often about the silent shout (see "Individual Practices," 39:23), and this was a practice he taught his disciples, where the crying out to God is not done audibly but imagined and "heard" within the mind. Rabbi Nachman also said that he could dance without moving a limb. In that context we can note this saying of Rabbi Menahem Mendel of Vorki:

> There are three things that are fine: upright bowing, silent shouting, and motionless dancing. (*Ha-Tzaddik ha-Shotek*, p. 151)

Just as Rabbi Nachman used the silent shout in audibilization, so can one dance before God or prostrate before Him in imagination (visualization), at times when physical dancing and prostration are impossible or inappropriate.[2] For example, such a service of imagination can be done in the synagogue during the *davvening*, and, as Rabbi Elimelech said, if the intention is true and sincere, it is accounted as real.

This teaching of Rabbi Menahem Mendel of Vorki (just quoted) is discussed at length in a hasidic book, which says:

> No one will know about your service of God in these three things—if you prostrate and cry out and dance within you. So your service will be greater because of that and you will be able to accomplish more spiritually; for there is nothing better than modesty and hiddenness in spiritual things. As it says, "And walk in modesty with the Lord your God." Moreover, when you dance within, you can dance by yourself whenever you want, and you do not need to wait for others to dance with you; and the wise person will understand. As is written in *Sichot ha-Ran* [by Rabbi Nachman], you can shout "loudly" in silence and no one will hear you—for you are imagining the shout within your mind. So here, too, you can stay seated and dance and sing and rejoice just as if you were dancing with others in the greatest rejoicing. So you can picture in your mind all the joy, and the dancing with many people, and no one at all will know that you are doing this. (*GMvGhTz*, II, p. 26)

20

Blessings

20:1 A blessing is a short meditation, and should be said with love and fear of God, and with *kavvanah* (directed attention) and *hitlahavut* (fervor).

See the discussion in Chapter 2, p. 37 on blessings for some general thoughts; here we will concentrate on the specifics of how to say a blessing.

> **20:2** Never just throw off a blessing without intention (*kavvanah*), and never say a blessing quickly. (*Derech Hayim* 5–35)

20:3 You should not do anything else while you are saying a blessing. (*Shulchan Aruch* 6–1)

20:4 When saying a blessing we should first think of what the blessing we have to say is, and then, with our full attention to God, say it. One counsel is:

> You should think of the translation and meaning of the words of a blessing *before* you say it and utter God's name, not after you say the Name. (*Yachin v'Boaz,* in *DhTvhY,* p. 9b, Kavvanat ha-Berachot #1)

20:5 When you make a blessing, direct your heart and mind to bless [praise and thank] God. (*Sefer ha-Yirah* of Rabbeinu Yonah, p. 193)

20:6 When you say the blessings of enjoyment, your intention should be to bless the King of the Universe and to praise Him, and not just to throw a blessing out of your mouth where it is obvious that your true intention is only your own bodily pleasure—to eat this fruit—and not to give praise to His name, blessed be He. (*Totzaot Hayim*, p. 15)

20:7 Rav said: When you make a blessing you must say, "Blessed are You, O Lord" . . . as it is written, "I have placed the Lord before me always." (*Midrash Psalms* 16–8)

When you say "Blessed are You" . . . you should think that He is standing before You, as it says, "I have placed the Lord before me always"; and you should have the fear of God on your face, and love of God within you, and speak with the full intention and concentration of your heart. (*Sefer ha-Rokeach*, quoted in *Reshit Hochmah*, Sh'ar ha-Kedushah, chap. 14, #32)

Although a blessing is something done in a very short time, it requires some preparation. Before making a blessing, you can take a deep breath and do a brief meditation on the *Shechinah* surrounding you in all six directions.[1] Then say mentally, "I have placed the Lord before me always," and think that the Holy One, blessed be He, is standing before you. Then say the blessing aloud.

20:8 Another rule for directing attention in blessings is that you should make it a habit when you are in your own house to say the blessings in a loud voice; for a raised voice arouses *kavvanah*. (*Totzaot Hayim*, p. 15)

20:9 You may also say blessings in a silent or whispered shout (see "Individual Practices," 39:23); this can be done outside your house as well.

20:10 Rabbeinu Asher suggests closing your eyes when making a blessing (*Orchot Hayim* 3–38).

Rabbi Alexander Ziskind:

You should say all the blessings with closed eyes. (*Yesod v'Shoresh ha-Avodah*, Gate 2, p. 28)

20:11 It is a traditional practice, emphasized in Hasidism, to give the Name of God great and overwhelming devotion and respect whenever uttered, in blessings or at other times.

> **20:11:1** Be careful to work at developing your fear and love of God, until you will merit being attached to Him, blessed be He, with both love and fear—and accustom yourself to tremble when you mention the Name, blessed be He. (*Darkei Tzedek*, p. 21)

> **20:11:2** You should bring your whole body to a state of arousal and shaking before you utter the Name. (*Derech Hayim* 1–77)

> **20:11:3** The meaning of the verse "to fear this glorious and awesome Name" (Deuteronomy 25:58)—is that when you mention the Name you should make all your body tremble; and when you make any blessing you should say it clearly and so that your whole body feels it. Do not just throw off a blessing quickly without attention, God forbid. (*Kav ha-Yashar*, chap. 41)

The point is that we should say the words with all our energy and with the utmost concentration, until our very limbs feel it.

20:11:4 Rabbi Moshe of Trani:

> You should bring some sort of feeling to your body. You should shake your body somewhat, as if trembling from the mention of the Name. (*Igeret Derech HaShem* [end])

This conscious act is what you do when you are on a lower level; the *tzaddikim* will naturally have an aroused bodily reaction when they mention God's name.

20:11:5 To what can this be compared? It is like a common person in awe of a great king who is about to visit his house. When he mentions the king's name his whole body tingles with awe.

Or it is like a young man who is madly in love with a beautiful young woman. Whenever he mentions her name his whole body thrills with his love for her.

So is it (making a distinction between holy and profane) with the Name of God. For when we mention the Name of the King of the Universe, who spoke and the world came into being—it should be with fear and awe, with trembling and shaking. And this is also the Name of our very own, the treasure of our hearts and the love of our soul—and when saying His precious Name we should also bring ourselves to an arousal of love.

20:11:6 A story is told about Rabbi Shlomo Leib of Lentshno and how he made the blessing over the wine in the *kiddush* on *Shabbat*:

> On the evening of the holy Sabbath, during the *kiddush*, I saw with my own eyes how when our glorious master and teacher and rabbi, may his merit protect us, said the Name in the blessing over the wine—a great fear of God came upon him so that all his limbs trembled and the cup of wine fell from his hand. It did not fall to the ground, however, because he caught it with his other hand. But the wine spilled, and he filled the cup again and finished saying the *kiddush* in a loud voice as was his holy way. From that time on the *rebbe* never held the cup by himself, but had his hands resting on the back of the chair with the cup on them, and someone else would hold the cup steady on his hands. And though we know that the *tzaddikim* have such fear and awe of God always, without a moment's cessation, yet they keep it hidden within themselves so that it not be seen—but this time the *rebbe* could not hold it in. (*Emunat Tzaddikim*, p. 87)

20:11:7 It is said of Rabbi Levi Yitzhak of Berditchev that:

> His way in holiness was actually like a seraph [a fiery angel] and an angel. It was said of him that when some food was brought before him to eat, and he had to make a blessing of enjoyment first, he would make the blessing with such fervor and with such a great fire of devotion that he would end up in one corner of the room and the food in the other corner.[2] (*Seder ha-Dorot ha-Hadash*, p. 36)

The Berditchever was famous for his amazing fervor, and when doing *mitzvot* and when praying he would throw himself about bodily and fall in the ecstasy of his flaming devotion.

To such as Rabbi Shlomo Leib of Lentshno and Rabbi Levi Yitzhak of Berditchev did the rabbis apply the verse of Proverbs 5:19, "In her [the *Shechinah's*, or the Torah's] love will you be ravished always"—where the word for "ravished" (*tishgeh*) is also understood to have another meaning, "err"; that is, due to their love of the *Shechinah* they will always make errors. For in the ecstasy of their great and overwhelming love for God the *tzaddikim* sometimes cannot control themselves and so err in their performance of the *mitzvot*.

> **20:11:8** Once the *gaon* and *tzaddik* Rabbi Shimon, the head of the religious court of Dobrimil came to Ropshitz. He was in the *Beit Midrash* and had started to say a word of Torah before the disciples of the Ropshitzer Rebbe, when the holy rabbi, Rabbi Hayim of Tzanz [who was then a young man and a leading disciple of the Ropshitzer] came out of the bathroom and was washing his hands [according to the *halacha*]. They stopped and waited for him to come over, and they saw how he began to say with great fervor the blessing *asher yatzar* ["who formed," the blessing said after leaving the bathroom and after having washed the hands: "Blessed art Thou O Lord our God, King of the Universe, who formed man in wisdom, etc."—praising the wondrous nature of the body created by God], but he was so enraptured in his fervor that although he had begun with the correct blessing, he continued [in error], "on the *mitzvah* of *tzitzit*" and then he said, "uh . . . on taking the *lulav*"—all this being in the way of what is said, "In His love will you be ravished always" [and err]—until he finally returned to the [correct] blessing of *asher yatzar*. And this was his usual way when making blessings. Rabbi Shimon, who had been watching all this, was amazed at how great his fear of God was. (*Mekor Hayim*, p. 153, #528)

> **20:12** If you did not have *kavvanah* [when making a blessing] . . . feel regret and sadness, and resolve to be careful and take it to heart [that you not let it happen again]. If necessary you must fine yourself a small amount of money [for *tzedaka*], according to your means, each time you fail to have *kavvanah* when making a blessing, for that will help you to have *kavvanah* the next time. (Rabbi Moshe of Trani, *Igeret Derech HaShem*, end)

20:13 The "minor" eating you do which only requires a blessing before and after should be done as a meditation, just as when you have a full meal. See the chapter on "Eating and the Holy Meal" for a complete description of such a meditation. Here we will just quote from *Yesod v'Shoresh ha-Avodah*, which, in its discussion of blessings, gives a summary of the matter:

> Make it your practice when you sit down to eat, or when you take the cup in your hand to drink, to think this valuable thought: that

there is in this food or drink holy sparks of a spiritual nature, and it is from them that you will taste the pleasure or life-giving goodness in eating or drinking. Also, when you meditate on this before you eat or drink, you will not lower or coarsen the pleasure to a material plane. Your intention should be to lift up the holy sparks to their root and source. After this make the appropriate blessing on "the fruit of the tree" or "the fruit of the earth" [vegetable], or "kinds of *mezonot*" [cereal products], and think to yourself, full of joy, How amazing is God's power! How amazing is God's power! [*Gevurot HaShem! Gevurot HaShem!*] in this creation, and how wonderful is His wisdom in bringing into being this fruit or this cereal with His word, blessed is His Name and blessed is His remembrance forever. And you should have this intention in all blessings of enjoyment, even when drinking water after making the blessing *sh'hakol* ["through whose word everything comes into being"].

And when you are eating the fruit or vegetable . . . and enjoying its sweetness and taste, you should meditate this way . . . thinking, "Is not this as sweet as honey to my taste? This is nothing but the holy sparks from the Upper Worlds that I am tasting. And if a little spark that is in this food or drink gives me such pleasure, how much enjoyment is there in the holy Upper Worlds themselves from which this pleasure is taken. O that I were on the spiritual level to experience the pleasure of the *Shechinah* always, and not just through the spark in this food or drink!" You should call to mind the amazing nature of God's power and his wonderful wisdom in creating this fruit or vegetable with its sweet taste. And especially when you are very hungry or as thirsty as a gazelle panting for the waters of the brook, and when your pleasure in the eating or drinking is certainly great . . . then meditate on this *kavvanah* with great joy, and intend by this *kavvanah* to give pleasure to your Maker and Creator, blessed and exalted is He.

Be careful with the *kavvanah* of the after-blessings of the blessings of enjoyment. When you finish the blessing "who has created many living beings and their needs . . . Blessed are You, the life of all worlds"—think, with great joy, "You [O God] give life and existence to all the worlds, and without the flow of Your holy goodness for one moment they would all disappear instantaneously as if they had never existed."

If you ate a number of kinds of food and afterwards drank some things also, and on all of them made one common after-blessing of "who has created many living beings, etc.," and your intention was to cover all the kinds of things you ate and drank, it is good to intend, when you say the words, "for all that You created with which You enliven every living thing," all the individual different

> things you ate and drank. For example, go over in your mind, giving thanks for each with great joy thinking, "I give You thanks for this food and that which I ate and enjoyed, for this and that drink that You created to enliven every living thing. And You have enlivened me with them so that I can engage in Your holy service." Then conclude, "Blessed are You, the life of all worlds," with great joy and *kavvanah.* And certainly it is proper for every one of Israel, the holy people, to give thanks to our Maker and Creator, blessed and exalted is His name and His remembrance forever, on each and every enjoyment by itself. . . and not to make do with one common blessing. (*Yesod v'Shoresh ha-Avodah,* Gate 7, chap. 10)

See "Eating and the Holy Meal" (10:17:5) about how Rabbi Nachman of Bratzlav followed this practice, not for regular blessings, but during the Grace After Meals.

Also see "Eating and the Holy Meal" for more about blessings.

21

Repetition of a Holy Sentence

21:1 The rabbis say about Hanoch (Enoch, Genesis 5:24):

> Hanoch was a shoemaker who would sew together the uppers and lowers of the shoes. With each and every stitch he would say, "Blessed is His glorious kingdom for ever and ever!"*[1] And he was able to bind together the Upper and the Lower worlds. (*Hedvat Simha*, p. 57)

Hanoch repeated this devotional sentence so that he would be linked to heaven in continual God–consciousness.

The sentence that Hanoch used is the answering response we make following the recital of the first line of the *Sh'ma*. The *Sh'ma* itself affirms God's oneness and our acceptance of Him as our God; the "Blessed is His glorious kingdom, etc.," which is its partner, inspires reverence for God's kingdom and consciousness of its presence. In saying it we declare our readiness to do His will at all times, and our desire to realize continually that everything that happens in this world is from God's hand and doing, the working of His kingdom, and that the Upper and the Lower Worlds are in reality one.

21:2 The phrase said to have been used by Hanoch is an important one in Judaism and powerful in utterance. The *Sh'ma* itself, also of course basic and potent, can be used as a repeated sentence—though the *halacha* limits this use only to the time when one is in bed, going to sleep.[2]

Indeed, this practice of repeating a holy sentence is especially helpful and valuable before sleep. One of the benefits of a repeated sentence is that the repetition tends to build up its own momentum. When a holy sentence is repeated before sleep the mind's inertia can keep it going subconsciously through the night, purifying one's thoughts and dreams, and even continue until the time of waking.

There is a story in the Talmud about Rabbi Shmuel bar Nahmeni that tells how he used the *Sh'ma* in repetition before sleep.

> When Rabbi Shmuel bar Nahmeni would go down to the town of Eburra, Rabbi Yaakov the Miller would receive him into his home. Once, Rabbi Zeira, Rabbi Yaakov's son, wanting to learn all the holy ways and practices of the great rabbi, hid himself among the large baskets that were in Rabbi Shmuel's bedroom, to hear how he recited the *Sh'ma* before sleep. And he heard that he said the *Sh'ma* and repeated it over and over, until he fell asleep while saying it.[3] (*Yerushalmi Berachot* 1–13)

Rabbi Shmuel's repetition of the *Sh'ma* was obviously audible. However, since it is hard to imagine falling asleep like that, perhaps he repeated it for a while out loud and then continued with the repetition mentally until sleep came upon him.[4] (See below 21:5 regarding the practice of Rabbi Alexander Ziskind.)

21:3 Rachmei ha-Av teaches that to maintain *d'vekut* you should accustom yourself to say continually, "Blessed is the One and Only One" [*Baruch Yahid u'miyuhad*][5] and Psalm 16:8, "I have placed the Lord before me always." (See Chapter 2, pp. 36–37.)

It should be noted that the declaration that God is the "One and Only One" is a traditional equivalent to the words of the *Sh'ma*, "The Lord is one."

> When you say the "*Sh'ma Yisrael*" you should concentrate on its meaning: Hear O Israel, that the Lord, who is our God, is one—the one and only one [*yahid u'miyuhad*] in heaven and on earth.[6] The (*Shulchan Aruch*, 17–3)

Thus, while one cannot use the *Sh'ma* as a repeated sentence (except before sleep), this phrase, "Blessed is the One and Only One," can take its place at other times. (In fact, since there is actually some question about the appropriateness of repeating the *Sh'ma* even before sleep, one could use this phrase then too. Rachmei ha-Av seems to suggest this;* see the quote referred to in chapter 2, p. 37.)

> **21:4** The rabbis, of blessed memory, said: "Let every soul [*neshamah*] praise God" (Psalm 150:6). This means: praise Him with each and every breath [*neshimah*]. So you can say at every moment and continually, "Blessed is the Merciful One, King of the Universe, Master of this time" or "of this moment."* (*Or ha-Ganuz l'Tzaddikim*, p. 45)

(In the Aramaic, this line, particularly with the second of the two alternative words, is very alliterative and rolls off the tongue: *B'rich Rachmana, Malka d'Alma, Marai d'hai Riga.*[7])

21:5 Rabbi Alexander Ziskind had a repeated phrase that he used regularly, and he joined it with a sentence in which he accepted God's kingship on himself. As with *Or ha-Ganuz l'Tzaddikim* (21:4), he thought of this practice as a fulfillment of the rabbis' teaching that you should praise God with each and every breath.[8]

> From the greatness of my continual joy and pride in the holiness of God's Being [*elohuto*], I would always mention Him, blessed be He, continually; even when I was not occupied in Torah study or prayer or doing *mitzvot*, I would say out loud, full of joy, these three [Hebrew] words: "You are my Maker and Creator" [*Yotzri u'Bori Ata*]. And I would say these three words many times, again and again, out of my great love and longing for His holiness.
>
> After these three words [repeating them many times] I would say, "My Maker and Creator, I believe with complete faith that You created all the worlds, the Upper and the Lower worlds, worlds without end or number, and I accept on myself that You are my God, and I accept it on my children and grandchildren to the end of all generations."
>
> [Rabbi Ziskind also used these three words as part of a stated intention before many of his actions. He continues in the text with examples. One is that before going to the synagogue he would say out loud, "My Maker and Creator, I want to go to the synagogue to

pray before You with the congregation."* After these examples, the text continues:]

When I had to go to sleep, I would immediately begin to say mentally these three words, "You are my Maker and Creator," until I fell asleep. And whenever I was walking somewhere I would repeat mentally these three words, and also would accept on myself His kingship, as above.

And I will tell you, my beloved children, that whenever I was not involved in Torah or prayer, these three words and the acceptance of God, blessed be He, as my God, was ever-present in my mouth and even more so in my thoughts. Except for the forgetfulness which is part of man's nature (according to God's will) . . . I can testify about myself, my beloved children, that there was not a minute during which my mind did not glory in God, blessed be His name and His remembrance forever, in the above language and language similar to it.[9] Due to forgetfulness this would sometimes cease briefly from my mind, but it would immediately be rearoused—and all this due to the greatness of my love for Him, blessed be He. (*Tzva'a Yekara* [the ethical last testament] of Rabbi Alexander Ziskind, #34)

21:6 About the hasidic *rebbe*, Rabbi Mordechai of Neshkiz:

Psalm 84:17 says "Lord of hosts, happy is the man who trusts in You!" When Rabbi Mordechai felt the need to strengthen his trust in God, he would repeat this verse over and over, so many times, until he became filled with trust in God, blessed be He.

The source of this practice of his is in the Jerusalem Talmud, *Berachot*, chapter 5, halacha 1, which says: "Let this verse never cease from your lips: Lord of hosts, happy is the man who trusts in You!" (*Admorei Neshkiz, Lechovitz, Kaidenov, Novominsk*, p. 34)

21:7 Let us consider the theory behind this practice of repeating a holy sentence or phrase.

First, there is the fact that the mind has a natural tendency to wander. As a result, holding onto God-consciousness is difficult, for the mind always jumps from one thing to another.

The value of a repeated sentence then is that the repetition, if persisted in for a period of time, easily establishes itself as a habit and becomes almost automatic. As a result, the mind is aided in its concentration on God and holiness by the steady and continuous flow of the sound of the repeated holy sentence.

There is the further benefit that once the repetition becomes habitual, the mind is led back to it even after a break or interruption. It is like a compass—you can hold the needle for a while, but when it is released it once again points to the north. Note how Rabbi Ziskind says that although he sometimes forgot to say his repeated sentence "it would immediately be rearoused."

For the sound of the repetition to aid you in your concentration, you should, when engaged in this practice, bend your ears to hear what your mouth is saying.

If there is some simple and appropriate tune available for the verse you want to repeat, so that it can be chanted, that will also help with the facility of the repetition, and with your concentration.

The repetition can be done loudly or in a whisper, depending on the situation and circumstances. It is also possible to chant silently to yourself, and this is in fact particularly effective, with moving lips or without. But this mental repetition is more difficult to maintain, for you lose the support to concentration provided by the sound.

The repetition of a holy sentence should be full of intention, not just mechanical, and infused with love and longing for God, as if you are calling to Him. It should be an emotional as well as a mental meditation. For this it helps if there is a name or designation of God in the sentence being repeated. For instance, in the verse that Rabbi Mordechai used, when you would say, "Lord of hosts," *call* to God, directing yourself to Him to get His attention. In the phrase used by Rabbi Ziskind there is not a name, but the appellations "My Maker" and "My Creator"; moreover, the whole phrase, "*You* are my Maker, etc.," directs his mind to God.

It is also very good just to repeat a name or appellation of God in the way just described, such as "Master of the World," or "Father in Heaven."*

> Rabbi Levi Yitzhak of Berditchev, who was always immersed in *d'vekut*, would not turn his mind away from the service of God, and he would call out again and again, "Merciful One! (*HaRachaman*!)."* (*Midor Dor*, I, #579)

(The Hebrew, translated as "again and again" [*t'chufot*] is not exact enough to know if the meaning is "one after the other" or just "frequently." See also "Eating and the Holy Meal," 10:7 and "Prayer," 5:1:18:3:2 and 5:2:4 for related practices.)

Even when you just call out God's name, there are many ways that a name can be uttered, but it should be called out with love.

The Maggid of Mezritch said that: "When you call out to a man by using his name, he leaves what he is doing and answers the one who is calling him, since he is as if bound to his name" (*Or ha-Emet*, p. 28). So when you call out to God by His name, He is drawn to you. As it says, "In every place where I cause My name to be mentioned, I will come to you and bless you" (Exodus 20:21). When you call out God's name in faith, He comes to you and is present with you.

From another perspective we can say that the "cause and effect" is even more intimate, since, as it says in the *Zohar*, "God and His Name are one" (*Totzaot Hayim*, p. 28). So when you say His name, He is there. This is a deep matter, but here is a thought as to its meaning: God's presence is everywhere, but the manifestation of His presence can be more or less. That which is holy and has an intimate association with God reveals a greater manifestation. Thus, there is a greater manifestation of His presence in synagogues, in holy books, holy people, etc. There is a particularly great connection, however, between God and His name, for the very purpose of the name is to call to mind His being and presence. So wherever His name is mentioned, He is there.

To avoid consciousness of self and ego in the repetition of a holy sentence or of a name of God, it is good to have an attitude of humility: "God, it is not my will, but it is by Your will that I am repeating this." Think that it is God who gives you the power of thought, speech, and movement.

As the verse says, "In every place *where I cause My name to be mentioned. . . .*" And as the Besht taught about what we say before the *Shemoneh Esreh*, "O Lord, open Thou my lips, and my mouth shall declare Thy praise."—that we should take it that it is the *Shechinah* which is present and says the prayer through us (*Keter Shem Tov*, p. 22b). Or as the Maggid of Mezritch said on the verse, "Lift up your voice as a *shofar*," you are like a *shofar*, and if the *Shechinah* does not blow the sound through it, there is nothing there (*Or ha-Emet*, p. 6).

Rabbi Levi Yitzhak of Berditchev taught that on the highest level of calling out God's name, one so separates himself from the body and materiality that he is altogether within the words he utters—he is clothed not in the body, but in the speech. It is his soul alone, which is a spark of the *Shechinah*, and not the body that is calling out. On this level, then, it is the *Shechinah* Herself who is doing the calling. Thus God calls to God, the *Shechinah* to the Holy One, blessed be He.

> A person should clothe himself in the holy words he says until he reaches the state of stripping off materiality and the bodily garment [*hitpashtut ha-gashmiyut*], and when he is nullified [before God] in his essence and loses consciousness of self, then he will be able to cleave to the letters [of his speech].
>
> And when he has stripped off materiality and the body, then it is the *Shechinah* who is speaking out of his throat. This is the meaning of the verse, "In every place where I cause My name to be mentioned, I will come to you and bless you." For should not it have said, "In every place where *you* mention . . . ?" But the meaning is that in every place where *I* mention My name, that is, I Myself mention My name, when you are in a state of *hitpashtut ha-gashmiyut* and you have nullified yourself before God—then the *Shechinah* Himself mentions His name out of his throat. (*Kedushat Levi,* Likkutim, p. 83)

The Berditchever continues that on this high level the Great Name of God, YHVH, can be used. But since that level is difficult to attain, especially in the time of exile, we use the name *Adonai* (Lord). Still, one can learn from this teaching that the correct way to call out *Adonai* or other of God's names, is with the consciousness that it is not you but the *Shechinah* that calls out.

Elsewhere, the Berditchever gives another related teaching, applying this thought to a scene in the Torah. When Moses was on Mount Sinai he asked God to reveal to him His inner nature and personality. God answered by revealing Himself and calling out the manifold aspects of His mercy—which the rabbis counted as thirteen: "*Adonai, Adonai* [YHVH, YHVH], a God merciful and gracious [giving and forgiving], patient, and abundant in faithful love; keeping steadfast love unto the thousandth generation, pardoning iniquity and transgression and sin . . ." (Exodus 34:6–7).

The beginning of the Torah verse here is: "And the Lord passed by before him [Moses] and cried out, '*Adonai, Adonai,* a God merciful and gracious, etc.'" Rabbi Levi Yitzhak of Berditchev interpreted the twice repeated name of God to be referring to the inner manifestation of God, the soul, as calling out to the outer manifestation of God. He understood it to read "And *Adonai* cried out, '*Adonai* . . .'" Here are his words:

> It is the *neshamah* [man's soul] calling to the Holy One, blessed be He. For the soul of man is an actual part of God [of the *Shechinah*] from above. Thus, when "The Lord passed by," that is, when the feeling of love and awe for Heaven passes over you and overwhelms you, then the divine within—"The Lord"—cries out to the divine above, "O Lord!" (*Siftei Tzaddikim*, Beshallach, p. 30b)

In these teachings of Rabbi Levi Yitzhak of Berditchev we see how, when calling out the name of God, we are to do so with humility, conscious that it is God's own power, the *Shechinah*, that gives us the ability of utterance; also, we are to call out His name with love and awe.

21:8 As with *davvening*, the repeated sentence may be in Hebrew, for the holy tongue has an inherent association with God, and because of the few words involved anyone can master their meaning. Further, the spiritual tradition of generations behind the Hebrew gives it an innate power. But for all that, speaking in a language other than our native one can be a barrier of sorts, and the sentence can also be said in English, or the language you are most familiar with. Either way is appropriate and you should choose what you find best.

21:9 As for what to say, you may take a name or appellation of God, such as Father in Heaven, and use that alone. Or, you may use it together with a Torah verse or another sentence that has a special meaning to you. You can, if you so desire, make up a sentence or phrase expressing your own feelings in devotion to God. Rabbi Ziskind's words, "You are my Maker and Creator," and the sentence he used with it were his own.

21:10 Our goal in the repetition of the holy sentence should be that in answer to our call and directed awareness, God will make His presence known to us. We should have faith that when we say His name with devotion, He is present, for He and His name are one. We want to experience His presence, however, and to see His glory with these eyes.

During the repetition, if it feels right, we can intersperse (mentally or verbally) little prayers. For example: "God, I am calling to You from the bottom of my heart; let me be aware of Your holy presence." Or we can make declarations such as: "I accept on myself that You are my God" (as Rabbi Ziskind in 21:5).

21:11 Another important aspect of the repetition is that we should meditate on those aspects of God which the sentence refers to—with the *Baruch yahid u'miyuhad* (Blessed is the One and Only One), on God's oneness and holiness and that there is nothing in existence but Him; with the *Baruch shem kavod* (Blessed is His glorious kingdom, etc.), that His kingdom is ever present and exists through all eternity; with Psalm 84:17 that Rabbi Mordechai used, that we should have complete trust in God; and so on.

21:12 In the Jewish tradition, for historical reasons, the use of the special name of God [YHVH] in actual utterance ceased. This custom is connected with the way of the fear of God, where our reverence and awe of God's Holy Name and the possibility of its misuse becomes so great that it is rarely or never uttered.

In the hasidic way of love, however, there is a deep attachment to God's name (all the different names of God). We are often encouraged to always have God's name in our mouth. Although according to *halacha* that Great Name of God cannot be used, the other names and appellations (Father in Heaven, Master of the World, etc.) can be spoken, and the love of God and His name would keep them always on our lips.

Because the special name cannot be repeated verbally, the hasidim of the Baal Shem Tov used instead a visual method of picturing the Name YHVH יהוה always written before their eyes, like watching a movie with that written on the screen. Having the Name before your eyes this way is considered a fulfillment of the verse, "I have placed the Lord [YHVH] before me always."

> You should continuously picture the Name before your eyes in the accustomed way. (Rabbi Moshe Teitelbaum, *Hanhagot Tzaddikim*, p. 50, #43; p. 49, #19)

As with the continuity of the sound of a repeated sentence, the continuity of the visual image aids the concentration of the mind on God.

Rachmei ha-Av teaches that you should continually say the verse "I have placed the Lord before me always" (*Shivitti HaShem l'negdi tamid*), at least the first word *Shivitti*. (See Chapter 2, p. 37.)

> It is told of the holy Rabbi Yaakov Koppel Hasid of Kolomaya, the disciple of the Besht and the founder of the hasidic dynasty of Kosov-Vishnitz, that he would verbally repeat at all hours of the day, nonstop, "I have placed the Lord before me always," even

> during the hours of work and business. And even the gentiles called him "The *Shivittinik.*" (*Tiferet Beit David*, p. 103)

Like Hanoch, Rabbi Yaakov Koppel repeated a holy sentence over and over during work. With the rabbi it is explicitly said that he repeated it continuously throughout the day, even during work; probably with Hanoch the same thing is intended.

One can, of course, combine the repetition of the verse, "I have placed the Lord [YHVH] etc.," with the visualization of the Name. Presumably that is what Rabbi Yaakov Koppel was doing.

21:13 Rabbi Nachman of Bratzlav taught the repetition of a single word or phrase, but he intended it primarily as a way to open oneself up in conversation with God when that is otherwise difficult. *Hitbodedut* ("aloneness" with God and intimate conversation with Him) is at the center of Rabbi Nachman's way in holiness. Regardless, he certainly believed that such repetition of a holy word or phrase is a valuable spiritual practice. The one phrase he particularly mentioned was the repetition of "Master of the World" (*Ribono shel Olam*).

Rabbi Nachman about daily sessions of *hitbodedut* and conversation with God:

> He said that if you cannot converse [with God], but can just say one word, you should be strong-minded and say that one word many, many times, without end or number. Even if you spend many days repeating just that one word alone, it is also very good. You should be strong-minded and determined, and continue to say that one word over and over, countless times, until God, blessed be He, has compassion on you, and opens your mouth so that you can converse with Him freely. (*Likkutei Moharan*, Tinyana, #96, quoted in *Hishtapchut ha-Nefesh*, p. 32, #4)

> He [Rabbi Nachman] said that when you were only able, during *hitbodedut*, to say the phrase, "Master of the World!" [*Ribono shel Olam*], it is also very good. (*Hayei Moharan*, Part 2, p. 15, quoted in *Hishtapchut ha-Nefesh*, p. 46, #45)

21:14 Some of the uses of a repeated sentence are more general, others more specific. For example, "Blessed is the One and Only One" is of a general significance. On the other hand, Psalm 84:17, used by Rabbi Mordechai to increase his trust in God is more specific.

Other verses can be selected and used for their different qualities. Sentences and verses can also be repeated for the purpose of instilling in ourselves an awareness of certain ethical teachings.

The program of the *Musar* (character development) movement uses repetition of sentences which inspire fear of God or cultivate particular character traits. The main practice is to recite passages from Torah books (the Torah itself, the *Midrash*, *musar* books, and so forth), or a saying or verse, in an emotionally charged way. This is typically done to a melody—taken from the kind traditionally used by *maggidim* (traveling preachers)—and at twilight or in a subdued light, so as to open one's heart to the wisdom of the teaching (*Encyclopedia Judaica*, *Musar* Movement).

Rabbi Israel Salanter was the great founder of the *Musar* movement. A book about his life and teachings says about his method in the study of *musar* books:

> Here Rabbi Israel innovated—for concentration in study alone [though important] is not sufficient. He taught that one must fix specific times for the repetition of certain verses with feeling and fervor. For only that kind of repetition makes a lasting impression on the soul and has the desired effect. (MiDor l'Dor, vol. 1, *Rabbi Yisrael mi-Salant*, p. 14)

Knowledge of Torah truth is not enough to bring us to soul realization and to action. For that one needs repetition, melody, and fervor—such is the belief of the *Musar* school.

> As we see with the power of musical instruments and the singing voice—a man's soul and his spirit become aroused, either to joy or to sadness.[10] [Note: The *Musar* movement concentrates on fear of God and sadness over sin, contrary to the hasidic movement, which emphasizes love of God and the joy of service. Note in what follows that this inclination of the *Musar* movement is not necessary for the method prescribed. The text continues:] So when you recite the sayings of the Sages, of blessed memory, [from the Talmud and *midrash*] and the words of *musar* books, which enflame hearts to the fear of God, blessed be He, with a sad and mournful voice, with an arousal of the soul, then your heart will begin to heat up within you, and your soul will become more and more awakened, until all your senses are affected—and then the words will strike root in the innermost part of your heart, to bring the fear of God within you. And how much more so is this true if occasionally this learning of

> *musar* with arousal brings you to tears, and streams of water flow from your eyes . . . then a new spirit will be put within you. . . .
>
> So it is good to repeat a saying of the fear of God and *musar* many times. Especially when you are studying a *musar* book and reach a saying of the Sages or some other word of *musar* that you feel you relate to . . . repeat it again and again with arousal, numbers of times, until it is engraved on the tablet of your heart, and is frontlets between your eyes. Then, even when you walk outside and when you lie down on your bed, it will ring in your ears like a bell and will not depart from your memory.
>
> Our master [Rabbi Israel Salanter] learned *musar* books with great arousal, with a sweet voice that would bring [holy] sadness to anyone who heard him, and sometimes he repeated one saying many times. (*Or Yisrael*, p. 33)

To employ this method, pick a saying of the Torah, or Sages, etc. that has a special meaning to you or that teaches in a powerful way something that you know you need to absorb. Then, sit down, perhaps in a dimly lit room with a candle burning, and repeat the saying for a defined amount of time in an appropriate melody or chant, with emotional arousal and fervor. If the saying or verse involves a character trait that you are working to improve, the same verse might be used for a period of time until there is improvement.

Rabbi Aryeh Kaplan, discussing this practice of the *Musar* movement, gives the example of using the Torah verse forbidding gossip:

> The method of breaking the gossip habit would be to take the biblical verse, "Do not go as a talebearer among your people" [Leviticus 19:16] and repeat it every day for a twenty- to thirty-minute period. . . . As one works on it, the message is gradually absorbed, and the self-control necessary to avoid gossip is attained. (*Jewish Meditation*, p. 163)

Rabbi Tzvi Elimelech of Dinov (a hasidic *rebbe*) recommended a similar method to his disciples, with regard to speaking truth always. He said:

> You should continuously picture the word אמת—truth before your eyes, and also remind yourself by saying over and over, "Truth, truth . . ." (*Hanhagot Adam*, #26)

(Note how he combines the visual with the aural aspects.)

As the quote from *Or Yisrael* (above) suggests, you can use the method of the *Musar* movement while reading a *musar* book or other

Torah book, repeating individual sayings and verses as you come upon them—or you can use it during special sessions exclusively devoted to repeating a particular saying or verse.

21:15 The repetition of a holy sentence or phrase is of great efficacy when used in the synagogue at times during the services when there are minor delays or breaks in the worship. The continuity achieved by this means allows a steady build-up of concentration and intensity way out of proportion to the ease of the practice itself. (See "The Synagogue and the Synagogue Service," 6:20 for more about this.)

21:16 The practice of the repetition of a holy sentence, phrase, or name can be used, as said, during work, when walking, even when you are otherwise occupied. It is relatively easy to do, and is therefore of particular value at times when you are somewhat fatigued, or when other, more demanding religious practices are impossible. See "Repetition of a Holy Sentence," Chapter 3, p. 66 for a discussion of some of its advantages, these being among them.

But one can also set aside specific times for such repetition, and sit before a *Shivitti* or card with the Name on it, and repeat for a period of time the phrase or sentence you have chosen, using it as the basis for a meditation.

22

Tzedaka and *Gemilut Hasadim*—Charity and Kindness

22:1 EVERY DAY

> **22:1:1** Try to fulfill some *mitzvah* of kindness every day . . . for as it says in the Talmud (*Avodah Zarah*): "Someone who engages in Torah study and does not involve himself in doing deeds of kindness is like someone who has no God." (*Totzaot Hayim*, p. 19)

If possible, have a specific time each day for this, just as you would fix a time for Torah study.

The Hafetz Hayim said:

> "You occasionally see a Jew who [in a praiseworthy way] learns Torah [as much as possible] and values his time [not wasting a minute]. But if he does not set aside part of the day to do deeds of kindness, what a lack of intelligence!" (*Michtivei ha-Hafetz Hayim ha-Hadash*, vol. 2, II, p. 85)

> [Rabbi Meir'l of Tiktin] would try to do some act of kindness every day before eating. He made a fence for himself not to taste any food

before he had done some kindness. And since God fulfills the will of His servants, an opportunity to do some act of kindness, or favor for someone, came to Rabbi Meir'l every day.

But one day no such chance came his way and he fasted the whole day. At night he did not go to sleep but went outside to the street. And behold, there was a wagon full of wooden boards in front of his house. So he ran to the house of the carpenter, knocked on his door to wake him up, and brought him back with him. The carpenter inquired of the gentile who owned the wood what it cost and found that the asking price was low, and the wood was just what he needed for his work.

But unfortunately, though at that price it was a real buy, he did not have enough money to pay for the wood. Since one *mitzvah* leads to another, Rabbi Meir'l had a chance to do another *mitzvah* of loaning the carpenter the money. He gladly did so, and then went into his house to eat his first meal of the day, full of joy. (*Shemen ha-Tov*, p. 111, #125)

22:1:2 Each day you should expectantly look forward that some opportunity for a new *mitzvah* of *tzedaka* or of kindness come your way; and immediately when God does bring it to you, you should do it happily, and should bless God and thank Him that He sent it to you. (Rabbi Tzvi Elimelech of Dinov, *Hanhagot Adam*, #15).

22:2 *KAVVANAH*— INTENTION IN GIVING

22:2:1 Be aware when you give charity and offer help that you are only serving God, and be grateful to the one receiving the help for having given you the opportunity to have the joy of the *mitzvah*. In this way you will be able to avoid pride and a patronizing attitude, which are often joined to attempts to help others.

The person who gives should be aware that he is really receiving, not giving, for "More than what the householder [who gives *tzedaka*] does for the poor person, the poor person does for the householder [in giving him the opportunity to do good and lift up his soul]." (Rabbi Yaakov Yosef of Polnoye, *Toldot Yaakov Yosef*, Noah, quoted in *L'Yesharim Tehillah*, p. 31)

22:2:2 When you give charity there are also other appropriate intentions, such as:

> **22:2:2:1** Not from my own have I given, but from what God has given to me. (*Derech Eretz Zutta*, 2:1)

As the rabbis also say elsewhere:

> Give Him what is His; for you and what is yours are His. (*Avot* 3:8)

Your possessions and money are God's, and He has given them to you for the purpose of sharing them, according to the Torah's teaching.

> The person who gives should be aware that it is not really he who is giving, but the Holy One, blessed be He, is the one giving. (*L'Yesharim Tehillah*, p. 31)

22:2:2:2 The various intentions connected with *tzedaka* can be said aloud before or even after giving, as stated intentions.

> Before giving the money for *tzedaka*, say, "I devote this to *tzedaka*, from what God, blessed be He, has bestowed on me. And I give it for the sake of His Name, blessed be He, to find favor in His eyes, so that in His mercy He will fill my heart with love and fear of Him, for He is all that I want for my efforts in this world." (Rabbi Yaakov Hagiz, Zichron l'Vnai Yisrael, #13, in *YHvT*, p. 41)

> **22:2:2:3** Whenever you give *tzedaka*, fall down before your Creator and say a short prayer that the Master of Mercy pardon, forgive, and atone the sins and transgressions and misdeeds you have done from the day you set foot on the earth until today. And pray that in His great kindness He join your soul to His service, and make your eyes shine with His *mitzvot*, and unify your heart to love and fear His great, mighty, and awesome Name. And pray that He find you worthy to learn His Torah in holiness, and to teach it to the Children of Israel, to keep, perform, and fulfill all the ordinances of His will. (Zichron l'Vnai Yisrael, #14 in *YHvT*, p. 41)

22:3 *KAVVANAH*—INTENTION IN RECEIVING

22:3:1 The Besht:

> When a rich person gives *tzedaka* he does a *mitzvah* . . . but when a poor person accepts *tzedaka*, at first glance it seems that he is not doing a *mitzvah*. But if the poor person receives it with this

kavvanah . . . that, "If I have to take, I am going to do so to give merit to the rich person who gives me the *tzedaka*," then he is doing a *mitzvah*. This is what our Sages, of blessed memory, said: "More than what the householder does for the poor person, the poor person does for the householder" [Leviticus *Rabbah* 34:10]. (*Keter Shem Tov*, p. 109)

22:3:2 Rabbi Zusya of Hanipol:

Certainly the one giving *tzedaka* can give for the sake of the *mitzvah*, and to unite the Holy One, blessed be He, with His *Shechinah*. But the Torah spurs on the one who receives the *tzedaka*, so that his taking should also be for the sake of the *mitzvah*. (*Menorat Zahav*, p. 63)

Giving the *tzedaka* for the sake of God is not so extraordinary. What is extraordinary is when the poor person, in receiving the *tzedaka*, thinks not primarily of his benefit, but . . . of serving God, blessed be He. And he should think that God is the one who is indeed giving this to him, and when he accepts the *tzedaka* he should think of his intention of him benefiting the person giving, by giving him a chance to do good. (*Menorat Zahav*, pp. 63–65)

This teaching applies also to receiving favors and other kinds of help. And though not many of us will have occasion to receive charity, all of us accept help from others. (See "Trust in God," 8:9 and 8:10.)

22:4 TITHE

22:4:1 Give a tithe of all your money [the capital], and from all the money that you make. (*Derech Hayim* 2–13)

22:4:2 Take out a tithe of all the money you earn. (Rabbi Moshe Teitelbaum, *Hanhagot Tzaddikim*, p. 51, #50)

22:4:3 The tithe is a *mitzvah*. The particular point of these two teachings is to make it a practice to set aside the money as it is earned.

22:5 A SPECIAL PURSE

22:5:1 Be careful about everything concerned with charity and give as much as you can, according to your ability. Have a special

> purse just for charity money. Take a tithe from all your savings, and afterwards give a tithe of everything you earn (after your own expenses). Put this money in the purse, which you should not use for yourself at all. Whenever you have occasion to give charity to the poor or to needy sages . . . give it from this purse.[1] (Rabbi Shmelke of Nikolsburg, his *hanhagot* in *Shemen ha-Tov*, p. 50)

22:5:2 In *Erech Apayim*, in the list of personal *hanhagot* of the author:

> I commit myself to try in every way to do more and more *hesed* [deeds of kindness], and not to turn away a poor man. To this end I will make it a rule to try as much as possible always to have money with me that has already been set aside for *tzedaka* and *hesed*, which will not be used for my own needs, but which will be on my person at all times. (p. 77)

22:6 A *PUSHKE*

22:6:1 Have a charity box [*pushke*] on a table in your house, so that throughout the day, and at specified times (see 22:8) you can give *tzedaka* and acquire the habit of giving frequently.

22:6:2 Have a charity box in your house, and label it as such, so that people who visit you can give some charity. If someone needy visits you, you can give him some of that money.

22:7 TRAIN YOUR HAND TO GIVE

22:7:1 A hasid once told his *rebbe* that he had a certain amount of money to give as charity and he asked him whether he should give it as a lump sum, or distribute it in smaller amounts. His *rebbe* told him to do the latter so that he would train his hand to give. (Source unknown)

22:7:2 There is a story of Rabbi Nachman of Bratzlav as a boy training himself in a somewhat similar way:

> As a young child, he would often take several silver coins and have them exchanged for coppers. He would then secretly enter the synagogue through the window, taking along his copy of [the prayer

book] *Shaarey Tzion.* He would then joyfully recite the prayer, *LeShem Yichud* ["For the sake of the unification of the Holy One, blessed be He, and His *Shechinah,* etc."], petitioning that the elements of God's Name be united through the good deed he was about to do. As soon as he finished the prayer, he would take one copper and place it in the charity box for anonymous donors. He would then distract himself, as if he had completed the deed and was ready to leave. Then suddenly, he would begin again. He would say the *LeShem Yichud* a second time and deposit another copper in the almsbox. He would then distract himself again and repeat the process. The Rebbe would do this again and again until he had placed every single copper in the donation box, each time repeating the *LeShem Yichud.* In this very simple and unsophisticated manner, he would perform not one, but many *mitzvos* with a single silver coin. (*Rabbi Nachman's Wisdom,* p. 13, Shevachey HaRan, #13)

22:7:3 The Holy Jew [Rabbi Yaakov Yitzhak of Pshischa] said that a person should train himself to be good-hearted and giving. Start with something small. For example, accustom yourself to giving others a little of your snuff tobacco; then do a little more, like letting them enjoy the use of your pipe, and so on by degrees, until gradually you are in the habit of being generous. (*Niflaot ha-Yehudi,* p. 58)

22:8 SET TIMES

22:8:1 Before eating give something for *tzedaka.* (Rabbi David ha-Levi of Steppin, *Hanhagot Tzaddikim,* p. 56, #19)

22:8:2 Before sex give something for charity, putting it into the special purse; do everything for the sake of heaven. (Rabbi David ha-Levi of Steppin, *Hanhagot Tzaddikim,* p. 56, #21)

22:8:3 Before prayer give something for *tzedaka,* and put it all in the special *tzedaka* purse. (Rabbi David ha-Levi of Steppin, *Hanhagot Tzaddikim,* p. 56, #20)

22:8:4 Give as much charity as you can, and give every day and before you pray. (Rabbi Aaron of Karlin, *Hanhagot Tzaddikim,* p. 4, #4)

22:8:5 Rabbi Yehiel Michal of Zlotchov says the same thing about giving before prayer, and adds:

> On *Shabbat* and *Yom Tov* [when you cannot touch money], state verbally what you will give, and give after the day. (*Hanhagot Tzaddikim*, p. 52, #7)

> **22:8:6** At the time of *Minha* give *tzedaka* before you pray. *Erev Shabbat* and *Erev Yom Tov* give double the amount. (Megaleh Amukot, by Rabbi Hayim Liberzohn, p. 17)

> **22:8:7** Before going on a journey, give some charity. (*Shulchan Aruch*, chap. 68)

22:9 GIVE WHENEVER YOU SPEND

We are told in the *Midrash* about Rabbi Tanhum:

> If he was going to buy one liter of meat, he would purchase two liters instead: one portion for himself and one portion for the poor.

A practice such as this can be adapted. You can, for example, give some charity whenever you spend any money on yourself. If you carry a special *tzedaka* purse with you, you can put this money in it. (*Kohelet Rabba* 7-2)

23

Speech

23:1 Speech is a world in itself, and many of the most important aspects of our lives are lived through speech. Whole books have been written about how to speak as a Jew should speak. The Torah teaches about the ethical dimensions of speech and how we should not tell lies, slander others, and so on. Frequently, in lists of *hanhagot*, one will be found that names these aspects of speech one after another, and says to be careful about them. For example:

> Stay far away from slander and lies and from flattery and informing and mockery, and also from idle conversation, and certainly from lewd talk, even between husband and wife. (Rabbi David ha-Levi of Steppin, *Hanhagot Tzaddikim*, p. 56, #23)

In a more general sense the goal of virtuous speech is given in the wisdom books of the Torah in such sayings as Proverbs 2:18: "There is one whose sharp words are like sword thrusts; but the speech of the wise is healing."

Most of us know people who fit the first half of this verse; happy are they who have met some whose speech fulfills the second half, for there are such holy people.

Along with the ethical side, the hasidic *rebbes* also emphasized teachings about purity in speech, and the avoidance of speech about unclean things or the use of unclean expressions.

> Never let anything unclean or ugly cross your lips, not even the word for excrement. (*Derech Hayim*, 5–16)

> Let nothing unclean be heard on your lips, such as the names of various kinds of idolatry . . . and let nothing lewd or licentious be heard from your mouth, as for example, mentioning prostitutes or similar things. (*Sefer ha-Yirah* of Rabbeinu Yonah, p. 200)

One should not only avoid undesirable types of speech, but more positively:

> You should make it a habit always to intermingle in your conversation something connected with a *mitzvah*, or some Torah or words of *musar*, in order to sanctify your speech. (Rabbi Natan Netta of Shinovi, *Hanhagot Tzaddikim* [III], vol. 1, p. 268, #10)

Not only is the content of speech important, but also how it is delivered. Many hasidic *rebbes* taught that you should speak softly and quietly, with humility. Rabbi Rafael of Bershad specifically emphasized that the tone of your voice should be gentle:

> He would teach us to be careful even about the tone of our voice. For example, if you have to tell someone in your family not to do something, you should not speak in an angry or strict tone, but softly and gently. And he would remind us of what is written in the Ramban's Letter, that all your speech with your fellow man should be spoken gently. (*Midrash Pinhas*, p. 40, #32)

(See "Anger," 37:1 for more about this.)

23:2 *D'VEKUT*

There is still another hasidic goal connected with speech, and it is that during conversation you should maintain your consciousness of God. This is always considered one of the most difficult attainments.

> You should see to it that every day you separate yourself for some time to be alone with God, with your mind just on Him, and draw

> on yourself fear of Him due to His greatness. Become accustomed to doing this until you reach the level where even when you speak with someone else you will not forget the Creator, blessed be He. (Rabbi Hayim Heikel of Amdur, *Hanhagot Tzaddikim*, p. 43)

Controling speech and maintaining *d'vekut* is so difficult that some pious people, in order to achieve holiness, almost give up talking. One hasidic story tells of how a hasid of the Holy Jew (Rabbi Yaakov Yitzhak of Pshischa) decided not to talk at all except when absolutely necessary, and to speak only words of Torah and prayer. He kept this up for three years until:

> His holy master, the Holy Jew of Pshischa, sent a message with some hasidim that he should come to him. So he traveled to Pshischa, and when he arrived close to the city at dusk, he came across his *rebbe*, the Holy Jew, who had gone out for a walk in the countryside with some disciples. When the hasid saw his master he jumped out of the carriage and ran to him to receive the greeting of peace. But when the Holy Jew greeted him, he said, "Young man, why don't I see any of your words?" [With his spiritual sight he did not see that this hasid had any hold in the World of Speech.] He answered simply, "Why should I speak unnecessarily? Isn't it better instead just to speak words in learning Torah and praying?" But his holy master responded, "If that's the situation, prepare a pipe for yourself, and get enough tobacco for the whole night; come to me after the Evening Prayers and I'll teach you how to speak." And he sat with him the whole night, teaching him how to speak. After this, he began to talk again. (*Ohel Elimelech*, p. 72, #172)

There are various ways to approach the goal of God-consciousness in conversation. On the one hand, due attention to the religious and ethical aspects of your speech and to its purity while you are engaged in conversation is certainly a service of God and a demanding one. Moreover, it can be a method of maintaining awareness of God. But the hasidic methods also include those that are more direct.

23:2:1 For a method which is direct but also "negative" in aspect, see the quote in Chapter 1, p. 12 that when you speak about worldly things, you should be like a man who leaves home and is thinking continually about when he will be able to return—to the Upper World with God. This kind of consciousness during speech will itself keep your mind on God.

23:2:2 A more positive approach is that when you talk to people you should somehow talk to, or before, God.

23:2:2:1 When you want to maintain your God-consciousness while talking with others, see to it that everything you say is directed to God; you can also think that all the words you speak are coming to you from God who gives you the power of speech [more about this below]—and as a result you will not forget God when you converse. (*Darkei Tzedek*, p. 4, #16)

23:2:2:2 The light of the living God rests above your head; so be silent in your awe of Him. When you speak, speak with Him and let the one who is listening [the person you are talking to] hear [by the way]. This way you will be able to cleave to Him, blessed be He, always in *d'vekut*. (*Sefer Haredim*, chap. 66, #14)

23:2:2:3 When you speak with your fellow man, let your intention be to speak with your Creator. (*Sefer Haredim*, chap. 66, #118)

23:2:2:4 You should also make it a practice, when you ask any favor of another person, that you have it in your mind as you ask that you are asking God.

This was the level of the earlier *tzaddikim*, and also of Daniel. See Rashi on Daniel 4:16 where, though Daniel ostensibly is speaking to Nebuchadnezzar, he is really directing a prayer to God. This is also what is said about Nehemiah, where he says "and so I prayed"—all these words were spoken to God and not to the king [see below]. And so too in the *Gemara* [*Avodah Zarah* 16b], the story in which Rabbi Eliezer, when brought before the court, says: "I have complete trust in the Judge." He was speaking to the Roman judge but directed his words to God.

And this is a very great thing, and a high level, and its attainment requires much practice. (*Darkei Tzedek*, p. 4, #17)

23:2:2:5 The Besht said that:

When talking to your friend, and just speaking about this and that, at the same time you should be doing unifications [meditations that unite the upper and lower worlds[1]]. The Maharsha, in his interpretation [on *Rosh HaShanah* 3b] said that when Nehemiah was conversing with the king Artahshasta, he was with these same words really praying to God, blessed be He. (*Sefer Baal Shem Tov al ha-Torah*, vol. 1, p. 253)

In *Rosh HaShanah* 3b, Nehemiah 2:5 is translated/interpreted as: "So I prayed to the God of Heaven, and I said to the King [of the Universe]." He seemingly spoke the words to the king Artahshasta, but his intention when he made his request was to speak to God, the King of the Universe.

23:2:2:6 Another method of attaining God-consciousness during conversation is to turn every topic, at least for yourself, to God, and be reminded of God and His service in everything spoken about:

> It is a good spiritual practice to "go upward" [to raise each thing to its spiritual root Above] when speaking with others. When the people you are with are talking about something connected with some kind of love for example, you should turn your mind to love of God, and think of how you should love only Him, blessed be He; or when the talk is about wealth, you should think here too that it is from God that wealth comes to a man, and so also honor. And do the same when the conversation is about anything relating to beauty, splendor, or glory. So too when the talk is about worldly fears, think that you should fear only God. And so with all other things. You should attend to what is before you, and as a result you will never cease from God-consciousness, even when you are conversing with other people. (*Darkei Tzedek*, p. 3, #15)
>
> Rabbi Israel Baal Shem said: "Sometimes when I am sitting among people who are conversing idly, I first attach myself in *d'vekut* with God, blessed be He, and then I bind all their words with greater attachment [to their spiritual roots]. (*Likkutim Yekarim*, p. 5a)

23:2:2:7 Some *tzaddikim* always saw that their words had some twist toward holiness and carried more than one meaning:

> The essence of the perfection of the *tzaddikim* is that they always have their minds on Him and attached to Him without any separation whatsoever, God forbid. Even when they speak of something about their worldly needs, they direct and form their speech so that they will not be separated from Him, God forbid. Their words are chosen to carry two meanings and to arouse some fear of God or *d'vekut* or unification. So too with what he hears from someone talking to him, he also understands his words as if they were holy words. . . . You have to teach yourself to be able to speak in your ordinary speech in a way that you are not separated from your *d'vekut*. (From *Divrei Moshe*; found in *Lev Sameah ha-Hadash*, p. 73, n. 1 and *Derech Emunah u'Maaseh Rav*, p. 31)

An example of speech with two meanings is this story about Rabbi Hayim of Tzanz:

> His daughter . . . died during his lifetime and on the first *Shabbat* after the seven days of mourning he asked that some English porter be brought to the table and he drank some of it. Then he said, "People say that porter is bitter. But the truth is that it's not bitter, it's just strong." And he repeated these words a number of times with great fervor. Everyone understood that he was speaking about the bitter experience he had gone through and was saying that everything is for good and not bad. (*Mekor Hayim*, p. 22, #63)

23:2:3 There are many stories of *tzaddikim* in great *d'vekut* while they seemingly engage in worldly conversation. Here is one report about the hasidic *rebbe*, Rabbi David Biderman of Lelov-Jerusalem (d. 1917):

> The *gaon* Rabbi Mordechai Girsh, the head of Yeshivah Hasdei Avot in Hebron and the leader of the *rebbe's* people there, said: "I have seen many *tzaddikim*, but another *tzaddik* like Rebbe Reb David'l I have not seen—a *tzaddik* who is in *d'vekut* with God even when he converses about insignificant matters. For I have seen him when he was talking about worldly matters of no import, and yet an inner conflagration was bursting out of him—his limbs were trembling and the arteries of his head were swelling up and sticking out, and his heart was pounding like a drum—from his supernal fear of God. (*Tiferet Beit David*, p. 104)

23:2:4 So far the teachings quoted have been mostly about speaking; but of course hearing is the other half of the world of speech.

The Besht:

> In all the . . . world there is nothing but the Light of the Infinite One, blessed be He, which is hidden within all things. And all the verses, such as "There is none but Him" and "I fill heaven and earth"—are to be understood according to their literal meaning that there is no act or speech or thought whose essence is not the Godliness that is hidden and contracted within it.
>
> So when one looks well, with his mind's eye, on all the things before his eyes, on their inner essence and their vitality, and not their surface and external side alone, he will not see anything but the Divine power within them, which gives them their vitality, brings them into being, and preserves them each and every minute.

And when he listens well to the inner voice which is within the material voice and sound that his ears hear, he will not hear anything other than the voice of God, which enlivens and brings into being, that very minute, the sound he hears. (Hadrachot ha-Besht, end of *Divrei Shmuel* [The teachings of Rabbi Shmuel of Slonim])

23:2:5 It is a hasidic practice to understand all things that happen to you (and everything that happens to you is from God) as a hint or message from God. This is particularly true of words spoken to you, regardless of how the speaker intends them. (This is briefly mentioned at the end of the quote from *Divrei Moshe* in 23:2:2:7.)

23:2:5:1 How should we understand the verse "A voice in the desert cries out: Clear the way of the Lord!" [Isaiah 40:3]? In every word you hear another speaking, even from ordinary people, from there too it is a voice calling out: "Clear the way to serve the Lord!"[2] So in what you hear there will also be something from God. And you should believe with perfect faith that everything that happens to you comes about through the Divine Providence of the Creator of the world, who has brought this to you, to hear these very words and no others, on this day and no other.

There is a time for every thing and for every purpose, and it is not in vain that God sent these words for you to hear, now and not on another day, to you and not to someone else. Because the thing is for *you* and it is for you to fix something spiritual here, not for someone else; that is why it was sent to you.

It is explained in the holy books that the way of the *tzaddikim* in all the things that they are involved in, is to separate out the holy sparks [focus on the spiritual aspect and separate out good from evil and holy from profane]. They see in every place the glory of God, for the whole world is full of His glory, and there is no place where he is not. So whenever people speak to them, even when ordinary people speak to them about ordinary and this-worldly things, the *tzaddikim* hear just the spiritual lesson for their own selves, whatever they can take from what they hear. (*DhTvhY*, II pp. 36b–37a, Dibbur #24 and 25; the first of these quotes is taken from *Or ha-Meir*, Beshallach, and the second from *Divrei Hayim*, Mikaitz)

23:2:5:2 When you merit to bend your ears to truly hear all the speech in the world, you will hear that all of it is crying out to you and giving you hints to return to Him, blessed be He, for from all the things and words in this world the glory of God cries out. . . . And when you accustom yourself to hear, in everything spoken, just the inside, the voice of God within it, the light of your soul will shine on you with the light of understanding, with an awesome and wonderful illumination. [*Tikkun Kriat Sh'ma al ha-Mitah mai ha-Arizal*, Bratzlav, p. 81)

23:2:5:3 There is no speech from which you cannot hear the voice of instruction in how to serve God, even in words spoken in the marketplace when one person speaks to another about buying and selling. . . . Perhaps this was a hint of David, in the psalm where he says, "I will hear what God says," that is, even from the words spoken in the marketplace. (*DhTvhY*, III p. 77, Tochachat Musar #1, from *Or ha-Meir*)

23:2:5:4 There are various hasidic stories that illustrate how the *tzaddikim* would hear the voice of God in what was spoken to them, or even overheard by them. Here are three examples:

23:2:5:4:1 The holy rabbi, the Rebbe Reb Elimelech of Lizensk, and his brother, the holy rabbi, Rebbe Reb Zusya [of Hanipol], were wandering for a number of years "in exile," sharing the fate of the Divine Presence which is in exile, so as to heal the spiritual breach in the world.

Once, they arrived in a certain village, and though the head of the village wasn't in his house, his wife took them in as guests. When her husband came home in the middle of the night, he lit a candle on the table as he worked to mend a rip in his fur coat.

The two brothers who were in bed but awake, heard how his wife called to him saying, "Hurry up and fix the coat while the candle is still burning." And one brother said to the other, "Did you hear what the lady of the house is saying to her husband?"

This is a great teaching, to fix yourself quickly and repent while your soul is still within you. (*Siah Sarfei Kodesh*, II, p. 80, #260)

23:2:5:4:2 Once, when the Holy Jew was taking a walk in the countryside with his disciples, they came across a hay wagon that had overturned. The gentile driver called out to them to help him put it upright and reload the hay. They went to his aid, but try as they could, they were not able to turn it over. "We can't do it," they said. But the gentile yelled at them angrily in Polish, "You can all right, but you don't want to!" Then the Holy Jew turned to his disciples and said, "Do you hear what this gentile is saying? He says we can lift up the *Shechinah* from the dust, but we don't want to." (*Sichot Hayim*, p. 9)

23:2:5:4:3 The holy Rabbi Moshe Leib of Sassov, of blessed memory, was, as a young man, very poor (may the Merciful One save us), and his house was next door to someone whose business was to travel to the market on market day. Once, his neighbor's compassion was aroused over the sad state of the holy rabbi and he said that he should come with him to market day and stand by his merchandise so it would not be stolen. For his trouble he would pay him enough to feed his family for the week. The holy rabbi agreed. But when he arrived in the city early in the morning, he went to the *Beit Midrash* to pray with a congregation, and he stayed so long in prayer that when he returned, the merchant, seeing that he would be no use to him at all in this job, did not give him any of the money he had promised him.

When the holy rabbi came home and his wife and children found out that he did not bring back any money at all, they cried out, "You didn't bring back anything from market day?" Hearing this the holy rabbi fell on the ground and began sobbing loudly. When they asked him why he was crying, he said, "Why shouldn't I cry? Wasn't I at the market for just one day, and you asked me 'What have you brought back?' But what about the other market day—that they sent me here from Above—and I've been here for twenty-five years. When I return they'll demand, 'What have you brought back with you?'—and I won't be able to answer them. Why shouldn't I cry?" (*Siftei Kodesh*, p. 84)

23:2:5:4:4 See the teaching of the Baal Shem Tov quoted in "Repentance," 14:5:3, where "hearing of the hints" is mentioned, along with related matters; 14:6 has other stories of this kind.

23:2:5:4:5 Even hearing the messages from heaven requires intelligence and discrimination. A hasidic story tells how a *misnagid* once came before Rabbi Shneur Zalman of Ladi and rebuked him for his supposedly haughty ways, in having a servant standing at his door, and so on. The *rebbe* put his head down on his hand on the table, and stayed that way for some time. Then he lifted his head and answered the man, explaining how a leader has to maintain some separation from the people. The explanation was, indeed, accepted, and the man left; but when he did, the *rebbe*'s son asked him why he had put his head on his arm like that, because for the answer he gave that [degree of meditation and concentration] was not necessary. His father then told him that at first he had to know if this man (regardless of his own motives) was delivering to him a heavenly message criticizing him for pride. So he put his head down to consider if there was pride and haughtiness in his actions. When he saw that there was not, he realized that this was not such a heavenly message and he answered what he answered. (*Sippurei Hasidim*, vol. 1, p. 354)

23:2:6 A great rabbi and *tzaddik* of our time has said that he feels that methods of direct God-consciousness in conversation (such as those discussed above) make it seem as if talking to people is not in itself good enough—but it is.

Perhaps one reconciliation of the two attitudes is to take the view that the person you are speaking to is in the image of God, or (much the same) a son or daughter of God, and that you should speak to him or her with the greatest love and reverence. As it says in *Or ha-Ganuz l'Tzaddikim*:

> You should speak with your fellow-man with great reverence and love, as if you were speaking with the Holy One, blessed be He [p. 31]. When you see any person, imagine the Being of God and His effulgent light flooding through him to you [p. 62].

When you see the fellow human you are conversing with as closely connected to God, you can talk with *him* with reverence and love, and yet maintain your awareness of *God*.

Rabbi Mordechai of Tchernobil suggested something like this also:

> The main thing is to believe with perfect faith that the Glory [*Shechinah*] of God fills all the earth, and there is no place where He is not. And when you look at the world you are looking at God, blessed be He. And when you converse with someone, you are conversing with the soul within him (for were the soul to leave his body you would not be able to talk to him at all, for he would be as lifeless as a stone). [So] you are conversing with the soul within him—it is just that you cannot see it, just as you cannot see God, Who is the soul of all souls. So you should believe this, and say to yourself: "He is here and present—I just cannot see him." (*Likkutei Torah*, Hadracha 6, p. 7)

(See the chapters on "Humility and Pride," 38:3 and "Loving and Honoring Our Fellow Men" [9].)

23:3 THE SPEECH OF THE WISE IS HEALING

As in the quote from Proverbs (23:1), our speech should not only be ethical but healing. We should train our tongues to speak well of others and to be accustomed to give blessings.

23:3:1 When we hear of others' worthy hopes or plans, we should bless them that God fulfill their wishes for good. (See "Pious Phrases," 26:11 for an example.)

23:3:2 Whenever you mention someone, anyone, in conversation, make it a habit to bless him, with a good eye and a good heart. (*Derech Hayim*, 7–8)

23:3:3 When you praise someone for his wisdom or his children, or speak about his great wealth, etc., you must then give him a blessing, to ward off the evil eye. (Rabbi Hayim Yosef David Azulai, *Hanhagot Tzaddikim*, p. 67, #15)

Regardless of what people in former times understood by the "evil eye," what it can mean to us in this instance is that praise arouses in the mind its opposite, or sometimes jealousy—and to ward this off we should bless the person we praise.

23:3:4 Be careful never to speak against the Jewish people; never say that a certain Jewish custom is no good, or any other bad thing, God forbid. But rather accustom your tongue always to speak good about the people Israel, and in their defense. (*Derech Hayim*, 7–43)

23:3:5:1 You should refrain from speaking derogatorily of any man, and even of any creature or animal. (Rabbi Moshe Cordovero, in the list of his *hanhagot*, #7, in *Reshit Hochmah*, H. Y. Walman edition, Jerusalem, vol. 1, p. 50)

23:3:5:2 Never speak derogatorily of any creature of God, not even a cow or a wild animal or birds. (*Derech Hayim*, 7–44)

23:4 FROM ONE SOURCE

It is a very high level when talking with another person to consider it as if you are talking with yourself, as if the conversation was all within one mind and self. For all souls have their root in the *Shechinah.* This is another way of maintaining *d'vekut* in speech (see 23:2:2:1). And if you do this you will not be as critical of what the other person says (a very common tendency and failing), and you will not disagree as readily and get angry.

It should be as if the thought the other person speaks had arisen in your own mind; then, even if it seems wrong or strange, your response will be sympathetic even in disagreement.

The Baal Shem Tov:

> When you speak, do not think that you are the one speaking—because it is the Divine life-energy within you, God, blessed be He, speaking in you. And by this [awareness] you lift up the act of speech to its Source. And equanimity is also included in this reflection; for just as everything you speak is from Him, blessed be He, so is everything that your fellow man speaks from Him. (*Tzavaat ha-Ribash*, p. 21)
>
> [To clarify the comment about equanimity:] You should have equanimity in whatever happens; everything should be equal to you, as in the matter of whether men praise you or abuse you. . . . And whatever occurs, say to yourself, "Isn't this from Him? And if it's acceptable in His eyes [certainly it should be so in mine]." (*Tzavaat ha-Ribash*, p. 2)

23:5 BEGINNINGS

Each day make a special effort with the first words you speak to another person, that they be spoken with the right awareness. And make a special effort with the first words of every conversation, to begin the right way.

23:6 AT PEACE

In Hebrew a conversation opens and closes with the blessing of peace (*Shalom*). So at the beginning and end of a conversation you should see that you are in the right relation with the other person.

The previous Lubavitcher Rebbe, Rabbi Yosef Yitzchak Schneersohn, after lamenting how too often today the *Shalom* exchanged in greeting is not what it once was, writes:

> But the Torah-inspired *Shalom Aleichem*—the *Shalom Aleichem* of bygone days—is a vehicle for the light of love. (*Likkutei Dibburim*, vol. 1, p. 4)

When you begin a conversation, make your opening a blessing in your intention, regardless of the expression used in greeting.

During a conversation there can be tension and offense (often without either party being fully aware of it). Knowing this, speak words of parting that reestablish the right relationship: say words of blessing or peace and, if necessary, at the end of the conversation, also humbly ask forgiveness in case of any offense. (See "Pious Phrases," 26:20.)

23:7 AFTERWARD

After a conversation it is good to go over in your mind the quality of your speech—and repair what needs fixing.

23:8 CONTROLLING YOUR SPEECH

Control over your speech is essential in holiness.

> **23:8:1** Never let anything be uttered by you unless you know that it is the will of God that you say it. (*Derech Hayim*, 2–17)

> **23:8:2** Twice a week you should have a set period for reflection and meditation on how you should be as careful in giving out words as in giving out money. (*Hayei Musar*, III, p. 89)

23:8:3 Just as it is good to gain control of your eating through interruptions, so is the same true about speech and conversation. In Chapter 3, pp. 60–61 we quoted how Rabbi Mendel of Premishlan "in the midst of a conversation would interrupt himself and stop for a while to break his talk-lust."

Along the same lines, it is possible to have a "fast" of words and speech, just as you can fast from food.

> It is better to fast by abstaining from talk than by abstaining from food—for when you fast from talking it will not hurt your body or your soul, and it will not weaken you [causing you to lessen your Divine service]. (*Rosh ha-Givah* quoted in *Or Yesharim*, p. 90)

> [Rabbi Moshe of Kobrin said:] Rather than fasting from *Shabbat* to *Shabbat* [as very pious people would sometimes do], it is better to fast from lies and untruths, and not speak a false word from one *Shabbat* to the next. (*Mazkeret Shem ha-Gedolim*, p. 196)

These two quotes should be considered as practical suggestions.

A fast of speech can be more or less strict. The Hafetz Hayim occasionally instructed people to engage in such a fast and "not speak during that day at all, except what is absolutely necessary" (*Michtivei ha-Hafetz Hayim ha-Hadash*, vol. 2, III, p. 74, #7). Another source, however, says:

> The difficulty involved in [a fast of speech] is that one must put a rein on one's mouth to refrain from speaking even about one's needs, and to be even more careful not to speak unnecessary things, and still more careful about entirely idle conversation. That day, you should use your speech only for Torah and prayer. (Rabbi Yitzhak Alfiyah, *Hanhagot Tzaddikim* [III], vol. 2, p. 836, #9)

23:8:4 Control of speech implies the avoidance not only of forbidden talk (lies, etc.), but of idle conversation.

> **23:8:4:1** As much as possible, avoid idle conversation. This was one of the ten pious customs of Rav [a famous rabbi of the Talmud], who in all of his life never talked idly. (Rabbi Moshe Cordovero, in the list of his *hanhagot*, #23, *Reshit Hochmah*, Walman edition p. 50)

> **23:8:4:2** There is nothing so good for purifying the soul as keeping a rein over your mouth and eschewing idle conversation. Not only is this the case, but it aids greatly in having *kavvanah* in prayer, as alien thoughts do not intrude and distract you.
>
> There is a story of a hasid who, after his death, appeared to his wife in a dream, and seeing the hair of his head and beard all aglow like a torch, in his glory, she asked him, "By what did you merit all this?" He answered that it was because he spoke as little as possible of things other than Torah and the fear of God—for the Holy One,

blessed be He, is sure to care for those who exert themselves to avoid profane talk. (*Kav ha-Yashar*, chap. 12)

23:8:4:3 Rabbi Tzvi Elimelech of Dinov:

> Keep yourself from empty conversation . . . and all the more so from forbidden speech. If you get involved in one or the other, fine or penalize yourself somehow and meditate immediately on turning back to God, and confess. (*Hanhagot Adam*, #20)

(See "Psalms," 16:15 about "fixing" sins of speech with holy speech, by words of Torah or the recitation of Psalms.)

> **23:8:4:4** Watch over your mouth and your speech, for this is an important fence in the service of God. Therefore, be very careful not to speak unnecessarily, and . . . each time you speak improperly or to no purpose, fine yourself and give something to *tzedaka*. (Rabbi Yaakov Hagiz, Zichron l'Vnai Yisrael #1 and 2, in *YHvT*, p. 38)

> **23:8:4:5** Rabbi Yosi Ber of Brisk always had a snuffbox on his table. When he was about to converse with someone, he would first open it up, glance within, and then begin to talk. One of those close to him could not overcome his curiosity, and took a look inside, where he found engraved the abbreviation W.K.H.M.A.T.K.H.F.T. Not knowing what this meant, he asked the rabbi about it, who told him: "It is from the verse of Scripture: '*W*hoso *k*eeps *h*is *m*outh *a*nd *t*ongue, *k*eeps *h*imself *f*rom *t*rouble'" [Proverbs 21:23]. (*Midor Dor*, vol. 2, #1619)

23:8:4:6 Although there is great value in avoiding idle talk, there is still a time to talk and a time to listen—for human brotherhood can be established through speech, and conversation can be a vessel for love. The rabbis say that when you are burdened with anxieties you should talk over your troubles with another and get them out. The Seer of Lublin said:

> You should receive every person with warmth, and bear his yoke, and treat him with gentleness, as if he were your king. It is part of human kindness to listen to him talk, even if he overdoes it; but at the very same time you should not forget the Creator, blessed be He, at all. (*Zot Zichron*, p. 3)

> Here is a story about the great *musar* teacher, Rabbi Israel Salanter:

Once our master and teacher and rabbi had a conversation with one of his relatives about worldly things, and he was speaking with him in a jovial way. One of his students, who was a God-fearing person, overheard the drift of this conversation and it seemed to him that the rabbi was talking needlessly. So later he spoke with him about the subject of avoiding idle conversation, and dared to ask him about the conversation with that man.

Our master, in his humility, did not take umbrage at the question, but answered him, telling him that this person was very depressed, and it was very much an act of kindness to try to cheer him up and remove his anxiety and sadness. "And," said Rabbi Israel, "with what could I bring him some joy—by talking with him about the fear of God and *musar*? No, the only way was to talk with him in a pleasant and amusing manner about things of this world."

From this story we can judge how carefully our rabbi weighed all his words in the scale of the fear of God. (*Or Yisrael*, p. 112)

23:9 CONTROLLING WHAT YOU HEAR

It takes intelligence and determination to control, to the extent possible, what you hear.

23:9:1 About Rabbi Shlomo Leib of Lentshno:

He never engaged in any idle conversation. Even from his youth he was careful to guard himself against hearing idle talk and, even more so, bad talk, God forbid.

When he was young, he was living with a tailor, and he never came back to the house until all were asleep. Once, during the winter, it happened that they closed the *Beit Midrash* for some reason and [not being able to stay there to study and pray] he was forced to return home.

When he approached the house, however, he heard the tailor, as usual, still at work with his young helpers, and, also as usual, they were talking about indecent and unclean things. As a result, Rabbi Shlomo did not go in, but stayed outside walking this way and that, for it was very cold outside. He became so cold that he almost died, and he lay down on the earth from weakness; but in spite of this he still would not go in—for he was determined that he would not hear idle conversation. And when he lay down that way, a miracle occurred and the one candle they had inside went out, so they were forced to finish for the night and go to sleep. Seeing this he went in.

> "And from then on," said the holy rabbi, "my ears developed the ability to hear what people are whispering even at far distances." (*Eser Atarot*, p. 21, #3)

Rabbi Shlomo Leib himself refrained from inappropriate speech, and did everything possible to avoid hearing it from others. What is one to do, however, if one does hear such things?

Rabbi Uri of Strelisk said:

> "You should guard your ears more so than all your other senses, even though what you hear is not completely in your control and sometimes something which damages your soul, God forbid, will penetrate into your ear. The main way to deal with this is to pray to God that it not damage you; then, certainly, it will not have any bad effect at all. This is a general principle, that you should pray to God that a [spiritually] hurtful thing not cause you harm." (*Imrei Kodesh ha-Shalem*, p. 15, #40)

23:10 WHAT TO TALK ABOUT

The best use of speech is to talk always about God, about Torah, about holy people, and about holy ways and good deeds.

> When you converse about wicked people you can, as a result, have thoughts of wickedness and draw evil into the world, God forbid; you should rather talk always about the good traits and deeds of the *tzaddikim*, and so bring good into the world. (*Darkei Tzedek*, p. 6, #40)

24

Song and Dance—The Service of Joy

24:1 Rabbi Eleazar Azikri says that love is the greatest service of God, and that:

> One of the main expressions of fervent love is that the lover sings songs of love—so should we sing before God. (*Sefer Haredim*, chap. 34).
>
> It is the way of one who loves passionately to sing. Since the love of our Creator is so great, even beyond the love of women, someone who loves Him with all his heart will sing before Him as sang Moses and the Children of Israel, and Miriam and Deborah and Joshua, and the sons of Korach, and David and Solomon, all with the holy spirit. (*Sefer Haredim*, chap. 9, #6)

24:2 When you sing a religious song, sing it before and for God, not for yourself or for others.

> "Then sang Moses and the Children of Israel this song for God" (Exodus 15:1). "For God" they sang it, and not for flesh and blood. (*Midrash ha-Gadol*)

However, it is also true that you will often, in a sense, first have to sing to your own soul (though also before God), to inspire yourself, before you can sing to God. As King David says in Psalms: "Bless the Lord, O my soul!"[1] (See 24:7.)

Although you sing for God, yet through song your soul can cleave to the soul of your fellow man, and one can raise up the other.

Rabbi Pinhas of Koretz:

> When a person sings and cannot lift up his voice, and another comes to help with his raised voice, then he too can lift his voice in song. This occurs because of the secret of the *d'vekut* of spirit to spirit. (*Midrash Pinhas*, p. 28, #36)

> **24:3** Hasidism sees the *niggun* [melody] as one of the branches of Divine service—as a way to show love of God, and to bind oneself to Him with cords of love and joy. (*Ish ha-Pele*, p. 69)

The Talmud:

> Which is the service of joy and happiness?—that is song. (*Arachin* 11)

It was the Baal Shem Tov who opened up the gates of hasidic music before his disciples and hasidim.

> "Through music," he once said, "you can reach joy and *d'vekut* with the Infinite One, blessed be He." (*Ish ha-Pele*, p. 69)

24:4 Rabbi Zusya of Hanipol, in his great love for God, served Him with song:

> When the holy Rabbi Zusya was permitted to join those who fear God, and was accepted as a member of the fellowship of hasidim who attached themselves to the holy teacher, the Great Maggid of Mezritch, he was still young. He would go off to hidden places and to the forest and pour his heart out in songs and praises of God, blessed be He, with fervor and great love and desire and yearning, until the words applied to him, that, "In her love you will be ravished always" (Proverbs 5); for he seemed like someone always wrapped up in his inner thoughts, and abstracted, due to his great *d'vekut* with God, blessed be He and blessed be His name, and from his great yearning to serve Him, may He be blessed and exalted. (*Mazkeret Shem ha-Gedolim*, p. 70)

See the story of Rabbi Zusya whistling for God in "Waking and Beginning the Day," 4:15.

24:5 The following three teachings are from Rabbi Nachman of Bratzlav:

> **24:5:1** Through holy music you can come to the level of prophecy. For the essence of *d'vekut* with God is through melody. (*Likkutei Aytzot*, Neginah, #3)
>
> **24:5:2** Melody and musical instruments have great power with which to draw a person to God, blessed be He. So it is good to accustom yourself to enliven yourself frequently with some melody, to bring yourself to joy, and through this to cleave to God, especially on Sabbaths and holidays. (*Likkutei Aytzot*, Neginah, #11)
>
> **24:5:3** The Rebbe said that it is good to make a habit of inspiring yourself with a melody. There are great concepts included in each holy melody, and they can arouse your heart and draw it toward God. Even if you cannot sing well, you can still inspire yourself with a melody sung to the best of your ability while alone at home. For the loftiness of melody is beyond all measure. (*Rabbi Nachman's Wisdom*, p. 399, *Sichos HaRan*, #273)

A story of Rabbi Shneur Zalman of Ladi illustrates Rabbi Nachman's words about the great concepts in each melody:

> The Ladier noticed an old man among his listeners who obviously did not comprehend the meaning of his discourse. He summoned him to his side and said: "I perceive that my sermon is unclear to you. Listen to this melody and it will teach you how to cleave unto the Lord." The Ladier began to sing a song without words. It was a song of Torah, of trust in God, of longing for the Lord, and of love for Him.
>
> "I understand now what you wish to teach," explained the old man. "I feel an intense longing to be united with the Lord."
>
> The *rebbe*'s melody became part of his every discourse henceforth, although it had no words. (*BeOhalei Habad*, pp. 49–50, quoted in *Hasidic Anthology*, p. 283)

24:5:4 Particularly when you are involved in *mitzvot*, such as Torah study or prayer, your soul within is inspired with the joy of a *mitzvah*. Be awake to that joy; let it out, express it, and expand it, until it becomes song, and even dance.

From the Bratzlaver *Seder ha-Yom*:

> *Joy*—You should accustom yourself to serve God with *niggunim* [melodies] and with joy and with dancing and hand clapping; and especially during the time of Torah study and prayer you should greatly rejoice.

24:5:5 It is wonderful when you can express in song and dance the joy in God you already feel, but it is also true that you can inspire joy in yourself by singing and dancing.

Rabbi Nachman of Bratzlav:

> Through dancing and the movements you make with your body, you awaken joy within yourself. (*Sefer ha-Middot*, Simha, #8)

24:6 It is a way among the hasidim to be happy for no apparent reason. There are many reasons, however, why a Jew who believes in God should be happy. But the point is that you do not need an excuse to sing and dance. This is something important to understand. The hasidim sing and dance spontaneously. You can do this also. For example, while you are studying Torah, or *davvening*, or even just doing some chore—without reason, sing a *niggun*, and if you are inspired, start dancing also. Perhaps you are tired or frustrated or at a low moment and feeling sad—just start singing to God, or dancing. If you are with someone else, take him with you.

> The Holy Grandfather [of Shpola] danced on Sabbaths and holidays—but not just then. Every occasion of a *mitzvah* and of inspiration became a time of ecstatic dancing—even while the fish were frying, when he himself cooked them in honor of the holy Sabbath. (*Ish ha-Pele*, p. 75)

(See 24:12 for a story about the dancing of the Shpola Zeyde on the Sabbath.)

> **24:7** Rabbi Nachman of Kossov [a disciple of the Baal Shem Tov] had a relative whose name was Rabbi Yudel of Tchodinov, and once he was together with Rabbi Nachman in the holy community of Ludmir, where Rabbi Nachman had built a *Beit Midrash* right next to the water; and so the *mikveh* was next to the *Beit Midrash*.
>
> On the morning of the holy *Shabbat* they both went to the *mikveh*. Rabbi Nachman was very quick in everything he did,

and while Rabbi Yudel was still taking off his clothes, Rabbi Nachman had immersed, gone out, dressed, and was already standing before the Ark in the *Beit Midrash* praying the Sabbath Morning Service. When Rabbi Yudel got out of the *mikveh* and was dressing, he could hear Rabbi Nachman, who was right next door, singing "*Ha-Aderet v'ha-Emunah*"—and he became so excited that he ran to the *Beit Midrash* in the middle of dressing, with just his pants and shirt on, and he danced there for two hours. (*Shivhei ha-Besht*, #109)

24:8 From Rabbi Kalonymus Kalman Shapiro, the Peasetzna Rebbe:

A person should make ladders for himself by which he can sometimes go up to heaven. The *niggun* is one such ladder, especially when you sing after experiencing the joy of a *mitzvah*, and with a broken heart. (*Tzav v'Zairuz*, #36)

Elsewhere he speaks about:

The arousal through song, which the hasidim engage in so much . . . The world of song is very high, but we, who are simple people, need just what is for a simple service of God. Once we investigate this, and, with the knowledge that we have, serve God, then also the exalted nature of song in the heavens will be drawn down to us even without our understanding its mysteries. . . .

But song is just a way of bringing the soul and its feelings out into revelation; there is still the matter of what a person does once he is aroused emotionally, and what he does with this part of his soul or inner self which is brought out.

For instance, there are two people who are happy—one then uses his joy to serve God, the other acts wildly. So also with song, which is one of the keys to the soul, and which awakens it and its emotions. One person can open himself up, bringing out a part of his soul, and not only does he not use this opportunity for something good, but he acts so as to do damage to this part of his soul, either through wildness, or through sadness and depression, until he even falls from his trust and faith in God and does things that should not be done, God save us from such.

Since we want to bring out [our emotions] and reveal our [lower] soul [*nefesh*] for the purpose of giving it rule over the body, binding it into the holiness of God and nullifying it and our own essence in our Godly soul [*nishmat Shaddai*], we should make it a regular practice to use song and melody for heavenly service. . . .

Taking a part of a *niggun* you know, turn yourself to face the wall, or just close your eyes, and think that you are standing before the Throne of Glory [on which God sits], and with your heart broken you have come to pour your soul out to God, with song and melody which come from the innermost part of your heart. Then you will certainly feel that your soul is coming out as you sing. If at first you were singing slowly before your soul in order to arouse it from its sleep, slowly, slowly, you will feel that your soul has begun to sing of its own. . . .

It will happen sometimes that as you sing, without intending it, you will spontaneously begin to speak words of prayer to God. If at first these words may be associated with the life and desires of the body, the more you become spiritually aroused, and your soul comes out of its sheath to fly upwards, the more will you leave this world and its concerns, and from the depths of your heart you will cry out in pure prayer to God. And lest you think that such prayers are somehow less important than those written down in the Siddur, you should know that prayers such as these come from the very same quarry from which the soul itself is hewn.

It will also happen sometimes that you will not be aroused to speak words of prayer, and you will not feel any need to ask for something from God; nevertheless, you will feel something hard to describe, a kind of throwing yourself at God to endear yourself to Him, like a child who in a sweet way is pestering his father—he does not want anything but is just moaning and sighing, "Daddy, Daddy." His father asks him, "What do you want, my son?" He answers, "Nothing," but he continues to moan and to sigh, "Daddy, Daddy." For with regard to knowing how to bring out the soul there are many things to be learned from children, for a child's actions are without conscious intention, and his soul just naturally expresses itself through actions and gestures.

So too here, with the endearing way that the child pesters its father, for what this is is an outflowing of the soul of the child to the soul of the father. You, too, will sometimes feel, as you sing a melody, this kind of restlessness and longing, without speech and without words, and with nothing to ask of God. It is just your soul that is murmuring and flowing out, with the unspoken chant, "Master of the World, Master of the World" [*Ribono shel Olam*].[2]

This is not only so with *niggunim* of the broken heart but also with melodies that express joy; you can use all of them for bringing out your soul. Such is the way of the hasid, that even when he is singing a joyful *niggun*, or when he is dancing, he will sometimes cry; and so, too, when he is crying, he rejoices.

So when you are in the company of hasidim when they are singing, whether during prayer or at a meal or some other time, sing

> along with them, and not just on the level of making your voice heard . . . but so as to bring out your soul and lift it up, on the level of what is said about Elisha the prophet, "And it came about, that when the musician played, the hand of God rested on him." Let your singing be like a marriage song, which is used to bring together and join in intimacy the bride and the groom. A word is enough for the one who understands.[3]
>
> Do not be restricted to those times when you are in the company of hasidim who are singing. Also in your own home, whenever you feel yourself in the right mood and are able to sing, do as described above. And you do not have to raise your voice either, for it is possible to sing in the merest whisper and have it heard in heaven. (*Hachsharat ha-Abrechim*, p. 46b)

To use hasidic melodies spiritually so as to draw out your soul, as the Peasetzna Rebbe suggests, it is good to be aware when a song comes to you. If you begin to hum or sing a little, notice this and do not let it go; develop it and allow yourself to sing fully. And if the spirit carries you so far, get up and dance to your song.

24:9 Though *niggunim* can be spontaneous and inspired, one can also, in a regular way, weave them into one's service of God by using particular melodies and songs at particular times.

The previous Lubavitcher *rebbe*, Rabbi Yosef Yitzchak Schneersohn, said:

> My grandfather [the Rebbe Maharash] used to sing certain *niggunim* to himself: in the course of *davenen*—during *pesukei dezimrah* and the blessings of the Reading of *Shema* and while putting on the *tefillin* of Rabbeinu Tam; while he was putting on his *Shabbos* clothes, and again after *Shabbos* as he took them off; and at the *Shabbos* table, by evening and by day. (*Likkutei Dibburim*, vol. 1, p. 214)

24:10 The Peasetzna Rebbe mentions melodies of heartbreak and joy. There are many different kinds of songs, of course, but some of the categories used by the Lubavitcher hasidim will suggest some of the different functions and uses of the *niggun*. There are (1) songs for gatherings, (2) dance songs, (3) songs of joy, (4) songs of spiritual arousal, and (5) songs of *d'vekut*.

24:11 Hasidic melodies often have no words. But many *niggunim* originally without words were given words at a later date. Perhaps the reason for this is that words can help in concentration when one begins singing.

But once a higher level of *d'vekut* is reached in the song, then they are a hindrance. Words are often dropped as the singing progresses. Of course, songs with words can be sung without them.

Another thing to know about the spiritual use of hasidic *niggunim* is that they are often sung for a longer period of time than would be natural in a Western, secular song. Sometimes *niggunim* are repeated over and over for a great length of time. This is because their purpose is different from that of a secular song.

It is told of Rabbi Hayim of Tzanz:

> Once on *Shabbat* evening he poured himself the wine for *kiddush*, took the cup in his hand, and began to sing, with fervor and holy awe, "O Creator, Thou art the Crown; O Creator, Thou art the Crown" for more than an hour, until the thick candles that were burning on the table went out—but he, with great *d'vekut*, still kept on singing. (*Rabbeinu ha-Kodesh mi-Tzanz*, p. 219)

24:12 Dancing was always the way of the hasidim, going back even to ancient times. The hasidim of the movement of the holy Baal Shem also love to rejoice in dance. And, just as with singing, dancing is also to be before God.

> **24:12:1** [The Baal Shem Tov] used to dance to attain religious enthusiasm (*hitlahavut*) and communion with God (*d'vekut*). He taught his followers that "The dances of the Jew before his Creator are prayers" and quoted the Psalmist, "All my bones shall say: Lord, who is like unto Thee?" (Psalm 35:10). [Rabbi] Nachman of Bratzlav, great-grandson of the Baal Shem Tov, believed that to dance in prayer was a sacred command, and he composed a prayer which he recited before dancing. (*Encyclopedia Judaica*, Dance, vol. 5, p. 1267)

24:12:2 The Besht:

> Dancing is to lift up holy sparks; and, in a holy dance, the lower rung of spirituality is to be lifted up to the higher. (*Keter Shem Tov*, p. 39)

24:12:3 Rabbi Nachman of Bratzlav wanted his hasidim to turn his teachings into prayers. Here are two such Bratzlav prayers, to pray to attain to holy dancing:

> **24:12:3:1** May it be Thy will that you have compassion on me and make me worthy to be always joyful, so that I'll always be happy

with the joy of doing a *mitzvah*, and I'll be glad and happy in You and in Your salvation always—for all the kindnesses that You've done with us.

O compassionate Father, help me and make me worthy to be always joyful, so that I'll merit to arouse myself always to great joy, especially on Sabbaths and holidays, and I'll merit that my heart burn with fire and flame in holy joy, with great desire and longing and fervor for Your Name and Your service—until the fervor of my heart be drawn down to my feet so that I'll merit to lift my feet with great joy and I'll merit to do holy dancing in great joy, especially on Sabbaths and on holidays and days when You performed miracles for Israel.

Guard me and save me, in Your great mercy, from the wine of drunkenness and from the fervor of heart and the dancing that emanates from the Other Side, God forbid . . . and make me worthy that I be able to arouse the source of the wine that rejoices, as it is written, "And wine, which rejoices the heart of man," and make my heart to rejoice always with great holiness, in truth, until I merit to do holy dancing.

And through dancing with a fervent heart from the side of holiness, and through the wine which brings joy, I'll merit, with Your compassion, to sweeten and nullify all the judgments that cling to the heels and the feet, and You'll give us the power to nullify and break and sweeten them, that all the judgments on us, and on all Your people the House of Israel, be nullified from now and forever. (*Ha-Niggun v'ha-Rikud b'Hasidut*, p. 81)

24:12:3:2 Another such prayer includes this:

May I merit, through Your compassion, that this holy spirit be drawn into my hands and feet until I become worthy to fix all the [spiritual] damage to my hands and feet, and to reveal and illumine the light that dwells within my hands and feet, until my heart awakens with great joy to Your Great Name, in truth, until this great joy spreads into my hands and feet and I merit to hand clapping and dancing in holiness, in a way that we'll be able to sweeten the judgments on us and on all Your people the House of Israel through holy hand clapping and dancing, and until, through Your compassion I can lift and raise and elevate my hands and feet so as to cleanse them of every fault and everything wrong with them.

And that You be my help, that I be able to do many *mitzvot* with my hands and feet, every hour and every minute, in a way that I merit to raise up my hands and feet to their holy source so that their great light be revealed, and I merit to hand clapping and dancing in holiness. (*Ha-Niggun v'ha-Rikud b'Hasidut*, p. 84)

Not only can we use these prayers for ourselves, but close study of the lines in them about dancing will provide us with a number of holy *kavvanot* for dancing.

24:13 The dancing of the *rebbes* in particular was not always a simple matter, and there are many stories about how each movement of theirs was with spiritual intention.

Once, Rabbi Shalom Shachna of Probitch, son of Rabbi Abraham the Angel and grandson of the Maggid of Mezritch, was visiting with Rabbi Arye Leib of Shpola, the Shpola Zeyde (grandfather):

> **24:13:1** On the night of the holy Sabbath Rabbi Shalom sat at the table, as was his custom, in great *d'vekut*, and he and the Shpola Zeyde did not speak at all. But when they finished eating, the Grandfather said to the holy Rabbi Shalom, "Can you dance?" He answered, "No." The Grandfather then said, "Grandson of the Maggid, look at how the Shpola Zeyde dances!" And he immediately jumped up and began to dance about the room.
>
> When he had danced once this way and once that way, he said, "Son of the Angel! Did you see the way the old man dances?" Then he said again, "Rabbi Shalom! Did you see?"
>
> This same sequence happened a number of times and when the dancing of the Shpola Zeyde became even more fervent, Rabbi Shalom, who slowly came out of his inward looking *d'vekut*, suddenly stood up and focused his gaze on him with wide-open eyes. After looking for a while this way, he turned to his hasidim who were with him, and said to them, "Believe me when I tell you that he has purified and sanctified all his limbs to such an extent that with each step of his holy feet he accomplishes holy unifications." (*Tiferet Maharal*, p. 10)

"Unifications" are mystical actions that unite the Upper and Lower Worlds, Heaven and Earth. Without entering into *kabbalah*, the following words of Rabbi Zev Wolf of Zhitomir help us to understand how one can dance with spiritual intentions. Talking about the gestures a person makes in fervent prayer, such as clapping or lifting the hands high, he says:

> Sometimes he will close his hand, with all five fingers in his palm. And there is no gesture without a thought behind it, and that thought expresses itself through the body. For example, the gesture just mentioned shows God's unity, how there is no place where He is not present, and the whole earth is full of His glory. He, Blessed be He, put it in our hearts to express this naturally through closing

> the five fingers together in one place, to indicate His oneness. So are all the other gestures that an intelligent person makes during prayer symbolic. (*Or ha-Meir*, vol. 1, p. 42b)

Rabbi Nachman of Bratzlav taught that hand clapping produces air like that of the Land of Israel; lifting the hands above the head means "going above [beyond] the intellect," and so on. The gestures for dance have the same kind of symbolic meaning as those for prayer, for the dances of a Jew are prayers.

24:13:2 About Rabbi Moshe Leib of Sassov:

> The spectacle of his dancing on the night of *Shabbat* was like a wondrous vision not of this world. Every Sabbath evening he took expensive new shoes, put them on, and began to dance for the honor of the holy Queen Sabbath. His dancing was dancing of *d'vekut*, of yearning and thirsting for God until expiration. With each and every movement he accomplished awesome and wondrous unifications until the whole house was full of light. All the heavenly host of angels danced with him, a great fire flamed around him, and, eye-to-eye, it was seen that the *Shechinah* came to rest in his *Beit Midrash.*
>
> He would be dressed all in white and his face was like that of an angel of God. For hours at a time he danced in *hitpashtut ha-gashmiyut*, utterly divorced from all materiality, without tiring. His dancing drew to him all the hasidim in Apta, where he was living, and they never tired of watching the revelation of the *Shechinah* that took place where he danced. (*Tiferet Banim Avotam*, p. 177)

Rabbi Moshe Leib, we are told, "danced in *hitpashtut ha-gashmiyut*, utterly divorced from all materiality." Rabbi Yitzhak Meir, the Gerer Rebbe,

> speaking about the dancing of men of deeds at times of joy, said, "Dancing separates the materiality of the body from the soul until one reaches the state of *hitpashtut ha-gashmiyut* [taking off materiality and the body from the soul as a garment is removed]." (*Ramatayim Tzofim*, Eliahu Zutta, p. 37b)

How does dancing, the most complete exercise of the body, result in divorcement from materiality? The answer is that when the body is used most completely in the service of God its materiality disappears, it is spiritualized—and we can then free ourselves of its weight. This thought can also provide us with *kavvanot* when dancing.

24:14 When you dance before God you should be aware of the Divine Presence. Holy dancing should not, God forbid, degenerate into wildness and an expression of animal energy. As you dance, dedicate all your movements and all your limbs to God. Think: "God, You have made all my limbs and by Your power they move. You have made me within and without, and I dedicate all my limbs and movements to You, O Holy One!"

> The limbs which Thou hast formed in us, and the spirit and breath which Thou hast set in our mouths, lo, they shall thank, bless, praise, glorify, extol, reverence, hallow, and assign kingship to Thy Name, O our King. And all my insides and reins shall sing unto Thy Name . . . and all my bones shall say, "Lord, who is like unto Thee!" (From *Nishmat*—Shabbat Morning Prayers)

There are, of course, many other possible holy intentions for dancing.

24:15 When it might otherwise be impossible or inappropriate to dance one can serve God by dancing "in imagination." Rabbi Nachman of Bratzlav used to say that he could dance without moving a limb. (See "Service of the Imagination," 19:13 about this.)

24:16 One can have a practice of simply listening (with devoted attention) to recorded *niggunim*. This is a good way to learn songs. Of course, it is also possible to sing and dance. Records and tapes of hasidic songs, such as those of Rabbi Shlomo Carlebach or of the Lubavitcher hasidim, are available in most Jewish bookstores. The best hasidic recordings are the authentic ones done by the hasidim themselves, rather than by professional singers.

24:17 If you do not know how to do hasidic dancing (the simplest dances are very easy), go among the hasidim where you will be able to see it.

24:18 For some beautiful teachings and stories about the singing and dancing of hasidic *rebbes*, see the sections about song and dance in "Prayer," 5:3:9 and 5:3:10 and in "*Shabbat*," 18:2:4:5:7. For more about the special level of singing and dancing until you sweat, see "*Mitzvot*," 11:3, and the important context there.

25

Sight

Control of all the senses is necessary for one who would achieve God-consciousness, for the senses ordinarily work to divide our attention and to draw us into the world of sense pleasure—and our goal is to achieve greater and greater concentration on God and heavenly things.

With regard to sight, looking at unclean things leads the mind in the wrong direction, while looking at clean things leads the mind to God.

What are holy and clean things, then? To some degree this depends on the person, his religious path and his spiritual level—but generally they are those things that easily remind us of God: servants of God, houses of God, holy books, and holy objects such as *tzitzit*, *tefillin*, and *mezuzot*. But of course one cannot go through life looking only at holy things. A person should work, then, on cultivating an ability to have the many things he sees in the world remind him of God. (See Chapter 2, "Everything That Happens," p. 30.)

What things are unclean and not fit to look at? Again, this depends on the person and his religious way and level. But sights that lead us to temptations certainly draw us away from God—such as gazing at the opposite sex. In our times, not only are we regularly exposed to provocatively clad people of the opposite sex, but even more so are we bombarded through the media. Violence and cruelty are also not fit to look at (except when there is a good purpose in the seeing). Can we gaze on such things, in the media for instance, without having our souls affected?

We could divide, then, the objects of vision into three broad categories: (1) those things that are holy and clean and actually good to look at; (2) those things that are "neutral," which we can look at when necessary for our worldly activities and which we should try to link with God and spirituality; and (3) those things that are unclean and whose sight we should make efforts to avoid.

Control of the glance is a sure sign of one who is spiritually advanced and whose mind is under his control.

> When we know that a man of Israel always guards his eyes and never gazes or rests his eyes except on holy things—although, of course, there are times when he has to look at something because of his necessary activities in the world. But if he never looks at something evil or unclean in any situation or circumstance, then he is on a level where it is certain that everything else about him needs no further investigation. (*Sh'ar ha-Tefillah*, quoted in *DhTvhY*, II, R'iya #3, p. 71)

> The holy Rabbi Hayim of Krasna [a disciple of the Baal Shem Tov] never lifted up his eyelids to look at something that had no connection with the service of God. (*Mishnat Hasidim*, p. 371, #35)

(This very thing is said of other *rebbes* too.)

> Rabbi Shneur Zalman of Ladi said of himself that once he went outside as evening was falling, and for a moment he looked in a place where there was no need to do so, and he felt great anguish that he had not guarded his eyes as he should have. So he went over to a nearby wall, put his face to the wall and cried and cried. But when he turned away from the wall he saw that night had already fallen and darkness covered the earth, and that the time for *Minha* had passed—and again he felt terrible because this touched his very soul. So he thought about what to do, and deciding on a course of action, he drew himself above time and prayed *Minha*. (*Shema Shlomo*, II, p. 12, #34)

In developing one's spirituality, the focus is often on inwardness, the opposite of looking around this way and that:

> Make it a practice not to look beyond your personal space, your four *amot* [cubits]. (Rabbi Yehiel Michal of Zlotchov, *Hanhagot Tzaddikim*, p. 54, #5)

> Guard your eyes so that you look only either up above or down at the ground. (Rabbi Moshe Teitelbaum, *Hanhagot Tzaddikim*, p. 48, #11)

It would seem that once your eyes are subject to your will and direction, the necessity for so closely limiting the scope of vision would be eased, for then you are able to use your eyes in the service of God. But there are different ways in this matter, and this is not always the case.

So a person should avoid looking at anything evil or unclean, and conversely, should seek to set his eyes on things clean and good and holy. If you look at something unclean, an unclean impression is made on your soul; if you look at something clean, a clean impression is formed.

> Just as it is forbidden to gaze at something evil, so is it a commandment to look at something holy, which will bring light and a wonderful illumination to your soul. (*Sh'ar ha-Tefillah*, quoted in *DhTvhY*, II, R'iya #2, p. 71)

Thus, it is forbidden to gaze directly into the face of a really wicked person, since the impression of his evil will enter into your soul. And, conversely, you should make every effort to look into the face of a holy man, even to stare, because it is as if you were looking at the Divine Presence, for the Divine Presence rests upon his face. So if you have the good fortune to sit before a teacher of Torah, for example, who is, as the rabbis say he should be, an angel of God, look well at his face and draw the holy impression into your soul.

Once a man came to the Rizhiner Rebbe to ask him to give him an order of repentance so he could return to God and atone for his sins. The *rebbe* told him, among other things, that while he was with him,

> whenever the *rebbe* would be sitting at his holy table, he should look at his face and not take his eyes off him. (*Eser Orot*, p. 128, #14)

Rabbi Elimelech of Lizensk taught:

> It is a great help in receiving illumination and encouragement to do *tshuvah* to see the face of a *tzaddik*, for since he has the fear of God on his face, whoever looks in his face receives a great illumination. (*Noam Elimelech*, Likkutei Shoshanah, p. 91b)

The Besht said of another *tzaddik* that at a certain time of the year the *Shechinah* was on his face and whoever saw his face was aroused to repentance (*Shemen ha-Tov*, p. 124, #167).

> The reason why we are not to look into the face of an evil person is that by doing so you receive an influence from the spirit of evil that appears in his face. And as a result your mind will be disturbed and you will be shaken from your *d'vekut*. (*Reshit Hochmah*, Sh'ar ha-Tshuvah, chap. 6, #48)

At the outset of our discussion we should note that there are different ways with regard to the holiness of the eyes. Whenever holiness is involved there are always those who will take things to the furthest limit. They are the *parushim* (Hebrew–separatists), those whose prime goal is to separate from the world and its temptations and from sin. Their path emphasizes fear of God and fear of sin. The other way is that of the hasidim, whose path is that of love of God. And thought both *parushim* and hasidim seek to sanctify their senses and their vision, the hasidim see that their *parush* comrades' tendency to extremes interferes with the Torah goal of holy involvement with the world and our fellow men. (For clarity, we must say that even among the "hasidim" of the movement of the Baal Shem Tov there are those who lean toward each of the two poles of *parushim* and hasidim.) We will have more to say about this subject and this divergence in ways at the end of our discussion.

Following is a selection of representative quotes which gives the basic teachings about the sanctification of vision.

25:1 In Chapter 1, p. 17 we considered the practice of seeing the spiritual aspect of all things and objects, and of "seeing" God.

We can add here one quote from *Yesod v'Shoresh ha-Avodah* about the service of the eyes:

> If you look at material things in the world, for example, trees or stones, whatever you see, you should think of the amazing wisdom of the Creator, blessed and exalted be He, in the growth of this tree and of its fruit, or in the creation of this stone . . . and you should say to yourself, "How wonderful is His power! How wonder is His power! And how amazing is His wisdom in this—that man's wisdom cannot even begin to fathom in the slightest!" When you have this *kavvanah* you draw the holy sparks from these material things [and raise them up—you draw out their spiritual essence and relate to that]. (Gate 1, chap. 6, p. 14)

> **25:2** Attach your mind to what is Above . . . and do not even look at the things of this world. Just try to separate yourself from

> materialism, for gazing on this world coarsens you. Our rabbis, their memory for a blessing, said: "Seeing leads to remembrance and remembrance leads to desire." So is it written about the Tree of Knowledge of Good and Evil that it was a delight to look at and good to eat (Genesis 3:6). And because she [Eve] gazed at it, it became desirable. (*Tzavaat ha-Ribash*, p. 2)

25:3 Controlling our vision will help us overcome our bodily lusts:

> The remedy for this is to separate yourself from materiality by not even looking at the things of this world except when necessary; nor should you think about them at all. Because when you look at the things of this world, even food and drink, not to speak of other things, God forbid, even though you only allow your mind to dwell on it for a while, you coarsen yourself. And how much will you rejoice and be glad when you can say about yourself that you have merited to reach the level of having subdued your lusts and desires for the glory of God, blessed and exalted be He. (*Yesod v'Shoresh ha-Avodah*, Gate 7, chap. 2, p. 134)

25:4 It is gazing upon members of the opposite sex that leads to lustful thoughts and imaginings rolling through the brain. Almost all the *rebbes*, therefore, speak of the need for men to avoid looking at women (or anything about them, even their clothes, that arouses sexual thoughts); similarly, women should avoid looking at men.

If you do not get control of your glance you will be pulled around like a monkey on a string every time an attractive member of the opposite sex enters your field of vision. But it is, indeed, only when you are already determined to achieve singleness in directing yourself to God that you even become aware of how often throughout the day you are aroused to no purpose by your straying eyes.

25:5 Rabbi Yitzhak Isaac of Komarna wrote about his early adolescence:

> I went through a short period when I experienced a great strengthening of *Samael* [Satan], may his name be blotted out, and I failed to guard my eyes, and there loomed before me two paths, one to *Gehinnom* and one to *Gan Eden* [Hell and Heaven]. Then the side of good was aroused in me, and one day I entered a synagogue alone, and cried my heart out before Him who created the world. The tears flowed from my eyes as from a fountain, until I fainted.

. . . And from that day until today, twenty-five years later, I have not looked at or seen, even at a glance, the visage of a married woman. Since then I have in this heavenly aid, that I will not see this even by chance. After that experience I returned to my service of God, to Torah and to prayer. (*Ateret Tiferet*, p. 32, #23)

25:6 Reb Arele Roth:

My soul, my soul, if you want to serve your Creator, I will tell you that the beginning of the acquisition of holiness is with the eyes. And if you guard your eyes as you should, you will merit to cling to the Light that shines from the face of the Living King. . . . You should know, my children, that . . . the power of sight is very great in drawing down all kinds of purity and holiness. Contrarily, great harm is easily come by through sight, and the effects are as mountains hanging by a hair. . . . So be careful and guard yourself when you have to leave your house to go about in the streets and in the marketplace. For if you fail to keep your eyes lowered, but look about this way and that, you can stumble, God forbid, with great and serious sins.

It is an important rule in guarding your eyes that you not desire to know who is walking on the sidewalk and who is riding in the coaches. . . . A counsel about this is that whenever you go out, pray and beseech the Creator, blessed be He, that He help you to guard the holiness of your eyes, that He save you from every bad use of your eyes, and particularly that you not stumble with lustful thoughts of women.

Especially in our time, when the wicked have broken all bounds of decency with chutzpah and arrogance, you need great mercy from heaven to be saved from this, so that you do not go after it, and your sight not bring you, God forbid, to lust. And the holy Torah is a lovely and graceful doe, and he who meditates on Torah is saved from all kinds of sins.

So happy is he who knows words of Torah by heart, that he can continually go over [as he walks about outside], for they will certainly save him from undesirable and low thoughts. . . . If you can accustom yourself not to look up as you go about, but just look in front of you and in a humble way keep your eyes on the ground . . . there will be drawn on you holiness, to save you from all evil, and you will merit through this to purity of mind.

And [to go from negative to positive] this will be even more so if you keep in remembrance the holy and honored Name of God [YHVH] or the other holy names before your eyes—then you will certainly be helped, and you will go up and up in spiritual level. For it is within the power of this image of the Holy Name to destroy all foreign thoughts, and to save your soul from all evil and harm. The image of the Holy Name will polish your soul until it shines in a state of great glory. Through this practice you will be able to make war on your evil inclination and also to direct your heart with great concentration in Torah and prayer. . . .

And so, my children, let not the matter of guarding the holiness of your eyes seem something unimportant to you. If you see to it that you always remember its importance and its value, undoubtedly you will have drawn on you much holiness and fear of God. (*Noam ha-Levavot*, pp. 40–41)

25:7 Be careful to keep your eyes from gazing at anything bad or evil, God forbid, and by this you will merit having the Divine Presence rest on you. (*Or ha-Ner*, #38)

25:8 Do not look [directly] in the face of a woman or at her clothes [so as not to be led to lustful thoughts], and do not look in the face of a heathen, or in the face of someone who is angry or an idiot or insane, or in the face of a wicked person, or someone who is lazy or in a nasty mood. But it is a *mitzvah* to look in the face of someone who is attached to God, for such will give rise to holiness in your soul. You should not look beyond your immediate personal space, nor at animals engaged in sexual intercourse. Do not look at unclean things or at that which is disgusting, or in the face of a dead person. . . . For everything at which it is permitted to look, think of the spiritual power that is in it. It is a *mitzvah* to look at the sky and at the stars at night. (Rabbi Tzvi Hirsh of Nadborna, *Alpha Beta* of Rabbi Tzvi Hirsh, Histaklut, in *YHvT*, p. 59)

This kind of list is very common in the *hanhagot* of the hasidic *rebbes*; that they all made a point of including such admonitions shows the importance they attributed to this matter of the holiness of the eyes.

Rabbi David ha-Levi of Steppin, in his list of *hanhagot*:

(28) Do not look at anything that will give rise to lustful thoughts, not at your own private parts nor at those of another, not at women or at their clothes, even when they are hanging on a wall. (29) Do not look at animals when they are engaging in sexual intercourse. (30) Do not look at the face of a wicked person. (31) If you happen to see a husband and wife showing affection for each other, do not allow yourself to dwell on it and have lustful thoughts. (32) Do not look at a bed in which husband and wife sleep together. (33) Do not even look at your wife's private parts or those parts of her body

that are ordinarily covered, so that the *yetzer ha-ra* will not incite you to lustful thoughts. (34) It is forbidden to look at your wife when she is in a state of *niddah*. (*Hanhagot Tzaddikim*, p. 57)

Rabbi Yehiel Michal of Zlotchov, in his *hanhagot*:

You should not look at any idol or other thing associated with foreign worship. (*Hanhagot Tzaddikim*, p. 54, #12)

We should note that when it is said not to "look" in the face of this or that person, it means not to gaze. As Rabbi Shmelke of Nikolsburg says:

Do not gaze at a wicked person . . . but just look (*r'iya b'alma*). (The Hanhagot of Rabbi Shmelke of Nikolsburg, beginning of *Divrei Shmuel*)

Although the rabbis regularly mention things that arouse lustful thoughts, such as women's clothing hanging on a wall, animals copulating, and so on—familiar sights in their world—with us the current equivalents would be lewd advertisements, certain things on television or in the movies, immodestly dressed people, and the like.

25:9 While some teachings emphasize limiting vision, others take a different approach and tell us rather to have what we see remind of us of God somehow. The following quotes speak of having what we see remind us of *mitzvot*, but there are other, broader possibilities, as we discussed in Part One (Chapter 2, p. 30).

It is an important rule in the service of God that for everything you see you should remember the 613 *mitzvot*, and think immediately of the *mitzvah* that relates to each and every thing you see. When you see a man, think, "And you shall love your neighbor as yourself"; seeing a woman, think, "You shall not covet or lust"; also remember not to covet or desire when you see another's money or property or house; and seeing a house, think of the *mitzvot* of putting on a *mezuzah* and making a parapet for the roof. And so with everything that you see, think right away of the *mitzvah* that depends on that thing and you will be saved from bad thoughts. (*Or ha-Ganuz l'Tzaddikim*, p. 43)

King David, peace be upon him, said in Psalms, "Keep my eyes from seeing evil! Enliven me in Your ways." A man should know that there are many things that depend on the eyes' seeing.

For this reason it seems to me that immediately upon awakening, if a man sees through his window other houses, he should think of how God gave us the commandments of putting a *mezuzah* on the entrance to a house and of making a parapet on the roof. . . . If he goes out of his house in the morning and comes across some clean animals fit for sacrifice in the Temple, he should think of how the Holy One, blessed be He, commanded us to offer sacrifices. If he comes across unclean beasts and animals, he should think of how it is forbidden to eat them. And if he meets some non-Jews, he should think how it is forbidden to intermarry with them.

Everyone should so meditate on what he sees, each one according to his Torah knowledge and his understanding, for it is a very important practice to put your eyes into holiness. . . .

We know that "The one thing equal and opposite to the other did God make" [Kohelet 7:14]—so that if someone who looks at holy things makes a garment of holiness for his eyes, in the same way, God forbid, it works on the other side, that if a man puts before his eyes forbidden things, and non-Jewish women, then he puts himself into great uncleanness. . . .

Our Sages, their memory for a blessing, established a fence and barrier to purity: that we should not look at things that are close to bringing us to sin, such as looking at women, even unmarried women, for looking at them will lead a man to an uncontrolled ejaculation of semen during sleep. . . .

There is an effective way to be saved from this sin, and that is that a man should always imagine before his eyes the four-letter Divine Name as if written in black ink on white parchment, as it is written, "I have placed the Lord [YHVH] before me always." [Psalm 16:8] . . .

You should know that for every sin there is a cause and a reason that brought a man to it; so there is a cause and reason why a man came to look at a non-Jewish woman. He began by looking at unclean things and feasted his eyes on them. . . . If a man looks at unclean creatures, then he draws on himself the aura of uncleanness that hovers over it, and it leads him later to look at something even worse, which will finally lead him to stumble and fall. . . .

And so also did the rabbis forbid us to look straight into the face of a wicked man. Instead, a person should accustom himself to look at holy things, and then he will draw holiness on himself. . . .

It is good for a man to look at the skies, to see the works of God, blessed be He. As it says in the *Zohar*, Rabbi Eleazar, the son of Rabbi Shimon bar Yohai, said that "Once I was on the seashore and Elijah came and appeared to me and said to me, 'Rabbi, do you know the meaning of that which is written, "Lift up your eyes to the

> heavens, and see who created these"?' [Isaiah 40:26]. I answered, '[The meaning is that] a man should gaze at the skies and bless the One who created them, as it is written, "When I behold the heavens, the work of Your fingers, the moon and the stars which You have established!"'" [Psalm 8:4] (*Kav ha-Yashar*, chap. 2)

Not every detail of the teachings in 25:8 and 25:9 is easy for the sensibility of our time. But I did not want to withhold these quotes, for their underlying theme is important. In fact, there are different paths in these matters. But let everyone understand according to his own lights.

25:10 It is a good practice, as mentioned previously, to look often at the sky, whose character as a unitary and awesome expanse is such that it suggests things we associate with God. Thus, the rabbis teach that the sky reminds us of God's glory (in their language, that it is similar to the Throne of Glory). Because of this, God came to be spoken of as dwelling in the sky/heaven, and as our Father in Heaven.

This practice of looking at the sky is particularly beneficial during prayer and Torah study, but is good at other times too, as when walking on the street.

> **25:10:1** It is good to look at the sky to see the works of God. (*Kav ha-Yashar*, chap. 2)

> **25:10:2** It is good to look at the sky often, as this helps to develop the fear of God. (Rabbi Hayim Yosef David Azulai, *Hanhagot Tzaddikim*, p. 66, #7)

25:10:3 Rabbi Elimelech of Lizensk also mentions the night sky:

> A person is drawn to reflect on God's greatness by looking at the sky and seeing the stars in their paths keeping their watches, and shining with their pure light. Through this he will come to the fear of God and to an appreciation of God's greatness, for this is the story which the stars tell. (*Noam Elimelech*, p. 6)

25:10:4 Rabbi Hayim Vital wrote of Rabbi Yitzhak Luria (the Ari):

> My teacher, may his memory be for an everlasting blessing, used to teach that it is beneficial for an individual to reside in a house with windows, so as to be able to gaze at heaven at every moment. It is

> especially good if he gazes upon God's wondrous creations of nature as did King David, may he rest in peace: "When I behold Thy heavens, the work of Thy fingers, the moon and the stars which Thou hast established," (Psalm 8:4). . . . Acting in this way imbues an individual with wisdom, endowing him with reverence for God and holiness. Therefore, it is good to gaze at all times at every moment upon heaven. (The Hanhagot of Rabbi Yitzhak Luria, in *Safed Spirituality*, p. 68, as taken from the appendix of *Sefer Toldot ha-Ari*)

25:10:5 *Or ha-Ganuz l'Tzaddikim* says that when looking at the sky you should imagine that it is a "screen" through which God's light is flooding to you (see "Individual Practices," 39:36 for the quote).

25:11 Just as you can meditate on the sky, which suggests God's greatness and glory, you can, when walking, for example, meditate on the earth beneath your feet and think of your own smallness. As God said to Adam, "For dust thou art and to dust shalt thou return." (Genesis 3:19)

This is what Rabbi Zusya of Hanipol (Rabbi Elimelech of Lizensk's brother) did. He would say:

> Earth, Earth, you are better than I, and yet how is it that I walk on you and trample you with my feet? Soon the time will come when I will lie under you and be subject to you. (*Derech Emunah u'Maaseh Rav*, p. 20)

The source of Zusya's meditation can be found in *Kitzur Shnei Luchot ha-Brit* where this is said about humility:

> When you walk, you should do so in great lowliness, with your head bent down and your eyes lowered, and you should not look beyond your four *amot*. Always remember the four *amot* plot of ground that every man has for his grave . . . and that you will eventually sleep under the ground, as it says, "For dust thou art and to dust shalt thou return." [The traditional instruction to keep your gaze within the four *amot* of your personal space is here fancifully interpreted to mean the four *amot* plot of your grave.] (Sh'ar ha-Otiyot, Ot Ayin, Anavah, p. 38)

Both brothers, Rabbi Elimelech and Rabbi Zusya, believed in meditating on God's greatness and also on our smallness (to achieve humility), but they started at different ends. Elimelech went from God's greatness to our smallness, Zusya in the other direction. (See the story of just this "argument" between them in *Mazkeret Shem ha-Gedolim*,[1] p. 73.) So it is remarkable to see how the one brother, Rabbi Elimelech, spoke of contemplating God's greatness in the sky (25:10:3), while the other brother, Rabbi Zusya, spoke of contemplating your own smallness and humility in relation to the earth (meditating on your death).

But there is another way to meditate on the earth or floor while looking down. Rabbi Simha Bunim of Pshischa used to explain the verse "The earth is full of Your possessions!" [in the Morning *davvening*] to mean that through every thing created on earth we can come to know, and, so to speak, "possess" the Creator.

The son of his disciple Rabbi Yitzhak of Vorki applied this verse and teaching literally to the earth beneath our feet:

> [Rabbi Mendel of Vorki] said that even from the dirt floor you can get fear of heaven, as the Scripture says, "The earth is full of Your possessions!" (*Eser Z'chuyot*, p. 47, #36)

The point is that even the dirt floor, the earth beneath your feet, is created by God, and through true vision one can become aware of the Creator. (See the story of Rabbi Shneur Zalman of Ladi and his son in "Prayer," 5:1:18:3:1; the words of the Peasetzna Rebbe in Chapter 1, p. 18; and of Rabbi Mendel of Ber in "The Synagogue and the Synagogue Service," 6:23.)

These teachings about meditating on the sky or the earth add to our appreciation of the word of Rabbi Moshe Teitelbaum mentioned earlier about guarding your eyes and only looking up above or down at the ground.

25:12 We should sanctify the first use of our eyes in the morning by looking at something holy or something that will remind us of God. And we should pray that God help us protect the purity of our eyes throughout the day. See "Waking and Beginning the Day," 4:9, the three sources quoted in *Derech ha-Tovah v'ha-Yesharah*, and the material that follows the quotes from that book.

25:13 In Chapter 3, p. 61 in the discussion about the value of interrupting worldly activities, a quote was given about Rabbi Mendel of Premishlan, that:

> The way he achieved his spiritual perfection was by means of such interruptions. . . . He would interrupt his vision [by turning away or closing his eyes while looking at something], and so on in many other things. (*Derech Tzaddikim*, p. 4, #21)

Elsewhere, there is this quote from Rabbi Mendel himself, wherein he instructs us to "fast" from unnecessary sights, and work at extending the period when we have control of our vision:

Rabbi Mendel of Premishlan said:

> What is this that people fast and weaken their strength for serving God? It is not mainly the stomach, but the other limbs and organs that are sinning—but they are blaming the stomach and concentrating all their efforts on it with their fasts!
>
> The correct way is to fast not from food, but with these other organs, like your eyes. For example, for one day do not look at anything except that which is absolutely necessary; afterwards extend this to three days at a time, and after that do it from one Sabbath to the next.
>
> Follow this same scheme with your ears and hearing, and so too with your mouth [that is, speech].
>
> And after all this, when you then fast from food for even one day, it will be very precious in heaven. (*Pe'er l'Yesharim*, p. 15a, #156)

As we can see from these words of Rabbi Mendel, the general pattern of everything that is taught about sight (which is most often spoken of) can be applied to the other senses and faculties, such as hearing. Just as with our eyes, our ears can be sanctified by using them the right way, for not everything should be listened to.

Some rabbis went to great extremes to achieve holiness in sight and hearing.

> Aaron, the son of Rabbi Hayim of Amdur was called the Deaf Reb Arele because he had stopped up his ears for a long time. Just as the Seer of Lublin covered his eyes for a long time until eventually his vision became poor, as is famous, so the holy Reb Arele stopped up his ears; and as a result he talked very little. (*Shema Shlomo*, II, p. 30, #58)

25:14 No one sanctified his vision more than the holy Seer of Lublin, and his spiritual greatness as a "seer" was attributed to the holiness he achieved with regard to his eyes. But his *rebbe*, Rabbi Shmelke of

Nikolsburg, tempered his excess, and the interaction between master and disciple is instructive in our desire to understand the differences with regard to sight between the way of the ascetics and those of the more moderate path.

> During his [the Lubliner's] youth he kept his eyes closed for seven years so that he would not see anything untoward [*ervat davar*: the suggestion is mainly sexual], except when he prayed or studied Torah, when he had to look in the book he was reading or from which he prayed. As a result of this, his vision was very poor and he was very nearsighted.
>
> From the age of 12 he kept a cloth tied over his eyes and kept his eyes closed; it was from this that he merited to see the Hidden Light.
>
> [As a young man the Lubliner studied for two years as a disciple of Rabbi Shmelke of Nikolsburg. When he was in Rabbi Shmelke's *yeshivah*] he never looked beyond his immediate personal space [four *amot*] and his eyes were always lowered.
>
> Rabbi Shmelke said of him that in those two years he attained all his spiritual levels. Because it was there that he taught himself that his vision and his speech should be dedicated to the service of God alone. (*Niflaot ha-Rebbe*, p. 50, #102, #104; p. 51, #106; p. 71, #185)

Another hasidic book gives us the important information of how Rabbi Shmelke tempered the excess of the Lubliner and taught him the true way with regard to vision.

> When Rabbi Yaakov Yitzhak of Lublin [the Seer] was 12 he accepted on himself not to look outside of his personal space [four *amot*]. He tied a handkerchief over his eyes so that he could not see more than what was below, around his legs. He went about that way for two and a half years, until Rabbi Shmelke told him to stop. He explained to him that avoiding the sight of evil is not the true service of a *tzaddik*; the essence of Divine service is when you withhold yourself from doing evil and overcome it. "And," continued Rabbi Shmelke, "a *tzaddik* has to refine his limbs and train them so that even with his eyes fully open he will not see evil, and with his ears he will hear no evil talk." (*Ha-Hozeh mi-Lublin*, p. 20)

> (Returning now to *Niflaot ha-Rebbe* with which we began:)

> [The Lubliner] taught his eyes not to see anything that had no purpose for his service of God.
>
> In *Derech Pikudecha* it is written [by the Lubliner's great disciple, Rabbi Tzvi Elimelech of Dinov]: "I saw with my own eyes how

> our holy master and *rebbe*, Rabbi Yaakov Yitzhak of Lublin, of blessed memory, had his eyes completely within his control, and though he could look right at something, he actually would not see it if it had no relation to his service of God according to the Torah. And, in truth, what I saw of this cannot even be described in print." (*Niflaot ha-Rebbe*, p. 92, #315; p. 94, #324)

Here is a story that shows this same level with the Lubliner's master, Rabbi Shmelke of Nikolsburg:

> When Rabbi Shmelke first came to Nikolsburg he was invited to the home of a wealthy hasid for coffee. When all the various dishes and vessels with coffee and milk were on the table, the *rebbe* asked, "Where is the milk?" The hasid pointed to the milk with his finger, but after a few moments the *rebbe* once again asked him where it was.
>
> Realizing that this strange behavior was not without meaning, the hasid quickly ran to investigate and found out that the milk was not kosher. When he returned he asked the *rebbe* why he had not just told him it was *treif*; why instead did he ask him where it was? The *rebbe* explained to him that since it was forbidden, he absolutely did not see it at all. (*Shemen ha-Tov*, p. 68, #30)

Here is a story of another encounter between the way of extreme asceticism and the more moderate path:

> Rabbi Simha Bunim of Kalish [in the Vorki line of hasidic *rebbes*] was once walking with the *tzaddik* Rabbi David Biderman of L'vov [of the Lelover dynasty], in the paths of Jerusalem. And, as was his way, his eyes were covered with a large cloth [when he went about outside], and Rabbi David had to lead him to their destination.
>
> When they arrived, Rabbi David asked him why he did this. Was it not it possible to keep your eyes from looking on bad things without covering them? "What!," said Rabbi Simha Bunim, shaking all over. "Is it not written, 'Be not wise in [with] your own eyes?' When it comes to the holiness of the eyes, you are not to consider yourself wise and clever." (*Ha-Tzaddik ha-Shotek*, p. 110)

A rabbi and *tzaddik* of our time gave a lesson about sight, which puts the issue into good perspective. He compared Korach, who wanted to take the high priesthood for himself, to Aaron, and said that Korach, too, was holy. But Korach was the type of the *parush*, the holy man who is separated from the world's temptations and from sin. When Korach went through the streets he was led around by two attendants, one at each arm, because he kept his eyes closed so as not to see anything bad. Korach, indeed, thought that because of this he was holier than Aaron.

But Aaron's holiness was of a different sort, and was actually higher than that of Korach. For Aaron was the type of the hasid (as opposed to the *parush* type) who loves people very much, even "bad" people, and wants to bring them back to God. So when he walked on the streets he always looked for "sinners" to greet and to show warmth to, so that he could turn them to *tshuvah* (see *Avot d'Rabbi Natan*, chap. 12).

So while Korach would not even look at wicked people, Aaron would actually seek them out.

From this teaching we can understand that there are different ways to sanctify your eyes—and one of the highest ways is to see that you have a "good eye" and that you see the good in your fellow man.

Some of the quotes in this chapter should be reconsidered in the light of this deep teaching.

26

Pious Phrases

It is a traditional practice to use various pious phrases in speech. These phrases, which should be repeated until they become habitual, will then direct our minds in the path of piety and serve to support the concepts that inform our beliefs. Here are some of the more important phrases, with a brief explanation of their use.

26:1 "Blessed be God" (*Baruch HaShem*): This is used when we are saying something about some good which has come our way, and we give recognition that God is its source and we offer thanks. For example: Someone asks us if we found the apartment we were looking for. We answer: "Blessed be God, I found just what I wanted." Many traditional Jews use the Hebrew (*Baruch HaShem*) even in English conversations, at least with other Jews.

Rabbi Meir Margulis, a disciple of the Besht, said:

> It is a *mitzvah* for a person to accustom himself to say "*Baruch HaShem*" about each and every thing. (*Sod Yachin u'Voaz*, p. 36)

The Baal Shem Tov, wanting to arouse mercy on high for Israel, would always ask Jews how they were, for he knew that they would answer,

"*Baruch HaShem,* all is well." For having the name of God on your lips, and giving recognition of His goodness to you is very praiseworthy.

Rabbi Shneur Zalman of Ladi said that

> he heard from the Maggid [of Mezritch] about the Baal Shem Tov, that one of his habits was to travel from city to city and village to village [teaching] and every Jew he met [whether men or women, young or old, Torah scholars or simple people] he would ask about their situation—their health, if they were making a living, and the like—and his purpose in this was for the praise of the people Israel, that they would answer "*Baruch HaShem.*" (*Tzavaat ha-Ribash,* Hosafot, Kehot edition, p. 82)

26:2 "Thank God" or "Praise God" (*Todot l'El or Tehillah l'El*).

"Thank God"—known to anyone who speaks English. *"Praise God"* can be used when referring to something of a larger significance than is typical with "Blessed be God." For example: "Praise God, Israel is at peace."

26:3 *"Blessed be He."* Whenever you mention God, bless Him. This is why you see in the words of the rabbis that whenever they mention God, as for example "the Holy One," they almost always automatically add "blessed be He."

26:4 When mentioning a good person or a *tzaddik* in speech, or when you hear his name mentioned, bless or praise him. For someone deceased we can say, "The memory of a *tzaddik* for a blessing" (Proverbs 10:7); for someone living we can say, "May his light shine" or, "May he live a good and long life" or some other variation of blessing or praise.

26:5 When you refer to holy things—the Sabbath or the Torah, for instance, or to holy people, speak about them in a way to arouse your own (and others') recognition of their sanctity.

> **26:5:1** Whenever you mention *Shabbat* you should always say "holy *Shabbat.*" (*Haghaot Mahartza,* quoted in *DhTvhY,* Hilchot Shabbat, p. 10, #22)

26:5:2 It is told about the Maggid of Koznitz:

> When he was learning the *Gemara* with his students, when he mentioned the name of a Tanna or an Amora [sages mentioned in

> the Mishnah and *Gemara* respectively] or even just a *posek* [a halachic authority], he would mention them with awe and reverence and say, "The holy Rava," "the holy Abaye," "the holy Rashi," "the holy Tosafot," and other similar language.[1] (*Eser Orot*, p. 69, #9)

So we should make it our habit always to speak of the holy Torah, the holy Sabbath, the holy rabbis, and so on.

26:6 "To make a separation" or "To make a distinction" (*L'havdil*). This is used when we compare something holy with something profane or even the opposite of holy. We want to compare some similar aspect to make a point, but in order to prevent our minds from improperly associating the two realms we qualify the comparison by saying "to make a separation." For example: "In both worship in the Temple and (to make a separation) idol worship, offerings are made on an altar." The Hebrew *L'havdil* is often used in English conversation.

26:7 "God willing" (*Im yirtzeh HaShem*).

> With every action that you do, say "God willing." (*Derech Hayim*, 7–24)

This expression is used to separate us from the false belief that our will is enough to bring something into the world, and to remind us that everything that happens happens only when it is God's will. For example, when making an appointment: "I will meet you at six P.M. on Wednesday, God willing." Whether or not the appointment can be kept depends not only on us but also and primarily on God's will. The Hebrew is often used in English conversation, its pronunciation usually slurred to make it sound like "MeertzHaShem."

26:8 "If God so decrees" (*Im yigzor HaShem*). This is essentially an alternative to "God willing."

> A man should never say that he will do something except according to God's decrees, as it says, "Many are the plans in the mind of a man, but it is the purpose of the Lord that will be established." (Proverbs 19:21) (*Midrash LiOlam*, chap. 12, in *Beit Ha-Midrash*, III, p. 116)

26:9 "With the help of God" (*B'ezrat HaShem*). This is essentially the same as the preceding two phrases, perhaps used more when your own efforts are more prominently involved. When you plan to do something, you give recognition that God's help is indispensable for your success. For example: "With the help of God, I'll collect all the money for charity by next week." This phrase is also used for past events. For example: "I completed the whole project successfully, with God's help." Again, the Hebrew is often used in English conversation.

> If you profited in some business, say "I profited with God's help." (*Kitzur Shnei Luchot ha-Brit*, Sh'ar ha-Otiyot, Ot Aleph, Emet v'Emunah, p. 19)

> **26:10** In all his actions, a man of Israel should always say first, "If God wills," and it is also good to say "If God so decrees with the living,[2] and the verse, "My help is from the Lord, the Creator of heaven and earth" [Psalm 121:2]. Even when doing something small, say, when you begin, "With the help of God, blessed be He." You should accustom yourself to say these kinds of phrases in every instance—"With God's help" or "With the help of heaven"—and then you will see success and a good outcome in all your doings. (*Kaf ha-Hayim*, p. 281, #2)

Excepting the psalm verse, the Hebrew phrases are, in order: (1) *Im yirtzeh HaShem*; (2) *Im yigzor HaShem b'hayim*; (3) *B'ezrato yitborach sh'mo*; (4) *B'ezer HaShem*; and (5) *B'siata d'shemaya* (Aramaic).

Note that these various phrases are said not only in conversation, but to yourself, and for your own benefit. Note also the promise in the final sentence that if you use these kinds of phrases you will see success in what you do, a thought that is relevant to the following story.

26:11 There is a lovely story about some of the phrases discussed above:

> A certain rich man had a lot of land, but he had no oxen to plough it. So what did he do? He took his wallet full of money and went to another city to the market to buy some oxen.
>
> Now, although it is true that this man was very generous, giving a lot of charity and always offering hospitality in his home—for all that his heart was not firm in believing in God's Divine Providence over all things. So he would often think to himself in a proud way that, "It is my own doing and ability which have brought me all this wealth," for he had made a great deal of money.
>
> On his way to the other town he was met by Elijah[3] the prophet, his memory for a blessing, who was also going to market (as his custom is to frequent the markets), and Elijah was disguised as a

merchant. Elijah then asked the man, "Where are you going?" And he answered, "To this particular market, to buy oxen." Elijah said, "You should say 'God willing,' or 'If God so decrees.'" But the rich man was obstinate and insisted, saying, "My money is in my wallet and it all depends on my will." Elijah said, "If that is your attitude, then you are not going to be successful in this."

Soon after this the wallet fell out of the man's pocket without his noticing it. Elijah picked it up and placed it on the crag of a large rock deep in the forest, in a place where no one ever passed.

When the man made a deal for some oxen at the market and reached for his wallet to pay, he realized that he had lost it on the way and went home in disappointment. Again he took more money and went to the market to buy oxen, and again Elijah the prophet who was also going to the market met him, this time appearing like an old man.

Elijah asked him, "Where are you going?" and the merchant answered that he was going to the market to purchase some oxen. The old man said to him, "Say 'God willing' or 'If God, blessed be He, so decrees.'" But the man gave the same answer as he did the first time.

Elijah then caused sleepiness to descend upon him and the merchant sat down to rest and quickly fell into a deep sleep. Then, without the merchant feeling anything, Elijah took from him his wallet with the money and left it in the middle of the forest in the same place where he had left the first wallet.

The merchant awoke and saw that his money was gone and said to himself, "It must have been that robbers came along and took my wallet." And again he went home in disappointment.

But on the way he thought to himself, "No, this must be God's hand causing all this to happen, because I haven't believed with complete faith in the Divine Providence of the Creator, blessed be He." So he decided then and there that from that day on he would always say "God willing" for everything he planned to do.

So the merchant tried a third time, taking a wallet full of money to go to the market to buy oxen. Again Elijah met him, this time in the guise of a poor youth who was looking to hire himself out for some work. And this boy asked the merchant, "Where is my master going?" He answered, "I'm going to the market to buy oxen, God willing." Elijah blessed him with success in his purchase and said to him, "Let me ask just one thing of you, master. When you buy the oxen and need a helper to drive them to your home, perhaps you'll be kind enough to hire me for the work; for I'll be at the market too, and I'm very poor and it's that kind of work that I'm setting my hopes on." The merchant said to him, "Fine. If God will help me,

> and I'll buy some oxen, come to me then and I'll take you on to help me drive them home."
>
> The merchant did buy good oxen, and cheaply too, and he hired Elijah to lead the oxen home. When they were on the road, they were passing alongside the large forest with the oxen, and in the middle of the journey the oxen stampeded and fled into the depths of the forest. The merchant and the boy chased after them, but the oxen went farther and farther into the woods until they came to a stop and stood in front of the crag of the large rock on which the two earlier wallets, with the money, were placed.
>
> When the merchant caught up with the animals and saw his wallets with the money still in them he was overcome with joy and gave full praise to God on the spot. After this his oxen went along calmly, listening to the commands of those leading them, until finally the merchant arrived safely at his home. Then, suddenly, the boy vanished into thin air, and the eyes of the merchant were opened to understand that it was nothing but Providence from Above that was behind all this, and he said about himself the verse, "It is an ignorant man who will not know, and a fool who will not understand this [Psalm 92:7]." (*Otzar ha-Sippurim*, V, story 8)

This story uses "God willing," "If God so decrees," and "If God will help me," essentially synonymously.

The point is also made that if you invoke God's help you will receive it, while if you neglect to do so you will not succeed in your undertaking. The merchant failed when he ignored God, but when he finally remembered his need for God's aid, he succeeded.

Note the custom, illustrated in the story, that if you hear of someone's plans, especially if he himself believes in Divine Providence, you should bless him with success; say, for example, "May God give you success."

26:12 "So be it" (*Y'hi kain*) or "Such was God's will" (*Kain haya ritzono*; *kain ratzah HaShem*).

> The holy Rabbi Yaakov Yosef of Polnoye, the author of the *Toldot* [and one of the greatest of the Baal Shem Tov's disciples], was once invited to be a guest of honor at a *brit milah* [circumcision], but since he was late in arriving they circumcised the infant without him.
>
> When he did arrive he became very angry at them, because it is well known that his holy way was full of fire; for this *tzaddik* was a flaming fire and anyone whom he disapproved of was in danger of being burned to a crisp.

But out of nowhere there appeared at the celebration feast that followed the *bris* a beggar, and when they asked him if he would like something to eat he just answered "So be it." When they asked him if he would like to sit down, he again answered, "So be it." And to everything he was asked, all he said were the words "So be it," until everyone thought it was quite funny.

But after the meal Rabbi Yaakov Yosef began to think about this and to wonder just who this man was, and he realized that there was more to it than met the eye. So he instructed a few of the men to investigate who he was and what he was about, but they could not find any trace of him. It was as if he had flown away, leaving no clue.

The rabbi was very disappointed at this result, and they revealed to him from heaven that this poor man was indeed Elijah,[4] and because of his irritation at their going ahead with the *bris* without waiting for him, and his many other fits of temper, they sent Elijah to him in the guise of this beggar to teach him that for everything that happens to him a Jew should say "So be it." As a result he will never get annoyed or angry and he will be spared from arguments and from sin. (Source unknown)[5]

This pious beggar recognized everything as God's will. When they asked him if he would like to eat or to sit down, he took their suggestions as God's will, and said "So be it," that is, "Yes, let it be so, for such is God's will." Such an attitude represents a very high spiritual level.[6]

The lesson found in the way of this holy beggar is applied to the rabbi's behavior regarding the *bris* performed in his absence: he should have accepted this frustration as God's will. But note that there is a slight difference in the way the poor man accepted things *as* they happen and were suggested to him (to eat, sit, etc.) and what is indicated as to how the rabbi should have accepted things that had *already* happened (the *bris*). So when something is happening *now*, say "Let it be so, for such is God's will"; once something *has* happened, say "Let it be so, for such was God's will."

It is interesting also to see how close this story is in general outline to the one in 26:11 about Elijah teaching the merchant to say (for the future), "God willing." Here the rabbi is taught to say (for the present or past), "So be it" ("Such is/was God's will").

Although "God willing" ("If such is God's will"), referring to the future, is a very widespread pious phrase, "Such is God's will" and "Such was God's will," referring to the present and the past, are not. Neither is "So be it" in a pious sense common. At least a partial suggestion to explain this is given in 26:13.

Note that in the story the poor man merely says "So be it," but in the lesson we learn from what follows, we can see that the unsaid continuation of his thought was "for such is God's will." We can take from this a suggestion of how to use this phrase unobtrusively. When we are "speaking to ourselves" and something happens, we can say, "So be it, such is God's will." When we are with others, we can just say, "So be it," and continue with the rest silently to ourselves.

To conclude with an example of use: If someone tells us that our application for a job was rejected, we can reply, "So be it," and continue the thought to ourselves by saying silently, "for such was God's will."

26:13 "This also is for the good" (*Gam zu l'tovah*); or a related phrase, "Everything that God does is for good" (*Kol ma d'aveed Rachmana l'tav aveed*). These phrases are equivalents, the first Hebrew, the second Aramaic.

> Accustom yourself to say, "Everything that the Merciful One does, He does for good." (*Derech Hayim*, 3–76)

These expressions are used when something happens that seems to be against our good and welfare, and we remind ourselves of our trust in God, that everything He does is for our good, even what seems otherwise.

It should be noted that the two phrases are essentially alternatives for what was suggested in 26:12 about the use of "Such was God's will." As said previously, although "God willing" (for the future) is in common use, "Such is God's will" (for the present) and "Such was God's will" (for the past) are not. Perhaps this is because the two phrases here (in 26:13) have taken their place. But the difference between them is this: although the sayings in 26:13 are basically used when bad things happen, the others are not necessarily so restricted. They can still have an important use, then, in many situations that are either neutral or good. For example, the beggar in the story, who goes along with what others suggest to him—"neutral"or "good" things, to sit, to eat, etc.—says "Let it be so (for such is God's will)."

It should also be noted that all these sayings basically are used for one's own benefit, and if they are said to others, it is still mostly for one's own ears. *Sefer Haredim* (chap. 35, #25), in fact, suggests we say, "This also is for good," silently to ourselves because the main thing is our inner belief. But, of course, saying it verbally can help to arouse our faith and trust in God.[7]

26:14 When something bad happens and you lose that which you value, say, in the words used by Job (1:21): "The Lord gave and the Lord has taken away; blessed be the name of the Lord."

26:15 *"Without a vow" (B'li neder).* When a person *says* that he intends to do a particular *mitzvah,* from a spiritual perspective it would ordinarily be considered as a vow even if he did not use the language of a vow. This is because *mitzvot* are themselves binding in a general sense (for example: you are obligated to study Torah), so a verbal statement of intent to do a *mitzvah* ("I'll study Torah tonight for two hours") is automatically taken as a vow. So to prevent your statement from having the force of a vow (and if it is a vow, you are bound by it and failure to carry through is a serious transgression), you should preface it with: "Without a vow . . . (*B'li neder*).

In this regard matters of personal choice are different from *mitzvot* (where you are obligated). But there are two situations with personal choices: when someone else is involved and when the activity involves no one but yourself.

In the first case, it is a good habit to say "*B'li neder,*" even with matters of personal choice. So, for example, when you tell someone you will do something for his benefit, you can state that you are not intending your remark as a promise or vow binding before God. The reason for this is that since a Jew's word should be true, and you should do what you say, this kind of statement of intention can be considered as equivalent to a vow. So it is necessary to make an explicit indication when you do not want your assurance to be taken as completely fixed. For, again, if your promise comes out as a vow, you have no leeway—and if you do not fulfill it, it is a serious transgression.

But if the matter of choice involves just yourself, you may simply say (without any concern with the issue of vows), "God willing" or "If God so decrees." For example, you may say to someone, "I intend to go to the library tonight, God willing."

> *Shulchan Aruch* (67–4):
>
> [When declaring your intent to do a *mitzvah*:] Even if you make a simple statement, not in the language of a vow or oath, it is counted as a vow. So you should be careful to say "*B'li neder*" when saying that you will do some *mitzvah*. It is also good if you accustom yourself to say this even when you say you will do something that is a matter of personal choice—so that you will keep yourself from stumbling, God forbid, by making a vow and not fulfilling it.

Rabbi Hayim Yosef David Azulai:

> When it is a matter of a *mitzvah* that you are speaking about, say, "Without a vow"; when it is a matter of choice, say, "If God so decrees." And if you succeed in something or make a good profit in business, say, "I accomplished this" or "I made this profit because of His goodness, blessed be He, and because of His help." (*Avodat ha-Kodesh*, Tziporen Shamir, 11–170)

The Hebrew phrase for "without a vow" is often used in English conversation, for example, "*B'li neder*, I'll bring you the books tomorrow."

26:16 "*May it be an atonement for you.*" This is said to others when something unfortunate (but not terrible) happens to them, blessing them that this slight misfortune forestall a more serious one by atoning for sins if it is accepted with love. This obviously should be said only to someone who is religious and will understand its use. This phrase has a close relation to what you are to say and do when such a mishap occurs to you; for that, see "Afflictions" (35).

26:17 *"May God fulfill your lack."*

> If your fellow man has sustained some loss [of money or property], say to him, "May God fulfill your lack." (*Hanhagot Adam*, Y. L. Lipshitz, p. 18)

26:18 A hasidic story makes use of the two previous phrases, but the person applies them to himself. It tells how one of the early *rebbes* of Lubavitch, Rabbi Shmuel, sent a hasid on an important mission to deliver a letter to someone near his home town. But when he returned home he got caught with his servants and his horse-drawn carriage in a great storm, and forgot.

> [Soon after arriving home:] his servant came to him and told him that one of the horses just died. "May it be an atonement for me," he answered. After a short while the servant came again and told him the second horse had died. This news made him unhappy, but he consoled himself, saying, "What can be done? May God fulfill my lack." Again, after a short while the servant came still a third time, and informed him that his mill was on fire. Hearing this he remembered about the letter [and realized that because of his failure to deliver it, and having forgotten such a holy commission from his *rebbe*, all these disasters had overtaken him one after the other]. (*Sippurei Hasidim*, vol. 1, #523)

26:19 *"God forbid."* In Hebrew the traditional phrase is "*chas v'shalom*," which means literally, "[May God] spare [you] and [give His] peace." There are a number of such phrases in Hebrew though, and this is not the only one. But all of them are used when speaking about something bad that might happen, and you pray that God forbid it from happening. For example: "If, God forbid, he fell, it would be a disaster." Another such Hebrew phrase is "*Rachmana litzlan*," literally, "May the Merciful One spare us from such!" This is used when you are referring to a misfortune, perhaps one that came to someone else, and you pray that it not strike you or whomever you are talking to. For example: "There was a terrible car accident (May God spare us from such!) on the highway this morning."

26:20 *"Shalom."* When you greet someone or leave him, say "Shalom" or "Peace." Although people may take this as just the conventional kind of formality, you can intend it as it was originally meant, as a real blessing that God's peace rest on them (see "Speech," 23:6).

26:21 It is easier, of course, to use phrases like the ones in this chapter when speaking to other religious people. It can be awkward to speak in a religious and pious way to people who may find your attitude incomprehensible, if not peculiar. There is a time for being forthright and a time for being discreet.

One of the *hanhagot* that the Seer of Lublin wrote for himself was:

> Be careful not to speak differently from the way people commonly speak, for example, using very pious language or even expressing a more than ordinary humility. (*Divrei Emet*, very beginning, list of *hanhagot*, #13)

(Of course the Lubliner certainly used the traditional phrases common among religious Jews.)

In many cases we can alter the phrases to make them unobtrusive even when speaking to nonreligous people, in situations where we do not want to make a point of our piety with people who would not understand it. As an example, in the situation mentioned earlier, where someone asks you if you found the apartment you were looking for, instead of using the traditional "*Baruch HaShem*" (Blessed be God), you might say, "Thank God, I found just what I wanted." The phrase "Thank God" is almost meaningless in spoken English, but it does not have to be so for us, especially if we use it with intent. Of course, how to deal with this whole matter depends on the wisdom of each person.

27

Bathroom

27:1 When in the bathroom we are forbidden to say any words of Torah aloud or even to think any holy thoughts. We must not, even unconsciously, associate holiness with uncleanness and bad odors.

> **27:2** It is forbidden even to think Torah thoughts in an unclean place, except when you do so to separate yourself from what is forbidden, as it says it the *Gemara*. For "His kingdom rules everywhere" [Psalm 103:19], and you can mention and call to mind words of Torah in order to subdue them [bad thoughts and the evil "external forces"]. (*Darkei Tzedek*, p. 14, #55)

27:3 Considering that the goal of hasidic practice is continual meditation on God, the necessity to turn one's mind from holy thoughts in the bathroom presents certain problems.

> Once when the holy *gaon* Rabbi Abraham David of Butchatch went to the bathroom [outhouse], one of this opponents locked the door on him from the outside so that he was stuck there for an hour. The holy *tzaddik*, of blessed memory, suffered very much from the unpleasant odor and also from the fact that he had to constrain his mind from thinking holy thoughts all that time; for he

never ceased for a moment from thinking holy thoughts in *d'vekut* with the Creator of all worlds.

When the people of the *rebbe's* household realized that he was missing, they found him and opened the door for him. And they told him that for the sake of the honor of Heaven and the honor of the Torah he should take revenge on his opponents and put them under a ban. He was about to follow their advice, and he had taken a *shofar* in his hand to blow in invoking the ban, when he said to himself, "Be truthful. Are you really concerned about the honor of God and His Torah—or perhaps is it that you are concerned with your own honor? How can you tell?" At that moment the heart of this holy man turned within him, he put down the *shofar*, and left off. (*Seder ha-Dorot ha-Hadash*, p. 10)

27:4 What should we think about then in the bathroom?

27:4:1 While in the bathroom it is forbidden to think of sacred matters. It is, therefore, best to concentrate on your business affairs and accounts, so that you may not be led to think either of holy matters, or, God forbid, indulge in sinful thoughts. On the Sabbath, when it is forbidden to think of business, you should think of interesting things you have seen or heard about, or something similar. (*Shulchan Aruch*, 4–4)

27:4:2 Rabbeinu Yonah:

In an unclean place such as a bathroom, think of money matters, your expenses, and similar things, and that will remove holy thoughts from your mind. As soon as you leave there, however, and purify yourself [by hand washing], return to your previous thoughts—what you should be thinking of continuously—of how to be diligent in the service of God. (*Sefer ha-Yirah*, p. 206)

27:4:3 In every place you should know your Creator. How then are we to know Him in a place where meditation on the Torah is forbidden?—by behaving modestly. And also, when you are in a bathhouse or bathroom, remember how much uncleanness and filth exits from your body, and be humbled. . . .

Two things, both forbidden, are common in the bathroom—thoughts of Torah and thoughts of sin. Now when you are able to learn Torah you should not spend your time instead thinking about such matters as your needs and your possessions. But when you go to the bathroom or bathhouse then you should think about those things so that you will not think Torah thoughts or be led to sinful

> thoughts. Moreover, since you are thinking about your needs in the bathroom, later, when you study Torah [or pray] your mind will be free of them and you will be able to learn with full concentration. (*Sefer Hasidim*, #545, #546)

27:4:4 Rabbi Elimelech of Lizensk echoes the foregoing words of *Sefer Hasidim*:

> In the bathroom you should be modest and you should think about what it is permitted to meditate on. For example, think how full of shame and filth [excrement] you are and how you are like an animal. (*Noam Elimelech*, Ki Tissa, p. 45b)

Rabbi Elimelech emphasized in his teaching a two-sided meditation on the greatness of God and our own lowliness; this suggestion of his (which follows one line of Talmud teaching) goes along with his general approach.

27:4:5 The bathroom, a place of uncleanness, where we are in touch with our lowest functions, is an appropriate place to subdue the influences of the realm of Impurity. Rabbi Shlomo of Karlin said:

> When I am in the bathroom relieving myself, all the chariot of Impurity is underneath me. (*Sifran Shel Tzaddikim*, p. 29, #8)

According to the Kabbalah (*Tikkunei Zohar*), while we are to bind ourselves to the *Shechinah* and make ourselves a chariot for the Divine Presence, we are also to bind the evil inclination below us, that it be a chariot on which we ride (*Reshit Hochmah*, Sh'ar ha-kedushah, chap. 16, #68). In other words, our lower nature should be a vehicle for our higher one. This concept seems to link with what both *Sefer Hasidim* and Rabbi Elimelech taught, that we are to meditate in a way that will subdue and humble our natural ego and animal nature. That also would seem to be the import of Rabbi Shlomo of Karlin's words. In the bathroom, where we are so occupied with the lowest functions of our body, there is, of course, a tendency for the body to fill our consciousness. The Karliner made sure that his spiritual purposes were predominant in his mind at that time, and that the lower influences were kept below.

27:4:6 They once told the Rebbe of Lublin a Torah teaching of another rabbi which made use of the latter's knowledge of botany.

> The *Rebbe* said that the teaching was good, but for all that, he sensed something of the odor of the bathroom in it. And the truth was that that rabbi, in order to avoid Torah thoughts in the bathroom, would take into the toilet with him a botanical journal written in Polish. And it was from that knowledge that he drew for his Torah comment.[1] (*Niflaot ha-Rebbe*, p. 123, #371)

This story provides us with a lesson about why we are not to think holy thoughts in the bathroom. But it also suggests that reading nonreligious books or newspapers is appropriate there.

27:4:7 There are many possibilities, of course, for what to think about or read in the bathroom. For instance, it would be appropriate to give consideration to bodily matters such as health, food, or exercise.

27:4:8 Although we are not to think of God and Torah in the bathroom, we can think of things concerning our fellow men. *Yesod v'Shoresh ha-Avodah* notes that our love for our fellow men and our heartfelt sympathy for their welfare does not have to cease in the bathroom or any other unclean place.

> If you see or hear that some good came to your fellow man you should be happy and rejoice in your heart, just as if it happened to you—and by this sympathy you fulfill the positive commandment of "you shall love your neighbor as yourself." And so also for the opposite circumstance, God save us [if something bad happens to another, you should be unhappy]. Thus, a person can fulfill this *mitzvah* even if he is in the bath or any other place considered unfit or unclean [for holy thoughts]. (*Yesod v'Shoresh ha-Avodah*, Gate 1, chap. 7, p. 15)

This teaching focuses on the fulfillment of the commandment of love by sympathizing with others. This lesson can be enlarged to other meditations on love of neighbor that are permissible in the bathroom—such as thinking about the problems and needs of others and how we can help, about what favors we can do for them, and so on. In other words, we can meditate in the bathroom not only on our own physical needs, but those of others.

27:5 Although we cannot have holy meditations in the bathroom, we should have holy intentions when we go there and before we enter.

27:5:1 One intention may be that we know that retaining wastes within the body longer than necessary makes the body disgusting and an unfit receptacle for holiness, and by doing so we violate the commandment "You shall not make yourselves detestable" (Leviticus 11:43).

The reason for this is that at the same time you have holiness in your thoughts, you also have in the back of your mind the consciousness of the wastes in your body. It is in the nature of the mind that when the excretory organs are full or near so, part of the mind is directed there. To that very extent, then, your mind will be distracted from loftier and holier matters. Moreover, insofar as your mind at that time is concentrated on holy things, its thoughts will be subtly influenced in a bad way by these other thought-waves that are turned to the presence of filth within you. For this reason, checking yourself and going to the bathroom if necessary is one of the preparations for prayer.

Getting rid of this negative influence of excrement in our bodies can be a motive used for going to the bathroom.

> **27:5:1:1** [By going to the bathroom] you separate the vileness of the Shells from that which is holy. So before going to relieve yourself, say this short sentence [as a stated intention]: "I am going to relieve myself, to separate the Shell from what is holy." (*Yesod v'Shoresh ha-Avodah*, Gate 2, chap. 1, p. 23)

Translating the kabbalistic language, one could say: "I am going to relieve myself, to separate the negative force and influence from what is holy." The "Shell" is that which surrounds and traps within it the essence, just like a nut; thus, the "Shell" of uncleanness and evil is what can stifle the inner essence of holiness and goòdness and prevent it from being expressed.

27:5:1:2 The Besht:

> When you go to the bathroom, think, "Am I not separating the bad from the good, and is this not a unification [of the Upper and Lower Worlds]?" (*Tzavaat ha-Ribash*, p. 4)

By removing the Shell, the negative influence of excrement, our soul, which is part of the *Shechinah*, and yearns to unite with God, comes closer to its goal. The Holy One, blessed be He, and His *Shechinah* are brought closer together, and there is a unification of the Upper and Lower Worlds.

> **27:5:1:3** When you go to the bathroom, have as your intention to burn out the thorns from the vineyard (to destroy the Shells so they will not keep you from serving God), and not to transgress the prohibition "Do not make yourselves detestable." (Rabbi Tzvi Elimelech of Dinov, *Hanhagot Adam*, #4)

27:5:2 Another holy intention in going to the bathroom is the general one that the body does not, so to speak, belong to us, but is God's, and is to be used for His service. As such it should be taken care of with that thought in mind. This holds true of all care of the body and of all cleansing, whether external or internal, through washing or excretion, in bath or bathroom.

> **27:5:2:1** All the limbs of your body . . . even each and every hair on your head . . . it all belongs to God. (*Sefer ha-Hayim*, Gate 5, section 15)

27:5:2:2 Rabbi Yitzhak of Vorki once rebuked someone who was overly ascetic, saying:

> When did you acquire ownership of your body so that you have the right to afflict it? Are your limbs your own that you can do with them what you please? (*Beit Yitzhak*, p. 162)

27:5:2:3 When we go to care for our body with the consciousness that it is God's, not our own, we can have the added thought that it is indeed the dwelling place of our soul, which is made in the image of God and therefore all the more deserves our reverent attention.

A story about Hillel teaches this:

> Let Hillel be your model, and let all your deeds be done for the sake of heaven. For when Hillel would leave to go somewhere his disciples would ask him, "Where are you going, master?" And he would answer, "I am going to do a *mitzvah*." "What *mitzvah*, Hillel?" "I am going to the bathroom." "Is that a *mitzvah*?" would come the astonished reply. "Yes," he said, "for it is a *mitzvah* to see that the body is kept in good health and is not brought to any harm." [According to the rabbis delaying excretion harms the body.]

On another occasion they again asked him, "Where are you going, Hillel?" Again he answered, "I am going to do a *mitzvah*." "What *mitzvah*, Hillel?" "I am going to the bathhouse." "But is that a *mitzvah*?" they asked. "Yes," he said, "for it is a *mitzvah* to keep your body clean."

"And I will tell you why this is so. Consider the statues of great and famous men that stand in the palaces of gentile kings. The person put in charge of them, to polish them and keep them clean, is well paid by the government; not only is he given a good yearly salary, but his work is prestigious enough that he is held worthy to mix with the most powerful people in society. How much more, then, will we be rewarded for cleaning and caring for our bodies—for we have been created in the image and likeness of God Himself, as it is said, 'for in the image of God did He make man [Genesis 9:6].'" (*Avot d'Rabbi Natan* - B, chap. 30)

The concepts discussed here can also be made into a brief stated intention when going to the bathroom. For example: "I am going to the bathroom to care for my body, which is Your creation and belongs to You, O God, so that it will be healthy for Your service." Or: "I am going to take a bath to keep my body clean, for the honor of my Creator; for my body is His wondrous creation, the house of the soul, which is made in His image."

27:6 As we go to the bathroom, and before entering, we are to have one of these holy intentions for the service of God. But since we cannot have holy thoughts in the bathroom itself we should pause before we go in and do something to put a stop to the wheels of our mind (which should be involved with holiness), so that such thoughts will not continue once inside. And we should caution ourselves then to be careful about this.

27:6:1 When the holy Rabbi Mordechai of Nadborna, the memory of a *tzaddik* for the life of the World to Come, spoke of the greatness of his holy father, Rabbi Bertzi of Nadborna, he said: "When my father had to do his preparations for entering the bathroom, he lowered himself from his *d'vekut* slowly. And I can tell you this," Rabbi Mordechai concluded, "when my father lowered himself completely from his *d'vekut*, there are many good Jews who would be blessed if they had such *d'vekut* when they said the *Sh'ma Yisrael*." (*Raza d'Uvda*, Sh'ar ha-Otiyot, p. 20, #3)

27:6:2 In the Talmud two suggestions are made about what to say before you enter the bathroom and in each case the words are directed to the two angels who, we are told, always accompany a man.

> Before you enter the bathroom say, "Remain in your honor, O honorable and holy servants of the Most High. Give honor to the God of Israel and leave me here until I enter and take care of my needs, and then return to you."*
>
> But Abaye said, "You should not say it that way, lest they leave you for good; rather, say, 'Guard me and help me and support me! And wait for me, until I enter and leave—for such is the necessity of men.'"* (*Berachot* 60b)

The *Shulchan Aruch* notes that: "Now it is not our custom to say this" (3-1). Perhaps this is because the belief in the accompanying angels is not much in use. The *Mishnah Berurah* says here that in our time we are not on the religious level where we have angels accompanying us so that we should ask them to wait for us. Regardless, the Ari ha-Kodesh and others after him renewed this practice.[2]

We too can say the words as in the Talmud; but if not, the situation still dictates that something be said for the purpose indicated—putting a halt to our mind's momentum toward holy thoughts.

There is a way to understand the sentences offered in the Talmud that suggests a "translation" in which they can be used. As with the angels whom we welcome in our homes on *Shabbat* (when singing *Shalom Aleichem*), the accompanying angels addressed before entering the bathroom can be understood as holy thoughts and feelings which God sends us[3] (see "*Shabbat*," 18:2:4:2).

If we make an appeal that these thoughts not come to us in the bathroom, it is not appropriate to speak directly to the Holy One, blessed be He, at the very doorstep of an unclean place. That is why the words of the Talmud are directed to the angels. Taking the lead of the Talmud, then, we can address ourselves to the thoughts themselves and, translating into a modern idiom, say: "O holy thoughts that come from the Most High, remain in your honor and give honor to the God of Israel and leave me here while I enter and take care of my needs, as is the way of men. And as soon as I exit, come to me again."

27:7 Before entering the bathroom you should also have something ready to read there if necessary, or determine what you will think about once inside.

27:8 After leaving the bathroom we ritually wash our hands. Our intention is that after being in an unclean place we remove the impression of uncleanness that tends to remain with us even after we leave (the "spirit of uncleanness" in the language of the rabbis), and by our action we also make a separation between the two realms of the clean and the unclean. As the water flows over our hands we should think of the removal of any trace of uncleanness from us. And afterwards it is good to raise our hands palms up, fingers slightly cupped as if receiving something—to symbolize the reception of purity and holiness.

> After washing and before making the blessing [*al netillat yadaim*], be sure to raise your hands, spread apart and above your head, and begin to make the blessing "[who has commanded us] on the washing of the hands." Raising the hands this way when saying this blessing has a spiritual effect in its own right. (*Yesod v'Shoresh ha-Avodah*, Gate 2, chap. 1, p. 24)

Immediately after this blessing we are required to make the following one:

"Blessed are You, O Lord our God, King of the Universe, who formed man in wisdom and created in him many orifices and vessels. It is revealed and known before the Throne of Your Glory that if one of these be opened, or one of those be closed, it would be impossible to exist and to stand before You. Blessed are You, O Lord, who heals all flesh and does wondrously."[4]

In this blessing the tradition accomplishes two things. On the one hand, it makes use of a natural feeling of relief and satisfaction after we relieve ourselves, and directs that good feeling, with our thanks, to our Creator, blessed be He.[5] As a result of this, the blessing makes us aware of God's wondrous doings for our benefit in the creation and workings of the body.

On the other hand, this blessing also provides us with a habit which will direct our minds back to God after having kept ourselves from all holy thoughts while in the bathroom. And as Rabbeinu Yonah said about what to do after leaving the bathroom:

> After you purify yourself, [by hand washing], return to your earlier thoughts of how to be diligent in the service of God. (*Sefer ha-Yirah*, p. 206)

28

Tiredness

28:1 There are two basic religious approaches to tiredness. The first is to fight it, overcome it, push yourself harder and harder to serve God without halt. Rabbi Shmelke of Nikolsburg, whose way this was, has in his list of *hanhagot*:

> Whenever your evil inclination incites you during Torah study to finish up a subject or shorten your learning because of *tiredness* [italics mine] or your lack of understanding or because there are distractions such as the noise of the children, rebuke the evil inclination and overcome it with force, break your lower nature and learn for even more time than is your habit, and learn with all your energy until you sweat; by doing this you will break the evil Shells and the External Forces and your sins will be atoned for. (*Shemen ha-Tov*, Likkutim, #171, p. 52, Hanhaga #52)

(See the stories about Rabbi Shmelke in "Sleep and Before Sleep," pp. 534f.)

This is one attitude. The second of the two religious approaches to tiredness is simply that when you are tired, rest. For your service of God when you are fatigued, and your mind and body dulled, is not what it should be.

Both of these attitudes are ancient, and a dispute where both sides act for the sake of heaven has no end. But it should not be thought that it is a matter of deciding which of the two ways is superior, for that is not necessary. According to the root of his soul a person chooses his way. And certainly, not giving in to tiredness, and pushing oneself at all times not to be separated from God, is an exalted path, as worthy as the other.

28:2 When you are tired, turn to God and say: "Master of the World! With my own strength I am too tired to serve you further; but if You want me to continue, You have to give me Your strength, as it says, 'Those who hope in the Lord will receive new strength' [Isaiah 40:31]. Blessed are You, who gives strength to the weary." Then, trusting in God's strength, continue Your Divine service.

> [Rabbi Israel of Koznitz] was very thin, and so sickly and weak that he was forced to be in bed almost all the time. And he had to wear garments of rabbit fur due to the sensitivity of his limbs. . . . But when the time for prayer came, he would blaze like a fire with holy fervor; he would leap and dance and roar like a lion in his prayer. He was as strong then as a youth of 20, who had no equal. And he said about himself, "I stand before God, blessed be He, like a serving boy, ready to be sent on an errand."
>
> Once he was honored at a *bris*, and when he was about to step into the carriage to take him to the synagogue, they wanted to help him get in; but he sharply rebuked them, saying, "Fools! Do you think I need your strength? I have, blessed be God, a better strength, as it says, 'Those who hope in the Lord will receive new strength [literally: exchange strength].' I exchange my poor strength for the strength of God. And He has strength to spare." (*Mazkeret Shem ha-Gedolim*, p. 120)

Or when you are tired you can say: "Master of the World! With my own strength I am too tired to continue. Let me then serve you in the way of a sacrifice."

We usually think that we are to do something when we seem to have adequate energy to do it; but recognizing that we do *not* have the energy, we can do the service anyway, acting from the special energy source of self-sacrifice. Going beyond yourself in this way is a true sign of devotion to God.

> If you have great difficulty doing some *mitzvah,* either because of the evil inclination, or because of embarrassment in front of other people, think of that *mitzvah* as being done for the sanctification of God's name, as a kind of martyrdom. For it is appropriate to die for the sake of doing His commandment. Certainly, then, it should be done although great difficulty is involved. (*Darkei Tzedek*, p. 20)

The same logic applies to tiredness (in fact, note how this quote speaks of the evil inclination, and in the quote in 28:1 it is said that tiredness often comes from the evil inclination).

If you finally do have to rest, turn to God and say: "Master of the World! In my heart I know that if I could continue to serve You I would, for that is my greatest desire. But if I do not rest my service will be confused and poor. I am going to rest now so that I can gain strength to serve You anew with vigor and freshness." (See Chapter 3, p. 56 about how to arrange this kind of rest.)

28:3 As noted in Chapter 3, p. 50, one way to decrease fatigue is by alternating religious practices. You can go from something harder and requiring more concentration to something easier. For example, if you reach an impasse studying Torah, or begin to feel dull, you can say some psalms, or you can repeat a holy sentence (see Chapter 3, p. 66). That may be enough to restore your clarity.

Since some practices do require more effort and concentration than others it is generally a good idea to adjust your activities to your capabilities at the moment.

It is a recurring theme with the Baal Shem Tov that the life-force ebbs and flows (*ha-hiyut ratzo v'shov*), and there are alternating periods of expanded consciousness (*mohin d'gadlut*) and constricted consciousness (*mohin d'katnut*). Sometimes particular practices are noted to be appropriate for one state or the other. Of course, tiredness is usually (though not always) associated with constricted consciousness.

According to the Besht, meditating on God's presence filling the world, and seeing the *Shechinah*, are services of small consciousness; expanded consciousness (for which this other service in small consciousness is a preparation) is to make a soul-ascent into the Upper Worlds. Thus, he says:

> You should meditate on how the Glory of God fills the earth, and His *Shechinah* is always present with you . . . and you should meditate in vision and think that just as you are looking at material things, so are you looking at the *Shechinah*, and She is present with you. This is a service for the time of small consciousness. (*Tzavaat ha-Ribash*, p. 23; cf. p. 9)

It is important to realize, however, that what is constricted consciousness for one person on a high spiritual level is expanded consciousness for another on a lower level. The meditation which the Besht recommended for the time of small consciousness would be a practice of expanded consciousness for many people.

> **28:4** As we find in *Erubin* [28b] . . . when Rabbi Zera would feel tired and weak and could not study Torah or do any other *mitzvah*, he would go and sit at the entrance of the house of Rabbi Yuda, the son of Rabbi Ammi, saying, "When the rabbis come to his house and leave, I'll be able to stand before them [to give them honor] as they go in and out—so I won't be idle without doing any *mitzvot*." [It is a *mitzvah* to stand up this way to honor Torah scholars.]
>
> And I have received a tradition from holy people, that if they were for some time unable to do any other *mitzvah*, they would handle their *tzitzit* and look at them—because looking at the *tzitzit* is something very deep, and raises up the *Shechinah* in exile. (*Kav ha-Yashar*, chap. 45, beginning)

(Of course, the Torah says about the *tzitzit*: "that you may look at it and remember all the commandments of the Lord, and do them" [Numbers 15:39].)

28:5 When you are tired, be sure to pray or study Torah or whatever other religious practices are to be done, *before* you put yourself in a situation where you will rest and then maybe end up falling asleep (see *Berachot* 3b). And this is a good time to strengthen yourself with vows.

For example, when you come home after work or late at night and know that you will be tempted to rest as soon as you enter the house, as you approach, say, "I vow to You, O God, that as soon as I enter the house I'll study Torah." See "Vows" [12] to learn about cautions to take in their use.

29

Sleep and Before Sleep

As with every other act of ours, sleep is to be a service of God. We are not to go to sleep just for our own needs, just because we are tired.

> For everything from which you derive benefit or enjoyment in this world, your intention should be not your own pleasure, but to serve God, blessed be He . . . and so with sleep; certainly when you are able to occupy yourself in Torah study and *mitzvot* you should not allow yourself to sleep for your own pleasure.
>
> Even when you are fatigued, and have to sleep to rest yourself from your labors—if you do so for your own pleasure, it is not praiseworthy. Your intention should be to give sleep to your eyes and rest to your body for the sake of the health of your body, and so your mind will not become dull and unfit for Torah study due to lack of sleep. (*Orech Hayim* 231 on *Shulchan Aruch* 31:1 and 31:4)

As with food and other aspects of our bodily existence, regulation of sleep can greatly affect our spiritual life. Too much or too little sleep can both be harmful.

There are two basic approaches to sleep: one is to sleep the least possible, because during sleep we cannot actively serve God, and our ability to have God-consciousness is diminished, if not extinguished altogether.

Rabbi Adin Steinsaltz, speaking of the greatest *tzaddikim*, characterizes the type as "the man for whom the Divine Presence is all. The one who is constantly consumed by love for God to the extent that he is unable to sleep at night, so agonized is he by the fear of losing conscious contact with the Beloved" (*The Long Shorter Way*, p. 240).

Rabbi Joseph Zundel of Salant said:

> Do not go to sleep except when it is impossible for you to be without sleep, for "Sleep is not good for the *tzaddikim*" . . . and in *Avot* 6:6 it is said [that Torah is acquired by] "minimizing sleep." Such should be your practice until it becomes second nature. Then it will be good for you in this world and in the World to Come. (*Hanhagot Tzaddikim* [III], vol. 1, p. 579, #9)

Rabbi Tzadok ha-Cohen of Lublin interpreted the rabbis' statement that "Sleep is not good for the *tzaddikim*." He said that if you have attained a higher state of God-consciousness by your efforts, sleep is not good because:

> Your expanded consciousness and the holy thoughts of the whole day disappear, and on the following day you have to begin again and make great efforts to regain that level once again—and all beginnings are difficult.[1] (*Tzidkat ha-Tzaddik*, #238)

But severely minimizing sleep can result in tiredness when awake, with its own problems.

The second of the two ways is to sleep moderately, just enough so that we are clear-minded the next day and can serve God with all our faculties.

Many holy people actually need very little sleep, since they are so unified in soul that little energy is expended in fighting psychic battles, and little energy needs to be recovered in sleep. Furthermore, their sleep itself is perfect, and being largely without internal disturbance is efficiently brief.[2]

Rabbi Shmelke of Nikolsburg was among those who believed that as long as you could ward off sleep you should do so. There are many stories about his own heroism in this regard.

> Our rabbi, the holy *gaon*, the Rebbe Reb Shmelke, the head of the religious court of Nikolsburg, the memory of a *tzaddik* for a blessing, was once studying Torah with his brother, the holy *gaon*, Rabbi Pinhas, the memory of a *tzaddik* for a blessing. The two of them had already been awake together for a number of nights with

no sleep, studying standing on their legs all the time. Rabbi Pinhas had no more strength to continue, so he went and got himself a pillow to lean on to go to sleep for a little while.

His elder brother, the Rebbe Reb Shmelke, reproached him, saying, "Brother! How can you cease from learning the holy Torah, leaving what is of eternal worth for a transient enjoyment?" His brother, Rabbi Pinhas, answered, saying, "Don't you see that I haven't the least bit of strength left with which to learn?" Rabbi Shmelke replied, "But I was talking to you about just this moment that you used your energy to walk over and get a pillow for yourself. With that energy you could have stayed standing and learning." (*Mekor Hayim*, p. 100, #333)

Rabbi Shmelke not only stayed awake as much as possible, serving God with Torah study, but when he studied Torah he maintained a state of continuous God-consciousness, without lapse (see the story about him in "Torah," 15:22:5).

The holy Rabbi Mordechai of Nadborna once said, "I have to give myself credit, that when I was young, as long as I had strength in my legs to carry my body I never lay down to sleep." (Because he only slept when he absolutely was falling off his feet and had no strength at all—and he would sleep once every two days.) (*Raza d'Uvda*, Sh'ar ha-Otiyot, p. 77, #2)

Though our weak generation has an attraction to what is easy, there is no question that the way of minimizing sleep, of pushing it away in an attempt to keep one's God-consciousness, is a holy path, and that holding to this path will result in attainment of the highest spiritual levels.

Here is an expression of the other way, the second approach. Rabbi Yitzhak Isaac of Komarna said:

When someone wants to serve God, blessed be He, with *d'vekut* and Divine light, and with joy and desire, he must have his mind clear and bright and undimmed, and his body vigorous. And if he is awake more than he should be, his vitality will decline and his mind becomes dulled. My holy father [Rabbi Alexander Sander of Komarna] said to someone who was making every effort to perfect himself and was exerting himself to the fullest and hardly sleeping, that it would be better if he would sleep the whole day and be a man for the two hours he was awake, rather than stay awake all the time and be a horse for ten hours, dully carrying the yoke. Because staying awake too much is very harmful. (*Ateret Tiferet*, p. 37, #49)

There is a lovely hasidic story in which Rabbi Shmelke again appears, that takes sides in regard to the two attitudes toward sleep.

> It was the way of the holy Rabbi Shmelke of Nikolsburg, not to sleep a fixed sleep in a bed, but only fitfully, when he had to; for he made his service of God fixed and continuous and it was his sleep that was occasional—not the other way around. So he always slept sitting in a chair at the table where he studied Torah, his head resting on his arm. In order not to sleep long, he held a lit candle which roused him when it guttered and the flame touched his hand.
>
> When the holy rabbi, Rebbe Reb Elimelech of Lizensk visited him he saw that the Torah study and prayer of Rabbi Shmelke were with such fervor and with such expanded consciousness, that if he would only sleep and rest himself, he would attain even greater heights, and he would go up in holiness ten levels. So he himself prepared the bed for Rabbi Shmelke and with great difficulty finally persuaded him to lie down and sleep in a bed. Then, Rabbi Elimelech closed and shuttered all the windows in the room so that Rabbi Shmelke would not realize what time of day it was and wake up, for Rabbi Shmelke usually was up long before dawn.
>
> Rabbi Shmelke slept until broad daylight. When he awoke in the morning, with the sun already up, his mind was clear as it never had been. As it was close to the time for prayer he went to the synagogue as usual and himself led the congregation in prayer, as was his holy custom. And all of his prayer in his Divine service was so powerful in holiness that he set all those who heard him on fire—to such an extent that when they recited with him the verses about the crossing of the Red Sea, where you are to imagine yourself there, they all lifted up the hems of their kaftans to keep them from getting wet. For it actually seemed to them that they had gone down into the Sea which had split before them.
>
> Later, the holy Rebbe Reb Shmelke said about himself, "I knew that I could serve God, blessed be He, with Torah study and prayer, but not until this day did I realize that one can also serve Him so much with sleep." (*Ohel Yitzhak*, p. 74)

Rabbi Shmelke himself saw how his service in the Morning Prayer was greatly affected, for good, by proper sleep. When you *davven* the Song at the Sea you are to imagine that you are at that moment yourself passing through the split Sea with Moses. And when he rested, his prayer was so alive, and so inspired the prayers of everyone present, that it seemed to them that they were actually there.

This story is written from the viewpoint of the side that holds that an adequate amount of sleep is a necessity. But as we know from another version, it seems that Rabbi Shmelke slept a full eight hours just this once, and afterwards went back to his old practice of two or three hours a night (*Ohel Elimelech*, p. 62, #146).

We see that while Rabbi Shmelke held that sleep should be reduced to a minimum, Rabbi Elimelech of Lizensk took the other view and in this he was supported by his holy brother, Rabbi Zusya of Hanipol.

Another hasidic story tells how, following the passing of the Maggid of Mezritch, the head of the hasidic movement after the Baal Shem Tov, the leading hasidim chose Rabbi Elimelech to succeed the Maggid.

After the funeral of the Maggid many of the hasidim went with Rabbi Elimelech to accompany him on his journey home. When evening came on they all stopped at a roadside inn, and because of his fatigue from traveling, Rabbi Elimelech took a nap and kept on sleeping for a few hours. The hasidim were shocked that the one whom they had chosen to lead them could sleep uninterruptedly this way for hours at a time. It seemed to them a serious lapse on the part of Rabbi Elimelech and they wanted to wake him.

But since it was improper for them to wake their *rebbe*, they asked Rabbi Zusya, his older brother, to do so. Rabbi Zusya went with them to the room where Rabbi Elimelech was sleeping, stood at the doorway and put his hand over the *mezuzah*. To the astonishment of all, Rabbi Elimelech immediately woke up.

They asked Rabbi Zusya to explain this, and he said:

> It is well known that you are supposed to picture the name YHVH continuously before your eyes, as it says, "I have placed the Lord [YHVH] before me always." How then can a man go to sleep, for during sleep it is impossible to do this? But he answered his own question, saying, "The answer is that we rely on the divine Name which is written on the *mezuzah* [the letter *shin* on the outside which stands for *Shaddai*, "the Almighty"]. So when I put my hand on the *mezuzah* and covered up the Name, Rabbi Elimelech had to wake up immediately to picture YHVH before his eyes." (*Ohel Elimelech*, p. 49, #124)

Of course, after seeing this, the hasidim no longer doubted the wisdom of their choice of Rabbi Elimelech as their *rebbe*.

Our interest in this story is the information it gives us regarding the different views about sleep. According to one view, the desire to have the highest and fullest consciousness of God always would lead you to decrease sleep to the very minimum—for when you slept you could not picture the Divine Name before your eyes nor could you be aware of the Divine Presence that it represented. But the other view, held by the two brothers, Rabbi Elimelech and Rabbi Zusya, was that the lack of sleep was what caused a decrease in the level of your God-consciousness when you were awake, and a person who would serve God must sleep adequately. But even so, it was difficult to "justify" sleep if that meant willingly removing the awareness of the Presence of God from your mind. The answer to the problem is that we are permitted to do this because we can rely on the Divine Name on the *mezuzah.* Furthermore, the story communicates the message that Rabbi Elimelech was somehow, through the *mezuzah,* connected with God even while asleep—and he was on such a high level that he was aware of this also, and immediately awoke when the Name on the *mezuzah* was covered, and that connection was broken and disrupted.

A good part of our life is spent in sleep and the great importance of sleep is due to its general influence on us and on our spiritual state when we are awake.

How we go to sleep and what kind of sleep we have will affect the way we are when we wake.

> If your lying down to sleep is done thoughtfully and properly, then your rising up will also be right. (*Seder ha-Yom ha-Katzar*, p. 7)

Rabbi Arele Roth said:

> Sleep is so important. For as the Rebbe Reb Elimelech, of blessed memory, said: "When you sleep like a horse, you also get up like a horse; but when you sleep like a man, you also get up like a man!" (*Igrot Shomrei Emunim*, Letter 32)

Rabbi Shmuel of Slonim said:

> It is an old adage that "As you make the bed, so do you sleep; and as you sleep, so do you wake; and as you wake, so do things go the whole day." If this is the case with material things, certainly it is so with spiritual things. And this is an important principle. (*Divrei Shmuel*, p. 202, #24)

29:1 PREPARATION FOR SLEEP

As everywhere in hasidic practice, with sleep too, preparation is seen as the key to true service of God. There are various preparations for sleep, with different purposes.

29:1:1 How Much to Sleep

Once, when the holy Rabbi Mordechai of Nadborna wanted to teach his hasidim a way in the service of God, he said that before he went to sleep he decided beforehand exactly how much time he wanted to sleep. And if he overslept even a little beyond what he had decided, he penalized himself by decreasing his sleep the next day. (*Raza d'Uvda*, Sh'ar ha-Otiyot, p. 77, #3)

29:1:2 *Tshuvah* and Taking Account

29:1:2:1 Before sleep you should be like a storekeeper who carefully goes over his books at the end of the day, to consider everything that you did that day for good and for bad. Then, confessing your sins of that day, turn in repentance to God. (Rabbi Moshe Teitelbaum, in *Hanhagot Tzaddikim*, p. 50, #35)

29:1:2:2 According to the rabbis, one is to be a "master of accounts" as they put it. This is one of the instructions in the Bratzlaver *Seder ha-Yom*:

> *Be a Master of Accounts*—Thank God for all the good that you merited to do that day, and make confession for all your failings—in thought, word, and deed. Pray to God for pardon, forgiveness, and atonement, and that He help you from now on to do as He wants.

29:1:2:3 I heard how once one of the young boys was lying down to sleep in the *rebbe*'s [Rabbi Nachman of Bratzlav] room, and he came over to the *rebbe* and began to cry before him, that he wanted to be a real Jew. The *rebbe* was already lying in bed, and he sat up on the bed and began to talk to him. He told him how to do this, and he gave him some things to study. He also told him that he should be a "master of accounts"—that every night before he lies down to sleep he should consider how the day passed. If he learned and prayed as he should, he should thank God, blessed be He, and offer Him praise and thanks—"to Your great and holy Name, that You made me worthy to learn and pray this past day according to

> Your will—at least a little bit. And I beg You, O Lord my God, that You help me tomorrow to increase in Your service with as much Torah and prayer as possible, with the greatest *kavvanah* possible." And if, God forbid, you did not learn and pray as you should on the past day, confess, and beg Him, blessed be He, saying, "Master of the World! I know that I transgressed today and didn't serve You as I should, neither with Torah nor with prayer, etc. But now I beg and pray that You forgive and pardon me for the past, when I did not serve You as I should, and help me tomorrow to do Your service with Torah and prayer, with *kavvanah* and perfectly according to Your will, as I should." (*Hayei Moharan*, #135)

29:1:2:4 *Kitzur Shnei Luchot ha-Brit* teaches that you should say a confession before sleep:

> Say "Our God and God of our fathers, let our prayer come before Thee, etc. We have trespassed, we have been faithless, etc. Naught is concealed from Thee, or hidden from Thine eyes"—as is found in the confession [in the *Shemoneh Esreh*] of *Yom Kippur*. And you can also say the *Al Het* ["For the sin"] prayer which is arranged according to the *Aleph Beit* [alphabetically]. (Inyan Kriat Sh'ma d'Lailah al Mitato, p. 104)

Both of these prayers are in the regular Siddur, and they are in the *Shemoneh Esreh* of *Yom Kippur*, one after the other. One or both of these confessions may be used and joined one way or another with a personal confession of sins.

29:1:2:5 It is a recommended practice that you always carry with you a little notebook in which you can record throughout the day failings and faults, so that at the time set for introspection and *tshuvah* (before bed being a usual time, but there are others) you can go over everything and fix what needs repair.

> During the day the Rebbe Reb Zusya [of Hanipol], may his merit protect us, wrote everything he did on a slip of paper. Before going to bed at night he read it, and wept until the writing was blurred by his tears; then he knew that his sins were forgiven him. And this shows how everyone should be a Master of Accounts every night before sleep. (*Knesset Yisrael*, p. 136)

(See "Individual Practices," 39:3 for a quote about the practice of keeping such a little notebook and its use.)

The Rebbe Reb Zusya, the memory of a *tzaddik* for a blessing, once told to those at his table at the third meal on *Shabbat* this story:

When I and my brother, the holy Rabbi Elimelech were in exile [wandering from place to place sharing the exile of the *Shechinah* according to the kabbalistic/hasidic practice], it once happened that we were on the road and it was very cold—a tremendous amount of snow came down on us, and there was also a very strong wind. Now this was on the third day of our intermittent fast [fasting every two days and eating on the third], and we said to each other that we had better make our way to some place of habitation so we can have at least something to eat by evening. We did so and arrived at some town by evening, and prayed *Minha* and *Maariv* there; and then had a little to eat.

I prepared myself to say the *Sh'ma* and then to lie down on the ground to sleep. But my brother, the holy Rabbi Elimelech called out to me and said, "Zusya, what are you doing? Don't we have to be Masters of Account?" "You're right," I said to him. Then my brother began to write down the transgressions he had committed that day. He found that he had committed 110 sins that day. So he began to do a complete *tshuvah* on them all, and he cried his heart out until the Holy One, blessed be He, had compassion on him and all the sins were erased—then he went to sleep on the ground.

[After explaining to one of his listeners that indeed his brother was a great *tzaddik* and had not committed great sins, he continued:] "The reason I've told you this story about how my holy brother found that he committed 110 sins that day, was so you would know how careful you have to be to turn away from evil and do good." (*Beit Pinhas*, p. 46, n. 30)

29:1:2:6 Do not lie down to sleep unless you have given full and thorough consideration to your sins. If you have sinned that day, God forbid, then set yourself some kind of fine or punishment, and make a fence for yourself so it will not happen again. (Rabbi Nahum of Tchernobil, *Hanhagot Tzaddikim*, p. 35, #10)

29:1:2:7 Before a person goes to sleep at night he should think over what he did that day, about his speech and other things; for whatever he did that was not right he should feel regret, and turn to God in repentance, and immediately make a fence for himself so that he will not do the same thing again. He should set for himself some kind of compensatory practice appropriate to fix what he has damaged by that sin. [For example, if you have sinned by shaming someone with your criticism, (beyond apologizing and appeasing that person) make it a point, for a certain period of time, to compliment everyone you converse with.] (*Derech Hayim*, 3–19)

29:1:2:8 The main thing before sleep, at the time when you say the [Bedtime Prayer Service with the] *Sh'ma Yisrael*, is to give thought to what you have done the whole day, and to confess your sins and cry and plead before God that He help you not to return to your foolishness. (Rabbi Asher of Stolin, *Hanhagot Tzaddikim*, p. 9, #19)

29:1:2:9 It is told of Rabbi Levi Yitzhak of Berditchev:

> Every night before going to bed he searched his actions of the day and went over them carefully. He considered them so closely, with such a fine tooth comb, that he always found faults in everything he did. And he did *tshuvah*, and he would say, "Levi Yitzhak won't do any of these things again!" Then he would say aloud, "But Levi Yitzhak—didn't you say the same thing last night?" And he would answer himself, "Yes. But yesterday I wasn't telling the truth; now I am!" (*Zichron l'Rishonim*, p. 96)

29:1:2:10 It is best when you begin this practice to do it for, let us say, five minutes. It is a general rule, when you begin new spiritual practices, not to overburden yourself. Once it becomes habitual and easy you can then lengthen the time according to your desire. But even when you start it is good to have one night a week when you engage in a lengthier self-examination. Thursday night is an appropriate time for this, when you can evaluate the events of your week (not only that day) before *Shabbat*, and do *tshuvah*. To succeed you will have to do this when you are still fresh; so plan your evening accordingly on that night.

29:1:2:11 If you have made a list of *hanhagot* to which you have committed yourself, before sleep is an appropriate time to read it.

29:1:2:11:1 Rabbi Moshe Teitelbaum, at the end of the list of *hanhagot* he made for his hasidim:

> Read over this little booklet of *hanhagot* every night before sleep. (*Hanhagot Tzaddikim*, p. 51, #56)

29:1:2:11:2 Rabbi Shmelke of Nikolsburg instructed his followers to read his list of *hanhagot* three times a day:

[once] after the Evening Prayers, before sleep. (*Shemen ha-Tov*, p. 52, #54)

(See "Individual Practices," 39:2 about making a list of *hanhagot* for yourself.)

29:1:3 Peace with Your Fellow Men: Forgiveness and Reconciliation

29:1:3:1 Before he gets into bed, a person should forgive anyone and everyone who sinned against him or hurt his feelings.

29:1:3:1:1 Every night before sleep, you should forgive those who have sinned against you. (Rabbi Moshe Teitelbaum, *Hanhagot Tzaddikim*, p. 51, #54)

29:1:3:1:2 You should say three times: "I forgive anyone who has hurt me," and then say: "Creator of the Universe, I forgive . . ." (*Shulchan Aruch* 71–3)

29:1:3:1:3 Forgive anyone who hurt or wronged you, and pray that God forgive him. Then, pray for his good.

The rabbis say:

> Where someone hurt his fellow, even though the transgressor does not ask it of the one hurt, he should pray on his behalf; as it says about Abraham with Avimelech, "And Abraham prayed to God, and God healed, etc." [Genesis 20:7,17] (*Tosefta, Baba Kama* 9–29)
>
> [The Holy Jew, the Yehudi] would not go to sleep until he prayed for those who persecuted him. (*Tiferet Banim Avotam*, p. 214)

29:1:3:1:4 Rabbi Elijah deVidas explained one aspect of forgiving those who hurt us:

> You should forgive anyone who abused you, so that Above they will forgive you your sins. (*Totzaot Hayim*, p. 35)

So after reciting before God your forgiveness of those who sinned against you, then ask Him to forgive you your sins.

29:1:3:2 If you remember at this time of accounting that you yourself hurt someone during the day, make a resolution to apologize first thing the next day.

> **29:1:3:2:1** If you remember that you sinned against someone by speaking to him harshly and abusing him, or if you slandered him somehow, or embarrassed him publicly, you should shed tears of regret and make a resolution that immediately the next day you will go to apologize to him, to soothe his hurt feelings and make up with him, and that this will be the very first thing you do the next day. . . . And if someone sinned against you by insulting you, forgive him immediately and say, "I forgive anyone who hurt me," and say the *Sh'ma* before sleep with concentration. (*Kav ha-Yashar*, chap. 55)

29:1:3:2:2 There is a lovely story about Rabbi Yitzhak of Drobitch that illustrates a number of teachings in relation to sleep, including the one about apologizing immediately:

> The holy Rabbi Yitzhak was on the level that as soon as he lay down in bed and said the words "Into Thy hands I commend my spirit," he immediately fell asleep. And if it happened that he did not immediately fall asleep, he would know that he had committed some sin, and they did not want to receive him in heaven until he had done *tshuvah*. For during sleep the soul of a good person ascends Above.
>
> Once this happened, and he considered his deeds of the day and did not find anything wrong—but when he continued, and scrutinized them very carefully, he realized that he had been together with some people [*misnagdim*] who made fun of the Baal Shem Tov, and he had kept quiet and did not protest.
>
> Without further ado he immediately got up from his bed, gave order to his coachman to prepare the coach, and immediately set out in the night for the holy community of Medzibuz to ask the Besht for forgiveness. Now the Besht had never met Rabbi Yitzhak, and no one at all in Medzibuz knew him. Rabbi Yitzhak arrived in the very early hours of the morning and went to the *Beit Midrash* to pray; and he was standing in the corner out of the way, praying. But when they took out the *sefer* Torah to read, the Besht called him up for an *aliyah* by name, addressing him as "Our master and teacher, Rabbi Yitzhak, the son of Rabbi Yosef." And he said to him with gentle humor and a smile on his lips, "Is it worth making fun of the

> Besht if you have to travel such a distance to make amends? But the Besht forgives you completely, from his heart."
>
> Look at how great was the holiness of Rabbi Yitzhak, and how careful he was about the least suggestion of slander. (*Mazkeret Shem ha-Gedolim*, p. 4)

(Rabbi Yitzhak of Drobitch, who was the father of Rabbi Yehiel Michal of Zlotchov, became a disciple of the Baal Shem Tov.)

We can learn a number of things from this story: (1) that if you are on the high spiritual level you should be, you should fall asleep immediately (for you will not have conflicting thoughts, desires, and motives fighting your intention to serve God through sleep);[3] (2) that sins prevent this and disturb our sleep (for we are not "received in heaven"); (3) that you should repent before sleep, and if you cannot sleep, investigate your deeds again; (4) that, if you realize that you have offended someone, go to apologize and appease him as soon as possible (the next day would be soon enough for all but the most pious—such as Rabbi Yitzhak!).

Rabbi Yitzhak of Drobitch himself taught:

> Many people have the false notion that they can stay angry at others until *Erev Yom Kippur*, and then they all go to apologize to one another and be reconciled. But that is not the way wherein light dwells, because each night before sleep you should forgive the other person for everything he did to you, saying, "God! Please forgive anyone who has wronged me." (*Mazkeret Shem ha-Gedolim*, p. 5)

So too, just like *Erev Yom Kippur*, we are to go each night, or the next day where that is impossible, to appease someone we have sinned against—as Rabbi Yitzhak himself did in the story.

Another story about Rabbi Yitzhak of Drobitch and his son, Rabbi Yehiel Michal of Zlotchov, was told by Rabbi Zusya of Hanipol, who had been a disciple of Rabbi Yehiel in his youth.

> When I was young and a disciple of Rabbi Yehiel Michal of Zlotchov, my holy *rebbe* once spoke to me harshly. Afterwards, however, he apologized and said, "Reb Zusya, forgive me for humiliating you!" I answered him, "Rebbe, I forgive you!"
>
> But before I went to sleep he came to me again, and again said, "Reb Zusya, forgive me!" And once again I answered, "I forgive you, Rebbe!"

> But when I had already lain down to sleep, the Rebbe's father, the holy Rabbi Yitzhak of Drobitch, of blessed memory, came to me from the Upper World [he was deceased] and appeared to me while I was still awake. And he said to me, "I have only one son in the Lower World, a precious and wonderful son; and you want to destroy him because he insulted you!" I answered him, "Rebbe! Haven't I already forgiven him with all my heart and soul? What more can I do?" He said, "That is still not a complete forgiveness. Come with me and I'll show you how to forgive!"
>
> I got up and followed him until we came to the *mikveh*. There Reb Yitzhak told me to immerse three times, and each time to say that I forgave his son. I did so, and when I got out of the *mikveh* I saw that his face was shining with such a great light that I wasn't able to look at him. (*Toafot ha-Rim*, p. 174)

We see from this story that (following the ways of his father) Rabbi Yehiel Michal, before he himself went to sleep, went a second time to apologize to Rabbi Zusya. We also see that Rabbi Zusya could not sleep because of his failure to forgive completely. This story is an important lesson about what is involved in really forgiving. Forgiveness must be from the heart. According to Rabbi Yitzhak Drobitcher and then Rabbi Zusya (the disciple of his son), one must even go to the *mikveh* if necessary to truly purify oneself from resentment. (Note that he immersed three times in the *mikveh*, each time saying, "I forgive." This is modeled on the three times you say before sleep "I forgive anyone who has hurt me," mentioned above.)

According to the rabbis, two ways to forgive completely and remove any traces of resentment from your heart are (1) to pray for the welfare of the person, and call down blessings upon him; (2) to do him some good. Thus before sleep you can pray for a person who hurt you (29:1:3:1:3) and also determine to do him some favor (29:1:18:2). (See "Loving and Honoring Our Fellow Men," 9:11 and 9:12)

29:1:4 Of course, what kind of sleep one has, that is, its spiritual level, depends largely on how a person acted during the day, what he was thinking of and what he did. As the rabbis say:

> What a man sees in his dreams is nothing other than what he thinks about in his heart. (*Berachot* 55)

As Rashi explains: "what he thinks about in his heart during the day." Another word of the rabbis is:

> Do not think about women and sex during the day so that you will not have a nocturnal emission during sleep. (*Avodah Zarah* 20)

Holy people who think of God throughout the day and are altogether pure do not dream of sex and violence; they see holy things and have visions of angels and converse with them.[4]

In his writings, Rabbi Yitzhak of Radevill (the Zlotchover's son) often says that a Torah teaching was revealed to him from heaven. For example, he says:

> My brothers, I will reveal to you a wonderful secret that I learned last night in the Upper Garden of Eden, in a dream. (*Toafot ha-Rim*, p. 236)

He also says:

> Let me explain to you what I mean when I say that I learned something in a dream in the Upper World. All dreams come from what we have been thinking about during the day, consciously or otherwise. And since I exert myself the whole day with supernal unifications [holy meditations], at night I see these things in a dream, and their secrets are revealed to me. (*Toafot ha-Rim* p. 237)

Therefore, the whole day is a preparation for sleep. But what one does shortly before sleep can also have a special effect. Repentance, seeking forgiveness from God for our sins, asking forgiveness from those we have sinned against, or resolving to do so, and forgiving those who have sinned against us, are all ways of purifying our hearts before sleep. We put ourselves at peace with God and man.

29:1:5 Torah Study

Torah study before sleep will also affect our dreams and sleep thoughts. During sleep your thoughts are largely freed from your conscious control. But if you immerse yourself in holy Torah thoughts before sleep, you will affect your sleeping mind for good. So study something appropriate for the time, like *aggadah*, hasidic stories, or *Zohar*, that will start the wheels of your imagination turning. Then meditate on what you have read as you lie in bed.

> **29:1:5:1** Be careful to learn every night before sleep, either *aggadah* or the holy *Zohar*. (Rabbi Yehiel Michal of Zlotchov, in *Zichron l'Rishonim*, p. 86, #21)

29:1:5:2 Among the *hanhagot* of Rabbi Yerahmiel Moshe of Koznitz we are told that:

> He learned *Midrash Rabba* before sleep, leaning on the table, not sitting; and he also learned *Beit Aharon* [the hasidic teachings of Rabbi Aaron of Karlin]. (*Sifran Shel Tzaddikim*, p. 84, #8)

29:1:6 The Prayer Service and Meditation

One of the main preparations for sleep is the prayer service called (after its central part): "The Recital of 'Hear O Israel' Before Bed." Most of the parts of this service have been selected because of the relevance of some of the individual verses to the time of night and to sleep. If you look and study, you will see this.

A hasidic meditation for *d'vekut* can be done during the *Sh'ma* of the bedtime prayer service.

> **29:1:6:1** The thought of the Divine Unity [that nothing else exists but God] is, therefore, the core of all [hasidic] contemplation. There is the story of the Chasid who, on a journey, stopped at an inn for the night. When he was asked if he desired to eat supper, he replied that he was far too tired and that all he wanted to do was go to bed at once, for he had to rise early. He was shown to his room, and there he briskly went about making his preparations for sleep. Among other things, as was his custom, he recited the bedtime prayers, and at the right place [the *Sh'ma*], he concentrated on the greatness and oneness of the Creator. In the morning, when the innkeeper came to wake him, he found the Chasid standing, with one foot on the floor, the other on the bed, still immersed in the thought of Divine Unity. (*The Long Shorter Way*, p. 222)

> **29:1:7** Before sleep (and after waking), Rabbi Yerahmiel Moshe of Koznitz would say three times in a loud voice: "I am God's and God is mine!" and then: "There is a God in heaven and on earth, and over all the worlds—One, Single, and Unique—Who Was, Is, and always Will Be!" (*Sifran Shel Tzaddikim*, p. 91)

These words express the meaning of the *Sh'ma*, that "The Lord is *our* God"—I am His and He is mine; "The Lord is One"—God is One, Single, and Unique.

29:1:8 Once you finish this short prayer service, and get into bed and say the blessing (*Hamappil*), it is customary not to converse anymore with anyone and to eschew any further activity. Now is the time for serving God with sleep, and you should not be distracted with anything else. Furthermore, you are to carry these final meditations and prayers right into sleep without allowing an interruption of other, foreign thoughts.

> Those whose truth-saying can be depended upon told this story [about Rabbi David Moshe of Tchortkov, a son of Rabbi Israel of Rizhin]: When he was about 7 years old a fire broke out in the house of the holy rabbi of Rizhin. The Rizhiner left his room and asked after his children. Immediately they all came around him, but he saw that one was missing—David Moshe. At once one of the attendants went into his room and found him lying in bed awake. The attendant asked him if he did not hear all the noise, that a fire had broken out. The holy child, without speaking, indicated to him that he had heard, but that since he had already made the blessing *Hamappil* ["He who causes the bands of sleep . . ."] he did not want to interrupt [by getting up again. He wanted to go to sleep immediately]. He signaled to him that God, blessed be He, would save him. The attendant told this to his holy father, and it was immediately seen that the fire went out. The holy Rizhiner said, "Don't be amazed that the fire was extinguished for his sake, for it's written, 'He fulfills the desire of those who fear Him,' and this son of mine is a pillar of the fear of God." (*Tiferet Adam*, p. 7)

29:1:9 *Mezuzah*

Before sleep it is a good practice to kiss the *mezuzah* of the room you are in (touch it with your fingers and then kiss them), and think of God's presence in the room and His protection.

> **29:1:9:1** Before going to bed [after the prayer-service], go over to the *mezuzah*, put your fingers on it and say, "God protects me and watches over me; God is the shade at my right hand; God will guard my going out and my coming in, now and forever." And afterwards say seven times, "Know Him in all your ways, and He will straighten your paths before you." (*Shulchan Aruch*, 71-4)

> **29:1:9:2** It is a practice received from the holy master Rabbi Aaron of Tchernobil that before sleep you should go over to the *mezuzah* and meditate on how it is a token of God's protection for the house. Put your hand on the *mezuzah* and think of how God is the true owner of the house and we are all His guests, and how God will guard all those in the household. It is an important obligation

to do this every night. And say this: "Bar Kapparah said, 'What is the smallest portion of the Torah from which all its basic principles can be derived?' It is 'Know Him in all your ways, and He will straighten your paths before you'" . . . and say this verse seven times." (*Megaleh Amukot*, by Rabbi Hayim Liberzohn, p. 11)

(Compare this to "Waking and Beginning the Day," 4:15:1:2. It is a practice of some to do and say this at the *mezuzah* before leaving their house in the morning. See also the story on p. 537 about Rabbi Elimelech of Lizensk and the *mezuzah*, which has a connection with this practice.)

29:1:10 Stated Intention

Your intention in sleeping should be to renew your strength for the service of your Creator—and if so, it is then accounted as being for the service of God.[5] (*Shulchan Aruch*, 71–4)

It is appropriate to say this as a stated intention.

Before sleep say: "My intention in going to sleep now is to strengthen my body for the service of God, blessed be He." (Rabbi Yehiel Michal of Slutzk, *Hanhagot Tzaddikim* [III], vol. 2, p. 716, #18)

Perhaps one can include a preceding general stated intention and say: "My Father in Heaven, I am going to sleep as a service, to do Your will and to give You pleasure in me. And I am going to sleep now to renew my strength and my clarity of mind, so that I can serve You with all my energy tomorrow."

Rabbi Alexander Ziskind wanted, it seems, to bring God's presence and witness in at the very moment when he felt the need for sleep, so that it would not be as if his motive was self-oriented, without regard to his Creator. For he would rather stay awake and serve God, but God was bringing sleep on him, and he was too tired to continue. If he did, his Divine service would be poor and with an unclear mind.

And when I had to sleep I immediately called to mind these few words, "My Maker and Creator, You are witness that I am descending into sleep." (*Tzva'a Yekara*, of Rabbi Alexander Ziskind, p. 20, #34)

29:1:11 At the very moment of lying down there are also various verses or lines of prayer that can be said:

29:1:11:1 "You know my lying down and my rising up." (cf. Psalm 139:2,3)

29:1:11:2 "In perfect peace will I lie down and sleep, because You alone, O God, will surely see that I rest in safety." (Psalm 4:9)

29:1:12 After lying down, the feeling of relief, safety, and thankfulness that normally come with this moment can be lifted up spiritually and expressed in prayer, along with other appropriate requests and resolutions. Here is an example of such a prayer, based on the traditional "He who causes the bands of sleep" (*Hamappil*) prayer said at this time (*Shulchan Aruch*, 71–4; Siddur—Bedtime Prayer Service):

> Blessed are You, O God, who has given me this bed and this place in which to rest and sleep in safety and comfort. You have created sleep for us so that we can be refreshed and renewed to serve You tomorrow with greater strength.[6] Let that be my portion and my resolve—to serve You tomorrow with renewed strength. And let my sleep be considered a preparation for tomorrow's divine service. For You know, O God, that I would rather stay awake now and serve You. But I cannot, since I am too tired [or: but if I did, my service would be poor and with an unclear mind. So too would my service tomorrow be poor if I do not have adequate sleep].
>
> My Father in Heaven, it is You who bring sleep upon us, and rouse us from sleep; let my lying down and my rising up be in health and in peace of soul. And while I am asleep, let all my thoughts and dreams be holy and pure, and dedicated to You.
>
> And to that end I resolve now that all my thoughts as I rest in bed and approach sleep be without sin and turned to You. I resolve that with Your help I will rise early, with speed and energy, to Your service, and that my first thought in the morning when I wake up will be to think of You and all Your goodness, to be aware of Your presence and to say the *Modeh Ani*, to wash my hands to separate myself from any bad thoughts or dreams I may have had while asleep (Save me from them!), and to prepare myself to serve You in prayer. If such is Your will. Amen.

(See "Waking and Beginning the Day" for the waking practices mentioned here.)

Such a prayer can be said in speech, or in thought alone, but perhaps because saying it aloud is harder, it expresses more determination.

29:1:13 To protect yourself from low thoughts during sleep:

> When you go to sleep, picture before you the special Name of God [YHVH], blessed be He, in big letters, as it says, "My eyes are always turned to God, and He will keep my feet from being trapped." [Psalm 25:15] (*Avodat ha-Kodesh*, Tziporen Shamir, p. 23b, #121)

This probably means that you are to do this as you go to the bed; but it would seem to be a good practice to picture the Name also while lying in bed, perhaps while repeating mentally the quoted verse or another psalm verse, such as "I have placed the Lord before me always."

29:1:14 Visualizations

Rabbi Elimelech of Lizensk suggested a Divine service through visualization: "When lying on your bed without being able to sleep you should imagine throwing yourself in the fire as a martyr." (See "Service of the Imagination," 19:4:1 for the full quote.) But other visualizations are also possible. For example, picture yourself prostrating again and again to God in the Temple in Jerusalem (as it will look when it is rebuilt, soon and in our days), or walking on a pilgrimage to Jerusalem.

29:1:15 Making the Bed

Some of the hasidic *rebbes* would take care to make their beds with special holy intentions in mind, for if the bed is made in holiness, the one who sleeps in it will be influenced to have holy thoughts and dreams.

> The two holy brothers, Rabbi Elimelech of Lizensk and Rabbi Zusya of Hanipol, once went to Nikolsburg for the express purpose of trying to get Rabbi Shmelke to sleep in a bed, for he never slept in a bed, but always slept sitting up in a chair. They succeeded with him one time, and they themselves made the bed for him, doing so with holy intentions. And that night Rabbi Shmelke slept for hours more than was his wont; and when he awoke, he felt a special clarity and an expanded consciousness in his prayers and in his service of God the whole day. But for all that, he said that he could not do this always and give up his own way. (*Ohel Elimelech*, p. 62, #146)

(This is another version of the story at the beginning of this chapter.)

Elsewhere, still another version of the story comes with an explanation:

> As is well known, the holy Rabbi Shmelke, may his merit protect us, never slept in a bed except once, when Rabbi Elimelech visited him and made the bed for him and urged him to sleep in it—and he did. The next morning he said that if Rabbi Elimelech was always with him to make the bed, he would sleep in one, because that night he reached higher levels in sleep than ever before. (*Ohel Elimelech*, p. 135, #342)

The lesson here is that when you make your bed you should have holy intentions (perhaps stated out loud) about your sleep.

(Although this matter of making the bed had more importance in times when the beds were of straw, and how they were prepared would really affect your comfort, still, even today this practice has relevance.)

29:1:16 One can put a holy object like a Psalm book or the Torah book you were studying before sleep beneath the pillow for the sake of the aura of holiness which it emanates—leading to holy thoughts and dreams.[7]

A tradition has it that when Jacob set out from Beersheba to go to Haran, he stopped at Mount Moriah (where Abraham was told to sacrifice Isaac), where he had his famous dream of the ladder going up to heaven. This is how *Pirke d'Rabbi Eliezer* (chap. 35) understands Genesis 28:11, "And he took of the stones of that place and put them under his head":

> Jacob took twelve stones from the stones of the altar whereon his father Isaac had been bound, and he set them for his pillow.

We can imagine that the holy stones of the altar, which lifted Jacob's head off the ground, influenced his dream of the ladder reaching up to heaven.

29:1:17 *Sefer Haredim* says that we should always be aware that we are in God's presence:

> You should not lapse for even a moment. When you speak with your fellow, let your intention be to talk to your Creator. When you are silent, direct your heart and mind to Him [in meditation]. When you lie down, lie down with love for Him, and make supplication to Him that your heart not turn away from Him during sleep. (chap. 66, #118)

So when we are in bed we can meditate on God's presence and our love for Him, and pray that even in sleep that love not cease.

29:1:18 When lying on the bed going to sleep it is good to make resolutions for the next day, and to express our determination before God to serve Him the next day. We can go over in our minds how we will begin that service and in what order, as soon as we awake (see "Waking and Beginning the Day").

> **29:1:18:1** [Rabbi Arele Roth:] Before sleep pray that you should be able, with your very first thought when you wake up, to cling to God and to have God–consciousness. (*Noam ha-Levavot*, Shomer Emunim, Letter 32. See also 29:1:12.)

29:1:18:2 Just as we can meditate on our love of God while going to sleep, so can we meditate on love for our fellow men:

> He who lies in his bed at night to go to sleep and thinks to himself, "Tomorrow I will get up early and do a favor for so-and-so," will one day rejoice with the *tzaddikim* in the Garden of Eden. (*Midrash Proverbs* on 12:20)

(See "*Tzedaka* and *Gemilut Hasadim*—Charity and Kindness" 22:1.)

29:1:18:3 In the morning we are to wake up to serve God with vigor; but to do this we have to make our resolution the night before.

> If a person's nature is to sleep a lot, he certainly has to overcome that. . . . But to do so in the very hour of battle, to rise in the early hours when it is still dark, as soon as you wake from sleep, is difficult, for the *yetzer* makes him sleepy and casts on him a net of laziness. For the time of waking is a time of war, and you have to plan a stratagem before the war—before lying down to sleep.
>
> If you are by nature lazy and accustomed to sleeping a lot . . . think with resolve before sleep, "When I awake, I will get up with speed and energy and make myself get out of bed immediately!" And it is also good for someone like this to pray a short prayer before lying down to sleep, in whatever language it may be, everyone according to his own level, that God help him, that he not fall into the hand of the *yetzer*, and that He strengthen him so that he can get up in the early hours. (*Nahalat Avot*, p. 12a)

29:1:19 Once in bed it is a good practice to:

> Try to see that you fall asleep while thinking over words of Torah, that your soul [which during sleep goes up to heaven] appears

> before the Creator of the world while meditating on Torah. (*Seder ha-Yom*, p. 29b)

It is easier to meditate on Torah as you fall asleep if you make it a practice to study Torah right before sleep, and meditate on what you have read as you lie in bed. (See 29:1:5.)

The effect of Torah study, particularly something that is repeated, can carry over even until waking.

Genesis 28:10–22, which tells the story of Jacob's dream of the House of God, with the ladder going up to heaven and angels ascending and descending on it, is the focus for a number of the rabbis' comments about sleep. Genesis 28:16 says: "And he woke from his sleep (*mishnato*)." On this the *Midrash* says that he woke "from his *mishnah*-study" (*mimishnato*).

Baal ha-Turim (in the *Chumash*) comments on this:

> Since he meditated on Torah during the day, his mind kept on doing so while he slept, in his dream.

The Hidushei ha-Radal (in *Midrash Rabba*) says:

> He fell asleep in the midst of words of Torah that he was repeating (*sh'shana*).

The intent of the *Midrash* is not fully clear. But the point seems to be that the Torah which Jacob was repeating as he went to sleep carried on through sleep, and went on until the time of waking. And it was because of this that he had a holy dream of prophecy.

In the personal *hanhagot* of Rabbi Yosef of Dubnow:

> I must be sure to fall asleep while thinking words of Torah, so that when I awake *my first word and thought will be directed to the Holy One, blessed be He*—in Torah and prayer or in song or praise—*since my last word* [*and thought*] *was in Torah.* (*Yesod Yosef*, p. 10, #42) (Italics mine)

We can mention here in passing the dream question. Before sleep you may also rehearse a question you want answered, and pray that God answer it in a dream in a way that you will remember on waking up.

29:1:20 *Hitbodedut*—Talking to God

While lying in bed you can have a quiet conversation with God, speaking your heart out to Him until you fall asleep.

> The *Rebbe* [Rabbi Nachman of Bratzlav] said (*Sichot ha-Ran*, #68) that the main time for King David's *hitbodedut* was when he was lying in bed before sleep, when he covered himself with the sheet. Then he spoke to God and talked his heart out before Him, blessed be He, as it says (Psalm 6) "All the night I make my bed to swim [I water my couch with my tears]."
>
> And Rabbi Abraham, the son of Rabbi Simon [a Bratzlaver hasid], said that this was also the *Rebbe*'s way. Before sleep he would seclude himself with God, blessed be He, and do *hitbodedut* for a long time until he fell asleep in the midst of *hitbodedut*.
>
> And Rabbi Abraham, the son of Rabbi Simon, used to speak about this, and he would say, "How can someone say [before God]: "I am going to sleep"?[8] Rather, you should say that you are going to do *hitbodedut*—and if you fall asleep while talking to God, what can you do? What you cannot help, God excuses."
>
> And they saw that this was always his way when he lay down to sleep; for even if there were people in the room, he would just turn his face to the wall and engage in *hitbodedut* until he fell asleep. (*Tikkun Kriat Sh'ma al ha-Mitah mai-ha-Arizal*, Bratzlav, p. 21)

(See "Talking to God and Being Alone with God—*Hitbodedut*" [33] for more about this practice and what it involves.)

29:1:21 Repetition of a Holy Sentence

One can, while going to sleep, repeat a holy sentence over and over.

29:1:21:1 Rabbi Alexander Ziskind used a three (Hebrew) word phrase as a repeated sentence throughout the day which he would say over and over, time after time. He says:

> When I had to go to sleep I immediately would repeat those three words over and over in my mind—"You are my Maker and Creator" [*Yotzri v'Bori Ata*] until I fell asleep.[9] (*Tzva'a Yekara*, #34)

29:1:21:2 One can repeat the *Sh'ma* until sleep comes.

There is a story in the Talmud of how:

> Rabbi Shmuel [bar Nahmeni would] say the *Sh'ma* in bed and then repeat it over and over until he fell asleep while saying it. (*Yerushalmi Berachot*, 1-13)

Rabbi Shmuel's repetition of the *Sh'ma* was obviously audible. But since it is hard to imagine falling asleep like that, perhaps he repeated it for a while out loud and then continued with the repetition mentally until sleep came upon him (cf. the practice of Rabbi Alexander Ziskind just mentioned; however, Rabbi Abraham, the Bratzlaver hasid, seems to have talked to God until sleep came upon him).

See "Repetition of a Holy Sentence," 21:2 and 21:3 for the full text of this story in *Yerushalmi Berachot* and its interpretation.

29:1:21:3 Any other appropriate one line verse or prayer can also be repeated while going to sleep. The *Shulchan Aruch* (71–4) makes various suggestions of verses to say if you are unable to fall asleep right away. They are: "A Torah did Moses command us, as an inheritance for the Congregation of Jacob" (Deuteronomy 33:4); "I hate them that are of a double mind, but Your Torah do I love" (Psalm 119:113); "Light is sown for the righteous, and joy for the upright in heart" (Psalm 97:11); "A continuous fire shall burn on the altar, it shall not be put out" (Leviticus 6:6).

This last verse alludes to the continuous flame of devotion that should burn in your heart for God even during sleep.[10]

There were many hasidic *rebbes* who reached this level, and whose hearts burned with love of God even while they slept.

29:2 HOW THE *TZADDIKIM* SLEEP

After telling us how Rabbi David Moshe of Tchortkov slept only two hours a night, a hasidic story goes on to say:

> Even during that time, he would continually call out while sleeping, "Holy Father!" "Holy Master of the whole world!"—just as was his holy practice during meals, when he sat at his pure table before God, in the company of his hasidim. (*Eser Orot*, p. 147, #8)

There is a similar story about Rabbi Yehiel of Mushe, a disciple of Rabbi Mordechai of Lechovitz:

> His holy way was to sleep every night about two hours, no more, and during the time of sleep he kept repeating sentences of the longing of his soul for God, such as "My soul thirsts for You," "Whenever I speak of your Glory my heart is aswirl with my love for You," and "My heart desires You in the night hours"—and

> others like this—all this while he was sleeping.[11] (*Torat Avot*, p. 284)

To understand these stories we should know that it is a holy practice to express longing for God verbally throughout the day. Rabbi David Moshe did this at the table during meals. Rabbi Yehiel must certainly also have been doing this during the day (though it was likely not known by others), but when he went to sleep, the same lines or their like would come to his lips—and then he could not hide what he was doing and saying, and people could hear it. It is also quite possible that Rabbi Yehiel was repeating these very verses as he was going to sleep.

Such behavior during sleep is not, however, merely a mechanical carry-over from the daytime; these holy people were burning up for God.

About Rabbi David Biderman of Jerusalem (in the Lelover line of *tzaddikim*):

> He slept little, and as [the Talmud says about] King David, he would "doze like a horse [dozing and waking on and off] until midnight, when he awoke and strengthened himself like a lion to learn the hidden teachings of the Kabbalah. He rarely slept in a bed, but many nights he sat learning in a chair and would sleep briefly at the table. And even during those moments of sleep he would burst out with longing for the holy *Shechinah*, and call out in a voice suffused with love and yearning, "Mother, Mother!" (*Tiferet Beit David*, p. 105)

(One especially interesting aspect of this is that the *rebbe* calls out to the *Shechinah* as his Mother.)

Here is another story about another disciple of Rabbi Mordechai of Lechovitz:

> Our master, the holy grandfather Rabbi Mordechai, testified about Rabbi Moshe Binyamin that five minutes would never pass without him thinking about *tshuvah* and turning to God. Once Rabbi Mordechai sent his great disciple Rabbi Moshe of Kobrin to Rabbi Moshe Binyamin, so that he could learn from him how a Jew should sleep. The Kobriner was with him in his bedroom and saw how while sleeping he would wake up every few minutes and cry out from his great *d'vekut*, "Master of the World!" and other things like that. (*Torat Avot*, Maasei Avot—Ha-Saba Kadisha mi-Lechovitz, 23)

The Kobriner was supposed to learn how to sleep; what is the lesson then? First, we are to see how even during sleep a Jew can burn with love for God; second, we see how the practice of Rabbi Moshe Binyamin during the day of continually turning to God ("every five minutes") carried over during sleep. During the day too he had intense *d'vekut*, continually turning to God and crying out, "Master of the World!" and similar things.

It is a holy custom in Israel, followed by some devout people, to wake at midnight or thereabouts every night to say the Midnight Service and to study Torah, along with other service of God. (See "*Tikkun Hatzot*" [31].)

As with any other physical activity, there is a spiritual benefit to be gained by the interruption of sleep. There are holy people who even interrupt their sleep continually. And *Tikkun Hatzot*, when they get up in the middle of the night to stay up in Divine service till the morning, is the "final interruption."

Hear what the rabbis say in the Talmud of King David, where they were certainly describing the practice of some of their own:

> David said, "I never passed midnight in sleep." Rabbi Zera said: "Until midnight he dozed as does a horse—which dozes off and wakes again and again; thereafter he strengthened himself like a lion to fight sleep and serve God until the morning." (*Berachot* 3)

This tradition became the model for *tzaddikim* and is alluded to again and again in describing their ways.

It is told of Rabbi Dovberish, the Maggid of Lublin, that:

> His holy way was to study Torah with his son from memory, and every *Shabbat* they would study together until the candles went out. When he went to sleep he would tell his son Eleazar also to go to sleep, and they would be side by side with a little partition between the two beds. There was water next to each bed so they could wash whenever they wanted [upon waking].[12] They would learn Torah together in the dark until they began to doze off a little, just like in *Berachot* 3b [about King David]. Then the Maggid would wash his hands and call out to his son in a loud voice, "Lazerka, Lazerka, you have already slept too much. Now is the time to learn!"
>
> And again they would learn until they dozed off. Again he would awaken, and wake his son and learn with him. And so did he pass the entire night in learning, with small interruptions of sleep. (*Shemen ha-Tov*, p. 100)

Note that their practice was to learn, with necessary interruptions for sleeping, rather than sleeping with interruptions for learning. We can also note that one can try this high kind of sleep on *Shabbat* if not other days. There are people who do not sleep at all on *Shabbat*, so as not to spend any part of the holy day, with its heightened spirituality, in sleep.

Rabbi Yehiel of Alexander stayed one night as a guest in the house of a hasid, Reb Shmulke Kossover, who reported what he saw to the author of *Eser Z'chuyot*:

> [At night] everyone went to sleep, but the holy *rebbe* did not lie down at all. He took some holy book or a Psalm book in his hand and paced back and forth in the room, reciting [softly] with awesome fervor, as was his holy way. Rabbi Shmulke lay on his bed and heard all this and his heart broke into pieces [in repentance at seeing the *rebbe*'s holy service of God]. This went on for about an hour or more.
>
> Suddenly he heard the *rebbe* say to himself, "*Oy vey*—I haven't any more energy at all!"—and he fell down on the bed and slept for about a quarter of an hour. Then he jumped up from the bed with a great commotion and cried out, "*Gevald*! What have I done? I lay down to sleep!" And he began again to learn and to pray. Again, in the middle, he said, "*Oy vey*—I haven't any strength left at all!"—and he fell down on the bed and slept. Then, after a short while, he jumped up again as before. This happened a number of times during the night, until before dawn, when he no longer lay down again. And this was his way of sleeping. (*Eser Z'chuyot*, p. 64)

> Our holy rabbi [Rabbi Yitzhak of Vorki] slept very little. Once he traveled from Sadigura to Vorki, and on the way he stayed over in the town of Kaminsk. He had to continue his journey in the morning and he only had three hours to sleep. This was after two days traveling without any sleep at all.
>
> When the rabbi went to sleep there were a number of people there who stayed up and were able to see the way he slept. He had had a big bucket and a vessel full of water and a cup for washing his hands put at the side of his bed. When he had slept twelve or thirteen minutes he got up, full of awe and fear of God, washed his hands three times and went back to sleep. After another twelve or thirteen minutes he again woke and washed his hands, and so on for the full three hours, during which time he woke up about fourteen times. (*Beit Yitzhak*, p. 181)

It is reported of the ways of Rabbi Yitzhak Isaac of Ziditchov:

> Our master's day began half an hour or an hour before midnight (if he did not stay awake all night) and ended at 9 P.M. . . . In his youth he would not go to sleep at all, but would just doze off briefly while

sitting in his chair [studying Torah, etc.]. Later, he strengthened himself like a lion, putting his feet in a basin of cold water to keep himself awake, and stood that way throughout the night studying Torah.

Even in his old age, when he was weak and was forced to sleep in a bed, even then he would only sleep in short spurts until midnight. After sleeping about fifteen minutes, he would wake and wash his hands three times, then go back to sleep for another sixty breaths [the rabbis said that a horse only dozes off for sixty breaths at a time] as at first, then he would wake up again and wash again. This was the way he slept till midnight. Then he awoke fully, got up from his bed, and began his Divine service. (*Pe'er Yitzhak*, p. 78, #1)

About Rabbi Menahem Mendel of Rimanov it is said:

He never passed midnight in sleep; and the time that he slept until midnight was in this manner. He had the books he was studying placed on the table by his bed. When he had slept five or ten minutes, he awoke and washed his hands (his personal attendant who sat near his bed handed him the vessel of water). And he would study for five or six minutes in a somewhat hurried way in the book he had ready. Then he lay down and fell asleep immediately. After sleeping for some more minutes, he woke, washed his hands, and studied another book—the *Zohar*, or *Mishnah*, etc. And thus did he do for the length of those hours he slept, until midnight. (*Ateret Menahem*, p. 35, #116)

It is hard to tell in every case what was behind the continual wakings of the different rabbis. Sometimes it seems that they purposely intended to wake themselves. With others it seems that they could not bear the lessened *d'vekut* of the sleep state, and so kept waking up spontaneously to reestablish a stronger connection with God, calling out, "Master of the World!" (Rabbi Moshe Binyamin); although sometimes they would call out in sleep without waking (Rabbi David Moshe of Tchortkov, Rabbi David Biderman). It seems with some of the *rebbes* that their *d'vekut* was itself of such intensity that they kept bursting out of the sleep state—like a man so much in love that, his heart afire, his sleep is continually disturbed.

Rabbi Menahem Mendel of Vorki (the son of Rabbi Yitzhak of Vorki):

He said many times . . . commenting on the words of the poem, "There is no sleep before Him" [whose simple meaning is that God does not sleep]—that someone who is before Him, blessed be He,

> and in His presence, is not able to sleep. (*Ha-Tzaddik ha-Shotek*, p. 131, #3)
>
> The way that Rabbi Levi Yitzhak of Berditchev slept was not like ordinary men. He would sleep in the middle of the bed, and on each side of him he had someone studying Torah. There were two men, one studying the *Zohar* and the other the *Ein Yaakov* or *Midrash*. And whenever he woke up, which he did again and again throughout his sleep, he would call out, "Master of the World, there is no sleep before You! And when I remember that You are by me, how can I sleep?" (*Zichron l'Rishonim*, last page Hashmatot)

It seems that the Berditchever, in having the two men sitting on his bed studying Torah, wanted to hear the holy sound of Torah even while asleep—so that even then he would remember God. And:

> Rabbi Elimelech [of Lizensk] testified that just as a man trembles who is suddenly surrounded by robbers while walking in a forest, so did the heart of Rabbi Levi Yitzhak beat within him out of fear of God, even when he was asleep. (*The World of a Hasidic Master—Rabbi Levi Yitzhak of Berditchev*, p. 166)[13]
>
> The Tzanzer Rebbe slept very little, and when he got up he did so with such vigor that he almost leapt out of bed. A number of times he got into bed, having taken off all his clothes, even his socks, and then, after having slept only two or three minutes, he got up!
>
> Once, a great rabbi expressed his frustration to him, saying that, try as he might, he could not overcome his need and desire for sleep. He asked the Tzanzer if there was some method he himself used, that he was able to do with so very little sleep. Since this rabbi knew about the Tzanzer's ways with sleep, it was understandable that he asked him what he could do to be like him.
>
> Our holy rabbi answered him, saying, "If you are able to sleep, how good. But as for me, I can't sleep." (*Mekor Hayim*, p. 101)

Now why was the Tzanzer unable to sleep? Was he afflicted with insomnia? Hardly. But, like the Berditchever and the Vorker, he was burning up with his devotion to God, and so aware of the presence of God, that he could not sleep.

What then is the meaning of his answer to the rabbi? Is he saying that we cannot learn to overcome sleep, as he did? It seems that the point of his answer is that conquering sleep depends ultimately on our reaching that high spiritual level where you cannot sleep—like a person who could not conceivably fall asleep in the presence of the king.

Help in understanding this comes from Rabbi Pinhas of Koretz who said:

> When you are joyful it is not possible to sleep because you are in a state of expanded consciousness, and sleep is the state of constricted consciousness. (*Nofit Tzufim*, p. 15a, #35)

Therefore, when you are in *d'vekut* and aware of God you cannot sleep.

Although it is true that for most people the goal in sleep is to be renewed for the service of God, there are *tzaddikim* on a very high level who can serve God during sleep itself. Rabbi Shmelke of Nikolsburg said that when he slept on a bed made by Rabbi Elimelech, he reached "higher levels" in spirituality—in other words, he was aware of his spiritual levels and doings in sleep (see 29:1:15).

Whereas for most people, even *tzaddikim*, their sleep is on a lower level of *d'vekut*, for others, their sleep can be higher than their waking, for the soul is able to free itself from the body. The soul goes up to heaven during sleep, and there are *tzaddikim* who are able to take advantage of that, so to speak.

> Our holy master, our teacher Rabbi Tzvi of Ziditchov, the memory of a *tzaddik* and a holy man for a blessing, used to say that if he accomplished in sleep just what he does while awake it is not a good sleep. For the service of God in sleep should be higher than the service during the time you are awake. (*Yifrach biYamav Tzaddik*, p. 104b, #18)

> [The Vilna Gaon] used to say that God created sleep to this end only, that a man should attain the insights then that he cannot attain, even after much labor and effort [in his waking state]. Because when the soul is joined to the body, the body is like a curtain dividing [man from the spiritual world]. But during sleep, when the soul is out of the body and clothed in a supernal garment [these insights] are revealed to her. (Rabbi Hayim of Volozhin, the Vilna Gaon's most important disciple, in his introduction to the Vilna Gaon's commentary on the *Sifra diTzniuta*, quoted in *Joseph Caro, Lawyer and Mystic*, p. 315)

The Vilna Gaon is known to have told one of his disciples that every night he experienced such ascents of the soul to the celestial academies, where wonderful insights were revealed to him (*Joseph Caro, Lawyer and Mystic*, p. 314).

In being a chariot for God, one level is that of the wheels, which are moved through outside energy (by the animals that draw the chariot); and a different level is that of the animals themselves, which pull the chariot and move through their own impetus (but directed by the hands of the charioteer on the reins).

> The holy *tzaddik* Rabbi Abraham Joshua Heshel [of Apta] said of his holy master Rabbi Yehiel Michal of Zlotchov that he would sleep according to one of two ways: as the holy animals that pull the Divine chariot or as the holy wheels of the chariot. In the former case when he wanted to ascend into heaven; in the other case when he was summoned to heaven and "The voice came to him and he was called."[14] (*Shema Shlomo*, II, p. 51, #6)

In either case these are very high levels.

Rabbi Tzadok ha-Cohen of Lublin:

> At night, when you lie down to rest and sleep, you also [as in the morning on waking] have to accept on yourself the yoke of the Kingdom of Heaven [by reciting the *Sh'ma*], so that "When lying on your bed [sleeping] you will know in whose presence you are,"[15] as is written in the comment of the author at the beginning of *Orach Hayim*.
>
> This is a greater service and more difficult to attain [than during the waking state]. I have heard this very thing in an interpretation of the verse, "And Jacob dreamed" (Genesis 28:12). For from a person's dreams is his spiritual level known. Thus, it is a very high level if even when he does nothing and makes no effort [being asleep], all his thoughts [and dreams in sleep] are still: "and behold, the Lord was standing over him" [the continuation of the verse].
>
> In this matter, only a few of the *tzaddikim* prided themselves that they reached this level. For that reason, there is an additional blessing in the Evening Prayer Service: "Cause us [O Lord] to lie down in peace" [that in sleep we should be in *d'vekut* with God]. (*Tzidkat ha-Tzaddik*, #3)

30

Men's *Mikveh*

30:1 Immersion in a *mikveh* is a hasidic custom and practice, though its regularity can vary. Almost all hasidim will go to the *mikveh* before *Yom Kippur*, many go before every holiday and every *Shabbat*, and some go every day before the *Shaharit davvening*. There are even those who have still more frequent uses of the *mikveh*.

> **30:2** It was said about the Baal Shem Tov that he attained his enlightenment and great levels of holiness because he very frequently used the *mikveh*. (*Keter Shem Tov*, quoted in *DhTvhY*, section on Taharah, p. 16b)

30:3 From the *Seder ha-Yom* according to the teachings of Rabbi Nachman of Bratzlav:

> *Mikveh*—A man should immerse himself every day, and through this he will sanctify himself and get rid of all the impurity of his sins and draw close to God in truth.

30:4 Rabbi Mordechai of Lechovitz said:

> You should always seek to purify yourself in the *mikveh*, especially

> when necessary, for the *mikveh* purifies the mind. (*Zichron l'Rishonim*, p. 32)

Sins cloud the mind, keeping it from perceiving God's truth and light. The *mikveh*, when joined with repentance, purifies from sin and opens the mind to enlightenment. "Especially when necessary" refers to the hasidic practice of men going to the *mikveh* the morning after sexual intercourse or after having an emission of semen during sleep. The involvement in the *mitzvah* of sex, as well as the uncontrolled sexuality during sleep and dream life, both require purification.

30:5 According to the ordinance decreed by Ezra, a man must immerse after any seminal discharge, whether from copulation or otherwise—and without this immersion he is not fit for prayer or Torah study. Although this ordinance has been abolished, it is observed by the pious.

Rabbi Kalman Kalonymus of Cracow:

> It is impossible to know what true fear of God is, learning Torah and praying with trembling and quaking, except by being careful to do the immersion decreed by Ezra . . . and Judaism was in a ruined state until those two great lights, the holy Baal Shem Tov and Rabbi Elimelech [of Lizensk] (may their souls rest in the Garden of Peace) came and opened a gate for the righteous to pass through—that a person should not even think any Torah thoughts at all until he has immersed and cleansed himself from his seminal emissions. The Sages of the *Gemara* only nullified this requirement because the majority of people could not comply with it. Otherwise, those who want to attain the truth of Torah and *mitzvot* should be most careful to perform this immersion. (*Maor v'Shemesh*, Emor)

30:6 It is good to stand in the water of the *mikveh* up to your neck and to pray: to repent, confess, and ask forgiveness of your sins.[1] Then immerse fully at least twice.

30:6:1 Rabbi Aaron of Karlin said that:

> He heard that the Besht, his memory for a blessing, had said that he would say Psalms while in the *mikveh*. (*Mazkeret Shem ha-Gedolim*, p. 139)

30:6:2 Of Rabbi Tzvi Hirsh of Ziditchov we are told that:

> It was his way to say psalms while in the water of the river he used as a *mikveh*, and to meditate deeply with his holy thoughts on the unification of God's name. (*Seder ha-Dorot ha-Hadash*, p. 77)

30:6:3 While you are standing in the water, say seven times, "Create in me a pure heart, O God, and renew within me a willing spirit!" [Psalm 51:12] . . . Through immersion in the *mikveh* the evil Shells and the Other Side are separated from you, and you should pray that God give you a pure heart . . . for this is when you become a new creation, by searching your deeds, confessing, and casting your sins from you, by doing *tshuvah* and immersing in the *mikveh* with holy intentions. (*Kitzur Shnei Luchot ha-Brit*, Mesechet Shabbat, pp. 150–151)

30:6:4 Immerse no fewer than two times—once to remove uncleanness and once to draw holiness on yourself. (Rabbi Aaron of Karlin, *Hanhagot Tzaddikim*, p. 3, #3)

30:7 There are various ways to think of immersion in the *mikveh* and the repentance that accompanies it.

30:7:1 I heard this about the *kavvanah* of the *mikveh*: when you go to the *mikveh* you should intend to remove garments and when you return you should intend to clothe yourself. The simple meaning of this teaching, which is, of course, about "soul garments," seems to me to be that when you go to the *mikveh* you should do *tshuvah* and feel deep regret over all the things you have done until now transgressing against the will of God. Through this you will remove the "filthy garments" from you. And when you come back from the *mikveh* you should think of how to accept on yourself, from now and forever, to do only good deeds, and to clothe yourself with them. (*Seder ha-Yom ha-Katzar*, p. 9)

30:7:2 Another hasidic *Seder ha-Yom* puts the intention this way:

> On *Erev Shabbat*, go to immerse in the *mikveh*, and have as your *kavvanah* that just as the water purifies your body on the material level, so on the more inner, spiritual level may the water purify your soul. (The *Seder ha-Yom* of Rabbi Shalom Shachna of Probitch, in *Sefer Tzavaot v'Hanhagot*, p. 92)

The point here is not to compare a physical and a spiritual purification. Rather, both are spiritual purifications, but one is the purification of the body, the other of the soul. As *Reshit Hochmah* explains, the water purifies his body, and the Presence of God that resides there purifies his soul (*Sh'ar ha-Ahavah*, chap. 11, #25).

> Everything in the physical world has a spiritual counterpart. Every action in this world likewise has its counterpart in the spiritual realm. The spiritual counterpart of physical man is his divine soul. When man immerses in a physical Mikvah [sic], his soul likewise becomes immersed in its spiritual counterpart. (Rabbi Arye Kaplan, *Waters of Eden*, p. 62)

There are a number of ways to understand the symbolic or spiritual "meaning" of water and immersion in water. One powerful aspect of water immersion is the entrance into a completely different medium, which surrounds you on all sides. This can easily symbolize the entrance into a new state of consciousness, where God's presence is revealed. Such a *kavvanah* is made even stronger by an awareness that the *Shechinah* is especially present in the *mitzvah* waters of the *mikveh*.

One way to view things according to this perspective is that the *mikveh* immersion can be thought of as an immersion in the Waters of Wisdom, whereby all reality reveals God's presence. Rabbi Asher of Stolin:

> Through *mikveh* you can come to unity. For *mikveh* immersion points to the truth, that there is no place where He is not—for the water completely surrounds you. (*Gan Hadasim*, p. 48)

Looking from another perspective, and according to another spiritual meaning, water is the agent of cleansing par excellence. So the *mikveh*, understood as a spiritual "bath," can purify and clean the soul from the "filth" with which it has been soiled. In the laws for the purification of vessels there are two kinds of purification: passing through fire and immersion in water. Sometimes the purification of a person in the *mikveh* is spoken of in this way, that the body is purified by the water and the soul is purified in the Supernal River of Fire, God's heavenly fire of purification. According to the *Zohar*:

> Souls cannot enter the Upper Garden of Eden until they have immersed in the River of Fire. (*Reshit Hochmah*, Sh'ar ha-Ahavah, chap. 11, #30)

So the purification of *mikveh* immersion is a means to enter the Garden of Eden in this life through *d'vekut*. (See 30:11.)

30:7:3 A hasidic book puts the intention for the *mikveh* in this prayer, to be said at the time of immersion:

> May it be Your will, O Lord my God and God of my fathers, that just as I purify myself here Below, so may You purify my soul Above in the River of Fire.*[2] (*Sefer Hayim*, Kochavei Boker, p. 13)

The point here is also that our spiritual cleansing requires God's help. As the rabbis teach: If you come to purify yourself, you are given heavenly help. If Below on earth you sanctify yourself a little, Above in heaven they add greatly to the power of your doing and you are sanctified much.

By our immersion in the *mikveh* with the right intention and with repentance, we can effect the purification of our body; but for the immersion to touch our soul and bring it to purity, we need God's action and help.

30:7:4 One interpretation of the *mikveh* relates it to an experience of death and resurrection, and also to the reentry into the womb and reemergence. Immersing fully, you are like the fetus in the womb, and when you come up out of the *mikveh* you are as reborn. The individual who has sinned and become impure is transformed; he dies and is resurrected and becomes a new creation, like a newborn child. (See *DhTvhY*, section on Taharah, p. 15b and *Reshit Hochmah*, Sh'ar ha-Ahavah, chap. 11, #29.)

But the condition for this transformation is that you repent and do so with self/soul-sacrifice (*mesirat nefesh*), by giving your soul back to God for purification.

> The Mikvah represents the womb. When an individual enters the Mikvah, he's re-entering the womb, and when he emerges, he is as if born anew. Thus he attains a completely new status. (Rabbi Arye Kaplan, *Waters of Eden*, p. 13)

Of course, being without clothes and surrounded by liquid is like the state of the fetus in the womb.

> The *kavvanah* for immersion in the *mikveh* . . . when you double yourself over . . . like a fetus within its mother and you are born as a

new creation—is *mesirat nefesh*, giving up your life to God. (*Maggid Ta'alumah*, quoted in *DhTvhY*, section on Taharah, p. 15b)

One practice related to this self-sacrifice is that at the *mikveh* you accept on yourself, in doing *tshuvah*, the punishment of death for your sins. Rabbi Hayim of Tzanz would do this:

> At midnight every day [before *Tikkun Hatzot*] he would go down to the *mikveh* near his house and immerse in the midst of intense Divine service. Before he entered the water he would accept on himself the four death punishments meted out in the Torah, in order. When he entered the waters of the *mikveh*, with his *yarmulke* still on his head, he would say, in a voice choking with emotion, "I accept on myself the four death punishments of the Torah: stoning, stoning—for the sake of the Infinite One, blessed be He; then he immersed for the first time. Then he received on himself the punishment of death by burning, and he would immerse himself; and also by the sword and by strangling. So he immersed four times, once for each punishment which he accepted on himself.[3] (*Rabbeinu ha-Kodesh mi-Tzanz*, p. 298)

This practice may seem somewhat harsh, but it has a beautiful gravity. Of course, you can accept on yourself the punishment of death for your sins without reference to the four kinds of punishment, which are not a necessary part of the intention. It is possible to consider yourself as if drowning when immersing; compare the prayer of Jonah in Jonah 2.

> When a person immerses himself in water, he places himself in an environment where he cannot live. Were he to remain submerged for more than a few moments, he would die from lack of air. He is thus literally placing himself in a state of non-existence and non-life. Breath is the very essence of life, and according to the Torah, a person who stops breathing is no longer considered among the living. Thus, when a person submerges himself in a Mikvah, he momentarily enters the realm of the non-living, so that when he emerges he is like one reborn. (Rabbi Arye Kaplan, *Waters of Eden*, p. 13)

30:8 From the various suggestions above you can choose what suits you as to how to conceptualize your own *mikveh* experience and what to say to express your intentions.

30:9 It is common for people to combine various holy thoughts and intentions in their meditation at the *mikveh*. For example, you can stand in the water up to your neck and say psalms to arouse your feelings of repentance. Then think of repentance and confess. Accept on yourself the sentence of death for your sins and immerse as if drowning. Pray for forgiveness of your sins. Call out seven times Psalm 51:12, praying that God create in you a new and pure heart, immersing after each repetition. Immerse once to remove your uncleanness. Call out the *Sh'ma* and *Baruch Shem Kavod*.[4] Immerse to receive holiness. Meditate on God's presence in the *mikveh* and in the water. Pray that your eyes be opened always to see His light everywhere, and then immerse with that intention. Before *Shabbat* one can add immersions, such as to remove the weekday (spiritual) garment, to take on the Sabbath (spiritual) garment, to receive the illumination of *Shabbat*, and the extra soul-power. (For examples of these various combinations of immersions and intentions, see *Kitzur Shnei Luchot ha-Brit*, Inyanei tevilah b'Erev Shabbat, pp. 150–151, and *Kaf ha-Hayim*, 27:16, pp. 369–371.)

30:10 Another level of understanding of the *mikveh* is that, as we all know from our experience in the bath or shower, or in the pool, lake, or ocean, immersion in water has a tremendous effect on the total body-feeling and mood. Complete immersion is the fullest expression of this. That is why swimming and bathing are so relaxing. On a simple level, then, various aspects of our body-feeling which have formed as a result of our sins and misdirections are, under the influence of the *mikveh* (together with repentance), washed away by the complete immersion. New and holy body-feelings replace the old ones and these are conducive to a new and different mind-set.

30:11 WHAT TO DO WHEN THERE IS NO *MIKVEH* AVAILABLE

A story about the holy Seer of Lublin gives insight into the *mikveh* and also suggests what to do when we do not have access to one.

> Once, when the holy Yismach Moshe [Rabbi Moshe Teitelbaum] was with the holy Seer of Lublin when the latter was in another city, he went to the *mikveh* and found that it was a ruin, so he went to immerse himself in the river. Afterwards, when he went to where his *rebbe* was staying, to greet him, the Seer noticed that water was still

> dripping from his beard and *payot*, and asked him how he went to the *mikveh*; was it not in ruins?
>
> When Rabbi Moshe explained that he had gone to the river, the Seer said, "And what is one to do if there is no *mikveh* and also no river? Then you can immerse yourself in the River of Fire." And he whispered into the ear of his disciple, "in the fire of *d'vekut*." (*Eser Orot*, p. 98, #66)

What the *rebbe* meant was that the purification of the *mikveh* immersion experience can be attained through other forms of Divine service (Torah, prayer, singing, dancing—but most particularly meditation) when they are done with intense *d'vekut*. (See "*Mitzvot*," 11:3 about the River of Fire and how to follow the Lubliner's advice about immersing in the fire of *d'vekut*.)

> The holy Rabbi Moshe of Kobrin was once praising the *tzaddik* [Rabbi Israel] of Rizhin in the highest way. Among other things, he told how he was once sitting next to him on *Shabbat*, close to nightfall, when suddenly the *rebbe* said to him, "A Jew must learn how to immerse in the River of Fire!" "And immediately," said the holy Rabbi Moshe, "the Rizhiner *tzaddik* bent over [as if immersing] three times, and when he straightened up, water was dripping from his *payot*!" (*Beit Rizhin*, p. 206)

There is another story about a hasid of the Kotzker Rebbe who had no chance to go to the *mikveh* before *Shabbat*, nor could he do so in the evening, and he was very upset about this:

> Then he decided what to do—he would use the kabbalistic intentions for the *mikveh*, meditating on them in depth as if he were immersing himself in the *mikveh*. "Because," he said to himself, "the essence of the immersion is the spiritual purity attained through purification in the Waters of Wisdom. So there is no absolute necessity for the actual material waters, and the movement of the bodily limbs in the water. The spiritual immersion can be accompanied by the stripping off of all materiality and the body from the soul as a garment [*hitpashtut ha-gashmiyut*], and together with it the fullest concentration of the mind in the intentions of the Upper Immersion."
>
> And so did he do—he concentrated all his powers to meditate on all the exalted intentions and thoughts connected with the *mikveh*, with the holy names of God related to it, and stripped himself of all external thoughts, because he was a person on a high spiritual level such that he was able to do this. So he paced back and forth in the

Beit Midrash until he felt within himself that he had completed his task, and that a new spirit had been born within him and he had become another man.[5] (*Shivhei Tzaddikim*, p. 43)

These stories and teachings tell us, on the one hand, what level we are to strive for in our use of the *mikveh*. On the other hand, they let us see the *mikveh* as one way of attaining a certain level of *d'vekut* and transformation which can be arrived at through alternate means, means that can sometimes substitute for the *mikveh* when one is not available.

One can also consider doing a service of the imagination in circumstances where use of a *mikveh* is impossible. See "Service of the Imagination," 19:14.

For more about *mikveh*, see "*Shabbat*," 18:1:2:2:3:2.

31

Tikkun Hatzot— The Midnight Prayer Service and Vigil

31:1 It is a widespread hasidic custom, which is praised to the sky by many *rebbes*, to arise at midnight or thereabouts to engage in Torah and prayer until dawn. The centerpiece of this devotional vigil is what is called the Midnight Prayer Service, *Tikkun Hatzot*, in which the destruction of the Temple is lamented, and prayers are offered for its rebuilding and for the redemption of Israel.

The Temple was the visible manifestation of God's dwelling on earth among men, and its absence symbolizes all that is spiritually wrong with the world. For now the Divine Presence is in exile.

When we mourn the destruction of the Temple and pray for its rebuilding, we also mourn over our own sins and our low state, for each man and woman of Israel is to be a Temple in which God dwells—and we pray that we will soon merit to have His light come and dwell with us.

31:2 The *rebbe* Rabbi Yitzhak Isaac of Ziditchov once said that for fifty-four years consecutively he never slept through midnight

> [except under duress], but always awoke and said *Tikkun Hatzot*. And this meant that he began this practice when he was about 14 years old. (*Eser Kedushot*, p. 73, #8)

The same thing is said for many hasidic *rebbes*.

31:3 *Tikkun Hatzot* is praised again and again in the *Zohar*, and Rabbi Elijah deVidas (the author of *Reshit Hochmah* and *Totzaot Hayim*, and the disciple of Rabbi Moshe Cordovero), who wrote much about this practice says:

> I have discussed this at length because it seems to me that this practice is a basic pillar for all the service of God. And it is not an accident that the Midnight Service is emphasized so much throughout the *Zohar*, innumerable times, more so than all the other *mitzvot*. (*Totzaot Hayim*, p. 23)
>
> The culmination of all the good practices—and happy is he who attains to it, for its value is immeasurable—is to awaken in the middle of the night every night in order to learn Torah and to be awake until dawn. (*Totzaot Hayim*, p. 19)

He goes on to say how the *Zohar* says:

> [Such a one] is called a son of the Holy One, blessed be He . . . and a son of the King's palace, and there is none who stands in the way when appeal is made on his behalf to the King's palace. (*Totzaot Hayim* p. 20)

31:4 After the *Tikkun Hatzot* service is said sitting on the ground as a mourner, a person should study Torah and sing songs and praises of God, and engage in *hitbodedut* [being alone with God] and repentance until the light of day when the time comes for the Morning Prayer. (See "Talking to God and Being Alone with God—*Hitbodedut*" [33])

> After finishing the *Tikkun*, sit elsewhere and learn Torah [the whole night, until the time of the Morning Prayers]. When it gets close to dawn, sing some holy songs and praises of God. And if you do not have a nice voice and cannot sing well, then recite some psalms in a loud voice, with great *kavvanah* on each word. (*Or Tzaddikim*, p. 15a, #7, see also #3; p. 15b, #23)

(For quotes about repentance and *hitbodedut* at this special time, see 31:5, 31:14, 31:15, 31:16.)

31:5 From the *Seder ha-Yom* according to the teachings of Rabbi Nachman of Bratzlav:

> A person should get up at midnight and mourn over the destruction of the Holy Temple . . . and over his own sins and transgressions and misdeeds, and over his bad character traits and bad desires—for all these delay the rebuilding of the Temple. He should identify with what he reads out in the *Tikkun Hatzot* and see himself in what he reads. So let him pray to God that He bring the redemption and salvation of all Israel, and also the redemption of his soul from its subjugation to the evil inclination, which always lies in wait to do him ill. The time for *Tikkun Hatzot* is from six hours after the stars first appear at night and lasts for two hours.

31:6 The holy Rabbi Hayim of Tzanz would go to the *mikveh* before saying the Midnight Service.

> When he came back from the *mikveh* he said *Tikkun Hatzot* with an outpouring of his soul and with such bitter crying that those who were outside his room would themselves break down and begin to wail. And after he said *Tikkun Hatzot* he learned in the *Zohar* with great *d'vekut*, and then he repeated *mishnayot* from memory, usually from the order *Zeraim*. (*Sefer Rabbeinu ha-Kodesh mi-Tzanz*, p. 250)

> **31:7** Pray to God before sleep that you will be able to get up at midnight. If your going to bed is with thought, and the way it should be, so will your getting up be well, and you will advance in holiness. Get up at midnight then, for this time is very good to consider why you came to this world and what your purpose in life is. Look to fix and mend that which you have damaged. Say *Tikkun Hatzot* and learn Torah, and when you say the *Tikkun* be careful to say it not by rote, but from the depth of your heart, in sorrow at the destruction of the Temple. (*Seder ha-Yom ha-Katzar*, p. 7)

31:8 When the Baal Shem Tov was a young man, recently married, he made his living by the labor of his hands and was very poor. Once, for a few days, he was on the farm of a charitable Jew who had a special house for poor people who needed hospitality and assistance.

> After the holy *Shabbat*, when Reb Baruch [the landowner] lay down to go to sleep, he suddenly and unexpectedly saw a light

through his window. He got up from the bed and went over to the window to see where it was coming from—and he saw that there was a bright light coming from one of the rooms of the poor people's house. Reb Baruch was very surprised at this and was also afraid, for he thought, maybe, God forbid, a fire had broken out. So he quickly dressed and ran to see what this light was from. He approached the door of the room carefully and looked through the keyhole—and saw the poor man [the Baal Shem Tov] . . . sitting on the ground and saying, with great trembling, *Tikkun Hatzot*. He was at the verse, "Why have You forgotten us for so long, why have You left us abandoned for such length of days?" and his hands were spread and raised, his face was shining brightly with a great light, and tears were running down his cheeks. (*Sippurei Hasidim*, Zevin, vol. 1, #268)

31:9 The order of the *Tikkun* is that after you wash and purify your hands [as always after waking] and dress and say the blessings, sit by the *mezuzah* [of the room you are in], remove your shoes, bow your head as a mourner and cry as much as you can. Then put wood ashes on your forehead on the spot where the box of the head-*tefillin* would rest, bend your head down as a bulrush, lowering your face almost to the floor [and begin the *Tikkun*]. (*Or Tzaddikim*, p. 16a, #5)

31:10 The Baal Shem Tov said:

[You] should turn the nights into days and you should sleep a few hours during the day so that just a little sleep at night will suffice. [And he suggests that:] When you get up at midnight and are sleepy, walk briskly around the room and sing devotional songs with a loud voice, in order to remove the sleepiness. And when you learn Torah do not concentrate all in one area such that it becomes burdensome, but learn many different things. (*Tzavaat ha-Ribash*, p. 4)

It is common for a person to have a regular order of different things to study during the night vigil.

It is elsewhere suggested that if sleepy you should not sit, but learn standing and with a loud voice to keep awake, also dabbing water on your eyes (*Seder Tikkun Hatzot*, p. 13; also *DhTvhY*, Din Hashkamat ha-Boker, #25).

31:11 Rabbi Yitzhak Isaac of Komarna:

There is nothing greater than learning Torah during the nighttime, specifically after midnight, for doing so causes the soul to shine and brings the Divine Presence to rest on a person, and he attains to a true holy spirit and many virtues without number. In fact, almost every aspect of Judaism depends on this. A person should, then, make every effort to sleep somewhat in the daytime, and also at night before the Morning Prayer Service, so that he can lessen his sleep at night—all according to every man's ability and according to the time and the circumstances. This is what our master, the holy Rabbi Yaakov Yitzhak of Lublin said, that he never passed midnight in sleep, but would always sleep two or three hours in the daytime, and also at night before the Morning Prayer Service, he would lie down to sleep an hour or so—so that his mind would be clear for prayer. (*Notzar Hesed*, quoted in *Seder Tikkun Hatzot*, p. 83)

31:12:1 See to it that you have a regular practice of waking up in the middle of the night. And if you can learn Torah after *Tikkun Hatzot* until dawn, that is very good. But if not, then after learning for half an hour or more you can go back to sleep; but wake up for about half an hour of Torah study before you go to the synagogue. (Tzavaat Rabbi Moshe Hasid mi-Prague, 1–11, in *Tz'vaot v'Derech Tovim*, p. 29)

31:12:2 And if you have to, [after saying the *Tikkun*] go back to sleep until the morning. (*Seder ha-Yom ha-Katzar*, p. 7)

31:13 [Rabbi Nachman of Bratzlav:] A Jew's main devotion is, in the winter, to rise at midnight (and say *Tikkun Hatzot*, the Midnight Service, and then study until morning) and in the summer, when the nights are very short [and we do not say the Midnight Service except in the Holy Land], he should be careful to wake up early in the morning, with the break of day [to engage in the devotional service of God]. (*Rabbi Nachman's Wisdom*, p. 415, *Sichos HaRan*, #301)

31:14 There is no better time for *hitbodedut* than from midnight until daylight, when all the world is sleeping. Then is the time when you can make your accounts with your Creator and search your ways. (*Seder Tikkun Hatzot*, p. 12)

31:15 Rabbi Tzvi Hirsh of Ziditchov says about the Midnight Service:

There is no more choice time for a man to seclude himself in *hitbodedut* than after midnight, to do *tshuvah*, and make confession for his sins and express his regret for them.

He should speak from his heart words just between himself and his Creator, words of love and pleading, and he should beg for his soul and be ravished with his Lover in the delights of love. And let him seek pardon and forgiveness and atonement for the past day if he in any way acted without the dedication and the separation from worldly things proper for servants of God.

He should also pray to his Creator about the coming day, that he should have full God-consciousness throughout the day and be immersed in the wisdom of the Torah and all her sweet ways—and that nothing whatsoever untoward, God forbid, should occur throughout the day, but that he should be inseparably attached to God and His Torah and with the love of God all the day; and that he should be spared from any foreign thoughts, and from the foreign flame of any ungodly desires, but should be full of the fear of God all the day. (*Sur maiRa v'Asei Tov*, quoted in *DhTvhY*, Hashkamat ha-Boker, #21)

31:16 Rabbi Tzvi Hirsh continues:

But know this too, my brothers, that I have received a tradition from our rabbis that *Tikkun Hatzot* arouses on High a special time of Divine favor, when a man's misdeeds will be forgiven him. . . . My brothers, there is no better time for *hitbodedut* and for separation from worldly things, when worldly thought will not disturb you, than at midnight. That is the time to arouse yourself to stand up and pray for the welfare of your despondent soul, which has become removed through her sins from the source of pure living waters and has become coarsened through involvement with the body which has its root in the lowly dust. . . .

At this hour you should search well to uncover those things that you have done which are worthy of shame, and you should speak from your heart to God, like a servant before his master, with bowing and prostrating, lying on the ground and spreading out your arms and legs, with soft words, humbling yourself, and with verses about God's mercy, to speak like a son before his father. All that he says in prayer should be in his native tongue that he speaks and understands, so that he can pour out his soul without hindrance and can express fully the pain of his heart over his sins and transgressions. He should beg pardon and forgiveness. . . . You should beg God who made you and formed you and created you that He come to your aid to bring you close to His service, so that you will revere Him with all your heart. . . .

This *tshuvah* is the whole purpose of arising at midnight. . . . When you consider all this before sleep, pray that from heaven they will wake you at midnight [that you will succeed in getting up then], and then you will go to sleep without worries and be at peace.[1] (*DhTvhY*, Hashkamat ha-Boker, #22)

31:17 Rabbi Yitzhak Isaac of Komarna:

It is a tradition handed down from the *tzaddikim* that after saying *Tikkun Hatzot* a person should say these verses: "O Lord, You are my God and I will exalt You and praise Your name, etc." [Isaiah 25:1]; "I will praise You; for I am fearfully and wonderfully made" [Psalm 139:14]; and other verses about God's oneness and about accepting Him as your God, blessed be He, such as "You have shown" [*Ata haraita la'daat—Shabbat, Shaharit,* before Torah reading in *Nusach ha-Ari*], and other similar verses. And after that he should say "None is like our God" [*Ein Keloheinu*] until "You will save us" [*toshiyeinu*; *Nusach ha-Ari*] in a sweet way and with a beautiful melody, and he should say "It is our duty to praise" [*Aleinu*], and when he reaches "and we kneel down," he should kneel and then prostrate fully with outstretched arms and legs as on Rosh HaShanah and Yom Kippur and should say "*Sh'ma Yisrael*" while he is prostrate and . . . seven times: "The Lord, He is God!—the God of Abraham, the God of Isaac, and the God of Jacob; the God of Israel, He is my God and my father's God—and to Him do I prostrate myself." And when he is worthy he will experience a great light when he is thus accepting on himself the yoke of His kingdom and His lordship and His fear and love. When he gets up he should say three times: "Blessed is His glorious kingdom for ever and ever!" in a loud voice, but sweetly. And lastly, he should [continue *Aleinu* where he had left off and] say: "He spreads out the heavens," until "There is no other." (*N'tiv Mitzvotecha,* quoted in *DhTvhY*, Hashkamat ha-Boker, #30)

31:18 A story that tells how Rabbi Naftali of Ropshitz hid his holy ways shows him prostrating as just described:

Once, when he was saying *Tikkun Hatzot,* prostrated fully with arms and legs outstretched on the floor, he had forgotten to close the door, and just then, although it was very late, one of the townspeople came to his room and discovered him like that. The *rebbe* immediately jumped to his feet to hide his holy ways from the man; but when he realized that he had already been seen, the *rebbe* said to him, "Certainly the people of the city don't know the greatness of their rabbi!" The man, thinking that the *rebbe* was saying this out of pride, spoke in disparagement of him to others—as the *rebbe* intended. (*Eser Tzachtzachot*, p. 88, #21)

31:19 To get at least a glimpse into one aspect of the deeper significance of the Midnight Service we can quote this word of Rabbi Natan, the great disciple of Rabbi Nachman of Bratzlav:

> Through arising at midnight, or at least before dawn, in order to join night with day by means of Torah study and prayer, the night, which is the level of Disorder, becomes included in the level of Order, which is the day. (*Seder Tikkun Hatzot*, p. 19, #8)

The night is the time when Disorder is strengthened. Breaking its power by rising at midnight when sleep is normal, and then engaging in devotional service until, and into, the day, attaches that time to the time of day and includes it in the whole of Order and service to God.

Reshit Hochmah explains it this way:

> One must accustom himself to rising every night at midnight and studying Torah until dawn. How many marvelous things do you merit by virtue of rising at midnight for the purpose of studying Torah! Among these is the subjugation of the evil Shells. . . .
>
> The confusion of mind that a person may experience while engaged in praying or in studying Torah is on account of his sins, insofar as he renders himself unfit for unifying God. His sins function as an evil accuser which comes between a person and God. But when an individual accustoms himself to rising in the middle of the night in order to study Torah, he subdues the Other Side and atones for his sins. Through such means he purifies his thoughts, and his efforts to unify God are not hampered.
>
> The reason for this is that night normally nourishes the forces of strict judgment. However, by the virtue of Torah study, the night is transformed from darkness into light, from the attribute of judgment to the attribute of compassion. And since the night becomes sweetened, so too are all those negative forces which are bound up with it. (*Reshit Hochmah*, Sh'ar ha-Kedushah, chap. 7, #19; translation based on *Safed Spirituality*, pp. 103–104)

In the darkness of night people's fears are naturally aroused. When we overcome our fears and attach ourselves in the middle of the night to faith in God, we ourselves are redeemed, and this also stands as a sign and harbinger of the Final Redemption, for the Exile is likened to Night.

> Once, when Rabbi Tzvi Hirsh [of Ziditchov] was in Lublin [at the court of his master, the Seer of Lublin], Rabbi Yaakov of Radzimin was there also. Before dawn the Seer asked Rabbi Tzvi Hirsh, "Rabbi Hirsheli, has morning come?" "The daylight has certainly

arrived," answered Rabbi Tzvi. The Seer then told Rabbi Yaakov to go outside and see. He went out and saw that it was still dark; but since they realized that the Seer wanted it, they agreed with him and said that it was already day. The Seer then commented: "It is still dark, but through the *Tikkun Hatzot* that we did we have clarified the darkness into day." (*Ha-Hozeh mi-Lublin*, p. 138)

As we see from the words of Rabbi Nachman above, the rabbis considered it a practice of special power to "join, or bind together, the day and the night" through Divine service.

The Baal Shem Tov:

> Be sure to do the Midnight Service and [continuing through dawn] bind together day and night [in Divine service]. (*Tzavaat ha-Ribash*, p. 12)

Rabbi Tzvi Hirsh of Ziditchov:

> Many of our early forebears, who had the holy spirit, told us to bind together day and night through Torah and prayer. (*Yifrach biYamav Tzaddik*, p. 39b)

This practice applies not only to dawn but also to dusk. (See "Individual Practices," 39:37.)

31:20 Keeping the Midnight Vigil as a regular practice is very difficult.

Rabbi Elijah deVidas:

> Your *yetzer* will argue that you should not get up lest you harm yourself and your health. [But he says that you should resolve to get up] even if you see that you get a headache from doing so. Do not let that stop you from keeping up the practice the next day and on. So keep on day after day, and help will come to you from heaven, for the Torah says that "He who keeps a *mitzvah* will come to no harm," and "That which is good will not be withheld from him who acts in sincerity"; for the Torah is only won through intense self-sacrifice. [And he says:] Before you go to sleep, or in the blessing "He who hears prayer" in the *Shemoneh Esreh*, you should pray that the Holy One, blessed be He, help you to get up at midnight and to stay awake until daytime. (*Totzaot Hayim*, pp. 22, 23, 25)

In the *Seder Tikkun Hatzot* there is a long prayer called "A Prayer to Be Worthy to Rise at Midnight Every Day."

Although various *rebbes* discouraged the practice, if a person finds it otherwise impossible, there are places where it is said one is permitted to stay up late, into the midnight time period, to say the *Tikkun* and study Torah, and then go to sleep.

> Nevertheless [although you are supposed to sleep earlier and then get up at midnight or thereafter], if it is altogether impossible to do so . . . and if you know that sleep is sure to overcome you and you will not be able to get up after midnight at all, you should then make an effort to at least stay up until after midnight, and say the *Tikkun* and learn Torah, at least a little Torah, during this time of special Divine favor. [Then go to sleep.] For God after all wants the heart, and if that is the best you can do, He will receive it. (*Birkat Hayim*, p. 52, n. 1)
>
> Of course it is best to say the whole *Tikkun.*
>
> [However,] if you do not have time [to say it all], at least say Psalm 137 and Lamentations 5 and "In Your Sanctuary" [*B'hechalecha*], or at the very least just the latter. And you can even say this before sleep if it is after midnight. (*Midrash Pinhas*, quoted in *Hanhagot Tzaddikim* [III], vol. 2, p. 817, #19)

"In Your Sanctuary" is a lamentation poem not available in translation. Since it is not even included in some versions of *Tikkun Hatzot*, we can learn from this teaching that if a person can only say some part of the *Tikkun* (such as Psalm 137 or Lamentations 5), it is still good.

> **31:21** Whoever cannot do this [*Tikkun Hatzot*] nightly should maintain an absolute minimum of once a week, before *Shabbat* [Thursday night]. (Rabbi Shneur Zalman of Ladi, *Tanya*, Igeret ha-Tshuvah, chap. 10)

31:22 There are two parts to the *Tikkun Hatzot* service: *Tikkun Rachel* and *Tikkun Leah* (named after the two wives of Jacob who were sisters).

Tikkun Rachel is the true lamentation on the destruction of the Temple and therefore cannot be recited on Sabbaths and holidays and other happy occasions (when we also do not say *Tahanun*). *Tikkun Leah*, which is more joyful and hopeful, and looks forward to Redemption, can be said on those days. But insight into the hasidic attitude about the lamentation of *Tikkun Rachel* comes from the following story:

> When the rabbi and *tzaddik* Rabbi Nahum [later the Rebbe of Tchernobil] was a young man and was with the Baal Shem Tov, he was once standing in the vicinity when the Besht was getting into his carriage for one of his excursions—as was his holy way. Rabbi Nahum wanted very much to be privileged to go with his holy master, so he walked near the carriage, hoping that he would be asked along. When the Besht got into the carriage he said to Rabbi Nahum, "Young man, if you are able to tell me the difference between *Tikkun Leah* and *Tikkun Rachel*, I will let you come with me." Without hesitation, Rabbi Nahum answered, saying, "What Leah accomplished with tears, Rachel was able to do with joy." Immediately the Besht took him into the carriage. (*Kerem Yisrael*, p. 27, #14)

What is the meaning of this? One *Tikkun* is named after Rachel because of the famous verse in Jeremiah 31:14 about Rachel weeping for her children, who are in exile. The other *Tikkun* is then named after her sister Leah. But the comparison of the two sisters has more to do with the story in Genesis. Jacob, we know, loved Rachel, but he had to marry Leah first. In Genesis 29:17 it is said that Leah's eyes were weak. The Midrash tells us that her eyes were weak because she cried incessantly when she heard people saying that there were two brothers, Jacob and Esau, and that her sister would marry Jacob, who was good, while she was to marry Esau, who was evil. So she cried and cried, praying that she would not fall to the lot of Esau. And her prayers bore fruit—she too married Jacob (*Midrash ha-Gadol*).

Rachel, however, was the true love of Jacob, and she won him not with tears (as did her sister Leah), but with joy—with her beauty and charm. The lesson from this for the recital of *Tikkun Rachel* is that: "What Leah accomplished with her tears, Rachel effected with joy"—and that even when reciting the mournful *Tikkun Rachel* we should say it out of joy also. Because, indeed, we cry for the exile of the *Shechinah*—as the rabbis teach: She is with us in our exile, and when Israel is low, She is low also—yet though She is with us *in exile*, there is joy, for She is still *with us*.[2]

There is a hasidic story about this important teaching.

> When [Rabbi Moshe Teitelbaum] first came to investigate the way of Hasidism it found favor in his eyes, but there still was one problem that troubled him. For the way of the hasidim is to be always rejoicing; but does it not say in the *Shulchan Aruch* that

everyone who fears heaven should be sad and mournful about the destruction of the Holy Temple?

Shortening the story for the point we need, he goes to his *rebbe*, the Seer of Lublin, who answered his question, saying:

> Believe me that we say *Tikkun Hatzot* with crying and lamentation; but with that, it is still all with joy. And this is what we learned from our holy master Rabbi Shmelke of Nikolsburg, of blessed memory, who told us a parable: There was a king who was captured in a war far away from his own country. And he was allowed to spend some time visiting with one of his devoted subjects [who was also in that country]. Now when this person saw that the king was in captivity he walked away crying without restraint; but with all that, he rejoiced, because the king was staying with him in his house. The application is understood easily: the *Shechinah* is with us [and although we cry for Her exile, we rejoice all the same]. (*Derech Emunah u'Maaseh Rav*, p. 94)

This teaching helps us to understand the meaning of the two *Tikkuns*. We lament over the exile of the *Shechinah* and the destruction of the Temple in *Tikkun Rachel*. But through this mourning itself we also begin the process of joining with the *Shechinah*, and tying ourselves to Her in love. So it is that in *Tikkun Leah*, and in the Torah study and other Divine service that follow it, we make ourselves a Temple for the *Shechinah*. In the words of Rabbi Yitzhak Isaac of Komarna quoted above: "There is nothing greater than learning the Torah . . . after midnight, for doing so causes the soul to shine and brings the Divine Presence to rest on a person, and he attains to a true holy spirit." This "personal redemption" of ours in the night hours looks forward to the future Redemption, of Israel and of all the world, from the night of the Exile.

Rachel and Leah, the two sisters, both wives of Jacob (Israel), represent two aspects of the *Shechinah*. And while one is the *Shechinah* in exile, the other is with (the people) Israel at all times. (Remember that while Jacob worked for his uncle to marry Rachel, he was already married to Leah and with her every night.)

> We have to do two fixings [*tikkunim*] at midnight—one to mourn over Rachel of *Briah* [the World of Creation], who went into exile; and the second is to mate Jacob and Leah. For both Leah and

> Rachel represent the *Shechinah*, which is sometimes called Rachel and sometimes Leah. And we have to do two fixings in relation to the *Shechinah*: one, to lament at midnight over the *Shechinah* who went into exile, in the way of "with him [Israel] am I [God] in his trouble." This *tikkun* is called *Tikkun Rachel*. In the second fixing we must learn Torah at midnight, and this is called the *Tikkun* of Jacob and Leah—for they mate and join together—Israel, who is called Jacob, with the *Shechinah*, who is called Leah—through involvement with Torah study at midnight. This is its simple meaning, but there are also deep secrets here—and he who knows will understand. (*Tikkun l'Nefesh*, p. 2)

31:23 Rabbi Elimelech of Lizensk instructed his disciples to memorize *Tikkun Rachel* and *Tikkun Leah* (*Tzetl Katan*, #17).

31:24 Of course, the Torah and Judaism have a special measure of compassion for widows. But it seems that some of the hasidic *rebbes* had a particular attitude to widows as representing the *Shechinah*, who is "widowed" from Her Husband (the Holy One, blessed be He).

Rabbi Yitzhak Isaac of Komarna writes about Rabbi Abraham Joshua Heshel of Apta:

> Once, I was standing at his side as he was conversing with a widow—and I realized that he was talking to her with hidden meaning about the exile of the *Shechinah*, who had become like a widow [Lamentations 1:1]. I started to cry, and he also cried. (*Zohar Hai*, quoted in *Ha-Rav mi-Apta*, p. 64)

It seems that comforting widows was a particularly sympathetic way of also "comforting" the "widowed" *Shechinah*.

> It was the custom of the Rebbe Reb Moshe Leib of Sassov every day after the Morning Prayers to go to all the widows of the city and to wish them a good morning. (*Menorah ha-Tehorah*, p. 51, #7)

> The story is well known and famous about a poor woman [separated from her husband who was in prison for theft] who had recently given birth during a cold winter. Rabbi Moshe Leib, putting on the clothes of a gentile peasant so that she would not recognize him, went to her in the middle of the night, carrying on his shoulder firewood he had chopped himself. He made a fire for her, and something hot to drink, and then he said *Tikkun Rachel* and *Tikkun Leah*. (*Menorah ha-Tehorah*, p. 51, #10)

So part of our *Tikkun Hatzot* devotions can involve giving help and comfort to widows and other vulnerable people, both men and women. For what is the Exile and suffering of the *Shechinah*? To a great degree it is the suffering of people. So we can help bring the Redemption not only through holy rituals expressing our devotion to God, but through service and love to our fellow man.

31:25 Unfortunately *Tikkun Hatzot* is not available in an English translation. Its essence, however, is selections from Psalms, the Prophets (particularly Isaiah), and Lamentations, which can be found in English. Below is a "core" *Tikkun* (for use by people with inadequate Hebrew) based primarily on the one given in *Or Tzaddikim* (p. 15a, #5) with some additions from the *Seder Tikkun Hatzot* version.

Tikkun Rachel: (1) The confession in the *Amidah* of *Yom Kippur*, the part that begins, "Our God and God of our fathers, Let our prayer come before Thee; hide not Thyself from our supplications" until "May it be Thy will . . . to forgive us for all our sins, to pardon us for all our iniquities, and to grant us remission for all our transgressions" (of course the English translation here can differ): (2) Psalm 137; (3) Psalm 79; (4) Lamentations 5 (repeat the last verse); (5) Isaiah 63:15–18; 64:7–11 (it would seem good to read from 63:15 until the end of 64); (6) then say: "Woe is me, for the exile of the *Shechinah*! Woe is me, for the destruction of the Holy Temple! Woe is me, for the burning of the Torah! Woe is me, for the martyrdom of the righteous! Woe is me, for the desecration of His Great Name and of His Holy Temple! Woe is me, for the enemy has conquered! Woe is me, for the anguish of all the worlds! Woe is me, for the anguish of the holy Patriarchs and Matriarchs! Woe is me, for the anguish of the prophets and the righteous and the pious in the Garden of Eden! Woe is me, for the anguish of the Messiah![3] It is our sins that have caused all this, and our transgressions that have set back the time of the End. Our wrongdoings have kept the good far from us. Woe to the children exiled from their Father's table! How long? How many years of suffering . . .? And every generation in which the Temple is not built, it is as if it was destroyed in their days." (From *Seder Tikkun Hatzot*, p. 51, taken from *Siddur Yabetz*); (7) Isaiah 62:6–9; (8) Then say: "Incline Thine ear, O my God, and hear; open Thine eyes, and behold our desolations, and the city called by Thy name [Jerusalem]; for we do not lay our supplications before Thee because of our righteous acts, but because of Thine abundant mercies." (From special prayers for Monday and Thursday in the Siddur); "Thou wilt arise and have compassion upon Zion; for it is time to be gracious unto her, for the appointed time is come; for Thy servants take pleasure in her stones and even her dust is pure and beautiful to their eyes [Psalm 102:14–15]; And God is the builder of Jerusalem, He will gather the scattered of Israel."

Tikkun Leah: (1) Psalms 24, 42, 43, 20, 67, 111, 51, 126; (2) Then say: "How long O God shall there be crying in Zion, and mourning in Jerusalem? Arise, and have compassion on Zion; build the walls of Jerusalem." Followed by: "Thou wilt arise, etc. as in #8 for *Tikkun Rachel*; (3) From the Morning Service, the special prayers for Monday and Thursday (in the Siddur), the one that begins: "Incline Thine ear, O my God, and hear" until "Thou doest wondrous things at all times"; (4) Chapter 1 of the Mishnah tractate *Tamid.*

> *Tikkun Leah* is said also on days when *Tahanun* is not said, even on *Shabbat* and holidays and *Rosh Hodesh.* But the preceding confession [as above in *Tikkun Rachel*, #1] is not said then, nor Psalms 20 and 51; but the rest is said. (*Seder Tikkun Hatzot*, p. 54)

If you study the nature of the selections from Psalms, Isaiah, and Lamentations given above you can add or make other selections from those sources—paying attention also to the difference between *Tikkun Rachel* and *Tikkun Leah* (see 31:22). Another source in English for such selections is the special prayers said in *Shaharit* on Mondays and Thursdays (beginning "*V'Hu Rachum*"—"And He, being merciful"). As said in *Yesod v'Shoresh ha-Avodah* (Gate 5, chap. 8, p. 101) about them:

> All these prayers were established to be said about the anguish of the *Shechinah* and about the destruction of the Temple—and to pray about our sins.

If you say the *Tikkun* in English, you can also lament that very fact, for that too (not knowing the holy tongue) is a part of the Exile.

32

Sex

Turning the sexual impulse in a spiritual direction is a central goal of Judaism. According to the Kabbalah, sexual matters are part of the aspect of reality called "Foundation" (*Yesod*). As the Torah teaches, spiritualizing sexuality is the foundation of a life lived for holiness.

Thus, the first covenant God made with Abraham, with its sign, circumcision, was sealed in the male organ of sexuality. The Midrash says:

> And so did God give the covenant of circumcision in the sexual organ, so that the fear of God would keep us from sexual sin. (*Midrash Tadshe*, *Beit ha-Midrash*, Jellinek, Part 3, p. 171)

Abraham and Sarah together put their sexuality to the service of God. This theme of the fear of God in matters of sex recurs throughout the stories of the Patriarchs and Matriarchs, for that was one of the marks of holiness that distinguished them from the peoples of the lands in which they lived.

> The very essence of the hasidism of our master and teacher and rabbi, the holy Baal Shem Tov, the memory of a *tzaddik* for a blessing for the life of the World to Come, revolves around the holiness of the attribute Foundation, as it is written how God,

> blessed be He, said to Abraham, on him be peace, "Go and make a path for your children!" (*Seder ha-Yom l'ha-Admor mi-Biala*, #137)

On the simplest level, the meaning of the Torah's concern with limiting sexuality is that the energy and attention devoted to lust (as all other bodily pleasures) are taken away from devotion to God.

On another level, it is not only that lustful activity takes energy away from spirituality, but that it undermines what spirituality there is. According to the Kabbalah, desires, lusts, and physical pleasures create opaque "shells," which prevent the light of the Divine Presence from reaching the mind, and the lust and bodily pleasure of sex is no different in this regard.

> You should know for a certainty that even if you never commit a [sexual] sin, but just fulfill your bodily desires willingly, and try to increase your pleasure, and yearn for such pleasures even when they are not before you, that is more than enough that, God forbid, you will never see the clear sky [of spirituality]. For all desires are the source of the Shells [which encase what is holy and darken the mind], and whoever is drawn after them will never be worthy of seeing light from the Face of the Living King. (*Be'er Mayim Hayim*, in *SKv'Tz*, p. 16b, #19)

So unrestricted sexuality and indulgence not only take away the energy that should be turned to God, but, like all lusts and bodily pleasures, undermine spirituality generally. Because of this, sex, one of the strongest of drives, must be given limits, and the sex which is permitted must be purified and sanctified and raised up into the spiritual realm.

The hasidic attitude to sex can be considered under two headings. First, there are the practices that are for the purpose of avoiding the temptations of sex, and second, the practices related to the sanctification of the sex act.

As for the former, with regard to unmarried people, many fences have been erected to stop the force of the sexual urge before it gathers strength. This generally involves avoiding contact with members of the opposite sex, and avoiding things that arouse sexual desires and thoughts, whether through sight or hearing or association or touch, or through uncontrolled musing (see "Sight" 25:4 and 25:8 where there are a number of quotes about this subject).

As for married people, many of the same things would apply to members of the opposite sex other than the spouse, and to the spouse also at certain times. Although a husband and wife are not, of course, to avoid each other, there are still sexual temptations within the relationship of marriage.

The hasidic way in sanctifying sexual intercourse revolves around the concentration of the couple on the spiritual aspect and reality of sex rather than the physical act. They are to have their attention focused on the presence of the *Shechinah* around them and between them.

As with other acts of Divine service, such as Torah study and prayer or eating, there is a special attempt made, through meditation, to experience God's presence in the surroundings, in the place where you are, for the whole earth is full of His Glory, and there is no place where He is not.

The *Shechinah*, however, is not only manifested in the place, but even more particularly and intimately in the relation between people.

> Our Sages, their memory for a blessing, said: When a man and his wife unite sexually in holiness, the *Shechinah* rests between them. (The Rambam, quoted in *Reshit Hochmah*, Sh'ar ha-Kedushah, chap. 16, #54)

There is always present a powerful energy between husband and wife, an energy particularly activated during the time of sex. When that energy is spiritualized, it reveals the Divine Presence; when it is material and expressed primarily in the bodily plane, it is a manifestation of the Other Side.

The tremendous energy between husband and wife can lead them very high, to great holiness and love, or very low—and all the teachings of the Torah about sex are directed to channeling it. The purpose is not to denigrate sex though, for not only is sex itself not low, but:

> When sexual union is done for the sake of heaven, there is nothing so holy and pure as it is. (*Igeret ha-Kodesh* of the Ramban, Siman 1, #10)

> Sexual intercourse is an action that is important, good, and valuable to the soul also, and there is no act of flesh and blood that compares with it—if it is done with a pure intention, and a pure and clean mind; then it is called "holy." (*Sefer Mor v'Ketziyah*, quoted in *SKv'Tz*, p. 9b, #9)

> The sexual union of man and woman has its root in the highest heights, in a place in the Upper World of awesome holiness; but if

> your mind and intention are unclean, the blemish you create is equally awesome and cannot be fathomed. (*SKv'Tz*, p. 61, #6)

What is the meaning of sex in religious and spiritual terms? What is its mystery? The rabbis say that a person without a mate is only half a person, and the Torah says that when a man marries he cleaves to his wife and they become "one flesh" (Genesis 2:24).

> A man without a woman and a woman without a man are but half a body. But when they join together and unite, they become actually one body. (*Zohar*, quoted in *SKv'Tz*, p. 7b)

The greatness of sex and its secret is that it is in their sexual union that the essence of the oneness between husband and wife is revealed.

Marriage is a paradigm for the human condition in that only in union with a fellow human are we whole; otherwise, we are just a half. For that reason, one of the deepest experiences of life is the experience of love. And in loving sex there is great wonder in realizing that our true completion comes to us in the form of another human. In that experience of love, of completion, God's presence can be recognized.

But the truth is that complete wholeness cannot be reached without clinging to God. Husband and wife are one, but only when they unite sexually in holiness, both aware of the Divine Presence, is that oneness fully realized. When husband and wife unite and become one they still remain (together) as a half and only in uniting with God do they truly become whole. Together the couple is as a woman, and God the man. The love of the husband and wife for each other is an expression of the *Shechinah* yearning upward. Thus it is the *Shechinah* that is manifested in their love, and She unites with the Holy One, blessed be He. The Holy One, the masculine aspect of God as transcendent, is to unite with the feminine aspect of God as immanent: heaven and earth, the Upper World and the Lower World join, and all reality becomes one.

The true aim of sex in holiness is then to intend not only to unite with your mate in love, but to unite with God. (According to the kabbalistic understanding and terminology, which is not for everyone, our intention should be to unify the *Shechinah* with the Holy One, blessed be He, in the union of the Supernal Lovers. Therefore, during sex we are to accomplish the two kinds of union, the lower one and the supernal one, together.)

The *Zohar*:

> Come and see. When a man joins sexually with his wife, and his intention is to sanctify himself as he should, then he is complete, and together they are called "one without blemish" (for a man without a woman is half a body, and blemished, and when he marries he is completed, and becomes one, without blemish). For this reason a man must make his wife happy before sex, to arouse her love and prepare her, so that they are of one mind . . .
>
> They should have the same intentions in sex, and when they are thus united, the two are one in body and soul. In soul—for they cleave to one another with one will and desire, and in body—for a person who is unmarried is only half a body. When male and female unite sexually they become one body. So there is then one soul and one body, and together they are called "one person," and the Holy One, blessed be He, comes to rest on that one.[1] (*Reshit Hochmah*, Sh'ar ha-Kedushah, chap. 16, #3, quoted in *SKv'Tz*, end)

The *Zohar* teaches that when man and woman, in sex, are both directed to the Divine Presence, the Divine Presence rests on their bed (*Reshit Hochmah*, Sh'ar ha-Kedushah, chap. 16, #6).

> [It is taught that a man should] make his house a Temple, and his bedroom a Holy of Holies. (*SKv'Tz*, p. 60)

It was in the most sacred place of the Holy of Holies that God revealed Himself. And He did so between the two cherubim who faced each other with their wings outstretched, for they were the Throne of God, and it was between them that His voice was heard.

Our rabbis tell us that:

> When the Israelites came up to the Temple in Jerusalem on the pilgrimage festivals, the priests would remove the curtain, and the cherubim were shown to them, their bodies joined together in an embrace. And they would say, "Look, you are beloved of God as the love between man and woman." (*Yoma* 54)

It is the goal of Jewish teaching that the sexual union of husband and wife be in such holiness, where the couple is concentrating on the presence of God around them, and between them, in their love, that their embrace becomes the very Throne of God, where His Glory is revealed.

How can a couple lift themselves up from the strong physicality of sex and into the spiritual sphere? How can they keep themselves from being overwhelmed by the experience of physical pleasure? Part of the answer is that the very pleasure itself is to be made the focus of meditation, for another aspect of experiencing the spiritual reality of sex is in having a spiritual relation to the intense bodily pleasure that sex involves. All pleasure and joy come from the *Shechinah*, and when the couple turns to the Source of their pleasure, they can come into the presence of God. (These various concepts will be clarified below.)

One way in which the sex act is sanctified is that it is surrounded with religious practices before and after.

32:1 PREPARATION

As with all other acts in the service of God, making sex something spiritual cannot be accomplished without preparation beforehand. Attaining *d'vekut* during sex requires building up to it slowly through a series of spiritual practices.

32:1:1 Washing Hands

32:1:1:1 Be careful that both of you wash your hands before and after sexual intercourse. (Rabbi David ha-Levi of Steppin, *Hanhagot Tzaddikim*, p. 57, #39; cf. Rabbi Yehiel Michal of Zlotchov, p. 52, #2 and p. 54, #17)

32:1:1:2 You should see that both of you have clean hands. And so you should have a vessel with water by the bed, to clean your hands before sex, for sanctification, and so also must you wash your hands afterwards, as is explained in the *Shulchan Aruch*. (*Avodat ha-Kodesh*, quoted in *SKv'Tz*, p. 25b, #12)

32:1:1:3 Washing hands is a frequent accompaniment of Divine service, and symbolizes a number of things: a desire for purity, washing off lower motives, and the separation of this act of service from what precedes and follows it. All these can be intentions at the time of washing. (See "Prayer," 5:1:5 and "Eating and the Holy Meal," 10:1:16.)

32:1:2 *Tzedaka*

32:1:2:1 Before sexual intercourse give *tzedaka*, as you are able, and not less than a single coin; and on Sabbaths and holidays specify verbally what you will give, and after the day do so. (Rabbi Yehiel Michal of Zlotchov, *Hanhagot Tzaddikim*, p. 52, #3)

32:1:2:2 Be careful to give some *tzedaka* before the sexual act, and on the morrow, during the day, give the money to the poor. (Rabbi Yehiel Michal of Zlotchov, *Hanhagot Tzaddikim*, p. 54, #15)

32:1:2:3 Giving *tzedaka* arouses the Divine mercy, which then protects us from bad influences in our spiritual endeavors. It also opens our heart to our fellow men, and that, in turn, helps us to open ourselves to God.

32:1:3 Arrange for yourself a fixed order of Torah study and prayer each time before you have sexual intercourse (just be sure that it will not be too much for you to fulfill always). It should be your practice that without this you will never engage in sex; this order should be inviolable, such that you never waive it.

The main thing is that you attach your mind and arouse your feelings during this learning and prayer to a holy *d'vekut*, immersing yourself fully, according to your ability so that you come to an awakening of love and fear of God, and of feelings of a holy and pure *tshuvah*.

You should also fix for yourself beforehand what to meditate on during the act of intercourse, such as various holy thoughts gathered from different holy books. This will help you to focus yourself and concentrate then on holy thoughts. (*SKv'Tz*, p. 62b)

This quote mentions prayer, Torah, *tshuvah*, and meditation. We will consider each of these four areas. (Under the category of prayer we will consider separately Psalms, the Prayer of the Repentant of Rabbeinu Yonah, and a personal prayer about sex itself.)

32:1:4 Torah

It is a practice of piety to learn Torah before sex, particularly those things that have to do with the sanctification of sex.

32:1:4:1 Rabbi Elimelech of Lizensk:

You should have as your rule before sexual intercourse to learn *Reshit Hochmah*, chap. 16 (Sh'ar ha-Kedushah) and the *hanhagot* of the Arizal. (*Tzetl Katan*, #14)

32:1:4:2 You can also learn other holy subjects—*Gemara*, Mishnah, *musar*, Hasidism—in order to prepare yourself fully, so that you can perform the *mitzvah* of sex as it should be done. (*SKv'Tz*, p. 25, #7)

32:1:5 Psalms

32:1:5:1 Before intercourse it is good to say Psalm 23, "A Psalm of David—The Lord is my shepherd, I shall not want, etc." Saying this helps to nullify negative spiritual forces (the Shells). (*Or Tzaddikim*, quoted in *SKv'Tz*, p. 23, #17)

32:1:5:2 Recitation of Psalms is frequently used in the tradition, in preparation for Divine Service, for the purpose of subduing negativity. (See "Psalms," 16:11 for an explanation.)

32:1:6 Repentance

32:1:6:1 Before sexual intercourse go over your deeds of the past, meditate on *tshuvah*, and give *tzedaka*. (*Shnei Luchot ha-Brit*, Sh'ar ha-Otiyot, Kedushah, quoted in *SKv'Tz*, p. 10)

32:1:6:2 The first preparation [for sex] is for a person to purify himself from his sins as far as possible, in a complete repentance before his Creator. (*Reshit Hochmah*, quoted in *SKv'Tz*, p. 23b, #1)

This is a good time to repent particularly for sexual sins.

32:1:6:3 It is good to say the Prayer of the Repentant of Rabbeinu Yonah [see "Repentance," 14:2]; on *Shabbat*, when confession is forbidden, meditate on repentance [from love], and say this verse: "And the Lord will circumcise your heart and the heart of your generations, that you may love the Lord your God with all your heart and with all your soul, in order that you may live" [Deuteronomy 30:6]. (*SKv'Tz*, p. 24a, #2)

32:1:7 Stated Intention

It is often suggested that you express your spiritual intention verbally before sex.

32:1:7:1 Each time before having sexual intercourse, say, "I want to have union with my wife [or husband] for the sake of the unification of the Holy One, blessed be He, and His *Shechinah,* with fear and love." (*Kitzur Shnei Luchot ha-Brit,* Inyanei Zivug, p. 76)

32:1:7:2 As discussed in Chapter 2, p. 45, intentions for actions (expressed mentally or verbally) can be either general or specific. The kabbalistic "unification of the Holy One and His *Shechinah*" is general (See "Leading Thoughts," 13:9, about the meaning of this intention; and see the quote from *Reshit Hochmah* on pp. 603–604 for how it relates to the sexual act.) There are other general intentions as well. The specific intentions in the sex act, both *mitzvot,* are to create a child and/or to foster love with your spouse. (See 32:1:9:2 for these stated intentions used in an example of a prayer before sex.)

32:1:7:3 The holy books say it is important that your original motive for sexual intercourse be pure, that you not be aroused by lust and then say that your intention is for the sake of heaven. Of course, this level is not easily attained, and trying to purify and elevate one's motives after being aroused is not to be despised.

Thus, if a sexual urge becomes demanding, and you decide to engage in sex, a part of a meditation beforehand can be on recognizing that this natural urge comes from God. A stated intention to this effect can help you to transform your motivation. "Master of the World! I know that having sex is to do the will of God and a *mitzvah*—and my intention is to engage in sex because such is Your will and You have created me this way, with these urges." (See 32:1:8:4.)

32:1:8 Meditation Before Sex

32:1:8:1 So it is good to compose yourself before the sexual act, to bind and attach your mind in meditation on the greatness of God, blessed be He, and your desire to do His commandments, so as to give Him pleasure, blessed be His name. (*SKv'Tz,* p. 21b, #12)

(See "Meditation" for an explanation of what is intended by a meditation on God's "greatness." Typically, such a meditation is directed to lead to an arousal of love and fear, and to an immediate experience of the *Shechinah.*)

> **32:1:8:2** Rabbi Tzvi Hirsh of Ziditchov, of blessed memory, wrote in his book *Sur mai-Ra*, "I heard from my master [the Seer of Lublin] that the main thing in the sanctification of the sexual act is to cleave beforehand with your mind to God, and attach yourself to Him, blessed be He and blessed be His name, as it is written in books about sexual holiness. But during the time of the act itself, it is impossible not to be taken up at least somewhat with the physical pleasure." (*Eser Orot*, p. 95, #47)
>
> For this reason, Rabbi Tzvi Hirsh taught his disciples:
>
> Before sexual intercourse they should give thanks to God, in their spoken language, for the pleasure that He created. (*Yifrach biYamav Tzaddik*, p. 48b)

When the source of the pleasure is recognized through this blessing and praise it is lifted up and spiritualized and does not pull you down. Some versions of this teaching of the Ziditchover say that you should give thanks for the pleasure beforehand; others, actually during sex. To do so aloud during sex seems somewhat unlikely. It would seem right to say this verbally beforehand, and during sex, a number of times mentally.[2]

One of the main aspects of a meditation before a bodily activity that involves pleasure is to fix firmly in your mind that the source and root of the pleasure is in God. This is true for the pleasure of eating as well as for the pleasure of sex. (See "Eating and the Holy Meal," 10:20:4). Because of the powerful nature of sexual pleasure, the Seer of Lublin and his disciple, the Ziditchover following him, emphasized making this connection before the act of sex.

32:1:8:3 In general, many things can be learned about hasidic practices connected with sex from similar teachings and practices associated with eating. As HaYabetz wrote in his Siddur:

> The main thing to understand is that sexual intercourse and eating are similar in many ways. (*SKv'Tz*, p. 3)

Sex and eating are the two great bodily lusts that must be turned to the service of God.

> When [Rabbi Isaiah Horowitz] the author of *Shnai Luchot ha-Brit* was about to be married and enter under the *huppah* [bridal canopy], he went to take leave of his rabbi, Rabbi Shlomo, the son of Rabbi Leibush, and ask for his blessing. He blessed him with these words, "I bless you that you shall be careful in the two things about which I command you—in the sanctification of eating and the sanctification of sex. And through sanctifying yourself in these two things, I promise you that in all your doings, you will be surrounded by an aura of light." (Rabbi Abraham of Slonim in *Yesod ha-Avodah*, quoted in *Zichron l'Rishonim*, p. 34)

> The "surrounding light" here is the light of the *Shechinah.*

> The *tzaddikim* intend to cling to God always in *d'vekut*, and even during the time of sex they are not separated from Him. The paradigm to understand this is to be found in the meditation when eating. . . . For while all the body is enjoying the food, the *tzaddik's* mind is attached above, in meditation on the spiritual reality of eating. So is this their way of having sex. (*Reshit Hochmah*, Sh'ar ha-Kedushah, chap. 16, #8)

Study of Chapter 10, "Eating and the Holy Meal," will give added insight into many of the hasidic practices discussed here about sex, particularly with regard to meditation.

32:1:8:4 Ideally, we are to initiate sex out of spiritual motives (see 32:1:7:3), but that high level is not easily attainable. It is desirable, then, if a sexual urge becomes demanding, that you make an effort to transform your motivation through meditation, by recognizing that this natural urge comes from God.

Rabbi Tzadok ha-Cohen of Lublin:

> All natural things are doing God's will. . . . So when a person does natural acts, which he must do according to his nature, it too is called "going to do the will of his Maker," and such an act is a *mitzvah.* This includes eating and drinking and sex, which are all natural, just as they are in animals which have no free will—so long as it is a matter of necessity, such as eating when you are very hungry, and sexual intercourse, as the Rambam wrote, when your nature demands it of you.

> An example of this is with Judah [in the Genesis story], where the rabbis said [Genesis *Rabbah* 85]: "He wanted to pass by [the "harlot," Tamar in disguise], but the Holy One, blessed be He, sent to him the angel who controls sexual urges." See *The Guide for the Perplexed* [of the Rambam] (Part 2, section 6) [that natural forces are called "angels" in the Torah because they are sent from God].
> So following your nature is considered doing the will of God and a *mitzvah*, when it is a matter of necessity, your nature forcing you to it—but only if your intention is that you are doing it just because your Maker willed it so and created you this way, with these urges. (*Tzidkat ha-Tzaddik*, #173)

Following this teaching of Rabbi Tzadok ha-Cohen, you can do a meditation on the Divine source of your urge even after being sexually aroused, when you feel compelled to have sex. Part of the transformation of that urge to a pure motive can be stating a religious and holy motive aloud as a stated intention.

We have noted the relation between sexual activity and eating. Developing the thought of the quote from Rabbi Tzadok ha-Cohen in line with another suggestion of his for eating, we can say that you should meditate before sex on how your mate comes to you from God (whose "main activity," according to the Talmud, is making matches), that your desire for sex comes from God, that He has created in you the senses of touch, sight, and so forth so that you have the ability to experience and enjoy sexual pleasure, and last, that He has created the pleasure itself.[3]

32:1:8:5 In Hasidism, a preparatory meditation on being in God's presence is often suggested for use before all the major spiritual practices. Such a meditation is used for Torah study, for prayer, and also for eating (see those chapters). Before sex also we can meditate on being in the presence of God.

Not infrequently, such a meditation is described as considering oneself to be in the Garden of Eden, where the light of the *Shechinah* is revealed. Carrying the thought a step further, we can note that the ideal of sexual purity is, according to the rabbis, Adam and Eve in the Garden before their sin; their sex was completely holy and pure.

> When you are always clinging in *d'vekut* to the Holy One, blessed be He, and are not thinking of fleeting and empty material realities, and your only desire is to cling to the Source of Life who gives life to everything, then your sex will be holy and will not be drawn after

> the *yetzer ha-ra* at all. You will be like Adam, the first man, before his sin. (*Reshit Hochmah*, Sh'ar ha-Kedushah, chap. 16, #8)
>
> The sexual union of man and woman is something holy and clean, when it is done as it should be, at the right time, and with the right intentions. Let no one think that there is anything shameful or ugly, God forbid, about it. And the clearest witness for this is Adam and Eve. (Igeret ha-Ramban in *Reshit Hochmah*, Sh'ar ha-Kedushah, chap. 16)

Before and during sex a couple can meditate on being in the presence of the *Shechinah*, in the Garden of Eden, where there is no lust or pride or anger, and everything is love and joy, where spirituality reigns. (See the quote from the Maggid of Mezritch in "Torah," 15:18:4:2.)

32:1:8:6 Rabbi Abraham Joshua Heshel of Apta taught that through intense *d'vekut* we can reach a level, even during sex, of complete separation from bodily lust:

> Although a man of Israel is commanded to fulfill the *mitzvah* of sex at regular intervals, as is known from the words of our Sages, of blessed memory, you should not have bodily lust during sex, but should be separated from it altogether. On the contrary, you should have holy thoughts then, to the degree possible, according to each person's level. Perhaps someone will ask, "How is it possible to attain the level needed for this *mitzvah* and its fulfillment? Does not lust overcome one's will? How is it possible to engage in sex and yet be separated from it and holy, and in a meditative state of mind?" There is a way, however, for a man of Israel to remove himself from animal lust and enter within the borders of holiness: you should have [God] engraved in your mind at all times and at every moment. Do we not know that the souls of the nation of the Children of Israel are quarried from under His Throne of Glory, may He be blessed and exalted, and they are each a part of God? So you should attach yourself in *d'vekut* to your Root, which is exalted in holiness, with love and fear. It is also known that the Creator, blessed be He and blessed is His name, who is awesome and glorious, fills all worlds and there is no place where He is not. Nevertheless, although He is within them, He is at the same time separate and apart from all the worlds. When a person truly attains to *d'vekut* with God, blessed be He, with love and fear, he is on the level that the Godly soul within him informs his consciousness, and he is able to reach this level and be like his Creator, so to speak, in being separated and holy [even while he is within materiality]. For he is a

> part of God from Above, and what is in the Root is also possible for the branches. (*Ohav Yisrael*, Kedoshim, quoted in *Ha-Rav mi-Apta*, p. 112)

The Apter is discussing here a state of intense *d'vekut* where you perceive God within as well as without, and you realize that the *Shechinah* fills you and moves you also, along with everything else in the world. On this exalted level, where you are in the Garden of Eden, there is no lust. Attaining this state involves a higher level of hasidic meditation on God's greatness, where one meditates on God being within as well as without. (See the chapter on "Meditation," particularly 17:10.)

32:1:9 Prayer

Before sexual union it is good for both husband and wife to state aloud before God their intention in this act for the sake of heaven, and to pray for its fulfillment.

32:1:9:1 *Zohar Hadash* (Bereshit, 15):

> Rabbi Yosi ben Pazzi said: Once I made a journey, and came to a town in the mountains of Ararat, where I took lodging with some people [a Jewish couple] who rejoiced in their portion. I stayed with them for *Shabbat*, and I saw how the innkeeper wanted to join with his wife; and they were standing in prayer, he in one corner and she in another.
>
> I asked them what they were praying, and they told me: "We have sexual union once a week, on *Shabbat*, and we pray that the Holy One, blessed be He, give us a son who will be a servant of God and sin-fearing, who will be occupied with the *mitzvot* and will not turn aside from what the Torah says, either left or right." (*SKv'Tz*, p. 21, #8)

32:1:9:2 The two main reasons for having sex are to have a child and to offer our love to our spouse and join with him or her in love. Both of these motives can be expressed in prayer (the former omitted when conception is not possible). Following is an example of a prayer before sex, based on earlier prayers of this nature and on teachings in holy books.

> *HaShem!*
>
> Our intention now is to serve You and give You pleasure in us, through sex which is in purity and holiness. And our intention is to

offer our love to our spouse and join with him/her in love, and to have a child who will be Your child and servant, following the ways of the Torah and turning aside neither left nor right.

We pray that You give us, through this union, a child who will be like our holy ancestors, like Abraham, Isaac and Jacob, Joseph, Moses, Aaron, and David; like Sarah, Rebecca, Rachel and Leah, Miriam, Deborah, Ruth, and Esther [add the names of other *tzaddikim* and *tzaddikot* throughout the generations for whom you feel a special admiration and attachment].

May I cleave to my husband/wife not in lust, but in love. Help me and my spouse to attain to purity, that we not fall into lust and become coarsened by our sexuality. Keep us from descending into what is low, but let us serve You through our sex, raising up what is of the body and material into the spiritual realm.

May we know, at this time, that we are always in Your Presence, surrounded by Your Light and Glory. And may we realize that we are in the Garden of Eden, where there is no pride and no hatred and no lust. Make us worthy that our sexual union be as pure and holy as that of Adam and Eve before the sin. And in the merit of our ancestors, may our union be like that of Abraham with Sarah, and Isaac with Rebecca, and Jacob with Rachel and with Leah—for the Light of the *Shechinah* was before their eyes every hour and every minute and every second, even during sex.

HaShem! I pray that I and my spouse be worthy in our love, so that the alien fire of lust not burn within us and between us, but that the fires of our love for each other be pure, so that the holy fire of the *Shechinah* surround us and fill us and shine before our eyes.

May we be aware of the Divine Presence at all times during our sex, and when we have pleasure in our contact and touch, may we realize that it is coming to us from the radiance of the *Shechinah*. And we give thanks to You, O God, for the pleasure that You created.[4]

32:1:10 Arousing Love

Before sex, a man and woman should speak words of gentleness and love to each other (though traditionally it is only the man who is so instructed).

32:1:10:1 Before sex he should speak sweet words to her, according to his ability . . . and he should soothe her and make her happy, so that they will feel love for each other. (*SKv'Tz*, p. 26b, #22)

32:1:10:2 He who joins with his wife must first speak to her soothingly, and make her happy . . . so that they are of one mind in desiring to have sex, and there is no coercion.

What are soothing words? Like what is written about Adam, the sweet words that he spoke to Eve, to bring her to love him, saying, "This is now bone of my bones and flesh of my flesh; she shall be called Woman [Genesis 2:23]." See how sweet are these soothing words that Adam spoke to his wife, to show her that they are as one body [Genesis 2:24], and that there is no separation at all between them. (Both of these quotes are from *Reshit Hochmah*, Sh'ar ha-Kedushah, chap. 16, #26, the first one itself a quote from the *Tikkunim*.)

32:1:10:3 There is no sexual intercourse without embracing and kissing preceding it. And there are two kinds of kissing: the first is before sexual intercourse, where the purpose of kissing is that the man soothe the woman and arouse the love between them; the other kind is during intercourse itself, where the purpose is to accomplish the two kinds of union, the lower one and the supernal one together. (*Siddur Yabetz*, quoted in *SKv'Tz*, p. 29, #28)

Before sex, kissing should express the love that unites the couple. During sex the kissing is to accomplish this and something more—it should unite the Holy One, blessed be He, and His *Shechinah*. When you kiss and embrace you should be aware that you are uniting in love with your spouse and that together, your love, which manifests the *Shechinah*, is a Throne on which the Holy One, blessed be He, comes to rest.

32:2 THE SEXUAL ACT ITSELF

32:2:1 The essence of Judaism depends on sanctifying yourself during sexual intercourse . . . and saying aloud [beforehand], "For the sake of the unification of the Holy One, blessed be He, and His *Shechinah*." Do not allow your *yetzer* to become too heated during intercourse, but cleave with your mind to the holy *Shechinah* in the unification of the Supernal Lovers. (*Heichal ha-Beracha*, quoted in *SKv'Tz*, p. 40, #33)

32:2:2 It has been said about our holy ancestors that when they were occupied with bodily necessities, all their intention was for the sake of heaven, and their minds were not separated from the Supernal Light for even a moment. As a result of this, Jacob

> merited being the father of the twelve tribes . . . for his mind was not separated from the Supernal Light, even during sex and during sexual intercourse itself. (*Menorat ha-Maor*, Section 184, p. 44)

A commentary on *Menorat ha-Maor* (Nefesh Yehudah)[5] explains the reference to the "Supernal Light": "That is, the Shechinah—for they would have the *Shechinah* before their eyes, for 'All the earth is full of His Glory [the *Shechinah*].'"

32:2:3 Meditations During Sex

32:2:3:1 A meditation during sex can be on the wonderful mystery of how in sex the couple become God's partners in creating a child, a new being in the world. As the rabbis said:

> There are three partners in the creation of a child—the Holy One, blessed be He, his father, and his mother. (*Kiddushin* 30)

One can turn one's attention to the presence of this third "partner," who is present at this wonderful and awesome time.

> Remember that from your loins will go forth a human being, in whom will be put a soul, a portion of God from Above. Then trembling and shivering will overtake you at this awesome event—and you will keep yourself from becoming involved in sexual union lightly. (Rabbi Moshe Leib of Sassov, *Likkutei Rabbi Moshe Leib*, Hanhagot ha-Simha b'Avodah, #25)

32:2:3:2 Another meditation can be on how the physical pleasure is coming from God, and is only a partial experience of the bliss of the *Shechinah*. *Huppat Eliyahu Rabba* says that the pleasure of sexual intercourse is similar to that of the World to Come (Gate 3, #6). The World to Come is here interchangeable with the Garden of Eden. The rabbis taught that you can experience the World to Come/Garden of Eden in this life. One should think: If this is a taste of the Garden of Eden, where the *Shechinah* is revealed, I should not focus on the physical pleasure, but on its Source (the *Shechinah*), where the delight, in its fullness, is certainly greater. (See "Eating and the Holy Meal," 10:14 about this kind of meditation.)

32:2:3:3 In the hasidic meditation for a holy meal, we are to concentrate, while eating, on the spiritual reality, of how the life and pleasure we receive from the food are coming to us from God, because of His love for us. So, during sex, we can meditate on the miracle of how life comes to the baby from God (and reflect also on our own similar creation)—and how God brings us all into being because of His love for us. We can also meditate on the source of the sexual pleasure as coming to us from God, drawing ourselves up from the bodily experience into the spiritual.

32:2:3:4 Still another meditation during sex can be on the love you share with your spouse, with the realization that God has brought her/him to you, and that He is the source of your love for each other. As said earlier, the experience of love is one of the deepest experiences a human can have. The realization that this taste of completion is from God attaches it to its source.

Such a meditation can also go beyond the immediate experience to reflect on how God is the source of all marital love, and further, that He is the source of all love and happiness and joy. This meditation is suggested by the words of the beautiful blessing said at a wedding: "Blessed art Thou, O Lord our God, King of the Universe, who hast created joy and gladness, bridegroom and bride, mirth and exultation, pleasure and delight, love, harmony, peace and fellowship." (This thought is taken from a talk by a great rabbi and *tzaddik* of our time.) We should also be aware that God brings us all this goodness and love because of His love for us.

32:3 AFTER SEX

> **32:3:1** Make it a habit for both of you to say the prayer *Ana b'Koach* [found in the Siddur in *Shaharit*, in *Korbanot*] after the sexual act, before sleep. Every night you should both accustom yourselves to say *Ana b'Koach*. (Rabbi David ha-Levi of Steppin, *Hanhagot Tzaddikim*, p. 58, #44)

32:3:2 The Bedtime Prayer Service (without the *Hamappil* "He who makes the bands of sleep to fall" blessing) is said before sex at night. Afterwards, after cleaning oneself, the first paragraph of the *Sh'ma* is repeated, and the blessing is said in bed as usual (*SKv'Tz*, p. 25, #8, with note **).

> After sex you should immediately wash and scrub yourself well with hot water, from your midriff and below [to remove any semen from your body]. (*Sefer Hasidim*, #509, quoted in *SKv'Tz*, p. 31, #6)
>
> You should wash the semen off, then wash your hands, and after that recite the *Sh'ma*. (*Mishnah Berurah*, in *SKv'Tz*, p. 25, note **)

Although these quotes are directed to men, women should also wash off any semen on the outside of the body.

32:3:3 One of the central practices for sexual purification for men is that after sexual intercourse (or after an uncontrolled ejaculation during sleep) a man go to the *mikveh* the following morning. The point is that this establishes in the mind that the sexual impulse is a great force which can be contrary to spirituality, and must be limited and restrained. Thus, the uncontrolled ejaculation must be mended; but even sex done in a holy way requires a barrier of *mikveh* immersion, so that adverse sexual influences on the body are controlled, and sexual thoughts do not roll on during the day as an unintended aftereffect. The pure waters of the *mikveh* can reverse these effects and restore the soul when it may have lost power.

If you cannot get to a *mikveh* you can stand under a shower for a time, according to the halachic measure, enough that about five gallons of water go over you (*SKv'Tz*, p. 32, #18).

32:4 SEX ON *SHABBAT*

Traditionally, the evening of *Shabbat* is particularly set aside for fulfilling the *mitzvah* of sex. Some of the most pious people have sex only once a week, on Friday night.

On the one hand, the pleasure of sex contributes to the joy of *Shabbat*; on the other hand, it is the holiness of *Shabbat* that helps to raise up the sex into the realm of spirituality, because *Shabbat* is the Day of Love, when love is lifted up to God.

> The enjoyment of sex is one of the pleasures of *Shabbat*, so the regularity with which Torah sages join with their wives is from one Sabbath to the next. (*Shulchan Aruch*, Orach Hayim, siman 280)

Rabbi Tzadok ha-Cohen of Lublin:

> [The Talmudic tradition that] the Torah sages engage in sex only from one Sabbath evening to the next, is because a person cannot attain *d'vekut* during sex as he should, except on *Shabbat*. (*Tzidkat ha-Tzaddik*, #167)

Certainly, on *Shabbat*, a couple should make every effort to lift up the spiritual level of their sex. By having sex on *Shabbat* with true *kavvanah* for the sake of heaven, lifting up the animal powers of their soul to God, blessed be He, a couple raise up spiritually whatever sex they have engaged in the other days of that week[6], and draw holiness to their sexual activity in the coming week.

Rabbi Tzvi Hirsh of Nadborna:

> On *Shabbat* see that . . . your sexual intercourse be in holiness, and that all your actions be for the sake of heaven, more so than on weekdays; and after *Shabbat* draw from this holiness into the weekdays. (*Alpha Beta* of Rabbi Tzvi Hirsh, Shabbat, *YHvT*, p. 66)

32:5 Another central aspect of Jewish spirituality related to sex is that of family purity and *niddah*. This important topic cannot be treated here, and the reader is advised to see *Waters of Eden—The Mystery of the Mikvah*, by Rabbi Arye Kaplan. Let us, however, just quote a paragraph from another of Rabbi Kaplan's books, *Jewish Meditation*, from the chapter on sexuality, "Between Man and Woman":

> Very important in making sex a holy act is keeping the rules of family purity. This involves the woman's counting seven days after the end of her period and then immersing in a *mikveh* (ritual bath). The monthly menses are seen as a cleaning process, and immersion in the *mikveh* as a process of rebirth. . . . In many ways immersion in the *mikveh* is more important in making sex a holy act than even marriage itself. (p. 158)

33

Talking To God and Being Alone With God—*Hitbodedut*

33:1 TALKING TO GOD

The origin of prayer is ancient, and the Patriarchs and Matriarchs continually talked to God. The fixed prayer services came later. They should not be seen as taking the place of the more basic personal dialogue with your Father in Heaven. Accustom yourself, then, to talk to Him all the time, in the language that you understand.

We are to have a continual conversation with God throughout the day. It is also a good practice to set a time during each prayer service when you speak to God in your own words—and this should be seen as a high point of the service (see "Prayer," 5:3:16). But we can, in addition, have fixed times other than during the prayer services to be alone with God and converse with Him. This latter practice is called *hitbodedut*, "aloneness" with God.

32:2 *HITBODEDUT*

Hitbodedut is a basic spiritual practice recommended by many hasidic *rebbes*. It is a centerpiece of the way to God taught by Rabbi Nachman of Bratzlav.

Hitbodedut literally means "self-seclusion," and is best accomplished in an isolated place where there are no people and where you can be truly alone with yourself and with God. Setting a specific time for this "aloneness" is of the essence, for we are saying, "God, I am now going to dedicate this amount of time to being just with You." Thus, Rabbi Nachman praises just sitting "with Him," even when you cannot open your mouth. If you dedicate some time to sit and be with God, then you are with Him even if you are silent.

The way the time is spent in *hitbodedut* can vary: "conversation" with God, prayer, meditation, self-reflection and spiritual account-taking, repentance, and confession are among the possibilities.

Traditional times for *hitbodedut* are before sleep (see "Sleep and Before Sleep" [29]), and during the night vigil (See "*Tikkun Hatzot*" [31]).

Various hasidic *rebbes* recommended doing *hitbodedut* once a day.

Rabbi Aaron of Karlin:

> If possible, it is good to separate yourself to be alone with God every day for some time, although not for less than an hour. (*Hanhagot Tzaddikim*, p. 3, #3)

Rabbi Shalom Shachna of Probitch taught that we should have three times a day for *hitbodedut*:

> You should set yourself a special time to be with God in the morning. So when you awaken, after going to the bathroom, see if your mind is clear and bright, and meditate on God's greatness and on your own lowliness.

He goes on to explain how it should be a meditation to arouse yourself to love and fear of God, to do His commandments, etc. (This is discussed at length. For a number of examples of such meditations on awakening, see "Waking and Beginning the Day," 4:4).

The Probitcher continues:

> You should do such *hitbodedut* mentally, or even verbally, in whatever language you want.

> Do *hitbodedut* once in the morning [this also serves as a preparation for *Shaharit*], and a second time before *Minha*, so that during that very day you can fix where you have begun to go astray, and a third time before sleep, when you should be a Master of Accounts to consider what you did wrong that day, God forbid, in thought, speech, and deed. . . . And these three times of *hitbodedut* each day should be for you a fixed obligation just like the three times of prayer. (*Seder ha-Yom* of Rabbi Shalom Shachna of Probitch, in *D'vir Yaakov*)

Rabbi Nachman of Bratzlav, who, as we said, made *hitbodedut* one of the main practices in his way of Divine service, taught that a person should have a set time of at least an hour a day for *hidbodedut*. There is a *Seder ha-Yom* (Daily Order of Divine Service) given according to the views and teachings of Rabbi Nachman,[1] wherein *hitbodedut* is included as one of the basic practices of the day:

> *Hitbodedut*—Strengthen yourself with all determination to seclude yourself with God each day, for at least an hour, and speak with Him at length about everything that is going on in your life. Confess to Him all your sins, transgressions, and failings, intentional and unintentional, and speak to Him freely, as one speaks to a friend. Tell Him about your troubles and everything that is causing you difficulty, and about any bad situation you find yourself in, and also that of your family and of the Congregation of Israel.
>
> You should speak at length, talk and talk some more, and argue with Him to convince Him to bring you close to Him, using every argument and every kind of persuasion you can think of. . . . You should call out to God and cry out for help; sigh and weep before Him, and also thank Him for all the kindnesses, spiritual and material, that He has done for you. Thank Him with songs and praises.
>
> Afterward ask of Him your needs, both spiritual and material, and believe fully that the pleasure that comes to Him from this your conversation—even if you are the least of the least—is greater than that which He receives from all the many other kinds of worship and service, and is greater even than all the worship of the angels in all the worlds. This is so even if you cannot open your mouth to speak. Just standing there before Him and hoping for Him, lifting your eyes on high and trying to force yourself to speak even one word during the whole hour—is so precious, and all of this is the fulfillment of your eternal purpose. (*Seder Tikkun Hatzot*, end)

One of Rabbi Nachman's greatest disciples, Rabbi Natan, writes:

> Another practice that he universally prescribed to all his disciples was for us to seclude ourselves in prayer each day. He told us to express our thoughts before God and ask that He have mercy and allow us to achieve true devotion. This secluded prayer was to be in the language we normally spoke. (*Rabbi Nachman's Wisdom*, p. 325, *Sichos HaRan*, #185)

Rabbi Natan gives us Rabbi Nachman's instructions about *hitbodedut*:

> The Rebbe once spoke to a youth and encouraged him to seclude himself and converse with God in his native language. The Rebbe told him that this is how prayer began. The main form of prayer was an expression of the heart before God in each man's native tongue.
>
> [Rabbi Natan continues:] Maimonides speaks of this in the beginning of his code on prayer [*Yad Chazakah*, Tefillah 1:2–4]. He states that this was the main form of prayer in the beginning, before it was formalized by the Men of the Great Assembly. It was only then that a formal order of prayer was introduced. But even according to the Law, the original form is still foremost. Even though we follow the order of prayer ordained by the Great Assembly, the original form is still the most beneficial.
>
> Make a habit of praying before God from the depths of your heart. Use whatever language you know best. Ask God to make you worthy of truly serving Him. This is the essence of prayer. In many places we discussed the importance of making this regular practice. This is the way all the Tzaddikim attained their high level. (*Rabbi Nachman's Wisdom*, p. 364; *Sichos HaRan*, #229)

This was how Rabbi Nachman, too, attained his own awesome holiness:

> The main way the Rebbe attained what he did was simply through prayer and supplication before God. He was very consistent in this. He would beg and plead in every way possible, asking that God have mercy and make him worthy of true devotion and closeness.
>
> The thing that helped him most was his prayers in the language he usually spoke, which was Yiddish. He would find a secluded place and set it aside to express his thoughts to God. Speaking in his own language, he would beg and plead before God. He would use all sorts of arguments and logic, crying that it was fitting that God draw him close and help him in his devotion. He kept this up constantly, spending days and years engaged in such prayer.

> His father's house had a small garret, partitioned off as a storehouse for hay and feed. Here the young Rabbi Nachman would hide himself, chanting the Psalms and screaming quietly, begging God that he be worthy of drawing himself close to Him. (*Rabbi Nachman's Wisdom*, p. 9, *Shevachey HaRan*, #10)

(See "Individual Practices," 39:23 about screaming quietly, the "silent shout.")

Some people have more difficulty than others in learning how to open themselves up to speak to God. Rabbi Nachman writes, in a discussion of the practice of *hitbodedut*:

> If it happens sometimes that you are unable to speak and cannot even open your mouth, the preparation that you are making by placing yourself before God with a desire and a yearning to speak, even though you are not able, is still very good.
>
> You can make this itself something to pray about and to converse with God about—and about this itself you can cry out and plead before Him, that you have become so separated from Him that you cannot even converse with Him. You should beg Him to have mercy and compassion on you, that He open your mouth so you will be able to converse with Him fluently and freely. (*Likkutei Moharan*, II, #25)

Rabbi Nachman wrote:

> It is good if for an hour you [just sit silently and] long to speak before God, and prepare yourself to speak, and then speak for an hour. (*Likkutei Aytzot*, quoted in *Erech Apayim*, 7:9, p. 100)

For a certain person who had a hard time opening himself to speak to God:

> The Rebbe prescribed that he spend two hours each day in secluded prayer. For an hour he was to meditate and prepare himself to speak. When his heart was awakened, he was to then speak to God for another hour. (*Rabbi Nachman's Wisdom*, p. 367, *Sichos HaRan*, #232)

Of course, if you are not devoting two hours, or even an hour, you can still apply this suggestion to whatever time you are doing *hitbodedut*. If you do have difficulty speaking to God, spend half the time in preparation, longing to speak and considering what to say, and the other half of the time speaking. (See "*Mitzvot*," 11:4 for further insight into this.)

Rabbi Nachman:

> When God helps a man in his secluded prayer, he is able to converse with Him extensively, like a person speaks with his friend. You should accustom yourself to speak with God as you would with your *rebbe* or with your friend. . . . How good it is that a man should be able to pour out his heart and mind to God, in requests and pleas like a child bothering his father about what he wants. How good when he can arouse his heart in his conversations with God until he can cry before Him as a child cries before his father. (*Likkutei Aytzot*, Hitbodedut, #20, #21)

Rabbi Nachman says the practice of *hitbodedut* is the greatest of all, and can bring you to everything in the religious life. He suggests setting a fixed time each day, and though he emphasizes that pleading and tears are the way for *hitbodedut*, sadness should be avoided at all other times.

The most propitious time for *hitbodedut* is, he says, at night, and if possible you should go to as secluded a place as you can find.

> The best time for *hitbodedut* is at night, when people are asleep, and the best place is one that is outside the city. [This was easier in those days of smaller towns.] A person should go out alone, to a place where people do not go even during the day. (*Likkutei Aytzot*, Hitbodedut, #7)
>
> It's best to seclude yourself and meditate in the meadows outside the city. Go to a grassy field, for the grass will awaken your heart. (*Rabbi Nachman's Wisdom*, p. 364, *Sichos HaRan*, #227; see there also #98, #144, #163)

Although the *rebbe* suggests a field as a good place for *hitbodedut*, he also recommends a secluded room (*Likkutei Moharan*, II, #25).

> It is good to have a special room set aside for Torah study and prayer. Such a room is especially beneficial for secluded meditation and conversation with God. (*Rabbi Nachman's Wisdom*, p. 401, *Sichos HaRan*, #274)
>
> The Rebbe said that it is very good even to sit in such a special room. The atmosphere itself is beneficial, even if you sit there and do nothing else. Even if you do not have a special room, you can still seclude yourself and converse with God. The Rebbe also said that you can create your own special room under your tallis. Just drape your tallis over your eyes and converse with God as you desire. You can also seclude yourself with God in bed under the covers. This was the custom of King David, as it is written (Psalm

6:7), "Each night I converse from my bed. . . ." You can also converse with God while sitting before an open book. Let others think that you are merely studying. [Remember that in Torah study the lips are moved. This can also be done in the synagogue, when you can talk with God while appearing as if praying from the Siddur.] There are many other ways to accomplish this if you truly want to meditate and express your thoughts to God. Above all else, this is the root and foundation of holiness and repentance. . . . There are many ways of doing this, but best of all is a secluded room. (*Rabbi Nachman's Wisdom*, p. 401, *Sichos HaRan*, #275)

Rabbi Natan says of Rabbi Nachman himself, when he was a youth:

The Rebbe lived in town and had his private room where he could practice his devotions. Still, he would often walk in the woods and fields and seclude himself in prayer. (*Rabbi Nachman's Wisdom*, p. 305, *Sichos HaRan* #162)

For other quotes about *Hitbodedut*, see "*Tikkun Hatzot*" (31) and "A Full Day Set Aside" (36).

34

The Service of Praise

The purpose and intention of all the creation is, in its essence, praise of God and prayer to Him. (Rabbi Yehiel Yehoshuah, the Rebbe of Biala, *Tefillat ha-Tzaddikim*, p. 4)

The service of praise is best learned from the words of that great *tzaddik* who was himself so much devoted to it, Rabbi Alexander Ziskind, the famous author of *Yesod v'Shoresh ha-Avodah*. The following selections are from *Tzva'a Yekara*, his ethical will and testament, written to teach his children the way of God.

34:1 I was very careful to give thanks and praise to God, may He be exalted and may His name be blessed, for everything bad (may the Merciful One spare us!) that happened to me, whether great or small . . . I would justify the judgment on myself with joy, and I also gave thanks to God, blessed be He, in these words: "My Maker and Creator, You are righteous in all that You have brought upon me, for You have acted in truth—and it is I who have done wickedly. And I offer You praise and thanks for this, my Maker and Creator, for certainly it is for my good that You have brought this upon me."

So too on everything good that happened, whether great or small . . . I thanked Him, blessed be He, for the good that He did to me—either for a *mitzvah* that He brought before me and gave me the opportunity to do, or just for the good that He did to me in my personal life.

Certainly everyone is supposed to do this, as it says in the mishnah (*Berachot* 9): "A person is obligated to bless God for the bad that happens, just as he blesses Him for the good." . . . The meaning here is that it is obvious that you have to praise God for the good—the purpose of the *mishnah* is to tell us that you also have to bless Him for the bad. And the One who knows our hidden thoughts can testify for me, my dear children, that even apart from the obligation that this *mishnah* speaks of, which is a *halacha* of Moshe from Sinai, I did this service of God continually, due to the great love of God deep in my heart. For I continually thanked and praised Him, blessed be His name and may He be exalted, for both the bad things as well as the good that he brought to me.

And now I will put before you, my dear children, some examples that come to mind, and from them you can yourselves know what to do in the many similar cases, for there are so many that it is impossible to speak about all of them. (p. 14, #26)

34:2 I have always been so grateful for the great kindness that my Maker and Creator, blessed and exalted be His name, did for me in giving me a special room for Divine service, since the day that I had a mind of my own (as you know). Such a room is a basic requirement for anyone who wants to reach perfection in this lowly world. So I gave Him thanks for this, blessed be He, every time it came to my mind what a great kindness He had done for me—even several times a day. I said this thanksgiving aloud, in these words: "My Maker and Creator, blessed be Your name, I thank You from the bottom of my heart for having given me a special room for Your Divine service—not according to my good deeds, but just because of your great compassion and Your kindness."

. . . Whenever I was returning from the synagogue, morning and evening, and approached my house, I always gave my deepest thanks aloud to Him, blessed be He, for giving me a house, for me and my family, and especially for its being so close to a synagogue. . . .

Whenever I went from my home to the synagogue I had to walk near the unstable wall of an abandoned house that was on the verge of falling. Even before I reached the wall I began to pray to God, blessed be He, that He "save me from the wall falling on me, or on any other person whom You have created." I would say a prayer in this language even a number of times, one after the other, whenever I passed the wall. After I had safely passed the length of the wall, I thanked and praised God, blessed be He, for saving me from the wall falling on me, in these words: "My Maker and Creator, blessed be Your name in the mouth of all who live, I thank and praise You, blessed be Your name, for saving me from the wall falling on me." And I prayed the above prayer and gave thanks even a number of times every day. (p. 14, #27)

34:3 When I put on my Sabbath clothes on *Erev Shabbat*, close to *Minha*, I gave thanks to God, blessed be He, with all my heart, and with great joy, aloud, in these words: "My Maker and Creator, blessed be Your name, I thank You that You have given me such good clothes, for the honor of the holy Sabbath—not according to my good deeds, but just because of Your great compassion and Your kindness." For I thought to myself, how many great *tzaddikim* are there, to whose ankles I do not reach, who do not have clothes like these. And I thought in my heart that certainly if I fail to thank and praise God for this, it would be, God forbid, an ill deed and rebellious of me—and so I gave thanks a number of times as I put on the clothes.

On weekdays, when I put on my good weekday clothes, I gave thanks in this way also.

During the cold winter days, I had a very warm sheep's wool coat, and every time I put it on I gave thanks to God, blessed be He, for giving it to me, for I thought that certainly, without this coat, I would be very miserable from the cold. (p. 16, #29)

34:4 Whenever I had a great need for something and I had that thing in my possession and did not have to search after it, or borrow it from others, I would joyfully give thanks to God, may He be exalted, in this language: "My Maker and Creator, blessed be Your Name, I thank and praise You for having given me everything that I need." I repeated this aloud, with joy, a number of times, one after the other, even with something that was just a benefit in my personal life, or that was very small—for example, when I needed to buy something insignificant, and had the money. I thought to myself, how many great *tzaddikim* are there, whose ankles I do not reach, who are not able to buy what they need, even a small thing for a few coins—and I am lacking for nothing.

Especially would I offer thanks for big things, for example, when I would travel somewhere and did not have to borrow clothing from others, or other travel needs. Even more so would I thank God when I could afford what I needed for a *mitzvah* . . . [Rabbi Ziskind goes on to tell how he gave praise to God when he had money to buy *tzitzit*, *tefillin*, and so on.] (p. 17, #32)

34:5 For every trouble and suffering that came upon me I justified God's judgment on me and said joyfully: "My Maker and Creator, You are righteous in all You have brought upon me, for You have acted in truth—but I have done wickedly [see 34:1]." So whether it was a matter of money loss, or of bodily suffering—for example, my teeth ached nearly every day (God spare us!), and even when the pain was so great that I could not learn Torah—I justified the judgment on myself almost every minute, saying "You are righteous, etc." And during prayer, when it is forbidden to interrupt, I would justify the judgment on myself in thought and in my heart with this language—and so with all other sufferings great and small.

For example, when I went somewhere and forgot to take something with me, and had to go back and get it, even a short distance, I justified the judgment on myself in this language, and so for all other bodily sufferings or discomforts. So also for any money loss, no matter how small. For example, if my snuffbox fell out of my breast pocket, and the snuff spilled out, even less than a coin's worth, I would justify the judgment on myself in this language—and so with other similar situations. The cases where I did this are so many that they cannot be numbered—where I suffered some monetary loss, or where I experienced the other kinds of trouble and all the situations similar to them—for all of them I justified the judgment on myself.

In the opposite case, where I enjoyed some satisfaction, or something good happened to me, whether great or small, I thanked and praised God, with much joy. I will give just a few illustrations because the multitude of instances where I did this cannot be described. For example, in regard to my aching teeth, which I wrote about before, whenever the pain would subside even a little, I would thank God with great joy, saying: "I thank You, my Maker and Creator, may Your name be blessed in the mouth of all who live, for sending me healing for my great pain." In the middle of prayer I would say this thanks in these very words, mentally and in my heart. In the case just mentioned, about forgetting something and having to return to get it, if I remembered after a short distance, and as a result did not have as much trouble in returning, I would thank God, blessed be His name, for this, aloud, with great joy, saying: "My Maker and Creator, blessed be Your name, I thank You for reminding me about this so soon, so that I would not be troubled as much in returning." In the matter of a small money loss that I mentioned before, for example, when my little snuffbox fell, [I justified the judgment on myself)]; but when it fell and did not open and I did not have any loss, I thanked and praised God for this, aloud, with great joy, saying: "I thank You, my Maker and Creator, blessed be Your name, for saving me from a loss."

I will put before you, my dear children, another example from which you can understand many similar incidents. For example, if a bottle rolled on the table and was about to fall and break, and I was quick enough to catch it before it fell, I would praise and thank God aloud, in the above language—and all the more so if it did fall and break; so too with my eyeglasses—when they fell and did not break—and you can understand from these examples many similar kinds of incidents.

Also, numbers of times it happened that I could not find my snuffbox, having forgotten where I put it. This caused me a certain amount of unhappiness, and so I justified the judgment on myself, as above. And when I found it later on, I thanked God, saying: "My Maker and Creator, blessed be Your name, I praise and thank You for returning to me what I lost."[1]

For with complete faith I realized the truth—that everything that happens to a person, whether something good and enjoyable, even something very small, or something bad, some loss or some suffering—it is all from Him, blessed and exalted be His name, by His Divine Providence over all men, every moment, and not according to "chance." . . . So I realized that I was definitely obligated, for every good that came to me, great or small (for it is from Him, blessed and exalted be His name, and by His Divine Providence), to give thanks and praise, in my heart and in my mouth. And for the reverse case, for afflictions and various losses, great and small, I was then obligated to justify the judgment on myself. (p. 18, #33)

(For more about the service of praise, see Chapter 2, "Remembering Him through Blessings and Praises," pp. 37, and for praising God when troubles come, see also "Afflictions" [35].)

35

Afflictions

35:1 We can determine in advance that we are willing to suffer in our service of God. For example, we can meditate on what we are ready to give up or to undergo, if necessary. A good time for such meditation is during prayer in the first paragraph of the *Sh'ma* when we speak of loving God with all our heart—understood by the rabbis as meaning willingness to give up our desires and lusts for His sake[1]; and with all our soul—understood as meaning self-sacrifice even to martyrdom; and with all our might—understood as referring to willingness to give up all our possessions and wealth. See "Service of the Imagination," 19:4 for some traditional meditations through visualizing these things. We can, for instance, use visualization to picture the suffering and difficulties we are prepared to undergo for our love of God, and how we give up these or those possessions most precious to us, which might bind us and keep us from a full readiness to do the will of God.

> **35:2** One summer, the holy Rabbi of Parisov, Rabbi Abraham, the memory of a *tzaddik* for a blessing, went for a walk with our master, teacher, and rabbi, the holy S'fas Emes, the memory of a *tzaddik* for a blessing for the life of the World to Come. While they were talking with each other, the holy Rabbi of Parisov said to the

> holy S'fas Emes, "It's very hot today." The holy S'fas Emes answered him by saying, "When a person commits himself to God's service and to the yoke of the Kingdom of Heaven like an ox to its yoke and like an ass to its burden, then, for an ass, even the hottest weather of the summer is cool because everything is accepted in advance." (*Siah Sarfei Kodesh*, II, p. 59, #207)

It is a high level to truly accept everything in advance. But we can all prepare ourselves in a specific way for likely suffering and hardships in a situation we are about to enter. See "Individual Practices," 39:15 for some instructive examples of this: of how Rabbi Yitzhak of Vorki prepared for the abuse he knew he would probably receive at the hands of a wagon-driver he was traveling with; or the teaching of *Reshit Hochmah* on how to avoid anger by preparing before you go to have business dealings with someone who you know is a difficult person.

35:3 Afflictions great or small are a regular part of a person's life. How you deal with them can be a daily practice directing you to God–consciousness. The main thing is to see that everything that happens to you, afflictions included, comes to you from God, and for a purpose. If we realize that an affliction comes to us because of our sin and that it helps us by humbling us and breaking down the ego shell that separates us from God, then we can receive it with love, and it serves an atonement, bringing us closer to our Father in Heaven. Of course, this is a very good thing, so the rabbis say:

> A person should be grateful to the Holy One, blessed be He, when afflictions come upon him. Why? Because these afflictions draw a man to God. (*Tanhuma*, Ki Taitzai, 2)
>
> A person should rejoice when afflictions come upon him more so than when good comes to him. Because when good comes to you, sins are not forgiven; but when you receive afflictions [with love], your sins are forgiven. (*Sifre*, V'etchanan, 32)

35:3:1 The Baal Shem Tov:

> "A righteous person lives by his faith" [Habakkuk 2:4]—When a person believes in God's Divine Providence, he knows that everything that happens to a man is from Him, blessed be He; and whether it is something great or small, everything adverse that happens to him is, he knows, a manifestation of the judgment of

> God, of the judgment of the Kingdom of Heaven, and is due to his sin. So when affliction comes upon him he immediately regrets his sins and is full of remorse and the fear of God, and then, as a result of this, in heaven they forgive him his sins. In this way a righteous person, who has faith that this all comes from God, "lives," that is, his sins are forgiven. Therefore, even when you just put your hand into your pocket for one coin and are bothered that another comes up, since you believe that this is due to your sins, and you regret them, it serves as an atonement for your sins. (*Toldot Yaakov Yosef*, Vayishlach, quoted in *DhTvhY*, Tz'ar, #3, p. 67)

> **35:3:2** What is said in the *Gemara* about the smallest affliction—that even if you reached into your pocket to get two coins and only one came up—our master, the Baal Shem Tov, his memory for a blessing for the life of the World to Come, explained that when someone believes that this is not by chance, but is all Divine Providence, and immediately has fear of God and trembles and repents—then these light afflictions are sufficient [and he will not suffer greater ones]. For that is the whole purpose of afflictions, that we repent wholeheartedly. (Rabbi Yitzhak Isaac of Komarna, *Notzer Hesed*, quoted in *Kerem Yisrael*, p. 7, #8)

35:3:3 In the Talmud (*Arachin* 16b) the rabbis discuss the smallest mishaps that are still considered afflictions. Since this teaching is regularly referred to in hasidic instruction on affliction, it is worth noting what is said there. Some of the opinions offered in the Talmud for what is the smallest affliction are: (1) If you were supposed to receive a hot drink (a cup of wine) and they gave you a cold one or vice versa; (2) If you put a piece of clothing on inside out, and had to take it off and put it on again; (3) If you wanted to take three coins from your pocket and you reached down and only two came up, and you had to reach down again. The rabbis teach elsewhere that even if you stub your toe, it was decreed in heaven. The point is that everything great and small happens by Divine Providence, and that even these small afflictions are sent from God as punishment, to get our attention, and that they too can make atonement for us.

The rabbis teach:

> The way the world works is that ordinarily a person transgresses, and for his sin deserves the punishment of death. How then is this atoned for? The answer is that his ox dies or his chicken is lost, his jars break or an egg breaks, or he stubs his finger or toe and loses a drop of blood. The rule is that a bit of the soul is accounted as the

> whole [one drop of blood or a little pain is like death, or—since your possessions become "parts" of yourself—when a possession is destroyed, that part "dies"]. So with a little here and a little there, these things add up to a full atonement for him. (*Pesahim* 118; *Yalkut Shimoni Kohelet* 977)

35:3:4 *Darkei Tzedek* makes it clearer what we should *do* at times of affliction:

> That which is said in the *Gemara*, that if a person puts his hand into his pocket to get one coin and another comes up, and so on, should be understood as follows: that he should take it to heart that even this minor frustration is from God's Providence and doing, and he should direct himself at that moment to hope and pray that this suffering will be an atonement for his sins. Then he should attach himself to God and meditate on repentance. (p. 11, #13)

35:3:5 Rabbi Tzvi Hirsh of Nadborna helps us to see the broad nature of this teaching:

> Everything that happens to you against your will and desire should lead you to rejoice as if it were according to your will, for by it your sins are atoned for. As the rabbis say: "What is the smallest thing that still counts as an affliction? If a man puts his hand into his pocket . . ." And as a result he is saved from more serious afflictions. (*The Alpha Beta* of Rabbi Tzvi Hirsh, Ratzon, in *YHvT*, p. 66)

35:3:6 The rabbis teach that you are to make a blessing on bad things that happen to you as well as the good. The blessing to make is "Blessed are You, O Lord our God, King of the Universe, the just Judge (*Dayan ha-emet*)."* We are taught that we are to receive the bad with love for God and make the blessing with joy—just as we receive good things (*Berachot* 60b; see comments of the Rif and the Aytz Yosef). The reason is that everything that God does is for our ultimate good.

This story is told of Rabbi Zundel (the teacher of Rabbi Israel Salanter, the great founder of the *Musar* movement):

> In his last years [in Jerusalem] a disaster came upon him, when one of his daughters, who was married to a great Torah scholar, died. The elders of Jerusalem testified that he made the blessing "the just Judge" with *kavvanah* and calmly, the same way that he would

praise and thank the Holy One, blessed be He, at the time of any other blessing of thanksgiving. For that is the *halacha*: "Just as we bless God for the good we receive, so are we to make a blessing on the bad."[2] (*Rabbi Israel Mi-Salant*, *MiDor l'Dor*, vol. 1, p. 10)

35:3:7 The goal of this way of sweetening the bitter (by seeing the good that is in what seems bad) is to be in that high state of consciousness called the Garden of Eden, where since everything is clearly seen as coming from God, there is only good.

The two brothers, Rabbi Shmelke [of Nikolsburg] and Rabbi Pinhas [of Frankfurt] asked their teacher, the Maggid of Mezritch, "Master, teach us. How is it possible for someone to fulfill the words of the mishnah: 'A person is obligated to make a blessing on the bad just as he does for the good?'" The Maggid said to them, "Go and ask Zusya" [also a great disciple of the Maggid]. They went to the *Beit Midrash* and found Rabbi Zusya of Hanipol there, sitting and smoking his pipe. And they told him why their master had sent them to him. "I do not understand," Rabbi Zusya responded, "why our master sent you to me. This question should be asked of someone who has had much trouble and suffering (May it not come on us!) in his life. But I've never experienced anything bad (God forbid) at all, just goodness and mercy all the days of my life." (*MiDor Dor*, vol. 1, p. 216, #575)

Now Rabbi Zusya had indeed lived in great need and poverty and seen much suffering in his life, as they knew—but he was on that high level.

35:3:8 Rabbi Arele Roth:

Every small thing that happens to you for ill, even if the sleeve of your shirt is turned inside out and you are bothered putting it on, or if you forgot to bring something with you and you are annoyed, and all small troubles that happen to you, or to your wife and children, God forbid, or to your possessions, say:

"I believe with complete faith that this trouble and these afflictions came to me from God and are a part of His providence, which is concerned with even the smallest matters of my life. And I receive it all with love for Him in my heart. All this came upon me because of my many sins, and You, O God, are just in all that You have brought upon me, because what You have done is in truth, and I am in the wrong. May it be Your will that these afflictions be an atonement for all my many sins. . . . According to what is right, I should repent and confess in detail before You all the sins and transgressions that have been the cause of these troubles coming upon me. But it is known and revealed before You that I do not even know all that I have done wrong. So may it be Your will, my Father in Heaven, that You wipe away and uproot every sin, transgression, and wrongdoing that caused me these troubles—and let all the judgments on me and on all Israel be sweetened, and let everything be turned to good, and let revealed goodness [rather than the goodness concealed in suffering and misfortune] be drawn on us and on all the House of Israel."* (*Shomer Emunim*, Maamar Hashgacha Pratit, chap. 14, p. 122b)

Rabbi Arele Roth continues here to explain how, if you say this, you will fulfill five *mitzvot*: (1) belief in God's providence in everything, however small, that happens to you; (2) justification of God's judgment on you; (3) repentance and confession; (4) the arousal of God's compassion on the Congregation of Israel; and (5) thanks to God for the bad as well as the good.

Reb Arele says that it is good to know this prayer by heart. Of course, something simpler is also appropriate. Sometimes someone might just say the blessing "the just Judge" (as Rabbi Zundel, p. 624), or they might say simply, "May it be an atonement for me." (See the story in "Pious Phrases," 26:18.)

35:4 When something unfortunate happens to another person, or you hear him tell you of such, it is traditional to say, as consolation and as a prayer of your own on his behalf, "May it be an atonement for you."

35:5 There are other pious phrases that should be in our minds and on our lips as we meet with suffering and difficulties. For example: "Everything that God does is for the good," or, "This also is for good." For losses we suffer: "May God fulfill my lack"—evincing your belief that everything comes from God, and your trust that He will again have mercy on you; or, in the words of Job, "The Lord gave and the Lord has taken away; blessed be the name of the Lord." (See "Pious Phrases," 26:13–14, 26:16–18; see also the *Shulchan Aruch*, chap. 59.)

35:6 One common enough form of affliction is the abuse we receive from our fellow men. The following teachings discuss how to deal with verbal abuse.

35:6:1 Rabbi Moshe Teitelbaum:

> You should not insist on your rights, and should be ready to receive hurt without response. If someone abuses you verbally, just remain silent and rejoice in affliction. You should say to yourself: God brought it about that this person would curse me so that my sins would be atoned for, if I received it all with humility and love for God. (*Hanhagot Tzaddikim*, p. 47, #4)

As noted above, your sins build up the walls, the shells of your ego, and regardless of the intention of the one who abuses you, if you receive abuse humbly, the shells are broken through, the strength of the "bad ego" is diminished, and your sins are atoned for—their effect in "thickening" your ego is removed.

35:6:2 Two holy books give different versions of a prayer that you can say at the time you are being abused:

> **35:6:2:1** When someone is abusing you, it is a good practice to say or think the following:
>
> "Master of the World! May Your name be praised for all the good things that You have done for me and that You do for me always—every day and every minute. And especially at this moment, for even though I am such a sinner, such a low and contemptible sort, who has so much sinned and rebelled against You—and I still have not done *tshuvah* as I should—even with all that, my dear Father in Heaven, You are seeking a way to help me out of the pit I dug for myself, through this light affliction and punishment—that I should hear myself abused and remain silent. For this is truly something light, and does not involve real suffering. And by means of this person who is abusing me You are scouring me clean of all my many sins, more so than could many hard afflictions. Through this You are saving me from all manner of harsh and bitter judgments in this world and the next, that I would have deserved because of my deeds. But through the humiliation of this abuse I will find Your favor and become beloved in Your eyes and You will accept my prayers, and I will become worthy of Your goodness and salvation. Selah."* (*Erech Apayim* 3:8 quoted in *K'tzait ha-Shemesh BiGevurato*, chap. 6, #12)

35:6:2:2 Rabbi Arele Roth:

> When someone is abusing you, say to God: "You are righteous, O Lord, in all that You have brought upon me, and You have acted in truth; and I believe with complete faith that these insults have come

> to me for my own good—so that the judgments on me be sweetened [by receiving light afflictions with love], and so that my sins be atoned for before You!"* (*Taharat ha-Kodesh*, II, p. 84, #1 quoted in *K'tzait ha-Shemesh BiGevurato*, chap. 6, #13)

Erech Apayim (in the place indicated in the quote on p. 627) says that as soon as someone begins to abuse you verbally:

> You should immediately begin to thank God in your native language (and if you cannot say this aloud, do so under your breath) . . . and you should not stop saying things like this until he stops abusing you.

35:6:3 It is sometimes suggested that we go beyond merely reacting (in the matter of abuse from others). Since abuse will bring us the great benefits of humility and atonement for our sins, as well as help us overcome our own worst nature, we should actually pray that God send tests our way. The following teaching is quite harsh, but that aspect is not a necessary part of praying for such tests.

> It is an important principle in the service of God to "seek humility" as the verse says [Zephaniah 2:3]—that you should *seek* in all your doings to try to be despised, and not have any importance at all, but rather to be on the level of nothingness. This should be your goal and you should say to yourself, "If only people would treat me badly and abuse me verbally, so that I would be debased in my own eyes and in the eyes of all, so that this would be an atonement for my sins." When you think about this well, you will not be bothered when people speak badly to you. On the contrary, you will be happy, because this is just fulfilling your own desire, so that your sins be atoned for.[3] (*Darkei Yesharim*, p. 13, the testament of one of the Besht's disciples, #1, See also "Individual Practices," 39:15)

Part of the value of praying for such treatment is that our normal reaction when receiving abuse is to return it; praying for this helps to prepare us for it so that we are able (with God's help) to accept ill-treatment in a religious way.

> **35:6:4** In Nikolsburg there was a very wealthy man, one of the leading men of the Jewish community, who was very much against the hasidic *rebbes*. The ways of Rabbi Shmelke of Nikolsburg were altogether strange to this man, and he wanted to humiliate him.

Once, on *Erev Yom Kippur*, he showed up at Rabbi Shmelke's house and in his hand he had as a gift a bottle of old wine. His intention was to get the *rebbe* to drink it, so by the time he got to the synagogue for *Kol Nidre* [the opening prayer] the strong wine would take its effect and he would be drunk.

To please him the *rebbe* did drink the wine, and the rich man kept filling cup after cup for him. Seeing this, the *misnagid* became quite happy, for it seemed to him he had indeed reached the goal he so long desired. He would show the whole community how worthless this Hasidism was; for if their leader could do this, what about the rest?

When the shadows of evening came on, the *rebbe*, as was his holy way, arrived at the synagogue as if he were the high priest himself, ready to do his service within the Holy of Holies. And the saying of the Sages, "Wine is strong but fear is stronger [and dissipates its effects]" was fulfilled with that *tzaddik*—for the fear of the Day of Judgment completely removed any effects of the wine on him.

Now the *rebbe*'s holy way was that he always spent the whole twenty-four hours of *Yom Kippur* in the synagogue. And after the Evening Service the *rebbe* would stay on to say psalms before the Ark. He would be the prayer leader and all the holy congregation would say the psalms verse by verse after him, in a loud voice. When he reached the verse [in Psalm 41] "By this I know that You have shown favor to me, if You will not cause harm to my enemy on my behalf,"[4] he repeated this verse many times, and he translated it into Yiddish many times. He said, "Even if I have enemies who desire my humiliation and shame, even so, forgive them—so prayed King David." The *rebbe* shouted this out many times until it entered the hearts of those praying, and they all began sobbing and crying.

Now the *misnagid*, who was by the eastern wall, knew well what the *rebbe*'s intention was and what his words hinted at—that not only did he not want revenge against those who hated him so much that they desired his humiliation, but he even prayed and pleaded for their welfare and success. He was so moved at Rebbe Reb Shmelke's righteousness and his humility that he came before him and fell down at his feet, crying and begging pardon and forgiveness. And he confessed publicly his evil design.

But Rebbe Shmelke said to him, "You think that I accepted the office of Rabbi of Nikolsburg for the crown and the honor. No, my friend, it is not honor I want. If you had indeed shamed Shmelke, how many benefits would you have done him by that. For how many of his sins and transgressions would you have washed clean with the shame and humiliation." The *rebbe* repeated a number of times that it was too bad that he had not come to humiliation for drunkenness, for it would have done him great good.

Hearing these holy words, the man cried even more as he begged forgiveness. And he became a friend and admirer of the *rebbe* for all his days. (*Shemen ha-Tov*, p. 77, #49)

35:6:5 When people abuse you, you should always seek peace and be humble, and you can make it a practice to bless them, and so overcome your evil inclination.

There is no one more humble than he who seeks peace with other men, for how can someone pursue peace except through being humble and lowly? What does he do? If someone curses him, he answers [with the blessing] "Peace be upon you." If someone argues with him, he remains silent. (*Kallah Rabbati*, 3)

The point here in real-life circumstances would be that when someone starts abusing you, seek peace and humility and bless him under your breath, so as to turn your heart to love and overcome your own urge to respond in kind. (See "The Synagogue and the Synagogue Service," 6:17:5 for the words of Rabbi Yoel Frumkin.) By bearing abuse humbly, you will find peace with your neighbors, peace within, and peace with your Father in Heaven.

35:6:6 Two years before his passing, the Hafetz Hayim was afflicted with a severe nosebleed on the night of the Passover seder, and he lay in bed for a number of days. When one of those close to him came to visit, the Hafetz Hayim said to him: "How good are afflictions [like his nosebleed] which purge a man of his sins, and so too the humiliations and abuse that a man suffers in his life, for they are a substitute for afflictions that cleanse him of his transgressions. But what a disaster it is then," he concluded, "for someone like me, who in his whole life has never been insulted!" (*Michtivei ha-Hafetz Hayim ha-Hadash*, vol. 2, II, p. 138)

Now the Hafetz Hayim, who had indeed been insulted enough in his lifetime, was so humble and lowly that he never felt humiliated by the abuse he received. He assumed he suffered his nosebleed because he had never been fortunate enough to be insulted.

See "The Service of Praise" (34) for more about how to praise God for the bad as well as the good.

36

A Full Day Set Aside

Considering all the normal distractions to concentration on heavenly matters, it is an excellent custom every so often to set aside a full day devoted exclusively to religious practice. If possible, this can be done regularly—once a week or once a month.

The Sabbath, of course, is a day for spirituality once a week but it is not really meant for hard spiritual *work.* Although the teachings quoted below emphasize fasting and repentance and fear of God, that particular character is not absolutely necessary to the idea of a weekday set aside for spiritual practice. However, there is something of a balance between the Sabbath, which is for service of God and repentance from love, and this one weekday set aside for repentance with the emphasis on fear.[1]

As Rabbi Moshe Leib of Sassov said:

> During the six workdays the attribute of fear is stonger, and on the holy Sabbath the attribute of love is stronger. (*Eser Tzachtzachot*, p. 54, #37)

36:1 You should seclude yourself one day a week when you can fast, pray, do *tshuvah*, make confession for your sins, and fix everything that needs fixing and attach your mind in *d'vekut* to God. (Rabbi Nahum of Tchernobil, *Hanhagot Tzaddikim*, p. 35, #7)

36:2 One day a week you should separate yourself from other people and be alone, just you and your Creator. You should attach your mind to Him as if you were standing before Him on the Day of Judgment [*Rosh HaShanah*], and speak to Him, blessed be He, as a son to his father and a servant to his master. (The Ari, quoted in *Tzavaot v'Derech Tovim*, p. 58, #2)

36:3 You should seclude yourself one day a week if possible, in a special room devoted to spiritual practice—where you can fast and do *tshuvah* and study Torah. . . . On the day of the fast, go to the *mikveh* and immerse yourself no fewer than two times—once to remove your uncleanness and once to draw on yourself holiness. During the whole day be especially careful not to engage in any idle talk—just involve yourself in Torah and the fear of God all day. See to it that everything you do be only for the sake of heaven, and with love and fear of God. You should cry before your Creator that He forgive you all your transgressions; be careful, however, that you do not have any insincerity mixed into your crying, God forbid, for that is dangerous altogether, God forbid. On the evening before the fast and on the one after the fast do not eat any meat.[2] (Rabbi Aaron of Karlin, *Hanhagot Tzaddikim*, p. 3, #3)

36:4 Every month separate yourself apart for one day, if possible in the synagogue or *Beit Midrash*, where you can be alone with God without distractions. Or, if that is not possible, then be in your house, but in a room with the door closed and locked. Do not talk with anyone, but divide the day into three: one part to search your actions and arrange to fix what needs fixing, one part for Torah study, and one part for prayer. Make this day go from one evening to the next, or if you are physically weak, just from morning to evening. And let this holy time be holy: do not think at all about worldly things but immerse yourself in holiness the whole day. (*Derech Hayim*, 2–27)

36:5 You should fast at least one day a week. On that day forget about all your other affairs, about everything else in the world, and stay by yourself. . . . Direct your thoughts to God, to cling to Him and to be embittered over how long you have rebelled against the Great King. You should cry and mourn with a broken heart, with many supplications and praises of God. . . . And do this all your days until you find favor in the sight of the King, blessed be He. (Rabbi Elija deVidas, *Totzaot Hayim*, p. 33)

Try to separate yourself and be alone with God one day a month, in the synagogue or *Beit Midrash*, to cling to your Maker; spend part

> of the day in going over your deeds, part in prayer, and part in Torah study. On this day that you go off alone, do not speak to any one about business matters at all. Try to fulfill on this day the *mitzvah* of "cling to Him" and the *mitzvot* of "do not turn to idols" and "do not turn your thoughts away from God." . . . If you can separate yourself this way one day a week, it is even better. . . . And during this whole day, when you are in the synagogue or *Beit Midrash*, have on *tallit* and *tefillin*, for this will draw holiness on you. (*Totzaot Hayim*, p. 62)

As to fulfillment of the three *mitzvot* mentioned in this quote, the Besht taught that your thoughts were either to God or not, there is no in between. If you turn your mind away from God, immediately you have turned to idols. So what Rabbi Elijah deVidas is saying is that you should try to have God-consciousness throughout the day ("to cling to Him" in *d'vekut*) without the least cessation.

36:6 One can also make this practice a regular and fixed one, committing yourself for a lengthy period.

> You can decide at the beginning of the year that every tenth day will be holy to God, with fasting and *tshuvah*, Torah learning and *tzedaka*—except when the tenth day falls on *Shabbat* or *Yom Tov* or on days when fasting is not permitted. Then you should devote yourself to more learning and *hitbodedut* [seclusion], not going outside. (*Kaf ha-Hayim*, 21:12, p. 286)

37

Anger

37:1 SPEAKING IN A LOW VOICE AND SILENCE

37:1:1 If someone you are with is provoking you to anger, be silent; if you have to speak to him, make it a point to speak in a low and gentle voice as this will keep anger from overcoming you. This is a good device to see that an argument that starts does not continue and get bigger. (Rabbi Hayim Yosef David Azulai, *Hanhagot Tzaddikim*, p. 67, #16)

37:1:2 About Rabbi Rafael of Bershad:

He told us to be very careful about anger and about being annoyed . . . and he was insistent even about the tone of our voice. For even when you have to give some order to those in your household, or restrain them from something bad, you should not speak with anger or irritation, but gently and softly. (*Pe'er l'Yesharim*, p. 7a, #54)

37:1:3 A great and wonderful method of avoiding anger is to accustom yourself to speak always in the lowest voice possible. This is more effective than any other method for attaining to the quality of patience. With other methods you are not able to work regularly on changing your nature, but just at those times when someone is insulting you or doing something against your will, and there can be a long period when something like that does not happen. As a result, it is hard to change yourself using those methods, because changing one's nature requires regular and consistent work to alter ingrained habits. . . . But this matter of speaking with a low voice *is* something that can be done consistently, and therefore, with enough effort it is easily possible to change yourself so that you get in the habit of always speaking in a low voice. As a result of this you will automatically be protected from anger.

Therefore, anyone who is an angry type by nature, and wants to overcome his fault, should put all his energy into this. He should always speak in the lowest voice possible. With God's help it will enable him to become patient and to move towards great lowliness and humility also. Furthermore, it is a wonderful aid in achieving purity of speech, because when you are always alert to be careful to speak in a low voice, you will also be reminded to be careful about forbidden speech [slander, for example] and idle conversation. . . . In *Or Tzaddikim* it is written that: "Someone who speaks with a low voice and favors silence becomes a chariot for the Divine Presence." (*Erech Apayim*, 4:13, pp. 83–84)

37:2 When you get into a dispute with someone, do not look into his face. This will cause your anger to dissipate. (*Derech Hayim*, 6–45)

37:3 If you see that you are becoming angry . . . look at the *tzitzit* on your *tallit katan*. Any time that you see you are falling into something that is not for the glory of heaven, and you want to be saved from it, look at the *tzitzit* and God will help you. But do this with intelligence and not so others will see you and say, "Oh, he's trying to be pious," and they will start up with you. For as it says, "Everyone who is wise acts with discretion." (Rabbi Tzvi Elimelech of Dinov, *Agra d'Pirka*, quoted in *DhTvhY*, Kaas, #13)

37:4 TURN TO GOD: PRAYER

Anything that helps you remember God at the time of anger helps in its dissipation. Looking at the *tzitzit* is one suggestion. It is also possible when you begin to get angry to (carefully) direct your anger to God, turn to Him and complain, "God, why are You letting this anger overcome me and control me? You know how much I want to be free of it!" Once you have remembered God, your deranged consciousness will start to return to a purer place and your anger will depart.

37:5 MAKE A VOW

When you find yourself in a situation where you are becoming angry, when someone is annoying you or you are being abused or insulted, make a vow to control yourself. You can vow not to answer a word, for example. Or you can vow that if you *do* become angry (after expressing your determination not to), you will fine or punish yourself in some specific way. The threat against yourself should be enough to restrain you.

Though it is not easy to directly vow at the time not to become angry, because that is not completely in your control, yet it is not altogether impossible.

But passing from the matter of making vows "on the spot," it is indeed taught that you can even vow not to become angry for a period of time. According to Rabbeinu Tam, when a person determines to do *tshuvah*:

> He should swear not to become angry . . . and when he makes a covenant for himself and a vow that he not become angry for a number of days, it will be like a medicine that is bitter as wormwood, but which he knows will save him from a severe disease, and so he vows to always take the medicine without fail. (*Sefer ha-Yashar*, Gate 6, Midah 2)

Reshit Hochmah refers to Rabbeinu Tam's teaching and adds that the vow should be that you will not get angry except in those (few) cases where the Torah permits anger (Sh'ar ha-Ahavah, chap. 3, #21).

37:6 FINES AND PUNISHMENT, MAKING FENCES, AND *TIKKUN*

You can make yourself fences, rules regulating your conduct in situations dangerous for you. For example, if you get into arguments with a friend over a certain issue, resolve that for a fixed period you will under no circumstances discuss that issue (see "Individual Practices," 39:17 about this). You can also set particular fines or penalties for yourself in the event that you become angry.

Rabbi Eliezer Papu, about someone who gets angry:

> He will never fix himself until he resolves that he will never allow himself to become angry, and that if he transgresses, he will penal-

> ize himself with some sort of affliction [fasting, severe exercise, reciting many psalms] or by giving money for *tzedaka*. Then, having [also] repented, he will be healed. (*Hanhagot Tzaddikim* [III], vol. 1, p. 485, #3)

What is suggested here is a *tikkun* (self-fixing) to repair the spiritual damage you have done to yourself by your anger. Penalties will train the body through distress, as one would train an animal. Bodily affliction and the loss of money affect the person on different levels. Other than the penalty aspect, the giving of *tzedaka* also serves to open one's heart when anger had closed it.

37:7 SAY PSALMS

It is recommended in many holy books that, having become angry, for a self-fixing and a self-punishment, you recite the whole Book of Psalms without interruption. This practice will dissipate the cloud of anger and the bad mood that hangs over you (see "Psalms," 16:16:5).

37:8 SONG

> If you have to break your anger the best advice is to sing. (Rabbi Yaakov Yitzhak of Makárov, *Sifran Shel Tzaddikim*, p. 52)

37:9 FIGHTING FIRE WITH FIRE

According to the hasidic scheme, most of our emotional modes can be divided between love and fear. Since love and fear are contradictory and in conflict, with cleverness they can be used against each other.

> When a man sees that the evil inclination is inciting him and he is becoming angry (and anger is on the side of the attribute of fear)—then he should cling to . . . the attribute of love, a "fire" that is an external and unspiritual love. For instance, he should arrange a meal for himself and he should eat. Through his desire for the food he will attach himself to the attribute of love, which though not spiritual is yet something permitted. And the evil inclination will let him do this without problems and without bothering him. As a

> result, the anger from the side of fear will be broken and dissipated through the contrary influence from the side of love. He should thus "make war with clever stratagems." Because if he was to just simply arouse the good inclination against the evil inclination immediately, and thus make war directly, the evil inclination would strengthen itself against him even more, God forbid. But here a permitted (but low) love is used to break a forbidden and low fear: anger. (Rabbi Tzvi Hirsh of Ziditchov, *Yifrach biYamav Tzaddik*, p. 91)

In a sense, the example mentioned is based on a natural inclination that at least some people have: to dissipate a bad mood through eating and the like.

37:10 THE TACTIC OF DELAY

> The Rabbi of Gastinin, of blessed memory, made it a practice never to express anger on the same day when he was upset or annoyed with someone. Only on the following day would he tell him, "Yesterday I was annoyed at you." (*Siah Sarfei Kodesh*, III, p. 29, #37)

There are many variations on this tactic of delay, so that an unjust anger dissipates completely, or so that a just anger can be purified of alien fire (such as pride).

37:11 BUY OUT YOUR ANGER

> **37:11:1** Rabbi Yaakov Yosef of Polnoye told of the Besht's teaching that, in money matters, someone who is afraid that he will stumble and violate the stricture against becoming angry, should choose to lose the money involved and not show any anger. (*Erech Apayim*, 6:1, p. 88)

> **37:11:2** A good method for avoiding anger in money matters is found in *Reshit Hochmah*: accustom yourself to be easygoing and on the pious side when it comes to money, and be ready to give it up. (*Erech Apayim*, 9:3, p. 104)

> **37:11:3** An important rule for someone who truly desires to guard his mouth and tongue and avoid arguments, slander, shaming others, and related serious sins, is to resolve to buy for himself the

attribute of always "passing over his measures," that is, not insisting on responding, or demanding your rights when they have been violated. In other words, for the purpose of acquiring this holy attribute, he should make a resolution to pay three or four shekels a year (and a rich man, according to his wealth).

Typically an argument starts over some small thing, where it seems to a person that he has been taken advantage of for a single gold coin or some such. Since no one ever sees himself as in the wrong, he determines to take a stand "for the sake of justice," and not give an inch. So he sets himself like an iron pillar before the other person, planted and immovable. . . . The result of this, of course, is an argument [and all the things that follow, such as shaming the other person, slander, and so on].

If you would add up what such arguments are over, you would see that for an average person for a whole year, it amounts at the most to only three or four shekels! . . . So the wise person saves himself from all these sins and from the ugliness of anger by deciding beforehand that in case of a dispute over money, he will give it up—those three or four shekels a year—and he will spend that money, as he would for other *mitzvot*, for the *mitzvah* of being saved from anger and its evil accompaniments. (Rabbi Yehiel Michal Rabinowitz, Peninei Yam, in *YHvT,* p. 100)

See also "Pious Phrases," 26:12 and "Individual Practices," 39:15 and 39:22.

38

Humility and Pride

38:1 THE LESSON IN FAILURE

There is a lesson of humility inherent in our failings and transgressions, and an awareness of this can be integrated into our religious life.

When we fail and get caught in transgressions, we should realize that we cannot succeed at anything, material or spiritual, without God's help. We cannot even come close to Him by our own efforts. So when we fall down spiritually, we should turn to God and pray for His help:

"God! I want to come close to You, but I know that I cannot do anything without Your help. Have mercy on me and strengthen me to always remember You and do Your will."

38:2 NOT ME: GOD

Do not be accustomed to say, "I did this," or "I will do that," for that is the way of pride. Say: "It was God's will that this succeeded," or "With God's help I will do it."

Whenever we do anything that brings us people's admiration we should realize that if we have accomplished anything it is only due to

God's help, and it was He who gave us whatever abilities we have. Avoiding pride we should feel that God directed us to do whatever it was that succeeded. (See "Pious Phrases," 26:8–12 and 26:18)

38:3 A LOW AND GENTLE VOICE

38:3:1 You should always avoid speaking in a loud voice because it inspires pride. (Rabbi Shlomo Hayim of Kaidenov, *Admorei Neshkiz, Lechovitz, Kaidenov, Novominsk*, 20, p. 123)

38:3:2 Accustom yourself to speak in the gentlest and sweetest way possible, in soft language and in a very low voice, as the meekest of the meek and the least of the least would talk to the sons of kings. Such should be the way you talk to every man. (Rabbi Tzvi Hirsh of Ziditchov, *Darkei Yesharim*, p. 13, #7; see also "Anger," 37:1)

38:3:3 This is the way to speak even with your family:

Do not speak loudly, even in your own house, but speak softly, as if you were talking to a king. (*Derech Hayim*, 3–42)

38:3:4 One of his hasidim writes about Rabbi Rafael of Bershad:

He would discuss this with us at length, how you have to treat your fellow man as if he were your king, and be gentle with him and not forceful. And his son, Rabbi Levi, told us how once the *rebbe* spoke with him about some matter, and he saw, while his father was talking to him, that he was as lowly as if he were a servant talking to his master. (*Midrash Pinhas*, p. 63)

38:4 SILENCE

Silence leads to humility. (*Hanhagot Tzaddikim*, p. 14, quoting *Hazal* [the Sages])

38:5 WELCOME HUMILIATIONS

Sometimes our errors can humiliate us before others. We should be happy when this happens, for it brings us to humility.

It is told about Rabbi Rafael of Bershad:

> We saw that he was always happy and enlivened when some kind of humiliation occurred to him, and he would consider it a great kindness from God, who sent this to him so that he would not be prideful.
>
> Once, on *Hoshanna Rabba* he made a mistake in the *hoshanna* [Save us!] prayers—he skipped over the *hoshanna* that the congregation was saying and accidentally said the one after it—until everybody realized what he had done, and he said it correctly with the congregation (and we remember that he seemed somewhat bothered about this).
>
> But later in his house he spoke about it, saying, "Thoughtless people become very worried when something like this happens because of the saying that 'When someone prays and makes an error, it is a bad sign for him; and if he is leading the congregation, it is a bad sign for them.' But they do not realize that it is really a great kindness to them from God."
>
> Once, he forgot to count the *Omer*, and from then on (as according to the *halacha*) he had to do it each and every night thereafter without the blessing, and he had to listen to the blessing said by someone else. When he led the congregation in the prayers he had to have someone else take his place when it came to counting the *Omer*, since he could not say it himself with the blessing. And this also he took as a great kindness from God, that he was able to have this experience of lowliness. (*Midrash Pinhas*, p. 62)

A particular reference for this helpful thought is our situation in the synagogue when we may not know how to do everything properly and may make mistakes (though of course that was not the reason for the *rebbe's* mistakes).

The humiliation we experience from our errors is similar to that which comes to us from the abuse of others. See "Afflictions" (35) about how we should thank God for this kind of suffering. And so we should also thank Him for the lowliness and embarrassment that our errors bring us.

38:6 TO THE OPPOSITE EXTREME

To conquer pride (and other bad traits) we are told to go to the other extreme:

> There is a fence that can help us avoid pride and other bad traits, for when someone wants to uproot arrogance from his heart com-

pletely, he should realize that this cannot be done through thinking alone.

At the beginning it is necessary to flee from pride by going to the opposite extreme. How? If a person is accustomed to dressing in expensive clothes and being particular about them, as is often the case with arrogant people, and if he wants to repent and separate himself from this falsity, if he will just limit himself to wearing nice clothes and caring for them in an ordinary way, he will not succeed in uprooting his pride.

Or if a person is accustomed to making much of himself in his conversation with others or is brazen in his speech and other actions, it is impossible to do anything about this until he acts toward himself in a contemptuous way.

Let him seat himself in the least honored place, wear worn-out clothes that are an embarrassment to those who wear them, and other such tactics, until he uproots his pride. (*Orchot Tzaddikim*, Gate 1, p. 18)

The continuation explains how going to the other extreme is the method to take with all bad traits, but once the trait is uprooted you should return to the middle way. (See "Individual Practices," 39:7.)

38:7 PUBLICLY REBUKE YOURSELF

The great hasidic *rebbe*, Rabbi Elimelech of Lizensk, speaking about the repugnant nature of pride, said:

I always rebuke myself and shame myself in front of people, in order to bring what is within me into the open. [By this the power of the *yetzer ha-ra* is broken somewhat and its ability to overcome you the next time is lessened. (See the *Tzetl Katan*, #13.)] (*Ohel Elimelech*, p. 140, #352)

Elsewhere, Rebbe Elimelech writes:

The way of a *tzaddik* is to always see sins in what he does, and he considers the slightest transgression a grave sin. He always humbles and lowers himself, and he rebukes himself in public, before others. (*Noam Elimelech*, p. 49b)

In describing the ways of the holy community gathered around Rabbi Elimelech of Lizensk, one of his disciples writes:

> They are always publicizing their faults, and shaming themselves in public. If they ever think a forbidden thought or if they speak one word without holiness or if they take a single step without holiness, they publicize and reveal it immediately to others to shame themselves, and they do a full repentance as if they had committed some grave sin, God forbid, of the sins of the Torah.
>
> And there is no difference between them at all about this, they always see fault in their own doings, and they always find justifications for whatever others do. (*Noam Elimelech*, Igeret ha-Kodesh, second letter)

This practice of Rabbi Elimelech, which he also taught to his disciples, is essentially following the teaching about going to the opposite extreme—here of breaking your pride by publicly humiliating yourself. (See "Individual Practices," 39:7:2 for another quote from Rabbi Elimelech which makes this clear.)

> The *tzaddik*, Rabbi Fintshi, the Rabbi of Piltz, was once pacing back and forth in the *Beit Midrash* of the Rebbe of Ger, the author of the *S'fat Emet*, and he was rebuking himself aloud with insults, revilings, and words of contempt—saying things that would not be said about one of the lowest of the low.
>
> When the Rabbi of Parisov, his uncle, heard him, he came over and said to him, "Listen, young man. You had better stop speaking ill of our Rabbi Fintshi, because to us he is somebody very important. And you had better be especially careful about our young hasidim, because if they hear you speaking like this about Rabbi Fintshi they will break your bones."
>
> Then he added, "If I said terrible things like that about you, you would certainly be mad at me. Who gave you permission to say such things about yourself?"
>
> Rabbi Fintshi answered him, saying, "It is true. If someone else would say such things about me I would certainly consider him an enemy. But when I say them, I am a friend to myself." (*Sippurei Hasidim*, vol. 1, #279)

38:8 SAY IT FIRST

When you are ashamed of something, be the first one to speak of it.

This is the line of teaching and counsel that the rabbis connected with the way Eliezer begins his conversation with Laban in Genesis 24:34—"And he said, 'I am Abraham's servant'" (*Yalkut Shimoni*).

38:9 GIVE WAY

A valuable practice with wide application can be learned from this about the Hafetz Hayim:

> In his advanced old age, the Hafetz Hayim called all his household together and said to them: "My children, I want you to know that all my life I was always careful not to make anyone defer to me; on the contrary, I would always defer to all and give way. And if someone takes this path, it is good for him."
>
> One time the Hafetz Hayim was walking on a narrow sidewalk and an army officer approached from the opposite direction. The rabbi immediately stepped down from the sidewalk to let him by. The officer, who was surprised to see this elderly man hurry so to defer to him, went up to him and asked him about it. The Hafetz Hayim replied: "All my life I have made it my custom to give way and to move to the side so others can pass." The officer responded: "Such a custom should assure that you will pass through life in happiness." (*Michtivei Hafetz Hayim*, Helek ha-Dugmaot, 35, quoted in *K'tzait ha-Shemesh b'Gevurato*, p. 203)

When walking on the street, it can be part of our meditation to remind ourselves to be ready to give way and learn humility. Another meditation for humility can be to reflect while walking on how one day we will be under the earth we trod on, for "Dust thou art, and to dust shalt thou return." (See "Sight," 25:11 for more about this.)

39

Individual Practices

39:1 SET TIMES— A DAILY SCHEDULE

39:1:1 The Peasetzna Rebbe:

Set a time limit for all your actions. If you are about to eat, set a time limit beforehand: "I will spend half an hour" or "fifteen minutes eating." If you are going to your friend's home to engage in conversation for a little while (if you cannot then study Torah), set a time limit beforehand: "I will spend this amount of time there and no more." This is excepting the case where you are going to have a discussion about religious things and Hasidism. In general, you should feel yourself to be like a soldier in the army, whose time is not his own—where each set time is followed by another, and where each activity is followed by another. (*B'nai Machshavah Tovah*, Seder Hadracha v'Klalim, #13)

39:1:1:1 The Peasetzna Rebbe:

If you care for your own life, set time limits for the whole day; every hour for its own worship. Even when you enter into a conversation,

> at the beginning set yourself a given amount of time that you will talk. Let no hour be neglected, but rather engaged in its own appointed worship. Write for yourself on a piece of paper a daily schedule and do not budge from it the least bit. (*Hovat ha-Talmidim*, p. 95)

Note that the use of a daily schedule does not necessarily imply exact adherence to it to the minute as the Peasetzner suggests. One may compose this written daily schedule in the morning, before or after *davvening Shaharit*, or it could be done the previous night during the time of the account-taking before sleep.

39:1:2 We are told about Rabbi Nachman of Bratzlav:

> He would plan out an order of devotion for each day, and often at the beginning of the day make a vow to fulfill it. (*Rabbi Nachman's Wisdom*, p. 15, *Shevachay HaRan*, #15)

(For more about Rabbi Nachman's way in this, see "Vows," 12:6:1–2.)

> **39:1:3** In his youth Rabbi Tzvi Hirsh [of Ziditchov] divided up the twenty-four hours of the day and put on a piece of paper when he would do each thing. For example, he set aside a specific amount of time for learning each Torah subject; similarly, he specified when he would not converse, and so too for other *hanhagot* for each and every part of the day. And when he came to the Seer of Lublin [who became his *rebbe*] he highly praised this practice of his. (*Ha-Hozeh mi-Lublin*, p. 138)

39:2 CARRY A LIST OF YOUR *HANHAGOT*

> You should write the main *hanhagot* that are necessary for you at the time, for the particular character trait you are laboring to fix, on a small piece of paper . . . for example, for anger, you might write: "Silence and speak in a low voice." If you want to write them so that others will not be able to read it, then write in signs and hints. This little notepaper should be before you or in your hand at all times. Continually look at it and read it with renewed feeling and determination to be careful about everything there. (*Erech Apayim*, 3:8, p. 68)

It is suggested that this note include only the bare minimum, because if you try to concentrate on remembering too much you remember nothing (*Erech Apayim*, 3:16, p. 72).

Though the suggestion here is about *hanhagot* relating to one particular character trait a person is working to improve, such a list is also valuable for *hanhagot* you are following in your general spiritual practice and daily order. You can then also have a fuller list of all your *hanhagot*, which you read over at set times.

Sometimes lists of *hanhagot* are arranged more or less randomly, but others are in the form of a daily order (*Seder ha-Yom*). You can construct your own *Seder ha-Yom* from waking to sleep, with various general principles and ethical matters you want to keep before you included (as is fairly typical in such lists).

Frequently in lists of *hanhagot* by hasidic *rebbes* instructions are given at the end to read it regularly at certain times. At the end of his list of *hanhagot*, Rabbi Abraham Kalisker says:

> And the right thing to do is to read these things over once a week. (*Hanhagot Tzaddikim*, p. 40)

Rabbi Yisrael Dov of Vilednik (a disciple of Rabbi Mordechai of Tchernobil):

> Read over this note every Monday and Thursday after *Shaharit*. (*Hanhagot Tzaddikim* [II], 4:20)

At the end of his list, Rabbi Yehiel Michal of Zlotchov wrote:

> You should read this over every day. (*Hanhagot Tzaddikim*, p. 53, #26)

Rabbi Moshe Teitelbaum:

> Go over this list every night before sleep. (*Hanhagot Tzaddikim*, p. 51, #56)

At the end of his list, Rabbi Mordechai of Lechovitz says:

> You should read this note three or four times [a day] so that every word of it is thoroughly familiar to you, so that you have it in your heart to do what it says fully. (*Hanhagot Tzaddikim*, p. 42, #13)

Rabbi Shmelke of Nikolsburg has at the end of his list of *hanhagot*:

> Read these things over three times every day. Make it a fixed rule for yourself, to be done always, without exceptions. And it is best if you read it once as soon as you wake up, once after the Morning Prayers and before you go out to work, and once after the Evening Prayers before sleep. (*Shemen ha-Tov*, p. 52, #54)

Rabbi Elimelech of Lizensk in his *Tzetl Katan* (Little Note [of *hanhagot*]):

> Every time before you study Torah, look first at this list of my *hanhagot*. (#16)

Each day before the Morning Prayers the author of *Tosafot Yom-Tov* would read aloud, together with the congregation, from a booklet of *hanhagot* (good practices of all sorts, ethical and otherwise). The booklet he used, *Orchot Hayim*, by Rabbi Asher (the author of the *Turim*) is organized according to the days of the week, with ten to twenty short, one-line instructions and reminders for each of the seven days (*Orchot Hayim*, p. 1 note; printed together with *Mai Ber Yeshayahu*). This is an excellent custom if for no other reason than because it adds a valuable practical and ethical dimension to the prayer service. You can easily create such a booklet for your own use.

39:3 CARRY A NOTEBOOK TO RECORD YOUR FAILINGS AND YOUR SOUL-ACCOUNTS

> You should become accustomed many times throughout the day to give a backward look over the time past to consider how you have behaved. . . . And if you have failed somehow, see that you immediately jot down what you have done in a little notebook that you carry with you for just this purpose, so when it is your set time to consider your conduct and faults and how to fix them [traditionally before sleep], you will remember what transpired.
>
> Do not be involved in any consideration of the thing on the spot, for that will only lead to your being depressed all the time, and the main thing in our service of God is that it be altogether full of joy. So on the spot, if you realize that you did something wrong, just jot it down, and also make a confession before God, committing yourself to reversing your course. . . . Then, trusting that God

> accepts your repentance, return immediately to a happy frame of mind.
>
> Later, during your fixed time for this, consider well what you have done and devise practices, fences, etc. to rectify your failings. (*Erech Apayim*, 3:8, p. 69)

The son of the Hafetz Hayim writes about his father as a young man:

> I remember . . . how he would often go by himself into the fields outside the town to make a soul-accounting of all his actions of the day. . . . He had a little notebook in which he wrote his "accounts" and the fences [rules of extra self-restraint] which he had made for things in which he had stumbled.
>
> I heard from him a number of times, many years later, how he wondered that people having even the smallest store keep a notebook to record their accounts . . . but as for the accounts of their soul, they make no effort to be aware of their situation [by having a notebook and making soul-accounts]. (*Michtivei ha-Hafetz Hayim ha-Hadash*, vol. 2, I, p. 7)

39:4 CARRY A LIST OF YOUR VOWS

If you have made vows to perform certain religious practices or good deeds, it is important to write them down so they are not forgotten. Such a list can be joined with the other list of *hanhagot* mentioned in 39:2, or with the booklet of your failings and soul-accounts mentioned in 39:3.

> So that you will not forget from one day to the next to fulfill any vows you have made, it is good . . . to make a little booklet to note down what you have accepted on yourself, and that it be with you always so that you remember everything. This path is the right one for everyone who wants to accomplish something in practice and deed. (*Reshit Hochmah*, Sh'ar ha-Kedushah, chap. 14, #22)

39:5 STUDY *MUSAR*

Many of the lists of *hanhagot* state that you should learn from a book of *musar* (inspirational literature dealing with ethics and character development) every day.

39:5:1 The Baal Shem Tov:

> It is a most important thing to learn *musar* every day, whether much or little, so that you are always developing in yourself good qualities and taking on new spiritual practices. (*Tzavaat ha-Ribash*, beginning)
>
> **39:5:2** Learn from a *musar* book regularly and in order [not skipping around] each day. (Rabbi Aaron of Karlin, *Hanhagot Tzaddikim*, p. 5, #10)
>
> **39:5:3** See to it that you learn from a *musar* book every day, and repeat what you learn two or three times [this could be on the same or successive days], and be sure that you get the lesson into your heart. (Rabbi Nahum of Tchernobil, (*Hanhagot Tzaddikim*, p. 34, #5)

For some thoughts about *how* to study *musar* see "Torah," 15:23:2 and "Repetition of a Holy Sentence," 21:14.

39:6 STUDY *HALACHA*

Each of the different branches of the Torah has its own character and virtue and we should try to study them all. For example, *Aggadah* is heart-learning, and according to the rabbis, *Aggadah* draws the heart, giving a man insight into God's ways and letting him know how to cleave to those ways. Rabbi Nachman of Bratzlav explained one important aspect of the virtue of studying *Halacha*, religious law:

> The Rebbe constantly stressed for us the importance of studying the codes of religious law. He emphasized this more than any other study.
>
> It is best to study all four sections of the *Shulchan Aruch* in order, from beginning to end. If you can also study its major commentaries, all the better. But you should at least cover the main work.
>
> This study is a great spiritual remedy. When a man sins, good and evil are intermingled. A legal opinion is a clear separation between the permitted and the forbidden, the clean and the unclean. When you study religious law, good is once again separated from evil and the sin is rectified.
>
> The Rebbe said that everyone must study the codes each day without fail.

If you are under duress and have no time, you may study any law in the *Shulchan Aruch*, even if it does not follow your regular course of study. You must go through at least one law every day of your life. Under normal circumstances you should have a fixed practice of studying the *Shulchan Aruch* in order, a given amount each day. Continue until all four sections are completed and then start again at the beginning. Continue this way all the days of your life. (*Rabbi Nachman's Wisdom*, p. 130, *Sichos HaRan*, #29)

39:7 FORTY DAYS TO CHANGE A TRAIT

39:7:1 If you have some bad character trait, God forbid, you should determine to overcome it for a period of forty days . . . and then you will attain a second and new nature, and it will be removed for good. (*Or ha-Ner*, #40)

39:7:2 A man was not created except to change the nature he was born with, so you should make every effort to improve yourself as soon as you can. . . . For example, if you were born with a stubborn streak—go against your nature for a period of forty days, so that you act just the opposite of what your normal inclination is. Or if you are naturally lazy, see that for forty consecutive days you do everything quickly and energetically—in going to lie down on your bed to sleep, in getting up from your bed in the morning when you wake up, in dressing quickly, doing the ritual washing of your hands quickly, and cleaning yourself [in the bathroom], in going quickly to the synagogue after getting up from your early session of Torah study, and so on.

If you are naturally shy, meaning the bad kind of shyness (not the religious kind), force yourself for forty days to pray in a *loud* voice, with vigorous movement of all your limbs, to fulfill "All my bones shall say—O Lord, who is like unto Thee?" and to make the blessing over Torah study in a loud voice, until help comes to you from heaven and they remove the bad shyness from you . . . for in everything habit is king. If by nature you are not inclined to be constant in Torah study, you should accustom yourself for forty days to study more than usual . . . and from then on you will receive help from heaven to have more and more success in breaking your born nature until you reach perfection. (Rabbi Elimelech of Lizensk, *Tzetl Katan*, #16)

(See also "Humility and Pride," 38:6.)

39:8 IF YOU HEAR OR SEE SOMETHING GOOD FOR THE SERVICE OF GOD, DO NOT LET IT ESCAPE YOU

If we hear any word of Torah, we will guard it in our hearts and go over it with our lips so that it will not be forgotten, especially something that relates to the service of God, blessed be He. If possible, we will write it down on the spot. Also, if we see something in a book that relates to His service, blessed be He, we will bind it in our memories and write it on the tablets on our hearts. (*Hanhagot Adam*, #14, the commitments of the *havurah* of Rabbi Tzvi Elimelech of Dinov)

(See also "Torah," 15:30:4 about Rabbi Uri of Strelisk.)

39:9 REPEAT HOLY SAYINGS

Accustom your lips to be always repeating religious sayings relating to piety, such as, "Be bold as a leopard, swift as an eagle, fleet as a deer, and strong as a lion, to do the will of your Father in Heaven" (*Avot* 5:23); "The end of the thing, all said, is: Fear God and keep His commandments—for this is the whole purpose of man" (Kohelet 12:13); "And now, O Israel, what does the Lord your God require of you, but to fear the Lord your God, to walk in all His ways, to love Him, to serve the Lord your God with all your heart and with all your soul, to keep the commandments and statutes of the Lord which I command you this day for your good?" (Deuteronomy 10:12); "Be very, very lowly of spirit." (*Avot* 4:4) You should accustom your tongue to repeating these and other sayings of this sort, and then you will not stumble. (*Sefer ha-Yirah* of Rabbeinu Yonah, p. 202)

A person can select favorite sayings like these, memorize them, and repeat them over and over during the day.

39:10 MAKE SIGNS FOR YOURSELF TO REMEMBER

In the book, *Pitgamin Kadishin*, it is written in the name of the holy rabbi, Rabbi Aaron of Zhitomir, of blessed memory, that:

> The main thing is that you not forget the service of God for even a minute. To this end you should make signs for yourself within your house to remind you to fear God—let each person do this according to his own intelligence—so that you remember to avoid pride, anger, falsehood and other sins. You should not rely on yourself to remember without this aid . . . for even great *tzaddikim* did not trust themselves, and there was a *tzaddik* in our generation who hired someone to be with him continually and remind him that he should fear God. This is an important principle in the service of God. (*Erech Apayim*, Hakdama u'Peticha, p. 12, Commentary Vayosaif Avraham, note 3)

39:11 EXERCISE

> If your custom is to take walks, you should intend it for the sake of heaven—in order to be healthy for the service of God, blessed be He. Your thought should be that you are exercising so that your mind will be relaxed and vigorous, so that you will see how to act in all your affairs as is proper [that is, psychological health]. (*Avodat ha-Kodesh*, Moreh b'Etzba, 3-123)

Something of this nature can be expressed as a stated intention before and during exercise.

39:12 NULLIFYING BAD THOUGHTS

> You should make it a regular practice to continually nullify your bad thoughts, that is, to say continually: "I hereby declare that I nullify all thoughts that come to my mind that are forbidden and low and vile, whether during Torah study or prayer, and whether during the day or the night. Let all of them be nullified and void completely, because I do not want them at all, God forbid."
>
> This practice has a wondrous efficacy. And you should also say the verse "*Sh'ma Yisrael*," together with "*Baruch Shem Kavod Malchuto l'Olam Vaed* [Blessed is His glorious kingdom forever and ever]." (Rabbi Aharon Roth, *Shomer Emunim*, Maamar ha-Emunah, p. 75b)

(For a particular application of this practice, see "The Synagogue and the Synagogue Service," 6:24 and "Prayer," 5:1:23.)

39:13 MEDITATION AND PRAYER IN BED

The Baal Shem Tov said that though others were in the house, you could pretend to sleep and yet be in *d'vekut* with God.

> You can lie down on your bed, and though it appears to others in the house that you are sleeping, you can be spending this time in communion [*hitbodedut*] with your Creator, blessed be He. (*Tzavaat ha-Ribash*, p. 23)

(See what Rabbi Nachman of Bratzlav says about secluding yourself with God under the covers in bed in "Talking to God and Being Alone with God—*Hitbodedut*," 33:2.)

39:14 TO OVERCOME TEMPTATION, NULLIFY YOUR WILL BEFORE GOD'S WILL

A comment of Rabbi Israel, the Maggid of Koznitz, about nullifying your will before the will of God:

> God, blessed be He, gave free will to a man to do as he wants, whether good or the opposite, in order to be able (as is well known) to give him a good reward when he fights off the various temptations and inclinations of his own self. In that case then, when something against God's will presents itself before you, and your evil inclination is pushing you that way, and your own will is leaning that way, then nullify your own will and say before God, blessed be He: "Master of the World, I nullify my own will completely. I do not want free will at all—neither it nor its reward. I just want Your will." Then God will answer and nullify the powers of the evil inclination pushing you to do wrong. (*Avodat Yisrael*, Likkutim p. 9, on *Avot* 2:4)

39:15 KNOW WHAT COULD GO WRONG BEFOREHAND AND PREPARE

Make it a practice many times each day, for example, as soon as you wake up in the morning, and every time you leave your house

> to go to the synagogue or the *Beit Midrash*, and whenever you leave there to go home, and especially when you leave your house to go to work or to be in the company of other people for any reason, that you go over verbally, speaking out loud, the difficulties that may arise and the bad things you could become involved in (regarding your own behavior) in the situation you are entering.
>
> You should resolve that you will be careful about all these things. And you should also make your heart long that you be tested in these things, and say out loud, "O that I be tested in this!" and even pray that God will bring these tests to you (where He knows you will succeed). (*Erech Apayim*, 3:8, p. 68)

The practice described here of verbally going over what awaits you as you pass to each new activity in turn is a very valuable one (and not necessarily linked to the matter of praying to be tested). The book from which this quote is taken emphasizes overcoming anger and acquiring patience, and the quote continues with an application to that matter by suggesting that you pray for a test:

> This is an important counsel in the service of God, for since you are expecting the test, and even ask for it to come to you, it will be easy to withstand when it does come. Not only that, but you will even be happy when people abuse and insult you, because this is actually what you wanted and prayed for.
>
> I found this in a testament from one of the disciples of the Besht, of blessed memory:
>
> "It is an important principle to 'seek humility,' as the words of the verse go, that you should seek in all your doings to be despised, and this should be your goal. You should say in your heart, 'O that people would insult and humiliate me, so that I become despised and lowly in my own eyes and in the eyes of all, so that it be an atonement for my sins.' And when you take this to heart, you will not be bothered at all when people do insult you, but rather you will be happy, for this is what you wanted."
>
> In the book *Hayim v'Hesed* by the holy Rabbi Hayka [Hayim Heikel] of Amdur, of blessed memory, he writes: "O man! Know that every day there will come to you some new test, either insults and abuse, or monetary loss, and you should see to it that you are prepared for everything before it happens, and then you will receive it with joy." (*Erech Apayim*, 3:8, p. 68)

Here are some other quotes, again particularly related to patience, which teach the value of preparing yourself beforehand for what you are about to encounter:

It says in *Reshit Hochmah* that the way to avoid anger when you have business dealings with a difficult person is to have it settled in your mind beforehand that you are ready to bear all his insults, in word and deed. For when a person is actually waiting for the other one to insult him, in word and action, and it does not come on him suddenly, he will not get angry. So should you do until you can be free of the person and then run away from him as from a black bull in the days of the month of Nisan. (*Erech Apayim*, p. 104)

The holy Rabbi Yitzhak of Vorki was once, in his youth, traveling with one of his friends, and their wagon driver was giving them a lot of trouble, for he did not want to wait for them when they wanted to say their prayers and so on. His friend was getting into continual arguments with the driver about this, but Rabbi Yitzhak bore it all in silence with a serene equanimity.

When his friend asked him how he was able to do this, he answered, "You didn't prepare yourself to suffer from the wagon driver because you thought that he'd show you respect and treat you well, allowing you to do as you like, so that you'd be able to take a lot of time to say your prayers and to act in a pious way as you desire. So now it's hard for you to bear it when he doesn't do as you want. But as for me, I'm already well familiar with the way that wagon drivers act, and how they can make their passengers miserable. So when I decide to take a trip with a wagon driver I prepare myself in advance to bear even much more than what we've gone through now. As a result, I don't get excited or angry about what he does because I'm prepared beforehand to suffer from him even a good deal more than this. And in fact, this driver still remains a veritable *tzaddik* in my eyes compared to what I expected." (*Derech Tzaddikim*, p. 51)

This practice of preparing yourself verbally as you go to each new activity can be joined with the other *hanhaga* mentioned in Chapter 3, "Transitions," p. 58) about repeating certain prayers or Torah sayings or verses as reminders when making a transition in place, activity, or posture.

39:16 A BOOK OF TORAH WITH YOU ALWAYS

The Holy One, blessed be He, commanded that the king have a *sefer* Torah with him at all times, "and it shall be with him, and he

> shall read in it all the days of his life, so that he learns to fear the Lord (Deuteronomy 17:19)." The Sages explained that a *sefer* Torah was with him always and therefore he was constantly reminded of how he should have fear of God. In the *Tosefta* it says: "He would go out to war, and it was with him; he would come back, it was with him; he would sit in his house, it was at his side; he would go to the bath, it would wait for him at the door. And so did King David say, 'I have placed the Lord before me always' (Psalm 16:8). Rabbi Judah said: The *sefer* Torah was at his right hand and the *tefillin* was on his left [both to remind him of the fear of God]." *Reshit Hochmah*, Sh'ar ha-Yirah, chap. 15, #82)

Though we cannot have a *sefer* Torah with us at all times, we can carry around a pocket-sized Torah book to be with us wherever we go—to study from and to remind us always of the fear of God.

> The *rebbe* [Rabbi Raphael of Bershad] told us that we should always have placed before us a little *Chumash* to look into each and every minute, together with Rashi's commentary—like what is said about the king: "and it shall be with him, and he shall read in it all the days of his life, so that he learns to fear the Lord." (*Pe'er l'Yesharim*, p. 31b, #94)

The Besht would often take his disciples with him in his coach on journeys, and:

> His holy way was that all during the trip he would have one of those with him recite Psalms out loud, or read out loud from *Ein Yaakov* [the *aggadah* of the Talmud]. (*Emunat Tzaddikim*, p. 6, #3)

It is a widespread Jewish practice when traveling to study Torah from a book or to recite Psalms from memory or from a small Psalm book.

39:17 FENCES

> You should make a fence [a rule of extra self-restraint] that keeps you far away from what is forbidden, until the time when you are certain that you will never again transgress in that forbidden thing. The fence should be according to the problem. If the problem is general and you see that in a certain area of behavior you are completely lacking and have not even begun to improve, then make the fence general and act the exact opposite of your bad nature.

For example, in the case of anger, which we are particularly dealing with in this book, if you see that you are always getting angry whenever people do or say something against your will, then accept on yourself the practice to be careful that whenever you talk to people you do so good-naturedly, in a pleasant way and with your voice as low as possible, and that you will not speak at all with those who are acting badly to you. If you become accustomed somewhat to bearing frustration and nevertheless you still become angry at a particular person and regarding a particular matter, then make a fence to accept on yourself that you will not deal with that person or with that matter again.

For example, if you became angry with your wife about the food, take it upon yourself not to talk with her at all about food until a certain time or date.

A wise person will learn from this example how to deal with many different matters and how to make a fence for himself according to the need of the hour and the matter at hand. (*Erech Apayim*, 3:12, p. 70)

39:18 PUNISH, PENALIZE, OR FINE YOURSELF

You may not always be able to prevent yourself from committing certain transgressions, but afterward when you are calm and realize what you have done and feel regret, you can then punish yourself, and in this way teach yourself a lesson.

It is like training an animal (for the body with its desires is basically like an animal)—you cannot stop the puppy from urinating where he should not, but afterwards you can indicate your displeasure to him, and he will learn from the reprimand.

Such punishments and fines can also be determined by you in advance: if I do such-and-such, I'll penalize myself this way.

39:18:1 Punish yourself for any transgression you commit, whether of a custom, or certainly of a *mitzvah.* (*Derech Hayim*, 4–82)

39:18:2 Do not lie down and go to sleep until you have made a reckoning of your transgressions and failings for the day, and if you did sin, God forbid, you should set for yourself a serious penalty or punishment and make a fence to protect yourself from it happening again. (Rabbi Nahum of Tchernobil, *Hanhagot Tzaddikim*, p. 35, #10)

39:18:3 For each and every transgression that you commit, whether it was done unintentionally or intentionally, as for example when you touch a lamp or light it, having forgotten that it is *Shabbat*, or if you touch it accidentally, you should confess and fast, at least Monday and Thursday. And so for all transgressions, great or small that you do, fast.

In this there are two benefits: first, the fast atones for the sin. And second, it will prevent you from transgressing because you will think: "If I do this I will have to fast," and as a result you will not do it.

The best fence to make to keep yourself from transgressing is to punish or fine yourself—either by giving *tzedaka* or by causing some distress to your body when you transgress. This is the way you should deal with all the sins that you are accustomed to, such as hating, taking revenge, enjoying others' difficulties, empty conversations that just waste time, slander, or not concentrating when you say blessings or when you pray. (*Orchot Tzaddikim*, Gate 26, p. 173)

The particular emphasis here on fasting may not appeal to you, but there are many possible adaptations of the basic idea. You may, rather than fasting, do strenuous physical exercise.

39:18:4 *Fines*—Resolve that if you transgress any practice to which you committed yourself, or any fence you made, you will fine yourself in some way that will cause you real distress, such as a fast, eating less by this or that amount; or with sleep, that you stay awake the whole night or not sleep in the bed one night [but on the floor instead]; or that you immediately give so much *tzedaka*; or learn so much in *musar* books that speak about the matter wherein you transgressed; or that you immediately say so many psalms, a number that is difficult for you, so you will be unhappy. And you should not eat until you fulfill this penalty. (*Erech Apayim*, 3:15, p. 71)

39:19 TORAH AS PRAYER

If you are in need of healing, learn in the *Gemara* and in the Torah all the stories of God's miracles having to do with healing. By doing so you arouse the power of God's mercy to heal. And so with all other things, such as situations where there is the necessity of

> overcoming enemies or for being saved, and for all situations where you need God's saving power. (*Darkei Tzedek*, #25)

To do this it might be helpful to make lists for yourself of where to find stories of a particular kind.

39:20 A HOLY PURCHASE

> Even when you are involved in conversation about worldly matters you should not, God forbid, lose your consciousness of and connection with God. Because if you see to it that you have this God–consciousness at that time, then holiness will adhere to the thing that you are involved with.
>
> For example, if you bought something, and when you were involved in conversation about the purchase you maintained your consciousness of God, you draw holiness to the thing you bought. Later, when you have occasion to use and handle that object, it will be easier to maintain God–consciousness then too. (The Holy Jew, *Tiferet ha-Yehudi*, p. 17)

39:21 HOLY OBJECTS

All holy objects, such as holy books, *tallises*, *tefillin*, *mezuzahs*, and so on manifest God's presence in a special way, and we are to treat them in a special way, with reverence and love. A customary expression of this is to kiss holy objects, and doing this also helps us to increase and cultivate that devotion in us. The more you put in, the more you get out. The more effort you make to express such devotion, the more benefit you will get in return from coming into contact with the holy things (and places and people).

It is also good to cultivate your sensitivity to the holiness of these objects and your ability to perceive their holiness and the Divine Light that shines through them. To this end, you can, at least briefly, when handling a holy object, meditate on this very thing.

> When you use holy objects with which *mitzvot* are done, such as the *tallit* and *tefillin* and *tzitzit*, you should have the intention and hope that the Light of the Infinite One who is clothed within them be revealed to you. . . . For example, when you put on a *tallit*, you should think that the Light of the Infinite One is hidden within this *tallit* that you wrap yourself in . . . and that when the wings of the

> *tallit* cover you, you are covered in the wings of the Light of the Infinite One. (*Or ha-Ganuz l'Tzaddikim*, pp. 36, 71, 73–74)
>
> When you kiss the *tzitzit* and the *tefillin* or the *sefer* Torah, say, "Let Him kiss me with the kisses of His mouth, [for Thy love is better than wine]" (Song of Songs 1:2), and have as your intention that just as you kiss the *tzitzit*, etc. so does the Light of the Infinite One and the Supernal Will that is clothed within this *mitzvah*, kiss you—the *d'vekut* of spirit to spirit. (*Or ha-Ganuz l'Tzaddikim*, p. 59)

There is a distinction between holy objects (*tallit*, *tefillin*, etc.) and objects used for a *mitzvah* (*ethrog*, *matzah*, etc.), but there is an obvious relationship.

It was said of Rabbi Levi Yitzhak of Berditchev that:

> When any object used for a *mitzvah* came to his hand, he would cover it with heartfelt kisses. The *ethrog*, the *lulav*, the *sukkah*, *matzot*, and so on—all these would he kiss with the utmost devotion and fervor. (*Seder ha-Dorot ha-Hadash*, p. 35)

Rabbi Levi Yitzhak was already on the highest level of devotion and when he did this it was not with forethought to cultivate his love for God and holiness. But care must be taken in these matters to avoid pretense.

The author of *Emunat Tzaddikim* writes about Rabbi Shlomo Leib of Lentshno:

> I must record for a memorial what I saw with my own eyes of his great love for the *mitzvot*. When he held the *ethrog* everyone saw how he almost expired because of his great love for the *mitzvah*. He kissed the *ethrog* again and again as he chanted the *Hallel*. During *Sukkot* he kept the container with the *ethrog* in it before him on the table, and he would stare at it with great love. And he did the same with the *shofar*, which he always had placed near him during the month of *Elul*. Again and again he took it in his hands and brought it to his lips as if wanting to blow it. So too on the holy *Shabbat* when he sat at the table, he looked at the *challahs*. And because of his love for the *mitzvah* he could not contain himself and he would kiss the *challah*. But once a certain rabbi was visiting him on the holy Sabbath, and when he saw this, this rabbi also took one of the *challahs* of the twelve on the table and kissed it; from then on the *rebbe* never again kissed the *challahs*. (p. 87)

39:22 PUBLICIZE AND PROCLAIM YOUR COMMITMENTS

A good method, tried and tested, to correct the trait of anger and all other bad traits that can be seen by other people, such as those involving speech, is . . . always to publicize before everyone in your house and other people too [presumably, common sense will determine to whom], that you have committed yourself to act in these and those particular ways, and you are determined to be careful about them.

You should always make it a point when speaking with people to let them know this. You should also write it in big letters in the beginning of your Siddur and other places where other people will see it too, that you have accepted on yourself to act in such and such a way from now on. Use other ways to publicize this to everyone.

By doing this you will be forced to fulfill these commitments so that people will not reproach you and mock you . . . and you will be forced to do it because of the shame. Eventually pure motives will replace these lower motives of shame, etc.

Do not worry about pride and self-advertisement, because you are doing this for the purpose of fixing your bad character traits. (*Erech Apayim*, 3:17, p. 72)

It is also possible to use this method in an even more effective way, so that with God's help you can repair all your bad traits that can be seen by others. This better version requires the service of a good friend.

If you can, get yourself a good friend who is also trying to serve God, and be with him at all times. Let each of you tell the other all the practices and religious commitments, about things that can be seen by others, that he has accepted upon himself. Let there be an agreement between you that each will watch over the other, and protest any deviation from adherence to those things.

And if you cannot find such a spiritual friend, then enlist those who are fit and appropriate for such a task from your own home or from the *Beit Midrash* to watch over you and rebuke you if necessary. (*Erech Apayim*, 3:19, p. 78)

The continuation here says that it is even possible for a parent to have one of his children fill this position for him, as long as care is taken that the commandment to honor one's parents is not violated. If a person has many children or others who are worthy to help him in this way he should use them all.

39:23 SILENT SHOUTING

Rabbi Nachman of Bratzlav taught the practice of silent shouting in personal prayer:

> You can shout loudly in a "still small voice" [1 Kings 19:12]. You can scream without anyone hearing you shouting with this soundless still small voice.
>
> Anyone can do this. Just imagine the sound of such a scream in your mind. Depict the shout in your imagination exactly as it would sound. Keep this up until you are literally screaming with this soundless "still small voice."
>
> This is actually a scream and not mere imagination. Just as some vessels bring the sound from your lungs to your lips, others bring it to the brain. You can draw the sound through those nerves, literally bringing it into your head. When you do this, you are actually shouting inside your brain.
>
> When you picture this scream in your mind, the sound actually rings inside your brain. You can stand in a crowded room, screaming in this manner, with no one hearing you. Sometimes when you do this, some sound may escape your lips. The voice, traveling through the nerves, can activate the vocal organs. They might then produce some sound, but it will be very faint.
>
> It is much easier to shout this way without words. When you wish to express words it is much more difficult to hold the voice in the mind and not let any sound escape. But without words it is much easier. (*Rabbi Nachman's Wisdom*, p. 118, *Sichos HaRan*, #16)

The note in the English edition from which this quote is taken specifically says that this teaching "does not apply to formal prayer, where one should worship in a loud voice."

Rabbi Nachman seems to have preferred that his silent shouting be wordless. This is prayer on the principle of the *shofar*, where the sound alone expresses the prayer, without the necessity for worded petition. This goes along with the teaching given by Rabbi Nachman on the use of wordless sighs and groans in prayer or as prayer (see "Prayer," 5:4:7).

What is the meaning of such a wordless, silent shout? It is a cry of heartfelt anguish at separation from God, it is a cry to draw His attention to us, it is a plea that He draw us close to Him.

We are told about Rabbi Nachman's practice of *hitbodedut* as a boy, that:

> His father's house had a small garret partitioned off as a storehouse for hay and feed. Here the young Rabbi Nachman would hide himself, chanting the Psalms and screaming quietly, begging God that he be worthy of drawing himself close to Him. (*Rabbi Nachman's Wisdom*, p. 10, *Shevachey HaRan*, #10)

The Baal Shem Tov himself taught not silent shouting, but that you should pray the formal prayers, as well as study Torah, in a *whispered* shout. (See the quote in "Prayer," 5:2:5:5.)

Rabbi Nachman, the Besht's great-grandson, had a different way than his illustrious forebear. On the one hand, he kept the loud voice in formal prayer; on the other hand, for personal prayer (at least sometimes) he went to this completely silent and usually wordless shout.

Rabbi Menahem Mendel of Vorki was a master of silence; the book of his life and teachings is called *The Silent Tzaddik* (*Ha-Tzaddik ha-Shotek*). He also believed in silent shouting for personal prayer:

> Jews! Brothers! Let us call out with a silent shout! For the true Jewish shout has its source in the heart, and therefore raising the voice has no connection with it. It is written, "I shall answer you from within the hiddenness of the thunder"—meaning that the thunder of prayer should be hidden within. And from where do we know that silent prayer, without sound or speech, is to God's liking? From Aaron the Priest do we learn this. For when he was in great distress and could not even speak or move his lips in prayer and all he could do was pray within his heart, God said to him, according to the *Midrash*: "I tell you, yours [your prayer] is greater than theirs [those who pray aloud]. (*Ha-Tzaddik ha-Shotek*, p. 67)

(See "Service of the Imagination," 19:13.)

39:24 BEGINNING ANEW

Writing about Rabbi Nachman of Bratzlav's devotional practice as a boy, Rabbi Natan, his great disciple, says:

> When the Rebbe was involved in his devotions, everything he did required great toil and effort. No form of devotion came easily, and the Rebbe literally had to lay down his life in many cases. Each thing required tremendous effort, and he had to work hard each time he wanted to do something to serve God. He fell a thousand times, but each time he picked himself up and served God anew.

The most difficult thing was to begin serving God and accept the yoke of true devotion. Each time he would begin, he would find himself falling. He would then begin anew and stumble yet another time. This occurred countless times, over and over again.

Finally the Rebbe resolved to stand fast and maintain his foothold without paying attention to anything else in the world. From then on, his heart was firm in its devotion to God. But even so, he went up and down very many times.

But by then he was determined that he would never abandon his devotion, no matter how many times he fell. No matter what happened, he would remain devoted to God to the very best of his ability.

The Rebbe became accustomed to constantly begin anew. Whenever he fell from his particular level, he did not give up. He would simply say, "I will begin anew. I will act as if I am just beginning to devote myself to God and this is the very first time."

This happened time and again, and each time he would start all over again. He would often begin anew many times in a single day. For even in the course of a day there were many times when he would fall away from his high level of devotion. But each time he would start again, no matter how many times it happened, even within a single day. (*Rabbi Nachman's Wisdom*, pp. 7–8, *Shevachey HaRan*, #5, 6)

The Rebbe often spoke about his childhood piety. He said that he began anew many times each day. He would begin the day with deep devotion, resolving that from then on he would be a true servant of God. Then the temptation of a tasty meal or such would get the better of him, and he would fall from his high level of devotion. But on that same day he would begin again, with new resolve toward true devotion.

The Rebbe would thus fall and begin anew several times each day. He often told us how he continually began serving God anew.

This is an important rule in devotion. Never let yourself fall completely.

There are many ways you can fall. At times your prayer and devotion may seem utterly without meaning. Strengthen yourself and begin anew. Act as if you were just beginning to serve God. No matter how many times you fall, rise up and start again. Do this again and again, for otherwise you will never come close to God.

Draw yourself toward God with all your might. Remain strong, no matter how low you fall. . . . Whether you go up or down, always yearn to come close to God. You may be brought low, but cry out to God, and do everything you can to serve Him in joy. (*Rabbi Nachman's Wisdom*, p. 151, *Sichos HaRan*, #48)

39:25 HOLY COMPANY

The company of those who believe in God and who strive to serve Him is very important, and so too is the avoidance of those who will weaken you in your belief and devotion.

You can seek out such good company as a conscious part of your spiritual practice and development.

> It is so important to be continually with people who believe in God and in the place where they gather, and where they do not engage in idle talk, and also to distance yourself from the opposite. (Rabbi David ha-Levi of Steppin, *Hanhagot Tzaddikim*, p. 59, #57)

> Association with bad people, even if they are believers, will, at the least, disturb and destroy the service we are obligated to give God . . . and all the more so will association with nonreligious business people and worldly people have this deleterious effect. . . . Just as association with wicked people destroys and disrupts our faith and service of God, so does association with *tzaddikim* and servants of God strengthen our faith and our service—for we will learn from their actions. (*Beit Avraham*, #21)

39:26 *TZADDIKIM*

39:26:1 There is nothing more important than meeting and coming into contact with holy people, with *tzaddikim*, and if possible becoming a disciple of a true *tzaddik*. Some people mistakenly think there are no *tzaddikim* today or that they only come "advertised." But sometimes you have to use your own eyes and judgment to know about a person. And there are many different levels of *tzaddikim*. Someone can be on a level to guide you, without being a perfect *tzaddik*.

39:26:2 When you are with a *tzaddik* or *tzaddeket* (a holy woman) it is important to observe all her ways closely, everything she does, even her most ordinary actions such as how she makes small talk. And it is good to look in her face, even stare (without being noticeable or rude of course) to absorb her holy influence into your soul.

It is said about Rabbi Menahem Mendel of Rimanov that:

> He would study the ways of his *rebbe*, Rabbi Elimelech of Lizensk, with a sharp eye, and as he later instructed his own disciples: "When

someone has come to a correct understanding, when he sees a *tzaddik* and looks carefully at each and every one of his limbs, he can learn Torah from them. When I was with my *rebbe*, I learned Torah from every one of his limbs. When someone is not on the level to do this, at any rate, if he will look well into his *rebbe*'s face, the *tzaddik* will shed light on him for each and every limb." (*Ateret Menahem*, p. 7, #7)

It was also said about the Rimanover:

> He was delighted whenever he was able to hear about some *hanhaga* from any *tzaddik*. (*Ateret Menahem*, p. 90, #22)

Some *rebbes* would rarely say [teach] Torah:

> Rabbi Leib Saras used to say about those rabbis who would say Torah: "What is this that they say Torah? Should he not rather see that all his doings and actions be Torah, and that he himself be Torah?—that his behavior should so clearly reflect the Torah's ways that people will be able to learn from him, from all his actions and movements, and from his *d'vekut* and speech. All his doings will be Torah to learn from, according to what is said in the verse, 'There is no speech, there are no words, their voice is not heard—yet their voice has gone out over all the earth, and their words to the end of the world [Psalm 19].'" Rabbi Leib, his memory for a blessing, used to say that his traveling to the house of his *rebbe* and master, the Great Maggid, Rabbi Ber of Mezritch was not to hear Torah from him, but to see how he took off his shoes and how he tied them and put them on—as just said. (*Seder ha-Dorot ha-Hadash*, p. 46)

39:26:3 When you pray the thirteenth blessing in the *Shemoneh Esreh* ("And on the *tzaddikim*") which ends, "and let my portion be with them forever," let come into your mind and before your eyes the faces of the *tzaddikim* that you know or know about and to whom you feel some connection.

In *Avodah u'Moreh Derech* we are told how as a preparation for the *Shemoneh Esreh*:

> [You should] link yourself lovingly with the souls of the *tzaddikim* of the generation whose faces you know, and should picture them in your mind at that time. (p. 25)

39:26:4 Reading, hearing, and telling stories of the beautiful and holy ways of the *tzaddikim* is a great spiritual practice and is itself a great service of God. Rabbi Israel of Rizhin said that praising the *tzaddikim* is equivalent to praising God Himself. The Besht said:

> When one tells stories in praise of the *tzaddikim*, it is as though he is engaged in the mystic study of the Divine Chariot [for the *tzaddikim* are the Divine Chariot].[1] (*Shivhei ha-Besht*, #194)

It is a common practice among hasidim to sit together in a group, perhaps with some liquor, to sing *niggunim* and tell stories of the *tzaddikim*.

Rabbi Menahem Nahum of Stepinesht (a son of Rabbi Israel of Rizhin) used to say:

> Do you think that a person has to tell a story or a teaching of a *tzaddik* to someone else? It is not so at all. Just as when you recite the *Sh'ma* it is between you and God, in the same way, when you tell a story about a *tzaddik* it can be between you and yourself alone. (*Beit Rizhin*, p. 328)

Rabbi Menahem Nahum would particularly recommend telling such stories to oneself (and before God) upon waking, or right before sleep.

There are a number of books of hasidic stories available in English. Such stories are very inspiring, providing vivid models of what a person should be. Their light can lead us into the Way of Life. From Rabbi Natan, Rabbi Nachman of Bratzlav's great disciple:

> I heard this from the Rebbe's own lips when he revealed the lesson speaking about the importance of telling stories about Tzaddikim. . . . The Rebbe said, "I myself was greatly motivated to serve G-d through stories of Tzaddikim. Many great Tzaddikim used to visit the home of my holy parents. We lived in Medziboz, and this had also been the home of the Baal Shem Tov. Many would come and visit the Baal Shem Tov's grave, and they would mostly stay at my father's house. It was from them that I heard many stories of Tzaddikim, and this moved me toward G-d." It was through this that the Rebbe attained the great things that he did. (*Rabbi Nachman's Wisdom*, p. 268, *Sichos HaRan*, #138)

The biographical story of Rabbi Nachman's own spiritual journey and his attainment of holiness is itself tremendously inspiring and includes probably the best record available of how a great *tzaddik* reached his high level, as well as a good description of his own spiritual practices. The book (just quoted) is available in English.

39:27 A SPIRITUAL FRIEND

Many *rebbes* give the counsel, following *Avot* 1:6, to "get yourself a friend" to be a companion in religious matters.

39:27:1 It is an important arrangement to make for your spiritual life, that you find a close religious friend, so that you can always take counsel with him on how to do the work of God in the right way. (*Derech Hayim*, 2–90)

39:27:2 You should see to it that you have a good friend with whom you can talk regularly about the service of God. (*Alpha Beta* of Rabbi Tzvi Hirsh, in *YHvT*, p. 61)

39:27:3 See that you have a good friend, someone who can be depended upon, and who is able to keep a secret. You should talk with him half an hour every day about everything in your heart and innermost thoughts that is from the incitement of the evil inclination. . . . And if you have worries, as the rabbis teach, you should talk them out with a friend, and if something good happens to you, then you should share your happiness with him. (Rabbi Asher of Stolin, *Hanhagot Tzaddikim*, p. 9, #13)

39:27:4 Everyone should see that he fulfills what the rabbis teach about "cleaving to your comrades." And you should choose someone whom you have tested, at least according to your ability, to see that he wants nothing but to reach the truth, and wants with all his heart to escape from the snares of evil—from illusionary desires and from falsehood. Then you should converse together every day for about half an hour, where each one should disparage his own bad traits in front of the other, exposing them before his friend. Then when you have become accustomed to this and your friend sees something ugly in you and rebukes you for it, you will not be ashamed before him and you will be able to admit the truth. As a result, falsehood will fall and the truth will begin to emerge. (Rabbi Menahem Mendel of Vitebsk, in *Or ha-Emet*, II, p. 52)

39:27:5 You should make it a practice to regularly tell your spiritual teacher, or even a close religious friend, all of the thoughts and feelings against the holy Torah that the evil inclination causes to come into your mind and heart—either during Torah and prayer, or when you are lying in your bed, or in the middle of the day.

You should not hold anything back due to your embarrassment. And as a result of your bringing these things from the potential to the actual through your telling them to another person, you break the power of the evil inclination, so that it cannot overcome you as it might otherwise do.

Of course, in addition, there is the good advice you can receive from the one to whom you tell all this—for such advice is the word of God. And this practice has a wonderful effectiveness. (Rabbi Elimelech of Lizensk, the *Tzetl Katan*, #13)

39:27:6 Join with one of our comrades to discuss matters of the service of God every day. Discuss with this friend every *Erev Shabbat* what you did that past week, and after this go to receive the Sabbath Queen. (The (*Hanhagot* of Rabbi Moshe Cordovero, #14 and #15, in *YHvT*, p. 11)

39:27:7 The Holy Jew [Rabbi Yaakov Yitzhak of Pshischa] had a friend who was one of the hasidim of the Holy Grandfather of Neshkiz, in the city of Ostrovtzi, close to Apta [where he lived as a young man]. They were bound together with cords of love and would get together every week on a fixed day, and would talk about Torah and high matters. (*Ha-Hozeh mi-Lublin*, p. 75)

(See also 39:22.)

39:28 THE SERVICE OF CONFESSION

Rabbi Alexander Ziskind used confession continually in his service of God. He writes in his spiritual testament to his children:

> If I felt that I did something unintentionally against the will of God, blessed be He, in deed, speech, or thought, I confessed immediately on the spot before my Maker and Creator, with a broken heart. And I resolved in my mind with complete sincerity that I would be very careful about this (whatever it was).
>
> And to put before you, my dear children, all the cases where I did this, confessing for my wrongdoing in deed, speech, and thought, is of course impossible; but I will give you examples of each kind, and from them you can learn how to act in all other situations.

For deed—for example, if I felt that I had eaten too much, so that I would end up sluggish and would not be able to study Torah and pray with *kavvanah*, or I thought that because of the overeating I would have to waste more time in the bathroom, I confessed immediately to my Maker, blessed be He, and I accepted on myself with complete sincerity to be careful about this from then on. And I did the same for all other actions when I realized I had done something wrong.

For speech—for example, if I felt that I had spoken words for which there was no necessity, either for doing *mitzvot* or for the fear of Heaven, even though there was not the slightest slander or talebearing in them, God forbid, just that they were unnecessary—I would confess immediately. And I accepted on myself, etc. (as above for the deeds). Or if I said any words of prayer or in the Grace After Meals or other blessings, without the proper intention of my heart and mind, I immediately mentally asked for atonement before the Lord of all, with great brokenness of heart. And I was very careful afterwards about this as I continued the prayer, etc. And after I concluded the prayer or blessing I confessed aloud about this. . . . [Rabbi Ziskind mentions that during the *Shemoneh Esreh* he would use the confessions that can be made in the "who hears prayer" blessing and at the conclusion of the *Shemoneh Esreh* to confess failings in his *kavvanah* during that prayer.]

In thought—if I became aware that I had been thinking of something that had no connection with any *mitzvah* or with the fear of Heaven, I immediately turned away from that thought, and I confessed aloud with complete sincerity, and resolved to be careful about this from then on.

So be very, very certain, my beloved children, that you always have such confessions in your mouth and in your mind continually. For then you will be careful in what follows about something you have already confessed before the Creator, blessed be He. Not only is that true, but the confession itself has a great effect in the Upper World [to atone for sin, etc.]. (*Tzva'a Yekara*, #6)

39:29 LISTENING FOR GOD'S INSTRUCTIONS

39:29:1 The Besht taught that if you are in *d'vekut* and dedicate your thoughts to God—that is, you recognize that they, as everything else, come from Him, and you desire that He send you your thoughts and that they be of His will—then the thoughts that come to you are messages from Him. (See "Prayer," 5:5:5 for a discussion of this practice and relevant quotes.)

> **39:29:2** The spiritual levels and attainments in wisdom of our *rebbe* [Rabbi Moshe Teitelbaum] are famous and well known. Already in his youth he merited that all his *hanhagot* (ways) were according to special instructions he received from heaven; for he heard proclamations that went out from heaven and saw true visions and clear dreams that gave directions according to the needs of the hour. (*Ha-Gaon ha-Kadosh Baal Yismach Moshe*, p. 59)

39:29:3 Though there are no teachings that discuss this as a practice per se, it seems possible to make it one.

So, sit down quietly, empty yourself of worldly thoughts, and do a meditation for *d'vekut* (see "Meditation" [17] and "Prayer," 5:1:18 for instruction on this). Then make a declaration that you recognize that God is Master of all that is and all that happens, even of your thoughts, and you give them into His hand to form as He will. Offer a prayer that He direct your mind and mental processes, and that He indicate to you what to do. Then just sit and wait. As directions come to you, jot them down to consider later. Of course, when you do go over them afterwards, they should be checked, if necessary, against your own Torah knowledge and with a spiritual friend or teacher, to determine if they are from Above.

But once you have concluded, to the best of your ability, that the direction you have received is pure—then do not fail to carry it out. And as you do so, have the *kavvanah* that you are doing this in obedience to the will of God, blessed be He.

This practice can be done three times a day, as a fixed obligation like the daily prayers, or just once a day. It can also be done at the time of prayer, either during the personal part of the *Shemoneh Esreh*, or after prayer, as its conclusion. (See "Prayer" [5] for more about its use then.)

39:30 IS IT GOD'S WILL?

39:30:1 From the author of *Shevet Musar*:

> I have received it from my masters that when they wanted to do something and were in doubt whether to do it or not, they would

take a *Chumash* or *Tanach*, open it and look at the first verse on the page to see at what it hinted. (*Keter ha-Yehudi*, p. 47, n. 1)

39:30:2 The Besht:

When you learn Torah, and later in the day you have to make a decision about some action and you do not know if you should do it or not, you can understand what course to take from the power of the Torah that you learned earlier—but this is on condition that you are always in *d'vekut* with God, blessed be He. Then He will arrange that you will always know what to do from what you studied that day. But if you just walk with God sporadically, then He, too, will do so with you. (*Tzavaat ha-Ribash* and *Likkutim Yekarim*, quoted in *Sefer Baal Shem Tov al ha-Torah*, vol. 2, p. 205)

See also 39:31:3 and the words of the Zlotchover Maggid in Chapter 1, p. 8.

39:31 BE CALM BEFORE YOU ACT

39:31:1 Be calm and deliberate before you do anything—whether in speech or action. This is an important principle: if you are in doubt, it is preferable not to do anything. And this is a pillar and foundation in the service of God. (Rabbi Asher of Stolin, *Hanhagot Tzaddikim*, p. 15; cf. p. 25, #1 from Rabbi Aaron of Karlin)

39:31:2 You should not do anything from which you receive pleasure or from which you benefit, without calm consideration beforehand—and not in a scattered state of mind. (Rabbi Mordechai Yosef of Ishbitz, *Mai ha-Shiloach*, p. 74)

39:31:3 The Ramban offered a rule of thumb to use in connection with your actions, when something arises and you very much want to do it, but do not know if it is proper in God's eyes. You should remove from the equation, from what you plan to do, every aspect of benefit or pleasure that will accrue to your body, and then see what it looks like; then you will be able to know if you should do it or not. (*Darkei Tzedek*, p. 16, #15)

39:32 A MEDITATION FOR ALL TIMES: GIVE HIM WHAT IS HIS

Meditations can be done on Torah beliefs and concepts, which should not only be understood intellectually, but drawn into our emotional "understanding" and assimilated into our life and behavior. Here is an example of one such meditation that can be done frequently and in all circumstances:

> If you will consider everything that is yours, you will not find the least little thing that is not in fact really God's. All the limbs of your body, even the soul within the body, even each and every hair on your head, your clothes, and all the utensils in your kitchen along with the food there—it all belongs to God.
>
> If He were to take away everything of His, what would remain? Not the least thing. And intelligence requires that we not become proud of something that is not of our own making and doing. . . . If you will put all this before your eyes, and if you put yourself and all your belongings and everything of yours at the service of God, and say clearly: "I myself and everything I have—it all belongs to God. Whatever He wants to do with me, let Him do. I accept everything that He decides." When you so connect yourself and everything of yours to God, then, with this meditation you are performing a holy service of God. . . . And you are able to perform this service at all times, continually, when you are sitting down, when you rise up, in your house, or when you are walking around outside. (*Sefer ha-Hayim*, Gate 5, #16)

Elsewhere, a similar suggestion is made:

> Give over into the hand of the Holy One, blessed be He, everything that is yours, because it is all His. And by doing this you will not be pained by any loss that comes to you. (*Or ha-Ner*, #42)
>
> Our Sages said: "Torah is preserved only in someone who kills himself on her behalf." The Torah greats throughout the generations have interpreted this to mean not, God forbid, that a person should kill himself, but that he should kill his egoism. In Pshischa, under Rebbe Simha Bunim, this teaching was fulfilled in practice, for his disciples gave up all their possessions. "No one ever stole anything from me," said the *rebbe*, Rabbi Yitzhak of Vorki [one of Rabbi Simha Bunim's disciples], "for each day I give up all my possessions, abandoning any claim to their ownership. So whatever anyone stole—it was from what was already without an owner." (*Ha-Admor Rabbi Hanoch mi-Alexander*, p. 31)

One can give up ownership of one's possessions by means of a stated declaration to that effect. (Note the somewhat different declaration suggested in the quote above from *Sefer ha-Hayim.*)

39:33 INVEST YOUR INSPIRATION

39:33:1 When some good thought or inspiration comes to you, use it to do a *mitzvah* or to learn Torah, and so clothe it in holiness. (The Ramban, as quoted by the Peasetzna Rebbe in *Hachsharat ha-Abrechim*, p. 45a)

39:33:2 If you have a moment of spiritual arousal during the day, do not just let it pass and dissipate, but immediately make use of it by investing it in some Torah study or prayer or in other *mitzvot*. (*Seder ha-Yom ha-Katzar*, p. 5)

39:34 THE USE OF INTOXICATING BEVERAGES

The Peasetzna Rebbe:

The hasidim have always tried to take their emotions and subdue them and put them to the service of God. They also sometimes use external means to arouse their emotions and then turn them to His service.

The custom among the hasidim of drinking liquor is an important matter, and it is like what we are told in Genesis 27:25 about Jacob going to Isaac for a blessing, that "he brought him wine and he drank"; for the wine helped to draw down the *Shechinah* to rest on our father Isaac when he blessed Jacob.

Liquor arouses the heart of a man and his emotions. A low person, even if he does not get drunk, will become more active in doing bad things and sinning. He will clothe his soul, his inner self that has been brought into revelation somewhat, with even more evil, God save us from such.

But the hasid, who is a spiritual person, one who searches with candles for his soul, which is hidden within, says, "Yes, it is true that it was only through liquor that I have been aroused, and part of my soul revealed. Regardless, my inner being has been revealed somewhat, and I will hold on to that part that has come into the open and will not let go, and with it I will serve God with a revealed soul. And I will not just do so with what the liquor brought out, but through my Divine service I will bring my soul out even more with emotion and arousal and even with fiery enthusiasm."

So should you do too; drink with your comrades and friends who are hasidim and who are spiritual people, with this purpose

> and in this way—to bring about the arousal of your soul and a more alive service of God with a revealed soul.
>
> Since it is for this purpose and with this preparation that you drink liquor and arouse your emotions, and do so in a gathering of friends who are also hasidim, from the very beginning you will feel, as your emotions become revealed, that they are enclothed in holiness. It will be an emotional arousal for the service of God, for faith, and for the fear and love of God. (*Hachsharat ha-Abrechim*, p. 46b)

Of course, such drinking is not to be engaged in alone, without the association of religious friends. And in our time, with all the abuse of alcohol and drugs, care should be taken in every regard.

39:35 THE SERVICE OF SELF-EXAMINATION

Various hasidic *rebbes* taught intense self-examination as a way to purity. On his first trip to Rabbi Menahem Mendel of Kotzk (then living in Tomashov), Rabbi Hanoch Henich HaCohen (the future *rebbe* of Alexander) was given this teaching by the *rebbe*:

> "A hasid of Tomashov searches and questions himself not only once, but a second and a third time, about everything he does." "From then on," said the Rebbe of Alexander, "I spent much time examining and considering all my actions, everything I did. When I returned home from my trip to the *rebbe*, for example, and went to have something to eat, I picked up the vessel for the hand washing and began to question myself: What will be if I do not wash my hands? And if I do wash, am I then prepared for eating? Let us say I wash my hands and make a blessing over the bread—what kind of blessing will it be? How will I let it out of my mouth, and to Whom will I utter it?
>
> "So there I stood, examining and considering my actions, for about two hours. Now my father-in-law [in whose house he was living], seeing me standing there was amazed, and asked me why I did not begin my meal—but I was silent and did not answer. I went deeper and deeper in self-examination until I had plumbed the depths completely, and then I washed my hands, and roared in a thunderous voice that was not mine, '[Blessed art Thou, etc. who hast commanded us] on the washing of the hands [*al netilat yadayim*]!' And I tell you, since then I have never merited to give forth

a blessing like that." (*Ha-Admor Rabbi Hanoch Henich mi-Alexander*, p. 34)

39:36 REMEMBERING JERUSALEM

We are always to remember Jerusalem, the Holy City (may it soon be fully rebuilt, with our Holy Temple), and the tradition gives us a number of ways to do this: for example, by saying Psalm 137 before the Grace after Meals (see *Shulchan Aruch*, chapter 126 for others).

It is told of the hasidic *rebbe*, Rabbi Hayim Shmuel Sternfeld of Chenshtyn, that he wore a wristwatch that showed the time in the Land of Israel (*P'ri Kodesh Hillulim*, p. 107). A *tzaddik* I know has for years kept his wristwatch on Jerusalem time. Though this particular practice may not suit everyone, it is a good example of how *hanhagot* can be created in the service of God.

39:37 SEEING GOD—AN ADDED NOTE

> Regarding fulfillment of the verse, "I have placed the Lord [YHVH] before me always," it is fitting to strive always to picture the four-letter Name before your eyes. But you can also fulfill the essence of the teaching through another verse, "The Lord [YHVH] of hosts is both sun and shield," which means that you are to always picture the great light mentioned here [the light of the *Shechinah* symbolized by the light of the sun] as flooding at you. . . .
>
> When you see any person, you are to imagine the being of God and His effulgent light flooding through the person to you. So too when you see a holy book or the holy letters and words within, or when you see the skies—imagine that they are the "shields" [of the verse] or "screens" through which God's light is flooding. They are the "hosts" [of the verse], the "armies" of material things through which "the Lord" [of the verse] is manifest. (*Or ha-Ganuz l'Tzaddikim*, p. 62)

In practicing seeing God (see Chapter 1, "In the Presence of God," p. 17; "Prayer," 5:1:18:3:1; "Torah," 15:18) there are different ways to begin. What is suggested in this quote is one way, where we start with those things that have a greater manifestation of God's presence (holy objects, holy letters, people [note this—for man is made in the image of

God], etc.), and it is therefore easier to see the Light in or through them. As one reaches higher spiritual levels one will see God's light everywhere, and will not need to work to have this vision.

As to the suggested way to "see" other people who are before us, compare "Speech," 23:2:4 and the quote there from this same hasidic book, about speaking with others as if you were speaking with God. Presumably the light-meditation here would be linked with that.

39:38 BINDING TOGETHER DAY AND NIGHT IN HOLY SERVICE

It is a traditional hasidic practice to bind together the two aspects of the day, day and night, in Divine service. What this means is that you are to be up before dawn and engaged in spiritual activity at sunrise; so too are you to be involved in spiritual practice at dusk and sunset.

> Bind together day and night with Torah or prayer. (Hanhagot of Rabbi Yehiel Michal of Zlotchov, #8, *Zichron l'Rishonim*, p. 82)

Traditionally, when *Minha* is said in the late afternoon shortly before *Maariv* and at the onset of evening, the time between the two services as the sun sets is spent in the synagogue studying Torah.

This practice of binding together day and night has various meanings and purposes. On the one hand, it connects God with these two daily events of great natural power—sunrise and sunset. It also joins God-consciousness to the regular mood change that accompanies these times. (For more about this subject, see "*Tikkun Hatzot*," 31:19.)

39:39 FOR ONE HOUR

> Fix one hour during the day when you will behave completely according to the Torah. (*Hayei ha-Musar*, III, p. 89)

Appendix

This section includes the Hebrew or Aramaic of those things in the text that some people may want to use in their own religious practice in the original language. Yiddish quotes have not usually been included; neither are quotes of Tanach verses for which there are references.

PART ONE

Chapter 1

1. My words: (p. 20)
"Master of the World" — רבונו של עולם
"Father" — אבא or אבי
"Father in Heaven" — אבי שבשמים

2. The Berditchever: (p. 20) הרחמן

Chapter 2

1. R. Yosef Sagish: (p. 29) אשרי איש שלא ישכחך, ובן אדם יתאמץ בך.
2. R. Hayim of Tzanz: (Aram.) (p. 29)
ליח אתר פנוי מיניה — ממלא כל עלמין וסובב כל עלמין

Rachmei ha-Av: (p. 37)

"Blessed, etc." — ברוך יחיד ומיוחד
"I have placed, etc." — שויתי ה׳ לנגדי תמיד

Rachmei ha-Av: "Blessed be, etc." (p. 38)

גלובט איז הש״י שעושה עמי חסד.

(The first two words here are Yiddish; the Hebrew would be ברוך הוא.)

Kitzur Shnei Luchot ha-Brit: (p. 44)

אם ירצה השם... בעזרת השם... בשביל השם אני עושה

Chapter 3

Hanoch: (p. 54)

ברוך שם כבוד מלכותו לעולם ועד.

PART TWO

Chapter 4

Kochavei Boker: (p. 80)

ומים חיים האילו נובעים ממקור טהור.

Berachot 60b: (p. 81)

ברוך המעביר חבלי שינה מעיני ותנומה מעפעפי.

Rabbi Yitzhak of Radevill: (p. 84)

אני הריני רוצה לקיים מצוה זו של ואהבת לרעך כמוך.

1. R. Tzvi Elimelech: (p. 85) כח הפועל בנפעל
2. *Rachmei ha-Av:* See p. 37 under Part One, above.

Ayin Zochar: (p. 89)

רבונו של עולם, הריני מוסר עצמי אליך בכל תנועותי ומחשבותי ודיבורי ומעשי, ותנועות ומחשבות ודיבורים ומעשים של בני והתלויים בי, שיהיו הכל כרצונך הטוב עלי...

1. R. Leibele Eiger: (Aram.) (p. 96)

אנא עבדא דקודשא בריך הוא

1. R. Hayim of Tzanz: (p. 97)

אין בעולם כלל רק בורא אחד, זה נראה לכל וצריכין לעבוד אותו ולמסור נפשו עבור הבורא, לית מחשבה תפיסא בך כלל ונותן להאדם בחירה להתורה, לית אתר פנוי מיניה ואינני רוצה כלום רק שתכלה נפשי עבור הבורא... ואינני רוצה רק לעבוד את הבורא...

2. *Derech Hayim:*

רבונו של עולם, חוסה נא אלי למלטיני מן יצר הרע וכל כת דליה אמן

3. *Kav ha-Yashar:*

ה׳ ישמר צאתי ובואי לחיים ולשלום מעתה ועד עולם... בכל דרכיך דעהו והוא יישר אורחותיך.

Chapter 5

Derech Moshe: (p. 102)

זה המקום אני בוחר להתפלל לשם יחוד קודשא בריך הוא ושכינתיה בשם כל ישראל להיות מקום קבוע להתפלל אני וביתי וכל ישראל ויהי רצון שתשרה שכינה במקום הזה כמו בכל בתי כנסיות שבישראל.

Or ha-Ganuz l'Tzaddikim: (Aram.) (p. 109)

בריך רחמנא מלכא דעלמא מארי דהאי שעתא... (דהאי רגעא).

R. Abraham Hayim of Zlotchov: (p. 125)

הריני שולח תפלתי מכאן לארץ ישראל ומארץ ישראל לירושלים ומירושלים להר הבית ומהר הבית לעזרה ומעזרה לאולם ומאולם להיכל ומהיכל לקדוש הקדושים ומקדוש הקדושים להיכל לבנת הספיר למקום שהתפללו אבותי אברהם יצחק ויעקב עם כל התפלות של בתי כנסיות ובתי מדרשות ויחודם של כל ישראל ובפרט עם בניך היודעים כוונת התפלה וסודותיה ועל כוונה זו אני מתפלל בדחילו ורחימו ודחילו בשם כל ישראל.

Kitzur Shnei Luchot ha-Brit: (p. 164)

אנא ה׳ חטאתי עויתי פשעתי לפניך מחול חטאתי וסלח עונותי כפר פשעי מכל אשר חטאתי ועויתי ופשעתי לפניך מיום היותי על האדמה עד היום הזה.

Chapter 6

Kav ha-Yashar: (p. 181)

נדבת פי רצה נא ה׳ ומשפטיך למדני יהי רצון מלפניך ה׳ אלהי ואלהי אבותי שתהא תפלתי צלולה וזכה וברורה מכל ערבוביא המבטלים כוונות התפלה.

Derech Hayim: (p. 186)
הרי אני מקבל עלי עול מלכות שמים ומצות ואהבת לרעיך כמוך.

My words: (p. 188)
"Master of the World" — רבונו של עולם
"Father in Heaven" — אבי שבשמים or אבא שבשמים

Derech Pikudecha (p. 191) (Hebrew from *Taamei ha-Minhagim,* p. 5):
רבונו של עולם, גלוי וידוע לפניך שרצוני לעשות רצונך דייקא. ובאפשר באמצע העבודה יסיחני יצרי הרע ויפול במחשבתי איזה מחשבה אחרת לעבוד העבודה באיזה פנייה, הנני מבטל אותה מחשבה והרהור ורעותה דלבא כי רצוני באמת עצור בעצמותי ודבוק במחשבתי לעבוד עבודה שלימה בלתי לה׳ לבדו.

Chapter 7

1. *Hanhagot Adam:* (p. 201)
...אני בוטח בה׳... בעזרת השם יתברך... אם ירצה השם... אני הולך לעשות זה ברשות השם יתברך... רבונו של עולם בדברי קדשך כתוב לאמר הבוטח בה׳ חסד יסובבנו וכתיב ואתה מחיה את כולם. חלוק לי מחסדך ליתן ברכה במעשה ידי... אני עושה פעולה זו לשם יחוד הקדוש ברוך הוא ושכינתיה... הנני הולך לישא וליתן באמונה. לשם קודשא בריך הוא ושכינתיה ואני בוטח בה׳ שיצליח לי פרנסתי וארויח מזה העסק... ה׳ אלהים אמת תן לי ברכה והצלחה בכל מעשה ידי ואני בוטח בך שעל ידי עסק זה תשלח לי ברכה וקיים בי מקרא שכתוב השלך על ה׳ יהבך והוא יכלכלך... מה׳ היתה זאת לי.

2. *Kitzur Shnei Luchot ha-Brit:*
אני הולך לעשות זה ברשות השם יתברך למען שמו.

Rachmei ha-Av: See p. 37 under chap. 2, above. (p. 205)

1. *Avodat ha-Kodesh:* See p. 29 under chap. 2, above. (p. 206)
2. Peasetzna Rebbe:
רבונו של עולם נמצא אני עתה במקומות המסוכנים לנפשי וקדושתי, אתה אל תעזבני, תמוך ושמור אותי שומר ישראל.

Chapter 8

The Baal Shem Tov: (p. 213)
הלא זה הוא מאתו יתברך ואם בעיניו הגון [בעיני לא כל שכן] וכו׳.

Chapter 10

1. R. Shmuel Valtzis: (p. 232)
רבונו של עולם זכיני שתהיה אכילתי בקדושה ותהיה כוונתי לשם שמים ותצילני מאכילה ושתיה יתירה.

2. *Totzaot Hayim* and *Kitzur Shnei Luchot ha-Brit:* (p. 233)
אתה הוא האלהים הזן ומפרנס ומכלכל בחסדך לכל ברואיו מקרני ראמים ועד ביצי כינים [הטריפני לחם חוקי והמציא לכל בני ביתי קודם שנצרך להם מזונותינו בנחת ולא בצער בהיתר ולא באיסור לחיים ולשלום משפע ברכה והצלחה משפע ברכה העליונה כדי שנוכל לעשות רצונך ולעסוק בתורתך ולקיים מצותיך ואל תצריכני לידי מתנת בשר ודם ולא לידי הלואתם אלא לידך המלאה והפתוחה והקדושה והרחבה] פותח את ידך [ומשביע לכל חי רצון].

Mishnah Berurah: (p. 235)
הנני רוצה לאכול ולשתות שאהיה בריא וחזק לעבודת השם יתברך.

R. Eleazar: (p. 249) טאטא (Yidd.)

1. My words: "I am eating, etc." "I am making, etc." (p. 250)
הנני אוכל סעודה זו לשם ה׳
2. Likkutim Hadashim: (p. 251)
הנני עושה עצמי מרכבה לשכינה
שד׳ ישמרנו ויצילני מיצר הרע שלא אתגשם מן האכילה.

Or ha-Ganuz l'Tzaddikim: See p. 109 under chap. 5, above. (p. 261)

Chapter 11

Derech Hayim: (p. 285)
הריני עושה מצוה זו לכבוד יוצרי.

1. *Beit Midot:* (p. 285)
הנני עושה זאת לקיים מצות בוראי שבראני לכבודו.

2. R. Elimelech: (p. 286)

הריני עושה זאת לשם יחוד קודשא בריך הוא ושכינתיה לעשות נחת רוח להבורא יתברך שמו.

3. My words: "I'm doing this, etc." (p. 286)

— הנני עושה זה כי ה׳ צוה אותו, באהבה ויראה.
— הנני עושה זה לתת נחת רוח לאבי שבשמים.

1. R. Tzvi Hirsh: (p. 286)

לשם יחוד קודשא בריך הוא ושכינתיה.

2. R. Shalom Shachna: (p. 287)

אני אוכל בכדי שיהיה לי כח לעשות מצותיו ויהיה נחת רוח ליוצרי ויהיה לי כח לעשות גם כן ולעסוק בפרנסתי בשביל דבר זה...

הריני מזמן את גופי להתלבש במלבושים נאים לקיים מה שכתוב הכון לקראת אלהיך ישראל.

בשביל בריאת גופי לעבודתו.

My sentence about making oneself a chariot: See p. 250 under chap. 8, above. (p. 287)

Chapter 13

Kitzur Shnei Luchot ha-Brit: (p. 298)

לשם ה׳... בשביל ה׳ אני עושה.

"For the sake, etc.": See p. 286 under chap. 11, above. (p. 298)

1. My words: "with fear, etc." (p. 300) —
באהבה ויראה, בשם כל ישראל
2. My words: "I am doing, etc." — See p. 286 under chap. 11, above.

Chapter 14

Prayer of the Repentant: (p. 304)

אנא השם חטאתי עויתי פשעתי וכזאת וכזאת עשיתי מיום היותי על האדמה עד היום הזה ועתה נשאני לבי ונדבה אותי רוחי לשוב אליך באמת ובלב טוב ושלם בכל לבי ובכל נפשי ומאדי ולהיות מודה ועוזב ולהשליך מעלי כל פשעי ולעשות לי לב חדש ורוח חדשה ולהיות זריז וזהיר ביראתך. ועתה ה׳ אלהי הפותח יד בתשובה ומסייע לבאים לטהר פתח ידיך וקבלני בתשובה שלמה לפניך וסייעני להתחזק ביראתך ועזרני נגד השטן הנלחם בי

בתחבולות ומבקש נפשי להמיתני לבלתי ימשול בי ותרחיקהו מרמ״ח אברים שבי ותשליכהו במצולות ים ותגער בו לבלתי יעמוד על ימיני לשטני ועשית את אשר אלך בחוקך והסירות את לב האבן מקרבי ונתת לי לב בשר: אנא ה׳ אלהי שמע אל תפלת עבדך ואל תחנוניו וקבל תשובתי ואל יעכב שום חטא ועון את תפלתי ותשובתי ויעמדו לפני כסא כבודך מליצי יושר להמליץ בעדי להכניס תפלתי לפניך ואם בחטאי הרב ועצום אין לי מליץ יושר חתור לי מקום מתחת כסא כבודך וקבל תשובתי ולא אשוב ריקם מלפניך כי אתה שומע תפלה.

Chapter 15

The Seer of Lublin: (p. 311)

רבונו של עולם אפשר כתוב עלי ולרשע אמר אלהים מה לך לספר חוקי (תהילים נ׳). הנני מקבל עלי לעשות תשובה מעתה.

R. Tzvi Elimelech of Dinov: (p. 315)

הריני מוסר מודעה, שכל מחשבה רעה והרהור רע ורעותא דלבא, אם יעלה בלבי ומוחי, בפרט בעת התפלה ותלמוד תורה, באיזה צד ואופן שאינו לכבוד ורצון הבורא ית״ש, מעכשיו אני מבטל אותן מחשבות והרהורים רעים ורעותא דלבא אשר הם נגד רצון קוב״ה ביטול גמור כחרס הנשבר, ומכ״ש אם אדבר איזה דבור רע ואיסור, מעכשיו יהיו הכל בטלים ומבוטלים. ועתה אני מגלה דעתי ורצוני בכל לבי, כי רצוני ומאויי וכוונתי לעבוד את בוראנו אלהי אברהם אלהי יצחק וישראל, עבודה שלימה עבודה תמה במחשבה ודבור ומעשה ויראה ואהבה ושמחה כדת מה לעשות, וכל מחשבה ודבור ומעשה שהם נגד רצונו יתברך מעכשיו בטלים ומבוטלים כי הם מצד יצר הרע והכל הבל באופן שכל עבודתנו להבורא יתברך שמו במחשבה ודבור ומעשה הכל הוא לעשות נחת רוח לפניו דוקא בלי שום פניה כלל, ועיקר הכל הוא לשם יחוד קוב״ה בדחילו ורחימו ורחימו ודחילו ליחד שם י״ה בו״ה ביחודא שלים בשם כל ישראל לדעת רבי שמעון בן יוחאי ורבי אלעזר בנו ולדעת רבנו יצחק לוריא אשכנזי, ה׳ ברחמיו יעזרנו על דבר כבוד שמו מעתה ועד עולם יהיו לרצון אמרי פי והגיון לבי לפניך ה׳ צורי וגואלי.

Or ha-Ganuz l'Tzaddikim: (p. 318)
See p. 109, under chap. 5, above.

1. My words: (making oneself a chariot)— (p. 332)

הריני עושה את עצמי מרכבה לשכינה ה׳ השרה שכינתך עלי, הקטן.

2. R. Elimelech: (p. 332) הריני עושה את עצמי מרכבה לשכינה.

Kav ha-Yashar: (p. 333)
רבונו של עולם זכני להיות כסא לשכינה.

R. Shmelke: (p. 338)
הנני רוצה ללמוד כדי שישיבני התלמוד לידי מעשה ולידי מדות ישרות ולידי ידיעת התורה... המאור שבה יחזירני למוטב.

R. Moshe Teitelbaum: (p. 345)
יראתי בפצותי שיח לגשת אל התורה הקדושה. כי ידעתי כי עונותי עברו ראשי וכמשא כבד יכבדו ממני ע״כ אני מתודה בכפיפת ראש ובכפיפת קומה כל החטאים ופשעים ועונות שעשיתי. דברתי לשון הרע ורכילות ושקר לצתי. דברתי במקום שאסור להפסיק. שחתי שיחת חולין בבהכ״נ ובבהמ״ד ואף בשעת התפלה ובשעת קריאת התורה ואף בתפילין על ראשי והסחתי דעת מהם. חללתי את שם הכבוד חללתי שבתות וימים טובים בדבור ובמעשה. הסתכלתי במקום שאין ראוי לראות. שמעתי מה שאסור לשמוע. פגמתי בכל חושי פגמתי בברית הלשון ובברית המעור חותם הקודש. דברתי דברים בטלים. בטלתי מהתורה. יעצתי רע. כבדתי ושמחתי בקלון חבירי. הלבנתי פני חבירי ואף ברבים כניתי שם לחבירי. שנאתי בני אדם מישראל ואף בחנם. שנאתי מי שראוי לאהוב. ואהבתי מי שראוי לשנוא. קנאתי. חטאתי בגאוה. חטאתי בכעס. הלכתי בקומה זקופה. נדרתי ונשבעתי ולא קיימתי. תקעתי כפי על שקר. גליתי סוד חבירי. דברתי אחד בפה ואחד בלב. גנבתי דעת הבריות. אכלתי ושתיתי דברים אסורים. מלאתי פי שחוק. לא ברכתי ברכת הנהנין והמזון כראוי. התפללתי בלא כוונה. חשבתי בעסקי בשעת התפלה ואף בדברים בטלים והרהורים רעים. נכשלתי בשוגג וכו׳. הוצאתי מרשות היחיד לכרמלית בשבת. למדתי תורה שלא לשמה. עשיתי מצות ומע״ט עבור שישבחו אותי בני אדם. חטאתי בחנופה. וכל שאר עבירות רעות עשיתי הן הידועים לי או שאינם ידועים לי. על הכל אני מתודה ומבקש בהכנעה ושברון לב מחילה וסליחה וכפרה מאל מלך מוחל וסולח. פגמתי בדבור ובמעשה ובמחשבה ובכל רמ״ח אברים ושס״ה גידים של גופי ונפשי ורוחי ונשמתי ונשמה לנשמתי. פגמתי בכל העולמות קצצתי בנטיעות. שברתי צינורות השפע והולכתים ממקור עליון למקום הטינופות רשת הזמה. אוי לי. וי לי. אהה עלי. אויה על נפשי. גדול עוני מנשוא. עצמו פשעי מכפר. ועל כולם אני מתחרט בלב שלם ואחרי שובי נחמתי ואחרי הודעי ספקתי והנני מתחרט על כל העברות שעשיתי. והנני מבויש ומבייש את עצמי. אוי לי לאותה בושה. אוי לי לאותה כלימה. אוי לי איך אשא פני לעמוד לפני מלך מלכי המלכים הקב״ה וללמוד תורתו הקדושה. ומה אעשה כי יקום אל וכי יפקוד מה אשיבנו: אוי לי מיום הדין.

אוי לי מיום התוכחה. והנני מתאבל על החטאים ועונות ופשעים שחטאתי ועויתי ופשעתי נגד אדון עולם בוראי יוצרי עושי אשר הטיב עמדי בכל מכל כל. ואני הרעותי. אוי לי מה עשיתי. איך מרדתי במלך מה״מ הקב״ה ובתורתו הקדושה. איך פגמתי בנשמתי והחלפתי עולם עומד בעולם עובר. ומה אעשה ליום פקודה ברדתי שחת אללי ולבי דוי עלי ביותר במה שמרדתי בממ״ה הקב״ה עילת כל העילות וסיבת כל הסיבות הוא טהור ומשרתיו טהורים עושים רצונו. ואני נבזה כלב סרוח חוטא מנוול איך טמאתי א״ע. הנני מתחרט בחרטה גמורה ואם פעלתי און לא אוסיף ולא אעשה עוד כן כל ימי חיי. ואף אוסיף גדרים וסייגים שלא אבוא לידי כך. ועתה הנה נשאני לבי לשוב לפניך והנני מודה ועוזב. [וע״כ יה״ר מלפניך ה׳ אלהי ואלהי אבותי תבא לפניך תפלתי ואל תתעלם מתחנתי שאין אני עז פנים וקשי עורף לומר לפניך ה׳ אלהי ואלהי אבותי צדיק אני ולא חטאתי. אבל אני חטאתי. אשמתי בגדתי וכו׳. מה אומר לפניך יושב מרום עד צורי וגואלי. יהי רצון מלפניך ה׳ אלהי ואלהי אבותי שתכפר לי על כל חטאתי ותסלח לי על כל עונותי ותמחול לי על כל פשעי. על חטא שחטאתי לפניך באכילה ושתיה. ע״ח ש״ל בבהמ״ז. ע״ח ש״ל בגאוה. ע״ח ש״ל בדברי נדר ושבועה. ע״ח ש״ל בהרהור עבירה. ע״ח ש״ל בויעוד המחלוקת. ע״ח ש״ל בזנות. ע״ח ש״ל בחרם ובנדוי. ע״ח ש״ל בטריפות ואיסורים. ע״ח ש״ל ביין נסך. ע״ח ש״ל בכבוד ת״ח. ע״ח ש״ל בלשון הרע ורכילות. ע״ח ש״ל במעשר. ע״ח ש״ל בנטילת ידים. ע״ח ש״ל בגלוי ובסתר. ע״ח ש״ל בעושק ובגזל. ע״ח ש״ל בפריה ורביה ובי׳ ובקרי. ע״ח ש״ל בציצית ותפילין ומזוזה. ע״ח ש״ל בקידוש השם ובחילול השם. ע״ח ש״ל בכעס וברוגז. ע״ח ש״ל בשקרים. ע״ח ש״ל בתורת משה. עברתי על מ״ע ועל מל״ת על כריתות וארבע מיתות ב״ד על תורה שבכתב ועל תורה שבע״פ. שמך הגדול שכחתי מלכותך ויראתך בזיתי ואתה צדיק על כל הבא עלי כי אמת עשית ואני הרשעתי:

והנני ירא וחרד להתחיל בלימוד תורה הקדושה כי פה הנפגם בכל מיני פגימות איך ידבר בתוה״ק. פה דובר נבלה איך ידבר בתוה״ק עינים הנפגמים איך יסתכלו וכו׳. אוזן הנפגם בשמיעת לשה״ר ובשאר פגימות איך ישמע כו׳. רעיון ומחשבה אשר נטמא בהרהורים רעים איך יחשוב כו׳. ויראתי אם לא נאמר עלי ח״ו ולרשע אמר אלהים מה לך לספר חקי וכ׳. זבח רשעים תועבה ושמא ח״ו אבד שברי ותוחלתי מה׳. אך לבי אומר לי מה לך נרדם קום קרא אל אלהיך כי חפץ חסד הוא ולא יחפוץ במות המת כי אם בשובו מחטאתו וחי. ולא על צדקתי אני מפיל תחנוני לפניך ה׳. רק על רחמיך המרובים כי אל מלך מוחל וסולח אתה וימינך פשוטה לקבל שבים. לכן יה״ר מלפניך ה׳ אלהי ואלהי אבותי שתחתור חתירה מתחת כסא כבודך ותקבל את תשובתי ותפלתי ותמחול ותסלח לי על כל פשעים וחטאים

שעשיתי מעודי עד היום הזה בין בגלגול זה בין בגלגול אחר. ואל תשיבני ריקם מלפניך ושמע תפלתי ברחמיך הרבים כי אתה שומע תפלת כל פה ושימה דמעתי בנדך. יהיה לרצון אמרי פי והגיון לבי לפניך ה׳ צורי וגואלי:

ומעתה הנני רוצה ללמוד בתורתו לשמו ית׳ לקיים מצותו שצוה ית׳ אותנו ישראל עמו להגות בתורתו הקדושה וכדי שיבואני תלמוד זה לידי מעשה ולידי מדות ישרות ולידי ידיעות התורה ע״מ ללמד לשמור ולעשות. ויה״ר מלפניך ה׳ אלהי ואלהי אבותי שבלימוד הזה שאלמד יתוקן כל הפגימות שעשיתי מעודי בין בגלגול זה בין בגלגולים הקודמים בעולמות עליונים ובנפשי ורוחי ונשמתי ונשמה לנשמתי. ותזכני ללמוד וללמד לשמור ולעשות ולהיות מיודעי שמך ומבני היכלא דמלכא ומבני עליה. והדריכנו בנתיב האמת שלא אכשל בדרכי הטועים ופתח לי מעינות ואוצרות החכמה והאר עיני במאור תורתיך למדני חכמני והראני נפלאות בתורתיך בנגלה ובנסתר ואהיה כמעין המתגבר וכבור סיד שאינו מאבד טפה שלא אשכח מכל מה שאלמד. ויחד לבבי לאהבה וליראה את שמך וטהר רעיוני ולבי לעבודתך לב טהור ברא לי אלהים. ורוח נכון חדש בקרבי. ותן בלבי להבין ולהשכיל ללמוד וללמד לשמור ולעשות ולקיים את כל דברי תלמוד תורתיך באהבה. והדריכני בנתיב מצותיך גל עיני ואביטה נפלאות מתורתך. ודבק לבו במצותיך ותן לי לב חזק ואמיץ בתורתיך ובמצותיך לעמוד כנגד יצרי הרע לב שאור שבעיסה. ותזכני לעשות חבילות חבילות של מצות בשרשיהם וכלליהם ופרטיהם ודקדוקיהם וכוונותיהם. והצילני מכל עבירה רעה ושום נדנוד עבירה ושום מכשול עון שבעולם ומחילול השם ותן לי לב אמיץ לרדוף אחר המצות בכל כחי ואוני ויכלתי ובזריזות. ותזכני לקיים כל המצות שראוי לקים בדחילו ורחימו ובשמחה גדולה שאין לה קץ וסוף ותכלית. ונזכה לראות בנחמת ציון וירושלים יהיה לרצון אמרי פי והגיון לבי כו׳. [קודשא בריך הוא ושכינתיה באהבה ויראה בשם כל ישראל.]

Chapter 18

1. *Or ha-Shabbat:* (p. 387)

הריני עושה זה לכבוד שבת.

2. *Hanhagot Adam:* (p. 387)

דבר זה אני עושה (מבשל) לכבוד שבת.

3. R. Menahem Mendel of Rimanov: (p. 387)

לכבוד שבת קודש.

Sefer Haredim: (p. 388)

זה לשבת.

Kaf ha-Hayim: (p. 394)

הריני טובל כדי לקבל הארת שבת... הריני טובל לקבל נשמה יתרה.

1. *Or ha-Shabbat:* (p. 412)

הריני אוכל לכבוד שבת.

2. R. Eleazar Zev of Kretchnif: (p. 412)

לכבוד שבת קודש.

1. My words: (p. 419)
"Holy Sabbath" — שבת קודש
"Peaceful Sabbath" — שבת שלום

2. R. Eleazar Zev of Kretchnif: שבת קודש (p. 419)

Ahavat Shalom p. 420, 18:2:11:2:
"For the honor, etc": לכבוד שבת

Chapter 19

Rosh HaShanah Musaf: (p. 424)

אתה נגלית בענן כבודך, על עם קדשך, לדבר עמם. מן השמים השמעתם קולך, ונגלית עליהם בערפלי טוהר. גם כל העולם כולו חל מפניך, ובריות בראשית חרדו ממך, בהגלותך מלכנו על הר סיני ללמד לעמך תורה ומצוות, ותשמיעם את הוד קולך, ודברות קדשך מלהבות אש. בקולות וברקים עליהם נגלית, ובקול שופר עליהם הופעת, ככתוב בתורתך: ויהי ביום השלישי בהיות הבוקר, והיהי קולות וברקים, וענן כבד על ההר, קול שופר חזק מאד, ויחרד כל העם אשר במחנה. ונאמר: ויהי קול השופר הולך וחזק מאד, משה ידבר והאלהים יעננו בקול. ונאמר: וכל העם ראוים את הקולות, ואת הלפידים, ואת קול השופר, ואת ההר עשן. וירא העם וינעו ויעמדו מרחוק.

Chapter 21

1. Hanoch: See p. 54 under chap. 3, above. (p. 443)
2. *Rachmei ha-Av:* See p. 37 under chap. 2, above. (p. 445)
1. *Or ha-Ganuz l'Tzaddikim* See p. 109 under chap. 5, above. (p. 445)
2. R. Alexander Ziskind: (p. 446)

יוצרי ובוראי אתה...

יוצרי בוראי אני מאמין באמונה שלמה שאתה בראת כל העולמות העליונים והתחתונים עולמות לאין קץ ומספר ותכלית ואני מקבל אלהותך הקדושה עלי ועל בניי ועל בני בניי עד סוף כל הדורות.

...יוצרי ובוראי אני רוצה לילך לבית הכנסת להתפלל לפניך.

1. My words: "Master of the World," "Father in Heaven": (p. 447) See p. 188, chap. 6, above.

2. The Berditchever: (p. 447) הרחמן!

Chapter 26

The Hebrew expressions in this chapter are listed by chapter sections.

(26:1) ברוך השם

(26:2) תודות לאל, תהלה לאל

(26:6) להבדיל

(26:7) אם ירצה השם

(26:8) אם יגזור השם

(26:9) בעזרת השם

(26:10)

אם ירצה ה׳ ...אם יגזור ה׳ בחיים... עזרי מעם ה׳ עושה שמים וארץ...
בעזרתו יתברך שמו... בעזר ה׳... בסייעתא דשמיא יהי כן... כן היה רצונו,

(26:12) יְהִי כן... כן היה רצונו, כן רצה השם

(26:13) גם זו לטובה, כל מה דעביד רחמנא לטב עביד

(26:15) בלי נדר

יהיה כפרתך

(26:17) המקום ימלא חסרוני

(26:19) חס ושלום, רחמנא ליצלן

Chapter 27

Berachot 60b: (p. 527)

התכבדו מכובדים קדושים משרתי עליון תנו כבוד לאלהי ישראל הרפו ממני עד שאכנס ואעשה רצוני ואבא אליכם.

(Abaye:) (p. 527)

שמרוני שמרוני עזרוני עזרוני סמכוני סמכוני המתינו לי המתינו לי עד שאכנס ואצא, שכן דרכן של בני אדם.

Chapter 30

Kochavei Boker: (p. 569)

יהי רצון מלפניך ה׳ אלהי ואלהי אבותי שכשם שאני מטהר את עצמי למטה כן תטהר את נשמתי למעלה בנהר דינור.

Chapter 35

Berachot 60b: (p. 624)

ברוך אתה ה׳ אלהינו מלך העולם דיין האמת.

R. Arele Roth: (p. 626)

אני מאמין באמונה שלימה שזה הצער והיסורים שבא לי הוא בהשגחה פרטית מעם ה׳, והנני מקבל עלי באהבה, וכל זה בא לי מסבות עונותי הרבים, וצדיק אתה ה׳ על כל הבא עלי כי אמת עשית ואני הרשעתי, ויהי רצון שיהיו אלו היסורים לכפרה על עונותי הרבים, (ואם בעת רצון יאמר גם כן ולהקל בזה צער שכינת עוזינו כביכול וצערן של ישראל), והנה מצד הדין הייתי צריך לפרוט ולשוב ולהתוודות על החטא ועון שבסבתם בא לי אלו היסורים, אבל גלוי וידוע לפניך שאין אתי יודע עד מה, לכן יהי רצון מלפניך אבי שבשמים שתמחוק ותשריש החטא ועון ופשע שגרמו לי אלו היסורים, וימתקו כל הדינים מעלי ומעל כל ישראל, ויתהפכו כל הצירופים לטובה, וימשוך חסדים טובים ומגולים לנו ולכל בית ישראל עד עולם אמן.

"Master of the World!" etc. (p. 627)

רבונו של עולם! ישתבח שמך על כל החסדים טובים שעשית עמי ושאתה עושה עמי תמיד בכל יום בכל עת ובכל שעה. ובפרט בענין זה שאפילו רשע כמוני גרוע פחות ושפל נבזה ונמאס, שהרביתי כל כך לחטוא ולמרוד נגדך ועדיין לא עשיתי תשובה כמו שצריך. עם כל זה אבי שבשמים, אתה מחפש דרך ואופן זה להטיב עמי בדבר קל כזה — שאשמע עלבוני ואשתוק, שאינו באמת כלום וזה בלא יסורים. ועל ידיהם אתה ממרק כל עונותי הרבים, יותר מכל סיגופים קשים, ותצילני על ידי זה מכל מיני דינים קשים ומרים הראויים על מעשי בזה ובבא. ואהיה בזה רצוי ואהוב לפניך ותקבל תפילותי ואזכה לישועות רבות ולכל טוב סלה.

R. Arele Roth: (p. 628)

צדיק אתה ה׳ על כל הבא עלי כי אמת עשית, ואני מאמין באמונה שלימה שבאו לי אלו הבזיונות לטובתי — כדי שימתקו הדינים מעלי ויתכפרו עונותי מחטאתי לפני ה׳!

When *Erech Apayim* quotes this he says to say it in your native language (see p. 627). But in one of Reb Arele's other texts of this sort he says to memorize the language (see p. 626); and since the text is in Hebrew one would think that meant: say it in Hebrew. However, certainly either way is good.

Notes

Chapter 1-*D'vekut*

1. The Torah speaks of *d'vekut* with God, but the first Torah use of this root (דבק) is in Genesis 2:24 where we are told of how man cleaves to woman.

2. "The *tzaddikim*—they are the Chariot" (*Sifran Shel Tzaddikim*, Preface, p. 7).

3. See how he was "driven": 1 Kings 18:12, 46; 2 Kings 2:16; and how God directed all his movements: 1 Kings 17:2, 18:1.

4. 613 is traditionally given as the number of the *mitzvot*.

5. R. Yitzhak of Vorki:

> There are two deficiencies in a transgression: one is the transgression itself,—you have rebelled against the King of the Universe; two, that it darkens the eyes of a man so that he cannot see the Face of the Living King and cannot come close to Him. (*Eser Z'chuyot*, p. 28)

6. In this quote *Reshit Hochmah* speaks of three levels of attainment: in action, speech, and thought. It is one level to separate from the things of this world, its pleasures and possessions, in action, and to act only from spiritual motives, doing what is according to the will of God. It is a higher level to separate from speaking about this world (except when necessary). It is a sign of a certain spiritual level in a person when you see that he only talks about spiritual things and about God. You never hear him converse about worldly things except when absolutely necessary. The final level is to think of nothing but matters of the spiritual world, about God and what is associated with God; then the person is fully absorbed into spirituality and is in the spiritual world.

7. We learn from *Kitzur Shnei Luchot ha-Brit* that there are two parts to the Garden of Eden, Upper and Lower. The Lower part is the "Garden," the Upper part is the "Eden." In other words, only when you serve God, not just continually but with deep love, do you receive the delight from your service (Sh'ar ha-Otiyot, Ot Kuf, Kedushah, p. 45; Sh'ar ha-Mitzvot, p. 233).

8. The grandson of Rabbi Abraham of Slonim quoted previously and seemingly commenting on his grandfather's words.

9. The Shells are also the illusionary screens and barriers of material reality which seem to separate us from the presence of God. See the parable of the Baal Shem Tov in "Prayer," 5:1:19.

10. Rabbi Pinhas of Koretz (using a traditional metaphor):

> All the created world is like a snail's shell, for its garment is part of itself. Thus, the world is the Holy One, blessed be He. (*Likkutim mi-Rabbi Pinhas mi-Koretz*, #94)

> Our Rabbi Dov of Mezritch, of blessed memory, taught how the fear of God, blessed be He, should be on our faces so that we do not sin. His words about this are among the essential principles of Hasidism as established by the Besht, of blessed memory . . . We are to recognize and see, eye to eye, the reality of Godliness, blessed and exalted be His name, for the whole earth is full of His glory and there is no place where He is not. For in each and every thing there is the Divine life-energy of the Creator, blessed be He, which has descended and flowed down from world to world until it reaches this lowest world. It is known that there is no thing existing in the world in which there is no life-energy; even in the most material of things like stones and other inanimate objects there is some Divine vitality. Except for the life-energy that is in them, without a doubt they would be nothing and nonexistent. It is only due to that life-force within them that they exist according to the form we see before our eyes. This life-energy within each thing is also the life-energy from the Creator, blessed be His name, which has descended from the upper to the lower worlds, from world to world, to the farthest reaches of all the worlds. For all the worlds are nothing but that which comes from the life-energy of our Creator and Former and Maker, blessed is He and blessed is His name.
>
> Not only is this true of things that have physical substance, but of things that have form alone, such as taste and smell and appearance, and also moods and emotions, like love and fear, etc.—they, too, are from God and there is nothing in the world that has not its counterparts in innumerable higher worlds which are the root and the life of what is here below. . . .
>
> But to know all this with your mind alone is not sufficient to develop from it a true fear of God, blessed be He. It is not enough to reflect intellectually that there is no place where He is not. We must develop an actual sense-awareness and see this reality with our actual eyes—like the sense of sight, where the eye sees everything that appears before it and the vision is not within our volitional control, for as soon as something appears before our eyes we see it without delay. In this exact way should you have this spiritual vision and recognition established, so that as soon as something appears before you, you will see the Divine vitality of that thing and how it is an emanation from the life-energy of God, blessed be His name. And you should know that this awareness and instantaneous recognition is the power of knowledge (*daat*) that is in a man. In truth, *daat* is awareness . . . and you should be aware, in each and

every thing you see, of the life-energy of the Creator of all the worlds, for the whole earth is full of His glory and there is no place where He is not. . . .

When a person strives for this and reaches this level, certainly he will be in awe and fear of God, blessed be He, for God is always before him and he will be quaking and trembling before Him, and he will be lowly and humble and will give thanks to God, blessed be He, for His great mercy in drawing him, and all of Israel, close to His service, blessed be His name.

Whoever has a brain in his head will see the great difference between someone who spends his time meditating on the greatness of the Creator of all the worlds through intellectual means alone, and someone who accustoms himself to perceive the spiritual reality through sense-recognition—as we have explained—to recognize in each and every thing that he sees the Godly power that is within it. In this way each and every thing he sees and that appears before his eyes, whether good or evil, he will be able to find the Divine vitality hidden within it. And this is the meaning of "Know Him in all your ways" in terms of knowledge: that you have this power of recognition. (*Seder ha-Dorot ha-Hadash*, p. 27)

By emphasizing the hiddenness of the life-energy and its descent from world to world, this quote loses some of the force of its point—the *immediacy* of the sense-perception of Divine vitality. The emphasis on fear (rather than love) differentiates it from some other quotes on this matter.

11. See "Prayer," 5:2:4 and "Eating and the Holy Meal," 10:7.

12. In *Pesikta Rabbati*, chap. 1, this verse is understood as speaking of both seeing the *Shechinah* and also being seen by Her. So too was Deuteronomy 16:16 understood in this double sense. See the second quote from *Sefer Haredim* in "Meditation," 17:7.

13. See pp. 17–18 for the quote of the Besht from *Midrash Ribash Tov* and the story from *Ikkarei Emunah* of the Besht as a boy. From these we can see that the quote here about the Light of the *Shechinah* "dwelling with you" alludes to an awareness of God's presence and the vision of His light.

14. In this quote even the yearning for *d'vekut* is called *d'vekut* and is said to be sweet. For *d'vekut* is not only the actual "cleaving," but also the yearning to cleave to God. Love is not only being together with the beloved, but yearning to be with him/her when separated.

15. These verses are, respectively, from Psalm 63:2, the song *Anim Zemirot* (*Shabbat* Morning Service), and Isaiah 26:9.

16. *Reshit Hochmah* quotes *Hovot ha-Levavot* here, but differently than in our version. I have combined the two versions in my translation.

17. There are exceptions, however. *Tefillin* often were worn when going from the house to the synagogue in the morning. In *Or Yisrael* (p. 111), about Rabbi Israel Salanter, there is mention of a hidden *tzaddik* who "worked as a sawyer, but people became aware that he was wearing *tefillin* the whole day [concealed under his clothing], and his lips were always moving [whispering holy words]." Another story, in *Midor Dor* (vol. 1, #634) tells about the time the Vilna Gaon was traveling incognito, in "exile" with the *Shechinah*. Once, when he had got a lift on a wagon, it was very hot and he took off his coat, and it was seen that he

had on *tefillin* underneath. Then, when the coachman took a nap, the Vilna Gaon took over the reins and drove the horses, with his *tefillin* on. Thus, it seems that there were hidden *tzaddikim* who did wear *tefillin* the whole day, but under their clothing while working.

18. Rabbi Nachman's saying (p. 26) that *tefillin* symbolize *d'vekut*, and that a person should continually "examine" himself to see if he has *d'vekut*, alludes to the custom of continually touching the *tefillin*. The word פשפש translated as "examine," more literally means "to touch again and again," every moment, and is the word used about this practice with the *tefillin*.

Chapter 2–Remembrance of God

1. Literally, "for things of the World to Come."
2. See "Repentance," 14:5 for more about this practice.
3. See "Sight," 25:10 about this practice.
4. For stories illustrating this teaching, see "Repentance," 14:6 and "Speech," 23:2:5:4.
5. At the beginning of this chapter we spoke of the teaching that the standard of action is to do those things that bring us to *d'vekut*. We are to refrain from doing anything that would disrupt our God-consciousness. There is a variation on this theme, where one does that which allows him to keep the four-letter Name of God before his eyes, that ability being an indicator of his *d'vekut*. In a story about Rabbi Zusya of Hanipol we are told that: "He was once on the road traveling, and he came to a fork in the road and did not know which way to go. So he looked to see in which of the two ways the name Havaya was before him, and that was the way he went" (*Zichron l'Rishonim*, p. 13, note 6, quoting *Daat Moshe*). The source of this practice is in *Sefer Haredim*, chap. 66, #135. There it is said that a person always has two ways before him, that of God and that of the evil inclination. He should open the eyes of his mind and see God and the four letters of His Name before him, and go *that* way with fear and trembling and holiness.
6. According to *halacha*, these improvised blessings, if said in the form of a blessing, should be without mention of God's name or kingdom. Therefore do not say "Blessed are You, O *Lord our God, King of the Universe*, who . . . ," but "Blessed are *You*, who . . ."
7. This comment was made specifically about the morning blessings, but its application is general.
8. This might also be translated, "and if he were to place the Name before his eyes, as if God were actually before him."
9. See "Afflictions" (35) about this.
10. Compare *Mechilta d'Rabbi Shimon Bar Yochai*, Beshallach, 16:4.
11. See "Pious Phrases" (26) for a discussion of these various expressions.
12. The Arizal and other holy men ordained that one should say before every *mitzvah*

> [the commonly used kabbalistic stated intention] "For the sake of the unification of the Holy One, blessed be He, and His *Shechinah*," because this is like a blessing. . . . But since (for example) after making the blessing on Torah study in the morning, one is not permitted halachically to keep repeating it throughout the day each time one studies, they ordained that, instead, one should say, "For the sake of the unification of the Holy One, blessed be He, and His *Shechinah*." (*Or ha-Ganuz l'Tzaddikim*, p. 46)

13. For more about general and specific stated intentions, see "*Mitzvot*," 11:6–8.

14. A person on the highest level immediately feels the deprivation of joy connected with forgetfulness of God. See the quote from *Likkutim Yekarim* on p. 15 in the text. See also "Prayer," 5:4:7 about the use of sighing and groaning when you feel yourself separated from God.

15. The point here is that what the farmer does forget can, according to the Torah, be taken by the poor. But a large quantity is exceptional, since it is assumed that the farmer might forget it for a short while, but he will certainly remember it later. So it is *not* considered abandoned and available for the poor to take.

16. See "Individual Practices," 39:24.

Chapter 3–Ways in Attainment

1. The following quote applies this principle of alternating activities to the matter of Torah studies:

> You should have many different fixed sessions in your daily schedule of Torah learning, and not concentrate too much in one area or on one thing, lest it become burdensome. Rather, learn many different kinds of things. (*Darkei Yesharim*, p. 8)

2. See "Tiredness," 28:3.

3. See "Eating and the Holy Meal," 10:14 about lifting up the holy sparks. Rabbi Elimelech's own attainment of this spiritual level appears in a story in which, after his death, the Seer of Lublin, one of his great disciples, asked another disciple, Rabbi Elhanan Plentscher, to what extent he knew Rabbi Elimelech.

> "I know that all of his involvement in this world was 1 out of 100." The Seer answered him, "If that is what you say, then you did not know him at all, because even that 1 was 99 parts out of 100 in the Upper World." (*Ha-Hozeh mi-Lublin*, p. 119)

4. Rabbi Abraham of Slonim says:

> The way of service of householders [those who cannot devote all their time to Torah and to God] should be in the manner hinted at in the verse: "half of them were doing the work, and half of them had their spears in their hands" [Nehemiah 4:10]. (*Torat Avot*, p. 198, #259)

Perhaps the intention here is to teach that householders should support and protect those who devote themselves to religious matters full-time. This suggested to me the use of the following verse (Nehemiah 4:11) for a similar point, and perhaps Rabbi Abraham also had that in mind. The text in *Torat Avot* gives Nehemiah 4:15, but 4:10 is the true reference.

5. The original here is literally: "Blessed is *the name of* His glorious kingdom"—but this use of "the name" is idiomatic in the Hebrew of the time when this was formulated and has no meaning at all in English.

6. In the text here, Rabbi Simha Bunim of Pshischa reports an interpretative comment of Rabbi Abraham the Angel on the tradition about Hanoch, a tradition referred to by many sixteenth-century kabbalists.

7. See "Work," 7:11.

8. See "Eating and the Holy Meal," 10:7.

9. These thoughts are based on the teachings found in *Ha-Rebbe Reb Tzvi Elimelech mi-Dinov*, I, pp. 211–212.

10. [Compare]: "You know my sitting down and my rising up" (Psalm 139)—There is no place where He is not. If so, when a person wants to change his posture, from standing to sitting or the reverse, or any other way, how can he do so? Does not His Glory fill the earth? Is not the *Shechinah* resting where he wants to sit or stand? So it is as if he wanted, God forbid, to push the *Shechinah* aside so that there would be room for him. Therefore, whenever a person wants to sit or stand he has to ask permission from God, blessed be He; for if not, it is as if he is pushing aside the feet of the *Shechinah*, like a man who does not get permission before entering the king's palace. And this is what King David, peace be upon him, said: "You know my sitting and standing"—that is, "Without taking permission, I never sat or stood up from my place." (Rabbi Yehoshuah of Belz, *Sefer ha-Hasidut mi-Torat Belz*, vol. 1, p. 63)

11. The Mishnah (*Berachot* 5:1) says that while praying: "Even if the king greets him he should not [interrupt his prayer and] return the greeting; and even if a snake winds itself around his leg he should not pause." The Talmud has two stories about hasidim, illustrating both of these teachings. Here is one of them:

A certain hasid was once praying by the roadside when a Roman officer came by and greeted him, and he did not return the greeting. So the officer waited for him until he had finished his prayer and then said to him, "Fool that you are! Is it not written in your own Torah: 'Only take heed to yourself and keep your soul diligently' (Deuteronomy 4:9)? And it is also written, 'Take therefore good heed of your souls' (Deuteronomy 4:15). When I greeted you, why did you not return my greeting? If I had cut off your head with my sword, who would have demanded satisfaction of your blood from me?"

The hasid replied to him, "Be patient and I will explain everything to you. If," he went on, "you were standing before an earthly king and your friend came and gave you a greeting, would you return it?" "No," he replied. He then said to him, "But if you would behave that way when standing before an earthly king who is here today and tomorrow in the grave, how much more so I, when I was standing before the Supreme King of kings, the Holy One, blessed be He, who is for all eternity."

Hearing this and understanding the truth of what was said, the Roman officer accepted the explanation, and the hasid returned to his home in peace. (*Berachot* 32b)

For the other story, see *Berachot* 9a about Rabbi Hanina ben Dosa.

12. The rabbi suddenly became aware of his own spiritual reality. This paral-

lels in a way the story in Chapter 2, p. 31 where Rabbi Eleazar of Koznitz saw as a goose the young man who had been immersed in his meal.

13. The Besht, however, taught that you are not to expel these thoughts but, if possible, try to elevate them. For example, if a thought of a low love like sex comes to you while praying, by reflection you should turn yourself to love of God.

14. The anguish of the Besht's grandson at traveling (and being forced to decrease his Torah study) is a typically *misnagid* attitude (and certainly holy). But the Besht's hasidic way was to get out into the world, and he often traveled, this being essential for bringing the new light of Hasidism to the people. God, according to the Baal Shem Tov, wants to be served in many ways, and in all your ways you should know Him and have *d'vekut.*

> He taught: When a man is traveling and cannot pray and study Torah as he is accustomed to . . . he should not trouble himself about this, for God wants us to serve Him in many different ways [and He has put us in this situation]. (*Tzavaat ha-Ribash*, p. 2)

15. There is no hard and fast line separating Torah meditation on Torah concepts and what we are calling meditation. The difference might be expressed by saying that in the former, even when there is extended and deep contemplation, it is on Torah and the focus is on knowledge, although the point may be to use that knowledge to transform your behavior. In the latter, meditation is directly on spiritual realities, and its primary purpose is to lead to *d'vekut* and immediate God-awareness.

16. As in the quote from *Darkei Yesharim* (note 1).

17. See, for example, the quote from Rabbi Meshullam Feibush of Zabrizha on p. 23.

18. See the quotes from the Peasetzna Rebbe on pp. 22–23 and 67.

19. See "Being a Son or Daughter of God," and particularly the quote from *Beit Middot* (p. 24) on p. 21.

20. See "Torah," 5:18:3 for the extensive quote from *Or ha-Ganuz l'Tzaddikim*, with the two parables of the fish in the sea and the drop of water in the ocean.

21. Unfortunately, the traditions particular to hasidic women's spirituality are hidden. I hope that some women will soon take on the essential task of bringing them to light.

Chapter 4–Waking and Beginning the Day

1. See *Yesod v'Shoresh ha-Avodah*, Gate 2, chap. 4, p. 29.

2. This list has, in all, nineteen items. After the first six, which I have quoted, they are that we are to remember (7) the Exodus from Egypt, (8) Amalek, (9) the Giving of the Torah, (10) *Shabbat*, (11) what happened to Miriam, (12) that there is no other God, (13) and (14) not to covet or envy, (15) not to forget God, (16) not to forget the scene at Mount Sinai, (17) not to forget what Amalek did, and to take revenge; and (18) and (19) not to hate a Jew, and to love every Jew.

Compare the list on p. 28 from *Sefer Haredim*, which gives six things, basically the same as the first six of the larger list here.

3. This is condensed and adapted slightly, changing the medieval concept of the *galgalim*, the conscious celestial spheres, to the stars, etc.

4. Rabbi Tzvi Elimelech of Dinov begins his *Hanhagot Adam* this way:

> When you wake up . . . do not lie there in laziness . . . but stir yourself to begin the service of your Creator, who has returned to you your soul and life-spirit—so that you give Him pleasure. How good is our lot that He took us for His servants.

If we are happy that He took us for His servants, how much more so that we are His children. As children we should want to give our Father in Heaven *nahas*, pleasure from us.

5. After leaving the bathroom in the morning, one is to say the blessings (four) on the Torah. (See the beginning of the Morning Service in the Siddur.) The latter two speak of how God chose us and gave us the Torah. The Tur associates this with Mount Sinai:

> "Blessed art Thou, O Lord, etc. who hast chosen us, etc. Blessed art Thou, O Lord, who givest the Torah"—you should think when saying this of the scene at Mount Sinai, that God chose us and brought us close [to Him], at the foot of the mount, and let us hear His words out of the fire. (As quoted in *Yesod v'Shoresh ha-Avodah*, Gate 2, chap. 4, p. 30)

One could, then, do this visualization after leaving the bathroom, and in conjunction with the Torah blessings.

6. Rabbi Nachman of Bratzlav would speak to each of his limbs, to persuade them to join in his spiritual plans.

7. The blessing about washing the face has been moved up from its place in the Talmud series. The blessing about "strength to the weary" is in the Siddur, but not the direction for saying it, which is mine.

Before going to the bathroom and removing the uncleanness from within, we are not permitted to mention God's name or His kingdom in blessings. So note that these blessings as recorded in the Talmud do not have "Blessed are You, O *Lord our God, King of the Universe* . . ." as in the Siddur, where they are written as said in the synagogue (after having gone to the bathroom earlier).

8. See "Service of the Imagination," 19:12:1, for a suggestion about the context of this story.

9. These words explain the *Sh'ma*: "The Lord is *our* God"—I am His and He is mine; "the Lord is One"—God is One, Unique, etc.

10. The Hebrew is "Forke, Forke!" referring to his last name. But in English translation this makes less sense, so I translated it as "David, David!"

11. See "Sleep and Before Sleep," 29:1:9. Some do, and say this same thing before sleep at the *mezuzah* of the bedroom.

12. This prayer is connected with going out the door in *Nahalat Avot*, p. 13a.

Chapter 5-Prayer—The Service of the Heart

1. See the similar statement made about the Besht's use of the *mikveh* in "Men's *Mikveh*," 30:2.

2. Rabbi Aaron of Zhitomir said that:

> When you go to appear before a king, you have to give thought to what and how to speak to him. So must you do before prayer. The preparation for prayer should, by rights, take more time than the prayer itself; but unfortunately, most of us do not have the mental ability or the energy for this, so we rely on the *tzaddikim* of the generation who rise in the middle of the night and make preparations for the Morning Prayer—like my own master, our lord and teacher and rabbi, the holy *gaon*, may his merit protect us, Rabbi Levi Yitzhak of Berditchev. (*Tiferet Beit Levi*, p. 8)

3. See "*Shabbat*," 18:2:1:1 about burning incense before *Shabbat* to give the room a pleasant scent.

4. See *Berachot* 60b: "When you put on your belt (or girdle), say: 'Blessed is He who girds Israel with strength.' When you arrange your head-covering [turban], say: 'Blessed is He who crowns Israel with glory.'"

5. Perhaps the motive for shoelessness was to show reverence for the synagogue. When God first appeared to Moses on Mount Sinai in the burning bush, He said to him, "Put your shoes from off your feet, for the place on which you stand is holy ground" (Exodus 3:5). The same was said to Joshua (in Joshua 5:15). The priests in the Temple wore no shoes. And the synagogue is a "Temple in miniature."

6. About "meditative smoking" among the hasidim, see *Hasidic Prayer*, Louis Jacobs, pp. 48–49.

7. See the fuller quote in Chapter 2, p. 35.

8. See the teaching of the Maggid of Mezritch about how the pleasure God receives from our actions is the "sweet savour of an offering made by fire"—from our fervor in its doing (in "Eating and the Holy Meal," 10:14).

9. Rabbi Yitzhak of Drobitch taught that we are not to wait until *Erev Yom Kippur*, but should forgive twice a day—once before sleep and once before dawn. He connects this with the two daily sacrifices in the Temple (on which the daily prayers are based) (*Mazkeret Shem ha-Gedolim*, p. 5). See the story about him fulfilling this teaching in "Sleep and Before Sleep," 29:1:3:2:2.

10. Traditionally, God's light was also thought of as shining above the head, as in Job 29:3: "When His candle shone [*hilo*] above my head." This is the origin of the halo pictured around the head of a holy person. The concept of a man as a candle with the light of the *Shechinah* as the flame above his head is in the *Zohar* (see *Sefer Haredim*, chap. 3, where this matter is discussed at some length, for the sources). The head is the residence of the brain, the site of consciousness, and, according to the Kabbalah, part of the soul is within the body, but part extends without and above. It is also true that the soul is a part of the *Shechinah*. So it is natural to think of the soul as extending above the head and, in a holy person, illumined (the halo). This matter is also explained at the end of the first part of

the *Tanya*, by Rabbi Shneur Zalman of Ladi, at the very end of the last chapter (53). Perhaps, combining this concept with the other, that God's light is everywhere, the practice was developed of concentrating first on the light of the *Shechinah* above the head, and then thinking of it as flowing around you and out.

11. Compare this to the prayer before sleep about the angel Uriel (the Light of God) being before you, while the *Shechinah* is above you. See also *Pirke d'Rabbi Eliezer*, chap. 4.

12. See the story in *Niflaot ha-Rebbe*, p. 27, #40, about how upset Rabbi Elimelech of Lizensk was when he once interrupted his prayers. See chap. 3, note 8 for Mishnah and Talmud traditions and teaching about this. A story tells about the father of Rabbi Tzvi Elimelech of Dinov:

> For a certain period, the meager livelihood of Reb Pesah was derived from one barrel of liquor which he owned. Once there developed a crack in the edge of the barrel and the liquor began to leak out. His wife, discovering this, ran to tell her husband, who was in the middle of prayer, so that he would act quickly to stop this loss of the lone source of their livelihood. But Reb Pesah, whose way was to pray slowly and with great *kavvanah*, paid no heed to this matter about which she told him, and said, "*Nu, nu*," to indicate to her that he could not interrupt his prayer. When he finished praying, the barrel was already completely empty and all its contents gone to waste. (*Rebbe Reb Tzvi Elimelech mi-Dinov*, p. 16)

13. The reference to this practice comes in the context of an objection to it, and the note says:

> I heard it said in the name of Rabbi Yehoshuah of Belz that for a simple person such a practice is accounted as a forbidden interruption of prayer.

But people on an advanced spiritual level are permitted, and, indeed, this practice was approved by other *rebbes* without such restrictions. See the story about the Kotzker Rebbe on p. 319 and also the parallel story about Rabbi Eleazar, the son of Rabbi Elimelech of Lizensk, in "Eating and the Holy Meal," 10:7 where in each case one rabbi approved while another felt that such was only acceptable for a person who was on the level of a "son."

14. See the stories about the Besht in *Kahal Hasidim he-Hadash*, p. 15, #26, and about the Seer of Lublin in *Niflaot ha-Rebbe*, p. 57, #145.

15. Cf. *Kitzur Shnei Luchot ha-Brit*, Inyanei Tefillah, beginning.

> 16. When you close your eyes [and pray from memory] you can achieve greater *kavvanah*. (*Nahalat Avot*, p. 13b)

17. For a parallel quote from Rabbi Elimelech of Lizensk, see "Service of the Imagination," 19:7. From the comparison with the topic and language of Rabbi Elimelech's *Tzetl Katan*, #1 it is clear that the intention here is to use your imagination to picture the scene, identifying yourself with Isaac.

18. No source is given for this quote in *Encyclopedia Judaica*.

19. Unclear. Either the *mitzvot* done previously, where one separated oneself from materiality, or the *mitzvot* involved in praying.

20. One might wonder—if one loses body-consciousness during the high point of prayer during the *Shemoneh Esreh*, how, then, does one bow at the specified times? However, the essence of *hitpashtut ha-gashmiyut* is that one is fully concentrated on what one is doing, on praying, and not aware of the outside physical world or of anything material, even one's own body. One can then still control the body to move it when necessary, or even selectively allow the senses to function, particularly when this is for the very matter of one's concentration, the requirements of prayer.

21. Where a man's mind and thought reaches, there all of him is. (*Darkei Tzedek*, p. 14, #59)

22. Some sources seem to speak of soul-ascent to the Upper Worlds as an imaginative experience of leaving the body and ascending upward. Other texts, however, say, "Where a man thinks, there he is," meaning that just by thinking about being there you are there, without any mention of an "ascent." In general, it seems that the idea of imagining oneself in heaven or the Garden of Eden was developed in different ways depending on the inclinations of the people involved.

23. *Beit Avraham*, #13.

24. Where I translated "all the limbs" the Hebrew has the traditional number of 248 "limbs" (including all organs of the body).

25. Abaye and Rava both did become famous rabbis; they are often associated as a pair, their disagreements constituting a major part of the Talmud.

26. For example, *Sefer Haredim*, chap. 16, #72, #73.

27. Note that Rabbi Akiba kneels as well as prostrates himself. There is no reason why this should not be used in Jewish private prayer, except, perhaps, if it has been "spoiled" by association with Christian religious practice.

28. Prostration was the "outside"; but the "inside" was *d'vekut* and *hitpashtut ha-gashmiyut*. At this time, as we can determine from Rabbi Moshe's own teaching about the *Sh'ma*, he attained a state of complete unity, and experienced the bliss of the World to Come (*Tefillah l'Moshe*, 29:11, quoted in *Ha-Gaon ha-Kadosh Baal Yismach Moshe*, p. 187, note 3). A story tells how:

> "Once, when his grandson, the [author of the] *Yetiv Lev*, realized that it had already been quiet for a very long time in the room where the *rebbe* was praying *Shaharit*, he opened the door and was startled to see the *rebbe* lying on the floor in a faint [he thought], and the head-*tefillin* were almost on the ground. When he felt no heartbeat he ran for a doctor who began to massage his chest. Immediately the *rebbe* came to and called out loudly "*echad*!" [the last word of the *Sh'ma*]. Then they realized to what extent *hitpashtut ha-gashmiyut* reached. (p. 188)

29. *Kitzur Shnei Luchot ha-Brit* says the same and says this is particularly true of the confession in prayer:

> Especially when you make a confession in prayer and beg for forgiveness and pardon, of course you should cry and supplicate. But if sometimes you cannot actually cry, you should still pray with a low and broken voice as if you were crying. (*Hanhagat ha-Tefillah*, p. 128)

30. In the Talmud (*Berachot* 32b) two different verses are given for the sitting meditation before and after prayer. The one for after the prayer is Psalm 140:14, which has "the righteous will sit in Your presence"—literally "with Your face" ישבו ישרים את פניך. This certainly is the source of the Maharsha's comment.

Chapter 6–The Synagogue and the Synagogue Service

1. See *Berachot* 3a for both of these aspects.
2. These words, from "my soul is love-sick," are from the beautiful hymn *Yedid Nefesh*. It is good to sing this hymn to plead with God that He reveal the light of His Presence to you.
3. For example, *Or Tzaddikim* (p. 5b) instructs you to say Psalm 55:15 when you get to the courtyard of the synagogue. The Rabbi of Alesk said it that way also. *Kitzur Shnei Luchot ha-Brit* (Inyanei Tefillah and immediately preceding, p. 111), however, instructs you to say this verse when you enter the synagogue. For still another version of what to say when coming to the synagogue and entering, see *Seder ha-Yom*, p. 4b.
4. As one can see (in 6:10) the tradition in *Shemen ha-Tov* at least has Rabbi Meir'l circling the synagogue, not the *bimah*. In *Rabbeinu ha-Kodesh mi-Tzanz*, I, p. 219, moreover, there is uncertainty about the custom of the Tzanzer, some saying that he circled not the *bimah*, but the dinner table three times before the meal (another hasidic custom). This latter tradition is supported by the otherwise unusual reference in *Mekor Hayim* about when he came to the *Beit Midrash* to make the *kiddush* and eat with the hasidim. And in *Or Tzaddikim* one is told to circle the *bimah* seven times, but just once on *Shabbat*. The Tzanzer is said to have circled seven times on *Shabbat*. But all these are details, and all of the various customs are traditional, regardless of exactly what the Tzanzer did.
5. Turai Zahav, *Orach Hayim* 660.
6. See the continuation of this quote in "Loving and Honoring Our Fellow Men," 9:11.
7. It is traditional to connect the acceptance of love of neighbor before prayer with the joining of your prayers with all of Israel. For example:

> After you sit down in the synagogue, receive on yourself the positive *mitzvah* of "You shall love your neighbor as yourself" to love every Jew; and through this your prayer will be joined with the prayers of all the Congregation of Israel. (*Or Tzaddikim*, p. 20, #4; see the same from the Vorker Rebbe in *Ohel Yitzhak*, p. 20, #46, and in many other places).

The original source of this custom is from the Ari (see *Minhagei ha-Arizal*, p. 3a, #2). As these quotes seem to identify love of neighbor only with love of fellow Jews, and could thus be misunderstood, I preferred not to use them. For though we are to have a special love for our fellow Jews, love of neighbor is not restricted to Jews but applies to all people. Perhaps these words of Rabbi Elimelech of Lizensk put the matter in perspective:

> The *tzaddik* loves God and also every person in the world. As Rabbi Yohanan said, "No one ever preceded me in giving the blessing of peace as a greeting when I was walking outside in the marketplace, not even a gentile." . . . Though certainly not all loves are equal and the same, for the love for one of Israel and for a gentile are not the same. The love for another Jew is a perfect love, while the love for a gentile is less than perfect. (*Noam Elimelech*, Vayishlach, p. 15b)

We could also say that our love for other Jews is like the special love we have for our family. Certainly that does not and should not detract from our love for others who are not of our family.

8. See Isaiah 6 about God sitting on His Throne, His feet resting in the Temple. In general, God's Throne is in heaven, and His feet, as it were, rest in this world as His footstool.

9. These teachings about the *tzitzit* are general. I am applying them to the time in the synagogue, though in both sources the instructions come in sections about prayer and synagogue, so perhaps that was the intention there, too.

10. A *shtibel* is a small room used as a synagogue and also as a place for Torah study. The smallness of the space, as well as the smaller congregation, provides a more informal and more intimate setting for worship.

11. Though the psalm verse speaks of real personal adversaries, *Sefer ha-Yirah*, in quoting it, probably means the impersonal forces of evil.

Chapter 7–Work

1. This is evident from a parallel anecdote in the context.
2. A commentary on *Kulam Ahuvim* published with that book.

Chapter 8–Trust in God

1. As in the short prayer in *Berachot* 29, where the Maharsha says: "Since a man does not really know what is good for him . . . the prayer [to be spared from what is bad] ends with: 'and what is good in Your eyes (for those who fear You), do.'" Note that the Besht's teaching does not itself suggest that a prayer of this sort be said each time you make a request from God.

Chapter 9–Loving and Honoring Our Fellow Men

1. [When Rabbi Shmelke of Nikolsburg was asked:] "If you see someone who is wicked before God, how is it possible to love him?" he answered, "Are not the souls of all men parts of God from Above? Therefore, you should have compassion for God,

blessed be He, that His holy spark [within the man, his soul] is trapped by the [evil] Shells." (*Shemen ha-Tov*, p. 18, #53)

To make this more understandable we could say that knowing the inner reality of men as goodness and holiness, you should have mercy on the good side of a man when it is being stifled and choked by his wickedness.

2. My understanding of this is that you are to greet (first) people with whom you have some acquaintance, and also strangers in those situations where it is appropriate.

3. The intention here is that he called all Jews "brothers" and this was an expression of his love for Israel. However, note in the *midrash* (which follows in my text) that Jacob calls these men (not Jews) "brothers" even before he knows who they are.

4. לפי כוונות הלב הן הן הדברים.

5. See the story in "Pious Phrases," 26:12.

Chapter 10–Eating and the Holy Meal

1. Rabbi Elimelech of Lizensk was once at the house of a hasid of his in the town of Zitlin, and the hasidah [pious woman] of the house gave him supper that evening. Since they were very poor all she had to serve him was a humble porridge made of flour and water. Nevertheless, Rabbi Elimelech enjoyed the meal immensely, and after finishing one bowl, asked, "Is there perhaps enough for another bowl?" She gave it to him and he ate it, too, with pleasure. In Rabbi Elimelech's later years he did not even experience any taste at all in the food he ate [he was so divorced from materiality and bodily pleasures]—and yet once he said to his wife, "If only you would cook for me a meal like that which I had in Zitlin, then I would enjoy it." His wife traveled to Zitlin and asked that hasidah what she had made. She replied that she had cooked just flour and water to make a porridge, but that all the time it was cooking she had asked God that He put the taste of the Garden of Eden into the food, so that that holy *tzaddik* would enjoy it. (*Niflaot ha-Rebbe*, p. 28, #42)

2. The same story is told about the Seer of Lublin, in *Niflaot ha-Rebbe*, p. 8.

3. This is taken from Sh'ar ha-Otiyot, Ot Kuf, Kedushah b'inyanei ha-seudah.

4. *Kaf ha-Hayim*, p. 327, #55 discusses the same problem as *Reshit Hochmah*, that is, what to do if there are no poor people, and offers the same suggestion. But he just says to donate *tzedaka*—not mentioning the equivalent of what a full meal would cost.

5. Cf. *Darkei Tzedek*, p. 18.

6. See the important related quote from Rabbi Tzadok ha-Cohen in "Sex," 32:1:8:4.

7. Text corrected according to *Menorat Zahav*, p. 32.

8. Going to the *mikveh* is always associated with the related practice of hand washing, and in Hasidism immersion in the *mikveh* is a frequent part of the purification and preparation for prayer. But we are told:

> The holy *gaon*, Rabbi Mendel of Premishlan [a disciple of the Besht], may his merit protect us, would go to the *mikveh* before eating and not before prayer—for eating in holiness is a greater service of God than prayer. (*Mishnat Hasidim*, p. 279, #25)

9. This thought is developed from *Midrash ha-Gadol* on Leviticus 2:13.
10. In a related practice, Rabbi Abraham of Slonim said:

> When a Jew is eating, he should imagine to himself that he is eating at the table of a *tzaddik*. (*Torat Avot*, p. 242, #52)

Of course, hasidim are familiar with the holy scene and atmosphere when eating at the table of a *rebbe* and this will help them feel God's presence at their own table.

11. See the story in Chapter 2, p. 36 about how Rabbi Yitzhak of Drobitch would usually have the four-letter name of God visualized before his eyes. When eating (and probably at other times) he used the little plate for meditation.

12. See *Kedushat ha-Shulchan*, pp. 120, 129.

13. He called out to God this way in Yiddish and German, so we can use the language most familiar to us.

14. *Ohalei Shem*, p. 6, quoting *Divrei Elimelech*.

15. Rabbi Moshe Leib of Sassov was a disciple of Rabbi Shmelke of Nikolsburg (who, as we noted, reported the parable in the name of Rabbi Elimelech) and was also a disciple of Rabbi Elimelech himself.

16. See "Service of the Imagination," 19:12:1 and 19:12:2 where one can see that this teaching from Rabbi Moshe Leib directly relates to a teaching of Rabbi Elimelech found in his *Tzetl Katan*. There is also a possible relation here to Rabbi Elimelech's use of Deuteronomy 32:7 as quoted in the text: "*Ask* your father and He will *tell* you," meaning call out to God and hear His response.

17. The intention to offer the sacrifice to the fire seems to mean that the fire is understood as the Torah-designated way for the offering to be received—as if it were God's "mouth," so to speak. The significance of the intention to offer for the scent is that God does not eat; He enjoys the "scent," something hardly physical—something spiritual. What is "pleasing" to God is that His will is done in the offering of the sacrifice.

18. Conversing while eating can be dangerous and cause food to go down the windpipe, resulting in choking. It is not advisable, therefore, to talk at this time, even if you do hesitate and make an interruption before swallowing.

19. It is a method of the hasidic *rebbes*, as with Rabbi Elimelech, to instruct others by verbalizing self-criticism that really applies to those others. As he says in *Noam Elimelech*, Shemini, p. 49b, the *tzaddik* "always rebukes himself publicly and by this arouses thoughts of *tshuvah* in those who hear him."

20. The Besht's teaching here basically comes from *Reshit Hochmah*. See the quote from that book in 10:1:11.

21. When you eat, you act like a spiritual being and you treat the food as a spiritual entity. You act on the level of your soul, which is your holy spark, which is part of the *Shechinah*, and you join your soul with the "soul" of the food, which

is its holy spark. This is the "food" the soul "consumes" in eating, and which gives it pleasure.

22. In a soul-ascent the body is stationary and inert, while the soul leaves the body and ascends to the different heavens.

23. See note 21.

24. He goes on about how one who is not a *tzaddik* can only accomplish this by fasting, not through eating, which is a higher level.

25. See the *Midrash Shir ha-Shirim Zuta*, on 1:15, where this saying is applied particularly to the sacrifices. It is quoted in *Reshit Hochmah*, Sh'ar ha-Kedushah, p. 424, n. 207.

Chapter 11-*Mitzvot*

1. See Daniel 7:9, 10.

Chapter 14-Repentance—*Tshuvah*

1. The text explains that a sage is, in the tradition, considered to be on the "level" of *Shabbat* and, therefore, desecrating his holiness by making him do some work for you is similar to desecrating the Sabbath.

Chapter 15-Torah

1. The *rebbe* here was following the teaching of *Reshit Hochmah*, Sh'ar ha-Tshuvah, chap. 2, #24, and #25.

2. *Yesod v'Shoresh ha-Avodah*, Gate 6, chap. 5 discusses in detail different *kavvanot* for the different branches of Torah.

3. To make this declaration more usable by the majority who are not involved in Kabbalah, I have omitted two short phrases (see the ellipses in each case): (1) "to unify the name Yud He with Vav He in a complete unification"; and (2) "according to the teaching of Rabbi Shimon ben Yochai and Rabbi Eleazar, his son, and according to our master, Rabbi Yitzhak Luria Ashkenazi."

4. The light of the *Shechinah* is traditionally thought of as being above the head and next to the Divine soul that resides primarily within the brain (see the *Tanya*, chap. 35 and 53). The rabbis, in a teaching about humility and posture, said:

> Whoever walks fully upright, even for four *amot*, is as if pushing away the feet of the *Shechinah*, as it says, "The whole earth is full of His glory" (Isaiah 6). (*Berachot* 43)

The Maharsha comments on this: "For man is a chariot for the *Shechinah* above his head. . . ." For more about the light of the *Shechinah* above the head, see

Chapter 2, note 10. And for the source of this kind of meditation, see Gershom Scholem, *The Messianic Idea in Judaism*, pp. 207–208.

5. When you sit down to learn, it is good to think that you are not in this world, but in the Garden of Eden, in the presence of the *Shechinah*. (*Or Tzaddikim*, p. 23b, #12)

6. In understanding this quote, remember what was said about how seeing God everywhere and in everything that happens puts one in the Garden of Eden while in this world. See the related quote from the Maggid of Mezritch, Chapter 2, p. 30. That quote's ending (not given there) is: ". . . and with this you will easily be able to strip yourself of materiality during prayer."

7. This may be different, then, from the general instruction not to look elsewhere when studying Torah.

8. Or perhaps what is meant in the Maggid's quote is not a direct meditation on your surroundings, but a meditation on what is before your eyes (the book, for example), and your peripheral vision.

9. The Ziditchover mentions this in the context of his own opposition to this practice. "Havaya," which has the same four Hebrew letters as the four-letter Name of God (though arranged differently), is used for that Name.

10. The "throne" idea, the Throne of Glory, is that God is glorified by you, that He comes to rest (sits) on you when you are doing His will. Also, note that in the *Darkei Tzedek* quote the expression about making oneself a chariot for the *Shechinah* is a stated intention; in *Kav ha-Yashar* the parallel expression is part of a prayer. In my own suggestion (at the beginning of 15:23) I combine both forms.

11. This thought, in these approximate words, is repeated again and again at the beginning of Torah interpretations, in *Or ha-Ganuz l'Tzaddikim*, for example, and is found frequently in other hasidic books.

12. The Peasetzna Rebbe gives an extended example of this kind of Torah meditation in chaper 7 of *Hachsharat ha-Abrechim*.

13. These are kabbalistic images of having done damage in the spiritual world by cutting off the growth of what is good and holy.

Chapter 16–Psalms

1. Literally, the tractates *Negaim* and *Ohalot*.

2. It is probable that this illiterate wagon driver did not know the meaning of the words he was reciting, as in the story referred to in 16:7:4, where it says explicitly that the simple people did not know the meaning of the psalms they were chanting.

3. This is how the kabbalistic/hasidic scheme in *davvening* understands the function of *P'sukei d'Zimra* (the section of psalms, and mostly, psalm verses in the Morning Prayer Service): to subdue the negative spiritual forces before you can rise to higher levels with the *Sh'ma* and *Shemoneh Esreh*.

4. *Kerem Shlomo*, quoted in *Taamei ha-Minhagim*, p. 104.
5. The story continues that the Besht tells him that to rip out the very roots, he would have to become his disciple.

Chapter 17–Meditation

1. The Scriptural verse alluded to here is Lamentations 3:28: "Let him sit alone and in silence, for he has taken it upon him."

> 2. You should remind yourself to think always of God's exaltedness and greatness, of all the miracles and wonders from the days of old, so as to put an awareness of His exaltedness and greatness in your heart. (*Noam Elimelech*, Haazinu, p. 85b)

Even here the point is just that one should see God's miracles in everything; it is only that with the "great miracles," this is easy and everyone can see them.

> There are *tzaddikim* who are always in *d'vekut*, and they are always meditating on God's exaltedness and greatness, even when the Red Sea is not splitting in front of them. For even on the dry land they see His wonders, which are without limit, in everything that exists in the world. (*Noam Elimelech*, Likkutei Shoshana, p. 96a)

> 3. Chabad Chassidus [Hasidism], being largely devoted to the study of G–d, insists that intellectual achievement per se is inadequate. The mind must carry out its conclusions in the heart (the seat of the emotions, as the brain is the seat of the intellect), in the arousal of emotions indicated in the subject under study. For example, meditation on the greatness of the Almighty might lead to Fear . . . of Him. Recognition of His Providence might lead to love of Him. The emotions in turn must affect actual deeds, that one act in the light of his understanding and feelings, continuing the unbroken sequence of mind, heart and deed. (*On Learning Chassidus* [Lubavitch], Translator's Explanatory Notes, p. 9)

4. See "Prayer," 5:5:2.
5. See "Prayer," note 10, and "Torah," note 4.
6. See note 1 above.

Chapter 18–*Shabbat*

1. This is taken from *Midrash Talpiyot*, quoting *Totzaot Hayim*.
2. A hasidic story describes Rabbi Aaron of Karlin reciting the Song of Songs late *Shabbat* evening (*Sippurei Hasidim*, vol. 1, #70). So if you cannot say it earlier, say it later.
3. See the quote from the Rambam, Chapter 1, p. 5.
4. See a good example of this in the hasidic story in *Gevurat ha-Ari*, p. 13, #7.
5. It seems that this custom is behind the refrain of *Lecha Dodi*, written by Rabbi Moshe Cordovero: "Come my *friend* to greet the Bride, let us welcome the presence of the Sabbath." The refrain was also suggested by the words of Rabbi Hanina and Rabbi Yannai in *Shabbat* 119a.

6. See "Prayer," 5:2:9 about Rabbi Yitzhak Isaac of Ziditchov using a snuff-box on *Erev Shabbat* and smelling the scent of the Garden of Eden.

7. When the extra soul-power is lost at the end of *Shabbat* and there is a constriction of consciousness, we smell the spices at *Havdalah* to restore the soul and expand our consciousness at least somewhat (*Or ha-Shabbat*, p. 204, #5).

8. *Zemiroth*, Artscroll, pp. 62 and 140.

9. See Gershom Scholem, *On the Kabbalah and Its Symbolism*, p. 142.

10. In the story, Rabbi Koppel says that he learned this practice from his interpretation of a verse of a Sabbath table song.

Chapter 19–Service of the Imagination

1. I have coined the word audibilization (imagining sound) to parallel the use of visualization.

2. There is no suggestion in Rabbi Menahem Mendel's saying of anything about visualization or audibilization.

Chapter 20–Blessings

1. For a discussion on this kind of meditation, see the chapter on Meditation.

2. A similar story is told of Rabbi Abraham David of Butchatch in *Raza d'Uvda*, Sh'ar ha-Otiyot, p. 45, #4.

Chapter 21–Repetition of a Holy Sentence

1. See chapter 3, note 5.

2. At other times it is forbidden to recite the *Sh'ma* and then immediately repeat it.

3. Presumably this refers to the first paragraph of the *Sh'ma*, although it is not impossible that it is just the first verse.

4. There is another possible interpretation of this story which takes away its relevance for our discussion. The *Shulchan Aruch* (71–4) understands it to mean that the *Sh'ma* is not repeated continuously, but only at intervals if one is unable to sleep. However, the story in the Talmud says nothing about not being able to go to sleep.

5. *Yahid u'miyuhad* can also be translated as "single and unique." Sometimes the phrase is used that He is "*ehad, yahid u'miyuhad*"—"one, single and unique."

6. See *Yesod v'Shoresh ha-Avodah*, Gate 4, chap. 5, pp. 69–71.

7. The Aramaic for "of this time" is "*d'hai shata*."

8. *Yesod v'Shoresh ha-Avodah*, Gate 1, chap. 6, p. 13.

9. In *Yesod v'Shoresh ha-Avodah*, Gate 1, chap. 6, p. 14, he discusses this practice and indicates there the seven (Hebrew)-word line to be repeated mentally: "I believe with complete faith that You are single and unique" (or, "the One and Only One"—"*yahid u'miyuhad*").

Chapter 22–*Tzedaka* and *Gemilut Hasadim*— Charity and Kindness

1. The same teaching, in almost identical words, is quoted in the name of Rabbi David ha-Levi of Steppin in *Hanhagot Tzaddikim*, p. 56, #18.

Chapter 23–Speech

1. In a technical sense "unification" usually means a kabbalistic meditation on one of the letter configurations of the Tetragrammaton, or on configurations of such names with different vocalizations (*Encyclopedia Judaica*, Kabbalah, p. 630). But the term can also have a broader meaning, as I have indicated.

2. In a fanciful hasidic interpretation, the vowels of the word מדבר (mdbr) are changed, so that instead of the usual reading of "desert" (*midbar*), the word means "the speaker" (*m'dabair*). The verse, then, becomes: "A voice [of God] cries out from the person speaking to you: 'Clear the way of the Lord! [Repent!]'"

3. Literally: "lift up the [letter] *he* of God's name."

Chapter 24–Song and Dance

1. Psalms 103, 100, and 146.

2. See the remarkably similar real-life story about Rabbi Wasilski and his son in "Prayer," 5:1:18:3:2. Perhaps there is some nonevident connection that explains the astonishing similarity.

3. What is alluded to here is the kabbalistic unification of the Holy One, blessed be He, and His *Shechinah*, the "male" and "female" aspects of God. The Holy One is above in heaven (transcendent) and the *Shechinah* is God's power in this world (immanent). The soul is part of the *Shechinah*, and uniting the soul with God (in Divine service, such as by song) is uniting the Holy One, blessed be He, and His *Shechinah*. This is a Supernal "mating" or "marriage"; thus, the "marriage song" that the Peasetzna Rebbe mentions.

Chapter 25–Sight

1. Translated in Buber, *Tales of the Hasidim*, I, p. 243.

Chapter 26–Pious Phrases

1. It is possible that when the Maggid was doing this he was fulfilling the Talmud directive that when we are studying Torah and mention the names of the rabbis in connection with their various teachings, we should consider that we are in their very presence. See "Torah," 15:23.

2. Perhaps "with the living" is added here because God's "decree" often has a suggestion of judgment. The added clause counters that by emphasizing the wish that the decree be for life and good.

3. Elijah, who did not die but went up into heaven alive, appears on earth, often in different disguises.

4. See note 3.

5. Another version of this is found in *Or Yesharim*, p. 217, note 101. There, the poor man's key words are in Yiddish, "*Zol zeyn azoy*," with the same meaning as the Hebrew, "*Y'hi kain*," in the version I used: "So be it."

6. There is another aspect to this, however. There were holy people in those times who would wander around in the guise of beggars—hidden *tzaddikim*. Often they would have a rule not to ask anyone for their needs, but wait until something was offered. Rabbi Tzvi Elimelech of Dinov gives instructions about this and connects it with the teaching of the Talmud about the way of Elijah (who would accept gifts but not ask for them):

> Since he [the wanderer] sees that men on their own [without his asking] seek to take care of his needs, he then understands that this is the will of God, blessed be He. (*Ha-Rebbe Reb Tzvi Elimelech mi-Dinov*, vol. 2, p. 406)

7. This is according to the note in *Sefer Haredim*, Jerusalem, 1984.

Chapter 27–Bathroom

1. There is a similar story about the Holy Jew in *Niflaot ha-Yehudi*, Hosafot, p. 17.

2. See the commentary Shaarei Tshuvah on *Orach Hayim* here. This practice is also recommended in *Kitzur Shnei Luchot ha-Brit* (Inyanei Tefillin, p. 88) and in *Or Tzaddikim* (Amud ha-Tefillah, 3:2).

> 3. [Rabbi Pinhas of Koretz] explained that "guardian angels" are holy thoughts. (*Imrei Pinhas*, p. 175, #55)

4. This is a literal translation. Perhaps the meaning of the final line would be more fully comprehensible if expressed in a freer translation: ". . . who creates the wondrous mechanisms of our bodies, and keeps them functioning in amazing ways; and You heal them, when needed, through natural means or through Your miracles of healing."

5. The tradition does the same with the feeling of satisfaction after eating, transforming it by means of the after-blessing or the Grace After Meals.

Chapter 29–Sleep and Before Sleep

1. On the other hand, he says that:

> Sleep is good [if you are on a lower level] for after sleep you can more easily make a new beginning and spiritually arouse yourself after the confusion of foreign thoughts

and an absence of holy thoughts and Torah; for on waking you have the potential to start anew and be a "new creation."

2. The Tzanzer Rebbe once answered a rabbi who asked him how he could do with so little sleep, by saying that just as with learning Torah some can learn in a short time what takes others longer, so he is able to accomplish in two hours of sleep what others do in six (*Rabbeinu ha-Kodesh mi-Tzanz*, p. 209).

3. When he was a young man, the Holy Jew was asked by a *misnagid* why he went to the Seer of Lublin, and what he learned from him, since according to the estimation of the *misnagid* the Holy Jew was a greater Torah scholar than the Seer.

> The Holy Jew, of blessed memory, answered him, saying, "What I learned from my master, the Rebbe of Lublin, is that the moment I lie down in bed I fall asleep." (*Niflaot ha-Yehudi*, p. 47)

4. For an example see *Ohel Elimelech*, p. 68, #161.

5. Another motive can be that you want to do kindness to your tired body, just as you would have compassion on a tired animal. As it says in Proverbs 12:10, "A righteous man takes cognizance of the needs of his animal."

> O man! Do kindness and charity always. Even when . . . you go to sleep . . . you should intend to do kindness, as in the story about Hillel the Elder (Leviticus *Rabbah* 34-3), which is connected with the verse, "He who is being kind when he does good to himself, is truly a man of kindness (Proverbs 11:17)." (*Sefer Haredim*, chap. 67, #124)

In the story, Hillel was being kind to his body (by bathing it, and the like).

6. When you lie down to sleep, think that God created sleep for man so that his body will rest and renew its strength and be healthy for the service of his Creator. (*Lekach Tov*, p. 24, in *Sifrei Hanhagot v'Tzvaot v'Divrei Musar*)

7. It is a hasidic custom to put Rabbi Elimelech of Lizensk's book, *Noam Elimelech*, beneath the pillow of a pregnant woman as a *segulah*, a practice of mystical efficacy, here for a safe birth.

One could also put a large *tallit* below one's pillow. See *Toldot Menahem*, p. 103, about the use of priests' clothes in the Temple as pillows. One can put *tefillin*, if covered properly, near one's head (not under the pillow, however).

8. Note here the difficulty in justifying sleep, as we spoke about above.

9. In this section of his Testament, Rabbi Alexander Ziskind explains his continual use of the phrase "You are my Maker and Creator"—three words in Hebrew, *Yotzri u'Bori Ata*—to keep the remembrance of God always before him. Here he mentions his use of these few words when he became sleepy.

10. Rabbi Elimelech of Lizensk:

> This verse tells us that holiness and the Supernal Light should burn within us always and never go out. (*Noam Elimelech*, Tetzave, p. 44a)

11. For the references of these verses, see note 11 in Part One, Chapter 1.

12. Acording to the *halacha*, you have to wash your hands whenever you wake up from sleep.

13. Source not given.
14. קול לו קול אליו See *Yoma* 4a.
15. Rabbi Tzadok takes this sentence to mean (as indicated by my insertion of the word "sleeping" in brackets) that he is to be aware of God's presence even during sleep. Perhaps he came to this understanding because the next words in the text are: "When he wakes up from sleep, he should rise . . ."—as if what preceded was about when he was still asleep. Regardless, the text there seems to really mean that: "When lying on your bed [*still awake*] . . ." The point, however, is not so much how Rabbi Tzadok interprets a verse and arrives at his position, but what his position about sleep is.

Chapter 30–Men's *Mikveh*

1. See the *midrash* about Adam's repentance in *Pirke d'Rabbi Eliezer*, chap. 20; see also, *Kitzur Shnei Luchot ha-Brit*, Inyanei tevilah b'Erev Shabbat.
2. Cf. *Kitzur Shnei Luchot ha-Brit*, Inyanei tevilah b'Erev Shabbat.
3. Cf. *Kitzur Shnei Luchot ha-Brit*, Inyanei tevilah b'Erev Shabbat.
4. Sources for this are *Kitzur Shnei Luchot ha-Brit* and *Kaf ha-Hayim*; see references below, in the text.
5. This story ends that the Kotzker Rebbe became aware of this through the holy spirit and, it seems, disapproved; why is not clear.

Chapter 31–*Tikkun Hatzot*— The Midnight Service and Vigil

1. This is also in the Prayer Book of the Ari as quoted in *Seder Tikkun Hatzot* p. 83; that seems to be the source of Rabbi Tzvi Hirsh's words.
2. The two *Tikkuns* are, in their character, the opposite of what is said in the Besht story about the two sisters. *Tikkun Rachel* is mournful and *Tikkun Leah* is happier—while of the two sisters, Leah cried and Rachel is joyful. It would seem, if my understanding of the teaching of the story is correct, that the application is not to *Tikkun Leah* at all, but only to *Tikkun Rachel*: that, though one is to recite it with crying and lamentation, one is to have a deeper joy, knowing that the *Shechinah* is with us.
3. According to some traditions, the Messiah is in the Garden of Eden (heaven), and suffers at the delay of the Redemption (at which time he will come to earth).

Chapter 32–Sex

1. The explanatory comment in parentheses is added by *SKv'Tz*.
2. See *SKv'Tz*, p. 25b, #9.
3. See "Eating and the Holy Meal," 10:1:8:1:3.

4. The thought of having a child who will be a child of God comes from the *Zohar*, as quoted in *SKv'Tz*, p. 11a, #16. *Pele Yoatz*, Ot Zivug, has this prayer for before sex:

> Merciful Father, give me holy children, who will be like Abraham, Isaac, and Jacob, etc., and this Rabbi and that Rabbi" (*SKv'Tz*, chap. 4, #7, p. 20b).

This suggested the similar motif in the prayer I composed. See *SKv'Tz*, chap. 4, pp. 21–23 for other stated intentions and prayers.

5. In the Eshkol edition (Jerusalem).

6. See "Eating and the Holy Meal," very end.

Chapter 33–Talking to God and Being Alone with God—*Hitbodedut*

1. This is found in the back of the booklet, *Seder Tikkun Hatzot*.

Chapter 34–The Service of Praise

1. I have changed the position of this paragraph slightly to make the excerpts from Rabbi Ziskind more readable.

Chapter 35–Afflictions

1. The rabbis say that "with *all* your heart" means to use your good *and* bad inclinations in the service of God. The bad inclination represents your selfish desires, lusts, etc.

2. For some reason not clear to me, it is rare to see the exact words of this blessing, "the just Judge," in the sources. See, for example, Rabbi Arele's formulation in 35:3:8; though he does say, "You, O God, are just . . .," often even that kind of reference is not present. It seems that the exact wording is not a necessity.

3. This teaching is taken from *Totzaot Hayim*, p. 9 (with minor changes).

4. Usually translated: "By this I know that You have shown favor to me, if my enemy shall not shout in triumph over me."

Chapter 36–A Full Day Set Aside

1. See how *Reshit Hochmah* compares the one weekday set aside for holiness with *Shabbat* (Sh'ar ha-Kedushah, chap. 2, #30).

2. Although the text is not clear in its meaning, this makes it sound as if the fast and the "day" set aside is to be only from morning to evening. See the quote following this one, in 36:4.

Chapter 39–Individual Practices

1. The final comment I have added in brackets is from the version of this saying given in the name of Rabbi Menahem Mendel of Rimanov in *Sifran Shel Tzaddikim*, p. 7.

Glossary

Admor–Title of a hasidic *rebbe*. Acronym for *Adoneinu moreinu v'rabbeinu*: our master, teacher, and rabbi.

Adonai–"The Lord." Used as a name for God in place of the not-to-be-pronounced four-letter name, YHVH.

Aggadah–Negatively defined as that portion of rabbinic teaching that is not *halacha* (religious law); includes the more imaginative side of Jewish teaching: parables, stories, and the like.

Aliyah–Being called up, during the synagogue services, to recite the blessing over the Torah before it is read.

Amidah–*See Shemoneh Esreh.*

Ari–Rabbi Yitzhak Luria, the great kabbalist (1534–1572); also called "the Ari," the Lion, or "the Ari ha-kodesh," the Holy Lion, or "the Arizal," the Ari of blessed memory.

Ark–The cabinet in the synagogue where the Torah scrolls are kept.

Avot–*See Pirke Avot.*

Baal Shem Tov–Rabbi Israel, son of Eliezer, the founder of the modern hasidic movement. "Baal Shem," "the Master of the Name," was a term used for faith healers who made use of Divine names. This practice was controversial and in some disrepute. Therefore, with Rabbi Israel (who, among other things, was a faith healer) it was combined with "Shem Tov," a "good name," meaning someone of good reputation. So the "good" faith healer (and holy *tzaddik* and Torah teacher) came to be called "the Baal Shem Tov." *B*aal *Sh*em *T*ov is often shortened to "Besht."

Baruch Shem Kavod–The initial words that stand for the prayer declaration that follows the *Sh'ma*: "Blessed is [the name of] His glorious kingdom for ever and ever!"

Beit Din–Rabbinic court.

Beit Midrash–The House of Torah Study, also often used as a synagogue for prayer.

Besht–*See* Baal Shem Tov.

Bimah–The elevated platform in the synagogue from which the Torah scroll is read.

Briah–See Four Worlds.

Bris–A ritual circumcision.

Challah–Fine braided bread for Sabbaths and holidays.

Chazan–Cantor.

Cherub (pl. **Cherubim**)–A type of winged angel; their exact appearance is unknown. Two images of *cherubim*, which faced each other on the two ends of the cover above the Ark in the Holy of Holies, formed the Throne of God.

Chumash–The Five Books of Moses.

Chutzpah–Impudence, brazenness.

Davven (v.)–To pray (in a Jewish manner); *davvening* (n.): Jewish prayer.

D'vekut–Cleaving to God, the Divine Presence, in love.

Erev–Eve. Generally used for the daylight hours before a holy day, as for example: *Erev Shabbat*, *Erev Rosh HaShanah*, etc.

Ethrog–Citron (a particular citrus fruit). See Four Species.

External Forces–Negative and evil forces and influences.

Foreign Thoughts–Inappropriate or bad thoughts; usually distracting thoughts during a religious activity such as prayer.

Four-Letter Name of God–See YHVH.

Four Species–Four species of plant ritually waved on the Festival of *Sukkot*: citron (ethrog), palm branches, myrtle, and willow branches.

Four Worlds–Kabbalistic scheme of worlds. In ascending order of closeness to God: *Asiyah*, the World of Action (which includes our lower world); *Yetzirah*, the World of Formation; *Briah*, the World of Creation; *Atzilut*, the World of Emanation (or Nearness).

Gaon–A title denoting exceptional rabbinic learning and genius.

Gartel–A twined silk belt worn by men during prayer.

Gemara–The commentary and discussion on the Mishnah (which is the earlier text), the two together making up the Talmud.

Haftorah–The selection from the Prophets read in the synagogue services immediately after the Torah reading (from the Five Books of Moses) on Sabbaths and festivals.

Halacha–Jewish religious law.

Hallel–A group of psalms recited in the prayer service at certain festivals.

Hamotzi–The blessing said over bread.

Hanhaga (pl. **Hanhagot**)–A religious practice of personal piety.

Hashem–Literally, "The Name" (the four-letter Name of God that cannot be uttered); this is a popular way of referring to God.

Hasid (pl. **Hasidim**)–A pious person; specifically, the term is used to refer to a follower of a hasidic holy man (*rebbe, tzaddik*) and a member of the hasidic movement of the Baal Shem Tov.

Hasidah–A woman hasid; a pious or holy woman.

Hasidism–Piety. There have been different pietistic movements throughout Jewish history, the most recent that which emanated from the Baal Shem Tov.

Havaya–The name used in conversation for the four-letter Name of God (which is not to be pronounced), and made up of those same four letters in a different order.

Havdalah–End-of-*Shabbat* ceremony—with blessings over wine, spices, and fire—that makes a separation between holy and profane time.

Havurah–A fellowship.

Hayot ha-Kodesh–Literally, the holy animals. A type of angel: the angels who carry God's Throne and move the Divine Chariot.

Hillul ha-Shem–"Desecration of God's name." An especially ignoble or unethical act by a Jew which lessens the esteem of the God of Israel and Judaism in the eyes of nonbelievers; the opposite of *kiddush ha-Shem.*

Hitbodedut–"Aloneness" with God. Religious devotions performed in seclusion for a specific period of time.

Hitlahavut–Fervor, inspiration, enthusiasm.

Hitpashtut ha-Gashmiyut–A state of elevated mystic consciousness where one is divorced from any awareness of materiality or the body.

Holy Sparks–Kabbalistic concept. In the primeval creation, which preceded the creation of our world, the unitary Divine Light was fragmented and sparks fell among the Shells (see Shells). On the simplest level it usually means the spiritual rather than the material aspect of a thing.

Hoshanna Rabba–The seventh day of the Festival of *Sukkot.*

Kabbalah–(1) The main body of Jewish mysticism; (2) with a lower case "k" can also mean accepting on yourself a religious practice you intend to follow (with no relation to the first meaning).

Kabbalat Shabbat–The beginning of the Friday evening prayer service where the Sabbath is "welcomed" and received.

Kaddish–A prayer said during the synagogue prayer service. There are a number of forms, the most well known being the one recited as a memorial for the dead.

Kavvanah–The intention directed toward God while performing a religious deed. Can also mean a particular intention (for a prayer, etc.); the plural in that usage is *kavvanot.*

Kedushah–A responsive prayer said during the synagogue service when the prayer leader repeats the *Shemoneh Esreh.*

Kiddush–The blessing over the wine, made when ushering in a Sabbath or festival.

Kiddush ha-Shem–"Sanctification of God's name." An especially noble or ethical act by a Jew which raises the esteem of the God of Israel and Judaism in the eyes of nonbelievers; often refers to martyrdom. The opposite of *hillul ha-Shem.*

Kittel–A full-length white garment worn by men on certain holidays; worn by the person who leads the Passover seder.

Lulav–A palm branch. See Four Species.

Maariv–The daily Evening Prayer Service.

Maggid–Title for a preacher. Some of the *maggidim* (pl.) in Eastern Europe were itinerant; others were regularly appointed community preachers. The word is also used in a mystical context for an angelic teacher who reveals Torah secrets to the aspirant.

Mezuzah (pl. **Mezuzahs** or **Mezuzot**)–A small parchment scroll in a container attached to each of the doorposts at the entrances to a house and to the rooms within. The scroll has on it Scriptural verses. The *mezuzah* sanctifies the dwelling and assures Divine protection.

Midrash–Exposition or exegesis of the Scriptures, often including parables, sayings, and stories.

Mikveh–Ritual bath.

Minha–The daily Afternoon Prayer Service.

Minyan–The minimum prayer quorum of ten.

Mishnah–Ancient collection of legal decisions of the Sages; the earliest part of the Talmud, it is the text to which the *Gemara* (the other part) is the commentary. With a lower case "m," a *mishnah* (pl. *mishnayot*) is one teaching from the Mishnah.

Misnagid (pl. **Misnagdim**)–An opponent of the hasidic movement of the Baal Shem Tov.

Mitzvah (pl. **Mitzvahs** or **Mitzvot**)–A commandment of God.

Motzai Shabbat–The "departure of the Sabbath." The period following the end of the Sabbath, Saturday night.

Motzi–See *Hamotzi.*

Musaf–An additional prayer service for Sabbaths and festivals.

Musar–Inspirational literature or talk on ethics and religious character development. The *Musar* movement refers to the movement that focused on the teaching of *musar*; begun in the nineteenth century, its most important early figures were Rabbi Zundel of Salant and Rabbi Israel of Salant.

Niddah–A woman in a state of ritual impurity due to menstruation.

Niggun (pl. **Niggunim**)–A melody.

Ofan (pl. **Ofanim**)–Literally, a wheel. A type of angel, the "wheel angel" of God's chariot.

Omer–Counting the *omer*: the forty-nine days from the second day of Passover to the holiday of *Shavuot* are ritually counted.

Other Side–A kabbalistic usage, popular in Hasidism, for the side of Evil.

Payot–Ritual sidelocks worn by men.

Pesach–Passover.

Pirke Avot–The Ethics of the Fathers, a tractate of the Mishnah; usually also printed in the Siddur. It contains wisdom sayings, ethical and religious principles, and rules of conduct.

Rashi–The acronym for *R*abbi *Sh*lomo (ben) *Y*itzhak of Troyes, France (1040–1105), the great commentator of Bible and Talmud.

Reb–A title of respect; Mister.

Rebbe–A hasidic leader who heads a following of hasidim; often used as a title, sometimes together with Reb, for example, the Rebbe Reb Elimelech. Note that almost all the *rebbes* were and are rabbis, but very few rabbis are *rebbes.*

Rosh HaShanah–The Jewish New Year and Day of Judgment.

Rosh Hodesh–The Festival of the New Moon/Month.

Seder Ha-Yom–A daily order of Divine service.

Seder of the Holy Guests–A kabbalistic service and order of recitation on the Festival of *Sukkot*, at the table in the *sukkah*, where various of the Patriarchs and Torah heroes are received as guests.

Sedrah–The weekly portion of the Five Books of Moses read on a Sabbath.

Sefer Torah–A Torah scroll.

Shabbat–Hebrew for Sabbath; in English and Yiddish also: *Shabbos.*

Shaharit–The daily Morning Prayer Service.

Shechinah–The Divine Presence in this world; God as immanent.

Shells–Kabbalistic term, popular in Hasidism, for the negative forces of evil that surround and stifle what is holy.

Shemoneh Esreh–The "Eighteen [Blessings]." The central prayer of the prayer service; also called the *Amidah* (the "Standing Prayer") or the "Whispered Prayer."

Shivitti–A card, a wall poster, or plaque on which Psalm 16:8 with the four-letter Name of God is prominently displayed.

Sh'ma (Yisrael)–The "Hear O Israel" prayer; the central faith declaration in Judaism: "The Lord is our God; the Lord is one."

Shofar–The ram's horn primarily blown in the synagogue on *Rosh HaShanah.*

Shulchan Aruch–The main code book of Jewish religious law and behavior.

Siddur–The Jewish prayer book.

Sukkah–The booth used as a "temporary home" during the Festival of *Sukkot.*

Sukkot–The Festival of Booths (Tabernacles).

Tahanun–A prayer of supplication and penitence recited daily, excepting Sabbaths and festivals, as part of the morning and afternoon prayer services.

Tallit (Tallis)–The prayer shawl on whose corners are attached the ritual fringes (*tzitzit*).

Tallit Katan–A "small tallit" worn throughout the day by men, usually under their shirt. It has *tzitzit* (fringes) on its four corners and a central opening for passing it over the head.

Talmid (pl. **Talmidim**)–Disciple, student.

Talmud–The compendious series of volumes, which is, after the Bible, the most authoritative text in Judaism. It is comprised of the (earlier) Mishnah and the (later) discussion and commentary, based on the Mishnah, called the *Gemara.* The terms Talmud and *Gemara* are often used interchangeably.

Tanach–The complete Bible containing all three parts; the acronym for *T*orah (the Five Books of Moses), *N*eviim (Prophets), and *K*'tuvim (Writings).

Tefillin–Phylacteries. Leather boxes containing Scriptural verses inscribed on parchment; following Deuteronomy 11:18 two separate *tefillin* (pl.) are bound by straps onto the arm and the head during the weekday morning prayer service and at other times.

Temple–The now-destroyed Temple on Mount Zion in Jerusalem; only the Western Wall remains.

Ten Days of Repentance–The ten days (inclusive) from *Rosh HaShanah* to *Yom Kippur.*

Third Meal–The third of the three Sabbath meals, eaten after the Afternoon Prayer; very important in Hasidism, for at this meal especially there is singing of table hymns and Torah teaching by the *rebbe.*

Tikkun Hatzot–The Midnight Prayer Service and Vigil.

Torah–The revealed teaching of God. Can mean the *Chumash* (the Five Books of Moses), the *Tanach* (Bible), or, more broadly, all Jewish religious writings throughout the ages; it can also refer to oral teaching given by a Torah teacher.

Tosafot–Critical and explanatory notes on the Talmud.

Treif–Forbidden food.

Tshuvah–Repentance; literally, "turning [back to God]."

Tzaddik (pl. **Tzaddikim**; fem. **Tzaddeket**, pl. **Tzaddikot**)–(1) A righteous or holy person; (2) charismatic leader of a hasidic group; a rebbe.

Tzedaka–Charity.

Tzitzit–The ritual fringes on the four corners of a *tallit* (prayer shawl) or a *tallit katan* (a small *tallit* worn by men under their shirts).

Unification–In a technical sense, usually a kabbalistic meditation on one of the letter configurations of the four-letter Name of God, or on configurations of such names with different vocalizations; also has a broader meaning of any meditative activity that unites the Holy One, blessed be He, with His *Shechinah*, the Upper and the Lower Worlds.

Western Wall–The section of the western supporting wall of the Temple Mount which has remained intact since the destruction of the Second Temple (70 C.E.). It is the holiest spot in the Jewish religion.

Writings–The third division of the Scriptures; those books that are neither the Five Books of Moses nor the Prophets, such as Psalms, Proverbs, The Song of Songs, etc.

Yarmulke–The Jewish skullcap.

Yeshivah–A higher Jewish religious school for the study of Torah.

Yetzer (ha-Ra)–The evil inclination.

YHVH–The special Name of God (the others being secondary); also called the "four-letter name," the four English letters standing for the Hebrew letters יהוה (*Y*ud *H*e *V*av *H*e). See *Adonai* and *Havaya*.

Yom Kippur–The yearly Day of Atonement.

Zemirot–Devotional Sabbath table songs.

Zeyde–Yiddish for grandfather.

Zohar–The "Book of Splendor," the central book of the Kabbalah, the Jewish mystical tradition.

Bibliography

ABBREVIATIONS

DhTvhY	*Derech ha-Tovah v'ha-Yesharah*
GMvGhTz	*Gedulat Mordechai v'Gedulat ha-Tzaddikim*
SKvTz	*Sefer Kedushah v'Tzniyut*
YHvT	*Yalkut Hanhagot v'Takkanot*

Abir ha-Ro'im. T. Y. Mamlak.

Adat Tzaddikim (1959). Jerusalem, Israel.

Ha-Admor mi-Ohel (1959). A. Y. Bromberg. Mi-Gedolei ha-Hasidut, vol. 8. Jerusalem, Israel: Machon L'Hasidut.

Ha-Admor Rabbi Hanoch Henich Ha-Cohen (1969). Y. L. Levin. Jerusalem, Israel: Daat.

Admorei Belz (1972). I. Klapholtz. Bnei Brak, Israel.

Admorei Neshkiz, Lechovitz, Kaidenov, Novominsk (1963). A. Y. Bromberg. Mi-Gedolei ha-Torah v'ha-Hasidut, vol. 20. Jerusalem, Israel: Machon L'Hasidut.

Admorei Tchernobil (1971). I. Klapholtz. Israel.

Ha-Admorim mi-Ishbitza. Y. L. Levin. Bnei Brak, Israel: Yahadut.

Alpha Beta. Rabbi Tzvi Hirsh of Nadborna. See *Yalkut Hanhagot v'Takkanot*.

Ateret Menahem (1968). Ed. A. H. S. B. Michelzohn. Israel.

Ateret Tiferet (1968). Ed. Y. A. Teomim-Frankel. Israel.

Avodah u'Moreh Derech (1957). New York.

Avodat ha-Kodesh (1975). Rabbi H. Y. D. Azulai. Israel.

Avodat Yisrael (1973). Rabbi Israel, the Maggid of Koznitz. Bnei Brak, Israel.

Ayin Zochair (1976). New York: Hasidim of Bratzlav.

Aytzot Yesharot (1975). Rabbi Natan of Nemirov, ed. Rabbi M. M. Kitzkovesky. Jerusalem, Israel.

Azharot v'Tikkunim v'Sayagim. See *Yalkut Hanhagot v'Takkanot*.

Beit Aharon (1972). Jerusalem, Israel.

Beit Avraham. Rabbi A. Danziger. In *Sifrei Hanhagot v'Tzavaot v'Divrei Musar*.

Beit ha-Midrash (1967). A. Jellineck. Jerusalem, Israel: Wahrmann Books.

Beit Middot (1970). Y. L. Margaliot. Jerusalem, Israel.

Beit Pinhas. Ed. P. Shapiro.

Beit Rabbi. H. M. Heilman. Israel.

Beit Rizhin (1987). I. Klapholtz. Bnei Brak, Israel: Mishor.

Beit Shlomo (the Life of Rabbi Shlomo Shapiro of Munkatch). Jerusalem, Israel.

Beit Yisrael (1973). Rabbi R. Zak. Israel.

Beit Yitzhak (1975). Jerusalem, Israel: Mosad ha-Rav Y. M. Levine.

Birkat Hayim (1974). H. Y. HaCohen. New York: Beit ha-Sefer.

B'nai Machshavah Tovah (1973). Rabbi Kalonymus Kalmish Shapiro of Peasetzna.

Butzina Kadisha (1957). N. N. HaCohen. Jerusalem.

Connections/Hakrev Ushma (magazine). New York: The Inner Foundation.

Darka Shel Torah. See *Yalkut Hanhagot v'Takkanot*.

Darkei Hayim (1968). R. Tzimetboim. Tel Aviv, Israel.

Darkei Tzedek (1965). Jerusalem, Israel.

Darkei Yesharim (1965). Jerusalem, Israel.

Darkei Yesharim. In *Torat Hasidim ha-Rishonim* (1981). Bnei Brak, Israel: HaSeder.

Derech Emunah u'Maaseh Rav. Y. S. H. Lipshitz.

Derech ha-Tovah v'ha-Yesharah (DhTvhY). S. Y. Klein.

Derech Hayim (1973). Jerusalem, Israel.

Derech Moshe. Rabbi Moshe. See *Sefer ha-Gan v'Derech Moshe*.

Derech Pikudecha (1967). Rabbi Tzvi Elimelech of Dinov. Jerusalem, Israel.

Derech Tzaddikim (1912). Ed. A. Yellin. Pietrokov, Poland.

Divrei Emet (1973). Rabbi Yaakov Yitzhak, the Seer of Lublin. Israel.

Divrei Shmuel (Teachings of Rabbi Shmuel Shmelke of Nikolsburg). Israel.

Divrei Shmuel (Teachings of Rabbi Shmuel of Slonim) (1964). Jerusalem, Israel.

Divrei Torah. (This book is a reprint of one originally published in Warsaw in 1874.)

Dor Deah (1977). Rabbi Y. A. Kamelhar. Israel: Adir.

Emunat Tzaddikim. Rabbi Shmuel of Shinovi. Bnei Brak, Israel.

Erech Apayim (1966). A. Yellin. Jerusalem, Israel.

Eser Atarot. See *Z'chut Yisrael*.

Eser Kedushot. See *Z'chut Yisrael*.

Eser Orot. See *Z'chut Yisrael*.

Eser Tzachtzachot. See *Z'chut Yisrael*.

Eser Z'chuyot (1974). Ed. A. H. Zamlung. Bnei Brak, Israel: Machon l'Hotzaot Sefarim v'Kitvei Yad d'Hasidei Alexander.

Even Shtiya (1977). Rabbi H. Kahana. Ramat Vishnitz.

Gan Hadasim. Ed. E. Dov, son of Rabbi Aaron of Koznitz.

Ha-Gaon ha-Kadosh Baal Yismach Moshe (1984). Rabbi Y. M. Sofer. New York.

Gedulat Mordechai v'Gedulat ha-Tzaddikim (GMvGhTz). Ed. G. E. H. Stashevsky.

Generation to Generation (1985). A. Twerski. New York: Traditional Press.

Hachsharat ha-Abrechim (1966). Rabbi Kalonymus Kalmish of Peasetzna. Jerusalem, Israel.

Ha-Maggid mi-Mezritch (1972). I. Klapholtz. Bnei Brak, Israel: Pe'er ha-Sefer.

Hanhagot Adam (pamphlet). Rabbi Tzvi Elimelech of Dinov.

Hanhagot Adam. Y. L. Lipshitz. Pietrokov, Poland.

Hanhagot Tzaddikim (1976). Rabbi H. Y. Malik. Jerusalem, Israel.

Hanhagot Tzaddikim [II] (1981). Sefarim Kedoshim mi-Talmidei Baal Shem Tov ha-Kodesh, vol. 28. New York: Beit Hillel.

Hanhagot Tzaddikim [III] (1988). H. S. Rothenberg. Jerusalem, Israel: Machon Shaarei Ziv.

Ha-Shvil v'ha-Derech (1986). Y. Greenstein. Israel: Pe'er.

Hasidic Anthology (1968). L. Newman. New York: Schocken Books.

Hasidic Prayer (1978). L. Jacobs. New York: Schocken Books.

Hayei ha-Musar (1987). Yeshivat Beit Yosef in Ostrovtza, Poland. Bnei Brak, Israel.

Hayei Moharan (1962). Jerusalem, Israel.

Hedvat Simha (1966). Rabbi Y. H. Eibeshitz. Tel Aviv, Israel: Nehedar.

Hishtapchut ha-Nefesh (1976). Jerusalem, Israel.

Hitgalut ha-Tzaddikim (1959). Ed. S. G. Rosenthal. Jerusalem, Israel.

Hovat ha-Talmidim. Rabbi K. Kalmish of Peasetzna. New York: Taryag Publishers.

Ha-Hozeh mi-Lublin (1985). I. Klapholtz. Bnei Brak, Israel: Pe'er ha-Sefer.

Igeret Derech HaShem (1967). Rabbi Moshe of Trani. Jerusalem, Israel: Eshkol.

Igrot Shomrei Emunim (1942). Rabbi Arele Roth. Jerusalem, Israel: Hevrat Shomrei Emunim.

Ikkarei Emunah (1961). New York.

Imrei Kodesh. Rabbi Y. Frumkin. See *Sifrei Hanhagot v'Tzavaot v'Divrei Musar*.

Imrei Kodesh ha-Shalem (1988). Ed. Y. S. Frankel. Bnei Brak, Israel: Mishor.

In Praise of the Baal Shem Tov (1972). Ed. and trans. D. Ben-Amos and J. Mintz. Bloomington: Indiana University Press.

Ish ha-Pele (1987). Menashe Miller. Jerusalem, Israel: Machon Zecher Naftali.

Jewish Meditation (1985). Rabbi Arye Kaplan. New York: Schocken Books.

Joseph Karo: Lawyer and Mystic (1980). R. J. Zwi Werblowsky. Philadelphia: The Jewish Publication Society.

Kaf ha-Hayim (1986). Rabbi Hayim Plagi. Jerusalem, Israel: Siah Yisrael.

Kahal Hasidim ha-Hadash. Rabbi Shmuel of Shinovi.

Kav ha-Yashar ha-Shalem. Rabbi T. H. Kaidenver.

Kedushat ha-Shulchan (1979). Ed. Y. U. Zilberberg. Bnei Brak, Israel.

Kedushat Levi. Rabbi Levi Yitzhak of Berditchev. Jerusalem, Israel.

Kerem Yisrael (1973). Rabbi R. Zak. Israel.

Keter ha-Yehudi (1955). Ed. A. M. Rabinowitz. Jerusalem, Israel.

Keter Shem Tov (1968). Aaron of Apt. Jerusalem, Israel.

Kitzur Shnei Luchot ha-Brit. Rabbi Isaiah Horowitz. Cond. Y. M. Epstein. New York: Zichron Tzaddikim.

Knesset Yisrael (1976). Rabbi Israel of Rizhin. Ed. R. Ostila. Israel.

Kodesh Hillulim (1978). Rabbi M. Y. Weinstock. New York: Ateret.

Kol Sippurei Besht (1976). Ed. I. Klapholtz. Bnei Brak, Israel: Pe'er ha-Sefer.

K'tzait ha-Shemesh bi-Gevurato (1979). Sidrat Tikkun ha-Middot, book 4, ed. A. Tobolski. Israel.

Kulam Ahuvim. Commentary within *Tikkun ha-Nefesh*, David Elimelech, son of Rabbi Moshe of Munkatch.

Lekach Tov. Rabbi A. Galiki. See *Sifrei Hanhagot v'Tzavaot v'Divrei Musar*.

Lev Sameah ha-Hadash (1963). Rabbi Hanoch Henich Dov of Alesk. Jerusalem, Israel: Machon Mayan ha-Hochmah.

A Life of Chessed (1989). Rabbi D. Fisher. New York: Mesorah.

Likkutei Aytzot (1974). Rabbi Nachman of Bratzlav. Bnei Brak, Israel: Or Zorayach.

Likkutei Aytzot ha-Meshulash (1959). Rabbis Nachman of Bratzlav, Natan of Nemirov and Nachman of Tcherin. New York.

Likkutei Dibburim (1987). Rabbi Y. Y. Schneersohn of Lubavitch. Vol. 1, trans. U. Kaploun. Brooklyn, NY: Kehot.

Likkutei Moharan (1976). Rabbi Nachman of Bratzlav. Jerusalem, Israel.

Likkutei Rabbi Moshe Leib (RaMaL) (1965). Rabbi Moshe Leib of Sassov. Jerusalem, Israel.

Likkutei Torah (1972). Rabbi Mordechai of Tchernobil. Jerusalem, Israel.

Likkutim Hadashim (1984). Rabbi Yehiel Moshe of Kamarovka. Sefarim Kedoshim mi-G'dolei Talmidei Baal Shem Tov ha-Kodesh, vol. 12, book 6. New York: Beit Hillel.

Likkutim mi-Rabbi Pinhas mi-Koretz (1984). Rabbi Pinhas of Koretz. Sefarim Kedoshim mi-G'dolei Talmidei Baal Shem Tov, vol. 12, book 3. New York.

Likkutim Yekarim (1984). Sefarim Kedoshim mi-G'dolei Talmidei Baal Shem Tov, vol. 12, book 1. New York.

The Long Shorter Way (1988). Rabbi A. Steinsaltz. Northvale, NJ: Jason Aronson.

L'Yesharim Tehillah (1976). M. H. Kleinman. New York.

Maasiyot u'Maamarim Yekarim. Y. W. Tzikerick.

Maggid Devarav l'Yaakov (1976). Rabbi Dov Ber of Mezritch, ed. R. Shatz-Openheimer. Jerusalem, Israel: Hebrew University.

The Maggid Speaks (1987). Ed. Rabbi P. Krohn. New York: Mesorah Publications.

Mai ha-Shiloach (1976). Rabbi Mordechai Yosef of Ishbitz, ed. G. H. Henich. Jerusalem, Israel.

Marganita Taba. Rabbi Y. Valliner. See *Yalkut Hanhagot v'Takkanot*.

Mavo ha-Shaarim (1966). Rabbi Kalonymus Kalmish of Peasetzna. Jerusalem, Israel.

Mazkeret Shem ha-Gedolim (1967). Ed. M. H. Kleinman. Bnei Brak, Israel: Bina.

Megaleh Amukot (1979). Rabbi H. Liberzohn. Jerusalem: Tefillot Yisrael.

Meir Einei ha-Golah (1970). A. Y. Levitt, A. Mordechai of Warsaw, and M. M. Levitt. New York: Tov.

Mekor Hayim (1970). A. H. S. B. Michelzohn. Israel.

Menorat ha-Maor. Rabbi Y. Abuhav. Jerusalem, Israel: Eshkol.

Menorat Zahav. Ed. N. N. HaCohen. Israel.

The Messianic Idea in Judaism (1972). G. Scholem. New York: Schocken Books.

Michtivei ha-Hafetz Hayim ha-Hadash, vol. 2 (1986). S. Artzi. Bnei Brak, Israel: Mishor.

Midor Dor (1968). M. Lipson. Tel Aviv, Israel: Ahiasaf.

Midrash Pinhas (1971). Rabbi Pinhas of Koretz and Rabbi Rafael of Bershad. Jerusalem, Israel.

Midrash Ribesh Tov (1927). Rabbi Israel Baal Shem Tov, ed. L. Abraham. Kecskemet, Hungary.

Milei d'Avot (1981). Ed. M. M. Vishnitzer. Bnei Brak, Israel: HaSeder.

Mindel, Rabbi N. The significance of chassidic dancing. *Wellsprings* 5:7. New York: Lubavitch Youth Organization.

Minhagei ha-Arizal (*Petura d'Abba*) (1975). Ed. Rabbi U. Strelisker. Jerusalem, Israel.

Minhagim Tovim v'Kedoshim ha-Nohagim b'Eretz Yisrael. Rabbi A. Galanti. See *Yalkut Hanhagot v'Takkanot.*

Mishnah Berurah (1977). Rabbi Yisrael Meir (the Hafetz Hayim). Jerusalem, Israel: Vad ha-Yeshivot b'Eretz Yisrael.

Mishnat Hasidim (1981). Ed. M. M. Vishnitzer. Bnei Brak, Israel: HaSeder.

Nahalat Avot. Rabbi Meir, son of Rabbi Eliyah. See *Sifrei Hanhagot v'Tzavaot v'Divrei Musar.*

Netta Shaashuim (1966). Rabbi Natan Netta of Chelm. Jerusalem, Israel.

Niflaot Hadashot. Ed. Rabbi Y. Moshe of Kamarovka.

Niflaot ha-Rebbe. Ed. M. M. Walden. Bnei Brak, Israel.

Niflaot ha-Yehudi. Y. K. K. Rokotz. Jerusalem, Israel.

9 1/2 Mystics (1971). H. Weiner. New York: Collier Books.

Noam Elimelech. Rabbi Elimelech of Lizensk. Jerusalem, Israel.

Noam ha-Levavot (1978). Rabbi Aharon Roth. Jerusalem, Israel.

Nofit Tzufim. (1929). Rabbi Pinhas of Koretz, ed. Rabbi A. Y. Kleinman.

Ohalei Shem. Ed. Y. A. Teomim-Frankel.

Ohav Yisrael (1973). Rabbi Abraham Joshua Heshel of Apta. Jerusalem, Israel.

Ohel Elimelech (1968). Ed. A.H. S. B. Michelzohn. Israel.

Ohel Naftali. Ed. A.H. S. B. Michelzohn. Bnei Brak, Israel.

Ohel Yitzhak (1968). Ed. M. M. Walden. Israel.

On Learning Chassidus (1965). Rabbi J. I. Schneersohn, trans. Z. Posner. New York: Kehot Publication Society.

On the Kabbalah and Its Symbolism (1969). G. Scholem. New York: Schocken Books.

Or ha-Emet (1967). The Maggid of Mezritch. Bnei Brak, Israel: Yahadut.

Or ha-Ganuz l'Tzaddikim (1966). Jerusalem, Israel.

Or ha-Meir (1926). Jerusalem, Israel: Or ha-Sefer.

Or ha-Meir (1988). Rabbi Z. Wolf of Zhitomir. New York: Ziv.

Or ha-Shabbat (1975). A. Y. Eisenbach. Jerusalem, Israel.

Or Tzaddikim (1889). Meir, son of Rabbi Yehudah Leib.

Or Yesharim (1967). Ed. M. H. Kleinman. Jerusalem, Israel.

Or Yisrael. Rabbi Y. Blazer. New York.

Orchot Hayim (1957). Rabbeinu Asher. Jerusalem, Israel.

Orchot Tzaddikim (1976). Jerusalem, Israel: Lewin-Epstein.

Otzar ha-Sippurim. T. Moscowitz. Jerusalem, Israel.

Pe'er l'Yesharim (1973). Ed. Rabbi Y. D. Rosenstein. Jerusalem, Israel.

Pe'er v'Kavod (1970). B. Ehrman. Jerusalem, Israel.

Pe'er Yitzhak (1968). Rabbi M. Brover. Jerusalem, Israel.

Pele Yoatz (1985). Rabbi E. Papu. New York: Yerushalayim.

The Pentateuch and Haftorahs (1969). Ed. J. H. Hertz. London: Soncino Press.

Peninei Yam. Rabbi Y. M. Rabinowitz. See *Yalkut Hanhagot v'Takkanot.*

P'ri Kodesh Hillulim (1978). Rabbi Moshe Yair Weinstock. New York: Ateret.

Rabbi Nachman's Wisdom (1973). Rabbi Natan of Nemirov, trans. Rabbi A. Kaplan, ed. Rabbi Z. A. Rosenfeld. New York.

Rabbi Yisrael mi-Salant. Midor l'Dor, vol. 1. Rabbi Dov Katz. Israel: Ha-Histadrut ha-Tziyonit ha-Olamit.

Rabbeinu ha-Kodesh mi-Tzanz, vol. 1 (1976). Y. D. Weisberg. Jerusalem, Israel: Keset Shlomo.

Rachmei ha-Av (1980). Rabbi Y. Katina. Brooklyn, NY: Ha-Machon l'Hotzi u'l'Hafitz Sifrei Kedusha.

Ramatayim Tzofim. Rabbi Shmuel of Shinovi. Jerusalem, Israel: Lewin-Epstein. (Commentary on *Tanna d'Bei Eliyahu*, printed in this edition of that work.)

Ha-Rav mi-Apta (1981). Y. Alfasi. Jerusalem, Israel: Machon Siftei Tzaddikim.

Raza d'Uvda (1976). Ed. Meifitzei ha-Sefarim l'Beit Kretchnif. New York.

Ha-Rebbe Rav Tzvi Elimelech mi-Dinov (1978). Rabbi N. Ortner. Tel Aviv, Israel: Ha-Machon l'Hantzahat Hasidut Galitzia.

Reshit Hochmah (1984). Rabbi Elijah deVidas, ed. H. Y. Waldman. Jerusalem, Israel.

Rishpei Aish ha-Shalem. Rabbi Mordechai of Neshkiz.

Safed Spirituality (1984). Trans. and ed. L. Fine. New York: Paulist Press.

Seder ha-Dorot ha-Hadash (1965). Jerusalem, Israel.

Seder ha-Yom (1973). Rabbi M. Machir. Bnei Brak, Israel.

Seder ha-Yom (Bratzlav). Rabbi Y. Breiter. See back of *Seder Tikkun Hatzot*.

Seder ha-Yom ha-Katzar. Rabbi Y. Moshe of Kamarovka. See beginning of *Niflaot Hadashot*.

Seder ha-Yom l'ha-Admor mi-Biala. Rabbi Yehiel Yehoshuah mi-Biala. Bnei Brak, Israel: Machon Nahalat Yehoshua.

Seder Tikkun Hatzot (1965). Ed. E. S. Braslaver. New York.

Sefer Baal Shem Tov. Ed. Rabbi S. M. M. Gorvachov. Jerusalem, Israel.

Sefer ha-Hasidut mi-Torat Belz (1970). Ed. I. Klapholtz. Israel.

Sefer ha-Hayim. (By the author of *Tzaida l'Derech*). Jerusalem, Israel.

Sefer ha-Middot (1978). Rabbi Nachman of Bratzlav. Jerusalem, Israel: Hasidim of Bratzlav.

Sefer ha-Yirah (1967). Rabbeinu Yonah Gerondi. Jerusalem, Israel: Eshkol.

Sefer Haredim (1984). Rabbi Elezar Azikri. Jerusalem, Israel.

Sefer Hasidim (1972). Rabbi Yehudah ha-Hasid. Jerusalem, Israel: Lewin-Epstein.

Sefer ha-Yashar (1967). Jerusalem, Israel: Eshkol.

Sefer Kedushah v'Tzniyut (1979). Rabbi D. Frisch. Jerusalem, Israel.

Shaarei Tshuvah (1974). Rabbeinu Yonah Gerondi. Jerusalem, Israel: Keren Sefarim Toraniyim.

Shema Shlomo (1974). Ed. Y. M. HaLevi. Jerusalem, Israel.

Shemen ha-Tov. A. H. S. B. Michelzohn.

Shivhei Tzaddikim (1959). M. Tzitrin. Jerusalem, Israel.

Shomer Emunim (1978). Rabbi Aharon Roth. Jerusalem, Israel.

Shulchan Aruch Shel Rabbi Eleazar ha-Katan. Rabbi Eleazar ha-Katan.

Siah Sarfei Kodesh. Y. K. K. Rokotz.

Sichot Hayim (1968). Rabbi Hayim Meir Yehiel of Moglenitza. Jerusalem, Israel.

Sichot Yekarim (1975). Ed. E. Z. Stern.
Siddur Shirah Hadashah. Ed. H. D. Rosenstein. Jerusalem, Israel: Eshkol.
Sifran Shel Tzaddikim (1959). Ed. E. Dov, son of Rabbi Aharon. Jerusalem, Israel.
Sifrei Hanhagot v'Tzavaot v'Divrei Musar (1983). Ed. M. Kleiman. Jerusalem, Israel.
Siftei Kodesh (1969). Ed. Rabbi Y. K. K. Rokotz. Israel.
Siftei Tzaddikim (1928). Ed. P. Dinovitzer. Bilguray, Poland.
Simhat Yisrael. Ed. Y. Horowitz. Jerusalem, Israel.
Sippurei Hasidim. Ed. Rabbi S. Y. Zevin. Jerusalem, Israel: Beit Hillel.
Sippurim Niflaim (1976). Ed. H. Y. Malik. Jerusalem, Israel.
Sneh Boar b'Kotzk (1980). Meir Oryan. Jerusalem, Israel: Reuvan Mas.
Sod Yachin u'Voaz. Rabbi Meir Margulis. Israel.
Taamei ha-Minhagim. Ed. A. Y. Sperling. Jerusalem, Israel: Eshkol.
Tales of the Hasidim (1973). Ed. and trans. M. Buber. New York: Schocken Books.
Tanya (Likkutei Amarim) (1969). Rabbi Shneur Zalman of Ladi, trans. N. Mindel. New York: Kehot Publication Society.
Tefillat ha-Tzaddikim (1988). Rabbi Yehiel Yehoshua of Biala. Bnei Brak, Israel: Machon Nahalat Yehoshua.
Tiferet Adam (1976). (Life and teachings of R. David Moshe of Tchortkov.)
Tiferet Avot (1961). Ed. D. M. Rabinowitz. Jerusalem, Israel.
Tiferet Banim Avotam (1969). Y. S. Weinstock. Jerusalem, Israel.
Tiferet Beit David (1968). Rabbi M. Y. Weinstock. Jerusalem, Israel.
Tiferet Beit Levi. S. Guttman.
Tiferet ha-Yehudi. Y. K. K. Rokotz.
Tiferet Maharal (Moreinu ha-Rebbe Arye Leib) (1975). Y. Y. Rosenberg. New York: Ateret.
Tiferet Mordechai. Ed. M. Ginzburg. (Life and teachings of Rabbi Mordechai of Nadborna.)
Tikkun Kriat Sh'ma al ha-Mitah mai-ha-Arizal (1976). New York: Hasidim of Bratzlav.
Tikkun l'Nefesh (1875). Ed. Y. Kushta. Livorno, Italy.
Toafot ha-Rim (1986). Y. M. Tannenboim. Jerusalem, Israel: Machon Zecher Naftali.
Toldot Kedushat Levi (1957). T. E. Kalish. Jerusalem, Israel.
Toldot Menahem (1950). Rabbi Y. D. Miller. Jerusalem, Israel.
Tomer Devorah (1967). Rabbi Moshe Cordovero. Israel.

Torat Avot (1979). Jerusalem, Israel: Yeshivat Beit Avraham.

Torat ha-Naum v'ha-Drasha (1981). Rabbi S. Y. Glicksberg. Tel Aviv, Israel: Tzion.

Tosefta l'Midrash Pinhas (1984). Ed. M. Spiegel. Sefarim Kedoshim mi-G'dolei Talmidei Baal Shem Tov ha-Kodesh, vol. 12, book 4. New York: Beit Hillel.

Totzaot Hayim (1971). Rabbi Elijah deVidas. Jerusalem, Israel.

Ha-Tzaddik ha-Shotek (1965). N. Benari. Bnei Brak, Israel.

A Tzaddik in Our Time (1978). S. Raz. New York: Feldheim Publishers.

Tzav v'Zairuz (1966). Rabbi Kalonymus Kalmish of Peasetzna. Jerusalem, Israel: Vaad Hasidei Peasetzna.

Tzavaat ha-Ribash (Tzavoas Horivash) (1982). Ed. J. E. Shochet. New York: Kehot Publication Society.

Tzavaat ha-Ribash v'Hanhagot Yesharot (1965). Jerusalem, Israel.

Tzavaat Rabbi Moshe Hasid mi-Prague. Rabbi M. Hasid. In *Tzavaot v'Derech Tovim.*

Tzavaat Rabbi Yaakov mi-Lisa. Rabbi Yaakov mi-Lisa. In *Tzavaot v'Derech Tovim.*

Tzavaat Rabbi Yehudah ben Asher (1975). Rabbi Yehudah ben Asher. Tzavaot Gaonei Yisrael. Jerusalem, Israel.

Tzavaat Rabbi Yonah Landsofer. Rabbi Y. Landsofer. In *Tzavaot v'Derech Tovim.*

Tzavaot v'Derech Tovim. Ed. Y. M. Bakst.

Tzavaot v'Hanhagot (1977). Ed. Y. D. Weintraub. Bnei Brak, Israel.

Tzva'a Yekara. Rabbi A. Ziskind. In *Yesod v'Shoresh ha-Avodah.*

Tzetl Katan. Rabbi Elimelech of Lizensk. In *Noam Elimelech.*

Tzidkat ha-Tzaddik (1973). Rabbi Tzadok HaCohen of Lublin. Jerusalem, Israel: Aleph–Machon l'Hotzat Sefarim.

Vayakel Shlomo (1984). S. Z. Rapaport. Sefarim Kedoshim mi-G'dolei Talmidei Baal Shem Tov, vol. 12, book 7. New York: Beit Hillel.

Waters of Eden—The Mystery of the Mikvah (1982). Rabbi Arye Kaplan. New York: National Council of Synagogue Youth/Union of Orthodox Jewish Congregations of America.

The World of a Hasidic Master: Levi Yitzhak of Berditchev (1986). S. Dresner. New York: Shapolsky.

Yalkut Hadash. (Reprint. Originally published Warsaw, 1879.)

Yalkut Hanhagot v'Takkanot (YHvT) (1985). Bnei Brak, Israel: Sifsei Chachamim—Institute for the Dissemination of Torah and Musar.

Yeshuot Malko (1974). Jerusalem, Israel: Mosad ha-Rabbi Y. M. Levine.

Yesod ha-Avodah (1979). Yeshayah, the *shochet* of Odessa. Shaarei Tefillah. Jerusalem, Israel: Tefillot Yisrael.

Yesod ha-Tshuvah. Rabbeinu Yonah Gerondi. In *Shaarei Tshuvah.*

Yesod v'Shoresh ha-Avodah (1978). Rabbi Alexander Ziskind. Jerusalem Publishing Co.

Yesod Yosef (1981). Rabbi Yosef of Dubnow. Brooklyn, NY.

Yesodot b'Avodat HaShem (1983). Hasam Sofer. Ed. Y. Weiss. Jerusalem, Israel: Machon l'Heker Kitvei-yad al-Shem ha-Hasam Sofer.

Yifrach biYamav Tzaddik (1976). Rabbi N. Hertz. Jerusalem, Israel: Imrei Shefer.

Yosher Divrei Emet (1974). Rabbi Meshullam Feibush of Zabriza. Jerusalem, Israel.

Z'chut Yisrael (1973). Ed. Y. Berger. Israel.

Zemiroth (1979). Rabbi N. Scherman. New York: Mesorah Publications.

Zichron l'Rishonim (1977). Ed. M. H. Kleinman. Israel: Or ha-Sefer.

Zichron l'Vnai Yisrael. Rabbi Yaakov Hagiz. In *Yalkut Hanhagot v'Takkanot.*

Zot Zichron (1973). Rabbi Yaakov Yitzhak, the Seer of Lublin. Israel.

Index